W9-DBB-014

"The authors offer a powerful vision of learning wedded to a clear and actionable framework. But, best of all, they bring the nuts and bolts of teaching to life with dozens of pictures of practices drawn from teachers and learners around the world."

—David Perkins, Professor Emeritus, Harvard Graduate School of Education

"It is a rare thing to find a book so beautifully accessible to the classroom teacher while simultaneously engaging the reader in discussions of the theoretical and research basis behind the practice. I can't wait to share this powerful resource with teachers - it is a must have in the professional library of the contemporary educator."

—Kath Murdoch, International Education Consultant,
Author of The Power of Inquiry.

"In *The Power of Making Thinking Visible,* Ron Ritchart and Mark Church illuminate how teachers can deepen learning by igniting student curiosity and engagement. It is a must read for educators across every grade level and subject area. The helpful advice and research-tested practices shared in this book truly have the power to transform schools and classrooms."

—Madeleine Hewitt, Executive Director, Near East South Asia
Council of Overseas Schools

The Power of Making Thinking Visible

PRACTICES TO ENGAGE AND EMPOWER

ALL LEARNERS

Ron Ritchhart
Mark Church

JB JOSSEY-BASS™
A Wiley Brand

Copyright © 2020 by John Wiley & Sons, Inc. All rights reserved.

Published by Jossey-Bass
A Wiley Brand
111 River Street, Hoboken NJ 07030
www.josseybass.com

No part of this publication may be reproduced, stored in a retrieval system, or transmitted in any form or by any means, electronic, mechanical, photocopying, recording, scanning, or otherwise, except as permitted under Section 107 or 108 of the 1976 United States Copyright Act, without either the prior written permission of the publisher, or authorization through payment of the appropriate per-copy fee to the Copyright Clearance Center, Inc., 222 Rosewood Drive, Danvers, MA 01923, 978-750-8400, fax 978-646-8600, or on the Web at www.copyright .com. Requests to the publisher for permission should be addressed to the Permissions Department, John Wiley & Sons, Inc., 111 River Street, Hoboken, NJ 07030, 201-748-6011, fax 201-748-6008, or online at www.wiley.com/ go/permissions.

Limit of Liability/Disclaimer of Warranty: While the publisher and author have used their best efforts in preparing this book, they make no representations or warranties with respect to the accuracy or completeness of the contents of this book and specifically disclaim any implied warranties of merchantability or fitness for a particular purpose. No warranty may be created or extended by sales representatives or written sales materials. The advice and strategies contained herein may not be suitable for your situation. You should consult with a professional where appropriate. Neither the publisher nor author shall be liable for any loss of profit or any other commercial damages, including but not limited to special, incidental, consequential, or other damages. Readers should be aware that Internet Web sites offered as citations and/or sources for further information may have changed or disappeared between the time this was written and when it is read.

Jossey-Bass books and products are available through most bookstores. To contact Jossey-Bass directly call our Customer Care Department within the U.S. at 800-956-7739, outside the U.S. at 317-572-3986, or fax 317-572-4002.

Wiley also publishes its books in a variety of electronic formats and by print-on-demand. Some material included with standard print versions of this book may not be included in e-books or in print-on-demand. For more information about Wiley products, visit www.wiley.com.

Library of Congress Cataloging-in-Publication Data

Names: Ritchhart, Ron, author. | Church, Mark, 1970- author.
Title: The power of making thinking visible : practices to engage and
  empower all learners / Ron Ritchhart, Mark Church.
Description: First edition. | San Francisco : Jossey-Bass, 2020. | Includes
  bibliographical references and index.
Identifiers: LCCN 2019052277 (print) | LCCN 2019052278 (ebook) | ISBN
  9781119626046 (paperback) | ISBN 9781119626190 (adobe pdf) | ISBN
  9781119626213 (epub)
Subjects: LCSH: Thought and thinking—Study and teaching. | Critical
  thinking—Study and teaching. | Cognition in children. | Harvard Project
  Zero.
Classification: LCC LB1590.3 .R3624 2020 (print) | LCC LB1590.3 (ebook) |
  DDC 370.15/2—dc23
LC record available at https://lccn.loc.gov/2019052277
LC ebook record available at https://lccn.loc.gov/2019052278

Cover Design: Wiley
Cover Image: © nicolas_/Getty Images

Printed in the United States of America
FIRST EDITION

CONTENTS

LIST OF FIGURES

ACKNOWLEDGMENTS

This book is the story of our learning as researchers about the power of making thinking visible (MTV) through years of research. But it is more than that. This book also brings together the voices of hundreds of teachers from around the world who joined us in this journey. These teachers were willing to take risks and try out new routines still under development. They shared their successes and failures with us, pushing us to explore new possibilities. Through their teaching practice and their individual inquiry into their students' learning, these teachers propelled our collective learning as a community. There are too many of these to mention by name. We do want to mention a few though who have taken extra efforts to document, reflect, share, discuss, and review their practice with us. We hope that our representation in this book does them justice.

Our research and development work on visible thinking began in 2000 with the support of the Carpe Vitam foundation and included work in Sweden as well as several international schools in Europe. Since then the number of international schools with whom we engage has steadily grown and we continue to learn from this diverse group of global educators. Specifically, we want to thank Tom Heilman and Emily Veres at Washington International School; Joyce Lourenco Pereira at Atlanta International School; David Riehl at Munich International School; Nora Vermeulin at International School of Luxembourg; Mary Kelly at International School of Amsterdam; Walter Basnight at

American International School of Chennai; Kendra Daly and Gene Quezada at International School of Beijing; Regina Del Carmen at Chadwick International School; Chris Fazenbaker, Marina Goodyear, and Tahireh Thampi at American Embassy School in New Delhi; Julie Frederick at American International School of Lusaka; Laura Fried and Paul Miller at Academia Cotopaxi in Quito; Matt McGrady at American Community School of Dubai; and Caitlin McQuaid at KAUST Garden Elementary School in the Kingdom of Saudi Arabia.

In 2005 we began what would turn out to be 13 years of partnership with Bialik College in Melbourne, Australia. Many of the stories in *Making Thinking Visible* (2011) emerged from this very productive collaboration. Since then the ideas have spread widely throughout Australia based on these efforts. Many other schools have now taken up MTV practices and moved them forward in rich and exciting ways. At Penleigh and Essendon Grammar School, Nina Bilewicz has nurtured these ideas and supported teachers to take risks and try out new practices in their teaching. We have benefited from these efforts and have been able to learn from the deep reflective work of Sheri McGrath, Amanda Stephens, Steve Davis, Darrel Cruse, Lee Crossley, Kate Dullard, and Peter Bohmer at the school. Similar efforts were supported by the Association of Independent Schools of South Australia and at Wilderness School in Adelaide where many teachers, including Alison Short, eagerly tried out routines and put them into practice. Others we wish to thank include Sharonne Blum at Bialik College, Michael Upton at Holy Trinity Primary, Nick Boylan at St. Francis Xavier Primary, Kathy Green at Australian Catholic University, Alice Vigors at Our Lady of the Rosary Primary, Pennie Baker at St. Philip's Christian College, Wayne Cox at Newington College, Alisha Janssen at Pacific Lutheran College, and Amy Richardson at Redlands School.

Over the past decade we have been engaged with schools throughout the state of Michigan through the long-range vision of Oakland Schools to develop a culture of thinking for the more than 200,000 students in the area. As a result, we have been able to see these ideas grow, deepen, and develop in the hands of talented teachers, coaches, and principals. For a decade, these efforts were led by Lauren Child, who was always looking for ways to develop teacher leadership and experience. This has resulted in a large network of teachers who were able to take the new routines we were developing and put them to use in their classrooms to maximum effect. These include Shernaz Minwalla, Jodi Coyro, and Michael Medvinsky at the University Liggett School; Alexandra Sanchez at Parkview Elementary; Jeff Watson at International Academy; Julie Rains at Delta Kelly Elementary; Steven Whitmore from Oakland Schools; Jennifer Hollander from Huron Valley; and Kim Smiley, Morgan Fields, Mary Goetz, Ashley Pellosmaa, and Jennifer

LaTarte from Bemis Elementary. We were also fortunate to be able to tap into the expertise and experience of Mary Beth Schmitt in Traverse City. Through the inspired professional learning offered by Katrin Robertson and Diane Tamblyn at Whole**mind**esigns in Ann Arbor, we have had the opportunity to work with and learn from teachers Connie Weber at Emerson School, Mary Beane at Hilton Elementary, and Trisha Matelski at Washtenaw International High School.

In Pittsburgh, Jeff Evancho has grown a network of educators deeply committed to using and sharing Project Zero ideas. We have benefited from these efforts, specifically those of Tara Surloff, South Fayette High School, and Matt Littell, Quaker Valley High School. In Del Mar, California, Superintendent Holly McClurg and Assistant Superintendent Shelley Petersen have committed to developing these ideas through the regular use of Learning Labs. Caitlin Williams and Andrea Peddycord at Ashley Falls School participated in these labs and shared their efforts not only with their colleagues but with us as well. We also want to acknowledge the contributions of Jessica Alfaro from the Summit School in North Carolina, Julie Manley from Bellevue School District in Washington, Natalie Belli from the Village School in Marblehead, Massachusetts, and Hardevi Vyas from Stevens Cooperative School in Newport, New Jersey.

The Tapestry Partnership in Glasgow, Scotland, has engaged Scottish local authorities in the ideas of *Making Thinking Visible* since 2012. Under the leadership of Katrina Bowes, Victoria McNicol, Marjorie Kinnaird, Lesley Robertson, and several others, teachers and head teachers across Scotland have worked diligently to create classrooms where thinking is visible, valued, and actively promoted within their local school contexts. We've learned a lot from the efforts of many of these leaders of learning including Madelaine Baker, Louise-Anne Geddess, Claire Hamilton, Gagandeep Lota, and Laura MacMillan.

In understanding the effects *Making Thinking Visible* has on student performance, we wish to thank all the schools and teachers who so generously shared data with us. These include Jim Reese from Washington International School; Jason Baehr at Intellectual Virtues Academy in Long Beach, California; Adam Scher from Way Elementary in Bloomfield Hills, Michigan; and Jeremy Whan from Bemis Elementary in Troy, Michigan. In Australia, Nathan Armstrong from Wesley College and Stuart Davis from St. Leonard's College, both from Melbourne, and Judy Anastopoulos from St. Philip's Christian College in Newcastle, New South Wales. In Chile, Yerko Sepulveda from Universidad Tecnológica de Chile INACAP.

We wish to thank our Project Zero colleagues who have, as always, been our intellectual partners in this work. Veronica Boix-Mansilla, Flossie Chua, Melissa Rivard, and the Interdisciplinary and Global Studies initiative and The Global Lens project shared the routines the *3 Y's* and *Beauty & Truth* with us and helped to deepen our understanding of how routines can engage and empower learners. Mara Krechevsky, Ben Mardell, Terri Turner, and Daniel Wilson continually spark our imagination and encourage our practice of documenting learning and supporting deep professional learning.

A special thanks to the instructors and coaches of the Creating Cultures of Thinking online course who were able to share with us their learnings from years of making thinking visible and coaching other teachers in developing a culture of thinking. Their observations and insights were invaluable to our understanding of the power of making thinking visible. Thanks to Cameron Paterson at Shore School, Erika Lusky at Rochester High School, Denise Coffin at Sidwell Friends School, Shehla Ghouse at Stevens Cooperative School, Erik Lindemann at Osborne Elementary School, and Jeff Watson at the International Academy. We are indebted as well to those who read early drafts of this book and offered edits, feedback, and suggestions. These include Julie Landvogt, Connie Weber, and Pete Gaughan.

This book would not have been possible without the generous support of the Melville Hankins Family Foundation, who have nurtured our research and development work most recently. Their funding has also facilitated a multiyear collaboration with Mandela International Magnet School (MIMS) in Santa Fe, New Mexico. At MIMS these ideas have been supported by the principals Ahlum Scarola and Randy Grillo and a group of inspiring coordinators including Natalie Martino, Nevada Benton, and Scott Larson working with a group of dedicated teachers, who are continually growing and sharing with each other. A special thanks to math teachers Rudy Penczer, David Call, Jessie Gac, and Anne Ray, who all were willing to try new routines in their classrooms and share their efforts when we needed examples of how these ideas might play out in a mathematics classroom.

ABOUT THE AUTHORS

Ron Ritchhart is a senior research associate and principal investigator at Harvard Project Zero, where his work focuses on the development of school and classroom culture as prime vehicles for developing students as powerful thinkers and learners. Ron's research and writings have informed the work of schools, school systems, and museums throughout the world. His research is largely classroom based and focused on learning from the best practice of teachers to understand how they create conditions for powerful learning. Ron's seminal research, presented in the book *Intellectual Character*, identified thinking routines as a core instructional practice and laid a framework for understanding group culture that is widely used by schools and organizations. His book *Making Thinking Visible,* co-written with Mark Church and Karin Morrison, has popularized the use of thinking routines to facilitate deep learning and high engagement. Ron's book, *Creating Cultures of Thinking*, takes readers inside a diverse range of learning environments to show how teachers create classrooms where thinking is valued, visible, and actively promoted as part of the day-to-day experience of all group members. Ron splits his time between Santa Fe, New Mexico, and Santa Barbara, California, when he is not working in Cambridge or with schools around the world.

Mark Church has been in education for over 25 years, first as a classroom teacher, then as a facilitator of learning for other teachers and school leaders. Mark is currently a consultant with Harvard Project Zero's Making Thinking Visible and Cultures of Thinking initiatives, drawing upon his own classroom teaching experience and from the perspectives he has gained working with educators throughout the world. He is passionate about helping educators dwell in possibilities—considering big ideas that will help them become not only students of their students, but students of themselves. Mark believes in the power of teachers who create classrooms where thinking is visible, valued, and actively promoted. Though Seattle is home for Mark, he travels the world to engage others with these ideas, which continues to enthuse him and bring him much joy. Together with Ron Ritchhart and Karin Morrison, Mark is coauthor of the book *Making Thinking Visible: How to Promote Engagement, Understanding, and Independence for All Learners* (Jossey-Bass 2011).

INTRODUCTION

During the 1998–1999 school year, I spent a year studying a group of teachers who were very adept at getting their students to think (Ritchhart 2000). These were teachers who had been nominated by colleagues, coaches, principals, or university professors as educators who cared about thinking and making it central to their teaching and were also effective at doing so. These teachers not only got their students to think in the moment but also developed their disposition to think, cultivating their habits of mind in the long haul and forging their intellectual character. My collaboration with this extraordinary group of teachers has resonated with me for years, informing over two decades of research and writing.

Traveling back and forth to these classrooms, which served a diverse range of students in different schools and different states, I began to notice a very powerful pattern emerging: these teachers who were so skilled at getting students to think never once taught a thinking-skills lesson. Rather than instructing students on thinking, each of these teachers with vastly different backgrounds and experiences made use of structures, generally of their own making and design, to carefully prompt, scaffold, and support students' thinking. What is more, these structures were used over and over throughout the school year so that they quickly became the *routine* way of learning and thinking. These routines became part of the fabric of the classroom and helped to create a culture of thinking.

Having seen the power of thinking routines to make students' thinking visible in the moment while also developing their thinking dispositions in the long term, my colleagues David Perkins, Shari Tishman, and I chose to make thinking routines a core practice of the Visible Thinking project conducted by our research group, Project Zero (PZ) at the Harvard Graduate School of Education (www.pz.harvard.edu). Whereas the teachers I had observed had created their own routines to fit their needs, our team set out to develop a collection of thinking routines that might be useful broadly. We sought to craft routines that not only could work across different subject areas but also with different age levels. As researchers we were not tasked with designing a program or an intervention but an *approach* to developing students as thinkers and learners. Our goal was to design an approach that would cultivate dispositional development and enhance students' intellectual character. For this approach to work, we recognized that teachers must first embrace the goal of making thinking visible (MTV) as a significant aim of teaching; only then would the practices come alive in their classrooms.

From the outset of the Visible Thinking project, we noticed that teachers gravitated to these tools because of their ease of use. Furthermore, students liked them and began to engage more actively in their learning. More important, the teachers with whom we were working began to appreciate what it meant to get students to think and to make their thinking visible. When we first asked teachers to bring evidence of students' thinking to share with colleagues, many brought student essays, worksheets, or flawless tests. They had simply assumed that thinking must be evident in students' correct answers or in their exemplary work. However, teachers quickly realized that thinking is more a process than a product. Although certainly products may contain evidence of thinking, sometimes products obscure students' thinking. Was that correct response a guess? A hunch? An error? Or was it simply a memorized answer? How had the student arrived at that destination? It is only by illuminating the often mysterious and invisible process of thinking that we can begin to answer those questions.

Of course we were pleased that teachers found thinking routines useful, appealing, and applicable. The original Visible Thinking website (www.visiblethinkingpz.org, 2005) and the follow-up book, *Making Thinking Visible* (Ritchhart et al. 2011) made thinking routines accessible to teachers all over the world. Now, almost a decade later, we feel we have much more to share. We have developed a number of new routines that we want to introduce. These in themselves warrant a companion volume to the original. However, we want to do more than merely share these new routines—as useful as we think they are. We also want to share what we have learned about the power of thinking routines to truly transform teaching and learning. We want to communicate what we have learned about how teachers can realize the power of MTV practices themselves. This theme of "power" frames this book. Because both this book and the previous one offer useful insights and valuable tools, they should be considered a companion set. However, this new volume will be particularly useful in understanding why and how MTV is an important set of educational practices and how teachers, working together or individually, can help to realize the power of these practices.

We begin by exploring six powers of MTV in Chapter 1. These "powers" emerge through our extensive research in diverse schools around the world. They represent the promise of MTV practices to reshape schooling and constitute our raison d'etre as researchers. Although teachers often share thinking routines as useful practices and helpful strategies with their colleagues, for effective schoolwide use we must have a good understanding of just where these practices can take students, teachers, and schools. For many teachers, understanding this potential is necessary before they can begin to institute the routines themselves. Seasoned educators are often skeptical of the latest fad or technique and need a good reason around why they should try a set of new practices.

In Chapter 2 we draw on our long history of research to share our understanding of MTV as both a goal of teaching as well as a set of practices. This background information helps us to use thinking routines well and to fully realize their power to transform learning. There are some basics presented about how thinking routines are designed and structured that may be familiar to those who have read *Making Thinking Visible*. However, our knowledge of how routines operate continues to grow and evolve through our current work. There are new ideas presented here that are likely to enhance the practice of even experienced users.

Today almost every new research project at Harvard Project Zero makes use of thinking routines. Sometimes project teams will draw on routines already created. Other times teams invent new routines that help to scaffold and support specific thinking moves that the project is trying to encourage. Often thinking routines are backward designed by examining a learning situation and identifying the kinds of thinking to engage effectively in that context. These efforts have resulted in an abundance of new thinking routines. Although our first instinct in writing this book was to share all the routines we had developed or adapted, we quickly found there were too many. Consequently, we have chosen to share the 18 thinking routines most widely applicable and powerful for "Engaging with Others" (Chapter 3), "Engaging with Ideas" (Chapter 4), and "Engaging in Action" (Chapter 5).

Our past two decades have taught us much about how to use thinking routines most effectively. We have learned from the skill teachers have exhibited in adapting and applying thinking routines to engage students in learning and thinking. We have learned as much from the moments where things have not gone smoothly, or even failed, as we have from the moments when things went seamlessly. In addition, we have learned from seeing teachers sometimes using thinking routines superficially as mere activities. Such superficiality is never any teacher's intent. Nonetheless, it caused us to think more about why and how this happens and how we might help teachers avoid such superficiality. As a result, we have come to understand the importance of planning for thinking, priming that thinking both in our own minds as well as in our students, pressing students' thinking in the moment so as to advance their thinking, and positioning thinking routines well within an instructional sequence. We share these learnings about how to use thinking routines effectively in Chapter 6.

Finally, we conclude by communicating what we have learned over the years about how teachers can learn from and with one another as they embrace the goal of making thinking visible. In Chapter 7, we share the tools and practices we have developed to help teachers learn from and with one another through professional inquiry, observation, analysis, and reflection. For those looking to connect with educators outside their school who are using these ideas to share and discuss further, there are conferences, institutes, and online courses offered by Project Zero at the Harvard Graduate School of Education (http://www.pz.harvard.edu/professional-development) that provide valuable professional opportunities.

As you read this book, we invite you now to join with us in the quest to realize the power of MTV. Take inspiration from the stories shared here, drawing on the learning of others even as you extend it into your own context to produce your own insights. Add your voice to the chorus by sharing your own learning with us through Facebook (https://www.facebook.com/MakingThinkingVisible), or on Twitter and Instagram using #MakingThinkingVisible, or #VisibleThinking or by following and tagging @RonRitchhart or @ProjectZeroHGSE. Many of the examples and voices shared here have come to us through these forums. Most important, make these thinking routines and MTV practices real patterns of behavior in your classroom and across your school so that you too can experience the power of making thinking visible.

Ron Ritchhart and Mark Church

PART ONE

LAYING THE FOUNDATION FOR POWER

CHAPTER 1

Six Powers of Making Thinking Visible

To really focus on making thinking visible fundamentally changes the role of student and teacher. As I utilize thinking routines and document our learning, I notice my students speaking up more and guiding our learning. Focusing on students' thinking places the power in their hands and fosters a teacher–student relationship built on mutual trust and respect.

Alexandra Sánchez, Third-Grade Teacher Parkview Elementary School, Novi, Michigan

When I make my classes' thinking visible, it's like putting a dipstick in to check the oil. I can immediately see what they do and don't understand. It's a cue to what I need to do next in my teaching. This is probably the biggest way that my teaching has changed since I started teaching 25 years ago. I'm now much more responsive to my students' thinking.

Cameron Paterson, Director of Teaching and Learning, Secondary History Teacher, Shore School, Sydney, Australia

Witnessing nonverbal students with moderate cognitive impairments shift from struggling to answer assigned reading comprehension questions to proudly displaying their thinking has forever changed my view of supporting learners with neurodiversity. Making thinking visible practices offer these students a path previously untraveled, giving them a voice, a purpose, and a sense of pride. I see a huge shift in attitudes regarding the learning outcomes and thinking abilities of these learners across our school.

Erika Lusky, Secondary Speech and Language Pathologist, Instructional Coach Rochester High School, Rochester, Michigan

Alexandra, Cameron, and Erika speak eloquently to the power of making thinking visible (MTV). Theirs are not isolated voices. In diverse classrooms from around the world, teachers have shared with us the difference MTV has made in both their own teaching and their students' learning. As researchers observing in classrooms, we have seen this for ourselves, witnessing a new paradigm of schooling emerge within the context of engaged, purposeful learning. This has propelled much of our research and development work since the original publication of *Making Thinking Visible* in 2011. In our ongoing collaboration with schools, we have sought both to capture the ways we have seen teachers engage students in thinking and make it visible, as well as to understand the difference these efforts have made. How do MTV practices change students and teachers? What makes this set of practices powerful? How do efforts to make students' thinking visible transform the traditional story of schooling we have known for so long?

In this chapter we articulate six ways in which we see MTV practices exert transformational change in classrooms. MTV has the power to:

- Foster deep learning
- Cultivate engaged students
- Change the role of students and teachers
- Enhance our formative assessment practice
- Improve learning (even when measured by standardized tests)
- Develop thinking dispositions

We explore each of these powers by drawing on the voices of teachers who have shared where they have seen the power of MTV practices in their teaching and in their students' learning. We expand on these commentaries by connecting them to relevant research. Finally, we explain exactly why and how these "powers" exist in visible thinking practices generally and thinking routines specifically. What is it about MTV practices that help establish this power? How can teachers realize that power in their own classrooms?

FOSTERING DEEP LEARNING

The Visible Thinking project, which began in 2000, built on the preceding Teaching for Understanding project from the 1990s. These two ideas – understanding and thinking – are core to conceptions of deep learning. While no single definition exists of deep learning, The Hewlett Foundation, a major supporter of research in this area, defines deeper learning as the significant understanding of core academic content, coupled with the ability to think critically and solve problems with that content (Hewlett Foundation 2013). These core academic competencies are joined by the interpersonal and intrapersonal abilities of collaboration, communication, directing one's own learning, and the possession of positive beliefs and attitudes about oneself as a learner that serve to motivate one's ongoing learning.

Based on extensive research in schools and classrooms where deeper learning was occurring, Jal Mehta and Sarah Fine (Mehta and Fine 2019) assert that deeper learning emerges at the intersection of:

- *Mastery*: the opportunity to develop understanding
- *Identity*: the opportunity to connect to the domain and develop as a learner with a place in the world
- *Creativity*: the opportunity to produce something personally meaningful

These opportunities are infused with critical thinking, grappling with complexity, challenging assumptions, questioning authority, and embracing curiosity – all core elements of what it means to learn deeply.

Erik Lindemann from Osborne Elementary School in Quaker Valley, Pennsylvania, sees these elements coming into play as he makes thinking visible in his third-grade classroom. "The story of our classroom learning is dramatically different when we use visible thinking routines. The routines build learners' capacity to engage with complexity while inspiring exploration. As my students begin internalizing and applying these thinking tools, I become a consultant in their ongoing investigations. Curiosity and excitement fuel deeper learning as my students take the lead," he observes. Erik's remarks attest to the transformative power of making students' thinking visible. They move teaching beyond the realm of transmission, focusing on transformation not only of the content but also of the learner.

Secondary math teacher Jeff Watson at the International Academy in Oakland County, Michigan, has also noticed this movement from transmission to transformation. "Math classrooms that I have visited have mostly been lecture-oriented, teacher-centered environments. Many times, the only interaction is a response to the question 'Are there any questions?'" he laments. In contrast, Jeff notes that "thinking routines are an incredible way to change the entire classroom dynamic, as learning naturally turns over to the students and places them in a more active role. The best part is that while the changes are so powerful, they don't cost any money, require any curriculum changes, or sweeping reform."

As we have identified, an agenda of understanding and thinking rests at the core of deeper learning and are both central to the effective use of thinking routines. In using a thinking routine, teachers need to situate its use within the larger context of building understanding: How does this particular lesson fit within the larger enterprise of understanding I am striving for? Teachers can then begin to focus on the goals of a particular lesson: With which ideas do I want students to begin to grapple? Where are the complexities and nuances that we need to explore? How can I push students' understanding and move it forward? With these questions answered, teachers are ready to identify the source material and the kinds of thinking that might best serve the exploration of that material. Only then are teachers in a good position to select a thinking routine as a tool or structure for that exploration.

CULTIVATING ENGAGED STUDENTS

Reflecting on the difference MTV practices have made in the learning of her third- and fourth-grade students, teacher Hardevi Vyas from the Stevens Cooperative School in Newport, New Jersey, notes the power of thinking routines to engage learners:

"The continued use of thinking routines when exploring primary and secondary sources, as norms of conversation, as prompts for thinking has been the driving force that moves students from a place of interest, to deep engagement, to a real desire to take action by identifying the steps to take to make a difference. Thinking routines emotionally engage students, leading to a high level of intellectual rigor and ethical reflection."

Hardevi's comments identify three specific types of engagement: (i) engagement with others, (ii) engagement with ideas, and (iii) engagement in action. In engaging with others, we recognize that learning unfolds in the company of others and is a social endeavor. We learn in, from, and with groups. The group supports our learning as well as challenges it, allowing us to reach higher levels of performance. At the same time, learning demands a personal engagement with ideas. Whereas we might be able to receive new information passively, building understanding is an active process that involves digging in and making sense. We bring ourselves to the learning moment. Sometimes this is identified as cognitive engagement, to distinguish it from mere engagement in activity. It is cognitive engagement with ideas that leads to learning. Exploring meaningful and important concepts that are connected to the world often means students want to take action. Providing opportunities and structures for them to do so encourages students' agency and power while making the learning relevant.

We found this three-part framing of the nature of engagement powerful for understanding the different ways thinking routines engage students. Consequently, we have used this framing to organize the routines we present in Part Two of this book. Of course these three types of engagement are not discrete, and neither are the routines we present under each of these headings. While a routine might provide a great way to engage learners with others, students are still engaging with ideas. Likewise, when thinking about taking action we may work with others, and ideas will still remain at the core.

It may be tempting to blame students for their lack of engagement. After all, it is their behavior (or lack thereof) that we are noticing. However, research by David Shernoff found that 75% of the variation in student engagement was attributable to differences in the classroom learning context while only 25% could be explained by students' own background characteristics (Shernoff 2010). Furthermore, Shernoff and colleagues found that involving high school students in thinking led to greater levels of student-reported engagement in classes (Shernoff 2013). These findings mirror those of other researchers assessing urban middle school students' perceptions of their teachers. When teachers engaged students in independent thinking, students recognized this as useful to their development of understanding and autonomy as learners (Wallace and Sung 2017). The importance of deep engagement and thinking opportunities for all students was also a common theme among the teachers Mehta and Fine studied in their dive into deep learning (Mehta and Fine 2019). They found that teachers who promoted deep learning viewed thinking and engagement as a necessary part of learning and as something *all* students were capable of. This was in contrast to those teachers who failed to engage students in deep learning consistently. These teachers were more likely to view understanding, thinking, and engagement beyond the reach of their students.

This phenomenon of thinking leading to engagement is not limited just to middle and high school students. Lecturer Katrin Robertson experienced it in her arts education classes at the University of Michigan. "For many years I used question prompts to engage my university students in discussing texts. These 'discussions' often ended up being ask-and-answer sessions where the students simply responded to me but didn't speak to each other. Engagement felt compulsory and sometimes like we were all sleepwalking through class," Katrin observed. Not being content to blame her students for this pattern of behavior, Katrin made a shift. "When I began using routines everything changed. Students were given space to make their thinking visible versus merely answering my prompts. The room became energized with conversations. Students' ideas blossomed, new perspectives were revealed, wrestled with, and shared in a multitude of forms. I wish I had done this way earlier in my career," she said. On the other side of the world at Australian Catholic University, Kathy Green experienced the same reaction to the use of thinking routines. After experiencing them, her students asked, "Why aren't our other university classes doing this? It's so much more meaningful and useful."

CHANGING THE ROLE OF THE STUDENT AND TEACHER

In the traditional transmission model of teaching, the roles for students and teachers are well defined. The teacher delivers, often through lectures, PowerPoint slides, or assigned readings, and the student is the receiver, taking in the delivered information. If classes are interactive, they often consist of little more than teachers questioning students to see if they know the material. In this model, "good" students are well prepared, so as not to be caught out by the teacher's questions, whereas so-called "poor" students merely disengage or participate only when required. Unfortunately, this parody is a well-documented reality for far too many students (Lyons 2004; Pianta et al. 2007; Ritchhart 2015; Mehta and Fine 2019).

When teachers embrace the goal of making their students' thinking visible and begin to make use of the associated practices, they begin to see shifts in the roles played by teachers and students. These shifts are small at first but over time have the potential to become seismic. To be sure, when many teachers start using thinking routines they may be merely tacked on to the traditional transmission model of teaching as ways to enliven learning. Even when this happens, teachers still may see glimmers of what's possible. Teachers must then embrace this potential and cultivate it through the regular, thoughtful application of MTV processes. They must adopt not only the practices but also the goal of visible thinking. This necessitates taking a new stance toward teaching, of changing the story of learning one is telling, and reconceptualizing the goals of education.

While teachers whose classrooms are most transformed do not abandon curriculum or preparing students for high-stakes tests, they see their role as teaching beyond the test toward preparing students for a lifetime of learning. The test is only one small marker along the way. Listen to Cameron Paterson: "While I want my students to do well on the tests, I also want them to develop the dispositions they need to thrive in a globalized world full of robots — to be able to think for themselves, create and question." Assuming this stance toward teaching, teachers don't aim to simplify challenging material and make it easier; they explore how to make those ideas accessible. Students' questions excite rather than distract. When they look at the many elements crammed into their courses, they recognize that not all content is equal and so eschew coverage. They know depth of understanding is good preparation for future learning (Schwartz et al. 2009).

When teachers make these mental shifts and adopt new mindsets, the practices of MTV can be transformative, and teachers notice changes in both themselves and their students. Third-grade teacher Mary Beane from Hilton Elementary School in Brighton, Michigan, recognized this transformation happening in both herself and her students. "Making thinking visible and focusing on developing a culture of thinking has taught me how to help children develop a voice for their thinking," Mary reflected. "In a classroom culture where student thinking is valued by all, students organically begin to take initiative in ways I never knew were possible. I now have students suggesting routines to be used to help uncover the complexities of a topic. I am able to step aside so students can sit in a circle together to consider various viewpoints. Shifting our roles has allowed me to observe not just what children know, but how they listen, think, engage, and respond."

Mary has shifted her role from that of deliverer to *orchestrator* who works hard to establish a supportive culture and to create conditions for inquiry and opportunities for meaningful exploration. The dominant voice in the class shifts from that of the teacher to that of the students. Her students are no longer passive receivers of knowledge but active creators, directors, and community members. Recognizing her students' capacity for initiative, Mary has to guard against the teacher tendency to pull in the reins and exert control. Instead, she celebrates this new level of engagement and seeks to promote it, empowering her students and creating a sense of agency.

The idea of agency and initiative resonates with kindergarten teacher Denise Coffin from Sidwell Friends School in Washington, DC. "In making their thinking visible I empower my students. They begin to demonstrate an intention to 'be bigger on the inside' – their words, not mine. This means that their ideas and plans for action can be as valid and as complex as those of their older school peers and adults."

Another way in which MTV changes the role of the teacher is that teachers become students of their students. That is, they become curious about their students' learning, how they are making sense of ideas, what they are thinking, and what ideas engage them. MTV both allows and asks teachers to know their students in a different way. Traditionally, we have known our students by their academic performance and the skills and knowledge they possess. Many school systems rely on end-of-school comprehensive exams to define students through a single reductive score. When we focus on students' thinking, we see them as much more. We become interested in how they come to know what they know, what questions they have, and what challenges they face. We no longer see these challenges as deficits but as interesting opportunities for exploration. This curiosity in our students' thinking further drives our efforts to make their thinking visible as a mechanism for better understanding them and providing more responsive instruction.

ENHANCING OUR FORMATIVE ASSESSMENT PRACTICE

As the education world has learned about the usefulness of feedback and formative assessment to advance learning (Black and Wiliam 2002; Hattie 2009), policy makers and program marketers have sought to embed and formalize the practice of formative assessment in schools. Unfortunately, this has too often taken the form of requiring teachers to design and give set formative assessment tasks. In some instances these tasks must be written down formally, even before the students have started their learning, as part of curricular plans. We have heard teachers announce to students, "This is a formative" before handing out formal, predesignated tasks. Most students hear this announcement as, "This doesn't count." Thus, the task meant to inform teaching and learning becomes meaningless in the eyes of the student and assessment is seen as something done *to* them rather than *with* them. The problem with efforts to formalize formative assessment is that formative assessment is not a task; it is a practice. If you rely on and design formal tasks for the purpose of providing yourself and your students with "a formative assessment," chances are you have a weak formative assessment practice from which your students benefit little.

True formative assessment is the ongoing and embedded effort to understand our students' learning. It is a two-way street actively involving students and teachers in dialog about learning. It doesn't reside in a task and is not the evaluation of one's performance on that task. Formative assessment lives in our listening, observing, examining, analyzing, and reflecting on the process of learning. Even then, our assessment becomes formative only when we use that data to in*form* our teaching and students' learning. Formative assessment then is driven by our curiosity about our students' learning and the desire to make sure our teaching is responsive to their needs as learners.

If we want to know not just what our students know, but how they know it, then we must make their thinking visible. Thus, making students' thinking visible is a formative assessment practice. As Stevens Cooperative School principal Shehla Ghouse explains, "Insights into student thinking provide teachers with invaluable information that can be used to plan next steps for individual students. It also helps us better understand the individual learner and ways in which to reach them more effectively to further their learning."

Speaking about the specific benefits of thinking routines as formative assessment tools, Katrin Robertson identifies their open-ended nature as being particularly useful with her university students. "By asking students to make their thinking visible through a thinking routine (as opposed to a quiz or some other predesigned tool), I not only can collect data about specific areas of their learning that I want to understand, but also am able to reveal students' learning in ways that I had not considered or anticipated." She adds that by providing both sought after and unanticipated information, thinking routines "help me design better learning opportunities that support and extend students' learning in rich and nuanced ways as we move forward in our learning."

In each of the routines shared in Part Two, there is a section on "Assessment." However, you won't find information on how to score or evaluate students' responses to the routine because doing so will quickly send a message that you are looking for a specific answer rather than their thinking. What you will find are general guidelines on what to look for and pay attention to both as you carry out a thinking routine and examine students' responses afterwards based on the thinking the routine is meant to promote. You'll also find suggestions on how to respond if you notice weak or limited responses or if students are struggling.

If you do need or want a summative assessment, we suggest that the thinking routine be used as a vehicle for building understanding, with all the messiness that entails, and then followed up with a more traditional assignment in which students share their understanding. A great example of this is Tom Heilman's use of *Peeling the Fruit* (see page 113). Tom's high school students at Washington International School (WIS) use this routine to work in groups to build their understanding of a poem. Students then write an individual critical commentary of the poem. Tom intervenes, questions, prompts, and supports students' learning as they use the *Peeling the Fruit* routine. This is formative assessment practice in action. He then grades students' critical commentaries based on the case they are able to build about the meaning of the poem based on the evidence from the poem. Thus, students value their time *Peeling the Fruit*, not as an ungraded formative assessment task, but for the opportunity for building understanding it provides (see Tom discussing his use of *Peeling the Fruit* and assessment at https://www.youtube.com/ThePowerOfMakingThinkingVisible).

IMPROVING LEARNING (EVEN WHEN MEASURED BY STANDARDIZED TESTS)

When we first began the Visible Thinking project we had a hard time getting schools in the United States to work with our research project, even for free, because our work wasn't specifically about raising test scores. This was at the height of the "Standards and Accountability" movement in the States. We explained that our project was about getting students to think, engage, and develop understanding, but still we had no takers. Later, when we began sharing the work of the project and the associated thinking routines more broadly, we continued to receive questions about how they related to students' test performance. To be honest, we couldn't answer those questions. We knew that the routines engaged students in their learning, got them to think, and helped them build understanding. We felt this would help them on standardized tests, but we had no evidence. However, in the intervening years we have been able to collect this data.

As third-grade teacher Erik Lindemann notes, "Today's standardized tests include more open-ended problem-solving components requiring more complex analysis. Making thinking visible helps students to understand these questions as well as the types of thinking necessary for completing the tasks. When students have a deep understanding of their own thinking process and how to apply them, they can perform with 'proficiency.'" Because we consider MTV to be a complex set of practices that need time and support to mature, we don't view it as a program one adopts and then evaluates the results. Therefore, to check the effects on students' performance we rely on the data from individual teachers and schools who have embraced MTV as both a goal and a practice and nurtured it at their schools or classrooms through sustained professional learning.

The results have been impressive. In 2010, the English department at Washington International School saw average student subject scores on the International Baccalaureate (IB) Diploma, both Higher Level (HL) and Standard Level (SL), increase significantly over the previous year (see Figure 1.1). These gains were especially dramatic for student in the SL

Figure 1.1 Washington International School's International Baccalaureate (IB) diploma scores on A1 English exams for years 2009–2011.

IB English A1 Higher Level				IB English A1 Standard Level			
Year	N	Average Score	Percentage scoring 7 or 6	Year	N	Average Score	Percentage scoring 7 or 6
2009	29	5.07	24.1%	2009	30	5.20	30.0%
2010	36	5.58	52.8%	2010	29	6.07	79.3%
2011	24	5.54	50.0%	2011	31	6.23	87.1%

English classes where average scores went from 5.2 (on the IB Diploma's 7-point scale) in 2009 to 6.07 in 2010. Furthermore, a full 79.3% of SL students received a top score of a 7 or 6 on their English subject area exams in 2010 compared with just 30% in the previous year. In 2011 scores held steady for students in the HL classes but continued to climb for SL English students, reaching an average score of 6.23 with 87.1% scoring a 6 or 7 and no student scoring below a 5. This was not only a strong uptick in performance but also one that was surprising due to the larger number of learning support students in the 2011 class. Teachers attributed this to the fact the 2011 cohort had experienced three straight years of MTV practices. While English performance was dramatic, other subject areas at WIS saw similar gains. Performance levels have remained fairly consistent over the subsequent eight years.

In Melbourne, Australia, when Nathan Armstrong began working with visible thinking and building a culture of thinking in his senior English classes at Wesley College, he saw the percentage of his students scoring in the top 10% on the Victoria Certificate of Education (VCE) increase 2.5 times, rising from 21% of his students in 2007 to 55% in 2008. This high rate of performance has remained steady over the subsequent years. At St. Philip's Christian College in Newcastle, NSW in Australia, parents even recognized the difference MTV practices were making for students. One parent wrote high school English teacher Judy Anastopoulos the following:

> Dear Judy,
>
> James [a pseudonym] was a below average English student in Year 10 with little ambition to achieve successful results in his HSC [Higher Secondary Certificate]. His application to English with the introduction of a new approach to learning using Thinking Routines has increased his spoken language and confidence but the off shoot of this is the written script that earns him a Band 6 [Highest level of performance] in his HSC for English. My thanks and ever grateful appreciation for my son's progress!!!!!!

St. Leonard's College, in Melbourne, Australia, has worked to build a culture of thinking by employing MTV practices for the past four years. Principal Stuart Davis knows that there is a tendency for schools to celebrate top performing students and to market themselves based on the number of students they can get in the top rank. However, when students are ranked against each other, as they are in Australia, this means only a very small percentage of students in the country can ever reach these levels. The top 1% is limited to just 1% of students in the country each year. Furthermore, by focusing excessively on top performers, schools neglect the vast majority of students they are charged with educating. Stuart believes the best way to assess the difference MTV practices have made is to look at what is happening to median scores (the point at which half the students score above and half below) and at the scores of students in the bottom quartile of the school as opposed to just top performing students. In other words, do MTV practices help lower and average students? At St. Leonard's, the median ATAR scores (Australian Tertiary Admission Rank representing a percentile ranking of all grade 12 students in Australia) have climbed steadily each year: 2015 = 81.55, 2016 = 85.58, 2017 = 87.4, and 2018 = 90.5. As have those for the lower quartile of students at the school: 2015 = 68.92, 2016 = 73.06, 2017 = 76.97, and 2018 = 78.24.

At the middle school level, the Intellectual Virtues Academy in Long Beach, California, a school that has made thinking routines a core since its founding in 2013, topped their district's performance on the 2015 Smarter Balanced Assessment (the first year of such testing) in both math and reading and dramatically outperformed state averages. The Mandela International Magnet School (MIMS) in Santa Fe, New Mexico, was founded in 2014 as a nonselective middle school magnet using the IB Middle Years Program. The school would eventually grow to include students in grades 7–12. We have worked with this school since its inception under a grant from the Melville Hankins Family Foundation. During the three years New Mexico administered the Partnership for Assessment of Readiness for College and Careers (PARCC) exam consistently, MIMS scores steadily rose in eighth-grade English with proficiency rates of 46% in 2016 (27% for Hispanic students), 60% in 2017 (41% for Hispanic), and 67% in 2018 (59% for Hispanic). In eighth-grade math, the scores have not been as consistent at 44% in 2016, 39% in 2017, and 49% in 2018. However, the scores do show long-term growth and are extremely strong when compared to the district average of 17% for this time period. It is also instructive to look at a cohort of students progressing through the school to see what happens to their proficiency levels over time. When following the 2016 seventh graders as a cohort, their English level proficiency rates as a whole went from 46% in 2016, to 67% in 2017, to 77% in 2018. Considering just Hispanic students in this cohort, scores went from 24% in 2016, to 41% in 2017, to 56% in 2018.

In 2010, Way Elementary in Bloomfield Hills, Michigan, saw students' performance on the new state writing assessment far outpace district peers who were using the same writing program with 82% of their students scoring proficient or above versus 66% in the district as a whole. The only difference was that Way was dedicated to being a "Visible Thinking" school starting in 2008. As a new assessment there are no data on prior years, but the comparative data between Way Elementary and schools having a similar student population in the district and using the same writing program provides a good quasi-experimental comparison. Likewise, Bemis Elementary in Troy, Michigan, had reached a rate of 85% proficient or above in English language arts in 2010 and saw that increase to 98% in 2013 by having visible thinking a regular part of their practice. Bemis also saw a dramatic increase in students scoring at the *advanced* level in mathematics with initial performance of 28% in 2010, 37% in 2011, 49% in 2012, to 50% in 2013.

These examples could be dismissed as nonevaluative and not rigorous as it is not an experimental research context (a rare occurrence in educational research). There is no way based on these data to measure what level of effect size one is likely to get if one "implements" MTV practices. Nor is it possible to see how it stacks up against more straightforward interventions or single-focused programs. Furthermore, we recognize that there are confounding variables in that these schools had a clear purpose and vision and were guided by strong leadership, which we know affects students' learning. What we think the data do tell us is that efforts to make thinking visible can, in the right hands and pursued over time, greatly enhance students' performance – even on standardized tests.

This is not surprising. When students are more cognitively engaged, we know that performance goes up (Newmann et al. 1992; Shernoff 2013). A recent study by physics professors at Harvard found students learned more from active learning methods than from more direct, passive lectures (Deslauriers et al. 2019), despite students feeling that they learned better from lectures. When students understand material deeply, they tend to recall it more easily, are better at transferring it to new contexts, and perform better in problem-solving situations (Newmann et al. 1996, 2001). And when students are engaged in thinking, their understanding increases. Therefore, we shouldn't be too skeptical that such efforts, even when not designed as a program to implement, would have an effect on students' performance. As Cameron Paterson states, "When I make students' thinking visible, it becomes shared, so it is 'our' thinking, bounced off each other, rather than locked inside their heads. This process of publicly sharing thinking builds our collective understanding. We all learn more AND they do well on the tests." Furthermore, we have never seen scores decline when schools or teachers embrace visible thinking. This is consistent with other efforts to engage students deeply in learning (Claxton et al. 2011).

For those interested in experimental data in which the use of thinking routines is used as a treatment to compare with the performance of a control group, a recent quantitative study by Yerko Sepulveda and Juan I. Venegas-Muggli at the Universidad Tecnológica de Chile INACAP is instructive (Sepulveda and Venegas-Muggli 2019). They studied 883 business school students taking a core Cost and Budgeting course (using the same syllabus, quizzes, and exams) distributed across 32 different course sections and three different campuses. The 152 students who were taught using thinking routines (five different routines were regularly used) achieved a final exam grade that was on average 1.3 points higher (on a 1–7 scale) than their peers taught using traditional methods identified in two separate control groups.

A related question we are sometimes asked about visible thinking is: What is the empirical evidence for their effectiveness? Although it may seem that this question is the same as the one about test scores, empirical evidence and experimental evidence are not necessarily the same. Empirical evidence has to do with what can be observed or verified from experience. The empirical evidence for MTV is accessible to all. When you use a thinking routine you can answer for yourself: How did this change students' engagement? Are students building understanding? How did the routine facilitate their exploration of the topic? Did students go deeper than with the more traditional approach I have used? What you see in the moment, from debriefing with students, and from your analysis of and reflections on students' work afterward, constitutes your own empirical evidence and should be valued. We shouldn't let test scores be the only story that is told of our schools and classrooms. It is time we provide much more robust evidence of learning to parents, students, and the community.

Although we have not focused on MTV practices as a means of raising test scores does not mean we have not done research on their effects. Since we designed routines to develop students' ability to think, this is what we evaluated in our earlier research. We found that regular use of MTV practices had a dramatic effect on the development of students' meta-strategic knowledge, that is students' awareness of the strategies they had at their disposal. One's meta-strategic knowledge is a key factor in one's ability to direct one's thinking and tell oneself what to do as a thinker. Thus, MTV practices facilitate students' development as thinkers and learners. See Ritchhart et al. (2009) for a full explanation of this research.

DEVELOPING THINKING DISPOSITIONS

The main goal of the Visible Thinking project was to develop students as thinkers and learners by cultivating their dispositions toward thinking. A disposition captures one's personal patterns of interaction with the world. Our dispositions are a part of our character. Our thinking dispositions reflect who we are as thinkers and learners. Of course, a disposition goes beyond merely having the skill or ability – it implies that an individual also is *inclined* to use those abilities, is *aware* of and sensitive to occasions for the use of those abilities, and is *motivated* in the moment to deploy the skills (Ritchhart 2002). Thus ability, inclination, awareness, and motivation must all be present for us to say one has a particular disposition.

When teachers use thinking routines, they help students develop their ability to think, building up a repertoire of thinking moves. This process is further enhanced when we explicitly name the thinking and cue it up in our introduction of a routine as a thinking tool meant to serve a purpose. By having the Understanding Map (see Figure 2.1) posted in the classroom or in student notebooks for easy reference, students have a repertoire of thinking moves at their disposal. Fifth-grade teacher Sandra Hahn from the International School of Bangkok remarked, "My fifth graders became quite expert in identifying the thinking moves they used and describing how it was used to help them find a solution to our weekly maths problem. Some went even further to create a personal question prompt they could use in another situation to access that thinking move."

When we make thinking visible as a regular part of the classroom through our use of thinking routines, documentation, questioning, and listening, we send a message to students that thinking is valued. It is infused in everything we do and becomes part of the fabric of the classroom. Students come to see the value in their thinking and become more inclined toward thinking as an important part of their learning rather than as an occasional add-on. This changes who they are as learners.

Bemis Elementary in Troy, Michigan, has a long history of using MTV practices. They have embraced both the goal and the practices widely across the school. Over the years, fifth-grade teacher Kim Smiley has observed the difference this has made. "As students bring more years of thinking routine experience with them, they are internalizing these routines. As a result, the way they approach conversations, and the language they use has changed. They talk about their thinking easily and effortlessly." Similarly, Denise Coffin has seen how regular effort to make thinking visible changes her kindergarten students. "Over the years, I have noticed that my learners take all of this with them when they leave kindergarten. The thinking continues to deepen and the routine becomes an innate habit or disposition. I see my learners take this newly formed learning identity, routines and all, to other disciplines and even to interactions with their families."

When it comes to dispositional development, our research has shown that often the biggest impediment to realizing a disposition is the failure of individuals to spot occasions for deploying their skills (Perkins et al. 2000). People often have the ability to think yet fail to identify those instances when they should deploy those abilities. In schools, the development of awareness can be problematic as teachers often tell students exactly when and where to deploy their skills. To develop awareness, teachers have to step back and allow students to step forward to make more of these decisions. Of course, if students fail to spot the opportunity, we can step in but doing so before students have had the chance to identify the occasion robs them of the opportunity for dispositional development.

University of Michigan lecturer Katrin Robertson began to see this awareness developing in her students. "Once students had internalized the structures of a variety of routines, they began suggesting which routine they wanted to use so that *their* thinking was the center of our learning and not mine. It was exciting to see them take the lead and make these choices for themselves rather than me being the one to plan all of the instruction." At the other end of the learning spectrum, kindergarten teacher Jennifer LaTarte from Bemis Elementary recognized that she needed to hand more control to her students to allow for their dispositional development. "By giving students a voice you send the message that their ideas and thinking are relevant to the learning that takes place and they begin to naturally take agency over their learning if we hand them the baton."

CONCLUSION

Based on the power of MTV practices we have articulated here, one might assume that we have identified a magic bullet to cure the ills of schools, lessen the burden of teachers, and dramatically increase students' learning. Sadly, this is not the case. What we have tried to do in this chapter is to show where the use of MTV practices might take you, your students, and your school. The six powers articulated here are based on our research in classrooms where teachers have been engaged deeply with MTV practices over time, in sustained ways, and with the support of their colleagues. It is only through such ongoing efforts that one is likely to realize any one of these powers, let alone all six. Teaching and learning are complex tasks and we must respect that complexity. There are no quick fixes in teaching, only meaningful efforts to create the conditions for learning. MTV practices exist as part of those important efforts.

Knowing what is possible and understanding the potential of MTV practices helps to avoid the biggest pitfall we have seen in the implementation of thinking routines: that they are just activities used to break up the monotony of school. As you read more about the practices in the coming chapters and work your way through the new thinking routines we share in the upcoming chapters, remember the potential we have laid out here. As you integrate these practices into your teaching, think about these six powers as forming a theory of action by which you can judge your success (City et al. 2009). A theory of action ties together teaching actions with expected outcomes emerging from the actions. Having an articulated theory of action, either for oneself or as a whole school, helps us to avoid the implementation trap in which we merely implement a set of practices and hope for the best. Theories of action provide us with the touchstones we need to evaluate our efforts.

What might it mean to use the six powers articulated here as a theory of action? One possibility is: *If* I/we use MTV practices to actively engage our students with each other, with ideas, and in action, *then* student will experience deep learning, be more engaged in their learning, assume more active roles in their learning, develop as thinkers and learners, and improve in learning outcomes. At the same time, we as teachers will become better listeners, learn to encourage student initiative, and gain new insights into our students' learning that helps us to plan responsive instruction. A theory of action need not include all six powers as we have done here. You might want to focus on one or two of the powers specifically for a period and then expand. We encourage you to craft your theory of action, drawing on the six powers, and to revisit it often throughout your efforts to use the MTV practices shared here. If you are finding that over time your sustained efforts and actions aren't leading to the expected outcomes, reflect with colleagues about why this might be happening. You'll find helpful troubleshooting suggestions throughout the book both with regard to individual routines and more generally about MTV practices. Revisit these as you work with MTV practices to guide your reflections.

CHAPTER 2

Making Thinking Visible

A Goal and Set of Practices

Making thinking visible is not a program, an intervention, or even a framework. Sometimes we have referred to it as an approach to help cast it as a wider enterprise that cannot simply be pulled off the shelf and implemented. We have come to feel that making thinking visible is best understood as both a broad goal of teaching as well as a set of practices for supporting that goal. Let us explore both.

MAKING THINKING VISIBLE AS A GOAL OF TEACHING

If we believe that learning is a consequence of thinking (Perkins 1992), then we want not only to get our students to think but also to understand that thinking process as it is unfolding so that we can support it, prompt it, and grow it. When we make thinking visible, it not only gives us a window into *what* our students understand, the product of their thinking, but also into *how* they are understanding it, the process of their thinking. Of course, uncovering students' thinking is as likely to give us evidence of students' insights as it is to reveal their misconceptions.

Teaching is not telling, and the delivery of content at a preprogrammed pace does not engender deep learning. Learning happens when students engage with ideas, when they ask questions, explore, and construct meaning with our guidance and support. Therefore, we need to make thinking visible because it provides us with the information we need to plan opportunities that will take students' learning to the next level and enable continued engagement with the ideas being explored. It is only when we understand what our students are thinking, feeling, and attending to that we can use that knowledge to further engage and support them in the process of understanding. Thus, making students' thinking visible becomes an ongoing component of effective, responsive teaching.

Making students' thinking visible serves a broader educational purpose as well, a purpose that goes beyond content to focus on the question: Who are our students becoming as thinkers and learners as a result of their time with us? This question speaks to a purpose of education beyond the test to a lifetime of learning, engagement, and action. It speaks to the very notion of identity. To develop this identity as a thinker and learner we need to demystify the thinking process and make it visible. When we do this we provide models for students of what it means to engage with ideas, to think, and to learn. In doing so, we dispel the myth that learning is just a matter of committing information in the textbook to memory. School no longer is about the "quick right answer" but about the ongoing mental work of understanding new ideas and information. In their seminal 1991 paper, Collins, Brown, and Holum tied the idea of making thinking visible to cognitive apprenticeship (Collins et al. 1991). They suggested that deep learning and mastery of a domain arises not merely from the acquisition of knowledge but rather from learning to think as people in that particular field think. This is accomplished when mentors share the processes of their thinking with apprentices in such a way that the process of thinking becomes a core piece of the learning.

Vygotsky (1978), writing about the importance of the sociocultural context of learning in providing models, stated, "Children grow into the intellectual life of those around them." This is one of our favorite quotes because it provides a powerful metaphor for what it means to educate. With what kind of intellectual life are we surrounding our students? Is it hardy, inspiring, and complex? How are we fostering their growth into intellectual life? What are our students learning about learning in our classrooms? How are we apprenticing them in the processes of thinking, learning, problem solving, designing, debating, and citizenship? How can we move beyond merely imparting knowledge and passing along tips for how to achieve high marks on external exams so that we are prepping students, not for tests, but for life?

MAKING THINKING VISIBLE AS A SET OF PRACTICES

Thinking is an internal process, something that happens in the workings of the individual mind. As such, it can seem mysterious and inaccessible – hence the need to make it visible. We use the term "visible" here not just to represent what can be seen with the eye but also what we can perceive, notice, and identify. When we make thinking visible it becomes apparent to all, teachers as well as students. It then becomes something that then can be analyzed, probed, challenged, encouraged, and advanced. Four practices are used to make thinking visible:

- Questioning
- Listening
- Documentation
- Thinking routines

Although each can be discussed, examined, and reflected upon separately, in reality they exist as integrative practices that enhance and complement one another.

Questioning

Questions not only drive thinking and learning, they are also outcomes of it. As we engage with new ideas and develop our understanding new questions emerge. Voltaire famously said to "Judge a man [sic] by his questions rather than by his answers" as they are likely to reveal a person's real depth of understanding as well as their engagement with the issue. The central role of questions is evident in almost all thinking routines. Many routines, such as *Beauty & Truth*, the *3 Y's*, the *4 If's* and *What? So What? Now What?* have specific questions embedded within them. These questions can help drive the thinking and learning. Other routines, like *Peeling the Fruit*, *ESP+I*, *Leaderless Discussion*, and *SAIL*, make the asking of original questions central. These questions allow students to be the drivers of their own learning and reveal their curiosity as well as their understanding in the manner in which Voltaire identified. We even have a routine for dealing with questions themselves, *Question Sorts*, which helps students to ask good questions to shape inquiry.

Beyond this embedded nature of questions within routines, we have found that one cannot be effective in making thinking visible without asking what we call facilitative questions. These probe students' responses, demonstrate our interest in their thinking, and provide the opportunity to go deeper. Our favorite facilitative question is: "*What makes you say that?*" We even presented this question as its own routine in our first book, abbreviating it as WMYST? Teachers have called it "the magic question" because of the way it unlocks students' thinking, often revealing unexpected thinking behind an answer. Teachers have remarked that through their regular use of WMYST? they learn so much more and have much deeper conversations with their students, friends, and family. We have found that the wording of this question seems to strike just the right tone with people and invites them to elaborate on and clarify their ideas in a nonthreatening way. Of course, questions like, "Tell me why?" or "What's your reason for that?" are also facilitative and serve the same role. They push for a fuller explanation, but depending on the tone and delivery may not communicate the same level of curiosity and interest as does WMYST?

In using facilitative questions, the teacher's goal is to understand the student's thinking, to get inside their heads and make their thinking visible. Thus, we switch the paradigm of teaching *from* trying to transmit what is in our heads to our students *to* trying to get what is in students' heads into our own. Research has shown that the majority of teachers' questions in traditional classrooms are review questions (Goodlad 1983; Boaler and Brodie 2004; Ritchhart 2015). These sound like a mini-quiz and tend to emphasize the recall of knowledge. However, our research has shown that when teaches embrace the goal of making thinking visible, the majority of questions they ask are facilitative in nature. When one is more curious about the thinking and less interested in hearing correct answers, this shift is natural. Teacher researcher Jim Minstrell even coined a term for this pattern of questioning, calling it the "reflective toss" (Van Zee and Minstrell 1997). In the reflective toss, the teacher's first goal is to try to "catch" students' meaning and understand their comments. If meaning can't be grasped immediately, then a follow-up question such as, "Can you say more about that?" or "I'm not quite following you, can you say what you were thinking in a different way?" is asked. Once the meaning is grasped by the teacher, then the teacher "tosses" back a question that will push the student to further elaborate and justify their thinking, both to the teacher and to themselves: "What does that tell you then?" "What do you think you were basing that on?" or again our favorite, "*What makes you say that?*"

Listening

Of course, there is no reason to ask good questions if one is not listening for the answers. It is through our listening that we provide the opening for students to make their thinking visible to us. It is only when students know that we are truly interested in their thinking that they have a reason to share it with us. Thus, listening is not only a practice in which we teachers must engage, it is also a stance we must assume in the classroom. This stance is reflected well in the Reggio Emilia's "pedagogy of listening." These educators feel that listening must be the basis of the learning relationship that teachers seek to form with students. Within such a learning context, "individuals feel legitimated to represent their theories and offer their own interpretations of a particular question" (Giudici et al. 2001). As the feminist poet Alice Duer Miller observed, "Listening is not merely not talking," it is "taking a vigorous, human interest in what is being told us." This vigorous, human interest allows us to build community in the classroom and develop interactions that pivot around the exploration of ideas.

Researchers English, Hintz, and Tyson (English et al. 2018) refer to this vigorous interest as "empathetic listening" in which teachers listen "to and for the learner's own understandings, feelings, and perspectives around an idea or situation, while actively setting aside one's own interests, needs, perspectives, and judgments." The intent of this kind of listening is to understand the learner's perspective and personal sense making. It resonates with Jim Minstrell's efforts to "catch" students' meaning. As we listen in this way, we may find ourselves reflecting on our understandings of the topic being discussed, and our students' thinking may change our own perspective.

This is not the only reason for listening, however, particularly in educational settings. English, Hintz, and Tyson also identify "educative listening" in which we listen for and attend to the struggles, challenges, and confusions of learners. Here we must strive to identify when a student's challenge can lead to a productive struggle with the ideas and eventually yield new insights for that student versus when the challenge is overwhelming and likely to cause a student to shut down. There is also "generative listening" in which we listen for ways students' thinking and ideas might generate new opportunities for exploration or expand our goals.

Documentation

The processes of thinking and learning can be elusive and ephemeral. Documentation is the effort to capture this process in as much richness as possible. But where does thinking reside? Is it in the answers students give us? The finished work they offer? Although these artifacts may contain residues of thinking, too often thinking and learning are obscured in the effort to get good marks and produce correct answers. We are more likely to find thinking in the messy process of working through ideas over time as we are in the final product. When we can capture this process it provides us with a vehicle for analysis of and reflection on the thinking.

Our Project Zero colleagues, Mara Krechevsky, Terri Turner, Ben Mardell, and Steve Seidel, have spent decades investigating how documentation supports students' learning and teacher growth. They define documentation "as the practice of observing, recording, interpreting, and sharing, through a variety of media, the processes and products of teaching and learning in order to deepen learning" (Given et al. 2010). Embedded in this definition is the idea that documentation must serve to advance learning, not merely capture it. As such, documentation includes not only what is collected but also the analysis, interpretations, and reflections of the thinking and learning that took place. In this way, documentation both connects to the act of listening and extends it. To capture and record students' thinking, teachers must be vigilant observers and listeners. When teachers capture students' ideas, they are signaling that those ideas and thoughts have value and are worthy of continued exploration and examination.

Documentation of students' thinking also provides a stage from which students may observe their own learning process, make note of the strategies being used, and comment on the developing understanding. The visibility afforded by documentation provides the basis for reflecting on one's learning and for considering that learning as an object for discussion. In this way, documentation demystifies the learning process both for the individual as well as the group, building greater metacognitive awareness in the process. For teachers, this reflection on students' learning functions as assessment in the truest sense of the word because documentation illuminates students' learning and understanding. To uncover this richness, we often need more sets of eyes than ours alone. Sharing documentation with colleagues can lead to meaningful discussions of learning and allow us to notice aspects of students' thinking and implications for instructions that we might easily miss when working on our own.

Just as questioning and listening are integral parts of using thinking routines, so is documentation. Sometimes students will self-document through their written work done as either individuals or groups. This becomes a vehicle for sharing thinking with others, not as proof that one was "on task" but as an artifact for others to examine and comment upon. Other times, teachers will need to document to capture students' thinking. An important guiding question in such instances is to ask, "What do I want to capture so that we as a class can return to it later for more careful examination and analysis?"

Thinking Routines

Thinking routines are a central practice for making thinking visible. They operate as *tools* to prompt and promote thinking, as *structures* that reveal and scaffold thinking, and through their use over time routines become *patterns* of behavior. We have found that in learning to use thinking routines effectively, it is useful to understand each of these three levels: tools, structures, and patterns. Although in the following discussion we present each as distinct, it is important to recognize that thinking routines operate on these three levels simultaneously. Even as we attend to the tool-like aspect of a thinking routine, we recognize it is also helping to structure and scaffold the thinking. At the same time, the routine is slowly becoming a pattern of behavior.

Tools.   As teachers we must first identify what kind of thinking we are trying to elicit from our students and then select the particular thinking routine as the tool for that job. Like any tool, it is important to choose the right one for the job. If a hammer is needed, a saw feels awkward and doesn't work very well. So what kind of thinking tools do we need? In what kinds of thinking do we want to support our students? If thinking routines are tools, what's in the toolkit?

Because the goal of developing understanding is of central importance to schools committed to deep learning, the thinking that will lead to understanding is particularly relevant. Therefore, most thinking routines are designed with this goal in mind. What thinking leads to understanding? As part of the Visible Thinking and Creating Cultures of Thinking projects, we identified eight specific thinking moves that seemed necessary for building understanding. If any one of these thinking moves were left out of the process, there would likely be significant gaps in understanding or it would be much more difficult to build a robust understanding of the topic. These eight thinking moves include: observing closely and describing what is there, building explanations and interpretations, reasoning with evidence, making connections, considering different viewpoints and perspectives, capturing the heart and forming conclusions, wondering and asking questions, and uncovering complexity and going below the surface of things. Taken together, these eight moves form what we refer to as the Understanding Map (see Figure 2.1).

Figure 2.1 Understanding map.

Observing Closely & Describing What's There
What do you see and notice?

Wondering & Asking Questions
What's puzzling about this?

Making Connections
How does this fit with what you already know?

Considering Different Viewpoints
What's another angle on this?

Building Explanations & Interpretations
What's really going on here?

Reasoning with Evidence
What are you basing that on?

Uncovering Complexity & Going Deeply
What lies beneath the surface?

Capturing the Heart & Forming Conclusions
What's at the core or center?

HOW DO WE BUILD UNDERSTANDING?

By specifying the kinds of thinking necessary for building understanding, the Understanding Map has proven very useful to both teachers and students. It can be used to identify a type of thinking needed to help students engage with a particular piece of content. Once identified, one can select an appropriate thinking routine for promoting that type of thinking. Thus, the routine becomes a tool to accomplish a goal. This is important in the way we introduce routines to students. Rather than announcing, "Today we are going to do the *Making Meaning* routine," which names an activity, one announces the purpose of the lesson and the types of thinking one is trying to activate and then presents the routine as a tool for accomplishing that purpose: "Today we want to pull all of our learning together, make connections, build off of others ideas, and raise some additional questions. The tool we are going to use to help us do that is the *Making Meaning* routine."

The Understanding Map can also serve as a useful planning tool to help teachers plan for understanding throughout a unit. Although one wouldn't typically plan to engage students in all eight thinking moves in a single lesson, over the course of a unit a teacher can easily ensure that students have engaged in each of the eight thinking moves. Likewise, students seeking to develop their own understanding can apply the various thinking moves themselves. For too many students the process of building understanding is a mystery. As a result, they continually seek to apply the tools they have for memorizing knowledge to the endeavor of constructing understanding – not surprisingly without much success. The understanding map demystifies the process of building understanding.

Structures. The thinking routines we have developed have been carefully crafted to support and structure students' thinking. In many instances, the steps of the routine act as natural scaffolds that can lead students' thinking to more sophisticated levels. For instance, in developing the *Making Meaning* routine, we sought to carefully sequence and scaffold a process of collective meaning making in which each step builds on the preceding one. Identifying key ideas related to a concept lays a foundation for elaboration, which then creates a robust assortment of ideas that can be connected, and from which new questions might emerge. Finally, to synthesize and pull this process together, we ask students to capture the heart of the process and write a definition of the concept being explored. Thus, the steps of the routine provide a natural progression in which each stage builds on and extends the thinking of the previous one.

In using thinking routines the goal is never simply to complete one step and move on to the next, but to use the thinking occurring at each step in the subsequent steps. This sequential aspect can be helpful as you begin trying out the routines in your classroom. Think about how you will use students' responses and connect them to the next step, constantly looking for how good thinking at one stage sets up good thinking in the next stage.

In addition to scaffolding students' thinking, routines also provide structures for the discussion of ideas being explored. Sometimes, teachers struggle with how to support students having worthwhile and meaningful discussions on their own. Such discussions may be inhibited due to a lack of listening or by an over focus on work completion. If students feel that the group's job is to fill out the worksheet, then they focus their attention on the worksheet rather than the discussion. Having a process or structure to guide a group's discussion can be highly beneficial. However, too often we ask students to discuss ideas without providing them a structure for effectively doing so. The routines featured in Chapter 3 in particular are designed as structures for interaction and discussion.

Finally, it is important to recognize that all thinking routines presented here have been designed as structures to make thinking visible. Although that may seem self-evident, it is an important tool for judging the success of any routine. Don't judge your success with how smoothly the lesson went. This improves with time. Judge your success by what is revealed about your students' thinking. The question we need to be asking ourselves as teachers after using a thinking routine is: "What have I learned about my students' thinking as a result of doing this routine?" If you can't answer that question then several things might be going on:

- A focus on correctness over thinking
- Approaching the task as work rather than an opportunity to explore
- Weak content that provides few opportunities for thinking
- A need for models of what thinking might look like in this instance

Let's examine these in more depth and think about how each might be moderated. Students might have not given you their thinking because they thought you were looking for a correct answer. The only way to combat this is to clearly show an interest in and valuing of students' thinking over their correctness. Teachers have a long history of validating correctness and so students often assume this is what we are seeking. Another reason for weak responses could be that students may have approached the task as work to be done and so provided answers simply to fill in the sheet or get things completed. To combat this we must clearly situate the use of any thinking routine as a chance to explore and make sense. The task has to be given purpose as was discussed earlier. A third culprit leading to weak responses is that the content itself was not very rich. Thinking routines are always a marriage between content and the structure of the routine used to explore that content. If the content itself isn't robust and complex, it is doubtful the thinking will be either. Finally, students might be unsure of what kind of response is appropriate. In other words they may lack models of what a response might look like. A natural tendency might be to think one needs to provide models at the outset. However, doing so can result in a plethora of imitative responses. What works best is simply to consider the first use of a routine as the opportunity to provide models. Make sure students have a chance to share and see one another's response. Ask them to identify what they noticed about responses that really revealed a person's thinking. Remind them of these qualities the next time the routine is used.

Patterns of Behavior. Thinking routines must be understood within the broader notion of classroom routines as culture builders. Our instruction takes place within a context, and routines contribute to the establishment of that context through the creation of socially shared, scripted slices of behavior (Yinger 1979; Leinhardt and Steele 2005). Effective teachers of thinking address the development of students' thinking in this way, by developing a set of routines that they and their students can use over and over again (Ritchhart 2002). Students are able to use the routines as "shared scripts" with increasing independence. The true power of thinking routines is only fully realized when they become patterns of behavior for students and teachers. When routines pass from effective one-off activities into the realm of "This is how we do things here," the transformation of students as learners begins. Of course this takes time.

Although the word, "routine," may conjure up images of rigidness, what we see in the classrooms we study is that with use, and over time, thinking routines become flexible rather than rigid, continuously evolving. We observe teachers constantly adapting thinking routines to better serve the learning at hand. One element of one routine may be combined with an element of another to create a unique hybrid that serves the needs of the moment. This is possible because over time it is the *thinking* itself that becomes a *routine* part of students' engagement with content.

When thinking routines are used regularly and become part of the pattern of the classroom, students internalize messages about what learning is and how it happens. Thinking routines and efforts to make thinking visible are not simply practices that one tacks on to the existing grammar of schools to freshen it up a bit. Rather, they are transformative practices that have the power to change the way we approach teaching and students approach learning. Through their effective and regular use, thinking routines help to craft a new story of school by sending the message that learning is not a process of simply absorbing others' ideas, thoughts, or practices but deep learning involves uncovering one's own ideas as the starting point for learning and connecting new ideas to one's own thinking. Questions become not something a teacher asks to test your knowledge, but as drivers of learning and inquiry.

ORGANIZING THINKING ROUTINES

There are many ways to organize and present a collection of thinking routines. In *Making Thinking Visible* (2011), we grouped the routines from those that tend to be used early in a unit, to those that come in the middle, and those that often serve a more culminating function. This reflected the way we often saw teachers using the routines in their planning. Originally the Visible Thinking team organized routines around four key thinking ideals: understanding, truth, fairness, and creativity. At various times and in assorted places, researchers at Project Zero have organized the routines around specific goals of instruction such as developing global competence, enhancing memory, exploring complexity, supporting maker learning, or fostering transfer. Many teachers have formulated their own organizational frames that match their particular needs.

In developing the collection of routines presented in this book, "engagement" was a recurring theme. We had particular thinking routines that worked well for engaging students with one another in active discussion, exploration, or giving feedback (Chapter 3). We also noticed that some our new thinking routines specifically centered on building understanding and engaging with ideas (Chapter 4). Finally, a new focus for our work was that as we began to think about empowering students to take an active role in the world, we found we were developing routines that supported engaging in action (Chapter 5). Consequently, we choose this as our organizational framework for this book (see Figure 2.2). This is not meant to be limiting in any way, and you will certainly find routines that easily fit in more than one category and can be used for diverse purposes.

As you read through the collection of routines presented in Part Two, think broadly about how you might use any particular routine. Even though we tried to capture a diverse range of examples, you still may not find an example in the "Uses and Variations" or "Picture of Practice" that matches your own content area or grade level. Take inspiration from the examples offered but think beyond to explore new possibilities. And don't wait to get started! If you have ideas for using a thinking routine as you read, put it into practice as soon as you can. This is the best way to learn the routine and explore its possibilities.

Figure 2.2 Thinking routines matrix.

Routine	Key Thinking Moves	Notes
Routines for ENGAGING with OTHERS		
Give One Get One	Brainstorming, explanation, sorting, and classifying	Use for idea generation and sharing. Gets students moving, talking, and explaining.
Ladder of Feedback	Looking closely, analysis, and feedback	Structure for giving oral or written feedback. Can be used by teachers and students.
Leaderless Discussion	Questioning, probing, and listening	Use with text to help students take ownership of discussion and learn to ask good questions.
SAIL: Speak-Ask-Ideas-Learned	Explanation, questioning, exploring possibilities, and design thinking	Use to share a rough prototype, plan or draft to further clarify, plan, and generate new ideas.
Making Meaning	Making connections, exploring complexity, and raising questions	Use to define a topic/concept. Yields a definition.
+ 1	Memory, connections, and synthesis	Alternative note-taking method focused on using memory and improving other's notes.
Routines for ENGAGING with IDEAS		
Question Sorts	Questioning and inquiry	Use to identify questions for inquiry and learning to ask better questions.
Peeling the Fruit	Noticing, wondering, explaining, connecting, perspectives, and distilling	Use to structure exploration of a topic to build understanding. Can be an evolving document.
The Story Routine: Main-Side-Hidden	Perspective, complexity, connections, analysis, and wondering	Use with visuals to explore different "stories" or as a structure for analysis and going deeper.
Beauty & Truth	Noticing, complexity, explanations, and capturing the heart	Use with visuals or stories to identify where beauty and truth reside and how they intersect.
NDA: Name-Describe-Act	Looking closely, noticing, and memory	Use with a visual to focus on noticing and describing while building working memory.
Take Note	Synthesis, questioning, and capturing the heart	Use as an exit ticket strategy or to encourage discussion of a topic after presenting information.

Routine	Key Thinking Moves	Notes
Routines for ENGAGING in ACTION		
PG&E: Predict-Gather-Explain	Reasoning with evidence, analysis, explanations, and prediction	Use within the context of experimentation or inquiry.
ESP+I	Questioning, capturing the heart, expectations, and analysis	Use to distill and reflect on an experience or problem-based situation.
Be-Sure-to	Analysis, planning, explanations, and connections	Use to help students analyze exemplars to identify personal or group goals and actions.
What? So What? Now What?	Capturing the heart, explanations, and implications	Use for taking stock, identifying the meaning of actions, and planning future actions.
3 Y's	Connections, perspective taking, and complexities	Use with an issue or problem to explore how it affects different groups from self to the world.
4 If's	Connections, perspective taking, and complexities	Use with an issue or problem to explore possible actions that might be taken.

PART TWO

EIGHTEEN POWERFUL ROUTINES

CHAPTER 3

Routines for Engaging with Others

Figure 3.1 Routines for Engaging with Others matrix.

Routines for ENGAGING with OTHERS			
Routine	Thinking	Notes	Teaching Examples
Give One Get One	Brainstorming, explanation, sorting, and classifying	Use for idea generation and sharing. Gets students moving, talking, and explaining.	• 1st Grade, Design/PBL. Ashley Falls Elementary, Del Mar, California • 12th Grade, English. Penleigh and Essendon Grammar School, Melbourne, Australia • 3rd Grade, Social Studies. Chadwick International, Seoul, Korea
Ladder of Feedback	Looking closely, analysis, and feedback	Structure for giving oral or written feedback. Can be used by teachers and students.	• 3rd-5th Grade, Student-Led Conference. International School of Luxembourg • 11th Grade, Physics. Quaker Valley High School, Leetsdale, Pennsylvania • 5th Grade, Writing. Village School, Marblehead, Massachusetts • Kindergarten, Art. Sidwell Friends School, Washington DC
Leaderless Discussion	Questioning, probing, and listening	Use with text to help students take ownership of discussion and learn to ask good questions.	• High School, Psychology. American International School of Chennai, India • High School, Literature. Mandela International Magnet School in Santa Fe, New Mexico
SAIL: Speak-Ask-Ideas-Learned	Explanation, questioning, exploring possibilities, and design thinking	Use to share a rough prototype, plan or draft to further clarify plan and generate new ideas.	• 12th grade, Action Research Projects. University Liggett School, Grosse Pointe Woods, Michigan • 8th Grade, Music. Penleigh and Essendon Grammar School, Melbourne, Australia • 2nd Grade, Design/PBL. University Liggett School, Grosse Pointe Woods, Michigan
Making Meaning	Making connections, exploring complexity, and raising questions	Use to define a topic/concept. Yields a definition.	• 3rd Grade, Social Emotional Learning. Parkview Elementary, Novi, Michigan • High School, Special Education. Rochester High School, Rochester, Michigan • 9th & 10th Grade, Computer Science. Atlanta International School, Atlanta, Georgia
+ 1	Memory, connections, and synthesis	Alternative note-taking method focused on using memory and improving other's notes.	• High School, Mathematics. International Academy, Troy, Michigan • 5th Grade, Social Studies. Bemis Elementary School, Troy, Michigan • 7th Grade, Visual Arts. American Community School, Abu Dhabi, UAE

GIVE ONE GET ONE

> ➤ Teacher poses a question or offers a topic for exploration and students individually generate several responses.
>
> ➤ Teacher describes what students will explain or discuss when they share ideas with each other.
>
> ➤ Teacher establishes a goal in terms of the number of ideas to collect or a designated time in which to collect ideas.
>
> ➤ Students stand up, connect with a peer, and listen to one another's initial responses. Each student then "gives" a new idea for their partner's initial list, elaborating the importance of this addition.
>
> ➤ Students find a new partner and repeat the process for the preset number of times or the predetermined length of time.
>
> ➤ Students return to their table groups and share their expanded lists.

The essential structure of this routine has been around for over 20 years. Although its origin is not entirely clear, it was most likely developed by Harvey Silver and Associates as part of the 1997 Thoughtful Education Project in Clayton County Public Schools. At its core, this routine is a process of group brainstorming and sharing ideas, engaging with one another. We thought this basic routine had the potential to become a powerful *thinking* routine by adding a discussion and elaboration component that would push students to go beyond simply sharing initial thoughts and, thus, encourage active discussion and processing of ideas. Adding an additional step at the end involving the processing of the shared responses, students would be encouraged to engage with one another with the intention of looking for links, uncovering complexities, and considering a variety of perspectives. This elevates the thinking aspect of this routine.

Purpose

Give One Get One (GOGO) is a routine to encourage students to listen closely to one another, contribute to others' ideas, and tune in to a variety of perspectives. We often hear teachers express great desire to build classroom cultures whereby students attend to one another's thinking, not as an act of compliance but as a critical action to develop understanding. Powerful learning unfolds within the collaboration of others. This routine functions as a tool and structure to initiate physical movement to meet others with the greater purpose of promoting perspective seeking, divergent thinking, and elaboration of a variety of ideas central to the topic being explored.

The process of sharing ideas *and* then explaining, justifying, or connecting those shared ideas helps students to deepen their understanding. Having to justify and explain one's thinking is key to building connections and locking ideas into memory. The processing of ideas at the close of this routine helps students to form connections, look for similarities and differences, and form a larger conceptual framework.

Selecting Appropriate Content

GOGO can be used with a wide variety of content. It is particularly useful when multiple ideas and perspectives are likely to arise. For example, when generating ideas for a design project, reviewing content for tests, describing a character in a book, or uncovering students' knowledge about a topic. Whenever a teacher asks students to brainstorm ideas, *GOGO* could be used.

One difference between the generating initial responses in *GOGO* and brainstorming is that a parameter is put on the initial idea generation in *GOGO*. For example, a teacher could ask students to list the three most important ideas within a topic under investigation, or four key descriptors of a book character, or the two things they care about most in relation to the question posed. It is critical that the prompt encourages multiple perspectives, ideas, or responses rather than one singular answer. The content should invite a variety of possible responses, creating a need for students to eventually give and get further ideas from one another.

In selecting content, imagine what students could do with the list of ideas generated, gathered, and shared. If the list is likely to be limited, then perhaps *GOGO* is not the most appropriate routine as there won't be much to share, process, and discuss afterwards. Consider the expanded lists of ideas likely to emerge for every student and the table groups with whom they will share. The intention is that these expanded lists become the basis of more elevated explorations of the topic and should be an important part of further planning.

Steps

1. *The Setup.* Begin with the whole group. The teacher poses a question or provides a prompt for students to respond individually. Students will need a place to document their initial ideas, whether that be paper or a device. These lists need to be portable. Because laptops can be cumbersome, teachers may want to allow students to use their phones for this purpose.

2. *Provide the initial prompt and have students generate responses.* Indicate a time frame within which students respond (e.g., three minutes) or designate a number of desired responses (e.g., three to four responses). Students construct an individual list of ideas, which may consist of single words, phrases, or a more elaborated response, depending on the prompt. Be aware that in order for students to have fruitful interactions with each other, they need time to articulate their own personal responses to the given prompt. Do not shortchange this time.

3. *Explain the Give One Get One process with a focus on what will be discussed.* Model the process of finding a partner, listening closely to each other, then offering an additional idea for your partner's list, and explaining the significance of this addition. The focus is engaging with one another in meaningful ways. Each partner will both give and get from one another, and these additions need to be individually recorded so that an expanded list emerges for each student. When initially introducing *GOGO*, be sure to clarify the purpose:

   • Listen closely to one another in order to be good contributors to one another.

   • Offer an addition to your partner's list that is new or not already represented. If both students find their initial lists are the same, then brainstorm together a fresh idea that both can document and take away.

   • Choose others beyond your own table group so that when returning to share your expanded lists with tablemates at the conclusion of the interaction, you'll have a variety of perspectives and ideas to consider.

4. *Establish parameters for sharing.* Once the first exchange of giving and getting ideas from a partner is complete, students thank each other and then find a new partner with whom to engage in the same process: *listening, sharing, elaborating, and recording.* Set a goal for either the number of exchanges (e.g., repeat this process three times) or for a length of time (e.g., we'll do this process for five minutes).

5. *Students exchange ideas.* As students engage in *GOGO*, pairs may conclude at different times. Although this can create a short lag in pairing up with a new partner, it is usually not an issue. Encourage students to meet and share with

students near and far, even walking across the room to encounter a wide variety of peers. If you notice there is not much redistribution, urge more movement so that a table group of students are not merely getting the same set of ideas from the same people.

6. *Table group sharing and discussion of ideas collected.* Once students have expanded their initial lists – collecting a certain number of new responses or the time for exchanging ideas expires – they return to their seats so small group sharing can begin. Establish a way for table groups to share their *GOGO* exchanges. For instance, each person in the group could share their favorite new idea, the new idea that greatly pushes their thinking, or the new idea that illustrates a key perspective. Whatever way students share their expanded lists, elaborating their choices is essential. The goal of this step is to encourage depth rather than sharing lists in compulsory, mundane ways.

7. *Sharing the Thinking.* As groups have already shared with one another at their tables, there might not be a pressing need to then share as a whole class. You might want to listen to the table sharing, collect key ideas that you feel are important to note, and then share these with the whole class to further provoke or inspire learning. If table groups noted highlights of their sharing on chart paper, a gallery walk might be effective – with students looking for commonalities or connections across the documentation or new ideas that didn't emerge at their own table discussion.

Uses and Variations

Kate Dullard, Head of Senior School at Penleigh and Essendon Grammar School in Melbourne, Australia, used *GOGO* with her senior English class to help students realize the power of engaging with others when working collaboratively. Kate's variation of *GOGO* asked students to first annotate an article, specifically identifying significant persuasive devices. She then used the routine to have students share and elaborate their individual annotations both to offer further ideas for others and gain ideas that they may not have initially noted. Kate believed that the documentation proved very useful as formative assessment. "I had my students e-mail me the 'before' and 'after' photos of their articles, and I could see that many of them had not commented on the image or the headline until they had interacted with others." Kate also noted that when students explained their annotations, they went much deeper than in their initial writing.

First-grade teacher Andrea Peddycord used *GOGO* as part of a design thinking project at Ashley Falls Elementary in Del Mar, California. All students at Ashley Falls were thinking about the school of the future and what it might look like. The first grade took on designing the outdoor space of an imagined future school. Andrea wanted students to think broadly about this design and what humans gain from outdoor activities, and not simply come up with fancier versions of their current playground equipment. Her prompt to students was to write down three things they enjoyed doing outside. The class discussed the difference between "going to the zoo," which is a place, and "looking at animals," which is an activity. If students wrote a place, Andrea asked them what they enjoyed doing there and advised them to write down that activity. After modeling the process of *GOGO*, Andrea explained that when they shared an idea from their list they needed to tell what was it about that activity that gave them joy or made them happy. When the class came back together in small groups, they shared their collected ideas and sorted similar ideas together. Categories emerged: games, relaxing and quiet things, being with family, being with friends, adventure, and climbing. Andrea and her students used these categories as foundational features for their future outdoor play space designs.

Assessment

As students interact with one another, document independently, and drive independent conversations in *GOGO*, listen closely and note what emerges. Specifically, pay attention to the ideas that come up repeatedly on students' lists and in their exchanges. What is new or surprising here? What is expected? What is revealed about students' interests, values, priorities, or understanding based on what you hear? Are students able to think broadly and divergently about the topic? If not, why might that be the case? Was the topic framed too narrowly or do students lack sufficient background on the topic to be able to think more broadly? What kinds of misconceptions seem to be present? What conflicting ideas could be worth developing further learning opportunities around?

Attend to common themes that appear in students' table discussions. For instance, is there a pattern in the way students discuss or even rank the importance of ideas? What similarities or variance do you notice among differing table groups? Are students flexible in their thinking and open to different perspectives or are they quick to adhere to their initial lists and hesitant to take on the ideas of others?

Tips

As with other thinking routines, it is very important that teachers name purposes and intentions before announcing procedures. In this routine, it is easy to get students up, sharing their initial lists with each other, copy down something from the partner's list, and then be finished – with no explanation or elaboration to the giving or getting. Beware of *GOGO* becoming a speed race for completion, or a hoop to jump through, giving the illusion of an active, engaged classroom. Explicitly draw attention to the purpose of *GOGO: We want to listen closely to others and share ideas because it gives us a chance to solidify our own understanding. And we build further understanding as we encounter new ideas and perspectives from others. Remember, listening to one another isn't about just being silent. Really listening means we attempt to understand what others offer and consider how their ideas connect to and expand our own thinking.*

A Picture of Practice

Feeling safe to share ideas publicly with other learners is important to Regina (Nina) Del Carmen, a third-grade teacher at Chadwick International in Incheon, South Korea. Because many of her students seem timid or vulnerable to express their ideas publicly, Nina desires to nurture opportunities that give voice to all students, promote engagement, and ensure greater equity.

Nina saw a great opportunity to nurture this engagement with one another when starting a social studies inquiry unit on Peace and Conflict. "*Give One Get One* provides both a tool and structure to get my students surfacing initial ideas, then exchanging and elaborating their initial thinking with each other," notes Nina. "It also allows me to observe and assess their prior knowledge." *GOGO* also supports a goal Nina has for her students: to be thoughtful listeners and to be open to new ideas.

Because *GOGO* is a new process she wants to introduce to her students, Nina decides to lay some groundwork. She asks her class to think of a time when they had given something of value or importance to someone and what that experience was like for them. A few students speak, and Nina asks them to elaborate, "So can you say a little more about what was that like for you? How did that make you feel?" Nina tries to set the stage for her students to tune in to the purpose of the routine so that students feel confident to engage in the *GOGO* exchange. "The idea of giving and getting ideas offers my students a new perspective on what they can do with their thinking and that of their peers to actually build new insights and take learning deeper. I don't want them just to bounce from idea to idea without truly taking note of what they can learn from one another."

After getting a conversation started among her students as to what a healthy exchange feels like, Nina hones in on her purpose, "Today I'd like for us to start working with a new thinking routine called *Give One Get One*. But instead of giving and getting something tangible, you will give and get ideas that you feel are valuable and of great importance." Nina gestures with her hands the sort of exchange she wants to begin promoting more among her third graders – giving and getting.

Nina projects a slide with today's prompt for her students to see: "Reflect on this question: What are the factors that create peace? Take your time to imagine peace. Have an image about times you are at peace. List three words to describe peace." Nina allows the students a few moments to write down their three words. She then projects another slide: "Reflect on this question: What are the factors that create conflict? List three words to describe conflict." Again, Nina gives her students a bit of time to generate their initial ideas.

With initial lists of words that describe peace and conflict, Nina shares the *GOGO* steps without trying to over-scaffold or instruct, "With your initial lists in hand, I'd like for you to stand up, find one other person to share a word from your list to your partner – either peace or conflict – and explain to your friend just why it is you chose that particular word." Nina explains that as they listen to each other's words and explanations, they should document these ideas, growing their own initial lists. Giving ideas to each other and getting ideas from each other. She reminds them, "You are getting this word and explanation from your friend – something of value and importance. So, make sure you write this gift down."

Nina also draws students' attention to making sure the exchange goes both ways. "You'll both give an idea to your friend and get an idea from your friend. And we'll expand our initial lists of words around peace and conflict. See what I mean? Give one . . . and get one?"

As the students get into the *GOGO* exchange, Nina listens in. She notices that a lot of children seem to think of peace as "being quiet" and conflict as "war." This doesn't particularly surprise her. Listening even more closely, Nina notices three big ideas on conflict emerging: physical conflict, emotional conflict, and elements of the two.

One student claims, "Sometimes conflict starts with your feelings, then it becomes physical and if it continues, then it becomes both." This interests Nina.

She notes the complexity students are beginning to explore and uncover by giving and getting ideas from each other. "As I am listening in to them, I hear some tensions emerging on the concept of peace. For example, I heard some students asking each other 'Is nature peace?' 'Is family peace?' 'Is paradise peace?'" Nina reflects. She is excited to notice these things because they give her ideas as to how to plan next steps for students in the upcoming inquiry unit.

Eventually, Nina asks her students to return to their tables. "Now that you gave and got lots of ideas from each other, I'd like you to share your expanded lists at your table. Then I'd like for you as a table group to try sorting out all the ideas into some categories," Nina announces. "What themes are there? What kind of overarching ideas do all your given and received ideas seem to bundle into?" Nina sees this as a further opportunity for students to engage with others to build upon what they initially conceived of their topic Peace and Conflict.

As the table groups talk, Nina notes that certain themes emerge in their responses: Peace as a Choice, Peace as Sharing, Peace as Family, Connections to Nature, Peace as a Place, Peace as a Feeling, Emotional Conflict, Physical Conflict, Both. Nina reflects, "Broadly I see that the children relate peace to something good, happy, love, quiet, and positive, while conflict strikes them as bad, painful, loud, negative. But this gets my own mind thinking. The idea that conflict is bad is interesting because we could discover that in fact, not all conflict is bad. And on the other side, being quiet does not always indicate peace." Already Nina begins to think about upcoming experiences that could connect these initial ideas of "peace" and "conflict," but more important, challenge these initial ideas and offer her students more complex ways of investigating this topic.

"My interest in GOGO stems from my desire to not only surface initial ideas about an upcoming topic, but lay the foundation of getting my students to listen with intention to one another and engage one another to help us inquire with depth," says Nina.

Over time, this routine has become a mainstay with Nina and her students — throughout the Peace and Conflict unit and beyond. "GOGO is a favorite routine in our class," says Nina. "As it has become routine, I have seen students willing to change and grow their ideas, have confidence in their ideas, and be more willing to interact in ways with each other that promotes deeper listening, complex elaborations, and more learning."

LADDER OF FEEDBACK

The presenter chooses a design, artwork, construction, piece of writing, or other item on which to get feedback regarding what is working and what can be improved.

Clarify   Ask "clarifying" questions aimed at understanding what the presenter is sharing, trying to do, or struggling to figure out.

Value   Express what is working, is strong, shows thought, or is engaging about the work using "I value . . ." statements.

Questions and Concerns   Raise questions, puzzles, or concerns about the work. Share what is not working, confusing, or could be improved using "I wonder . . ." or "It seems like . . ." statements.

Suggest   Offer ideas for improving the piece. What could be changed, added, subtracted, or reworked? Be specific. Use "What if . . ." statements to suggest possibilities and not absolutes.

Thank   Presenter(s) thank their feedback partners by stating what they have taken away from the conversation. Feedback partners thank presenter by stating what new insights they gained through the process of giving feedback.

The *Ladder of Feedback* was developed by our colleague David Perkins and other Project Zero researchers (Perkins 2003). It emerged as part of an action research project they conducted with university managers in Colombia. In this setting they set out to develop tools and structures for communicative feedback, that is, feedback that is grounded in clarity and is fair and balanced in terms of attention to both the positives as well as negatives. Communicative feedback also focuses on improvement and deeper understanding of the issues at hand. In communicative feedback not only does the person getting feedback feel respected and valued, but the community as a whole grows in collaborative and reflective spirit.

Purpose

A long line of research has shown the importance of feedback to performance and learning (Black and Wiliam 2002; Hattie and Timperley 2007; Hattie 2009). However, feedback too often fails to achieve its potential. This can happen when people feel attacked, devalued, or personally criticized or when the feedback is vague and not action oriented. One reason for this is that when we respond in the moment we tend to engage primarily in two types of feedback: negative feedback in which we highlight what is wrong and needs to be fixed (this feels efficient) or conciliatory feedback in which we try to be vaguely positive and try to avoid criticism. However, good feedback, the kind of feedback that leads to improvement and learning, needs to emerge from conditions of mutual learning and collaboration, to focus on strengths as well as weaknesses, and be action/solution oriented. The *Ladder of Feedback* provides a structure for this. As such, it can be useful for teachers giving feedback to students as well as for peer-to-peer feedback.

Selecting Appropriate Content

The *Ladder of Feedback* can be used with almost any work in progress, such as writing drafts, design plans, project work, presentations, visual artworks, and dramatic and musical performances. The *Ladder of Feedback* often works best when there is enough completed "work" to respond to and the presenter is interested in refining or polishing. Research shows that individuals are not likely to take on feedback unless it is seen as useful and meaningful at the time (Wiliam 2014). This usually means that feedback is something that is requested and that there is an opportunity to revise or otherwise make use of the feedback. It is also important to recognize that the type of feedback being given when using The *Ladder of Feedback* is not merely highlighting things to fix but is more substantive in that it identifies things to rethink and consider. It aids the learning process because the learner stays in control of the thinking and decision-making process (Wiliam 2016).

Steps

1. *The Setup.* The routine can be done in pairs, small groups, or as a whole class. The steps can be timed, as is common in conversation protocols, or left open ended. In determining timings, consider the length and complexity of the work being presented (more elaborate projects will take more time), the age of the students (younger students generally take less time), and the size of the group (larger groups will require more time for the sharing of questions and ideas). As a rough guide, consider allowing approximately 2 to 5 minutes for each step. The protocol can be done in as little as 10 minutes or as long as 30.

2. *Present the Work.* Have the presenter share his/her work in progress, giving the audience enough information so that they can be helpful in asking good questions and offering meaningful ideas. If there are any sticking points, challenges, or problems that the presenter is encountering, those may be shared as well.

The responding audience, whether it be an individual or a group, then needs time to look closely, read, and examine the work carefully. This phase of the routine should take no more than three or six minutes depending on the complexity of the work. If the class is giving feedback on a common assignment with which everyone is familiar, it might not be necessary to present the work formally.

3. *Clarify.* The audience of responders is invited to ask clarifying questions to ensure they fully understand the work. Clarifying questions are designed to clear up confusion or provide missing information. They are not about offering suggestions. Thus, the question, "Have you thought about . . .?" is really a suggestion framed as a question and should be saved for the suggestion phase of the routine. As questions are asked, the presenter responds. Sometimes there are no clarifying questions, which is fine. However, if you are modeling this for the first time you might want to model what a clarifying question might be. For example, "Can you clarify who the intended user would be for this product?" This phase of the routine will be quite conversational in nature.

4. *Value.* The audience is now poised to express statements of value in the form of "I value" statements. These draw attention to what was positive, strong, thoughtful, or effective in the work. Valuing builds a supportive culture of understanding and helps the presenter to recognize strengths. These statements of value need to be specific in nature. So, if a student says, "This part was really good," there should be a follow-up question, "Can you be more specific? What are you noticing in the work that makes you say it is 'good'?" During this phase the presenter is silent but takes notes on what is shared.

5. *Questions and Concerns.* At this step, questions, puzzles, confusions, and concerns are raised. Avoid absolute statements of judgment, however. Saying "What's wrong is . . ." or "This part needs to be fixed," can put people on the defensive and cause them to shut down. Instead use more conditional language: "I wonder if you could . . ." "From my perspective it seems like . . ." "What would happen if you . . .." "You might want to look at . . ." "Is it possible that . . ." During this step, the presenter must avoid the temptation of responding. Doing so often creates a defensive posture and can derail the process.

6. *Suggest.* Responders provide concrete suggestions on how to improve the work. Use sentence stems such as:

- What about adding . . .
- Perhaps you could rework this part in order to . . .

- Something that might make this part stronger is . . ..
- It might be useful to consider . . .

Sometimes the "suggest" step is blended with the "questions and concerns" as it is quite natural to raise an issue and then provide a possible solution. If a particular suggestion is not clear to the presenter, they may ask questions to help clarify what is being suggested.

7. *Thank.* The presenter shares briefly what is being taken from the feedback session and one's current thinking. This might include sharing an action step or something they want to think more about. The responders also thank the presenter for the opportunity to give feedback. The learning in the *Ladder of Feedback* should be a two-way street in which the process of giving feedback also helps one understand more about one's own learning and work.

Uses and Variations

At the International School of Luxembourg, French language teacher Nora Vermeulin adapted the *Ladder of Feedback* to use with student-led conferences conducted by her third, fourth, and fifth graders with their parents. Students shared examples of their learning in French class, drawing from their portfolios, books, and materials. As they did so, they focused on their individual learning struggles and success. Parents, coached by their child, were then prompted to (i) clarify by asking questions to gain a deeper understanding of their child's learning, (ii) value by pointing out qualities of the students' reflection, (iii) identify an area for future growth, and (iv) suggest a possible strategy for moving forward with the child's learning. Because Nora's students had used the *Ladder of Feedback* on a regular basis to give peer-to-peer feedback on their personal writing (copies of the *Ladder* were placed in the students' notebooks), the transition to use it in this new context was quite smooth and helped to facilitate rich parent–child conversations in which parents' comments were more constructive and less negative and judgmental.

Quaker Valley High School teacher Matt Littell used the *Ladder of Feedback* with his 11th- and 12th-grade physics students as part of a project to design a rubber band–powered vehicle. When students arrived at Matt's class they gave their prototyped car to an assigned peer without providing any further explanation. Students were to take a full 30 minutes to look closely at the vehicle, documenting everything they could about its design, construction, and performance. This documentation would be presented to the designer for use in refining and modifying their prototype. Students drew sketches from multiple perspectives; identified the parts and their purposes; analyzed materials used and their effectiveness; made quantitative measurements of size, speed, and acceleration; conducted experimental testing; asked questions/wondered; and identified what was working and what needed to be improved. After 30 minutes, Matt gathered all students around two desks where he sat with one student and their prototype for a fishbowl observation. Matt directed students to pay particular attention to what he was doing throughout the discussion: his body language, the phrases he used, and the kinds of questions he asked. Matt then proceeded to model the *Ladder of Feedback* (without actually naming it) with the chosen student. Afterwards, there was a discussion among the "observing" students about what they noticed. The students naturally identified the main moves of the routine. Only then did Matt present the *Ladder of Feedback* as the structure he had been using, connecting it back to what students had noticed. Students then formed groups of three to give feedback using the *Ladder*.

Assessment

Learning to give good feedback takes time. At every phase of this routine teachers should look for and support growth over time in the responders. During the clarifying stage, can students identify potential points of confusion or elements that need further clarity or do they just assume they know? In the valuing step, look for and help students to be specific in their statements. Are they able not only to identify what was good or strong but also explain why it is so? If not, prompt them for a more elaborate response or ask someone else to provide the evidence. Learning to support one's statements with evidence easily becomes a learned behavior when it is insisted upon over time.

Raising questions and concerns in a way that is not negative can be tricky. Although you want students to be able to identify weaknesses, you also want them to be able to share those in a respectful way. Pay attention to the language students are using and help them reframe if necessary. If you are using sentence starters (see the "Tips" that follow), pay attention to see when these stems become automatic in students' vocabulary. Finally, being able to offer useful and practical suggestions is key to giving good feedback. At first students may be vague in their responses, suggesting only things that need to be changed. Again, push for specificity in how it might be changed. Also, look for students to move beyond simple corrective feedback, which identifies quick fixes: "Make the title bigger," and toward solution-oriented feedback that ties directly to issues and concerns: "I wonder if you made your title into a question if it would help grab people's interest more. Because when you stated the question you were researching I found myself much more interested." In the latter example, a possibility is presented along with implications of what it might accomplish. This puts the presenter in the decision-making seat with a goal to be considered.

It is equally important to pay attention to the presenters over time. Are students able to make good use of the feedback they receive? Do they see these as decision points to ponder and weigh versus just implement? Are presenters more open to feedback and comfortable receiving it? Do they actively seek out feedback? Does the language of the *Ladder of Feedback* begin to creep into other situations?

Tips

Initially, it can be useful to begin with a general discussion of what feedback is and why it is important to learning. Such a discussion might begin by asking students to recall a time when they received feedback that was really useful and then helping to identify the qualities of effective feedback. This helps clarify the goals of the routine and identifies how it supports learning.

Learning to give good feedback needs practice. The first time through the *Ladder of Feedback*, you may want to do the routine as a whole class with one presenter (chosen in advance) so that students can become familiar with the process. Alternatively, it could be done using the fishbowl technique in which a pair works through the routine in the center of the room while the rest of the class observes in an outer circle (watch Natalie Belli use the fishbowl technique to introduce *Ladder of Feedback* to her fifth graders at https://www.youtube.com/ThePowerOfMakingThinkingVisible). Once students are familiar with the routine the steps can be reviewed briefly at the outset by writing them on the board or giving students a handout.

The next transitional step is to use the *Ladder of Feedback* with a whole group. This allows you to act as a facilitator who can monitor the language students are using and prompt when evidence or specifics are not given. Finally, the last step in the gradual release of responsibility model is to have students practice individually, often with each partner taking a turn as both a presenter and a responder. As students work through the *Ladder of Feedback*, walk around the room and listen in on pairs. Take notes on both strengths and struggles. You might want to note the effective language you were hearing. After this individual work, debrief the protocol and have students share their reflections. What were they finding easy? Challenging? What needs more practice? Share your own observations as well.

Providing students with specific sentence starters can support learning to use more open and conditional language. In each of the steps outlined previously there were examples of language that might be useful. You can adapt this for your subject area and grade level. Sentence starters provide a very concrete scaffold for language use. These sentence starters can be incorporated into a simple graphic such as Figure 3.2.

It can also be useful to ask students to gather their thoughts in writing either before the feedback session begins or right before each step. This ensures that they will in fact have something to say.

Figure 3.2 *Ladder of Feedback.*

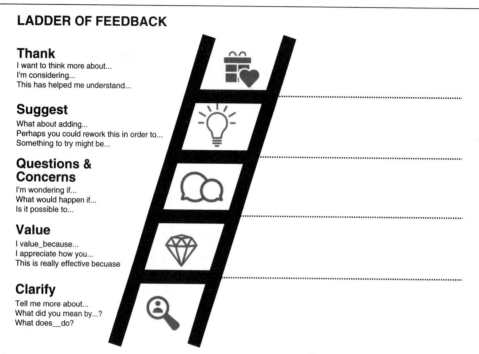

LADDER OF FEEDBACK

Thank
I want to think more about...
I'm considering...
This has helped me understand...

Suggest
What about adding...
Perhaps you could rework this in order to...
Something to try might be...

Questions & Concerns
I'm wondering if...
What would happen if...
Is it possible to...

Value
I value_because...
I appreciate how you...
This is really effective becuase

Clarify
Tell me more about...
What did you mean by...?
What does__do?

A Picture of Practice

Kindergarteners in Denise Coffin's class at Sidwell Friends School in Washington, DC, learn to use the *Ladder of Feedback* early in the school year. Denise carefully structures the process by first examining work others have created so that the process is safe and no one is likely to be upset by judgmental comments, as students are first learning to use the *Ladder of Feedback*. Denise begins by having students look closely at Egg Beater No. 2 by Stuart Davis on the screen (this work can be viewed at https://www.cartermuseum.org/collection/egg-beater-no-2). They then work their way through the steps of the ladder to give Mr. Davis feedback with Denise helping students to understand the language of each step and its purpose. During the next two weeks, Denise brings in a few more of Stuart Davis's paintings to look at and provide feedback on. In the work, *New York Elevated, 1931*, it seems almost as though the artist has taken on some of the class's feedback regarding the use of colors and defined shapes.

Having practiced the *Ladder of Feedback* three times with works by others, the kindergartners are now ready to put it into practice to give some peer-to-peer feedback. Denise continues to guide the whole class through the process as the class looks at towers that teams of students built during a math challenge. The challenge was to work as a team to build the tallest possible tower using a preselected assortment of items. Denise gathers the class together to commence the process of giving feedback to the first group composed of Aiden, Riley, and Maya. "We will use our *Ladder of Feedback* to help each other build a new, taller tower. We'll try to find out what's working well and what might be improved upon. What is the first step on our ladder?" Denise asks. Riley quickly responds, "Questions about the tower."

"Okay, does anyone have any questions?" Denise begins. Morgan asks, "How did you get the (round) block to stay put?" Aiden responds, "It kept rolling on the table." Maggie asks about the team dynamics, "Did you argue?" To which Aiden responds honestly, "I didn't agree with the other ideas," and then Riley chimes in, "We didn't argue, but we did have to glue our ideas together. It was hard."

Denise moves the class forward by asking, "What is our next step?" Maya offers her understanding when she states, "We should give out compliments," to which Denise adds, "Compliments or noticing what we value." Several quick comments are offered: "I like that they put the big squares on the bottom. I didn't do that. I like that it looks like a pattern here." When Morgan states, "I put value in the stability," Denise follows up with, "Can you say more about that?" Morgan responds, "It's not wobbly. When I build the bridge (at home) I have to make sure it has stability or it'll get too wobbly."

"Does anyone know which step we're on next?" Denise asks. Looking at the ladder that Denise has drawn on the whiteboard, a student offers, "I think it's challenges." To which another student adds, "It's concerns." Denise asks the class, "What might we have as a concern or worry?" Drawing on their experience as both builders and people giving feedback, the class expresses several concerns in an open way: "I wonder what would happen to the tower if all the flat blocks were on the bottom and the round ones there" (points to top). "I'm worried it won't get taller if they don't use the blocks like I did" (points to her tower).

"Our final step on the ladder is sharing our ideas or suggestions," Denise states.

Aiden, who is on the team receiving feedback, raises his hand, "I have an idea to put these square columns on the tall way. I don't want them to fall over." "Do you think that would make the tower taller?" Denise asks. Aiden nods, yes. "Are there other suggestions?" Denise asks. "I think they should try to put those blocks on the top," Kai says as he points to the rounded blocks. Devon adds, "and those too," pointing to small blocks at the bottom that are holding the round blocks from rolling away.

As the school year progresses, the *Ladder of Feedback* becomes a true routine in the classroom. Denise notes, "Its simplicity allows five- and six-year-olds to access the thinking that the routine is asking of them. I can lead young learners through some fairly complex thinking easily which allows it to become routine quickly. It is also inherently kind which lets learners practice interacting around their own thinking and ideas without feeling that they are being made 'small.' Its simplicity also means that it becomes part of their language quickly. Over the course of the year, I hear them using the *Ladder of Feedback* language independently and in a variety of contexts. Using the *Ladder of Feedback* really helps us build our learning community. It becomes part of their identities as learners and stays with them as they leave kindergarten."

THE LEADERLESS DISCUSSION

Group members read a common text or watch a video in advance. Individuals create two questions they are interested in discussing. Individuals reflect on how they might respond to their questions and why they find their own questions interesting or thought provoking.

Discussion Process:

➤ One person reads his or her question and explains why it is particularly interesting.

➤ Members respond to the presented question and share their thinking about the question, taking no more than five minutes total for the discussion.

➤ When time is up or the discussion over, the person who asked the question summarizes the discussion in a sentence or two.

➤ Subsequent Rounds: These steps are repeated until all have shared at least one question.

➤ The group reflects on the discussion and how it developed their understanding of the text and/or individuals write about how their ideas and thoughts have changed or developed and what new questions the discussion has raised.

Seventh-grade teacher Heather Woodcock at Shady Hill School in Cambridge, Massachusetts, created the *Leaderless Discussion* in an effort to nurture independence in her students (Ritchhart 2002). Heather frequently conducted earnest text-based discussions in class, but two things bothered her. One, she noticed that it seemed she was doing most of the work. She asked the questions. She moved the group along. She brought up new points. She chose who would talk. In essence, it was her discussion, not the students'. Two, although these class discussions were lively, in reality it was the same students who spoke up. Heather had to work to pull other students into the discussion. She created the *Leaderless Discussion* as a structure to encourage more student ownership and to create roles for all students to get involved. Additionally, Heather created this process to help her students generate good questions.

Purpose

The *Leaderless Discussion* creates an opportunity for students to own and drive the direction of a conversation about important topics and concepts. It also gets more students involved, bringing their thinking to the learning and actively engaging in discussion.

The *Leaderless Discussion* also provides the teacher ways to listen to and observe students, determining just what ideas and concepts are coming to the surface for them in their efforts to develop understanding.

Another central component of the routine is learning to ask good questions. Questions are not only drivers of learning but also outcomes of it. As we develop deeper understanding, our questions often become more insightful. Learning to frame good questions that engage others in discussion is not easy. It takes time to develop. As students work with the *Leaderless Discussion* over time the skill of formulating good questions emerges.

Selecting Appropriate Content

As a discussion structure, the *Leaderless Discussion* requires content worthy of discussion. This might be a work of fiction students are reading, or works of nonfiction, historical accounts, or scientific findings that take either textual or video form. It is even possible to use this routine after hearing from a guest speaker, listening to a presentation, or watching a demonstration. The best kinds of source material to use for the *Leaderless Discussion* are ones that present debatable ideas or can be reasoned from multiple points of view. Source material that contains a variety of stances and perspectives provides plenty of entry points for questions to be formulated, posed, and discussed rigorously.

Steps

1. *The Setup.* Identify the text, video, or other source material in advance. Allow time for students to read or watch the material beforehand, either in class or as home preparation for discussion. Students will have their discussions in small groups of usually four to five. When the time comes, selecting students randomly is often the best way to form groups (Liljedahl 2016), though there are times when students could be grouped more strategically depending on the dynamics of the group and the needs of the teacher.

2. *Preparing Questions.* Group members each create and record two questions they believe will be interesting for their discussion. These are not close-ended comprehension questions that are easily answered, but questions that will be useful in developing a more nuanced understanding through discussion with others (see the "Tips" section for advice on helping students generate good discussion questions). Along with generating two questions, each student briefly reflects upon the chosen questions and how they might personally respond. Students articulate why they find their questions interesting and useful for the *Leaderless Discussion*.

3. *Selecting a Timekeeper.* The group appoints an individual who will keep time and ensure that the group does not spend longer than five minutes discussing any one question.

4. *Initiating the Discussion.* One person reads his or her question and elaborates why this question is interesting for the group's consideration. At this point, if others believe they have a question that connects with the presented question up for discussion, they can suggest combining their question with the presented question. However, the decision should rest with the person asking the original question.

5. *Discussing the question.* Members of the group respond to the question and share their thinking. Students may elaborate on a point, offer another perspective, suggest a connection, or reveal another layer to the question under discussion. When listening to another's response, students should be encouraged to ask, "*What makes you say that?*" or to seek out further elaboration, evidence, or clarification in some way. The person who asked the question should pay attention to who is speaking and invite others into the conversation while making sure no one is dominating.

6. *Closing a round of discussion.* When the question seems fully examined or the timekeeper indicates that five minutes have passed, the person who originally posed the question, and anyone else who added a question, summarizes the conversation in a sentence or two. This allows the original question poser to add a final thought while also acknowledging the contributions of peers.

7. *Repeating the rounds.* Another member reads their question and the steps repeat until individuals have all shared at least one of their questions to their peers.

8. *Sharing the thinking.* Once the entire group has shared and several rounds of discussion have transpired, the group reflects on the discussion as a whole and identifies main ideas, themes, or connections that emerged. Here group members articulate how their understanding of the source material was enriched by the conversation and/or individuals write about how their ideas and perspectives have grown, changed, or developed. The group should identify which questions seemed to spark the most conversation, consider what new questions have emerged, or reflect on what point might have been left out of the conversation and why that might be.

Uses and Variations

Walter Basnight, a psychology teacher at the American International School of Chennai, India, discovered that a great use of the *Leaderless Discussion* was when moments of tension emerge while exploring ethical issues. "When polarities come up, then we have a thinking tension where students wish to debate all sorts of questions," said Walter. "For example, when we consider psychological behaviors and how they manifest in the consumer world or in the workplace. Other examples would be when we ask ourselves to what extent is it ethical to test on animals in order to advance knowledge." When such issues arise, Walter asks students to formulate questions in preparation for a *Leaderless Discussion*. In these discussions, Walter particularly attends to students' abilities to listen to one another, to paraphrase what they heard, and to press into each other's thinking safely, and with confidence with questions such as "*What makes you say that?*"

Walter reflects, "It's about culture building and giving students the capacity to push beyond 'serial sharing' and move to inquire into what is being explored in class." Walter explicitly teaches students how to dialog with each other with generative and facilitative questions early in the school year. He models the kind of questioning and reflection that happens in his subject area aloud with his students. These experiences set students up to engage in a *Leaderless Discussion* where Walter is then able to listen closely to his students and notice what resonates most with them.

Assessment

Notice the kinds of perspectives, links, or complexities students' questions reveal. Do they exhibit depth and nuance, or hover on the surface of the text? The nature of questions is often indicative of where a students' understanding of a text or topic presently stands. If you notice that students find it difficult to come up with good questions, it could indicate that the text or topic itself is not the most suitable choice or that students need help in developing their capacity to inquire into issues. They may also need more models of what complex questions might look and sound like.

During the *Leaderless Discussion* resist the urge to focus only on which students are "getting it" and which are not. It is more beneficial to situate yourself as an observer, noting which students are responding to each other's questions and how. Are students enhancing their understanding by incorporating perspectives brought forth by others? Are they able to build upon others' comments or do they offer thoughts disconnected from the ideas that have been shared? Do they elaborate on ideas that have been shared and press each other to do so? Do students revise their thinking based on the conversation?

Notice the connections students make, noting links and themes that emerge. Capture the questions students pose during the rounds. In what ways do they go to the heart of the topic or are they superficial? Are the students posing questions that might warrant further investigation once the *Leaderless Discussion* has concluded?

Make note of participation in the discussion. Who speaks and who doesn't? Does someone dominate? Is the group sensitive to this dynamic, and do they attempt to pull quieter students into conversation? Do students listen to one another, giving each other their full attention, or are they distracted? Do the questioners listen with interest as others discuss their contributions?

Tips

Do not shortchange the prediscussion process. The questions students generate for the *Leaderless Discussion* matter greatly, and thus the time investment to help students identify and articulate significant questions is worth it. Coming up with powerful, thoughtful questions will get better over time and with practice. Students do not naturally know what makes for an engaging discussion question, especially when this routine is unfamiliar. Consequently, pairing this routine with the *Question Sorts* routine (page 98) could be useful to provide students with some questions prompts to help them generate possibilities. Some examples are:

- What do you think the speaker/author means by . . .?
- What's another example of . . .?
- What do you think the author/speaker is assuming when they say . . .?
- What evidence and reasons are there for . . .?
- Who might have an alternative point of view on . . .?
- What's the consequence or effect of . . . likely to be?
- What's the take-away lesson from . . .?
- What's the core idea being expressed by . . .?
- How would things change or be different if . . . were to happen?
- What are the strengths and weaknesses of . . .?

However, don't let these stems limit students' thinking. They are intended only to spark ideas about where questions might go.

Expecting too much too early might undermine students' interest in joining in a *Leaderless Discussion*. One way to navigate this is for students to process with you, or with peer-partners, their initial ideas for questions and find the one or two that might feel "right enough" for now. Use past discussions to identify and discuss good discussion questions. There is often much to be learned by identifying the qualities of effective past questions. Over time, once this routine is established, the prediscussion process ought to feel more streamlined.

Students may also need support in listening to one another and building on others' ideas. Here again sentence stems and starters can be useful:

- I agree with . . .
- Could you say that again, it was unclear to me.
- What I think you said was . . .
- Building on _____'s idea, I'd like to add . . .
- What _____ just said reminds me . . .
- I would like to elaborate on to what you just said because . . .
- A connection I am making with what's been said is . . .

A Picture of Practice

Nevada Benton, a high school teacher at Mandela International Magnet School in Santa Fe, New Mexico, strongly believes in promoting equity of voice in her English language arts classroom. She feels teenagers always have a lot to say, and she wants them to feel that her classroom is a place where their ideas, opinions, and insights have great value.

Because getting students to do a lot of the talking is her firmly held conviction, Nevada makes great efforts to get students engaged in small group discussions frequently and has done so for a number of years. Nevada's worry with that, though, is that she often sees those with strong opinions run the discussion while other students remained silent. She wonders if perhaps an underlying cause for the silent students is that they need more time to process. Without much structure or guidance, maybe the quiet students find it easier to simply ride on the coattails of those students who are more verbose.

Previous attempts to address this issue have left Nevada feeling a bit dissatisfied. "I've tried the popsicle stick method. You know, the idea of having every student name on a popsicle and then pulling out a stick and calling on that student when we come back together as a class," reflects Nevada, "And while that does get more students talking, I worry this creates more angst than confidence in my quiet students."

Because small group discussions are already a mainstay in Nevada's practice, she feels the Leaderless Discussion offers a structure for students to get closer to her dream of getting them talking with one another and pushing the conversations forward themselves. Every student having created at least one or two questions ready to add to the conversation, coming from their own experiences and perspectives, appeals to Nevada. And the steps strike her as creating a sort of safety net. Every student can know what the flow of the conversation is going to be like, so they do not have to worry about being caught off guard by an uncertain step that makes them feel self-conscious or afraid to participate.

Nevada readies her first use of the *Leaderless Discussion* by selecting content that could feel slightly difficult or unfamiliar upon first glance to her students. She chooses a poem that is new for everyone and hopes for the best. However, in this first attempt, Nevada doesn't give her students a lot of time to generate their questions and assumes the steps of the routine will automatically make for a deeper conversation. This isn't the case. "Some of my students really got into the conversation," reflected Nevada, "But for others, the poem I had selected was so inaccessible that I found myself doing a lot of redirecting and explaining. I think I reached too far for that first attempt."

But rather than giving up after this first attempt, Nevada persists some days later. This time, Nevada decides to ready the *Leaderless Discussion* by first raising students' awareness as to what makes a conversation high quality. They tell Nevada things like when they're able to have dialog with each other in focused ways, when they cooperate with each other, and when different points of view get offered up for debate. Nevada makes a working list of the students' suggestions as to what constitutes a good discussion and invites the students to think of these as their norms. "As we get into our next round of *Leaderless Discussions*, I think we can all hold these norms up to ourselves," Nevada shares with her students. "We can all take responsibility for bringing these qualities to the discussion."

Nevada also decides that the material for discussion needs to still feel new but also accessible – something the poem she'd used the first time with students did not embody. Nevada presents a video clip from a foreign art film to her students that has animated characters trying to balance on a geometric platform with great difficulty. Without narration or text, the symbolism and imagery are intriguing and mysterious and a variety of possible interpretations and meaning-making naturally comes up. Nevada finds that her students can't help but raise questions as to what is going on. The students seem ripe to invite into a question formulating phase.

She hands her students a list of question starts and asks students to each write two questions that they personally wanted to bring to their *Leaderless Discussion* group based on the video they just watched. Nevada reintroduces the steps of the process, pointing out various points along the way where they should listen, respond, and share. She also reminds them of the norms of good conversations that they had just developed together.

The process seems to go better this second time in Nevada's mind. "Some students just can't help themselves from being able to contribute. They have so much to say," reflects Nevada. Sure, there were moments that didn't run as smoothly as Nevada hopes, but she has made peace with those rough edges. Nevada knows that putting the *Leaderless Discussion* in place as a matter of routine, rather than a one-off activity, will require further attempts with heightened attention to detail. "Getting the process up and running, without expecting perfection, is what's most important to me at this stage in establishing this as a new way of interacting and conversing in my class," says Nevada.

Indeed, as the *Leaderless Discussion* became more routine for Nevada and her students over the course of the school year, she honed in on various aspects of the process that she believed could enrich patterns of powerful interactions. "I started to get the students to turn their questions in beforehand, for example," recalls Nevada. "I didn't do that so that they felt I had to give them the go-ahead. In fact, I was wary of sending that message. But I did feel that I could get a sense of the kinds of questions students felt essential to discuss and look for places where I could coach or guide students into formulating more debatable, discussable questions rather than those which could easily be answered."

Nevada still hosts mini-lessons from time to time with her students, such as conducting a fishbowl experience and asking students to reflect upon what makes a good question interesting. She asks students to notice and name places in their *Leaderless Discussions* that feel like turning points or moments of great insight. She invites them to think about where they can push or prompt each other more to reason through claims when they come up in their *Leaderless Discussions*. "I don't want students to think things have to be perfect to be wonderful," says Nevada, "But I do want to convey a sense to them that as we develop the habit of engaging with one another and developing an elaborated conversation together, there will be parts of the process that we can always make stronger."

Nevada wants students to feel at ease and to have ownership of this routine. The goal isn't to run without falter or flaw, but that sticking with this process and leaning into each other's ideas is what makes this process more enriching for everyone. "I think it all starts with believing that students are capable of much more than we give them credit for," Nevada reflects, "If we give them tools and structures, and strive to put them into play routinely, students will amaze us with their insights and thoughtfulness."

SAIL: SHARE-ASK-IDEAS-LEARNED

The presenter chooses a plan, project idea, piece of writing, speech, or other item on which he or she wishes to get additional clarity, input, or feedback.

Share	The presenter shares his or her plan/project idea/piece with the group.
Ask	The group asks "Clarifying" and "Probing" questions of the presenter.
Ideas	The group offers ideas for improving the plan/project idea/piece. Presenter writes down what is offered but does not specifically accept, reject, or evaluate any suggestion.
Learned	The presenter states what he or she has learned or is taking away from the conversation, stating any new thinking about the plan/project idea/piece.

Working with teachers, we often use protocols as tools for helping colleagues generate new ideas for plans and projects or to solve problems of practice (see www.schoolreform initiative.org for examples). However, many of these adult protocols have a lot of steps or require extensive time to complete. We felt it would be useful to have a more streamlined protocol for use in the classroom for when students are engaged in project work or design thinking. Drawing on the best ideas of professional learning protocols, we created the *SAIL* routine.

Purpose

This routine provides learners with a structure for giving and receiving ideas from peers and suggestions for early project development when new ideas can easily be integrated and may be useful in shaping the work. Although this can certainly be thought of as feedback, the *SAIL* routine is a bit more open ended and suggestive of possibilities than how we sometimes think about feedback. In addition, typical feedback is more likely to occur near the end of a project to help students polish and refine. The *SAIL* routine is more commonly placed early in the process when students are still in the planning stages. When situated at the beginning, the *SAIL* routine helps learners to think through ideas, generate options, and consider alternatives that can be used to shape their work. Another key purpose of this routine is to create a community of learners in which students see one another as learning resources. This means that the group responding to the presenter is not just an attentive audience but is active in terms of questioning and offering of ideas.

Selecting Appropriate Content

The *SAIL* routine works most effectively in the development phase of a project, plan, or design. For instance, students may be planning a personal research project or inquiry and need ideas for where it might go. Students might be seeking to design or build something in a maker space and have only a vague idea of what they want to accomplish but would benefit from talking it through with others to help them clarify purpose and objectives. In a writing classroom, students may have ideas for a story or even characters that they want to incorporate but haven't really thought through where their ideas might go or what they need to consider in creating their story. A teacher might have an initial idea for a unit or activity that they want to think through with colleagues or even their students.

Steps

1. *The Setup.* The routine can be done either in small groups (as small as three) or as a whole class. The steps can be timed, as is common in conversation protocols, or left open ended. In determining timings, consider the complexity of the project/proposal being presented (more elaborate projects will take more time to explain but this should never exceed 4 minutes), the age of the students (younger students generally take less time), and the size of the group (larger groups will require more time for the sharing of questions and ideas). The protocol can be done in as little as 5 minutes or as long as 25. The first time through *SAIL*, you may want to do the routine as a whole class with one presenter (chosen in advance) so that students can become familiar with the process. Alternatively, it could be done using the fishbowl technique in which a smaller group works through the routine in the center of the room (the fishbowl) while the rest of the class observers are in an outer circle surrounding the group.

2. *Share.* Have the presenter share his or her plan/project idea/piece with the group. This phase of the routine should take no more than three or four minutes at a maximum. The idea here is to give the audience enough information about the project so that they can be helpful in asking good questions and offering meaningful ideas. It is often useful to explain:

   - The "why" of the project/piece, that is, the personal motivation behind it
   - The "how" or how the presenter is proposing to tackle or approach the project
   - The "what" in terms of what has been done so far
   - Any sticking points, challenges, or problems that the presenter is encountering

3. *Ask.* The audience is then invited to ask questions. As questions are asked, the presenter responds. This phase of the routine will be quite conversational in nature. Depending on the project, this phase of the routine might take anywhere from 2 to 10 minutes. The routine identifies two types of questions that listeners should be asking: clarifying and probing (Allen and Blythe 2004):

   - **Clarifying questions** are asked for the benefit of the questioner. They provide background information and context to help the questioner better understand the situation. Clarifying questions do not take much thought to answer and can typically be responded to in just a few words. For instance, questions like: "Have you ever written a story like this in the past? How many players will be needed for your game? Who have you interviewed already on this topic?" can all be answered quickly and will help the questioner better understand the context better.

   - **Probing questions**, on the other hand, are asked for the benefit of the presenter. They are designed to encourage greater reflection and introspection and require more thought to answer. They may even become a dialog. For instance, questions like: "Why is that feature important to you? How will you know if this has been successful?" require much more thought and may yield greater clarity for the presenter. Sometimes, probing questions cannot be answered on the spot and require further thought. If so, the presenter simply says they need to think.

4. *Ideas.* Having gained a better sense of the project through questioning, the audience is then poised to offer suggestions. These are offered in brainstorm mode, meaning the presenter doesn't evaluate them on the spot but merely takes them in. However, if an idea or suggestion is not clear, the presenter asks questions so that they fully understand what is being offered. Documentation of some type can be useful. Older students might record the suggested ideas for themselves. Younger students might use an iPad video to capture the conversation and then listen to it later. This phase of the routine might take from 3 to 10 minutes.

5. *Learned.* This step provides for closure of the sharing session. The presenter's learnings and takeaways from the session are briefly recapped. For instance, there may have been a question to mull over, or there may have been a suggestion to pursue. The presenter should also thank the group for their contributions. This step usually takes just a minute or two.

Uses and Variations

Each year at University Liggett School in metro Detroit, grade 12 students embark on a yearlong Academic Research Project (ARP) on a topic of their choosing. The idea is to give students an opportunity for individualized inquiry that is both substantive and complex. The ARP is a chance to develop an area of curiosity and passion beyond the school's walls (to learn more about the ARP project, watch the video at https://www.youtube.com/watch?v=iLxPt6k-Z2w). Topics range from an investigation of fly-fishing to the feasibility of zero emission communities to the design of adaptive sports equipment for disabled players. Because of the diversity of topics, Senior Project Coordinator Shernaz Minwalla knew that she could not be the only person helping students shape their projects. She wanted students to see one another as valuable colleagues in the process, so she decided to use the *SAIL* routine at regular intervals throughout the year. Working in groups of three in intervals of 20 minutes, each student took a turn being the presenter. Students felt it was not only invaluable to learn about the projects of others but found that the ideas and resources shared by their peers were useful in shaping their own projects.

In Peter Bohmer's eighth-grade music class at Penleigh and Essendon Grammar School in Melbourne, Australia, the *SAIL* routine helped students explore composing original music designed to evoke emotion. Peter began by giving students different images of storms at sea (a connection to Benjamin Britten's interlude to *Peter Grimes*) and asked them to do a quick *See–Think–Wonder* (Ritchhart et al. 2011) on their image. Students were then set a task of designing a musical work that reflected their observations, thoughts, and wonderings emerging from their image. Peter directed students to take 10 minutes to jot down ideas for their proposed work. Working in groups of four, students took turns as presenters using *SAIL*. Observing the groups, Peter was struck by students' comments during the "learned" portion of the routine, noting that many students offered ways in which their own thinking had changed from their initial ideas as a result of the activity. This connected to Peter's goal of helping students to understand how music could evoke emotion.

Assessment

Look for and support growth over time in both the presenters and audience. In the *Share* phase of the routine, look to see how students are able to present a developing project in a way others can understand. Are they able to organize their presentation in a meaningful sequence so that it is easy to follow? Can they anticipate what needs to be explained? Are they able to anticipate and raise issues with which they might benefit from help?

Both the *Ask* and *Ideas* phases of this routine put students into an active role of engaging with another's content. Are they able to assume this role or do they sit back as listeners? Who needs encouragement and support to become a more active contributor? Are students able to ask both clarifying and probing questions that demonstrate that they have listened to the presenter? (See the "Tips" section for how to facilitate this.) Note: if lots of clarifying questions are being asked, it can be an indication that the project has not been explained well during the *Share* phase of the routine. As students offer ideas, look for an ability to assume a perspective other than one's own. Are students offering suggestions based on what they would do or are they able to keep the presenter's goals and potential audience in mind? Do the ideas show respect for what has been done already and allow the presenter to build on rather than abandon their work?

The *Learned* phase of the routine is a chance for presenters to show that they have listened to their audience. Are students able to remember and recount ideas that were useful to them? Can the presenters summarize others' ideas in a way that shows understanding? Is the presenter able to present a plan for next steps based on the conversation?

Students may have difficulty accomplishing all the aforementioned actions the first time. In fact, students may struggle at every step. As part of your assessment, it is useful to call attention to what was done well in addition to what still needs to be improved. By using the *SAIL* routine repeatedly over time and providing regular feedback on performance, teachers can expect to see improvement.

Tips

As with most conversation protocols, it can be useful to do a round with the group before expecting students to do it independently. This also allows you to assume the role of facilitator as you guide the group through the stages. As facilitator, you can remind students about the difference between clarifying questions and probing questions and help them to identify what kind of question they are asking. You can also model these questions yourself. Finally as facilitator, you will debrief the routine in terms of what worked, what was challenging, and what might be improved next time. Consider using the fishbowl technique described on page 55.

Documenting the questions, particularly the probing questions, is useful. If documented, then at the conclusion of the routine you can ask the presenter which probing question was most useful and why. Repeating this technique several times helps a group to identify what makes a good probing question. This can help students in their future uses of the *SAIL* routine, and in many other learning situations.

Figure 3.3 SAIL routine diagram.

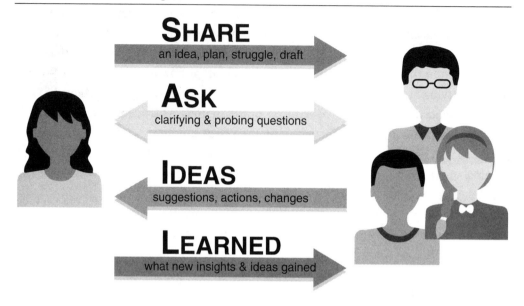

To help students understand the flow of the routine, consider using a simple diagram with the presenter on one side, the audience on the other, and arrows showing the flow of conversation (see Figure 3.3).

A Picture of Practice

Jodi Coyro recognized an opportunity for an authentic inquiry for her second graders at University Liggett School in Detroit when a student asked if she could create her own board game during exploration time and other students quickly followed suit. Jody had already anticipated a future exploration of the world of play and wanted to move the unit up to capitalize on students' interest in making board games. As the game creation evolved, Jodi sought support from Dean of Pedagogy and Innovation, Mike Medvinsky, who thought the games project provided a perfect opportunity for students to explore 3D modeling and printing and for using the *SAIL* routine.

The class has just settled in for the morning as Jodi announces, "We are going to start our day with our project work and another round of the *SAIL* routine. Yesterday we finished with Sonia having a turn. Today I think we have two people who are ready." Glancing across the faces of the group, Jodi checks to make sure her assessment is correct. Jodi asks the two boys who stepped forward to share to figure out who will go first. A quick game of rock, paper, scissors determines Max will start. "It is going to be hard to lift it," Max states as he starts to move his game, "King versus King," to the table in the center of the room.

"Okay, our first step is sharing, right?" Jodi confirms. "Everyone. Give your attention to Max so we can hear him share and so that we can understand his game." Max begins explaining his game, which uses black and white chessboard pieces and a 20-sided die. "It's like chess but the dice tells you how many spaces to move. The pieces move in the same directions and shapes as chess but the number of spaces is based on dice roll. If you land on a special space on the board, your piece is out," Max explains. He elaborates further, "landing on certain squares will cause you to be hit by natural disasters such as tornados or tsunamis that knock you out, but if you land on a meteor then you get to throw the meteor at your opponent and knock them out."

Acknowledging that several students' hands are already raised in anticipation, Jodi guides the discussion forward. "Let's think about asking our questions. I can see some of you are thinking about your questions already. Before you start, I want you to remember to use our language: 'I have a clarifying question for you' or 'I have a probing question for you.'" Before allowing Max to call on his classmates, Jodi encourages students to move back off the top of the table where several students have crawled to get a closer look.

Katya asks the first question, "Can the knights still go in the L shape?" To which Jodi gently prompts, "Katya, what kind of question are you asking?" "I think a clarifying question." Max responds affirmatively and demonstrates the movement of the knight piece.

Max then calls on Jason. "I think I have a probing question," he begins. "So, if you roll a number you get to move as many spaces into the game?" Recognizing that Jason actually has a clarifying question, Jodi softly elaborates, "So you are clarifying what the rules are." Max explains that that is indeed the way the rules work.

Aaliya offers another question, announcing with a bit of hesitation, "I think it is a probing question. Are you going to add more squares on the board?" pointing to the black cutouts on the board.

"No," Max clarifies, "those are jails. I'm going to ask if I can make a 3D jail. I'm thinking of changing the form of some of the squares."

Aaliya's question and Max's response shows that clarifying questions and probing questions are not always distinguishable on the surface. Although Max's quick response of "No" would indicate that it is a clarifying question, his elaboration and thoughts about modifying the game board would indicate that a new area of thought opened up for him. Max continues to call on his peers, who mostly have clarifying questions aimed at developing their own understanding of how the game is to be played. At one point, one member of the group comments, "I'm getting the hang of this."

After about 10 minutes of questioning and explaining, Jodi moves the conversation forward: "It's time to think about your ideas and suggestions for Max." Hands go up. Jason offers a suggestion framed as a question, "I was wondering if the 3D piece you made with 20 sides is that the right kind of piece for your game? It seems like if you roll a 20 then the game is over right away." Max immediately responds, "Okay, I will change it." Jodi jumps in, "You don't have to change it. It is just a suggestion." To which Max responds in a way that shows he understands the spirit and implication of the suggestion, "I know what you are saying. It is about whether you want the game to go on further or be over right away."

Another student offers an idea, "You could make it so that with the jail something happens, and you have to go somewhere but there is some way you can get out." Max likes this idea: "I will make a way for something to get out. I still need to make some adjustments. I will put a special key on the board where if you land there you can get out." This discussion prompts other ideas about the jail: making it bigger so it can hold more players and creating more of them. New ideas continue to be shared over the next few minutes.

Sensing students are getting anxious to conclude and begin work on their own games, Jodi wraps up by asking Max what he has learned from the discussion. "I want to think more about the jail and how that will work in the game. Also the dice and how long the game should go on. Maybe I need to play it a few times to see what will be best."

Reflecting on the session, Jodi feels that the *SAIL* routine was useful in providing a structure for students to think through their games and get new ideas for improvement. "There is still some confusion about clarifying versus probing questions," she notes. "I think the reality is that there are just a lot of clarifying questions because second graders have a hard time explaining a game in words, and this just naturally sets up the need to clarify the rules of the game. Students really want to ask probing questions, so I think in their quest to do that they sometimes mislabel their questions." Even with the preponderance of clarifying questions, Jodi felt that the process of listening to and responding to questions is helpful. "The *SAIL* routine offers this group of learners an avenue to grow their ability to share their thinking and practice truly listening to one another. Engaging in rich dialog with one another so early in the school year allows our classroom culture to grow exponentially."

MAKING MEANING

Choose a concept, idea, topic, or event to build meaning around. Guide the group through the following prompts one at a time. Record responses on chart paper:

➤ Taking turns, each person **responds** to the chosen focus with a single word. Each person's word must be unique so that it adds to the collective meaning.

➤ Each person **adds on** to someone else's word with an additional word or phrase so as to elaborate in some way.

➤ Collectively, the group **makes connections** between ideas that are already written on the chart paper, drawing lines and writing on those lines to illuminate the connections.

➤ Each person **records a question** about the focus topic based on what has emerged thus far.

➤ Based on the group's "Making-Meaning discussion" on chart paper, each individual now **writes their own definition** of the idea, topic, concept, or event being explored on a sticky note and reads it aloud to the group before sticking it on the chart paper.

The *Making Meaning* routine emerged, as many routines do, from our experience in facilitating the learning of a group. Working with teachers in the Learning to Think, Thinking to Learn Project, we wanted them to explore the meaning of the concept of *engagement* and raise questions and ideas about it before we launched into methods of engaging students. The word "engagement" is sometimes overused and can mean different things to different people. Initially, we considered using the *Chalk Talk* routine (Ritchhart et al. 2011), but that routine was quite familiar to the group, and we wanted something new. In addition, we thought that to really drill down into the meaning of the concept, we needed to facilitate deeper discussion. We decided to combine the idea of communicating on paper collectively with a focus on steps to push people to think deeper together and trialed a process of doing this with the group. Over the next year of trialing with teachers and students, we refined the steps and process to create the *Making Meaning* routine. Because this routine is such a visual one, we present an example of it here (see Figure 3.4) in the hope that the graphic will be orienting as you read further.

Figure 3.4 Grades 9 and 10 computer science class's *Making Meaning* of "Machine Learning."

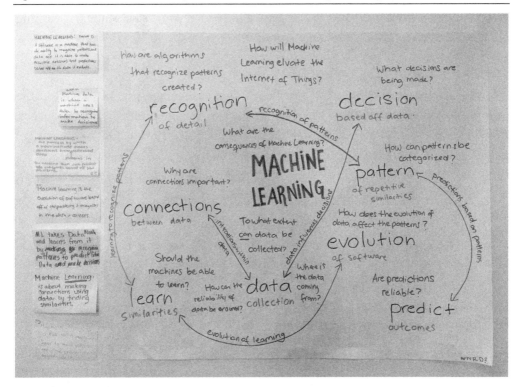

Purpose

This routine asks learners to explore an already familiar topic, concept, idea, or event through connection making, wondering, building explanations, and synthesizing in order to achieve deeper meaning. The topic may be familiar in the sense that students bring a lot of prior knowledge, or it may have become familiar through the group's exploration of the topic over time. The *Making Meaning* routine highlights the notion of building understanding in a collaborative way through putting forward ideas, adding to what others have said, raising questions, and synthesizing. The routine begins with simple one-word associations with the topic. By collecting different associations from each group member, key aspects of the topic begin to emerge. The group's initial associations are then expanded upon as people add on to one another's first words. At this point, a large map of key features and associated ideas emerges. However, these ideas are floating freely on the page and they need to be connected.

Once the group has exhausted the connections, they raise questions about the topic based on what has emerged in the documented discussion. Finally, as a way of distilling and synthesizing their new learning, students write a personal definition of the topic. By documenting all these processes and engaging in them step by step, students' learning and thinking are scaffolded and made visible.

Selecting Appropriate Content

Whereas *Chalk Talk* is often used to explore a provocative question of inquiry at the beginning of a unit, the *Making Meaning* routine focuses on defining a single concept, idea, topic, or event. Thus, this routine requires that students bring a lot of knowledge with them to the routine. For this reason it is often used:

- to unpack familiar ideas, such as community, bullying, or learning, in order to gain deeper insight into them and develop more of an agreed upon meaning, or
- as a way to conclude and pull together learning at the end of a unit on a topic, such as sustainability, revolution, or fractions.

In either case, students must have substantial ideas about the topic, and there must be something that can be defined.

Steps

1. *The Setup.* Place a large sheet of chart/butcher's paper on each group's table. Alternatively, the chart paper could be hung on walls. Place five to eight markers of a single color at each table (for example, one table gets blue, one red, one orange, and so on). Have one sticky note per student ready for the final round. Place students in groups of at least five and a maximum of eight. Be prepared to write each step of the routine on the whiteboard when it is time for that step.

2. *Present the Making Meaning Topic.* Have one student write the word/concept, topic, or idea being explored in the center of the page. Invite learners to think about what words come to mind when they hear this word.

3. *Respond with a Word.* One at a time, have each group member record the word that comes to mind when they hear the initial word. Each student's word needs to be different. Students can say their word aloud and write it when it is their turn. Space the words all around the page so that they are not all gathered in one place or in a list. Once everyone has written his or her word, collect all the markers from the group and pass them to the next table so that each group begins the next round using a new color marker.

4. *Add on.* One at a time, each member adds on to someone else's word. The addition could be another word that comes to mind when one thinks of that

particular word or one could add on to the word by turning it into a phrase. There does not need to be a one-to-one correspondence of responses here. That means two people could add on to the same word and some words might not have anything added on to them. If students are used to creating concept maps, they may automatically start drawing lines to their additions. Because lines are used for connections, ask students to make their additions either above, below, or on either side of the original word without drawing any lines. Once everyone has written his or her word, collect all the markers from the group and pass them to the next table so that each group begins the next round using a new color of marker.

5. *Make Connections.* Instruct groups to discuss the connections they see between the ideas on the page. As connections are identified, someone in the group should record the connection by drawing a line between the connected ideas and writing on the line what the connection is. Because this is a group process, not everyone will be making a written contribution in this phase. Once it feels like groups have exhausted their ability to make connections, collect all the markers from the group and pass them to the next table so that each group begins the next round using a new color.

6. *Record a Question.* One at a time, each member records a question about the original topic based on the exploration so far. Questions don't need to be connected to anything on the page and can just be written in the white space. Students can say their question aloud before writing it.

7. *Write a Definition.* Pass out one sticky note to each student. Instruct students to write their current definition of the topic/idea/concept based on the group exploration. Encourage students to make use of the ideas that have emerged in their groups. Stress that this is an individual definition that captures their understanding and not a dictionary definition. Once everyone in the group has written his or her definition, each member of the group reads their definition aloud and sticks it on the chart paper.

8. *Sharing the Thinking.* Conduct a gallery walk. Ask students to look for similarities between their group and that of others as well as differences. Alternatively, you might focus students on one aspect of the routine such as the words that came up, look for any additional connections they would make on other group's posters, or the questions that were asked that they find most interesting. Debrief what was noticed as a whole class.

Uses and Variations

Alexandra Sánchez from Parkview Elementary in Novi, Michigan, discovered that the *Making Meaning* routine could be done with a whole class of young children with the teacher acting as scribe. "A problem with gossiping had slowly been building in my class and one day at recess it boiled over. I found a text that I could share with my students to get everyone on the same page. Then, I had the class remain at the carpet and told them I thought a thinking routine might help us better understand the idea of gossip," Alexandra recounted. Using a blue marker, Alexandra recorded single words: bad, rumor, spreading, sad, unkind, and so on (Figure 3.5). Once it felt like the class was running out of new words, she invited them to add on to the words already on the page before them, which she recorded in pink. As the class moved on to explore connections, Alexandra was impressed with their engagement. "They took it very seriously," she said. Students' questions revealed their concern with stopping the behavior. For the last step, Alexandra had students return to their seats and write their own definitions of gossip. She then read each definition aloud. Alexandra concluded with a conversation about gossiping and its impact. "I felt like my students really appreciated that I took the time to help them understand their problems more deeply and to build their capacity to solve those problems," she reflected.

Working with a group of students with severe language and learning challenges, special education teachers Renee Kavalar and Erika Lusky at Rochester High School in Michigan felt that the scripted approach to teaching vocabulary provided in their designated program didn't engage students. They decided to try out the *Making Meaning* routine as an alternative. After the first experience with the word, "instinctively," which took them 30 minutes, both Renee and Erika felt that the routine sparked much more discussion and interaction than the scripted approach. "We were pleased with some of the vocabulary words the students came up with on their own," Erika reported. "They don't always include these in their unstructured oral expression or in their writing. We were surprised by the lively debate with plentiful reasoning that transpired." Renee Kavalar and Erika Lusky both felt *Making Meaning* was a more meaningful way for their students to learn the vocabulary than the scripted program, but was it really better? They decided to run an experiment comparing the two approaches over a two-week period. They found that once they and students became familiar with the routine, they were able to complete it in 10–20 minutes, depending on the word. This was comparable in time to the scripted approach. However, in the scripted approach, 80% of the time students did not achieve mastery of the vocabulary the first time through. This resulted in the need for reteaching and retesting. In the class that used the *Making Meaning* approach, all students achieved mastery when tested the first time.

Figure 3.5 Third-grade making meaning: Gossip.

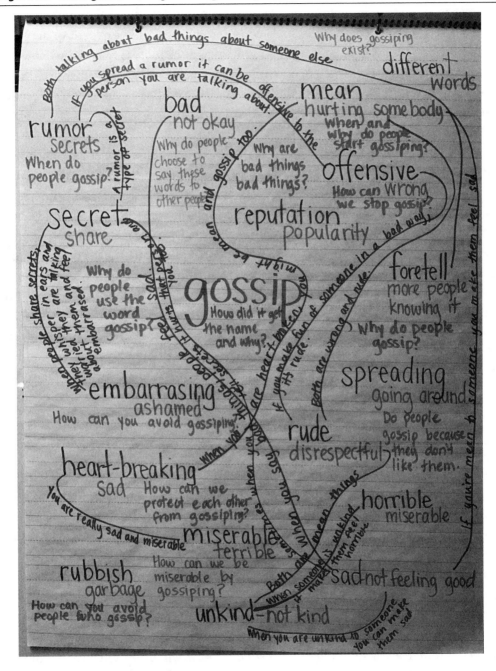

Assessment

As learners respond with initial words, look for what kinds of vocabulary they bring to the topic. Are their contributions related to the concept being explored or are they peripheral? If students have adequate background and the topic is rich, the vocabulary should represent this. If many students struggle to come up with words other than those others have offered, it may indicate this wasn't the best routine to use as the concept is not yet clear. In students' additions, see if their contributions provide layers of complexity and depth rather than just a restatement.

Students' connections will reveal the extent to which their knowledge of the topic is integrated or if it is discrete. How are they responding to the postings of others? Are they enhancing their understanding by incorporating ideas stated by others, or do they find it difficult to integrate others' ideas? See if students are able to identify connections that go beyond surface features. Having identified a connection, can they articulate it? Looking at the questions students pose, do they go to the heart and substance of the topic, or are they tangential? If the topic is familiar, are there questions that might warrant further investigation? If the topic is one the class has just finished studying, are there questions that show they are going beyond and extending the topic into new areas? Are there misconceptions that appear in the words, add-ons, connections, or questions that warrant future discussion and exploration? When examining students' definitions, explore whether students have made use of the group's discussion to go beyond what they might have been able to do before the routine.

Tips

If students are familiar with *Chalk Talk*, it is useful to acknowledge the similarities between that routine and *Making Meaning*. Both work on chart paper in groups and with markers. However, in a *Chalk Talk* the group remains silent whereas group members can talk in *Making Meaning*. A major difference, of course, is that *Making Meaning* is more structured and occurs in rounds or steps that the teacher facilitates. Rather than telling students all the steps at once, it is better to reveal one step at a time. This avoids cognitive overload.

Color-coding of each step makes it much easier to see how ideas develop during the routine. If each group has their own color to begin and then passes their markers after each round, every resulting *Making Meaning* page will have each step in a different color, though not in the same color in which others completed that step. In terms of group size, five is the minimum number as smaller groups don't have enough initial ideas down on the page in the first two steps, making it harder to identify connections later on.

It is important that this routine be approached in an open-ended and exploratory way so that students don't shut down or worry about giving the correct answer. In addition, the collaborative nature of the routine should be stressed so students get comfortable using and building on other's ideas. The discussion of connections as a group is particularly important. This stage of the routine is key to developing students' understanding and shouldn't be rushed. Allow students to write only once connections have been thoroughly explored.

A Picture of Practice

Joyce Lourenco Pereira of Atlanta International School decided to use *Making Meaning* to help her grade 9 and 10 computer science students consolidate their understanding of the concept of machine learning at the conclusion of their unit of study. "I've always found this to be a complex and challenging topic for students to understand as it involves how machines learn and interpret information," Joyce explained. She felt the *Making Meaning* routine would provide an important opportunity to both connect and synthesize all the learning students had done.

"Today we're going to use a routine to help us construct our collective meaning of 'Machine Learning.' I want you to draw on all the learning opportunities we've experienced up to this point in our study as you go about this process. You're going to work with your table groups to complete this routine together as a co-construction of meaning," Joyce announces. She then reads the instructions for each of the first four steps of the routine from the whiteboard and ask students if they have any clarifying questions.

"Is it okay if just one person does the writing?" a student asks. "Can we hang it on the wall so it will be easier to see?" another inquires. Joyce tells students that both options would be okay if any groups want to try it that way. She is curious to see how these adaptations play out.

Because she is working with older, more independent students, Joyce decides to allow groups to pace themselves. She gives each group a copy of the steps to refer to as needed and instructs the class that they will have 15–20 minutes to go through Steps 1–4 of the routine. Joyce then projects a digital timer on the board for students to refer to and puts on instrumental music to play softly in the background.

As students begin putting down words, group members are quick to point out if a word has already been used. Although there is a small bit of frustration when this happens, students support each other to find new words if anyone has trouble doing so. As Joyce walks around the room listening in she notices that there isn't much conversation happening. She encourages groups to ask one another "What makes you write that?" to better understand each person's contribution. Her suggestion is taken up immediately. Joyce overhears one student questioning another about the word, "decision." The student responds, "Computers have to sort through large amounts of data and that decisions were made based on that data." This prompts the student posing the initial query to write the phrase "based off data" to further elaborate on the word, "decision."

In another group, students are discussing the word "evolution." One student wonders about the specific evolution of software in improving machine learning while another wonders about the evolution of data and its impact on the patterns discovered. By talking about the different ways the word evolution might apply to machine learning, students are finding connections they were unlikely to have realized without the discussion. As Joyce continues her unobtrusive monitoring, she reminds the class that they have about five more minutes left.

As students move into the questioning phase of the routine, Joyce notices that many of the questions could easily be answered with "yes" or "no." She suggests that students try to open up their questions. "I wonder how your question might be asked in a way that encourages others to explore possibilities rather than just to answer 'yes' or 'no'?" she poses. As a consequence, a student modifies his original question from "Does machine learning have important consequences?" to "What are the consequences of machine learning?" Joyce notices that this simple suggestion generates a lot of interest among the members of each group, and there is an eagerness to respond to and engage with one another's questions.

As the clock winds down, Joyce notes that all groups have completed the first four steps. "Would someone from each group bring your group's page to the front and hang it up, please. We want to see if we can identify and share out similarities observed between the various group's posters."

"The word 'data' is everywhere. It keeps coming up," one student notices. "The questions are the most different of anything," another says. "Yeah, we really went crazy with the questions," another student adds. "It looks like every group had questions about the ethics of machine learning." Following the whole class talk, Joyce passes around sticky notes to complete the final step of developing personal definition of "Machine Learning." As students write, many come up to the posters to find vocabulary that they want to use. Once everyone has written their definition, students share them aloud and add the definitions to their group's chart (see Figure 3.4).

Reflecting on her and her students' first experience with the *Making Meaning* routine, Joyce feels that the routine has served her goal of helping students to pull together and synthesize their learning. "The students had a shared, deep understanding of 'Machine Learning' and were able to talk about it in a more thorough and thoughtful manner." The questions generated also provided an avenue to push the class's learning even further. "I was completely surprised by the questions the students developed. They were rich and made for excellent prompts that we used in future class discussions."

+1 ROUTINE

After reading a text, watching a video, listening to a lecture, or being presented with new information, a group of learners does the following:

Recall   In two to three minutes, working from memory, individuals recall key details, facts, and ideas from the presentation.

Plus 1   Learners pass their papers to the right. Taking one to two minutes, each student reads through the lists in front of them and *adds one new thing* to the list in hand. REPEAT this process at least two more times.

Review   Return the papers to the original owner. Learners read through and review the additions made on their sheets. They may also add any ideas picked up from reading other's sheets that they thought were important to note.

As researchers, we spend time in classrooms observing teaching and learning to better understand these processes. One practice we see in many classrooms, particularly secondary, is that of students taking notes. Although this is not a bad thing, there are several issues with students' note-taking. First, when students take notes, class participation often decreases. Students focus on compliantly recording material, not on discussing and questioning ideas within the material. Second, in many instances, students record everything being said or written on the board without any filtering mechanism, even when assured they will have access to the notes following class. A third issue, not directly observed, but identified through research, is that note-taking or reading one's notes is not generally an effective memory strategy, though students often think it is (Brown et al. 2014). To lock things into memory one needs to retrieve information, not simply record and read it (Karpicke 2012). To address these three issues – increasing in-class participation while engaging with ideas, facilitating effective filtering of information, and promoting the constructing of memories, we developed the *+1 Routine*.

Purpose

This routine cultivates retrieval practice by identifying important ideas worth remembering. Megan Smith and Yana Weinstein, cognitive psychological scientists who write for the blog, *The Learning Scientists*, describe retrieval practice as "recreating something you've learned in the past from your memory, and thinking about it right now. In other words, a while after you've learned something by reading it in a book or hearing it in a class or from a teacher, you need to bring it to mind or retrieve it" (Smith and Weinstein 2016). They suggest that retrieving noteworthy ideas *after* one has taken in information and held it for just a little bit makes one more likely to remember that information and work flexibly with it in the future. We do not want learners to be simply passive recipients of information but active processors of notable information through retrieval and application.

Retrieval practice happens through sketching notes, drawing illustrations of key ideas, or mapping noteworthy concepts. Our version of this practice provides learners with a structure for identifying key ideas and recalling them. Then, through engagement with others, learners build upon each other's notes. Throughout this process, students hone in on meaning making and relevance.

The benefit of post-experience note-taking is that students are required to retrieve and identify key ideas, an important processing move. This is significantly different from attempting to take notes during the actual experience, where it is easy to get lost in details and superfluous information. This routine harnesses the power of the group to enhance everyone's notes through specific steps of making additions to one another's initial recall lists, which leads to further conversations with depth and substance. At the same time, individuals each create written documentation for future reference. A video example of this routine can be found at https://www.youtube.com/ThePowerOfMakingThinkingVisible.

Selecting Appropriate Content

This routine can be used as an alternative to traditional note-taking. As such, it will work with the same content. Any scenario where students encounter new ideas and information provides opportunities for the use of this routine. These moments could be a lecture, a guided tour on a field trip, a text, a short video presentation. Whatever the stimulus, the important thing is that the information conveys a variety of facts, ideas, or concepts to recall and find key points worth taking note of.

Steps

1. *The Setup.* Students will need paper to write on that can be passed. A notebook or blank paper works easily. A computer will not work well. Have students write their names on the page so that their upcoming notes can be returned to them after they have been passed around. If students sit at tables, they can pass their papers in a

clockwise fashion. If they sit in another configuration, organize groups so that each person gains easy access to a classmate's list. Students need to respond to at least two or three other students. The paper will not be needed until after the stimulus has been presented, so it is best to wait until it is needed so as not to become a distraction.

2. *Recall.* After the stimulus, ask learners to recall what they just experienced individually. In two to three minutes, each person generates a list of ideas recalled from the presentation. Lists can include facts, statements, or bigger concepts from the presentation. It is not necessary that students evaluate these ideas at this time.

3. *Pass notes and make additions – "plus 1."* Once time is called for the recall and retrieval step, students pass their notes to the person on their right. Now, ask students to take one to two minutes to read through this new list and do whatever they can to add at least one additional note. This might be an elaboration, a new detail, a further point, something that was missing, or a connection between ideas. Although this routine was originally designed so that students add a single new idea on to each other's page before passing it along, it is possible that students could add much more than a single item. The goal is to use each other's thinking to build a robust set of notes. You can decide based on the stimulus, your goals, and your students what you feel will work best.

4. *Repeat the +1 step.* Pass the notes at least one or two more times, so that every student has contributed to at least two or three others' original recall list. During this stage, as students encounter new sets of notes, they will need time to read them and determine what further thinking can be added.

5. *Return the notes to the original creator for review and elaboration.* Students review their original recall lists with all the additions documented. Then, they add any further item they can to their own set of notes. One final "plus 1," so to speak. This step takes just a few minutes.

6. *Sharing the Thinking.* With robust sets of collectively created notes in hand, students now enter into discussion with one another. They may wish to raise questions for further consideration, synthesize what truly feels to them to be the heart of the presentation topic, or uncover complexity in the material with each other. To conclude, small groups might rank the facts and ideas in terms of importance in order to determine what is most salient. Groups or the class could use their notes to come up with a *Headline,* or as a first step in the *Generate-Sort-Connect-Elaborate* routine to begin creating a group concept map (Ritchhart et al. 2011).

Uses and Variations

Jeff Watson, a high school mathematics teacher at International Academy East in Troy, Michigan, has used the *+1 Routine* a number of times with his mathematics students. "Anytime I want to see what key ideas the students remember from certain activities, and how well they have committed those ideas to memory, I have them close their laptops and put away their source material and ask them to simply retrieve the most important ideas they think to be relevant to our learning right now." The notes Jeff's students recall and then collectively build on the spot spark generative student-to-student interactions. "The *+1 Routine* provides a great recap of our most recent learning, and the conversations lead to more ideas yet to be discovered being brought into view."

Elementary school teachers, though not usually known for having students take notes, have also found interesting uses and variations for the *+1 Routine*. Kim Smiley, a fifth-grade teacher at Bemis Elementary School in Michigan, has used the *+1 Routine* with social studies videos. She also used this routine with her students after an all-school assembly focused on Native Americans. "Students were able to sit down and immediately begin to write out notes on the 'big ideas' they had learned," said Kim. Students even told her that they thought this was a good routine because it forced them to really listen and concentrate. One student said to Kim, "I liked this better than taking notes while being there at the assembly. I think this is because I could really focus on the presentation."

Assessment

As students compose their initial lists, circulate to see what kind of things students recall, how many things they recall (an indication of working memory), and in what detail they construct their notes. Notice how students process. Do they work rapidly to get ideas down so that they don't forget them or do they work more methodically using one idea as a springboard for another? When students pass their lists, notice what students add. Do they add the same idea to each list or do they carefully read through the list and look where they might add detail or elaboration in response to this close reading? Do students offer challenges or questions to other's lists?

When the notes have been returned and you've invited students to converse with one another about key ideas worth noting, listen for what kinds of points students raise. Have groups uncovered a few important takeaways that the learning experience was designed to have them consider? What other ideas do students consider important? If their selections surprise you or feel off the mark, ask, "*What makes you say that?*" or "Which other group would like to add on to that idea or perhaps challenge it?"

Tips

For older students who are well versed in taking notes as a regular feature of their class activity, it can be helpful to talk about why you are asking them *not* to take notes initially but rather "take note" or seek relevance. Explain some of the brain science of memory and retrieval practice and that taking notes in the moment to capture everything simply isn't a useful learning technique. You can also explain that you want students to be more focused, more engaged, and more mindful during the presentation of material and not be caught up in copying down every utterance. Assure students that they will leave with a good set of notes and that their memory of the material will be enhanced.

Some students have a negative reaction to others writing on their papers or in their notebooks. If this is the case, then sticky notes can be used for the additions. Sometimes students find it useful if the additions are made in a different color so they are easy to spot. This holds true for the additions students make to their own page at the end of the process.

Some teachers might want to figure out a way to do the passing of the notes electronically. Although this is feasible, make sure the process doesn't inhibit the sharing and discussion the routine is meant to activate. Studies have also shown that physical representation itself enhances memory in a way that electronic note-taking does not (Perez-Hernandez 2014). If electronic means are being used to pass the notes, consider how the passing of the notes can happen so that everyone has focused attention on one list in front of them at a time in order to make contributions.

A Picture of Practice

Just looking around Matt McGrady's middle school visual arts classroom at the American Community School in Abu Dhabi, it is easy to see that making his learners' thinking visible is a prominent feature of his teaching. Students' ideas, processes, and projects are documented throughout the environment. It is important to Matt to create a space in his art studio where it is both safe and encouraging for students to take on others' perspectives when they're thinking about and constructing art. Matt is concerned, though, that at times his students' ideas flow so freely and quickly that interesting perspectives get lost or ideas are not always fully explored as much as they could be. He wonders if there could be a way to capture students' thoughts so that they can take on more prominence for the class and not simply disappear when the moment passes by. Matt also worries that quiet students don't always have as much of a chance to get their perspectives considered by those who tend to be more vocal. Matt believes the *+1 Routine* could be a great benefit to address his slight concerns, with every student having the opportunity to offer perspectives, suggest further points, challenge ideas, and collaborate with each other.

Matt introduces his seventh-grade students to the *+1 Routine* at the launch of a unit on abstract art. As with any new topic, Matt knows there will be wide range of preconceived notions about abstract art, many students thinking that it is just a bunch of splatter paint, without intention or reason. Matt plans an initial entry into the topic for his students that will both surface their initial ideas, whatever they may be, and immediately begin to provoke new ways of thinking about this genre.

The students will watch a video that gives a brief introduction to abstract art and its history over time. There is a lot of information in the video for his students to consider. Before it begins Matt tells his students, "I don't want you to worry about trying to get all the information down. Rather than taking notes during this video, I'd just like for you to take mental notes of what is important here. What are some of the key elements of abstract art that seem to be worth noting, in your opinion?"

Matt prepares his students by having them get out their art journals and prepare a blank page ready for them to recall big noteworthy ideas after the video is over. He then asks them to push their journals to the side, just a bit out of reach.

"So, we're not taking notes in our journals during the video?" asks a student.

"No, no, I don't want you to get lost in taking notes that you miss out on noticing what you feel are big ideas," Matt replies.

"We're just going to sit and listen?" questions another student.

"Not exactly," Matt responds as he checks that the students have organized their journals to get ready. "I do want you to sit and listen, but more than that, I want you to take note of key ideas. What do you hear? What seem to be the critical points the narrator is trying to get us to understand about abstract art?"

Another student asks hesitantly, "But what if I forget stuff by the time the video is over?"

Matt assures his students. "You won't be able to get everything down in your mind. That would be quite a difficult thing for anyone to do. But, I think there is value in us practicing our working memory, taking note of what strikes us as important, and then engaging in a new routine I'd like to share with you today called the *+1 Routine*." Matt explains the overall steps to the new routine in short form: they'll have a moment to recall what's important in their journals, then add ideas to one another's recollections, and after a few rounds of passing their notes to others, the journals will come back to their original creator so even more additions can be made. Matt says, "In a way, we are going to create a collective thought about our initial ideas of abstract art. And we are going to revisit this initial thinking a few times over the course of the unit. We may add to our thinking, we may change our thinking, our goal is to use each other's perspectives to keep growing our understanding of abstract art."

Once his students have a clear enough idea of how the process works, Matt plays the seven-minute video for them outlining, chronologically, the origins of abstraction in western art. When the video ends, Matt asks his students to quietly retrieve big ideas they noted on the blank page in their art journals. After two minutes of private recall time, Matt asks his students to pass their list to the person on their right. He asks them to have a quiet read of the notes just passed to their hands and do whatever they can to add to this list. He suggests they add details or elaborations or more noteworthy information. "Do whatever you can to add to these notes – as much as you can," Matt encourages.

At the end of the first round of making additions, Matt asks the students to again pass their notes to the right and repeat the process. He draws their attention to the fact that the list is more robust now, so they should dig deep to add anything else they can that they believe is significant. "You could even draw something or make a connection from your own ideas about the content we heard on the video. Try adding a simile or a metaphor to flesh out an idea. But try your best not to repeat an idea that is already there," suggests Matt.

After three rounds, Matt has his students return the notes to the original author for further examination (Figure 3.6). He asks students to take a few more minutes

Figure 3.6 Seventh-grade student's +1 notes on abstract art.

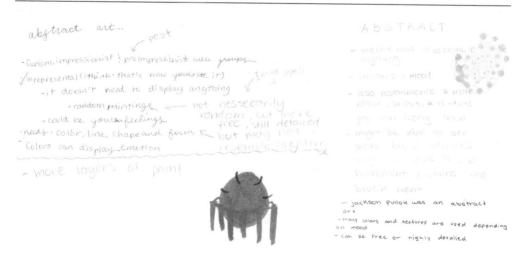

of quiet to read over their own list and make at least one more addition. "What do you remember clearly and why do you think that was the thing you remembered most? And what did others seem to pick up on that you didn't, but you could document now?"

Having built their set of notes, Matt then asks small groups to converse about their initial thoughts about abstract art and what it is. The notes generated by the *+1 Routine* act as an anchor for these interactions. Matt notices that students are really listening to one another and having interesting discussion. They debate ideas brought up in the video and ask questions of each other confidently. Matt is pleasantly surprised at the ease with which this process feels familiar and accessible even this very first time.

Reflecting on his students' initial use of the *+1 Routine*, Matt says, "One thing I noticed was a sort of frenzy of students reading over and focusing in once a new set of notes came their way. It's as if they all wanted to get right in there and see what else they could add. This was exciting to observe." Matt mentions that he saw a few students write the same thing every time they got a new set of notes, which he tried to discourage. Matt shares, "I think they may have written the same thing each time because they felt a sense of confidence with that particular add-on. This was a new process for both them and me, so I figured as long as they are making contributions to others, then we can keep working to make this process better."

CHAPTER 4

Routines for Engaging with Ideas

Figure 4.1 Routines for engaging with ideas matrix.

Routines for ENGAGING with IDEAS			
Routine	Thinking	Notes	Teaching Examples
Question Sorts	Questioning and inquiry	Use to identify questions for inquiry and learn to ask better questions.	• 1st Grade, Science. American Embassy School in New Delhi, India • Adults, Professional Learning. Association of Independent Schools of South Australia, Adelaide • 3rd Grade, Science Inquiry. Academia Cotopaxi, Quito, Ecuador
Peeling the Fruit	Noticing, wondering, explaining, connecting, perspectives, and distilling	Use to structure exploration of a topic to build understanding. Can be an evolving document.	• 9th Grade, Robotics. Penleigh and Essendon Grammar School, Melbourne, Australia • Kindergarten, Reading. Bemis Elementary, Troy, Michigan • 10th Grade, Poetry. Washington International School, Washington DC
The Story Routine: Main-Side-Hidden	Perspective, complexity, connections, analysis, and wondering	Use with visuals to explore different "stories" or as as a structure for analysis and going deeper.	• 5th Grade, Counseling. Oakland County, Michigan • 9th Grade, History. Penleigh and Essendon Grammar School, Melbourne, Australia • 12th grade, Accounting. Penleigh and Essendon Grammar School, Melbourne, Australia
Beauty and Truth	Noticing, complexity, explanations, and capturing the heart	Use with visuals or stories to identify where beauty and truth reside and how they intersect.	• 5th Grade, Science. Garden Elementary School KAUST. Thuwal, Saudi Arabia • 11th Grade, Literature. American International School of Lusaka, Zambia • 5th Grade Library/History. St. Philip's Christian College, Newcastle, Australia
NDA: Name-Describe-Act	Looking closely, noticing, and memory	Use with a visual to focus on noticing and describing while building working memory.	• 4th Grade, Social Studies. Bemis Elementary, Troy, Michigan • 12th Grade, Spanish. South Fayette High School, McDonald, Pennsylvania • 1st Grade, Science. Bemis Elementary, Troy, Michigan
Take Note	Synthesis, questioning, and capturing the heart	Use as an exit ticket strategy or to encourage discussion of a topic after presenting information.	• 12th Grade, Science. Washington International School, Washington DC • 3rd Grade, Science, Osborne Elementary, Quaker Valley, Pennsylvania • 9th Grade, History. Munich International School, Germany

QUESTION SORTS

Individually or as a group, brainstorm a large set of questions on the topic and write each question on sticky notes or note cards.

➤ **Sort by generativity.** How likely is the question to generate engagement, insight, creative action, deeper understanding, and new possibilities? Discuss and place each question on the horizontal axis of generativity.

➤ **Sort by genuineness.** How much does the group care about investigating this question? Discuss and move each sticky note vertically up or down on the vertical axis of genuineness.

➤ Decide as a group how each quadrant of questions will be handled and taken forward.

Many of the routines we developed (Ritchhart et al. 2011) invite students to generate questions: *See-Think-Wonder, Think-Puzzle-Explore, 321 Bridge*, and so on. As a result, teachers have asked, "What do I do with all the questions students come up with?" *Question Sorts* was created to help with this, specifically by putting the ownership of the questions back into the students' hands.

Purpose

Productive inquiry depends on good questions. But posing good questions is not always easy. To help students learn to formulate and identify the kinds of questions that can guide their learning, they must practice doing just that. Of course, there is not one single way to handle student-generated questions. Some questions might be worthy of extended investigation and easily worked into a unit of inquiry. Others might be explored only briefly. But how does one determine which questions to pursue? This routine helps students sort their questions and identify those which are truly generative and genuine to explore.

Selecting Appropriate Content

The most appropriate use of *Question Sorts* is when you want to help students to formulate generative, genuine questions about overarching concepts and ideas that are of interest to them. It works well with project-based learning, various inquiry models (Murdoch 2015; MacKenzie and Bathurst-Hunt 2019), or any of the culminating investigative experiences, such as those found within International Baccalaureate (IB) programs.

Something helpful to reflect upon when considering the use of this routine: "What is the bigger idea that our topic is a great example of?" Often this bigger idea is where the richest opportunity for question development is found. For instance, generating questions specifically about the "invention of the printing press" is a different opportunity from generating questions about *"how technology and innovation influence the ways we live."* The former focuses on a very particular object, the latter focuses on a broader concept about human ingenuity and the role that plays in affecting humanity. This is where good questions often begin and flourish. Of course, a topic also needs to be of interest to students and could need some early, guided exploration to develop such interest.

Steps

1. *The Setup.* Introduce the topic around which you wish students to develop questions, then have them brainstorm a healthy set of questions on the topic individually or in small groups. Have sticky notes or note cards nearby so that they can be used to document all the questions that come up and can be easily moved around in subsequent steps. Once a large bank of questions recorded one-per-sticky-note has been accumulated, the class is ready for sorting to begin.

2. *Sort by Generativity.* Draw a long horizontal line on the whiteboard or use masking tape on the floor or table as your horizontal line. Label this line "Generative." Write "high" on the right-hand side of the line and "low" on the other end. Explain to students that this horizontal line represents a continuum for them to sort all their questions according to the generativity of each question in relation to the others. That is, with each question, students decide how likely it is to prompt engagement, insight, action, or new understandings on the topic in relation to others in this bank of questions. Every question is valid. The goal is not to dismiss questions but to sort them. Allow students time to discuss the questions and their reasons for placement along this horizontal "Generative" continuum.

3. *Sort by Genuineness.* Now create a long vertical line bisecting the horizontal axis. Label this vertical line "Genuine." Write "high" at the top of this vertical line, and "low" at the bottom end. Ask students to consider their own genuine interest in each question, that is, how much they personally care about and are invested in pursuing any of these assembled questions previously sorted on the horizontal line. Students move each question directly above or below its current placement to indicate how genuinely interested they are in it, though careful to retain its horizontal placement as it moves up or down. Allow students to discuss the questions and their reasons behind their placements in either direction of this vertical "Genuine" continuum.

4. *Sharing the thinking.* Have the group step back and size up the sorting. Each question now resides within one of four quadrants. The upper-right quadrant (Quadrant 1) contains all the questions the group has decided are the most generative to investigate and that they most genuinely care about. These questions are the "best bets" for meaningful inquiry. The upper-left quadrant (Quadrant 2) contains questions that the group doesn't feel are all that generative in relation to other questions but still represent a lot of genuine interest. These are often brief, answerable questions. The group decides how they want to handle the questions in this quadrant, perhaps asking for volunteers to investigate and report back to the group in following class sessions. The bottom-left quadrant (Quadrant 3) holds the questions the group believes to be the least generative and the least genuine. In terms of ongoing inquiry, this set of questions is not likely to yield much new learning. The bottom-right quadrant (Quadrant 4) contains all the questions that seem generative in spirit but the group currently seems to have little interest in. Inform the group that these questions are on hold at the moment but are open for further consideration in the future should their inquiry bring them back into the foreground.

Uses and Variations

While teaching at the American Embassy School in New Delhi, India, Tahireh Thampi used the *Question Sorts* routine with her first graders in efforts to help them develop questions that weren't too big or vague to handle or only elicited "yes/no" responses. With a general set of questions her students had previously produced in their study of invertebrates, Tahireh asked her students to use four question starters to reframe this previous list of questions in a more creative way: *What would it be like if . . .? How would it be different if . . .? Suppose that . . .? What would change if . . .?* Once the class produced about a dozen revised questions, Tahireh made copies of these questions on cardstock so pairs of students could have a deck of cards each. In the next lesson, she distributed each pair a deck of the class questions on cards and asked them to decide together how to sort their questions along two different continua. Tahireh renamed the horizontal axis "possibilities and pathways," explaining that she wanted them to sort the questions according to how they would offer either "few" or "lots" of possibilities to study. She renamed the vertical axis "interest" and asked the students to line the questions up or down according to how interested they were in each question. Because every pair of students had the same set of 12 questions to sort, Tahireh and her assistant could easily listen to the first graders discuss their sorting choices and how they were making placement decisions.

An interesting variation on this routine is *Action Sorts*. Instead of working with questions, a group works with a set of possible actions they have produced. Ten school teams working with the Association of Independent Schools of South Australia in a three-year project to build a culture of thinking across their schools used *Action Sorts* to help them identify their "best bets" moving forward. Previously the group thought narrowly about their actions and often only in one dimension. Or only a single idea would be considered and discussed so that there was little time to explore alternative ideas. The school teams wanted to escape this pattern. After brainstorming a large set of possible actions, writing them on sticky notes, and without critiquing them, each school group then began to sort them. They labeled the horizontal axis, "Power," representing the power to move the school forward and to disrupt the status quo. They labeled the vertical axis, "Manageability," considering the time, resources, and energy to execute these assembled actions. Actions that got placed in the first quadrant were "good starting points." The second quadrant was "worth considering," the third "not worth the effort," and the fourth "long range." Using *Action Sorts*, school teams were able to plan with what struck them as more thoughtful, considered actions to put in place.

Assessment

Asking a question that has some teeth takes practice and experience. As students get more comfortable with formulating questions, notice if they shift away from what one might consider superficial questions and toward those that call for more nuance and investigation. If you notice their questions feel somewhat hollow, a list of question starters like those used in preparation for a *Leaderless Discussion* (page 59) could help.

As students sort along the two axes, listen for the reasons they give for where they place questions. What makes a question generative for them? What makes a question genuine for them? Are they interested in the history or complexity of ideas, the people involved, the influence, the purpose, or other things? How do students determine what kinds of questions seem to offer new perspectives beyond the obvious? Do the questions require a wide variety of thinking moves to investigate, such as looking closely, making connections, or uncovering complexity? Or do they require only information gathering?

Tips

Early on, discuss what makes for a good question and elicit students' ideas. This draws their attention to considering the quality of the questions they ask, rather than simply manufacturing questions. Books such as *Make Just One Change: Teaching Students to Ask Their Own Questions* by Rothstein and Santana (2011) and *Creating Cultures of Thinking: The 8 Forces We Must Master to Truly Transform Our Schools* (Ritchhart 2015) have been very helpful to teachers we work with to support students with question formulating, processing, and pursuing.

Many of the thinking routines, both those in this book and in *Making Thinking Visible* (Ritchhart et al. 2011), include opportunities for questioning, wondering, and puzzling. Rather than introducing a topic and then brainstorming a new set of questions, a teacher could easily take what has already come to light from other thinking routines as a starting list of questions to use with *Question Sorts*. The Understanding Map (Figure 2.1) can serve as a springboard for students to develop questions for sorting at the start of a research journey.

When *Question Sorts* documentation is prominently displayed, teachers and students can revisit and reference this over the course of an entire inquiry cycle. Students can add to the questions, elaborate on perspectives, or even come to see some questions take on more meaning than originally conceived. Teachers can use the documentation to plan future lessons and experiences. The dynamic nature of being able to move around, add, discard, or elaborate on sticky notes is a key documentation feature of this routine.

A Picture of Practice

Paul James (PJ) Miller, a third-grade teacher at Academia Cotopaxi, an international school in Quito, Ecuador, observed that when he asked students to brainstorm questions for a new topic, they tended to produce questions that were broad, vague, or meandering. "Sometimes some of their questions are in such far-off places, I don't really know what to do with them. And then, once we have all of these questions, I am not always sure what to do with them all," said PJ. Like many teachers, he knows answering each and every question students come up with is an impossible feat. There would never be enough time for that. Nor would that be the most worthwhile way to model good habits of research. PJ and his instructional coach, Laura Fried, felt that *Question Sorts* could be promising to help students develop meaningful inquiry.

To begin, PJ and Laura decide to focus students' attention on all the places they had previously been asked to develop questions. They lead a conversation about why learners even ask questions and what could make them powerful for learning. Together, PJ and Laura feel this conversation helps students view questions less like a checklist to complete and more like an exciting, dynamic set of curiosities that grow the more they learn. "We don't want students to think that we pose questions and answer them and then we're done. Finished." says PJ. "I want questions to feel more alive than just a mad race to get them complete."

The following day, PJ launches a new unit of inquiry on ecosystems, briefly introducing the topic and sharing a few images to get his students' imaginations engaged. He then asks them, "Remember yesterday how we talked about the importance of asking good questions to help our learning? Do you think you could create a few questions you believe will be good for us to ask about ecosystems on these sticky notes we have here?" He tells them he wants them to try their best to write what they feel are good questions and that they want to produce a lot of them.

"Do I write just one question on each sticky note?" a student asks.

"Yes, that's right, just one question per sticky note. So, if you have two questions you think could be good, then use two sticky notes. One for each question," PJ replies. At first the room is a little quiet, then the students get busy writing many questions.

Once he sees that every student has a handful of questions, PJ asks everyone to post them on the class whiteboard. Quite a large group of questions is immediately visible to everyone. The children gather around and begin to look at each other's sticky notes. PJ jumps into the emerging conversations, "Wow, just as I thought, you have a lot of questions about ecosystems. Look at all the questions we have!" The children nod in agreement. He continues, "Let me share what I think we can do with all these questions." The students turn their attention to him and PJ proceeds, "Now, every question up here will generate some thinking for us. You wouldn't have asked the question if it wasn't going to help our learning. But with so many questions, it's hard to know where to even get started, so I'd like us to do a little sorting."

"Sorting? What do you mean?" asks a student.

"Well, by sorting, I mean that we're going to try to figure out a way to find the questions in this big pile that will take our learning so much further and deeper about ecosystems," PJ tells them. He is careful to assure them that all the questions are helpful and important. However, some of these questions might produce opportunities for a lot of thinking, while other questions might only take them a little way.

Taking a marker and drawing a long horizontal line on a wide section of the whiteboard, PJ writes "Generates A Lot of Thinking" on the right-hand end and draws a quick image of a large industrial type of factory engine. On the other end, he writes "Generates a Little Thinking" and sketches a quick image of a small battery next to that. He explains he wants them to sort the stack of questions along this line. Questions that seem to have a lot of power go more toward the right. Questions that provide a little power go more toward the left.

"Now, I didn't have you put your names on these sticky note questions for a reason. Can you guess?" PJ asks his students.

"So you don't know whose it is?" a student responds.

"Well, yes, something like that," PJ explains. "But more important, now that we have all these questions in our class bank, the bank belongs to all of us. Together, we can make good decisions for our class inquiry rather than worrying about each and every specific question. Do you want to give this a try?"

He invites the students to come up to the bank of questions in pairs to pick one to handle, not necessarily their own, just any question. The pair then decides where to place it along the line of generativity. "Remember," PJ says, "the questions that you and your friend think could be like this big engine over here, you'll want to place more toward this side of the line. They have a lot of power. And those questions you think give us a little power, like this battery, just place them on that side of the line."

Soon there is a lot of movement and discussion. Admittedly, PJ is a little concerned some of his students would focus only on their own individual questions, and he worries about students getting their feelings hurt in some way. However, he is surprised that the process goes a lot better than either he, or his coach Laura, expect. PJ's students take on the sorting invitation quite seriously. Among the pairs, there is some debate as to where to place certain questions, but PJ sees them quickly come to consensus. This pleases him. He wonders if had he sold them short in the past by withholding opportunities to take ownership of creating questions and determining which ones could make for good learning. PJ, with a little coaching on the side from Laura, decides for a first attempt at this routine, sorting along the generativity continuum is good enough for today.

They revisit *Question Sorts* the following day. PJ introduces the vertical axis using the language: "really care to investigate" and "not a big interest to investigate." Logistically, PJ and Laura had anticipated that the sticky notes could go flying about thus wiping away yesterday's generativity sorting. So, PJ asks his students to imagine each question on the horizontal line as if it has its own swimming lane. He explains each question will either swim up toward "really care to investigate" or swim the opposite direction toward "not a big interest to investigate" (see Figure 4.2). This second day of sorting, along the Genuine continuum, goes just as well as the first day of sorting.

On the third day, the class looks together at the four quadrants of sticky notes. PJ asks his students, "If we are going to focus our inquiry to reach the furthest places

Figure 4.2 Third-grade students sort their questions on ecosystems.

possible, does anyone have an idea where we ought to get started?" They quickly identify the highly generative, highly genuine section as a good starting place for their research on ecosystems. It seems like a naturally good set of questions to start with.

Now they examine the other quadrants and decide that the low generative/highly genuine (Quadrant 2) section could be handled in quick rounds over the following days. PJ asks different students to volunteer to do some independent mini-research on this set of questions so everyone's interest is satisfied. For the questions that wound up below the horizontal line, the class decides to let them stay put – like in a holding tank. "Sometimes we don't know which questions will really be important and interesting until we start investigating," PJ says, "So having a holding tank seems like a good plan for these for now."

Reflecting on the experience, PJ shares, "I suppose in the past, I was afraid I wouldn't know what to do with students' questions if I weren't completely in charge. I think I am finally getting the idea of what my role can be in creating a thinking classroom. I have to believe in what my students can do!"

PEELING THE FRUIT

Select a topic, concept, or issue for which you want to map your understanding.

➤ Introduce the "Peeling the Fruit" graphic. Explain that one way to think about the process of developing understanding is to think of it as a piece of fruit.

➤ Start with the **SKIN** or outer layer of the fruit. *Describe what you see and notice.* Record any features or aspects that you see and notice immediately. Record what you already know about the topic, your prior knowledge.

➤ Get under the skin to the **MEMBRANE** of the fruit. *Raise questions, puzzles, and wonderings.* Record your responses.

➤ Enter the meat or **SUBSTANCE** of the fruit. Here you will develop or track your understanding as you: *Make connections, build explanations and interpretations, identify and consider different viewpoints.* As you are recording these, be sure you are *reasoning with the evidence* at hand to back up your claims.

➤ Define the **CORE** of the fruit. *Capture the essence or heart of the topic, concept, or issue.* What is it really all about?

➤ Now **STEP BACK**. Identify what new *complexities* are emerging as you look at the topic as a whole. What's getting complicated, nuanced, or layered? What new mysteries or puzzles are emerging?

When the Visible Thinking Project developed the Understanding Map (see Figure 2.1) as a means of articulating the kinds of thinking necessary to build understanding, people asked if the map itself could be a routine. While we stressed that there is not a sequence to the thinking moves and that constructing understanding can take many different paths, we acknowledged that one could propose a sequence for thinking that might prove quite useful. David Perkins took on the task of developing that sequence, and the *Peeling the Fruit* routine was born.

Purpose

Understanding is a major goal of our instruction. And yet, our students often don't have tools for developing their understanding or know how to go about the process on their own. Memorization of information is relatively simple but building understanding can be quite a challenge. The *Peeling the Fruit* routine offers *one* way to sequence the process of developing understanding. This routine has many steps and, thus, can take much longer than is typical

Figure 4.3 *Peeling the Fruit* graphic.

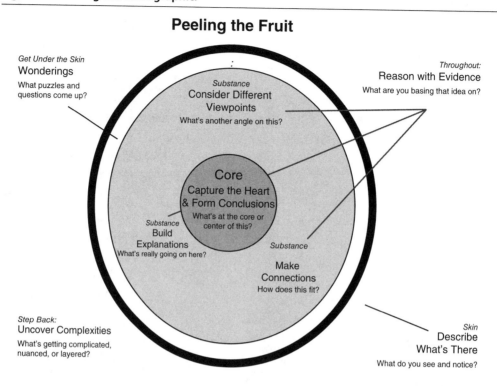

for a thinking routine. The graphic shown in Figure 4.3 can be useful both to recall the steps and the metaphor of *Peeling the Fruit* and in introducing the routine to students.

If the object of understanding is relatively small, say a poem, essay, or artwork, then the routine might be done in one setting with students working together in small groups. If a broader topic is going to be the focus, say understanding democracy, functions, or electricity, then this routine can be used as a graphic organizer to track the sequence of learning over time. Finally, the routine can be used as a synthesizing tool at the end of a unit to pull one's learning together and make sense of it all. In this way, the routine helps to integrate and make sense of the knowledge and information gained so that it can in fact lead to understanding.

Selecting Appropriate Content

This routine requires that there is something to understand deeply versus just gain knowledge about. The object of understanding can be relatively self-contained or an entire unit of study. For instance, students might work in groups to try to understand a passage of text, a current event, or a primary source document. If working with such defined source materials, the material itself should be rich enough that students can use what is actually there on the page, screen, or document to build their understanding and not have to rely on googling to "find the answers." In other words, the source material should afford one the opportunity to build some level of understanding through careful analysis and exploration alone.

If the routine is to be used as part of a unit of instruction, then one is not identifying a single piece of source material but is thinking about an entire sequence of instruction and all the materials that will be used. Whether one is working on understanding a topic (e.g., World War II) or a concept (e.g., sustainability), an important first step is to identify what it is we want students to truly understand versus just know about. Having clarified our understanding goals, we then can use the *Peeling the Fruit* routine to help sequence our instruction. In this case, we will have a lot of source material that students will be exposed to and use. At various points in our instruction, we will stop and engage students in building understanding based on the content to which they have been exposed. For example, after reading a text and watching a short video we might ask student to make use of that material to help them explore connections that will help to illuminate the concept or topic we are seeking to understand.

Steps

1. *The Setup.* Share the *Peeling the Fruit* graphic as a model of building understanding. Talk students through the metaphorical sequence of beginning with the skin and working through to the center. Place students in groups of three or four (you may want to do the routine first as a whole class) and have them read through and carefully examine the content with which you are trying to build an understanding.

2. *The Skin.* Working on a large sheet of chart paper, have students draw a large circle filling most of the page. On the outside of the circle students record what they are noticing. What is immediately apparent? What do they know already about the piece they are examining?

3. *The Membrane.* Have students draw a smaller circle about 1–2 inches inside the original circle. Inside this ring students record their wonderings, questions, and puzzles about the topic, concept, or piece they are exploring.

4. *The Substance.* Have students draw a small circle of about 3 or 4 inches in diameter in the very center of the paper. This will create a second much larger ring.

Inside this ring students record the connections they are making, the explanations they are building, and perspectives they are examining. This process will take a lot of discussion and examination of the piece and should be allowed sufficient time. Remember, this is a process of constructing understanding, not reporting back answers previously provided. This means there may be misconceptions and errors to be dealt with through future discussion and teaching.

5. *The Core.* In the center circle, students record a statement that synthesizes the central idea, message, or meaning they are making of the topic or piece. What is it really all about?

Uses and Variations

Drawing on the fruit metaphor, middle school teacher Sheri McGrath from Penleigh and Essendon Grammar School in Melbourne, Australia, created paper spheres resembling pieces of fruit from six sheets of different colored paper. Each group received a sphere and a piece of chart paper to use as they pulled together their learning from their unit on robotics. Students peeled back the first sheet off the sphere to find the directions: "What did you know about robotics at the beginning of this unit?" Students drew a large circle on their chart paper and recorded their responses on the outside. Next, students peeled off the second sheet of colored paper from their sphere to receive the directions for the next step of the routine: "What questions and puzzles did you have at the beginning of the unit? What additional wonderings or questions have emerged from our study of robotics?" Students recorded their responses inside the circle they had drawn. Sheri then instructed students to draw the 3-inches inner circle in the center or the page. She explained that responses for the next three layers from the fruit sphere would be recorded in this large ring on the chart paper. Working at their own pace, groups progressively peeled back the sheets of their paper fruit sphere to reveal directions to record connections between robotics and other topics they had studied in science as well as other subjects. The next sheet invited them to explain some of the scientific principles at work in the field of robotics. The fifth and next to last sheet asked students to consider different perspectives on robotics: "How might others feel about the topic?" The final sheet of paper asked students to record: "In a single statement, how could you summarize what robotics is all about?" Sheri thought the step-by-step process of unfolding the sphere to reveal the next set of directions helped to make the routine manageable for students and keep them focused.

Morgan Fields, from Bemis Elementary in Troy, Michigan, used the *Peeling the Fruit* routine as a means of documenting her kindergarteners' evolving understanding

Figure 4.4 Kindergarteners build their understanding of fairytales using *Peeling the Fruit*.

of fairy tales as they explored this genre. However, instead of using circles to resemble a piece of fruit, Morgan drew the outline of a castle with three towers on a piece of chart paper (see Figure 4.4). She then recorded what students thought they knew about fairytales on the perimeter of the castle outline. Next, Morgan drew a smaller outline of the castle inside the first to suggest a moat. Here Morgan recorded students' questions about fairytales. This document was then hung on the wall at the front of the classroom. Over the next week the class read and discussed a variety of fairytales. As students made connections between fairytales, "Both these stories have talking animals," these were recorded in one of the towers. Students were also asked about the various features in fairytales, "they often begin with 'once upon a time,'" and why these features might exist. As a class they looked at fairytales from different countries to gain new perspectives. At the conclusion of the unit the class composed their collective definition of fairytales and recorded this in a heart drawn in the middle of the castle: Fairytales are "made up stories with magic and happy endings. They have royalty or talking animals. They teach kids a good lesson!"

Assessment

Peeling the Fruit yields a wealth of assessment information. As students complete the "skin" portion of the routine, make note of what prior knowledge students have about the topic. Pay careful attention to what students are able to notice and name if they are looking at a piece (poem, image, essay, document). As we become more knowledgeable about any topic, our ability to see and notice new features is enhanced. Thus, whatever a student notices tells us what knowledge they have been able to integrate into their understanding of the topic. For instance, if in looking at an image a student notices the artist's use of chiaroscuro, then, we know that student understands that technique and is able to recognize its use. On the other hand, if a student has been taught about chiaroscuro but remarks on "lots of contrast between light and dark," we know the student may understand the concept but has not yet fully integrated the term used to describe it into their functional vocabulary.

The questions students raise can give us important formative information on which to base future instruction. Are students' questions basic and informational or do they reflect depth, curiosity, and nuance? What questions emerge that might form the basis for future instruction? For instance, in Morgan Fields's study of fairytales, students raised the question, "Does every fairytale have magic?" and "Is there always a good guy?" Morgan used these questions to select specific fairytales that might allow students to find answers.

As students make connections, build explanations, and consider different perspectives, they are actively building their understanding. This is a messy process and misconceptions, errors, and mistakes are often made. Make note of these as possible discussion points, either with individuals or with the whole class. This might be facilitated by having students go on a gallery walk to look at what other students have produced and asking them to identify any differences they see in the work of various groups or any ideas or comments they might question. This allows students to confront differences as a point of discussion and exploration rather than one of simple correction from the teacher.

In capturing the essence of any work, concept, or topic we want students to come to their own understanding. This means they might not always give the textbook definition we would like to see. This is okay. Once again, the class might talk about similarities as well as differences between their core statements and those of other groups.

As with all routines, we don't formally assess or grade them. However, having engaged in the process of building understanding collectively, students will be in a good position to engage in more formal assessments that can be graded. In the picture of practice that follows, Tom Heilman has his high school students write an analytic essay as homework following their in-class exploration of a poem using *Peeling the Fruit*.

Tips

Because of its many steps, this is a routine that is often done with the whole class the first time through. In which case, the focus is more likely a single object (poem, image, document, or artifact) rather than large topic or complex concept. When done as a whole class, the teacher acts as documenter, recording students' responses at each step. Alternatively, students could write responses on sticky notes to add to the class document. The "substance" of the fruit can be broken into three separate stages: connections, explanations, and perspectives, as Sheri did with her students exploring robotics. This might be useful to do the first time through when working with the whole class so that you can specifically direct students' attention to each of these different areas of thinking. However, in practice on their own, students often bounce back and forth between these three types of thinking, and it might be too constraining to feel that one must be finished before going to the next. Furthermore, there isn't really a logical order between these three thinking moves.

A Picture of Practice

Tom Heilman has always loved teaching poetry to his high school students at Washington International School in DC. However, he knows that students often approach poems with a bit of trepidation. "Students run away from poetry, and I had that experience when I was younger. I'm determined to make sure students here find a way in because it's a very, very rewarding experience. The most rewarding thing that I get is when a student finally understands a poem, and by that I don't mean that they have found some message that the author put in there. I mean understand it in that they can convey their understanding through an argument that they build on the facts of the poem."

To facilitate this process, Tom regularly engages his students in analyzing poems using *Peeling the Fruit* (watch Tom's video at https://www.youtube.com/The PowerOfMakingThinkingVisible). Tom stresses that the goal is for them to develop their understanding of the poem. "I don't care what you use but what I do want you to do is to develop your core understanding. You'll work from the outside and the surface features in until you come to that core understanding," Tom explains.

As Tom reads aloud Beth Ann Fennelly's poem, "I Need to be More French. Or Japanese." one hears a barrage of American references: to Wrigley Field, to

Mississippi, to magnolias, and to firecrackers. There are references to color: yellow, gray, celadon, brown, and red; and nature: bees, mockingbirds, buds, leaves, and blossoms. Throughout, the phrase "If I were" repeats though not in a rhythmic way. As Tom reaches the last sentence, a sense of wistfulness enters his voice:

> ...If I were French,
> I'd prefer this, end with the red-tipped filaments
> scattered on the scorched brown grass,
> and my poem would incite the sophisticated,
> the French and the Japanese readers –
> because the filaments look like matchsticks,
> and its matchsticks, we all know, that start the fire.

Stepping back into his role as teacher, Tom comments, "Now that's a long poem and it's an interesting poem in terms of the imagery. When you're in your groups you'll start to dig into that imagery."

Familiar with the process of unpacking a poem using *Peeling the Fruit*, students instantly move into groups and obtain a piece of chart paper from the supply at the front of the room. Immediately students draw three concentric circles on their paper and begin by naming and recording outside the largest circle the various features of the poem that they recognize: it is written in free verse, the speaker is the author, only one long stanza, no rhyming, and so on.

As Tom moves around the room, he notices that a group of girls have used their noticings as the basis for raising questions. Katie has written that the poem has "no rhyme" on the "skin" but another member of her group has drawn a line from that into the "membrane" and written "effect?" Likewise, someone in the group has recorded "sarcasm" on the skin, but someone else has drawn a line into the membrane to raise the question, "Not exactly sarcasm, but what?"

Tom notices that another group has not raised any questions in the second circle or membrane of the chart. Instead, they have merely expanded or given an example of what they identified. One student has written "reference to nature" on the skin, and inside the circle another student has given examples such as "mockingbirds, rose, blossoms." Tom presses the group, "What questions or puzzles are coming up for you around this poem?" The group goes blank. They are used to dissecting a poem and identifying all its parts but not questioning it or engaging with it personally. Tom suggests the group have a look at the questions other groups are raising to see if that might spark some ideas for them.

As groups move to explore connections, perspectives, and explanations the conversations become more intense and recording responses takes a back seat to students discussing their tentative ideas. "It seems like as the poem goes on the imagery becomes more elaborate," Katie offers. "Yeah, it is almost more tranquil too, more calm," Elise adds. Tiffany makes a counter point, "I'm not sure it's elaborate in the sense that it is bigger or more showy though. It's more like she's taking these very simple ordinary things and making them more complex."

All of sudden Katie perks up, "Hey that's a connection with the free verse and there being no rhyme. On one hand you think that is simple because it seems so casual and ordinary but then it's not really. There are also these simple, ordinary objects that aren't really. They become more complex." Tiffany builds on this connection, "Yeah, free verse only seems simple. But then you look at the punctuation and the line breaks and you realize how much is going on."

Forty minutes into class, Tom calls students back and asks a few groups to present (see Figure 4.5). He tells them, "You don't need to take us through everything you did step by step, but perhaps some of your richer points of discussion and what you found particularly interesting." John, Thomas, and Marie bring their chart paper to the front and hang it on the whiteboard. "One of our big discussions was around the use of stereotypes," John shares. "Mostly stereotypes against Americans," Marie adds. "It's like she is saying Americans are just loud, big, and crass. But then we noticed that this was more just a contrast she was setting up and it was almost more tongue-in-cheek." "Yeah," Thomas echoes, "she says she wants to be more reserved but there is almost this celebration of the big and then she ends with that last line 'it's matchsticks, we all know, that start the fire.' So, it's like she's embracing that bigness in herself."

The rest of the class erupts in discussion at this point with some agreeing with the group's interpretation and others arguing that they saw the focus not on the big but on the sophisticated versus the simple and that there was actually sophistication to be found in the simple. "This is great," Tom says. "This is everything that I am looking for in your critical commentaries that you'll write tonight as homework. I want you to take ownership of the poem and build the case for your interpretation based on the facts of the poem."

Figure 4.5 Grade 11 students' *Peeling the Fruit* for "I Need to Be More French. Or Japanese."

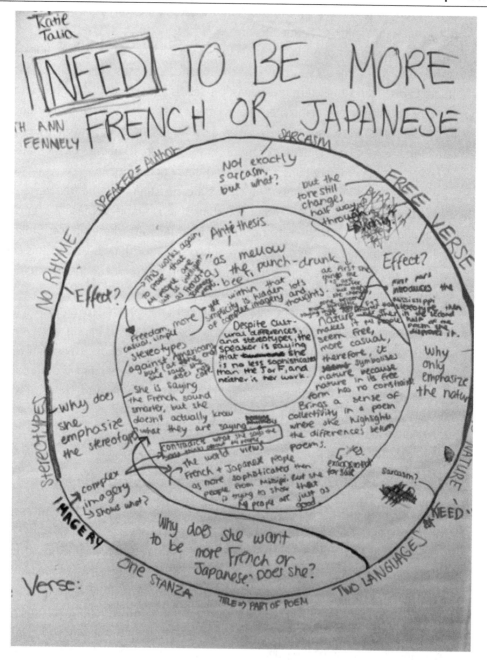

THE STORY ROUTINE: MAIN-SIDE-HIDDEN

After closely examining the source document or material, identify and explain:

- ➤ What is the **main** or central story being told?
- ➤ What is the **side** story (or stories) happening on the sidelines or around the edges? This may not necessarily involve the main characters.
- ➤ What is the **hidden** story, that is, the story that may be obscured, neglected, or happening below the surface that we aren't readily aware of initially?

Densho, a Seattle-based organization dedicated to preserving, educating, and sharing the story of the World War II–era incarceration of Japanese Americans, were looking for new ways to extend learners' understanding beyond the central story of the historical events of the period to explore the deeper issues and implications of these events both at the time and for today. Having accumulated a vast array of primary source documents on their website (densho.org), the question was how to get students to go deeply and look beyond the surface. This was particularly important as many of these documents were propaganda used to justify the internment to the American people and the world. The *Main-Side-Hidden* story emerged as one such vehicle.

Purpose

This routine helps students analyze events and explore documents in more depth by constructing a set of narratives around those events. Learners begin with the main narrative to capture the core or central story being told but then are asked to move beyond that. By looking at side stories, learners are encouraged to consider other actors, factors, and influences that may be at work that are complicating the more basic main story or adding an additional layer. This process may give rise to new questions of inquiry and wonderings. Furthermore, in looking for side stories, students are encouraged to identify additional points of view, which might not be fully represented or portrayed. Looking beneath the surface of events to uncover the hidden story, learners are invited to explore the complexities of the situation. This step pushes learners to think beyond the given and show insight.

Selecting Appropriate Content

Source material should embody depth and some degree of complexity. It might be a primary source document from a historical archive, a complex work of art, a news event or photograph, a particular event from a story or novel, a case study, a data set, or even a social problem or situation. Because the routine is a type of analytic framework, it is often possible to use this routine on the fly as situations come up that would benefit from deeper exploration. For instance, a teacher may recognize that the class's discussion has focused on recalling and becoming clear about the main story and then move the class's discussion deeper by asking what the possible side and hidden stories might be.

Steps

1. *The Setup.* Introduce the source material and invite students to examine it carefully. This could be done individually or in pairs. By attending to details and nuance, students will be more likely to find evidence for their side and hidden stories. This slow looking (Tishman 2017) shouldn't be rushed, and students should be explicitly encouraged to take time to notice things that aren't immediately apparent.

2. *Main.* After careful examination of the source material, invite students (working individually or in pairs) to identify the main story that captures the central ideas that are most apparent.

3. *Side.* Prompt students to identify possible side stories. What else is going on here around the edges? Who are the other actors that might be contributing to the main story but are not the major players?

4. *Hidden.* Finally, ask students to consider the hidden or untold story. What is not immediately apparent but might nonetheless be important in understanding what is actually happening? What might be obscured or left out, either intentionally or unintentionally?

5. *Sharing the Thinking.* Once students have a chance to identify their main, side, and hidden stories, turn to whole class sharing. Often there is agreement regarding the main story, and thus this doesn't need much elaborated discussion. A class will often generate a wide variety of side stories, and students' understanding of the situation can be enhanced be hearing these. As students share, ask them for elaboration, explanation, and evidence, perhaps by using the routine, *"What makes you say that?"* Discuss the hidden stories. It is not uncommon for some students' side stories to be others' hidden stories, and this is okay. As students share their hidden stories, you might follow up by asking, "So what is it that is making you wonder about this situation?" or "Why do you think that story has been hidden?"

Uses and Variations

Steven Whitmore from Oakland County and Jennifer Hollander from Huron Valley School District in Michigan both use the *Main-Side-Hidden* routine as a vehicle to further social and emotional learning (see Figure 4.6). Steven recalled one example of using the *Main-Side-Hidden* routine in a counseling session with a fifth-grade boy. The boy's father traveled frequently, and when the dad returned, the boy would have major meltdowns. After an incident, Steven brought the boy into his office and asked him to draw a house on a piece of paper. "I told him I wanted him to draw what happened inside the house," Steven said. "I just told him that mom said things had been a little rough lately. I didn't instruct him to tell me about a specific incident." The boy drew himself shredding his journal and messing up his room. Steven then asked him to draw to the side of the house "the side story." He drew a kitchen counter and a water bottle on the floor. Finally, Steven asked him to draw underneath the house "the hidden story." The boy drew a number of contrasting images between love and hate. Once all the drawings were complete Steven asked the boy to explain his pictures. The main story was that he had trashed his room and had ripped his journal up because he was angry. The side story was that his water bottle had fallen off the kitchen counter, and his mom blamed him, triggering the

Figure 4.6 *Main-Side-Hidden* **counseling template developed by Jennifer Hollander.**

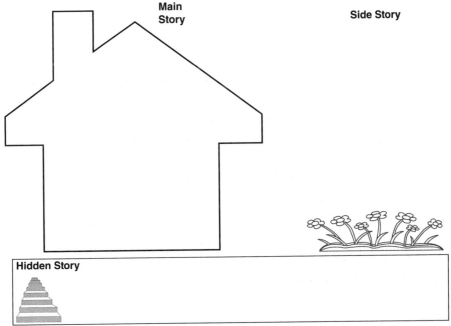

meltdown in his room. When Steven asked the boy to tell him about the hidden part, he said that he had "a love-hate relationship" with his mom and dad. He went on to explain that when one parent is gone, the other parent treats him better. They talk to him like an adult, he is allowed to tell his sisters what to do, and he can make decisions for himself. However, when both parents are home things change and he's treated like a kid. It makes him mad. Not only did the *Main-Side-Hidden* routine provide a vehicle for uncovering the issues behind the boy's behavior, Steven noted that the process of revealing the hidden story had an effect on the boy's behavior, noting that he hadn't had a meltdown since their session together.

Middle school history teacher Amanda Stephens from Penleigh and Essendon Grammar School in Melbourne, Australia, has found the *Main-Side-Hidden* routine works very well in helping students to learn from primary source documents. During a unit on indigenous rights with her ninth graders, Amanda brought in several of her own family's documents from the 1940s. One document, from the Commission on Native Affairs, clarified the classification of a mother's children as quadroons, explaining that as such they were not considered "natives" as long as the children did not live or associate with "natives." Her students uncovered the side story of total control over the lives of indigenous people and the associated condescension from those in power. The hidden story revealed what Amanda and her students identified as the "ugly truth" of racism and genocide in the systemic efforts to impede family connections with relatives and thus interrupt the passing on of indigenous identity.

Assessment

Identifying the main story shows students' ability to grasp the central idea or basic plot of the source material. Sometimes students may even overlook the main story and try to jump to a deeper level, as the main story seems too basic or superficial to them. It may be important to ask students to slow down. In identifying the various side stories, look to see if students are able to identify characters or events that are related to the main story and extrapolate from them to begin fleshing out peripheral issues and concerns. If students know a lot about an event or historical period, they may know of other general concerns and issues affecting events and identify these as side stories. Such connections can be very useful and shouldn't be discounted; however, do encourage students to make direct links to the source material as much as possible, asking: "Where in the image, story, or document does that show up?"

The hidden story is by its nature speculative as it asks students to think about what is not apparent. The question, "What might be going on that we are not seeing directly?" invites this. Are students able to think flexibly about possible hidden stories and influences? Can they then make a case for those hidden motives and influences by tying them back to the main story? For instance, "How does that hidden story help us to understand the main story better?" Can students identify reasons why that story might be hidden? For example, people don't often admit to racism as a motive for their behaviors and often try to hide it behind other, more acceptable motives.

Tips

To help students identify the *Main, Side, and Hidden* stories, it can be useful to develop specific questions that directly connect to the particular source material being used. For instance, in a mathematics class's examination of a data table a question to get at the main story might be: What does this data tells us? What's the table trying to show us or help us see? The side story then might be: What else is going on here with this data if we look a bit deeper? Then finally to get at the hidden story the question might be: What are some of the things we don't see in this data table that we would need to understand to fully make sense of this data? Are there hidden issues or concerns not immediately addressed in the table itself? Those questions would be quite different if we were examining a soliloquy from one of Shakespeare's plays, looking at a primary source document announcing the internment of Japanese Americans, looking closely at a work of art, or exploring a personal event.

To help students understand that hidden stories are not just fanciful imaginings but are built on and extrapolated from evidence, it may be worthwhile to watch an excerpt from Tracy Chevalier's Ted Talk on finding the story inside the painting (https://www.ted.com/talks/tracy_chevalier_finding_the_story_inside_the_painting). In this talk Chevalier, author of *The Girl with the Pearl Earring*, walks the audience through her process of looking closely at paintings to identify important and curious elements that she can then link to historical context and finally build a story around.

A Picture of Practice

When Steve Davis and Darrel Cruse from Penleigh and Essendon Grammar School first encountered the *Main-Side-Hidden* routine, they assumed it would not be one that they would use in their grade 12 accounting course. However, as they watched it being put to use in a senior English class as part of a Learning Lab (discussed in Chapter 7) something clicked. "As we watched this class unfold, we discussed a few things we liked about the routine and realized that we could use it in a particularly hard topic for our subject: discussion questions. These have been an area of concern for us, and something a lot of students struggle with, as there is no set criteria for marking on the end-of-year examination," Steve noted.

Specifically, Steve and Darrel thought the routine would be useful as a structure to help students formulate responses to discussion questions that required students to show an understanding of accounting as a whole and not just familiarity with a single topic or procedure. This is one of the big ways that accounting as a subject has changed across the state of Victoria. The end-of-year state exams have moved from a focus on recounting rules and applying procedures to the application of accounting in real-world contexts. Because these new types of questions focus on depth of understanding, students were often at a loss how to approach them. Darrel and Steve noted that many weaker students merely repeated information given to them without interpreting it.

Recognizing that applying the routine to looking at data would be different from interpreting literature, Darrel and Steve began by identifying the questions they would ask to link the routine to their subject of accounting. They came up with the following:

- *Main:* What can you take from the data or information provided, what does it directly tell you?
- *Side:* What core assumptions or characteristics of accounting apply to this area? How does each relate?
- *Hidden:* What is the effect of these? How does it affect decision making for the owner?

Steve and Darrel initiated the routine by using some familiar data around which students had a lot of context, the Australian Football League (AFL). Steve explained the task. "I'm going to give you some data on AFL teams' performance over the years. Please create three columns labeled Main, Side, and Hidden on a separate sheet of paper." Using the prompts Steve and Darrel crafted, students began to make notes within each column. As students finished, Steve explained the next task, "Use the notes that you have before you to craft your response to the discussion question I've posted on the whiteboard. This is quite similar to what you will be asked to do for the course exam." Steve noted that the writing process seemed much easier than it had with past questions. Students found the structure of organizing their initial analysis of the data in three columns using the Main, Side, Hidden framework helpful in jump-starting their writing.

The next day, both teachers repeated the process but with a table of raw information regarding historical cost, depreciation, carrying value, and estimated market worth for a business over a four-year period. Darrel wrote the discussion question prompt, one quite similar to what they might encounter on the test, on the whiteboard: "Using this data, discuss the impact and importance of recording depreciation for a business." Darrel reminded students to make use of the process from yesterday and create their three columns of Main, Side, and Hidden, or simply "the table," before beginning their writing.

Reviewing students' written responses after class, Darrel noted, "This approach gives a form and structure to students' writing and makes sure that they address implications of accounting and went beyond reading the table." Steve commented, "This seems to help the weaker to middle students the most. In the past, these students have struggled to find the links between why a business would depreciate."

Both Steve and Darrel continue to use the *Main-Side-Hidden* routine with each of the concept areas in the accounting course, seeing gradual improvement and success by the students. Although initially they thought the routine was of most help to their weaker students, over time Steve and Darrel noticed that improvement was happening across the board. "As Victoria Curriculum assessors of external examinations, we would be lucky to mark one or two student papers at the level of a 100% response out of the 300 odd papers we mark each year," Steve notes. "However, in our classes now we have at least 2–3 students per assessment task reaching that level out of our combined group of 55 students, which is astounding. We are also seeing significant increases for our lower to middle range who are now averaging scores in the 60–75% range rather than the previous averages of 40–55%."

BEAUTY & TRUTH

After reading a text, viewing an image, considering a complex issue, or reflecting upon an event, ask:

Beauty   Where can you find **beauty** in this story/image/issue/event? What are all the things that strike you as rather beautiful or appealing?

Truth   Where can you find **truth** in this story/image/issue/event? What are all the things that strike you as the fact of the matter, the reality of things?

Reveal   How might beauty **reveal** truth? Where does something of beauty illuminate some element of truth or bring it to light?

Conceal   How might beauty **conceal** truth? Where does something of beauty obscure some element of truth or make it hard to see?

For a number of years, our Project Zero colleagues, Veronica Boix Mansilla, Flossie Chua, and their team members, have examined what it means to develop and support global consciousness and global competence among youth. They are deeply invested in creating learning environments that cultivate the habits of mind with which students come to understand the complexities of the world and live and work in it successfully. Working with the Pulitzer Center education team as part of the Global Lens project supported by the Longview Foundation, Veronica and her colleagues set themselves the task of creating new routines specifically tailored to journalism. *Beauty & Truth* emerged as a result of these efforts, and we share our version of it here. This routine engages students with exploring big issues while fostering the dispositions of moving beyond familiar notions to engage with new points of view openly, discerning local and global significance, understanding places and contexts, taking cultural perspective, and challenging stereotypes.

Purpose

The types of thinking brought to the foreground in this routine include looking closely, considering viewpoints, making connections, and uncovering complexity. *Beauty & Truth*, in many ways, comes alongside previously published routines such as *Step Inside* and *Circle of Viewpoints* (Ritchhart et al. 2011). This family of routines provokes learners to move outside their own way of thinking and challenges them to take on a variety of differing perspectives in order to understand the nuances and complexities of an issue, an event, or a concept more broadly. When one considers an issue or event from seemingly different points of view, interesting opportunities to uncover complexities emerge that support critical engagement with global themes, current controversies, or timeless issues.

Selecting Appropriate Content

This routine explores the complex interaction between distinct points of view: beauty and truth. It was developed initially to explore complexities of global issues in light of the overwhelming quantities of information students have access to in our visually informed, media-saturated world. Educators in both schools and museums have found this routine useful when exploring journalism, both print and photographic, and also with works of art. It invites students to learn about how high-quality journalism uses beauty to engage us to learn more about an issue and seek truth, while causing students to reflect how journalists and artists comment on and invite us to consider our world.

We've seen teachers enact this routine with other content contexts, such as debating an ethical issue in science, analyzing poetry, or even looking into issues of anthropology, geography, or literature. One important ingredient in all these contexts is that the source material should be complex, rich, and nuanced. There needs to be enough present that one can "read into it" rather than staying on the surface. In choosing content it is useful to quickly apply the routine yourself. Are you able to find many instances of beauty? Can you find many features that reveal truth?

Steps

1. *The Setup.* Prepare the source material or provocation. If it is an image, it is best to have good quality, vivid reproductions or projections. Allow enough time for students to look at and experience the provocation closely before leading into the next steps. Often this initial looking is done silently with the simple direction to notice as much as possible, considering how to document ideas that come up. If the routine is done as a whole class, then the teacher might be the one documenting. If students will be working in groups, a group document might be created. Having a list of where beauty and truth reside in the source material can be useful as students begin to think about how beauty might reveal or hide truth. In some instances students might be asked to individually document their initial ideas before sharing out in their groups or with the class.

2. *Where can you find beauty in this story, image, issue, or event?* The word "beauty" is purposely broad and can be interpreted as features that are aesthetically or otherwise pleasing, attractive, or appealing. It is not necessary to overly define this word. Allow students to bring their own interpretations and follow up with, "*What makes you say that?*" Have students identify all the ways, great or small, in which one might conceive of beauty in the story, image, issue, or event in front of them.

3. *Where can you find truth in this story, image, issue, or event?* The word "truth" is also purposely broad, allowing students to interpret it in a variety of ways. Truth could be a fact, a reality, or a universal. Again, it is not necessary to overly define the term before beginning. Have students identify all the ways that truth – or fact of the matter, or reality – is represented within the story, image, issue, or event.

4. *How might beauty **reveal** truth?* Where does something of beauty illuminate some element of truth, or especially bring it to light? How so? *What makes you say that?* Students will need time to think, explore, or discuss with a partner before responding to this question. Often students' responses lead to compelling opportunities for exploration and discussion in which others join in. Welcome these interactions.

5. *How might beauty **conceal** truth?* Where is there something of beauty in this story, issue, image, or event that obscures something of truth and makes it hard to discern? How so? In what ways? *What makes you say that?* The questions of revealing and concealing do not have to be done sequentially. It is possible to consider them together and allow the conversation to bounce back and forth.

6. *Sharing the Thinking.* If the routine has been done as a whole class and students' observations documented, then much of the thinking has been shared. If the routine was done in small groups, have them share the most insightful points of their group conversation. In both instances, asking where they uncovered things that at first might not have been apparent can be a useful way to close the conversation. In addition, you might ask: "How was your understanding of the issue/topic illuminated by this routine?" "How has your understanding of the concepts of beauty and truth changed, grown, or deepened in some way?" "What might your '*I Used to Think . . . Now I Think . . .*' responses be?"

Uses and Variations

Caitlin McQuaid, a fifth-grade teacher at the Garden Elementary School at the King Abdullah University of Science and Technology (KAUST) in the Kingdom of Saudi Arabia, used *Beauty & Truth* with her international students during a unit of inquiry on various types of energy sources. Students read Allan Drummond's picture book, *Energy Island: How One Community Harnessed the Wind and Changed Their World* (2011). This book tells the true story of a small Danish island community coming together and reducing their carbon emissions by 140%, thus becoming almost completely energy independent. The inspiring story shows that with a little hard work and a big goal in mind, ordinary people can achieve extraordinary things. But this change didn't come without challenges. Caitlin asked her fifth-grade students to consider all the beauty conveyed in this community's journey to harness the wind. Then students turned their attention to the realities of making their dream come true. By thinking about this community's story from the vantage point of beauty, then truth, Caitlin found the level of discourse became nuanced.

Julie Frederick, a high school English language arts teacher at the American International School of Lusaka in Zambia, used *Beauty & Truth* when listening to a recollection from the critically acclaimed StoryCorps Project (https://storycorps.org). Julie's 11th-grade students listened to "Saint of Dry Creek," a story told by a gentleman as he recalled an interaction with his father when he was a teenager struggling to understand his sexual orientation growing up in the 1950s. In the story, the young man faces a moment of fear with his father that turns into a moment of unconditional love. Julie thought this afforded the opportunity to consider the story elements and literary features of a personal essay through the perspectives of both beauty and truth. Julie felt that scrutinizing these dual perspectives, beauty and truth, led to more complex conversations about identity, family relationships, fear, and love.

Still other teachers, like Alisha Janssen of Pacific Lutheran College in Queensland, Australia, have used *Beauty & Truth* with geography concepts when looking at technology, innovation, and the earth's resources. *Beauty & Truth* serves as a structure to help students develop a strong pattern of behavior to navigate complex, nuanced wide-ranging global concepts, from self-identity to energy independence.

Assessment

As students explore *Beauty & Truth*, pay attention to their responses in the first two prompts to understand how they are implicitly defining these terms. When students share elements of beauty, what aspects of beauty seem to be coming to the surface? Are students considering aesthetics, ideals, or benefits? When students share elements of truth, what aspects do their responses reveal? Are students considering practical realities and matter-of-fact items? Do they identify universal truths? Which aspects of truth could be called into question, meaning they might not be as inevitable as one would think at first?

Pay attention to students' perspective seeking, connection making, and complexity uncovering capabilities as they engage in this routine. Do their responses indicate that they recognize people can understand beauty and truth in different ways? Are they able to place themselves in the position of the actors or characters depicted in the sources to identify beauty and truth from their perspective? Do students connect and build off one another's ideas? As the discussion progresses, are students able to identify tensions, ambiguities, and complexities in the subject matter or do they attempt to simplify and draw easy conclusions? Over time, look for how beauty and truth become complex but useful touchstones in students' conversations and explorations.

Tips

As mentioned, don't be overly concerned about defining the terms beauty and truth at the outset. The terms are broad and have a multiplicity of meanings and applications. We notice students bring much more to these concepts than teachers might expect. For instance, Nellie Gibson engaged her kindergarten class in a months-long investigation of beauty that yielded rich conversation and insights (see Ritchhart, 2015). However, if you see that students struggle with how they understand beauty or how they articulate truth, you can create a future opportunity for exploration. For example, develop a list of criteria together over time as to what makes something strike us as containing "beauty" or representing "truth." Look for beauty and truth in the everyday experiences of students. Point out where you see beauty and truth. Once a list develops representing several angles on these notions, you can prompt students to broaden their initial perceptions and take on even more perspectives, a key goal for developing this type of global thinking disposition.

Rather than going through all four steps at once with a group of students, and then having a conversation, it is often useful to break the routine into two parts. Steps 2 and 3, the exploration of beauty and truth, can be done together as a whole class and documented. This expands everyone's understanding of what is in the source material and illuminates various perspectives of viewers. Then turn to Steps 4 and 5, the discussion of revealing and concealing truth. This step tends to be more conversational, nuanced, and complex. Students often try out various ideas aloud to see how they hold up. You can encourage this tentative exploration by having students first discuss in small groups or with a partner before turning to a whole class discussion. Teachers have also inverted the phrasing of Steps 4 and 5, asking, "How might truth reveal beauty?" or "How might truth conceal beauty?" rather than the other way around.

Facilitative questions can be key in better understanding the layers of complexity students grapple with in this routine. For example, *"What makes you say that?"* or "So how do you see this idea linked with this other idea?" offers students an opportunity to elaborate their responses and explain their reasoning. This also conveys a message that you're listening closely to them and following their line of reasoning, rather than trying to get them to land on a predetermined answer.

Other routines such as *Give One Get One* (page 42) or *Headlines* (Ritchhart et al. 2011) pair well with *Beauty & Truth* to create rich interactions for students to make connections and synthesize ideas. For example, students could be asked to identify three things of beauty and three things of truth in an image and then discuss these initial lists with others through the *Give One Get One* routine. In concluding the *Beauty & Truth* routine, students could be asked to create a headline that distills their new understanding of the issue/image/problem.

A Picture of Practice

Pennie Baker, a primary trained teacher working as a teacher-librarian at St. Philip's Christian College in Newcastle, Australia, has used the routines *See-Think-Wonder* and *Step Inside* for some time, and her students have become quite familiar with them. As a teacher-librarian, Pennie has multiple classes for just a lesson or two a week, rather than her own single homeroom group. Because it is a real challenge to continue threads of thinking over time, Pennie relies on the use of thinking routines to help document ideas to carry learning forward from lesson to lesson, especially because large gaps of time pass between sessions. *Beauty & Truth* struck Pennie as a promising routine that could build on her already established thinking routines and looked for just the right place to introduce it.

In a series of library lessons connected to their social studies curriculum, Pennie's Year 5 students watched a video, *Australia: The Story of Us*, originally airing on Australia's Seven Network (2015). This presentation featured several prominent Australians examining some of the people, places, and events that shaped Australia over the last 40,000 years. Pennie felt this experience could be processed by using *Beauty & Truth*, giving students an opportunity to think of their country's history, and global/universal issues embedded within, from multiple perspectives.

Pennie focuses on one particular event highlighted in the video, the Eureka Stockade. In 1854, gold miners in Victoria revolted against what they deemed to be unfair authority by the British colonial forces in the region. They strongly objected to severe regulation and taxation. Sadly, a fierce battle was fought and lives were lost. But this event is viewed by many as a defining moment in Australian history as the revolt of free men against imperial tyranny, paving the way for basic democratic rights.

Rather than asking her students if they agreed with the miners' actions or not, and perhaps just eliciting superficial opinions, Pennie replays a short segment of the video for the class. Then she asks, "I'd like you to take a moment and consider this: Just where was there something you saw in this clip on the Eureka Stockade that you believe is worthy of mentioning? You consider it as being beautiful, powerful, special, valuable or inspiring?" Pennie gives her students a few minutes to gather their responses, then asks the class what came to mind.

One student replies, "I think something beautiful was the miners standing up to the troops."

Pennie asks, "Why do you say that? What was powerful or beautiful about the miners and the troops?"

The student elaborates, "Well, they were willing to give up their lives and fight for their freedom."

Another student adds her voice to the conversation. "Something I thought was beautiful was that the miners stuck up for one another."

Pennie again asks a facilitative question. "Can you say a little more? Where did you see an example of that in the video?"

The student responds, "When the troops picked on one miner for not having the proper license, all the other miners started pushing the troops away."

Another student joins in, "Yeah, like they were a community. That was kind of beautiful."

Pennie reflects back to them, "Community. I see. And how does that show a sense of community?"

The student continues, "Well, they helped each other. They were willing to take a risk to help another friend in need."

Another student jumps in, "Well, the troops also stood up for each other like a community and they were actually just trying to do the job they thought was the right thing to do in service of their country. So maybe that was a thing of beauty too?"

Pennie feels this particular response really takes the conversation to another level of depth. Considering giving service to their country as a thing of beauty is a rather unconventional response that she had not expected students to surface. However, it actually reveals some great tensions and complexities to understanding revolts, uprisings, battles, and rather complex events like these. This pleases Pennie.

The conversation around beauty continues for some time. Then Pennie asks the students to think about the same video clip from another point of view: Truth. She asks, "Okay, so there are many things of beauty in this event, but now could I get you all to think about where you found truth in this video about the Eureka Stockade? If you had to make a list of just the facts or the reality of things in what you just saw, what would be on your list?" The students take some time to jot down their responses, then they begin to share when Pennie asks.

Some students mention the truth that neither side was willing to give up, thus the battle broke out. Other students mention that even though the miners standing up for their rights was a thing of beauty, the truth of the matter is that this led to violence and lives were lost because of this.

Pennie was blown away by the students' responses, just using this routine for the very first time. "In the past, I know that I would have just told them all the information about this, or any other event, with the belief that if I just tell them, they'll get it. But when given a tool and structure, along with time and interest on my part, my students can do so much more than I ever dreamed," Pennie reflected after the lesson.

Given that this was the first time Pennie had used *Beauty & Truth*, and also knowing that the library period was coming to an end, Pennie decided in that moment to hold off asking about where beauty reveals truth or where beauty conceals truth. "I do wonder what they might have said there," said Pennie. "I actually think they would come up with something interesting. I mean, already they articulated the fact that the colonial troops, though perhaps cast as bad guys in this video presentation, could have some interesting tensions and complex perspectives to explore. It's not so black and white!"

Pennie led other class sections in exploring the Eureka Stockade with the *Beauty & Truth* routine. "The students told me that when they heard each other's nominations for beauty and truth, they told me it gave them ways to see the same event from someone else's eyes. I think that's a powerful thing," Pennie reflected. "Once again, I was astounded by my students when I dedicate time for them to make their thinking visible. Going forward as *Beauty & Truth* becomes routine, I know I'll want to talk and direct even less so that the students can talk more. They have such depth in their responses, I think I just need to give them the agency they deserve. They have a voice and my job is to create a place for that voice to come out."

NDA

Choose an image to examine closely. Look at it for one minute and then remove it from sight. Now, working from memory . . .

Name Make a list of all the parts or features you can remember. These will most likely be nouns, things you can point to and name.

Describe For each of the things you have named, add a description. What adjectives could you add to the nouns you have listed?

Act For each of the things you have named, tell how they act. What are they doing? What is their function? How do they add or contribute to the whole? How are they related to other things you have named? These may be, but don't have to be limited to, verbs.

One of the most frequently used routines from *Making Thinking Visible* (Ritchhart et al. 2011) is *See-Think-Wonder*. This is a powerful routine because it fosters both close looking and deep analysis. We were looking for additional ways to foster close looking while also enhancing expressive vocabulary and developing working memory. We noticed that when we removed an image from sight and students had to recall what they had seen from memory, students often saw the value of looking closely and noticing in a way they might not have previously, thus, deepening engagement with the ideas. In addition, when students began with naming objects in the image and then were encouraged to progress to description (adjectives) and action (verbs) their expressive vocabulary was enhanced. This seemed to be particularly useful for second language learners who may have a limited vocabulary.

Purpose

This routine emphasizes the importance of careful observation and close looking as the basis for thinking and interpretation. Working with an image, the routine helps students notice and describe an image in ever increasing layers of detail. For young children or for students learning another language the routine can also help to build language proficiency. It can be done in groups or individually, but only when done individually is it likely to help boost working memory.

This routine can be a stand-alone activity (even as a game) to enhance students' ability to look slowly, observe closely, and utilize memory. It provides an opportunity to talk with students about how the brain works (Briggs 2014; Schwartz 2015). For instance, when asked to recall after the image is taken away, students have to rely first on their working memory, the stuff we are able to hold in our heads. Our recall from memory is one of the things that begins to lock short-term memories into long-term memory. This is why retrieval practice is a good study technique (Note: the *+1 routine* on page 86 focuses on retrieval practice). In recalling information about the image students are also making use of visual memory, recreating the image in their head. Visualization and imagery can also be powerful study techniques. Finally, students are utilizing "chunking" as they group associated objects together, which reduces memory load. This is why people in the US memorize telephone numbers as a series of three, three, two, and two numbers rather than 10 individual digits.

Although useful as a vehicle for talking about and developing memory, *NDA* is more powerful when the content is integrated within more purposeful learning. Used at the beginning of a unit, *NDA* can help to create what Alison Adcock calls a "motivated brain state" by fostering curiosity and a desire to know more about the image at hand (Briggs 2017). If information on the image is provided after the initial *NDA* routine, students are more likely to retain it and be motivated to learn more. This assumes of course that the image is one likely to spark interest and curiosity. When used with a topic that has been studied, the routine helps to solidify students' understanding as they identify the very parts and pieces of that topic. Finally, the routine provides an accessible framework for analysis as we will see in the "Uses and Variations" section.

Selecting Appropriate Content

Although the term "image" is used for this explanation, what the learners are asked to look at carefully may be a painting, photo, artifact, excerpt of text, political cartoon, chart, found object, in fact, almost anything that can be observed and interpreted. However, selecting an evocative, engaging stimulus is critical. A good test is to ask yourself whether the image/object engages you. Can you look at it for several minutes and notice new things? Does it spark your curiosity? Since the first step of the routine focuses on close looking and naming things, there needs to be a number of elements in the image to see and notice to ensure the routine is relevant. Likewise, because students will be asked to describe the things they have named, the objects should have a bit of variety. It may seem that the ability to describe how objects are "acting" would require the image to portray some kind of event or action; however, this need not be the case. Using a variety of verbs to describe similar actions can be useful in extending both vocabulary and thinking. For instance, a standing figure could be described as waiting, pausing, contemplating, lurking, menacing, directing, overseeing, pondering, and so on.

This routine can also be used to review a unit of study or text (see "Uses and Variations" below). In this case there should also be a degree of richness of things to name and identify, describe, and identify actions and/or interactions. In some cases, such a review may present too many things to recall, and you will want to narrow down the range of possibilities for recall.

Steps

1. *The Setup.* Present the chosen image for one minute in a way that allows students to see the image/object in as much detail as possible. Projecting the image on a screen in a darkened room works well. Because the observation period is timed, it is often helpful to create a blank slide in your presentation both before and after the image. Direct students to look closely and notice as much as they can in the one minute of observation. Remind students not to talk or share just yet. After one minute, remove the image from view.

2. *Name.* Ask learners to name in writing and from memory as many things as they can from the image. A useful prompt is to name things that you could actually put your fingers on within the image. Tell students to focus on just specific objects, that is, soldiers, guns, flames, and so on rather than "a fight" or "war." Students can write their responses in a list or divide their sheet into three columns at the outset and have them label each: Name, Describe, and Act.

3. *Describe.* Ask learners to describe each of the objects they named using one or two adjectives or an adjectival phrase. Stress the use of adjectives. For instance if there is a man in the image sitting at a table and students name "a man" as one of their objects, they should use adjectives to describe him such as tall, large, imposing, and so on rather than to write an elaborate description that focuses on actions: "Well the man is in the left hand corner and he is wearing a hat and a green coat, and he is sitting at a table, and it looks like he is waiting for someone." Learners can write their adjectives beside the things they have named. It generally is not necessary to put the image back up before this stage, but you could allow another viewing if you think it is needed. However, note that memory is enhanced and built through its use and a bit of struggle to recall is not necessarily a bad thing.

Note: An alternative way of handling the describing phase is to pair students. One student reads off of the list something that was named, and the student's partner describes it with an adjective. They repeat this process back and forth until both have exhausted their lists. If person A names something that person B did not see, then person A is responsible for describing it.

4. *Act.* Ask learners to tell how each of the named objects is acting. This might simply be assigning a verb to the object. If so, instruct students not to use the same verb more than once. This will stretch their vocabulary. Depending on the image or instructional intent, the focus on action might extend beyond the question, "What are they doing?" to consider: What is their function? How do they add or contribute to the whole? How are they related to other things you have named? How are they interacting with the other named objects?

   Note: If students are working with a partner, have them switch their focus to identifying actions. Student A names something from their list and student B assigns it an action by using a verb (or identify some other form of action, function, relationship, interaction). This continues with each partner taking turns naming something and the other assigning it an action.

5. *Put the Image Back up.* At this point, students are often eager to see the image again to confirm their observational memories. Put it up and allow students to talk informally. Typically, there is a lot of pointing and animated discussion. If you have selected an image to pique interest, ask students what they are still wondering about the image and what questions they have. This would be a good time to share any information with students about the image to capitalize on their motivated brain state.

6. *Sharing the Thinking.* If students have done this routine individually, provide an opportunity to share responses, in pairs or small groups. As students look at others' responses ask them to look for commonalties as well as differences: Did others name things you didn't see? Did others use the same or different words for the "Describe" and "Act" phase? Could you come up with even more words? If students have been doing the routine with a partner, then they have already been doing a lot of sharing. You might want to pull the whole group together and ask: Were there things your partner named that you didn't? What was the most interesting thing to try to describe? Which objects from the image do you think would have the most potential adjectives to describe them and which the least? *What makes you say that?* What was your favorite word for capturing how something was "acting"?

If this is the first time through with the routine, you can use it to talk about working memory, visual memory, and chunking. You can also inform students that our working memory is enhanced through our use of it as we did here.

Uses and Variations

Mary Goetz, a fourth-grade teacher at Bemis Elementary in Troy, Michigan, used *NDA* at the end of a unit on early Native American tribes in Michigan. Working as a whole class, Mary asked students to "name" as many things as they could recall from their study. "It was interesting to note that as we 'named' things in this routine, it was like a domino train being knocked down. One idea fell to another idea and so on and so on." After naming 57 things, Mary asked the class to put the list into categories. Students created groups for names of tribes, artifacts, food, government, and families. Because of the sheer number of items, Mary focused students on describing only a few. Picking an item from each group, Mary asked the students to describe or tell something about it. For instance, a student described a "longhouse" as being up to 200 feet long by 20 feet wide. When it came to actions, students said that the longhouses acted to create community but also an action was a loss of privacy.

At South Fayette High School in Pennsylvania, Tara Surloff used *NDA* to engage her AP Spanish Language and Culture students with short stories in lieu of traditional comprehension questions. After reading Carmen Laforet's short story *Al Colegio* as homework, Tara paired students and told them they would be having a structured conversation based on some simple prompts. Students had large sheets of paper and markers to document their discussion. First, Tara asked students to work together to name all the objects and characters they could think of that played a role in the story. At first students listed only the two main characters, but Sara pushed them, "What are the items in the story that played a role in the relationship between the two main characters?" The students looked at each other, puzzled at first, but then quickly began naming items: taxi, ice cream, braids, crosswalk, desk, chalkboard, and so on. Next, Tara moved students on to describing each of these things. Because this is an advanced Spanish class all discussion and description was done in Spanish. Finally, the pairs of students were asked to explain how each of the characters/objects acted throughout the story. It was during this portion of the routine where the students' misunderstandings of the story came out. As one pair was talking about how the relationship had changed during the story, they discovered they had a different understanding of the timeline. Afterwards students said that the routine "helps them understand the material better because they are looking at the story as a whole, rather than simply searching for the answers to the comprehension questions."

Assessment

In students' "Name" responses, look for improvement in their ability to notice details that take them deeper into the image rather than getting stuck on immediate surface features. In addition, pay attention to how many things students can name. The number of items students can recall is a rough indicator of working memory. Although research has put the number of unrelated items we recall at seven, give or take a few (Miller 1956), we are able to recall much more through chunking and use of visual memory. If students are struggling, additional efforts to engage working memory may be beneficial.

In the "Describe" step, students often use visual memory to recall details. Their responses here can indicate their richness of vocabulary as well as provide an opportunity to develop their vocabulary further. Similarly, the "Act" phase can be about vocabulary if the focus is solely on verbs. If it extends further to explore relationships, interactions, and functions there is the opportunity to assess students' deeper understanding, as Tara demonstrated. Finally, assess students' level of engagement with the image or other source material. Has the routine helped to activate a motivated brain state as evidenced in their questions, discussion, and curiosity about the material?

Tips

This routine has a game-like quality to it, so use that to have some fun and engage students. Doing it as a game can lessen anxiety about the number of items that can be recalled. Sometimes teachers don't like to see students struggle and so want to aid their recall by showing the image again or allowing them to go back to their books/notes. These practices, while helping to generate responses, actually undermine the purpose of the routine, to develop memory and enhance engagement with the source material. It is better to initially give students more time to view the image if you think that would be helpful. It is also fine to let students work with the information they can recall and to accept that as perfectly okay. Expect them to develop over time.

With young students the entire routine can be done verbally. After removing the image from view, students can pair with another student and take turns naming things. Afterwards, you can ask the whole class to name things they saw while you record them. Working from the list, you can read an object and call on several members of the class to describe it, each with a different adjective. One way of handling the "Act" portion of the routine is to have students "act out" or "act as if" they were that object. In one kindergarten classroom each student selected an object and then silently walked around the room as if they were that object.

A Picture of Practice

First-grade teacher Ashley Pellosmaa at Bemis Elementary in Troy, Michigan, thinks a lot about how she will begin a unit of inquiry with her students. In thinking about her science unit on rocks Ashley commented, "Having taught this unit in years past, I know that launching it is going to be the most challenging part because hooking the learners is essential. First graders are naturally inquisitive, so this unit generally layers quite nicely once we start the investigations, but kicking off the unit requires finesse. *Name-Describe-Act* is a routine that grabs an audience's attention and requires the mind and voice to play an active role. As a first-grade teacher, I knew this routine will not only engage my students but also give them a platform to convey and make sense of scientific images."

Ashley searched for two images on the Internet: one of the rock cycle and one of the water cycle. She thought that by having students look at images of both cycles together they might make more connections. In making her final selection of images, Ashley chose two that had vivid colors, many clearly delineated components, and some labels and arrows that helped to convey a sense of action. She felt that these components would support her students' development of scientific knowledge and relationships.

Ashley begins the lesson by gathering students in front of the interactive whiteboard. She explains to the class, "I found two images that came in our science kit, but I was having a hard time making sense of them and need your help." At this point, she opts not to tell students the focus of the science kit, instead using the *NDA* routine to garner interest. Ashley then reveals both images together on the interactive whiteboard, allowing about two minutes for students to look closely at the images and make mental notes. As students gaze silently at the images, Ashley asks the class, "What do you notice?" and instructs them to "Try and remember as much about these two images as possible so that we can discuss it later."

After two minutes, Ashley mutes the whiteboard and tells students to "Turn and chat with a friend about what you saw. Take turns naming items like having a ping-pong match. Go back and forth with one person naming something and then the other names something else." As students' conversations wind down, Ashley brings the class back together and explains, "I want to capture all of the things you just named on this chart paper so we can think more about them. Can someone tell me something they saw and named?" The students name water, rain, hill, trees, sky, sun, volcano, lava, rock, clouds, and mountains.

Next, Ashley tells students she wants them to think about all the items they named but take it one step further. She writes the word "DESCRIBE" at the top of the chart. She then provides an example of description, "If I were to describe a child in the class I might say, brown eyes, brown hair, green shirt, blue pants, and so on. I want you to do that with the items from our 'NAME' section. Turn and talk with your partner about the items we just named. How might you describe them with adjectives?" After a few minutes, Ashley brings the class back together and asks for their descriptions. Students offer a wide variety of adjectives for each of the items and offer lots of color, shape, and size words such as blue, pointy, oval, round, curved, gray, brown, green, gigantic, and big.

Finally, Ashley moves students to the "Act" phase of the routine. "Now we want to tell what each of these things we just named and described are doing." She writes the word "ACT" on the top of the chart and offers further clarification, "If we were truly watching these images in real life or if it were like a movie, then what would each thing be doing?" After sharing with their partners, Ashley collects their words: falling, dropping, standing, feeling, wet, shining, reflecting, erupting, bursting, taking care of everything, and so on. Closing the lesson, Ashley asks the students what the two pictures have in common. A quick response is that they are both about the earth, land, water, and sky. Ashley informs students that their next science unit will engage them in learning more about the earth, specifically the earth's rocks and that they will become geologists.

Reflecting later, Ashley comments, "I was thrilled that vocabulary and information surfaced. Had I merely launched this unit with Investigation #1 from the kit as is common, I don't think the discussion or vocabulary would have been as rich. I was blown away with their engagement with this routine and their working memory. When the opportunity was given to 'NAME' items in the picture, I noticed students digging to cover all bases. When it came time to 'DESCRIBE,' I was amazed at how students connected items to prior knowledge and abstract items." Looking over the documentation from the lesson, Ashley notes the words chosen to describe items – fluffy, curved, rounded, pointy, dull, white, and like cotton candy. "These words were refreshing to hear. It will be interesting to see how students connect these to more scientific words that we will learn. The students are now super curious. This routine really enhanced their confidence. Students walked away saying, 'We are geologists' and 'We are going to discover more about the earth and rocks because we already know so much!'"

TAKE NOTE

After a lecture, film, reading, or discussion learners "take note" of ONE of the following:

➤ What is the most important point?
➤ What are you finding challenging, puzzling, or difficult to understand?
➤ What question would you most like to discuss?
➤ What is something you found interesting?

This routine emerged from our research into helping students engage actively with ideas. In too many classrooms, we see students dutifully copying down notes during lectures rather than actually thinking about the material being presented. A similar problem can occur when students prepare readings for class. They may read but not really engage with the material. Harvard physics Professor Eric Mazur addresses this by asking students to respond to a short, online prompt after reading the material for his flipped classroom. He uses these responses to help shape his in-class teaching. We formalized Professor Mazur's technique into a set of four prompts, from which students choose one, as a simple technique for both engaging students with the material at hand and providing teachers with useful information on which future instruction can be built.

Purpose

Our learning and memory are enhanced by the regular distillation of key ideas as well as our identification of emerging questions and puzzles. In addition, the sharing of ideas and questions supports the group's learning by facilitating continued exploration, discussion, and synthesis as well as providing the instructor with feedback. This routine can be used after an instructional episode, before it, or in the midst of it. When used after an episode of instruction, the routine offers a chance to capture students' thinking. For instance, *Take Note* can be used as an exit ticket that teachers collect and review before the next class. Alternatively, *Take Note* can be used as a flipped classroom strategy in much the way Eric Mazur and others who employ "just in time teaching" strategies have done. Students could submit their responses on a Google doc, an online platform, through e-mail or text, or by using index cards that students bring with them to class. Teachers then organize students' responses as they prepare for the next class to ensure important points are addressed and questions explored. For this strategy to work in the long term, it is important that students see that teachers actually make use of students' responses and build their teaching around the issues and questions students raise.

Used during a lecture or content-heavy class, teachers might stop at regular intervals (every 10–15 minutes) and ask students to respond to one of the *Take Note* prompts. These breaks in the lecture provide moments of reflection and attention through what Professors Stephen Brookfield and Stephen Preskill call "structured silence" (Brookfield and Preskill 2005). They see such silences as a crucial element in conversation, even though students often feel initial discomfort. Therefore, it is important to provide experiences so that students become accustomed to such silences and learn to use them as part of their learning. Such lulls help to keep discussion grounded and focused as well as provide opportunities for new voices to emerge in conversation.

Selecting Appropriate Content

As with all learning, content matters. Meaningful discussions emerge from meaningful content. Likewise, significance can be found only when there is something of importance on the table. The possibility of differing perspectives on complex issues also adds to the richness of discussion. Therefore, this routine will work best with rich content that has a degree of complexity, nuance, and controversy. That content might come from a reading, a lecture, video, speaker, or podcast. However, if you know what you want your students to say in response to that content or think the range of potential responses to the content is likely to be limited, then *Take Note* is unlikely to yield anything substantive on which discussion or future teaching can be built.

Steps

1. *The Setup.* Explain that learning and memory are enhanced by regular distillation of key ideas as well as identification of emerging questions and puzzles. Encourage learners to participate actively in the learning episode without taking notes so as to fully engage.

2. *Respond.* At regular intervals (if there is a lot of content) or at the end of the lesson, pass out index cards (or use one of the technology platforms listed above) and ask each student to respond to any one of the *Take Note* prompts listed previously. The variety of prompts is designed so that every student can find something to which to respond. You may want to write these on the whiteboard or have a slide ready with the prompts. Have students record their thinking *anonymously*.

3. *Sharing the Thinking.* Whether done at intervals or at the end, there needs to be some kind of sharing. This could be done in a number of ways:

- Small groups share and discuss what they have written.

- One table group collects their index cards and passes them to another group. Upon receiving the new cards, the cards are randomly distributed, and each student reads and responds to the card they receive. Cards are recollected and passed back to the group from which they came.

- The teacher collects all note cards and redistributes them randomly. Students read aloud the note card they receive. The teacher may document and organize the responses. Alternatively, the teacher selects a few cards to discuss with the class.

- As an exit ticket, the teacher collects, reads, and summarizes the *Take-Note* cards as a form of formative assessment and begins the next class by sharing or in some way making use of them.

Uses and Variations

Secondary science teacher Emily Veres used the *Take Note* routine with her IB Diploma, higher level biology students at Washington International School in DC. The class was exploring the connection between human evolution and migration. Specifically, students examined maps that showed the global distribution of lactase persistence, human migration shown through mitochondrial DNA, movement of climate refugees, and human migration traced through DNA mutations. In pairs and small groups, students analyzed one of these maps as well as links to relevant articles presenting additional information. As groups explored these materials, they documented their collective responses to all four of the *Take Note* prompts. Emily repeated this lesson with her other biology class. The next day she posted both classes' work in a gallery walk and asked students to walk around each group's documentation and post a comment or question. She noted that some students made connections, some asked questions, and some simply posted general thoughts.

Exploring issues and solutions around reducing pollution, third-grade teacher Erik Lindemann used a similar strategy as Emily with regard to *Take Note*. He gathered a collection of grade-appropriate articles on pollution reduction for his students at Osborne Elementary in Quaker Valley, Pennsylvania. Because students would be working independently, Erik produced a one-page recording sheet divided into quadrants with one *Take Note* prompt in each quadrant (see Figure 4.7). As students read, they used the sheet to record their interactions with the text. Erik set a purpose by letting students know that their responses to *Take Note* on their recording sheet would frame the class's discussion the next day. Following that discussion, Erik used the *3 Y's* routine (page 178) to help students think about global, local, and personal connections.

Figure 4.7 Erik Lindemann *Take Note* recording sheet.

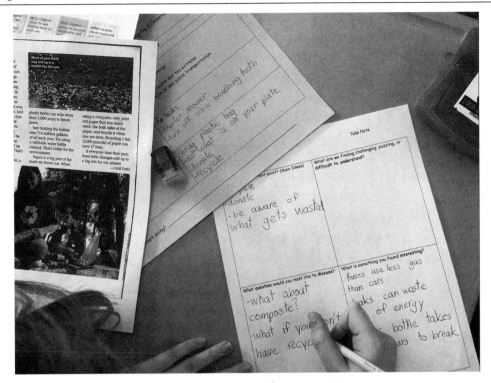

Having used this routine several times, Erik has observed that *Take Note* "is allowing kids to reveal how they are reacting to the ideas on emotional levels. These are the pieces they want to share, and often do in whispers and laughs. This routine captures those powerful bursts of reaction and uses them to shape discussions of interest. We also support a safe platform to unearth misconceptions."

Assessment

Take Note provides an opportunity for teachers to better understand how students are engaging with text, information, and ideas. Pay attention to students' puzzles, challenges, and confusions. Often students won't share their confusion in class because they fear looking silly. By making *Take Note* anonymous and synthesizing a class's responses, you are more likely to find out the things about which students are confused. As senior English teacher Lee Crossley from Penleigh and Essendon Grammar School in Melbourne, Australia, observed, "The great thing about this [routine] is it gave me feedback about areas we needed to work on as a class. It also generated discussion and allowed me to assess what proportion of the class was struggling with these things."

Similarly, the question prompt opens the door for exploration of the topic in a way that will address students' interests and needs. These questions also can be useful in planning future lessons. Pay attention to the kinds of questions students ask over time. Are they able to engage with the content in a meaningful way that will deepen their understanding? Are their questions open and inquiry based? If not, then some discussion of closed and open-ended questions might be useful. You might also use the *Question Sorts* routine (see page 98).

In students' responses to the most important and interesting prompts, don't just look for correctness. Instead pay attention to what is resonating with students. These prompts are to promote engagement with the ideas/information/text and not as tests. If you feel that students are missing the point, follow up with discussion along the lines of: "Several people said _____ was the most important, while others said _____ was. I'd be interested in hearing your reasoning behind those."

Tips

Students will give us their thinking only if they think we are interested. Therefore, it is important to value the responses students give to the source material and to make use of it in some way. As Erik Lindemann noted, "I think emphasizing how their contributions are directly related to the upcoming discussion motivates students as they know they are shaping the upcoming pieces of the day."

Although you may allow students to respond to all of the prompts, as was mentioned in the variations by Emily and Erik, one goal of this routine is to make the process of providing responses accessible for every student. Each of the four prompts provides an alternative way into the source material. If you have to respond to every prompt, every time, then the routine could become just another worksheet. In addition, responding to all four prompts can slow down what is meant to be a quick process.

A Picture of Practice

Ninth-grade history teacher David Riehl from Munich International School tried out the *Take Note* routine the first day his students returned to school after their fall break. David had learned about the routine at a Project Zero conference and was eager to try it. "I wanted to give myself the challenge of trying something new right away in our class. We value thinking and use a range of routines, so I was not inserting this routine out of the blue. I also hoped that some kind of product would emerge to make a bridge to the next lesson."

David's class had been studying the Indian Mutiny of 1857, which is also referred as the Sepoy Mutiny because it was led by Indian infantrymen known as sepoys. As historians, students were looking at both the causes and consequences of this mutiny. After reviewing material from previous sessions, David asks students to independently read an excerpt from their history text on the aftermath of the mutiny. He then directs them to another section of text about the actions taken by Britain to make India an official colony. This passage also details the intellectual and political roots of Indian opposition to colonization.

As students finish their independent reading, David writes the four *Take Note* prompts on the whiteboard. Once most of the class finishes reading, David explains the routine, "The purpose of this routine is to help cement our key understandings of the day and to identify key questions that might remain unanswered. You can respond to any of the prompts you want. It is okay to respond to more than one if you feel inclined. We're going to write these on index cards. You don't need to put your name on them. I'm interested in how the entire class is processing this new information. I am going to collect the cards as exit tickets and give feedback for your efforts to begin the next class."

Because David's students are used to using index cards and sticky notes to record their thinking, students seem clear about what they are being asked to do. As students exit, they hand David their cards. David notes that most students responded to more than one of the prompts and a few even responded to all of them.

At the end of the school day, David sits down and sorts through the cards. As he reads, he notices that many students identified both causes and consequences of the mutiny as important points. For example, that increased education and exposure to western traditions may have contributed to anti-British sentiments and that after the mutiny there was a shift by the British to allow more political involvement of Indians. In addition, broader themes such as power and justice emerge as students note the many ways the British were able to project power as well as the way they justified the killing of Indians.

Looking at the questions, David notices that some reveal a degree of confusion and misunderstanding about events. For instance, a student wrote, "Why did the sepoys [Indian infantrymen] get artillery in the first place?" Thus, the student had not fully understood that as an occupier the British army in India was largely made of British officers but required extensive use of local infantry men to fill out the British military force. Some of students' questions were basic, though important in under-standing the cultural context of the mutiny. For example, "Why were both Muslims and Hindus offended by handling the cartridges?" David knew that he could quickly answer such questions. However, he was most excited by the questions that showed insight into the complexity of the situation and the historical context. For instance, one student's question linked the issue of Indian infantrymen to the larger context of British occupation, asking, "How did 20,000 British control over 200,000,000 Indians?" Another student addresses the historical framing of the event in her query, "Could the events be described as both a 'mutiny' and as 'The First War of Indian Independence?'"

With his synthesis of students' *Take Note* responses, David feels he has the open-ing for his next discussion. He photocopies the synthesis he has created and makes plans to use it to dive back into the content from the previous lesson. "My plan is to have students recall their responses on the *Take Note* routine and to make connec-tions with my synthesis, looking to see where their own responses are represented. I then want to use students' questions to open up the discussion to explore why the uprising failed and examine its immediate impact on both the British and Indians. That will be my goal for the next class."

CHAPTER 5

Routines for Engaging in Action

Figure 5.1 Routines for engaging in action matrix.

	Routines for ENGAGING with IDEAS		
Routine	Thinking	Notes	Teaching Examples
PG&E: Predict-Gather-Explain	Reasoning with evidence, analysis, explanations, and predictions	Use within the context of experimentation or inquiry.	• 3rd Grade, Physical Education. United Nations International School of Hanoi, Vietnam • 5th Grade, Geography/Earth Science. Our Lady of the Rosary Primary School, Central Coast NSW, Australia • 2nd Grade, Mathematics. Holly Trinity, Melbourne, Australia
ESP+I	Questioning, capturing the heart, explanations, and analysis	Use to distill and reflect on an experience or problem-based situation.	• 5th Grade, Computer Science. St. Francis Xavier Primary, Montmorency, Victoria, Australia • 5th Grade, STEM. Wilderness School, Adelaide, South Australia • 3rd Grade, Mathematics. Summit School in Winston-Salem, North Carolina
Be-Sure-To	Analysis, planning, explanations, and connections	Use to help students analyze exemplars to identify personal or group goals and actions.	• 8th Grade, Language Arts. Chinook Middle School, Bellevue, Washington
What? So What? Now What?	Capturing the heart, explanations, and implications	Use for taking stock, identify the meaning of actions, and planning future actions.	• 12th Grade, Mathematics. Mandela International Magnet School, Santa Fe, New Mexico • Adult, Professional Learning. • 11th grade, Music. Redlands School, Sydney, Australia
3 Y's	Connections, perspective taking, and complexities	Use with an issue or problem to explore how it affects different groups from self to the world.	• Whole School, Literacy. Delta Kelly Elementary, Rochester, Michigan • 5th Grade, Mindsets/SEL. Emerson School, Ann Arbor, Michigan • 10th Grade, Spanish. Washtenaw International High School in Ypsilanti, Michigan
4 If's	Connections, perspective taking, and complexities	Use with an issue or problem to explore possible actions that might be taken.	• 3rd Grade, SEL. Parkview Elementary School, Novi, Michigan • 12th Grade, History/Jewish Studies. Bialik College, Melbourne, Australia • 6th Grade, Design/PBL. Ashley Falls School, Del Mar, California

PG&E: Predict–Gather–Explain

Consider the investigation, problem, or situation before you:

➤ What do you **predict** the outcome, results, or findings are likely to be? What are you basing those predictions on?

➤ Design and conduct your inquiry to **gather** data and information. What information do you need to collect? How will you go about getting it?

➤ How can you **explain** and make sense of the data before you? How do you know it can be trusted? Why did you get the results you did? How does it relate to your initial prediction?

This routine developed out of discussions with science and math teachers about ways to structure investigations to push students to do more than carry out the steps of an investigation. As with many routines, we designed the process backward by asking ourselves: What kind of thinking do learners need to do through the investigative process? To first engage with the investigation and activate their prior knowledge, we said that students needed to predict outcomes and justify their predictions. Learners then needed to design and carry out the investigation to gather the pertinent data and information. Finally, once we have data from an investigation, we have to make sense of it and reconcile it with our initial prediction.

Purpose

This routine can be used to guide an inquiry, investigation, or experiment, whether short or long term. Its initial step focuses on the thinking connected to theorizing and predicting and then asks students to engage in planning and carrying out an investigation or inquiry. Finally, the routine directs students to analyze their data to reason with the evidence collected as they build explanations and interpretations. This process may give rise to new questions of inquiry and wonderings.

Selecting Appropriate Content

Select a novel situation in which there is something new to discover and learn. Investigations that have some ambiguity and nuance invite more thinking than do tasks that merely require verification of an expected outcome. Don't be afraid of ill-structured or messy problems as these provide students with the opportunity to devise meaningful plans for data collection. Such investigations may even offer surprises and discrepancies that make learning engaging. Questions and problems for investigation may arise from the students themselves. Although well suited to scientific and mathematical experimentation, this routine also can be used in less-structured investigations, such as making a prediction about what might happen in a work of fiction, reading to gather data, and then making sense of the data you did collect.

Steps

1. *The Setup.* Pose and discuss the question, investigation, problem or inquiry. Make sure students are clear what is being asked in the investigation as well as any constraints that might be part of the problem.

2. *What do you **predict** the outcome/results might be for this problem/investigation/ inquiry?* After asking the question, give students time to think, gather their initial ideas, and draw on past recollections and experiences. It is useful for students to write down their thoughts and ideas so that they can refer to them later. Ask students to explain their thinking by using the prompt, "*What makes you say that?*" in conjunction with their prediction. Depending on the investigation, you might want to share initial predictions in pairs, table groups, or as a whole class.

3. *How might we **gather** our data?* This is a chance for students to plan an inquiry. Teachers have a tendency to tell students how they will conduct their inquiry or investigation. Thus, the task becomes one of carrying out directions, and important opportunities may be lost. Giving your students an opportunity to plan, even if those plans might not fully work, can provide important learning. You can always stop the process midway to evaluate how it is working, allowing students to redesign. In addition, if small group data is going to be merged into cumulative whole class data, then students will quickly become aware of the need for standardization.

4. *How can we **explain** our results? Why did we get the results we did? Why do the data look like this? If we did it again would we get the same or different results?* This phase of the routine asks students to interpret and analyze. This does not necessarily mean that they have all the answers, however. For example, a student doing an investigation on electricity might say, "It looks like you always have to have the wires going in a circle for the bulb to light," indicating some understanding of a circuit. However, there is still more to understand about what makes a circuit work using batteries, wire, and bulbs. Questioning, further investigation, and direct teaching can be important at this stage.

5. *Sharing the Thinking.* Much of students' thinking is shared when this routine is being done as a whole group. If it is done in small groups, you might have groups report out, perhaps focusing on how they collected and organized their data and how they are explaining it. Alternatively, you might ask students to review the class's cumulative data before analyzing it.

Uses and Variations

Physical education teacher Matt Magown used the *PG&E* routine with his third graders at the United Nations International School of Hanoi to explore forces in motion. Using the guiding question, "How can adding or taking away forces affect our high jump?" students collectively generated predictions as Matt documented their responses on chart paper. These initial predictions, such as "It will depend on the force" and "Speed and spring will help us jump higher," showed students' developing understanding of forces. In the "gather" phase of the routine, the class identified the various types of experiments and trial runs they might undertake. After conducting multiple trials and collecting data, the class understood that "adding momentum helps us jump higher" and that momentum could be gained through running or by using a springboard such as a trampoline.

Alice Vigors from the Central Coast, Australia, used *PG&E* to help her fifth graders at Our Lady of the Rosary Primary School examine the quality of water samples collected on a geography excursion. Using red cabbage juice as a natural pH indicator, students made predictions about the acidity of each of their various water samples, based on their experience in the excursion. They then tested their water samples and arranged them in order from most to least acidic. At this point, Alice used the *See–Think–Wonder* routine (Ritchhart et al. 2011) as a way to help her students in the "Explain" phase of the routine. Students were able to give reasons for and draw conclusions about their results based on the evidence in front of them.

Assessment

The listening, reading, and/or documenting of children's responses in the first step of this routine, "predict," provides an opportunity to become aware of the misconceptions students may have about a topic as well as their emerging understandings. You'll want to monitor whether students are able to revise their misconceptions based on the data that emerge.

In the "Gather" phase of the routine, assess to what extent students are able to plan an investigation. Can they identify the variables that they should attend to? Do they have ideas about how they might organize and record their data? Allowing students to work through the messiness of real data can provide significant learning, and we shouldn't short circuit it for the sake of efficiency. That said, once issues are identified, it can be useful to show students organizational methods and techniques that help them to arrange data in such a way that it can be easier to identify patterns and build explanations.

The "Explain" phase provides an opportunity to see if students are able to detect patterns, build explanation, and identify causal factors. This is not always easy to do, and many times it is necessary to plan additional investigations or do research to identify what is really happening in any situation.

Tips

To some science teachers, the *PG&E* may strike them as the same as the routine *Predict–Observe–Explain* (White and Gunstone 1992), and indeed two of the steps are the same. However, the focus on deciding what data to gather, how to gather it, and how to record it marks a distinction between these two routines. This distinction makes PG&E an appropriate routine for larger investigations and inquiries as well as smaller scientific experiments. Therefore, with *PG&E*, expect the gathering phase to be the longest as it requires time to carry out the investigation and record the data. In addition, explaining phenomena often requires us to go beyond observing. We frequently need to organize data in various ways so that patterns and relationships emerge. This is another reason to focus on the gathering and organization of the data. Consequently, this phase may require students to revisit their data and try out various methods of representation.

A Picture of Practice

At Holy Trinity Primary in Eltham, Victoria, second-grade teacher Michael Upton writes a new investigation question on the whiteboard, "What sum would come up most often if we rolled three dice 100 times?" Michael asks a student to read the question aloud and then asks the class, "What does that mean? Let's look at each part of this so that we can really understand what is being asked." The class proceeds to discuss the meaning of the word "sum," "most often," and "100 times." To make sure students understand, Michael holds up three dice and asks, "So I have my three dice. What do I do now?"

"Roll them," the class chants.

Michael rolls them on the floor and asks the class, "And what do I do now?"

"Add them up," Simon shouts, and then eagerly offers, "It's 10."

Michael makes sure the rest of the class agrees that the sum is 10 for the 2, 3, and 5 he has rolled. He then clarifies, "So what we want to find out is if I roll 3 dice, 100 times, what number is going to come up the most often." He then adds, "There are three things we are going to do today. We are going to *predict*." He pauses and turns his head quizzically to the class, "What does predict mean?" There are many shouts of "guess" from the class.

"Is there a little bit of difference between a prediction and a guess?" Michael asks, looking across the sea of faces.

Jemma raises her hand, "You are thinking what is most likely."

"Oh, so you have a bit of knowledge you are basing it on," Michael clarifies. He continues to explain the routine, "So first all we are going to make a *prediction* about what we think will happen. Then we are going to *gather* some data. We are actually going to do this. We are going to roll our dice 100 times. Then we are going to explain what happened and why it came out that way."

As the class discusses the investigation further, it becomes clear that some students think the goal is to reach a total sum of 100 rather than roll 100 times. This is clarified. Michael then demonstrates rolling three dice repeatedly and asks students what needs to be done after each roll. The class is clear that the sum needs to be written down. For now, Michael leaves the issue of having enough time to roll 100 times untouched, recognizing that it will soon come up and the need to combine data will then emerge. This moment will provide an opportunity to further discuss how to organize the data.

"So, we need to think about what number, what sum, is going to come up the most often," Michael continues. "That is our prediction. Take 10 seconds of thinking time. What sum do you think will come up the most? How will you work that out? Turn to someone next to you and share what you predicted and why you predicted it." As students pair and discuss, Michael moves around the room listening to the conversations. He is interested to see if students are able to identify a reasonable range for an estimate. Do they recognize that 18 is the largest possible sum? Are they able to begin thinking about possible combinations of sums? Next, Michael directs students, "What I want you to do is to go and write your prediction down in your maths book and then return to your seats on the floor."

Once everyone is seated, Michael begins to collect predictions, "What prediction did you make, Lindsay?" "13," she responds. Michael records Lindsay's predication on the whiteboard and calls on others for their predictions. Students' predictions range from 1 to 19, indicating that not everyone has been able to identify the maximum and minimum range but most had. Indeed, the vast majority of responses ranged between 9 and 13, indicating that many were beginning to think about the possible ways of combining three dice.

To ensure that students see this activity as an investigation and not a game, Michael locates the learning. "If we roll these dice 100 times and your prediction comes out to be correct has that taught you anything?" he asks. Students shake their heads. Michael elaborates, "So, it doesn't matter if your prediction is way off or spot on, that's not where our learning is today. Our learning will be in learning to gather our data and explain our results. Let's think about that now. How will we gather our data because looking at the clock we are going to run out of time? Riley, how are we going to do this?"

"We could each roll and then you write it down on the board," Riley offers.

"Okay," Michael responds. "We could do it altogether. How else might we do it?"

"Well if you did it like 10 or 20 times or even 50 you would figure out the answer you are going to get," Sandra suggests.

Michael recognizes the clear logic behind Sandra's suggestion but also knows that as a probability exercise a limited number of trials is likely to yield skewed results. To address this, he returns to the investigation prompt. "If we do it that way have we actually answered the question? Have we figured out what will come up in 100 times?"

"No," Sandra admits, "But you could change the question." Michael chuckles at the quick thinking, "I see. You are going to change our question. I do like the idea though because 10 or 20 rolls might be more reasonable to roll. So how can we do that and still get to 100?"

After several minutes exploring possibilities, the class determines that by breaking the investigation up into smaller chunks, with each pair doing 10 rolls, they will be able to reach 100. Michael quickly forms pairs by pulling student's names randomly from a jar. He has left the organization of the data up to students, recognizing that this is an important question for them to work through. He merely offers the prompt, "Talk with your partner about how you will record and keep track of your rolls so that you both can understand your results."

After 10 minutes, Michael stops the activity. "I've gone around the room and seen so many cool and different ways to record data. We are collecting data. What I notice is that some of the ways are so different that I am wondering if you will be able to share your data with someone else and have them understand. What I want you to do now is join with another pair and explain your data to them to see if you can combine your data." By asking students not only to explain their data recording but also look at how different methods can be combined, he hopes students will go beyond just sharing to really think about data organization.

After five minutes, Michael again interjects, "We've had a little discussion, but now we want to return to see if we have 100 rolls. Do you think we do?" The class responds that they think there were 100 rolls in the class altogether. Michael gives them another task. "Can you work out your data so that you know how many of each sum you got so that we can combine that together as a whole class?" Again, Michael allows students to deal with the messiness of the data rather than telling them how to organize it.

Calling students back to the carpet, Michael gestures to chart paper on the whiteboard. "I need to write down your numbers, but how am I going to do this? What is the best way? How can I do it when I need to get everyone's data?"

"Some people will probably have the same numbers as other people so you can write those down and put the ones that have the same together," Simon suggests.

Jesse adds, "You could put tally marks for each one. You could like put down 9 and then put down tally marks for those."

"Will that allow us to see which sum came up the most?" Michael asks the class. Collective heads shake, "Yes."

Because one of the earlier predictions had been 1, Michael asks the class how many rolled 1s. When he asks about 2s, Maria raises her hand, "You can't because you have three dice and you can't get a 1 or 2. The smallest number would be 3."

"Okay," Michael acknowledges and then moves to discussion of the maximum. "What is the largest sum I could get?" Many students, though certainly not all, respond with 18. Michael then records the numbers 3–18 and begins calling on groups to tell him how many times they rolled each sum. For some this is quick and straightforward data, but others quickly realize that they cannot readily answer how many of each sum they got and need to reorganize their data.

Once all the class data are recorded, Michael asks, "Have a look at this data and think about how you can explain what is happening. What is it telling us?"

Oscar offers the first response, "We can answer our question of what number will come up the most. It's 12."

"Thanks for that observation, Oscar" Michael responds. "Does everyone else agree?"

Heads shake and Rebecca adds, "And 10 was next."

"Okay," Michael acknowledges. "Why was 12 the most popular number? Why was 10 the second most? Why was 3 and 4 the least? Have a think. Why did that happen? That big question of 'Why?' Why does our data look like this? Have a think and talk to the person sitting next to you." Michael moves around the room and stoops to listen in to the pairs' conversations.

After two minutes, Michael pulls the class back together. "So, our big 'Why' question. Why does our data look like this? That big, big 'Why' question, Kera?"

"Because it's unlikely to get a 1, 1, 1. You're more likely to get other numbers. But like with 12. Well 12 is 6+6 and so you could roll a 6 and then you just need the other two numbers to add up to another 6 to make 12," Kera explains.

"I love that word 'unlikely,'" Michael says to help draw attention to this important conceptual idea of probability. "And you talked about lots of different ways or combinations for making 12. Scotty?"

Referencing the shape of the data, Scotty shares his observation, "Well like 10 and 12 are more in the middle of the numbers and those middle numbers happen most." Colin adds to the conversation, "We talked about that there were lots of ways to make 12 but in like 18 and 4 there aren't many ways."

Noticing the bell is about to ring, Michael sums up the conversation and suggests the next steps. "So, lots of people are talking about combinations and the ways we make numbers and saying that that might have something to do with why we got the data we did. That's something we can investigate further in our next maths lesson."

ESP+I

After completing an extended task, project, experiment, inquiry, or investigation, use this framework to reflect on the experience

Experience   What were some of the key actions or activities in this endeavor that moved your thinking and learning ahead?

Struggles   What were some of the things you struggled with or found challenging that you had to overcome?

Puzzles   What new questions came up for you along the way about your topic or area of focus?

+ Insights   At this point, what additional or new insights do you have on the topic or process?

When we researched ways to help students develop as thinkers as part of the Visible Thinking project in Sweden, we surveyed students on the types of thinking they were asked to do in schools and the types of thinking they felt were most useful to them in their lives. One of the findings was that the type of thinking they did most in schools was "reflection." However, they also told us that the type of thinking they found least useful was "reflection." Why the discrepancy? It wasn't hard to figure out. It seemed that what passed as reflection in many instances was merely reporting what one did. Students didn't find this very useful as it felt redundant. Our question became: How can we make reflection more beneficial and useful? The *ESP+I* routine (Experience, Struggles, Puzzles, and Insights) emerged from breaking down the important components of meaningful reflection.

Purpose

When students complete a project, investigation, exhibition, or some sort of extended endeavor, it is natural for them to express feelings about the undertaking. Perhaps they feel quite accomplished and positive about the experience. Or they may feel relief that the experience is over and they can move on to other things. Although this expression of affinity or aversion is typical, it is not necessarily helpful. Reflecting on one's actions in order to learn from them and plan future actions involves much more than expressing emotions. This routine asks students to reflect on their learning by looking closely at key areas that moved their understanding forward and by identifying questions and puzzles that remain. When students are able to describe their actions – both productive and challenging – they are much more likely to develop a sense of self-awareness and independence in regard to future choices they could make in extended learning opportunities that require self-direction.

Having a space to express one's puzzles and insights creates an opportunity to speak to and control their learning, often a missed opportunity in classrooms where students become accustomed to teachers administering directions up front, then telling them whether they've learned or not at the end. Stating lingering puzzles and fresh insights helps students become aware of themselves as learners, building trust in their own self-reliance and capabilities.

Selecting Appropriate Content

If reflection is to be a valued part of learning, then students need something meaningful and worthwhile to reflect upon. Trips, events, or projects are possibilities for this reflection. Frequently, appropriate content is any type of extended process of inquiry or investigation. Appropriate content could also be something smaller in scale, such as a less-involved problem-solving or coding task. Whether the task is large or small, appropriate content for this routine typically has multiple steps, requires students to make choices and take measured risks, and involves adjustments over time. These qualities set up good opportunities for reflections that affect learning. Too often, teachers design projects with such fine-tuned directives, timelines, and requirements that what materializes is very little opportunity for students to make any kind of decisions for their actions upon which to then reflect. If there is no opportunity for students to take a variety of actions to achieve their goal, or if there is no need for them to rethink or redirect themselves, then it is difficult for students to reflect in any substantial way other than reporting out what they have done and the feelings that arise from that.

Steps

1. *The Setup.* Typically, the individual, pair, or team involved in the process does this routine. If the project was undertaken by an individual, then the individual undertakes the *ESP+I* process. However, if a pair or team did the project collaboratively, they do the *ESP+I* reflection together. We suggest the reflections elicited from *ESP+I* get written; therefore, students will need paper, a computer, or notebook. Some teachers create a template or have students divide a paper into fourths and label the sections: Experience, Struggles, Puzzles, and Insights. The time needed to reflect will mirror the complexity of the project or task.

2. *Experience.* Ask students to reflect upon their experiences over the course of the project and identify the major actions that moved the work ahead. Please note, this differs from just listing "what we did." Here students are urged to identify key actions, steps, and choices that seemed important in advancing their learning. Ask students to elaborate on what made these actions particularly significant.

3. *Struggles.* Ask students to identify the challenges they faced along the way. These may be points at which they experienced difficulties, confusion, or missteps. They might also be more practical challenges such as finding resources or materials. Again, rather than merely listing the struggles, encourage students to reflect upon how those struggles were overcome or dealt with.

4. *Puzzles.* Ask students to raise and share any lingering puzzles, wonderings, or questions that emerged – questions that they still have after the investigation or task is over.

5. *Insights.* Ask students to name their key insights or takeaways from the task or project. Students think about what was learned about the process of research and inquiry, about the topic itself, or about themselves as learners.

6. *Sharing the Thinking.* When reflections are meaningful and new insights have been gleaned, people are often eager to share. This can be done with a partner or small groups. The *Microlab* routine can be a useful structure (Ritchhart et al. 2011).

Uses and Variations

Alison Short from the Wilderness School in Adelaide, South Australia, found that *ESP+I* was a useful way to have her fifth-grade students reflect on a STEM (science, technology, engineering, mathematics) project in which students created simple machines for a public exhibition. Students' individual reflections using *ESP+I* were displayed alongside their built machines. Some of the students shared how the experience of working with others and having to think quickly with others was both helpful for their designs, yet challenging to navigate. When different ideas were shared, they had to struggle together to find a way forward. Some students shared that they were still puzzled as to why some of their initial designs failed. At the same time, they posed theories as to why that might have happened. Many of the insights that students came away with were the idea that they had to sometimes go slow to go fast. Really thinking deeply and considering a variety of viewpoints took time, but when they took one another's ideas seriously, the results were much better. Alison also had students video record their insights for a class webpage as a way of documenting the class's learnings. She has been pleasantly surprised to see her students independently choose this routine when reflecting on their own on other occasions.

In Nick Boylan's "Hour of Code" at St. Francis Xavier Primary in Montmorency, Victoria, Australia, he regularly gives his students a coding challenge to work on with a partner. Nick uses *ESP+I* to have students quickly reflect on their learning at the end of the class. Students discuss with their partner and record their responses in an online document. Before class concludes, Nick invites pairs to share any aspect of their *ESP+I* reflections they wish with the whole class. As students share, many heads nod in agreement, having had similar reflections. Most student responses are short and to the point: "The struggle that we solved was that our cat went off the page then didn't come back on." At the same time, their responses often show key insights into coding: "Not all blocks connect together like other blocks do. Also, that you can do a lot more with coding than we thought we could do before." Or, "That coding does not always go right, but that's ok, you just try again." Frequently the puzzles students share illuminate their interest in coding and a desire to learn more, such as when Olivia shared that she and her partner were still puzzled by "making the bat stay one way up while chasing after the cat. We can solve this problem by doing trial and error, and to look at all of the possibilities."

Assessment

The thinking required in this routine provides a lot of opportunities for students to become self-aware, confident, and independent. In students' reflection on their experiences, look for their ability to identify key learning moments or actions rather than just reporting what they did. If you notice students approaching the task in a perfunctory manner with generalized statements like, "I really learned a lot," or "I got stuck because I didn't know something, but then a website helped me," it may be that they do not see the value in reflecting. It may help to restate the goal of becoming more independent as a learner and to communicate how these reflections help you as a teacher. If you notice students responding with generalities, push for specifics. You could also share some of the things that you noticed in terms of their experiences, struggles, or insights as a result of your close observation of them.

In identifying struggles, pay attention to how students express these moments, both in writing and in their conversation with their partner or team. Do they do so with frustration? If so, this may be a sign of impatience or their concern with being wrong. Do students recognize struggles as productive moments, followed by a sense of accomplishment and joy in their learning once overcome? If students are unable to recognize a struggle, then perhaps the task was not challenging enough. Ask,

"What would have made this more challenging for you so that you would have been more likely to experience some productive struggles? What could we do next time to make sure that happens?"

As you think about students' future learning, either as a class or individually, pay particular attention to their puzzles. It is here that you will discover what interests them, what next steps might be, or how you can challenge them. If students have no puzzles, questions, or wonderings, it may be that they completed the project as a piece of work for the teacher and were more concerned with getting it finished than actually learning.

Students' insights demonstrate where they found learning. This might not be directly related to goals of the task, however. Do students have personal insights into themselves as learners? Look to see if students' insights go beyond the task and touch on core ideas in the discipline. These collective insights can be a powerful form of classroom documentation to celebrate and use as a springboard for further actions. Remember that getting students into the habit of being self-reflective so that they become more independent and self-directed as learners is the primary driver of this routine. This won't happen with one experience, but look for students' growing self-awareness over time.

Tips

The distinction between struggles and puzzles often comes up, as the words are similar. Think of struggle as something one works through, resolves, and finally triumphs over. If you have talked with students about "productive struggle" then this framing of the word may already be in place. Frequently insights and acumen arise from persisting through struggles. If it is smooth sailing, there is not much to learn. By contrast, even when we have learned quite a bit and gained some real insights, we often still have puzzles, wonderings, and questions. These represent directions for future learning. Thus, we can identify a struggle by the fact it has been resolved and we identify a puzzle by the fact that it is still lingering.

As the "Uses and Variation" section demonstrated, this routine can be used in short problem-solving contexts such as Nick's coding challenge or with big ventures such as Alison's STEM project. It is useful to try the routine out in varied contexts to get students in the habit of reflecting via *ESP+I* and not simply another big assignment tacked on to the end of a project. Reflection need not always come at the end of things, however. Consider using *ESP+I* somewhere in the middle of a learning trajectory, in order to take stock and encourage students to find their next best actions. This variation is actually illustrated nicely in the following "Picture of Practice".

A Picture of Practice

Each December the third-grade team at Summit School in Winston-Salem, North Carolina, engages students in a multistep, open-ended design project that serves as a culminating understanding performance for mathematical learning. Specifically, The Santa Workshop Expansion project, developed a few years ago by third-grade teachers Jessica (Jess) Alfaro and Amanda Deal, is used to both assess and deepen students' understanding of math concepts, including area and perimeter, numeracy, measurement, and the use of mathematical tools such as rulers, calculators, and graph paper. The project challenges students to think creatively, approach a multi-part problem situation like one might encounter in the real world, and justify and defend their decisions and choices.

Jess found in previous years that students often lost momentum in the multiday project. At times it felt like her class was starting anew each day. The students had lost their way. She found herself constantly reminding students what they had done, what they had learned, what they needed to do next. This was too teacher directed for Jess's liking. "I believe students need to feel ownership of their learning so they can plan next actions. I knew *ESP+I* could be useful at the end of their project to reflect, but I thought perhaps it could be a great midpoint check in for them. The routine could help my students get clarity and self-direction, and also provide them with a few more ideas to take on. This routine could basically become a re-energizer for them," Jess recalled. She was excited to try placing reflection opportunities via *ESP+I* while students were in the midst of the project, rather than at the end, which was usually the case.

Written as a news article, the Santa Workshop Expansion task challenged the third graders to come up with designs using multiple approaches and drawing upon a variety of skills. Once students understood the challenge, Jess allowed them to work over the next two days, getting the project well under way.

On the third day of this weeklong project, Jess introduces *ESP+I* to launch their math lesson. She explains that she has been pleased with their big ideas, creative solutions, and diligent efforts to approach all of the facets of the design challenge so far. Then Jess reflects aloud, "But you know, one of the biggest opportunities for learning and thinking happens when we 'take stock' partway through something like this, check in with ourselves, organize our ideas, and manage the bits that still feel unclear or frustrating." Jess continues, "So, today I want to introduce you to a process for us to start doing just that! It's called *ESP+I*."

Jess distributes a sheet for students to record their responses. Together with the third graders, she spends a few moments talking about how each of these four components will help them take stock in their actions and reenergize their efforts to make some really great designs.

Jess explains the "ESP" sections, but not the "I" yet, and allows her students some quiet, unhurried time to independently record their own thoughts on their sheets. After some moments, Jess asks the various table groups to take two minutes to discuss what came up for each of them in each section. After that, Jess asks each group to share some highlights of their table conversations and gets ready to document what comes up for the whole class's benefit.

"Do we each have to share an idea?" asks a student.

Jess replies that it is best if the table decides on one big idea that came up during discussion at their table as they listen to one another. As the students share, Jess jots down some of the big themes she hears on a recording sheet taped to the whiteboard. She decided that she would invest time to create this class recording sheet, partly because it gave her a personal moment to simply listen and hear just what each table group had to say about their experiences, struggles, and puzzles so far.

Jess also believes that documenting student thinking communally models for students that taking stock in actions helps learners find key insights that shape direction for taking next actions. Even in this first use of *ESP+I*, documenting student responses conveys a powerful message that their reflections keep ideas alive and influence next steps.

As Jess listens and documents, she notes the language of thinking her students are using. Jess finds it fascinating and quite exciting when she hears them say how a friend's experience has connected to a puzzle they had, or that someone else's struggle is helping them clarify a puzzle they want to take on when they get back into planning their workshop expansion designs.

Jess also notices how quickly students could articulate their experiences, struggles, and puzzles. She finds it interesting that even though this is the first experience with *ESP+I* the students seem to be talking about struggles as if they are normal and not to be feared. Jess pauses the group from time to time to ask what kinds of things they did or could do to help overcome the struggles going forward.

In the final step of this routine, Jess has her students go back to their individual sheets and fill in a few more ideas under the "I," the insight portion. She says to her students, "Based on your table group discussions and our class discussion, what further insights have come up for you that you believe will help you with your next steps for our design challenge? How can you use all that we've just discussed and documented to help you move forward and come up with a pretty solid proposal for Santa and his new, expanded workshop space?" After individually jotting down some insights and then spending a little more time sharing these ideas with their table group, Jess' students got back to the projects that they had been working on for the past few days.

Looking back on the experience, Jess reflected, "Although we had not engaged with this particular routine before, many of the thinking moves and prompts in *ESP+I* are very similar to the thinking routines we use 'routinely,' as part of our normal class interactions." Jess was impressed by how naturally most of the students fell into this sort of reflection and thinking, which reminded her that they have become used to thinking about their thinking and using these sorts of structures to scaffold their understanding. Routines give students a way to navigate and process, not just equip them with more knowledge.

Jess elaborated, "If I want my students to be able to reflect on their learning process, organize themselves, take a variety of perspectives, and come up with next actions that make sense to them, then I have to create opportunities, establish routines, and allocate time for them to get good at this. *ESP+I* is a routine that gives us authentic ways to take stock of an experience of sort of a seamless way."

Some months later, at the end of the school year, Jess recounted how *ESP+I* became a fixture in her classroom. "This routine has become a great way to reflect and give students a moment to gather their thoughts at various points along the way of their project work. We've used it several times. It gets them noticing what has happened for them so far, naming their thinking moves, clarifying what still puzzles them, and creating plans for moving forward. It's become really easy for us to have this conversation and I've seen my students become more empowered to use their *ESP+I* reflections to chart next steps."

BE-SURE-TO

> *Review sample work, an anchor paper, previous student work, a model project, or an exemplar or rubric*
>
> ➢ *What features are there that you need to be-sure-to incorporate in your own work, project, writing, or approach?*
> ➢ *What features, problematic aspects, errors, or mistakes are there that you want to be-sure-to avoid or not do in your own work, project, writing, or approach?*

Be-Sure-To is a perfect example of a routine designed by an educator who identified a particular pattern of behavior she wanted to develop within her students. A number of years ago, Julie Manley, a middle school language arts teacher for the Bellevue School District in Washington State, worked with colleagues to develop lessons for rigorous English language arts instruction for SpringBoard, a College Board instructional program featuring student materials, teacher resources, and formative and summative assessments to help both teachers and students address state standards. Julie felt confident in her own familiarity with standards to address them in her daily classes, but she also worried that students might get lost in all the benchmarks and be unable to articulate for themselves the actions they needed to take to move their learning forward. The *Be-Sure-To* routine emerged from this concern.

Purpose

Teachers frequently teach students skills essential to producing final pieces of high quality. However, if these skills exist in isolation and students have very little understanding of how, when, where, and why to use these discrete skills when it matters, then they may become lost, overwhelmed, or unable to proceed without teacher direction. This routine is designed to promote self-reflection and self-direction in students so that they develop for themselves a sense of how, when, where, and why to apply their acquired skills.

Be-Sure-To also helps students keep their eyes on overarching goals and outcomes, reflect upon their experiences and efforts, and plan their next moves in order to achieve results. Getting students to adhere to a list of success criteria in completing a given task is one thing but inviting students to make sense for themselves what the big goal is and then to articulate and internalize it as a set of directions that makes sense to them is another thing altogether. This routine requires students to analyze work samples and detect patterns and markers of quality of a finished product. Awareness of these features then becomes the basis for students setting specific direction, taking action by asking themselves what it is they want to be sure to do to achieve their goal, and ultimately transferring their skills and knowledge independently in new situations, at their own direction and will.

Selecting Appropriate Content

Be-Sure-To is an especially beneficial routine to use when students have acquired a variety of new skills and are working toward a demonstration in which they evidence those skills and make choices about their application. For example: composing an argumentative essay, giving a persuasive speech, conducting a complex mathematical investigation, designing and carrying out a project, preparing for an arts exhibition, and so on. Frequently these are culminating, summative tasks or exhibitions.

The routine is designed so that students identify *for themselves* and develop their *own* understanding of the essentials of quality work. To help students do this, they need to examine and analyze examples of high-quality work as well as lesser quality examples. Therefore, you will need work samples of varying quality. It is best that these be authentic rather than produced by a teacher. You might use past student work or work you have from other classes or that you have found online.

Steps

1. *The Setup.* The setup serves to remind students what they are working toward on the far horizon and surface all the possibilities for getting there. It is typically done with the whole class. There are various ways this might be done:

   - Generate or review with your students the skills needed to reach a particular goal. For instance, critical elements that make a good argument, ways mathematicians reason with evidence, or key design parameters to consider when delivering a product.
   - Examine exemplars of high-quality work related to the goal or outcome and identify the qualities and features of good work.
   - Review assessment criteria or rubrics (*see* the "Tips" section for some of the limits of this last approach).

However this step is done, it is useful to produce a piece of whole class documentation with the skills, elements, thinking, qualities, and actions that have been identified.

2. *Articulate personal Be-Sure-To statements.* Have students consider the documentation and ask themselves, "What must I 'be-sure-to' do to achieve this goal or outcome?" Allow students time to craft and record their personal *Be-Sure-To* statements. These statements should specify a clear action.

3. *Articulate Be-Sure-To-Avoid statements.* Students identify particular problematic features, likely errors, or mistakes to avoid as they proceed. They ask themselves "What do I want to 'be sure to avoid' or not do as I try to achieve this goal or outcome?" Allow time for students to articulate and document these statements that specify clear actions.

4. *Sharing the thinking.* Though this is a personal process aimed at setting personal direction, students benefit from hearing the goals and actions others have set for themselves. This could be done through a quick go-around the classroom where every student chimes in briefly, as a think-pair-share, or a discussion in table groups. Sharing provides students an opportunity to reassess their own actions and both contribute to and gain ideas from the community of learners.

Uses and Variations

Though this routine was initially developed to help students articulate and plan actions for written work in the language arts classroom, it lends itself to any moment where a complex, multifaceted task lies ahead for students to take on. A first-grade class could use *Be-Sure-To* in a morning meeting gathered around the carpet when considering the best actions they could take to turn fairytales into short plays to perform for the preschool. IB Primary Years Program teachers could use this routine as a frequent check-in with upper primary students as they put together high-quality exhibitions, helping them to not lose sight of the big ideas, concepts, and skills that need to be a part of that process. A faculty sponsor could use *Be-Sure-To* with the student council to plan a series of viable actions for community-wide school improvement that has a lot of complexity to carry out successfully. A senior school world language teacher could use *Be-Sure-To* as a routine for helping her students prepare for oral examinations.

Assessment

As students devise and share their *Be-Sure-To* commitments, pay attention to what actions students identify as being personally relevant, worthwhile, and contributing to their success. Do their statements reflect personal struggles and needs as opposed to merely feeding back general actions? Are they taking ownership of their own learning by stating a meaningful action plan? Pay attention to students' self-awareness. Are they able to identify where they need improvement and where they are likely to make errors?

Listen for the kinds of skills and actions students consider important. Do their *Be-Sure-To* statements strike you as key and essential or minute and tangential? Which students seem to recognize how various skills work together to produce something of high quality? Which students seem to be stuck in the weeds of isolated details and may need guidance or working with them one on one or in a small group? What misconceptions are represented in student *Be-Sure-To* responses that could be addressed in a subsequent mini-lesson or class discussion?

Tips

It is important to give students time to individually articulate their own *Be-Sure-To* statements and to not get in a rush about this. Students need to see the value you are placing on getting them to set their own course of actions. The actual writing of the *Be-Sure-To* statements can be done on sticky notes distributed to each student, or this can be done in the margin of the exemplar, rubric, project assignment, or essay in the students' hands. This will take time, especially when first introduced, but the investment is important in developing a culture of self-management and self-direction. If enough time is not provided, students may simply agree with what others believe is the right next step and not take ownership of their own learning.

Although it is possible to do this process by examining assessment rubrics or success criteria, approach this with caution. Often these documents, especially if created externally, present a list of things that a scorer is looking for and easily become a list of things students quickly check to see they have done before turning in their work. The key to using these kinds of documents is to focus on actions. Take an element of the rubric and have students explore what it takes to do that. What kind of thinking is needed? What specific actions might be necessary? Remember, the goal is to develop self-directed learners able to make decisions, not simply rule followers. For this reason, it is also important that teachers not simply dictate to students their *Be-Sure-To* statements. While tempting, that defeats the purpose and does nothing to empower learners.

Similarly, resist the temptation to use the *Be-Sure-To* routine as an exit ticket to be collected. Although this certainly would offer the teacher a way to check in on the class, the unintended result could easily be that writing *Be-Sure-To* statements comes to be seen by students as an act of compliance done for the teacher's benefit rather than one's own. It is best to keep the *Be-Sure-To* statements in the students' hands at all times if possible and plan other ways to notice the individual responses as well as general trends or patterns on which you might base further instructional interactions.

A Picture of Practice

Working with other English language arts (ELA) colleagues to create rigorous lessons embodying Washington State standards for the College Board's SpringBoard ELA instructional materials program, Julie Manley was enthusiastic. At the same time, she was a little worried. "While we, the teachers, were getting so familiar with the state standards and translating them into lesson learning targets, I kept thinking about my middle school students," Julie recalled. "On the one hand, we teachers were becoming clearer about the skills and concepts we wanted to cover with our students in deep and meaningful ways. But if the students still experienced this focused instruction merely as a set of procedures to follow, might we actually be taking the power out of their hands? These standards could just live on paper and never feel authentic or purposeful for my middle schoolers."

Julie welcomed well-aligned learning targets. Her concern, though, was about students feeling ownership of their skills and abilities. Julie figured that even the best lessons teachers create could be experienced as a set of procedures to simply follow, that is, unless teachers somehow put students in the position to translate these standards into their own words, for their own purposes.

"I suppose something that has always been important to me is that my students get a sense that we are always working towards something. An essay, a speech, a drama production of a Shakespearean scene," Julie reflected. "And I feel pretty good about giving my students the skills with which to do these things successfully. But I'm not so sure I ever pause to ask them what they think the best next steps might be towards this larger thing we are working towards. I tend to just tell them what to do next." And this is how *Be-Sure-To* emerged, as a structure for developing an empowering, action-oriented pattern of behavior in her students that they could own.

When teachers have a lot of curriculum to teach and time feels tight, it's easy for them to articulate what students need to be sure to do. If students are encouraged to bring their voice out at all in these moments, it's often just to mirror to the teacher the very thing the teacher just told them. "While that could please my ears in that very moment," recalled Julie, "I had to face the fact that just because I told them to be sure to include this or that element, and they repeated that very same thing back to me, doesn't necessarily mean they find meaning in including that element or taking that action. *I knew* what made a particular skill or action powerful, but *did my students?*"

Julie began to wonder if she could make a slight yet distinct shift to this pattern of discourse. She decides to ask the students themselves what they think they should be sure to do in order to make a piece stronger or develop a skill more deeply to increase overall quality.

Getting started with this routine, Julie finds a place where the students had already been in the thick of learning a variety of skills and draws them back to the bigger purpose. "We are working on argumentative writing," Julie states. "We have practiced a variety of skills that go into writing an essay that presents arguments from both sides of an issue. And I know that my middle school students are ripe for this writing, considering their typical early adolescent obsession with truth and fairness."

Julie begins by asking, "Okay, in light of all the work we've been doing lately and skills we've been practicing, let's regroup a bit and ask ourselves what actually makes for a good argumentative essay? Can we brainstorm a quick list of all the elements of argumentative writing – especially when it is good? What are all the parts?"

After a few moments, the students brainstorm features they believe to be critical for good argumentative essays, such as finding ways to rephrase the thesis statement and major points, calling the reader's attention to underlying issues, developing concluding remarks that highlight major themes, and so on. Julie documents this. She then prompts, "Okay, let's think aloud a bit here. Now that we have this chart that represents all these features that good argumentative essays exhibit, what do *you* want to 'be sure to' do next in your own work to really get closer and closer towards this list?" Julie wants this invitation to serve as a scaffold, a tool and structure that helps her students determine their own next actions. Julie knows that this exhaustive list of quality features could be overwhelming to take in all at once, so she wants students to have the opportunity to point out the two or three things they feel they can practically and manageably attend to with intention in the next phrase of their writing.

"You mean we can just pick something from that list?" a student asked.

"Well, yes and no," replied Julie, "Of course, all of these features represent the skills I want you to develop as you strive for excellence and quality, but as you look over this brainstormed list, I want you to articulate for yourself, just what will you 'be sure to' do next that will give yourself, personally, something to work on, practice, and get better at. Knowing what you want to be sure to do next will help me get a better sense where I can be of most help to you and to the class."

"Do we just write these things anywhere?" another student wondered.

"Good question. If you have room in the margin of your drafts, why don't you write your two or three *Be-Sure-To* statements there? Highlight them, sort of like a note-to-self. Or you can use a sticky note to put on your draft. That will work too," Julie responded. "But the big idea here is for you *to tell yourself* what it is you will 'be sure to' do so you have a sense of where you're going next, what actions you'll want to take as we continue working towards writing some really high-quality argumentative essays." It did not take long for students to pull out what they wanted to work on next. (You can view a video of Julie's student's sharing their *Be-Sure-To* responses at https://www.teachingchannel.org/video/student-goal-setting).

Over time, this ritual for writing *Be-Sure-To* statements started to become routine, and Julie found all sorts of benefits from consistent use of this structure. "I knew I wanted to give them voice in and ownership of the skills we were developing as we worked towards something larger, but what I started to notice is that students' first *Be-Sure-To* statements often reflected the skills they already felt somewhat confident in. This actually allowed me to honor what students already felt they had a handle on. I could celebrate that with them. And then I could look for places to push them along into what some of them felt could be 'riskier' moves in their writing."

Julie sometimes looked for places to nudge in the moment, addressing something specific and focused with an individual student in one-on-one conversations based on what the student had brought to the table. At other times, Julie would look for trends among several students and use her next mini-lesson time to press into a skill that needed some clarity or more practice. Making their thinking visible via their *Be-Sure-To* statements gave Julie a chance to engage in formative assessment naturally in real time. Julie stood ready to help her students. But her help came from a place of students articulating their goals, rather than Julie imposing expertise they might not have really been able to assimilate.

Because the nature of the *Be-Sure-To* routine is so open ended, it allowed Julie and her class to talk about skills, qualities, and features in integrated ways. "It didn't pigeonhole us into focusing solely on one thing," recalled Julie. "Sure, we could practice skills during specific moments in time, but we kept asking ourselves how these skills build towards something bigger. It helped me convey a message that skills taught, practiced, deliberated, and discussed in context are the skills that stick. My students found empowerment with that."

Once *Be-Sure-To* became routine for both Julie and her students, she was reminded how much her students really do know. Julie reflected, "If I stop talking and give them multiple opportunities to process their own thinking, they've got much more in them to work with than I might see if I'm too directive and always calling the shots. It seems so simple to say now, looking back. But I just needed to listen to them first rather than directing them. If I could actually give myself the chance to hear from them what they think their next viable actions should be or what goals they set for themselves, I could then reflect upon what skills I needed to get in front of them next, in a better situated way."

WHAT? SO WHAT? NOW WHAT?

> *Recall an episode of learning, an experience, an observation, or a concept the class has been exploring. Have students write:*
>
> **What?** Describe what you did or what happened.
>
> **So What?** Make meaning of what happened, your actions, or observations.
>
> **Now What?** Plan forward and identify actions and implications.

Originally developed by Gene Thompson-Grove, formerly co-director of the National School Reform Faculty and more recently a founding member and leader of the School Reform Initiative, this protocol was designed to encourage whole faculty study group participants to connect with one another and to each other's work. Thompson-Grove invited teachers to identify current challenges or successes in their practice, then articulate just what it is they were working on and why this work was important to them in their teaching and leading. By attending to one another's reflections around these prompts, colleagues could then come up with the next steps in their work to elevate their actions. We thought that a version of *What? So What? Now What?* could become a tool and structure to help students develop habits of reflection and taking action.

Purpose

The purpose of this routine is to develop greater self-awareness and responsibility in students. It begins with reflecting on and analyzing an experience or event to notice what is happening or what was done. Once identified, these actions are evaluated to help clarify why they mattered, their purpose, and their effect. Often connections are made between the various events, parts, or actions identified in the initial step. When actions are understood and their purpose, intent, and meaning become clear, it is possible to learn from these actions, plan forward, and take next steps. These next steps become less reactionary and more imbued with meaning and purpose, as learners become more sensitive to intent and effects. When students are able to see what kinds of things stood out for them and why those things matter, they are more likely to feel confident in self-directing.

Selecting Appropriate Content

What? So What? Now What? can be used on any occasion where one wants to learn from an experience in order to make plans for future action. For instance, it could be used to reflect on a challenging or difficult incident that needs analysis so that performance next time is different. If the situation is problematic or one of conflict, the "What?" step helps to clarify what actually happened among the various participants.

Alternatively, this routine could be used to draw upon an observation to develop one's own actions. It is easy for observations to simply wash over us. This routine allows for the careful analysis by identifying key events or moments and then making sense of them. Why did they happen? What did they mean? What was their effect? Then one can consider personal actions based on this analysis to carry out new ideas and practices rather than simply learning about them.

This routine can also be used to explore text, either fiction or nonfiction. Here events or ideas are identified as interesting, important, or worthy of deeper consideration. These constitute the "What?" and may be highlighted directly in the text. The "So what?" portion of the routine is an opportunity to make sense of those ideas and why they matter. Finally, the "Now what?" phase is the opportunity to think about putting those ideas into action in the case of nonfiction or to make predictions if one is working with a fictional text.

Steps

1. *The Setup.* Return to the source material to be explored. This might take the form of reviewing what has been studied, experienced, observed, or read. Often the first phase is done individually and then moves into a more collaborative conversation with students discussing in groups or as a whole class. Consider when, if, and how you might move students from the individual to the group. Decide what and how you would like students to document their reflections. In documenting, it is always important to think about how the documentation might serve learning in the moment as well as in the future.

2. *What?* Identify and describe several concrete actions, ideas, quotes, moments, or observations depending on the source material. What happened? What was observed? What actions were taken? What key idea resonated? The purpose of this step is for students to identify and describe these "whats" from their learning. Additional prompts might be: "Of all the things we've done to date, what's the one thing that stands out to you?" Or "What is something that resonates with you most, given all we have been learning?"

3. *So What?* Once the "whats" have been identified, now ask: "So *what* about that key idea you just listed is rather significant or important?" or "So *what* about what you've done so far has been rather powerful for you in your learning?" The goal of this step is for students to put their thumb down on meaning, purpose, or significance. Additional prompts could be: *So what* does that tell you? *So what* seems rather important here? *So what* can be learned from that? *So what* does this say to us about why this matters?

4. *Now What?* After a discussion of the "whats" and their significance has taken place, ask students, "*Now what* actions are worth taking given all you have just discussed?" Actions could include self-management strategies, setting new goals, identifying next steps in research, implementation plans, or clarifying what still needs to be understood. The goal in this step is to have students identify and shape concrete actions for moving onwards.

5. *Sharing the thinking.* If these steps have all been done individually, students might pair up or form a small group to discuss what they've written. Students listen vigorously to one another, reflecting on big ideas or actions taken thus far and dwelling in future possibilities for action. Considering the experiences and perspectives of others is beneficial for both community building and for helping individual students broaden their own thinking beyond their particular points of view.

Uses and Variations

This routine can be utilized as a loose conversation structure to promote reflection on learning. For example, Rudy Penczer, a high school mathematics teacher at Mandela International Magnet School, used it with his seniors when wrapping up a study of bivariate inference. Rudy prompted his students: "*What* are the important ideas of bivariate inference?" He gave them four minutes to write their own responses, then asked them to share their thinking on the whiteboards around the classroom for all to see. Rudy and the class then took a look at what was documented around the room, and then he moved the group into a free-flowing conversation by asking them, "*So what* is important about these ideas?" Students made connections and drew out particular associations between ideas. He then asked his students, "*Now what* questions remain?" Rudy found this routine to be useful primarily for review but also to communicate a message to his students that just because they are finished with a unit doesn't mean they have reached the end of an idea.

Following along its original intent to create reflective moments for teachers, learning facilitators have used this routine to help move along professional inquiry action groups. In these groups, teachers identify a personal area of inquiry into their own teaching and then take actions that will inform their understanding. Inquiry questions lead to action, which lead to insights, which lead to further action. Making sense of the actions one takes is crucial to allow for the formulation of meaningful next steps. *What? So What? Now What?* can be useful in helping teachers begin this process. Members of the group may present their actions to the group. Then in conversation with the group, they can explore the meaning of those actions – the "So what?" Once this is clarified, the group collectively explores possibilities for the teacher's next actions by thinking aloud together the "Now what?"

We have also heard of this routine being used as a form of coaching, counseling, or collaborative sense making in which one person begins to recount experiences and the listener(s) probe by constantly asking "So what?" and "Now what?" when appropriate. This encourages the presenter to make sense of their actions in an ongoing, conversational way. In a counseling situation, the focus is on helping individuals understand the meaning of actions and events and move forward in a healthy way that leads to achieving one's goals. In a collaborative coaching situation, the roles may be switched so that the probing questioner becomes the presenter and vice versa.

Assessment

Virtually the entire set of thinking moves from the Understanding Map (see Figure 2.1) come into play in this routine and provide an opportunity to pay attention to students' thinking. As students write and share their responses to "What?," do you have a sense that they are looking closely, noticing, and describing in detail their actions or ideas? Or are their responses more global and superficial? As students respond to "So what?" there are many opportunities to build explanations, reason with evidence, consider various perspectives, make connections, and capture the heart. Pay attention to the kinds of thinking students are employing. Are they considering actions and events from multiple perspectives as they seek to understand them or are they locked in their own perspective? Where and how do they find meaning in the events? Are they able to find and use evidence as they build their explanations? In thinking about the effects of actions, are students able to make causal connections? Do you have a sense that students are trying to capture the essence of why the details of these actions or ideas matter or hold significance? Finally, as students start to articulate their "Now what?" next steps, do their suggestions seem to uncover another layer of depth and complexity that has potential to enrich and deepen their understanding?

Tips

Although the routine can be done completely orally, it is often useful to do some writing in combination with discussion. For example, ask students to review the situation and record the "What?" This might include what happened, what they observed, what actions they took, their role in the incident, the responses of others, what was good or bad about the experience. Having had time to gather one's thoughts, these ideas can then be shared as a whole group, in a small group, or with a partner. If done as a whole group, it is useful to document the individual "What?" responses so that the group can feel ownership of the entire list.

The "So What?" phase naturally builds on "what" was identified. Often this is a discussion. It could also be done in writing, in which students attempt to interpret and make meaning of the situation. Until they get used to this routine and experience it on several occasions, it can be useful to supply additional prompts that might aid students' exploration of meaning. As with any attempt to put thinking routines in place, language needs to be unpacked for students. In this case, your language might include: *So what does this tell me? So what is my understanding of the situation? So what can I learn here? So what are the implications? So what does this say about attitude, my feelings, or me? So what might have been done differently?*

The "Now What?" step asks learners to take their learning forward into implications. If a problematic situation is being examined, this may involve identifying actions to be avoided or changed so that the situation doesn't reoccur. If the situation is one in which a student can find inspiration, such as an articulated observation, then personal implications and actions are identified to carry one's learning into action. If the situation is about reflecting on one's actions to date, then next steps are identified. Doing this stage as a group is often helpful as it expands the repertoire of actions beyond what one might think of on one's own. *Action sorts*, a variation on *Question Sorts* (see page 101) could be used to decide what actions to move forward.

A Picture of Practice

Amy Richardson, a music teacher at Redlands School in Sydney, Australia, knows that nearing the end of their high school years, 11th-grade students have the capacity to be reflective but can sometimes be a bit judgmental toward things they don't particularly see value in. Amy had overheard some whisperings, a negative grumble, from one of her students. He didn't quite see the point of studying the history and development of jazz, a topic they had been studying for some time. From the student's point of view, American history was irrelevant to him as he lived on the other side of the world. Amy also knew this student preferred rock music over jazz and suspected other students, too, didn't feel much of a connection. Amy began to wonder If students can't see value or relevance in the topics they study, then how deep could their next actions really go? Amy worried her course could feel like an act of endurance for students. And she desired to figure out a way for her students to find meaning and significance in their topics so that deeper connections could be made.

In their study of jazz, Amy's students had looked at the migration of African Americans, and with them their musical ensembles, along the Mississippi River. In the late nineteenth and early twentieth centuries, this migration led to the development, advancement, and dissemination of jazz forms all over America. The class had considered what life might have been like for African American musicians in a time where segregation was widespread and poverty a reality for many. They studied how African Americans became musicians with viable careers in such tumultuous times. Students discussed and enacted scenarios. They explored creative situations. They studied historical venues and made concert billboards. Students even investigated what inflation and cost of living was like at the time as well as what earnings could be expected by these early jazz musicians. To really understand the development of musical genres, Amy believes one has to consider the perspectives, the complexities, and the context of the times in which they develop. Amy wants her students to see that jazz isn't just the notes – it's history, it's voice, it's story, it's identity. Because she wants students to see the complexities and connections of their topic, Amy decides to have a classroom discussion using *What? So What? Now What?* She feels this will help her students not only consolidate the class activities but to seek significance of bigger ideas.

Initially, Amy uses the routine's prompts orally, in a conversational way. She figures this could be a light, informal way to introduce this structure to her students that feels accessible to them. Without making a big deal about it, Amy asks her students to step back and consider *what* in their study seemed most important to take notice of in terms of jazz and what it represents. She then asked them to share *so what* about that most important thing was rather significant in terms of what they were learning about jazz, its history and evolution. This reflective conversation is new for her students, yet an exchange of ideas slowly begins to take place. After some time, Amy asks her students, considering what they'd just discussed, *now what* implications could these significant elements influence what they need to explore more in this study or more broadly as they consider this art form and its implication for them and humanity at large.

Amy is amazed at how quickly the classroom dynamic shifted once the discussion opened up. She notices their attitudes immediately shift, as students start sharing about the moral imperative for understanding this topic, even beyond the potential musical applications available to them within their own practice as student musicians. The conversation proceeds better than expected and Amy doesn't want to lose the richness of what had just happened or the momentum for beginning to embed a routine that the class could draw upon in the future. She decides to see how much more she can draw from her students.

In seeking to formalize the in-class conversations after the close of the class period, Amy decides to e-mail the class and ask them to reply with their individual responses to *What? So What? Now What?* She sends them this class e-mail (see Figure 5.2).

Figure 5.2 E-mail to 11th-grade music students asking them to reflect on their learning about jazz using *What? So What? Now What?*

Dear Year 11,

Thank you for your amusing and interesting insights this afternoon in class – the culmination of our last few weeks looking at the migration and development of Jazz Music – particularly the music of the African American people around America!

Whilst a fun activity with scope for creative embellishment and story-telling, there is always – inherent in any learning activity – scope to reflect and apply deeper meaning to our endeavours. To dig and find our 'take home' for ourselves. How is this relevant to me? At the end of our lesson we did a quick thinking routine as a group, but I am really curious to hear from you as individuals as to what you might be able to 'take home' from our current learning unit.

In your home learning time, I'd like you to take a couple of minutes to ponder and respond to the following questions. (Hit reply with your answers!)

WHAT?
What can I take away? / What have I learnt while looking at this topic?

SO WHAT?
Why might this be important?

NOW WHAT?
Where can these understandings take me or humanity more broadly? What can I do with this new knowledge? How can these ideas and new learnings shape my life, musical practice and ideas for the better?

I look forward to hearing from you.
Thanks everyone! Have a lovely weekend!

Mrs Amy Richardson
Music Teacher

The replies really please Amy. Some students mention that what struck them as relevant takeaways were that all of the contextual information around the development of jazz helps to shed light on the effect music has on people. Others mention that they came to appreciate jazz as an art form and that the ambitions of jazz musicians came from a place of resistance and resilience to the prejudice and discrimination they experienced in their lives. Some students articulate the significance of reflecting upon past societal wrongs and how that gives shape to people finding their voice through music. Others spoke of how understanding context and its role in developing musical forms informs their own cultural appreciation of music, where it comes from, what it embodies, and what it offers. It strikes Amy that her students are indeed understanding that music is so much more than notes on a page.

In terms of planning actions forward with their *Now What?* comments, some students wrote:

> "When listening to and responding analytically to Jazz in future, I will be able to reference and incorporate what I now know of the Jazz genre's development and context."
>
> "This really helps me think about how music shapes the view of our human experience and how I might capture that in my own pieces."
>
> "Music can become an escape to help deal, express, and overcome situations. I can take that with me in both my consumption and creation of music. Plus all of this is going to be very useful for my History and English exams as well."

Amy has since used *What? So What? Now What?* in a variety of contexts and with various age levels from 12- to 18-year-olds. "For our youngest secondary students, music is mandatory. I have found that *What? So What? Now What?* is a great routine to get them into the habit of seeking relevance, perhaps giving them a vision of themselves as students who wish to pursue a study of music further when it becomes an elective subject," said Amy.

Amy has come to love this routine, partly because of its immediate workability, and how it gives a space for negative attitudes students may hold to be addressed in a nonaccusatory or shaming way. "If showing signs of disengagement, which can happen among adolescents, *the 'So What?'* stage gives voice to their disgruntlement, while encouraging students to consider an alternative point of view that they might not take on naturally: *Why might this be important or relevant to me?"* Amy likes the way the routine is structured enough to help students reflect and engage with the curriculum material, while open enough to invite exploring different viewpoints, making connections, and uncovering complexity – all habits she wants of her student musicians and learners more broadly.

THE 3 Y'S

After an initial examination of an issue or topic through video, reading, or discussion, individuals or the group consider the following:

➤ Why might this topic, question, issue matter to me?
➤ Why might it matter to my community?
➤ Why might it matter to the world?

Our Project Zero colleagues Veronica Boix Mansilla, Flossie Chua, and their team developed the *3 Y's* routine as part the Interdisciplinary and Global Studies initiative, which received financial support from Independent Schools Victoria in Australia. In addressing both the opportunities and challenges of teaching for global competence, the issues of significance and empathy loom large. How do we understand and make sense of events happening in unfamiliar places? How do we see ourselves in the plight and dilemmas of others? In an increasingly interconnected world, how can we help students see that problems, issues, and events that they might not control nonetheless have impact on their lives? The *3 Y's* routine and its companion *the 4 If's* are designed to support teachers interested in preparing students not only to understand our world but also become active agents in shaping it.

Purpose

This routine helps students make connections between events, issues, or topics and themselves, their community, and the world. Such connections call on an empathetic response in which one considers causal relationships and impact of events as well as long- and short-range implications. By first connecting to the personal, one must place oneself in the context of the problem as someone who is affected by it in some way. If there are not direct impacts, then one may need to look for secondary and tertiary influences. In this way the routine pushes into uncovering complexities and nuances of the situation. This process can help students to own the problem and see themselves and their community in it. The expanding nature of the routine to consider self, community, and world helps students to identify different types of impact while locating themselves as members of those groups as well.

Selecting Appropriate Content

This routine can be used to examine current events, global issues, local controversies, ethical dilemmas, medical breakthroughs, historical events, environmental issues, and so on. Sometimes these topics may have a degree of controversy and complexity to them. Although such topics can be sensitive to address in the classroom, by focusing on students' personal responses and the significance of a topic through their own eyes, it can open up a window for safe discussion and further exploration. Of course, not every topic needs to be a global issue or controversial in nature. The routine can be used at the beginning of almost any new topic of study to help students think about significance and why the topic is worth studying, for instance, beginning a study of weather, the water cycle, writing a story, listening to a speaker, or reading a biography.

As you select content it can be useful to identify what types of significance one is likely to find in the event, issue, or problem. For instance, sometimes an idea is significant because of its *universality* and broad reach. It applies to everyone in some way. In other instances, the significance can be due to *originality* or *novelty*. These instances help us rethink the status quo. Significance can often be quite *personal* in that there is an emotional or cognitive connection. Sometimes the significance is of *insight* or exploratory power in that it provides a new angle or perspective that adds to our understanding. Or the significance can be *generative* in nature, providing new questions and lines of inquiry.

Steps

1. *The Setup.* Introduce the topic. If it is one that students are not yet familiar with, it is often useful to identify source material that can provide an interesting provocation. This might take the form of a short video, image of a painting, photojournalistic piece, provocative quote, or short story. This routine can certainly be completed at the individual level; however, often a richer discussion emerges if after giving students some time to think, they form small groups to share, discuss, and combine their ideas. Students can record their ideas in a number of ways: making three columns, using a Y chart, or writing in concentric circles with the inner circle being the self, then community, and outer circle the world.

2. *Why might this topic, question, issue matter to me?* After a careful examination of the source material or provocation, invite students (working individually, in pairs, or in small groups) to identify why the issue matters to them. Depending on the topic, you might want to acknowledge that the issue appears at quite a distance to them and so it may take some investigating and following a path of connections to identify ways the issue directly connects to them. Sometimes this might take the form of students identifying how their actions, though indirect, contribute to the problem.

3. *Why might it matter to my community?* In this step you will need to define the word community. It has many possible connotations so choose the one that best fits your needs. Community could be your classroom, your school, the people with whom you regularly interact, your town, or even your nation.

4. *Why might it matter to the world?* Direct students to think about the possible ways the topic might matter to the world both now and in the future. How does this issue affect everyone around the globe?

5. *Sharing the Thinking.* If students worked individually, they might pair up or share across table groups. If they worked collaboratively to complete the routine, then a gallery walk might be an appropriate way to share. Ask students to look for commonalities across the various groups but also to see if there are unique ideas and connections that other groups discussed that their group did not. One of the outcomes of this routine is that it tends to build interest in the topic once students have explored potential significance. If you are using the routine at the beginning of the unit, explain what additional ideas, background, and contexts you will be investigating. If you are doing this routine at the end, and you want students to begin to think about actions they can take, you might want to do the *4 If's* routine.

Uses and Variations

At Delta Kelley Elementary School in Rochester, Michigan, media specialist Julie Rains and her colleagues chose to use the *3 Y's* as part of an assembly to culminate their celebration of Reading Month. The team was hoping to create an assembly that went beyond talking at students and instead involved them in sharing their thinking as a community of learners. In preparation, Julie engaged all 570 students at the school in their media classes by reading and discussing Oliver Jeffers and Sam Winston's book, *A Child of Books*. They carefully looked at the book's images and interpreted them. Julie connected the discussion to the topic of literacy and asked students to do Google image searches using the term literacy. With older students, she explored social justice issues around literacy. At this point, Julie introduced the *3 Y's* routine to each of her classes and students completed it individually. Younger students made drawings to demonstrate their ideas and English language learners were offered the option of writing in their mother tongue. Students brought their recording sheets (see Figure 5.3) to the assembly where the whole school engaged in the *Give One Get One* routine (page 42) to share ideas about why literacy matters.

Figure 5.3 *3 Y's on literacy.*

Like many teachers around the world, Connie Weber has recognized the power in developing a growth mindset (Dweck 2006). She knew she wanted students not just to learn what the growth and fixed mindset are but also to think deeply about the implications of this theory for themselves and for the class community. Connie chose a brief two-page excerpt from Carol Dweck's book on the growth mindset for students to read to introduce them to the theory. The reading was presented as research on how students grapple with hard problems and challenges they encounter. After the reading and a brief discussion of the growth versus fixed mindset, Connie introduced the *3 Y's* by drawing a series of concentric circles on the board (Figure 5.4). In responding to the prompt "Why does the mindset matter to me?" students wrote: "It gives you a positive attitude. It makes you feel better. You have more experience by trying more things. It may affect how I work. I used to think if things didn't come easily it meant you were not good at it. Now I know you have to practice for things to come easily." In response to "Why might it matter to the people around me?" students responded: "If you have the wrong mindset it may change how you act to other people. It makes people think better of you. You would give

Figure 5.4 Connie Weber's fifth graders use the *3 Y's* to explore growth mindset.

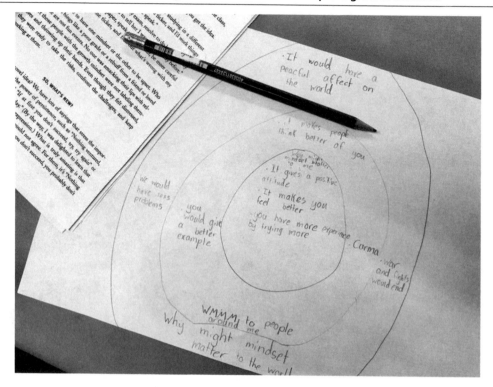

a better example." Finally, in considering "Why might it matter to the world?" students replied: "We would have less problems. It would have a peaceful effect on the world. It could change the way everyone does things, the way they act and the way they speak."

Assessment

Are students able to think beyond the here and now to consider long-range implications? Are they able to consider the consequences of actions to identify various degrees of impact? Are students able to connect with events in ethical, moral, behavioral, and cognitive dimensions? How does this ability to connect relate to the abstractness of the topic? Are students able to do this with familiar issues but not with new ones? How does the power of the provocation support students' ability to think of implications?

In considering the impact on communities and the world, one has to consider different perspectives of people not necessarily like them. Look for students' ability to do this. At the same time, one has to move from an individual perspective to a communal perspective to consider effects beyond oneself. Pay attention to students' ability to take on this communal perspective. Another issue is that often one must consider indirect influences and changes in attitudes as well as actions. Here look for more nuance and subtlety in students' responses. If students struggle with this, one potential prompt is: If we all embraced this idea or took it seriously, what might change in our community? How would we be different as a group? How might it change our thinking, our actions, or way of interacting with each other?

Tips

It would be wonderful if students always saw the significance of ideas they were studying and were able to relate their studies to their lives. However, this is easier with some topics than others. For that reason, you may want to initially use this routine with issues that clearly affect students' lives using engaging provocations. Then over time look at students' ability to make connections with less directly impactful situations and content.

Typically, this routine moves from the personal outward to the broader world. However, it is possible to reverse this order depending on the content. For instance, in considering a historical event, begin with the impact on the world but then take that down to the community level and finally to the personal level. Likewise, students considering a proposed development project in a state wetland area might find it easier to consider why the issue is important to the local community first and then the world before turning their attention to thinking about its impact on them. It is important that students work one step at a time so that they give each prompt careful consideration rather than taking all three questions at once. That said, once one has progressed through all three levels, new ideas may surface for any of the previous levels. In general, we recommend giving students individual thinking and writing time to identify responses rather than immediately moving to group or pair work. This ensures that individuals have thought personally about the prompts and have something to contribute before pairing up or joining a partner.

A Picture of Practice

Spanish language teacher Trisha Matelski felt the *3 Y's* routine would be perfect for helping her grade 10 students (second-year Spanish for most) at Washtenaw International High School in Ypsilanti, Michigan, think more about the global context of their learning. This is an important component of the International Baccalaureate's Middle Years Program (MYP), which strives to situate learning in an international setting. "I felt like the three questions posed by the routine would help get students invested in why they should think about health issues beyond their immediate community and encourage them to have a global perspective when discussing the topic. On their reading and listening tests, they have to make a personal connection with the text as well as give a global perspective and I thought that went along really nicely with this routine. I also thought using this routine would set that tone for the rest of the unit."

In introducing the routine, Trisha ties it to the course MYP expectations of being able to read or listen to texts and form both personal as well as global connections. She explains, "We are going to use the *3 Y's* routine to help us think about how to respond to the issue of malaria on three levels: personally, community-wide, and globally." She then gives the class an infographic on "el dia internacional de la malaria," the "International Day of Malaria." The graphic, all in Spanish, includes statistics on the prevalence, costs, and effects of malaria worldwide along with three paragraphs of text. Trisha gives the class 10 minutes of silent reading in which to highlight and annotate the text.

As students complete their reading and notation, Trisha moves the class forward, "Take five additional minutes to write your responses to the 3Y's. Remember to do this in Spanish." Next, Trisha pairs students up to share their responses in Spanish, "Be sure and talk to your partner if there was something that they say that you don't understand." Trisha walks around the room, listening. "What amazed me was that students were answering the prompts in a very deep and meaningful way. I also noticed that many times one partner learned new things from the other in terms of the content."

Following the partner share, Trisha invites anyone who wants to share with the large group. Immediately, it is clear that students connected to the content on a very personal level. For instance, in considering how malaria might affect them, one student connects the statistic on mortality of children under five to the fact that she has a sibling who was quite young and thus would be at risk. Another student connects the issue of malaria on a moral level, "Because with privilege comes responsibility." Even in considering the community, personal connections continue to emerge, with students sharing that they have family that live in India and that they take malaria medicine when they visit; another that his grandmother once had malaria. As students move into sharing the effects on the world, the concerns are both practical and moral, "Because people need to be able to travel safely, as well as ethically," "We need to work together to eliminate it," and "Because people in developed countries have a responsibility to help other countries."

Reflecting after the lesson, Trisha feels she has learned a lot about her students and their desire to be global citizens. Furthermore, she feels the *3 Y's* was a natural fit for her subject. "I see this routine becoming part of my lesson plans on a regular basis, especially when introducing a new unit and trying to get students to come to the global perspective that I always want them to get to when interacting with text, and this routine does that."

THE 4 IF'S

Choose an issue, ideal, or guiding principle to consider on 4 fronts:

➤ *If **I** take this ideal/principle seriously…* what are the day-to-day implications for how I live my life? What might my personal actions and behaviors look like? What might I choose to do differently? When and where might I find myself speaking out?

➤ *If my **community** takes this ideal/principle seriously…* what are the implications for our collective action and behavior? What new actions would we take on? What current actions or behaviors might we need to change?

➤ *If our **nation/world** takes this ideal/principle seriously…* what are the implications for our country/world? What current and future policies and proposals are needed? What wrongs need to be righted?

➤ *If I/we **don't do anything**…* what will happen?

The *4 If's* was developed to build on students' exploration of an issue and move them into consideration of actions that they and others might take. It is a natural companion to the *3 Y's* routine. The *3 Y's* uncovers students' passion for a topic and helps them to see its complexity and importance; however, we don't want students to feel overwhelmed by what might now seem an immense problem or issue. By assisting students to think about actions, we can help them to feel more empowered as citizens. The first three prompts mirror those of the *3 Y's*. We added the fourth because it is also important to consider the consequences of inaction. We want students to see that inaction on a topic is in itself a choice. However, it is not a benign choice but one with consequences.

Purpose

Students often study and learn about the world but find it hard to take action, or they may think their actions are too little to make a difference. After the exploration of an issue or topic, students can use the *4 If's* routine to generate possible courses of action based on their convictions. Beyond the generation of actions, the *4 If's* encourages two specific types of thinking: perspective taking and uncovering complexity in the form of cause and effect relationships. Identifying actions at the community, national, and world level requires us to think about the issue from new perspectives. Even when identifying actions we might take as individuals, one needs to consider how others might experience and respond to those actions. As we seriously consider and begin to weigh actions, we uncover their complexity and identify issues of causality. This often takes the form of considering motivation: Why is this a worthwhile thing to do? And we evaluate the results of actions: What will happen as a result?

Selecting Appropriate Content

Begin by identifying and clearly articulating a principle or ideal stemming from the class's study, reading, or inquiry. Current events, global issues, local controversies, ethical dilemmas, medical breakthroughs, historical events, environmental issues, and so on are ripe for consideration. For example, after studying issues of water scarcity and the importance of clean water to well-being, the class may identify the principle that "Everyone deserves access to clean water." When studying the constitution or founding documents of a particular country, one will find ideals laid out as guiding principles for that country. In studies of health, students learn about the lifetime benefits of remaining active and this might be framed as a guiding principle: "An active lifestyle contributes to one's well-being." In physical education classes the ideal of "sportsmanship" may be explored. Having identified and clearly articulated the principle or ideal for the class, it is useful to write it on the board or display it for clear reference throughout the routine.

Steps

1. *The Setup.* This routine might follow the *3 Y's* routine. In that case, inform students that having explored the significance of the topic or issue, we now want to look at actions we and others might take. Ask the class how the issue might be framed as a guiding principle for action. It is fine to frame this for students the first time. For instance, if the science and effects of climate change have been explored, then the guiding principle emerging might be: "Climate change poses a threat to the planet."

   Inform students how they will work: individually, in pairs, or in groups. Note: It is often useful to have student do some pre-thinking before joining a pair or group. At the same time, idea generation is often facilitated as we have the opportunity to build on one another's ideas. Determine how students will record. If students will be working in groups, provide a big surface, such as chart paper or whiteboards, on which to write. This ensures that everyone can see and that multiple people can write. Placing this on vertical surfaces can further enhance visibility and access while promoting discussion (Liljedahl 2016).

2. *If **I** take this ideal/principle seriously…* Invite students to identify actions they might take. Additional prompts such as *What are the day-to-day implications for how I live my life? What might my personal actions and behavior look like? What might I choose to do differently? When and where might I find myself speaking out?* can be useful in helping students generate actions.

3. *If my **community** takes this ideal/principle seriously…* In this step you need to define "community" in a way that best fits your needs: as your classroom, school, the people with whom you regularly interact, your town, or even your nation. Many times, we want students to investigate and engage with issues at the school-wide level, in which case we would choose that as our community.

4. *If our **nation/world** takes this ideal/principle seriously…* Here again, you will need to make a choice on whether you want students to consider national or global actions. As nations often have their own laws and policies to effect change, this frequently is a natural choice for considering action. Of course, you may choose to consider both national and global actions by simply adding a fifth *If*. With some topics, such as plastic contamination of the oceans, this might make sense.

5. *If I/we **don't** do anything…* Move students' focus to the consequences of inaction. Ask them to think about the current trajectory of causal factors related to the issue to consider what effects are likely to expand, dissipate, evolve, or change and what the impact of these is likely to be. *Who will it affect? How? To what degree?*

6. *Sharing the Thinking.* If students have worked in pairs or groups on chart paper or whiteboards, then a gallery walk might be appropriate. Give students something to look for such as commonalities across the various groups as well as unique and potentially powerful actions that other groups identified. If you truly wish to move forward into concrete actions, the work of the various groups might be combined into a master document that can then be discussed with an eye to identifying actions that are both doable and are likely to have a high impact. See the "Tips" section for more ideas on how you might move forward in considering actions to take.

Uses and Variations

As much as we would like to protect our students from distressing events, the most shocking tragedies and horrors of the world have a way of quickly dominating the media landscape so that there is often no escape from them. This was true on October 27, 2018 following the shooting at the Tree of Life synagogue in Pittsburgh, Pennsylvania. Third-grade teacher Alexandra Sánchez from Novi, Michigan, knew her students were troubled by the news and that they were likely to feel overwhelmed. "When tragic events like this happen, we feel helpless and wish there was something we could do. With this routine, students find agency and realize there are things they can do in their own lives that will have far-reaching impacts."

Alexandra read a short age-appropriate article about the event to the class, skipping over aspects that were sensational, graphic, or developmentally inappropriate. The article focused on the antisemitic motivation of the shooter and the fact that this was a hate crime against a particular group. Working through each prompt of the *4 If's*, students wrote their ideas on sticky notes and posted them on a sheet of chart paper. As they thought about their own actions, they considered actions such as being nice, reaching out to other people not like yourself, not being a "hater," smiling at people, speaking out against hateful comments, and so on. Some students' comments did reflect their very real fear of unexpected events with comments such as "lock my door." In considering their community, most of the actions related to being a powerful example for others. If as a community they could show how to get along and respect people, then others could see respect for others is possible. When thinking about the nation, students struggled with specifics and often spoke in generalities, "Stop hurting people." There were quite a few comments about restricting access to guns. Finally, the consequences of inaction were a recognition that more violence and death were likely to occur. By the end of the discussion, Alexandra felt that students had realized that they can fight against hate in the world by spreading love in their own lives.

In 2017 Australia held a plebiscite to gauge the public's opinion on whether or not same-sex couples should be allowed to wed. The ensuing debate had made it into the hallways and classrooms of the seniors at Bialik College in Melbourne, Australia and history and Jewish Studies teacher Sharonne Blum wanted to help students think about actions they might take even though they were not yet old enough to vote. Sharonne began by having students read an article on the Jewish case for marriage equality that appeared in the public broadcast news service, SBS. Sharonne was clear; students need not agree with everything the author said and encouraged them to raise issues and questions. She then had students individually respond in writing to the *The 4 If's*. Realizing this was a hot-button topic with members of the community holding diverse views, Sharonne didn't have all students share their response but merely opened the conversation for anyone who wanted to share actions. A theme that emerged was that beyond being LGBTQ allies by attending marches it is important to engage others with different perspectives and talk about the importance of acceptance as a guiding principle for society. "*The 4 If's* routine was so perfect for empowering students. It provided a really helpful framework to think about issues in a really heartfelt way."

Assessment

This routine requires students to think beyond themselves to consider others' perspectives, influence, and roles. Even when considering actions for oneself, one has to be aware of how one's actions will affect others and how such actions might be perceived. Look for students' ability to consider such consequences and perspectives. If students are working in groups, are potential actions discussed with regard to their effect and influence? Are the perspectives of others brought into the discussion?

There is a long history of schools engaging students in indirect actions around issues. For instance, money might be collected or fundraisers held so that a monetary contribution can be passed on to an agency that will do the direct work. Similarly, students are often asked to create posters to inform others about an issue. While such efforts can certainly be worthwhile, they keep students at a distance. Pay attention to see if students are able to think beyond indirect actions to consider direct actions, particularly as they consider the "I" actions. Occasionally this might be prompted by asking, "Are there things that you yourself could do that would help so that you don't have to rely on anybody else to do something?" If students' responses are general – "be helpful" – push for specifics, "What might that look like?"

In generating strong and effective actions, students also have to think of cause and effect relationships. That is, how do specific actions contribute to solutions, change, or improvement? As students discuss possibilities, listen for whether students are able to project forward what the consequences of certain actions might be. If you hear students simply responding with, "That's a good idea," you can ask, "What is it about that idea that you think might make it effective? How do you think it might improve or change the situation?" These prompts give students a chance to explore causal relationships if they haven't already.

With some topics you may need to pay attention to students' ability to extrapolate beyond themselves to consider an issue at scale. For instance, the issue of bullying can be quite easy to think about in terms of the community and on an individual level, but can students see how this issue plays out on the large national or world stage in terms of how people are treated?

Tips

Typically, this routine moves from the personal outward to the broader world. However, similar to the *3 Y's*, it is possible to change this order. What is important is that students work one step at a time so that they give each prompt careful consideration rather than taking all four prompts at the same time. That said, once one has progressed through all four levels, new ideas may surface for any of the previously considered levels.

Working in groups can encourage great discussion and exploration as well as prompt idea generation as students build on one another's responses. To make sure that all students come to the group with thinking to contribute, we recommend giving students individual thinking and writing time to identify responses rather than immediately moving to group work. This ensures that individuals have something to contribute before pairing up or joining a group.

Once students have generated ideas for taking action at various levels, you might want to do some evaluation, sorting, or elaboration on the ideas. This could take the form of having students select an action (at any level) that most intrigues them and then putting students in groups based on their choices to explore and shape these actions further. To help students identify the effectiveness of actions, students could choose an action at each level that they think has the most potential to effect change and discuss, reflect, and/or write about why they think this is true, and then present their case to the class for consideration. Alternatively, the *Tug-of-War* routine (Ritchhart et al. 2011) could be used to explore the benefits and problems associated with a particular action. Another way to process the actions generated is to have students sort their actions (either their group's or the entire class's) into direct (engaging in action) and indirect (advocating and promoting) actions. The idea is not to denigrate indirect actions, but there is less to explore and develop with such actions.

A Picture of Practice

At Ashley Falls School in Del Mar, California, all students were engaged in a large-scale project focused on the design of a school for the future. At each grade level, classes choose some aspect of the project they wanted to explore. For sixth-grade teacher Caitlin Williams and her class the choice was applying eco-friendly principles to school design. The class had spent a lot of time exploring environmental issues and the idea of sustainability, and this seemed like a natural extension. Working with a team of teachers from across the Del Mar school district in a collaborative Learning Lab (see Chapter 7 for more information on Learning Labs), Caitlin began the process of designing an introductory lesson.

As Caitlin shared her focus and goals for the project, it became clear that broadening students' thinking on the topic was a central goal. Caitlin was concerned that jumping too quickly into the idea of designing an eco-friendly school might push students to consider only standard solutions, such as adding on solar panels. Everyone felt that a better understanding of the importance and application of eco-friendly design before actually moving into issues of design would be beneficial. After much discussion, the collaborative planning team decided that the *3 Y's* routine, followed by the *4 If's* routine, would provide a good way for students to think about both the importance of eco-friendly design as well as its broad application prior to immersing them in the design challenge.

Caitlin begins the class by introducing the *3 Y's* routine and having students select a partner or a group of three with whom to work. Students record their responses on large paper divided into thirds. Some students create horizontal sections while others chose vertical. A few create a Y-chart on the page. Once students have captured their thinking around each prompt, the class does a silent gallery walk, looking for themes. Themes emerging were (i) a focus on the future, that eco-friendliness is something that contributes to a more secure future; (ii) sustainability, that eco-friendliness protects endangered plants, animals, and eco-systems; and (iii) harm, that not being eco-friendly harms plants and animals in ways we are just beginning to understand.

Building on this discussion, Caitlin introduces *The 4 If's* routine. "We're now going to move our thinking about eco-friendliness forward to consider actions. To help us do that, we are going to use *The 4 If's* routine. This is a similar structure to the *3 Y's* with one new addition." She reads through the four prompts, providing additional questioning and framing around each prompt. As she talks, Caitlin draws a rectangle on the board and divides it into fourths. She then writes each of the prompts in one of the sections. "In the *3 Y's* we really thought about the idea of importance. Now we are thinking about actions. Each of the boxes on your page will have actions written in them."

"So it is not about what will happen if we make use of eco-friendly design, but it is actions we will take to actually use eco-friendly design?" a student asks.

"Yes that is right. It is what actions you would take in your everyday life or in our everyday lives."

"Oh, so not the impact?" the student confirms.

"That's a really helpful clarifying question. Thank you for asking that," Caitlin concludes before directing students back into their groups. "We have about 15 minutes left here. That will be enough time for us to get our thinking really started on this issue."

Students return to their groups and divide their new sheet of paper into four quadrants, mirroring what Caitlin has drawn on the whiteboard. They label these I/we, Community, World, and Nothing. The conversations are lively and specific as students identify actions for themselves. In their responses, some students identify not only actions but also the results of or reasons for those actions. For instance, "We would use containers that are reusable *to lower plastic bag usage.*" Or, "We would make a garden and use the fresh produce to make school lunches instead of having fast food brought in." The class's actions tend to contain a mix of direct actions, such as those mentioned previously, and indirect actions or advocacy, such as "sharing ideas with friends and family" or "spreading the word."

Many responses reflect previous learning about sustainability, invention, and design thinking. There are lots of references to solar panels, drinking fountains with water bottle refill capabilities, using eco-friendly materials, and limiting overpackaging. One student mentions the creation of chewing gum recycling stations as something the community could do. He had read about a British inventor who designed chewing gum recycling stations that both addressed the problem of litter (chewing gum is the second most common type of street litter after cigarettes) and found a way to recycle the polymer base used to produce chewing gum into usable products such a soles of shoes and drinking cups.

As students think about "World" actions, they identify actions that reflect the idea of going to scale. For instance, the idea of creating buildings out of eco-friendly materials is mentioned both in the "world" and "community" categories. The idea of scale is also reflected in such actions as "plant billions of trees." Some students reference policy decisions such as "Make gas cars illegal."

As students move to consider the consequences of inaction, most mention the growing concerns associated with global warming and climate change as general concerns. Some identify specifics such as extinction of certain species and running out of natural resources. One student comments that the idea of "If we do nothing" is "a current possible scenario for our future."

In debriefing the lesson as part of the Learning Lab experience, Caitlin comments how "these two routines fit beautifully with where my students are. It allowed them to draw on their previous learning and passions around eco-friendly design but also move it forward into real actions. As we move into our design of a future school, I really want them thinking out of the box and not just sticking solar panels on the roof. I think they now have some ideas about how to do that."

PART THREE

REALIZING THE POWER

CHAPTER 6

Using Thinking Routines for Maximum Effect

In the previous section, we shared a collection of thinking routines designed to help students broaden their habits of engaging with others, engaging with ideas, and engaging with taking actions. As you read, we hope you found these tools and structures applicable and that at this point you may have even tried several routines in your own work with students. Although the barriers to getting routines into classrooms are quite minimal, putting them into practice in ways that are both compelling and influential to both student and teacher learning is another matter.

In our ongoing work, we consistently hear teachers say they realize thinking routines are being used for maximum effect when they veer away from simply "doing the routine," and steer toward making thinking moves a regular and ordinary part of their teaching. Gradually, the routines feel less like activities to complete and instead take on a role of igniting, driving, and capturing student learning in dynamic ways. As students' thinking is made visible, it becomes a reservoir for next questions and actions. When this happens, teachers and students alike begin to utilize thinking routines with greater flexibility and agility, maneuvering like a seamless dance.

With consistent use over time, teachers recognize major shifts in their students and in the culture of their classrooms as we set forth in Chapter 1. As teachers take on the language of routines, they find their students doing the same. Students begin to use thinking routines spontaneously. The nature of students' and teachers' questions grows deeper and more complex. Students become more willing to participate in conversation. Students contribute confidently to the classroom community as they recognize the class centers around their thinking rather than their correctness.

These shifts represent many of the qualities and functions that thinking routines are intended to advance. But how do teachers get there? What choices do they make to support the goal of making thinking visible? What takes these teachers from their initial use of thinking routines to using thinking routines for maximum effect?

We've found there are four key areas to which teachers attend that help them move from using thinking routines superficially to embedding them for most effective use:

- *Planning*: Identifying where and when thinking is needed and how it will happen. Asking, for example, "Where can I plan for students to look closely, make connections, and uncover complexity while engaging with ideas and one another?"

- *Priming.* Anticipating and being on the lookout for thinking as it emerges. Asking, "How will I recognize thinking as it unfolds in real time?"

- *Pressing.* Moving thinking forward in the moment. Asking, "How can I best interact with my students around the thinking they are making visible, in this moment and beyond this moment?"

- *Positioning.* Making thinking routine is a position we stake out, a stance we take, a goal we embrace. Asking, "How can I position myself to make thinking more routine in my classroom?"

In this chapter, we explore these four key, top-level areas and their associated practices in order to maximize the power of making thinking visible. Along the way, we'll hear from teachers who have put these practices in place and are committed to their classrooms being places where student thinking is visible, valued, and actively promoted.

PLANNING FOR THINKING

Unit planning is familiar territory for teachers. And two focal points often dominate teacher-planning conversations: activities and efficiency. Often, when teachers come together around a curricular topic, they begin to suggest activities they've conducted in previous years that might be good to do once again. They engage in what one might call an "activity dump." They amass a large stack of activities, and then they whittle the stack down so they can deliver a manageable set of activities over the course of the topic. Another typical planning tendency is the "efficiency approach." Given a lot of curricular items to cover, with too little time to feasibly cover everything, teachers often take the curriculum and divide it by the number of days in the term. What results from this becomes each day's lesson target between now and the finishing date.

A focus on activities and efficiency comes from a place of good intentions. However, the problem is that neither approach depends on the thinking of students for the ongoing learning experiences. The ideas, connections, curiosities, and perspectives students hold have relatively little influence for the direction of the learning. How then, can teachers move away from these common, yet limiting, planning tendencies? The following tools and practices can be helpful in planning for thinking:

- Use the Understanding Map
- Keep tomorrow in mind, and plan for "to-be-continued" moments

- Plan for interactions, environment, and time
- Plan where and when to listen
- Don't overplan

Use the Understanding Map

The Understanding Map, introduced in Chapter 2, is an orienting framework for planning (see Figure 6.1). We use the word "map" purposefully. Consider what maps offer us: They help us orient ourselves within a space. They help us get to a particular destination.

Figure 6.1 Understanding Map, courtesy of St. Phillip's Christian College.

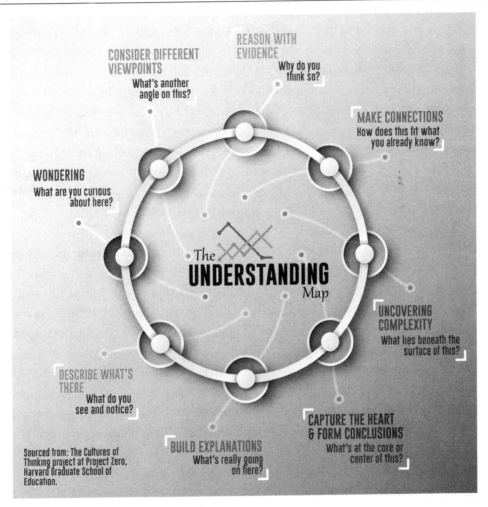

CONSIDER DIFFERENT VIEWPOINTS
What's another angle on this?

REASON WITH EVIDENCE
Why do you think so?

MAKE CONNECTIONS
How does this fit what you already know?

WONDERING
What are you curious about here?

The UNDERSTANDING Map

UNCOVERING COMPLEXITY
What lies beneath the surface of this?

DESCRIBE WHAT'S THERE
What do you see and notice?

CAPTURE THE HEART & FORM CONCLUSIONS
What's at the core or center of this?

BUILD EXPLANATIONS
What's really going on here?

Sourced from: The Cultures of Thinking project at Project Zero, Harvard Graduate School of Education.

They help us begin to assess the features that make up the surrounding terrain. Just like maps help us see that our environment is neither flat nor uniform, the Understanding Map helps teachers perceive learning in multilayered, multidimensional ways. Although the Understanding Map resonates with most teachers upon introduction, there is a tendency to get caught up with the implementation of Making Thinking Visible (MTV) practices. When "doing the routines" becomes the main focus, many teachers lose sight of the overall terrain. Remember, the goal is making thinking routine, not simply to do thinking routines.

The Understanding Map can be used by teachers and students to orient themselves as to what kind of thinking move they might act upon in any given moment. It can help students and teachers get a sense of the territory they are in – noting where they've come from and where they are going. The Understanding Map helps identify direction – charting what to move toward and what to move away from as the learning of a particular concept unfolds. Kendra Daly, an elementary literacy coach at the International School of Beijing, uses the Understanding Map to make interdisciplinary units more cohesive by focusing on thinking. "My teammates and I have found that identifying different types of thinking we would like to highlight in a unit is a great way to find points of integration between disciplines. Although lots of different kinds of thinking happens throughout an integrated unit, finding one or two thinking moves – and connecting these to routines – has helped my teammates and me grow more consistent in our practice. I am not constantly wracking my brain for activities, but instead, I approach my daily lesson plans by asking myself, 'What kind of thinking am I going for?' and 'What routine will help us access that thinking?'"

When teachers, like Kendra, determine there are certain types of thinking moves in which they want their students to become skilled, they begin to map that thinking across the day-to-day and week-to-week terrain of their classroom experiences. For student thinking to grow and develop, there have to be regular, ongoing opportunities for students to routinely engage in that kind of thinking. Referencing the Understanding Map, ask yourself: Is there a certain type of thinking I want my students to get a better handle on? Where do this week's tasks create opportunities for students to engage in that kind of thinking? Looking at the exam or end-of-unit project, what types of thinking will students need to be able to activate to get great results? Where in this week's regular, ongoing assignments will there be a chance to highlight that thinking, encourage it, and feature it in prominent ways?

Keep Tomorrow in Mind, and Plan for "To-Be-Continued" Moments

One of the six powers of making thinking visible is deeper learning. But it is hard to attend to depth if one is constantly in the habit of only planning through daily to-do lists. Teachers we've worked with often start with the thinking moves they wish to grow and develop more broadly, say, over the course of a unit or school year. They ask themselves, "What's the thinking move I want my students to get empowered with in this unit?" Then they ask, "So where will today be an opportunity to make that thinking move?" Also, they ask, "Where will the thinking moves that we make today lead toward the thinking moves we'll make tomorrow?" We see teachers planning for near-term experiences, with their eyes always on the far horizon of developing students' thinking dispositions as a primary goal.

This near-term and far-horizon attention to thinking moves is something Walter Basnight, an International Baccalaureate (IB) psychology teacher at the American International School of Chennai, India, considers deeply in his practice. He reflects, "I've become more specific in the type of thinking I am looking for and wanting to develop. And I think about how to scaffold that thinking over the course of a semester's or year's experiences. This is important as it helps me to identify thinking routines and articulate to my students the type of thinking these routines support."

Decades ago, there were certain television shows that were beloved in many American households. *The Brady Bunch*, *Gilligan's Island*, *Little House on the Prairie*, and the like. Most of the time those series presented an episode that transpired and wrapped up in a rather formulaic way. However, every so often, there were some episodes where at the end of the 30 or 60 minutes, the words "To be continued . . ." flashed up on the screen. Oh, how could they do that to the faithful audience? Viewers would have to wait an entire week before that show came on again. There was no Internet to fuel conversations among them. The anticipation as to what would happen drove the audience crazy. Although no one enjoyed having to wait, there was a level of satisfaction when an episode was so complex and rich (as far as those kinds of programs were at that time) that there was a "To be continued . . ." moment. The resolve was more nuanced. Viewers felt drawn into figuring out what would come next.

Teachers who have found great success with making thinking visible in their classrooms plan for "To be continued . . ." moments. Not in a cliffhanger sort of way, but in a "today's thinking plot will find its way into the next episode" sort of way. They surface student thinking via routines and documentation in such a way that there is always something that comes up in today's experience that will continue into subsequent learning opportunities, whether the very next day or in the coming days.

Mary Beth Schmitt, a middle school mathematics teacher for the Traverse City Area Public Schools in Michigan, believes greatly in "To be continued . . ." connectivity. "Developing a series of connected problem experiences that build from one lesson to the next, and one unit to the next – even with one grade level to the next – makes a positive difference in the depth of understanding for all students, I believe. I want what we learn today to continue on into what we can build with that learning tomorrow," says Mary Beth. Teachers who plan for "To be continued . . ." moments find themselves keeping today's learning in mind with their eyes always on that far-horizon goal of developing thinking habits. When planning, ask yourself, "Just what kind of thinking will be made visible today that can be woven into future experiences, investigations, or prompts so that the thinking can continue?"

Plan for Interactions, Environment, and Time

It is easy for teachers to look at the week ahead and rattle off the activities that students will do. But planning for lessons alone will not in and of itself ensure students' cognitive engagement and deep learning. Beyond planning daily lessons, teachers that create a culture of thinking also plan the interactions they envisage having with their students and how they will encourage interactions among students. Teachers also take into consideration the physical environment, planning just where and how students will engage in valuable thinking moves. Also, they are conscious to plan time for thinking to actually happen, rather than expecting quick responses that gloss over student thinking.

The Tapestry Partnership in Glasgow, United Kingdom, works together with many Scottish local authorities to engage educators with MTV practices. Laura MacMillan, a secondary music teacher and leader of learning, reflects on how her planning has moved well beyond any single lesson as a result of her participation. "My planning now considers time for pupils to think rather than to just complete tasks. Pupils now value this time and have noticed the difference to their completed work when given structure and time to prepare." Another Tapestry Partnership leader of learning, secondary drama teacher Claire Hamilton, states, "When planning lessons previously, I would think about the information I wanted to give students and how best to do that. Now I look for opportunities for pupils to interact with each other to discover and problem solve in order to make their own conclusions." Considering the classroom environment itself in her planning, Marina Goodyear, a fifth-grade teacher at the American Embassy School in New Delhi, India, shares, "I find that planning with intention about what will actually go up on the walls in the classroom environment helps me to be more aware of and responsive to my students' developing understandings so we can have further, even deeper, interactions with one another." When planning, ask yourself: "What time do I need to invest so that student thinking is not rushed? What interactions do I imagine students having with one another that will lend itself to deeper thinking? What thinking might students generate that could be physically featured on the classroom walls to invite further opportunities as the unit continues?"

Plan Where You Will Listen

As your week's learning experiences start to take shape, have you considered where you will listen? Where will there be moments when students are discussing, exploring, and grappling with ideas that you might use as opportunities to gain understanding of their learning? As we have emphasized, the listening that we do as teachers in classrooms matters. It is one of the four main MTV practices. However, if we are not deliberate about allotting time for listening to our students and trying to make sense of their thinking, our teaching becomes more about transmission and less responsive.

Many of the teachers we work with have noted that if they don't consciously make an effort to be an observer and listener in their classrooms, they are likely to fill up the space with their own voices. It is a given that teachers have expertise to bring, but this becomes a slippery slope when we jump in, perhaps with excitement, and take over the class conversation. Over-zealousness on the part of teachers to fill classrooms with their ideas can easily shift the power dynamic back to the adults and unintentionally cast students in the role of being passive recipients of their teachers' grand wisdom. What is needed is more empathetic and educative listening (English et al. 2018) in which we pay attention to our students' perspectives as they grapple with ideas in the process of sense making.

This tension is summed up perfectly by Wayne Cox, head of learning and teaching at Newington College in Sydney, Australia, and former secondary health and physical education teacher. He acknowledges, "The hardest thing I find is not being lost in or overengaged in my own learning. When these critical thinking moments arise in my plans and rich learning appears in my students, I can tend to railroad the whole concept and begin to give my own reflections and thoughts an increased voice and importance." Wayne is wary that his excitement could actually decrease his students' voice and take away their opportunity to develop their thinking at a deeper level. He continues, "I want to share my thinking, of course, but with intention to listen to students much more than I talk. I really try to stay very aware of this and plan to avoid doing too much talking as much as I can."

Don't Overplan

Some years ago, Mark Church and his colleagues were in charge of organizing an extended overnight field trip for fifth-grade students. They planned. And planned. And planned. Every minute of time was accounted for. They were meticulous so that everything would run like clockwork. Upon return, Mark remembers overhearing one of the parents greeting her son and asking about the trip. "It was nice, Mom. But we really didn't do much," said the student. Mark and his colleagues were disheartened. Students had done so many activities and had so many experiences. Every minute of time was planned for right down to the second. Reflecting years later, Mark thinks the student expressed something profound. The students really did *NOT* do much. They were passengers for their teachers' well-intentioned agenda. They were audience members for well-meaning experiences. Their role was truly that of bystander to the illusion of a lot of learning through activities.

Many of the teachers we work with have come to understand that overplanning activities can be just as detrimental as underplanning. Too much to do with too little time causes students to get into work completion mode and teachers to get into manager-in-chief mode. A tendency toward overplanning can also lead teachers to take rather complex ideas and break them down into small chunks or polish them up in such a way so that students can easily "get it." However, when all the rough edges to topics are scrubbed up and ready to digest, the bulk of the thinking opportunities have already been completed – but by someone other than the learners themselves. Powerful moments of connection making, digging deeper, considering alternative points of view, and generating questions occur when there is a tension, a dilemma, or where something has a bit of an edge. More often than not, these circumstances need time, space, and processing, much more than a long list of more activities.

Having defined goals for the development of students as thinkers can help teachers avoid overplanning. When teachers determine that getting students to make connections between ideas or consider perspectives of others is not just a lesson goal, but an overarching goal, then creating space for students to do those things routinely becomes what is most important to promote. Teachers may very well have activities poised and ready to go, but when they notice that students are bringing a lot of thinking to the learning that actually advances and deepens understanding, then they are less stressed to "get through activities" and more inclined to stay present in that moment. They try to mine all the power there is to be had in students demonstrating and developing thinking dispositions.

BEING PRIMED FOR THINKING

Teachers who use thinking routines for maximum effect not only plan for thinking, but also are *primed* for thinking. They are on the ready for thinking to happen. Everywhere. All the time. It's as if they cannot escape these thinking moves being ever present. There is a distinction, in our opinion, between teachers who strive to make thinking routine and those who simply try to add in thinking routines on occasion.

What does it mean to be primed for thinking? To illustrate this point, consider this common occurrence. Have you ever had the experience of purchasing a new car, say a sporty little MINI Cooper, and then the next thing you know you start seeing MINI Coopers all over the place? There's a couple of them in the grocery store parking lot. There's another one in the opposing traffic lane. One pulls up next to you at the stoplight. Just where did all these MINI Coopers come from? Or, have you ever come across a new word that you'd never seen or heard before? A word that's been part of your language for centuries, but this was the first time that you personally had ever come across it. Then, in the following two or three weeks, you begin to hear and see this word a half dozen or so times. It's popping up everywhere. Just where has this word come from and why is everybody suddenly using it now?

Most all us have experienced this effect, something cognitive scientists call the frequency illusion. There are a couple of processes at play. First, selective attention: Your brain has come across something novel (a MINI Cooper, a new word), and it is on the prowl to find it everywhere. Second, there is a process of confirmation bias going on. You just saw that new car or word. Then you saw it again. And then you saw it once more. Soon your brain starts to believe these MINI Coopers or new vocabulary words have come out of the woodwork and are showing up more frequently than before. Well, the truth is that these cars or words were likely already present in the world around you. It's simply that your brain has become sensitized to them and notices them with what seems to be more frequency. It is an odd, yet interesting phenomenon.

Turning back to being primed for thinking, getting familiar with thinking sometimes takes on that feeling in the best kind of way. When teachers decide that looking at issues from a variety of perspectives is powerful for students' learning, they start to see "perspective seeking moves" everywhere. When teachers point out to themselves that connecting ideas and looking for relationships provide great insights for students, they begin to see places where "connection-making moves" could potentially be made. Teachers who create classroom cultures of thinking are primed for thinking moves to happen routinely – in both explicit and subtle ways. While they plan for thinking opportunities through the use of routines, they are primed for thinking moves to be made in real time and then set about creating conditions for that to happen. The following tools and practices can be useful in priming thinking in ourselves and our students:

- Display the Understanding Map
- Let students know that their thinking matters
- Play detective in your own (and others') classroom(s)
- Honor the unplanned moments

Display the Understanding Map

Visibly display the Understanding Map in your classroom and refer to it habitually – at the start of an investigation, during a learning experience, when sharing the thinking and learning. Have it large enough to be in your line of vision as well as in students' (download a version of the Understanding Map in different languages and formats at ronritchhart.com). Be able to physically point to it, as if you're double-clicking on a particular move, when the moment for that type of thinking is advantageous. Use the visual of the Understanding Map *as an anchor and launch pad for your interactions with students*. Of course, posting the Understanding Map up in the physical environment, in and of itself, will not make the magic. In fact, it could just become a poster on the wall that gets lost in the day-to-day shuffle. The power lies in integrating it in your day-to-day instruction so that you highlight these thinking moves as part of the regular experience of learning in your classroom.

Gene Quezada, a middle school English language arts teacher at the International School of Beijing, shares his insights on how the regular use of the Understanding Map sets expectations for learning. "Since I use the Understanding Map in my planning, I also use it in my teaching. So, my students are aware of what we are doing. I want everything to feel pretty transparent and purposeful, but it starts with me being primed of where we want to go. The key thing that has changed in me is that I now see the importance of my role in naming and noticing the thinking my students are doing. In other words, during discussions or conferences, I find myself saying, 'Oh, so you are making connections with . . .' or 'I notice that you are thinking of another way to see this . . .' Students are always thinking, but am I primed to notice it, name it. The expectation being: we think in here!"

Let Students Know That Their Thinking Matters

When students realize their thinking forms the basis of your interactions with them, they are more likely to experience thinking routines as purposeful patterns of behavior that have meaning for their learning. At the same time, students won't give us their thinking unless they feel we are generally interested in it and not just looking for the correct answer. Indeed, one of the early hurdles teachers sometimes face when first using thinking routines is students asking "What are we supposed to write?" as if the routine is a work exercise. As Gene pointed out, any time you surface students' thinking, it is useful to identify a student comment or example you can use to create a further experience, conversation, or provocation. In the Cultures of Thinking project we say that thinking must be valued, visible, and actively promoted as part of students' day-to-day experience. We show the value of thinking by recognizing it when we see it, naming it as Gene did, and using it to take the learning forward.

Tahireh Thampi, a primary level educator at Magic Years International School in Bangkok, Thailand, highlights the importance of taking our lead from students. She writes, "Now I let students influence the direction of our learning. For example, when we are tuning in to a new unit, I am less fixed to where we will go next with activities. Rather, I think about what students are connecting to, what their perspectives are, and what misconceptions they bring to light. I then use this data to inform my next moves. I take their thinking seriously as a researcher of my own students. I believe my students start to see that the thinking that we do together has tremendous value because it shapes where we go." Gene and Tahireh's reflections point to three ways we can show students their thinking matters:

- Name and notice students' thinking to show it is something you value.
- Use students' thinking to shape the direction of your teaching.
- Identify student misconceptions and make plans to address them.

Play Detective in Your Own (and Others') Classroom(s)

Have you ever come across one of those picture books where the illustrator has filled the pages with all sorts of oddities and intricacies, such as what you might find inside an antique store or deep within grandma's attic? There is often an accompanying list of things to be found hidden within the illustration to challenge the reader. Can you spot a perched owl? A golden timepiece? A vintage Hawaiian postcard? It often takes a good while to find the various items, but once spotted, it seems plain as day. There it is, right there in front of your eyes. Being primed for thinking requires teachers to approach each day as if these thinking moves are going to be hidden in plain sight among their students and their job is to find them.

Play detective in your own and others' classrooms to look for where and when you notice thinking, opportunities for thinking, and unexpected thinking. You will soon get good at scanning, listening, and searching. You will also develop a sense of when to step away and move to another part of the picture to explore with fresh eyes. If thinking opportunities are intentionally planned, then students will likely be making valuable thinking moves frequently, both when prompted to do so and of their own accord. Your job is to try to spot these thinking moves in action when they occur in your classroom. Likewise, observe in other classrooms when possible to see what you notice about students who are older, younger, or in a different subject area other than your own. Spot thinking as a matter of consciousness in your own practice until doing so, too, becomes routine.

It takes a lot of close listening and staying in the moment to be able to find these thinking moves happening in real time. But, when noticed, the experience can be exhilarating. When you do spot thinking, consider framing an interaction around what you just witnessed. For example, you could say something like, "So you're really trying to step inside the viewpoint of the antagonist in this story?" or "It seems you're trying to make a connection between the likelihood of this result based on the experiences you conducted in these trial runs." If nothing more, teachers can mirror back to students what they just observed and ask, "Did I notice that correctly? Can you say a bit more about what you're trying to do there?"

Honor the Unplanned Moments

When teachers are primed for thinking, unplanned thinking moments come up with regularity. Those who have firmly established thinking routines seem to have a newfound respect for these unplanned moments. They no longer see them as distractions from classroom endeavors but as avenues for getting closer to the goal of developing and deepening students' thinking dispositions while deepening their learning. In these unplanned moments, there could be a thinking gold mine to be unearthed. Louise-Anne Geddes, a secondary English teacher and Tapestry Partnership leader of learning, honors these moments. She says, "I have found that unplanned thinking has produced some of the most authentic learning for my young people. I naturally find myself asking '*What makes you say that?*' when a pupil makes a contribution which shows insight or real understanding. Digging deeper into that thinking often takes the lesson in directions I hadn't planned for. I feel these are the most organic opportunities for learners to think deeply." Similarly, Mary Kelly, a middle school science teacher at the International School of Amsterdam in the Netherlands, shares, "I do not worry too much about where it is going to take us. If there is collective interest, it will almost always be to somewhere interesting. If it means stopping the lesson that was planned, then, so be it. Many students will say afterwards that the most interesting and life-changing lessons are the ones where we go 'off script' because something unexpectedly interesting came up that caused us to make many thinking moves."

Make no mistake, it can feel risky and like a leap of faith to pursue these unplanned moments – at least at first. After all, everyone has "stuff" they need to teach and get through. A key to making both happen is the recognition of where and when learning is happening and a belief that student engagement and empowerment are important goals. When we are able to capitalize on these unplanned moments, we send a clear message to students that we put their learning above our agenda.

PRESSING FOR THINKING

Being both planned and primed for thinking comes with a blessing and a curse. The blessing is that there are more places for thinking moves to be made than most teachers would ever dream possible. This is exciting news! The curse, though, is the real quandary a teacher experiences. With such amazing potential for thinking to be cultivated, how do we respond or press into this thinking?

Pressing into students' thinking lets them know that we take their thinking seriously. Yet to press into their thinking comes with challenges. Sometimes teachers don't know whether they should step in and say something when a seemingly rich thinking opportunity comes to light, or whether they should let it go for now and trust that there will be other opportunities to harness. This dilemma is one our Project Zero colleagues Tina Blythe and David Allen discuss in their book, *The Facilitators' Book of Questions* (Allen and Blythe 2004). They write that good facilitators are always asking themselves, "What's going on here with my learners? What, if anything, should I do? And what can I learn from what has just happened?"

We think these same reflective questions support the successful use of MTV practices. Once student thinking has been made visible via a thinking routine, questioning, listening, or documentation, teachers scrutinize the thinking and decide, what, if anything, they should do in that immediate moment. There is not a hard and fast rule to follow here. This is what makes this kind of work both exciting and daunting. We think pressing into students' thinking is a bit like a jazz musician (a metaphor we also borrow from Blythe and Allen) who at times takes off on a solo improvisation and really soars to new heights with the tune. Yet, so too is the case that this same musician takes off on a solo on other occasions and unfortunately meanders way off key. This is natural. But teachers should take heart. Rarely are any moves they make so disastrous that can't be redirected or reframed. Some techniques and tips for pressing into student thinking are:

- Pause, and then decide whether or not to speak
- Be on the ready with facilitative questions
- Step out before stepping in
- Don't turn watering holes into mini-versions of campfires

Pause, and Then Decide Whether or Not to Speak

Find a place to listen closely first and be reflective before being reactive. Giving oneself just 15 seconds of pause is not an eternity, though it can sometimes feel like it in our busy lives. Often a brief breath or two is just the break teachers need to formulate interactions or questions so that it feels like they are coming alongside a student's thinking rather than commandeering it. A good rule of thumb: Reflect before you react as much as possible.

Chris Fazenbaker, a high school IB Spanish teacher at the American Embassy School in New Delhi, India, believes in this power of taking pause and being present. She shares, "When a moment for thinking comes up, I often like to pause, stay in that moment, and explore it deeper. I have the unit Essential Questions in my mind, and most often the thinking that comes up relates to the unit in some way. Staying in the moment helps me see that. Something that I have needed to grow accustomed to is the idea of not structuring class too much, pausing, and letting the thinking during our conversation guide our learning."

Be on the Ready with Facilitative Questions

In Chapter 1, we discussed questioning as one of the key practices in making thinking visible. We introduced the idea of facilitative questions and the reflective toss as a particularly useful technique to prompt thinking. Facilitative questions follow up on students' initial responses to our questions and promote elaboration of the learner's own thinking. Facilitative questions request elaboration, reasons, evidence, and justification. Facilitative questions can also generate discussion among the class so that different perspectives and ideas can be surfaced. It doesn't take much for teachers to ask, "Can you say a little bit more about that?" "So, what's the question behind the question, really?"

or even, "So *what makes you say that?*" Presented here, these questions may not seem to carry a lot of weight. However, when posed in a well-situated learning moment, they can be transformational. When planned and primed for thinking, teachers find themselves ready and eager to press into it.

Step Out Before Stepping In

Consider the start of any class lesson. Teachers frequently recap where the group has been and where it's heading. They next provide a key prompt, or place an idea in front of students, to get the wheels of learning in motion. Although these practices are rather ordinary, teachers who are good at putting thinking routines to use in power-ful ways tend to look for places to get the wheels spinning, and then step out to let the students take on the thinking. They share a common belief that Kendra Daly perfectly states, "If the learning falls apart when I, the teacher, step out of the center, then I am doing too much of the legwork."

Stepping out does not imply looking for places to go off and attend to administrative work, follow-up on e-mails, or just sit passively on the sidelines, however. Stepping out means finding those opportunities to get off the metaphorical microphone and open up one's eyes and ears. To press students' thinking in meaningful ways, teachers' actions need to be responsive to something observed and can benefit from a gentle nudge. It is important, though, not to press or nudge because you are nervous about the silent spaces. Poet Judy Brown writes that it is the space between the logs where the fire grows (Brown 2016). Stepping out before stepping in – and doing so with flexibility, fluidity, and finesse – seems to be a distinction of teachers who truly make thinking routine. Jeff Watson, a high school mathematics teacher at International Academy in Michigan, captures this idea beautifully. He believes knowing when to step in and step out is the true art of great teaching, and becoming good at it takes time, patience, and a solid class-room culture. "I have certainly talked at times when I should not have, and have stood silent when I should have stepped in. I think, for me at least, the best thing I can do is reflect each and every day when moments like these happen, and then decide if the move I made was best for the kids, and if not, what could I do differently?"

Don't Turn Watering Holes into Mini Versions of Campfires

David Thornburg suggested that campfires, watering holes, and caves are key arche-typal environments for learning (Thornburg 2004). Many teachers have used this as a framework for thinking about the spaces for learning in their classroom or for structuring various learning activities (Ritchhart 2015). A campfire setting is where the group convenes around an individual leading the conversation so that all have a shared experience. There is a distinct interaction that occurs in a campfire setting that has a storyteller, of sorts, and a participating audience. In contrast, a watering-hole setting is where smaller groups of participants convene in a less hierarchical, more equal setting. Here empowered interactions happen among the group members. It feels different than a campfire gathering. In the classroom, there are times and places for learning to happen around the campfire. There are times and places for learning to happen around the watering hole. Each situation casts the participants in certain roles and power dynamics.

One of the missteps we have observed related to pressing into student thinking is when, having directed students into watering holes and empowered them to take the learning forward, a teacher suddenly comes in and presses into the conversation. This has the effect of immediately shifting the power dynamic. We call this occurrence turning the watering hole into a mini-campfire. When this happens, students tend to shift into being a passive audience and the teacher suddenly emerges as the campfire storyteller, albeit now in a small group scenario.

This move, though well intentioned, can extinguish student thinking rather than encourage it. Most certainly, intervention is an important and a necessary part of teaching. But premature intervention or rushed intervention can smother students' thinking. Sometimes teachers wonder if they should say something in response to thinking being made visible by students in a given moment, or if they should not say something. We think the better question isn't whether to say something or not but rather ask, "*When might I say something to press into this thinking? And how can I engage in this conversation that honors and empowers my students?*"

Another issue with turning waterholes into mini-campfires is that students are shortchanged the opportunity to solve problems for themselves or to be the ones that press each other on their thinking. If the teacher is the only one in the room who can press into the thinking of the community of learners, what motivation is there for the students to develop habits of engaging with one another to press, push, consider, challenge, or build upon their classmates' thinking? It is only when we step back that students can step forward. Over time, students will begin to press one another as a pattern of behavior. When this happens, teachers find more time to be observers in their own classrooms and to document important learning moments that can be mirrored back to the group for future opportunities.

POSITIONING FOR THINKING

As we mentioned in Chapter 1, making thinking visible is not a set of activities to enhance lessons, a curriculum to follow, or a program to implement. It is a goal. Making thinking routine is a position we stake out, a stance we take. And a stance is orienting. It allows us to see things in perspective. A stance is also grounding. It solidifies our beliefs and what we care about, providing a firm foundation from which to make decisions. Of course, no one hands you your stance (though they may try to). Our stance toward teaching emerges over time from our deep understanding of what matters and what is important. Like mindsets, which we explore in the next chapter, our stance reflects our core beliefs and what we value. As Mehta and Fine found in their study of teachers who were effective at promoting deep thinking, the teacher's stance, the position they take toward the enterprise, is not only the factor that insulated them from distracting, contradictory, or meaningless teaching practices, but it is also what empowered and energized them in moving forward (Mehta and Fine 2019).

We often hear teachers ask with great consternation, "With all I have to do, how can I do thinking routines, too?" This question, coming from good-hearted teachers, represents a stance they've taken, perhaps unwittingly. This position being: I either teach for content, or I teach for thinking. This dichotomy, though false, feels very real and thus creates anxiety for a teacher that doesn't need to be there. Not to be dismissive of the very real pressure teachers feel when asked to do things that seem like additions, however, we need to recognize the positions we sometimes take as teachers are often laden with blind spots. Where might we be unwittingly getting in the way of promoting thinking to maximum effect? A helpful reframing of "the coverage dilemma" might be: "With all we're trying to achieve in terms of student learning, how might promoting students as thinkers serve their learning?" Rather than asking, "How can I use thinking routines?," we could ask, "Just what kind of thinking do I wish to make so routine in my students that they effortlessly bring it to all their learning?" Specifically, positioning oneself to make thinking more routine entails taking the following stances:

- This is the right place and right time.
- The curriculum or program isn't my foe, nor is it my master.
- I can learn from my students.
- Making thinking visible *is* the plate.

This Is the Right Place and Right Time

Believe that your subject area or grade level is THE right place and right time where thinking is ideal and offers great promise. We have witnessed teachers who believe themselves to be so fortunate in the subjects and grades they teach. They seek us out and tell us, "I feel so lucky because my subject area is perfect for students to think. In fact, that's the heart and soul of my subject area." They whisper this in hushed tones, as if they take pity on the other teachers in the room because they must not be nearly as fortunate. We've heard secondary mathematics teachers whisper this to us. We've heard preschool teachers pull us aside and tell us this. We've heard arts colleagues, world languages colleagues, science colleagues, and physical education colleagues all tell us this same thing.

We've also heard teachers (sometimes the very peers of the ones who just confided in us) from these same subject areas or grade levels insist that it's impossible to promote thinking as a goal in their subject area because of the content, or the theoretical nature of their course, or that their students don't yet know enough, or the practical nature of their subject. This phenomenon is interesting – one mathematics teacher insists their subject area is perfect for thinking routines, whereas another mathematics teacher vocalizes the impossibility of thinking routines.

What distinguishes one of these teachers from the other isn't necessarily goodwill, hard work, or enthusiasm. It's belief. When one believes there isn't room for thinking, then obstacles are generally what one tends to see. When one believes there are bound to be thinking opportunities laden throughout, one tends to find possibilities everywhere. This belief is a stance we take, a position we hold, that allows us to see opportunities for us and our students, rather than impediments to our practice.

The Curriculum or Program Isn't My Foe, nor Is It My Master

Sadly, just as some teachers see their subject or grade level as an impediment to thinking, some also see their curriculum or program this way. Many schools we work with have set curriculum mandates, such as state standards, benchmarks, or the International Baccalaureate program. Other schools we work with have specific pedagogical practices they subscribe to: project-based learning, workshop models, inquiry, or design thinking. The goal of making thinking visible is compatible with all these and it generally enhances, elevates, and makes them more powerful. That is, unless a teacher feels it doesn't. Some teachers think of the curriculum or the programmatic approach they are using as a contractual obligation to fulfill or a strict orthodoxy they must follow. Some readily accept this master–servant relationship whereas others fight against it and see it as their foe or the reason why they can't do any of this. An alternative position we suggest is to consider how advancing students as thinkers and learners works *in service* of the curriculum, program, or approaches already in place, rather than in opposition to it.

I Can Learn from My Students

Debriefing the learning experience with students communicates an expectation that you believe that the experiences you're providing actually have some impact on their learning and understanding. Teachers who use thinking routines for maximum effect debrief with students regularly, probing with curiosity to find out what students are actually processing, linking, or uncovering as a result of the day's lesson. They believe there is much that they can learn from students. This debrief is not simply, "Tell me what you learned today." Rather it is being inquisitive about where there were and still are, what misconceptions arose, where did students get stuck, how did they get themselves unstuck, where were the hot spots of learning, and so on. Some teachers even use a thinking routine, like *Connect-Extend-Challenge* (Ritchhart et al. 2011) to structure this check-in: What *connections* did you make? What *extended* your thinking here? What are the *challenges* in all of this? When it becomes a ritual to check in with students – to genuinely hear what it is they are taking away – it communicates that their thinking is a priority for you and for them. Again, a very intentional position to take.

Making Thinking Visible Is the Plate

In concluding this chapter on how to use thinking routines for maximum effect, it seems fitting to address the bigger picture of just where does making thinking visible as a pedagogical undertaking sit in the grand scheme of our teaching. Sometimes, teachers first encountering these ideas may consider thinking routines as adding one more thing to an already full plate. A more helpful stance is to view the enterprise of making students' thinking routine and building a culture of thinking as the plate itself. All the other classroom agendas sit, then, upon these goals. Teachers we work with who take this position begin to ask, "So how do class projects look and feel when placed on the plate of engaging in thinking as opposed to work completion? How do assignments, tasks, daily interactions, and exhibitions feel when consumed on the plate of rich thinking?" To fully maximize the effect of thinking routines, take the most foundational stance of all: that making student thinking visible is THE plate, not another addition to the plate.

CHAPTER 7

Learning to Support One Another as We Make Thinking Visible

The act of teaching is itself a constant learning process. As much as we may know our content and be skilled in its presentation, creating the conditions for learning among an ever-changing group of students can be daunting. It requires us to know our students as individuals with their own unique interests, challenges, motivations, questions, and desires. It requires us to constantly look for ways to connect our students with content, being responsive to the diversity of their learning needs in any given moment. It requires us to look beyond curriculum documents negotiated by committees to identify the threshold concepts and ideas that are truly important for our students' understanding. It requires us to manage the demands of time needed to cover content with the need for time to actually learn that content. Because learning is complex, sometimes mercurial, and frequently nuanced, teaching is complex.

If teaching were not so challenging, we could easily master it in a few years and be content with deploying a set of well-worn techniques for the rest of our careers. However, as it stands, we must honor the complexity of teaching and learning by devoting ourselves to continuing our efforts to understand it. We must embrace the intricacy of our craft and eschew quick fixes. Doing so is not an individual endeavor, however. We grow and develop most fully as teachers by being in a community of other teachers who are equally curious about learning and teaching. In such a community we push and challenge one another, inquire together, experiment, and learn from our individual and group actions. If we cannot find such a group of teachers in our school, we find them outside of it and create our own community and build our own culture of thinking. These communities of inquiry develop greater understandings and insights by treating "their own classrooms and schools as sites for intentional investigation *at the same time* that they treat the knowledge and theory produced by others as generative material for interrogation and interpretation" (Cochran-Smith and Lytle 1999, p. 250).

In this chapter, we explore what the agenda for such teacher learning groups might look like. What kinds of things need to be explored through our collective inquiry? What do we want to get smarter around and better at doing? Where and how do we want to develop and grow? This book certainly presents many tools to be tried out, experimented with, and used; however, deep professional learning around the enterprise of making thinking visible must extend beyond merely acquainting ourselves with a set of tools. This is the shortcoming of a lot of professional learning; it focuses on training teachers in a set of tools or practices but ignores the deeper learning of the skill set and cultivation of mindsets needed to deploy those tools most effectively. In the following section, we articulate the set of skills needed in making thinking visible. Next, we explore the mindsets that motivate the whole enterprise of making thinking visible, expanding on the notion of "stance" presented previously. Finally, we look at the kinds of processes, supports, structures, and tools that can support this type of professional learning.

BEYOND THE TOOLSET: DEVELOPING OUR SKILLS AT USING THE TOOLS

Traditional professional learning opportunities in schools often seek to introduce teachers to a new set of tools meant to help in achieving a desired outcome. Typically, the idea is to "train teachers up" in the new practices so that they are familiar with them and put them to use. However, merely deploying a set of tools is rarely ever enough to achieve success in the outcomes one seeks. Tools are not silver bullets. Furthermore, all tools will eventually fail in some way. Therefore, to really learn how to make thinking visible, we must go beyond merely acquainting ourselves with the *toolset* and focus on developing the *skill set* needed to use those tools effectively.

We have not tried to hide the skill set needed to make thinking visible. It has been woven throughout this book. You'll find it in the rich "Pictures of Practice" accompanying each routine. You'll find it in the discussion of making thinking visible as a goal as well as a practice. You'll find it in the learnings from teachers' effective use of routines presented in the previous chapter. You'll find it in the explication of the six powers of making thinking visible with which we began. You'll find it in all voices of teachers shared throughout this book. We restate them here in explicit form to drive home the idea that these are not merely tips, suggestions, or useful practices but essential skills that we must develop over time, with our students, and in concert with our colleagues. To be effective at making thinking visible and utilizing thinking routines skillfully, we have found that teachers must hone their skills in:

- Listening to students so as to seek to fully understand their responses
- Identifying the key understandings sought in a unit of instruction
- Connecting student learning to the thinking they are asked to do

- Maintaining a formative assessment lens
- Being instructional responsiveness and flexible
- Analyzing students' learning responses

Listening to Our Students

We articulated listening as a key practice of making thinking visible in Chapter 1. Listening was also a thread that ran through each of the four areas of attention – planning, priming, pressing, and positioning – needed to use thinking routines to maximum effect. We emphasize it here as an express skill that supports the effective use of thinking because we have found it is something that we all need to develop and enhance. If students sense we are not listening, if we are not really interested in their thinking, then they won't give it to us. They will instead play the familiar game: Guess what's in the teacher's head. And genuine listening, as the poet Alice Duer Miller reminded us, is more than being quiet and giving the other space to speak. Real listening is "taking a vigorous, human interest" in the other. Thus, when we listen we often follow up with questions that demonstrate our interest.

As teachers, there are three things in particular that commonly stand in the way of our listening:

- Our rush toward quick judgment and evaluation. When students speak we often find ourselves judging the correctness of their response against what we are looking for. When we do that, we may stop listening once we have judged the response to be correct. Consequently, we miss what students are communicating.
- Our tendency to predict what students will say before they say it. Thus, we find ourselves listening for confirmation and may miss what students are actually saying.
- Our desire for closure. In our press for time and the need we feel to move the lesson forward, we may conclude our students' statements for them rather than allowing them to finish. We assume we know their thoughts.

Battling these tendencies takes awareness, practice, and time. We can develop greater awareness of both good and poor listening through observations of others. When we witness good listeners, we can learn from their example. When we witness poor listeners, we can learn to recognize the signs and actions associated with poor listening. Developing the practice of listening in the classroom requires one to become comfortable with silence, curious about our students' thinking, and a less dominant presence. Of course, unlearning the barriers to listening and embedding a new way of being takes time. We need to respect that and be kind to ourselves as we develop our skills.

Identifying the Key Understandings

As we have emphasized, thinking routines are clearly situated within the enterprise of teaching for understanding. It is within this context that they are most powerful. But identifying what it is we really want students to understand can be tricky. Often curricular guides and textbooks are of limited use as they present skills, knowledge, and facts as things students need to "understand." These documents may use the word "understanding" in a superficial way and not as we are using it here. When we talk about understanding, we are talking about the core ideas and concepts with which we want students to grapple. If we can just tell them, then it isn't real understanding; it is just a bit of knowledge. Furthermore, if your curricular documents list three or four things for students to understand in a single lesson, then again, the expectation is that there will be no depth, exploration, or grappling and that such understandings can be easily conveyed. In this context, the ideas are more likely to be just bits of knowledge.

Identifying key understandings requires us to take a broader view. Within this unit where is the core? What are those two or three big ideas that seem foundational that we will keep coming back to over and over? Are these ideas worth understanding? What will students be able to do with their understanding? How will this understanding serve them well in their future learning? What other ideas and concepts will it help them unlock? Answering questions like these is best done with colleagues so that we can make and defend proposals while considering alternatives. It can be hard work. However, once identified, key understandings for instruction are incredibly orienting. They help us sequence instruction, plan opportunities, and select thinking routines for maximum effect. Key understandings add a sense of flow and direction to our instruction as opposed to a series of episodes.

Connecting Student Learning and Thinking

Learning is a consequence of thinking. Therefore, we need to get used to making that link as strong as we can in our planning and instruction. As we identify our content, we need to ask ourselves: What is the thinking I want my students to do with this content? What thinking is needed to help my students explore and build understanding? The Understanding Map (Figures 2.1 and 6.1) is one tool that will help us to answer these questions. Once we have identified the thinking we need, it is possible to choose the best thinking routine as a tool for facilitating that thinking.

With foreknowledge of the thinking we are trying to motivate, we can also draw students' attention to it as a key feature of their learning. For example, rather than beginning a class with only an introduction to the content, we should highlight the learning and the thinking we want students to do. Instead of announcing: "We're going to begin class today by watching this excerpt from the series 'War on Waste' and then we'll discuss it," identify the thinking and learning students will be doing: "Today, we are going to continue to think about the issue of waste, and we will begin to explore some solutions and actions we might take. To help us do that, we're going to use the *What? So What? Now What?* routine to help us think through the issues presented in this excerpt from the series 'War on Waste.' After you watch the video, we'll spend some individual time naming the issues and problems the video presents; this is the '*What?*' portion of the routine. Then you'll think about the '*So What?*' Why does this matter? Finally, you'll move to '*Now What?*' as you think about possible actions we might take. Once everyone has some ideas, we'll use those to jumpstart our collective discussion."

Maintaining a Formative Assessment Lens

As we discussed in Chapter 2, formative assessment is a practice and not a task. As we use thinking routines and strive to make thinking visible, we are constantly attending to what we are learning about our students' thinking and understanding and where to go next in our instruction. Formative assessment, of which listening with intention is a part, is driven by our curiosity about our students' learning, our desire to understand how they are making sense of ideas, where they might be confused, and what new ideas they might have about the topic that we hadn't considered. Two questions can be useful in this process: What am I learning about my students' thinking and understanding through this thinking routine? How will I use that information to plan my next steps?

It can be difficult to focus on maintaining a formative assessment lens in the midst of trying a thinking routine for the first time. Often, we are too preoccupied with negotiating the steps of a new routine and making sure our language is right that we have very little mental resource left for much else. In this case, our formative assessment will take place as we look at students' responses *after* the lesson.

To truly maintain a formative assessment lens, whether in the midst of a lesson or in looking at student work afterwards, we have to learn to suspend judgment. If we look at students' responses in an evaluative mode: Who got it? Who performed as expected? Is that what I wanted to see? Did they hit my target?, then we will miss much of their thinking. To help avoid this trap, we should ask ourselves: Where do we see students' thinking present in their responses? Are there patterns across the class as a whole?

What is surprising, unexpected, or new here? How have students gone beyond what I expected? Where is there thinking or new ideas I can share back with the class to advance our collective understanding and exploration? The *Looking At Student Thinking* (LAST) protocol discussed later can be a useful tool in developing a formative assessment lens.

Being Instructional Responsiveness and Flexible

Formative assessment is a responsive act in that we have an obligation to use what we have learned about our students to shape our future instruction. Therefore, we shouldn't treat formative assessment as a purely diagnostic tool as it is so often portrayed by those invested in the old story of schools. Many reductionist models of teaching as transmission use formative assessment "tasks" as tools to diagnose deficits in learning so that information can be retaught in much the way computer instructional software does. Our argument is not that we should ignore these deficits and not attend to them, but rather that we should broaden our understanding of formative assessment so that it is responsive to a much wider array of learning needs. For instance, how might we push the students who have a rich understanding so that they are challenged further? How can we help students to confront their misconceptions? What new avenues for instruction do students' responses open up? Thus, the goal is always to advance learning rather than merely check to see if students "got" what we taught them.

In the effort to pace content and assist planning, we have witnessed schools that require teachers to include their use of thinking routines in their unit plans. While it is certainly worthwhile thinking about one's instruction in advance and considering which thinking routines might help student to explore specific content, we worry that such prewritten plans may not allow much room for responsiveness and flexibility. We must be willing to rework our plans and make adjustments in the service of student learning. Furthermore, if our interest is to develop learners and thinkers, empower them, and engender a sense of agency, then schooling cannot be something that is merely done to them. Our instruction must be responsive to both their needs and interests.

Analyzing Students' Learning Responses

Formative assessment practices that allow us to be flexible and responsive in our teaching rest on our ability to analyze students' learning responses. As mentioned, this means suspending judgment and rejecting a purely evaluative lens when we look at student work. Instead we need to seek to understand students' responses and identify their thinking. Learning to analyze student work in this way is a shift for teachers who are used to scoring and evaluating work for correctness and accuracy. Therefore, it is important to recognize this for the shift in perspective that it is. We are trying to develop new ideas for looking at our students' work, and this too takes time to develop. It takes time to learn to document and capture real learning and thinking so there is something rich and nuanced that is worth looking at. It takes time to unlearn past judgments. It takes time to recognize evidence of thinking. All of this takes support as well. As with each of the skills presented here, we don't suggest that their development is an individual enterprise. Rather, it is best viewed as a collective endeavor in which we engage with our colleagues.

BEYOND THE SKILL SET: THE MINDSETS THAT MOTIVATE ACTION

Have you ever been part of a change initiative and witnessed that some people were able to just grab on to the new tools and practices and immediately put them to use? They seem to just "get it." These individuals' effective and deep use of the tools seemed to outpace that of the rest of us. Often it is not that these individuals necessarily understood the tools better; it is that they already had the mindsets, that is, the beliefs, attitudes, and stances that were needed to motivate the use of the new tools.

In education we too often treat the tools as infallible. Just do this and learning will improve. We believe in the quick fix and often seek it out. We are given lists of best practices to merely implement. However, without having the mindsets that motivate the use of any particular toolset, teachers will struggle to understand how the tools are meant to work, have faith in them, or use them as designed. With regard to making thinking visible, these mindsets relate to our:

- Perception of our students
- Understanding of the goals of teaching
- Conceptions of thinking and learning.

Perception of Our Students

A long line of research initiated by Rosenthal and Jacobson's groundbreaking 1968 work, *Pygmalion in the Classroom*, has documented the effects of teacher expectations on student learning. Joseph Onosko, in his study sponsored by the National Center on Effective Secondary Schools, found that an important distinguishing characteristic of successful teachers of thinking was they were optimistic about their students' ability as thinkers (Onosko 1992). They didn't dismiss challenges or difficulties, but they had a belief that their students were capable of rich, deep thinking and that with time and support their abilities would not only emerge but would flourish. In comparison, over half the teachers who were less accomplished at getting students to think had a defeatist attitude in which they wrote off whole groups of students as incapable.

Erika Lusky has helped other teachers at Rochester High School in Michigan to see the potential of her students with learning challenges as thinkers and learners. By using thinking routines to tap into what students think and help them to build understanding, her group of neurodiverse learners often surprises teachers with their ability to think. Likewise, Jennifer LaTarte from Bemis Elementary identifies that teachers' perceptions of young students can often be an impediment to making thinking visible. She notes, "A roadblock to harnessing the true capacity of the thinking of young children can often be a teacher unknowingly putting limits on students. The power in making thinking visible lies in our acceptance and eagerness to tap into the ideas of even our youngest learners, knowing that they can think. Consequently, what we get from them is truly valuable."

Understanding of the Goals of Teaching

The way we think about the enterprise of teaching will define what we do as teachers (Schoenfeld 1999). It will determine what we find time for, our instructional practices, and the kinds of opportunities we design for our students. If we view the primary goal of teaching as transmitting our knowledge to students and preparing them for tests, then making thinking visible can seem a distraction that takes away from this agenda. Indeed, this was secondary history teacher Ryan Gill's initial reaction when introduced to these ideas. "I used to think making thinking visible and creating a culture of thinking in my senior classes would take more time." However, by focusing on making thinking visible, he has changed his view, "Now I think by continually teaching for understanding we actually buy ourselves more time in the long run as it results in my students being able to make connections between content areas and make more sense of what they're learning."

As we have mentioned throughout this book, making thinking visible rejects the transmission model of teaching in favor of a more transformative model in which students are engaged in deep learning that supports not only subject mastery but also identity formation as a learner who has the power to create, implement, and engage. A key mindset for making thinking visible then is the recognition of the importance of depth over breadth, of making sure students are engaged in true learning as opposed to just doing work for the teacher, of embracing complexity and ambiguity rather than aiming to simplify, and of encouraging originality over reproduction.

Conceptions of Thinking and Learning

Do you value thinking? If so, what kind of thinking are you seeking to promote in your students? Joseph Onosko found that effective teachers of thinking were able to answer these questions and offer more elaborate, detailed, and precise answers regarding the kinds of thinking they were trying to nurture in their classrooms and how these thinking moves related to students' learning in the discipline. These teachers were also able to clearly articulate the dispositions they sought to develop in their students, such as curiosity, skepticism, intellectual rigor, and open-mindedness. This relates to the teachers' understanding of their disciplines not as just a knowledge base to be imparted but as a collection of processes and ways of thinking in which students apprentice.

With regard to conceptions of learning, making thinking visible challenges the notion that learning happens through the delivery of information. Learning happens when the learner does something cognitively with that information. Too often though, learners have been left on their own to figure out what to do with the information they receive. High-performing students seem to just naturally do this, but far too many learners lack the wherewithal of how to think through and explore new and challenging ideas on their own. When teachers view learning as an active cognitive process of exploration and sense making that can often be complex, nuanced, and unique, then thinking routines, documentation, questioning, and listening do not feel like additive practices but become central to the enterprise.

SUPPORTS FOR DEVELOPING SKILL SETS AND MINDSETS

In our work, we have always eschewed the notion of "training" teachers. Although we certainly present workshops and speak at conferences, we consider these only the start of much grander conversations that must be continued and built upon in schools over time. We recognize that the real learning, the development of the skill sets and mindsets, is an ongoing, embedded endeavor. Furthermore, we recognize that teachers have much to learn from one another and from their students. This is not a mere sharing of ideas and solutions, however. Rich professional learning occurs in a spirit of inquiry in which teachers do more problem-posing – "What if we . . .?"—than problem solving – "What you should do is. . . ." Rich professional learning is built on teachers' questions and is more connected to uncertainty and possibility than assuredness and implementation. To facilitate this process, we have developed a number of tools and structures that can be useful, all designed to help teachers generate new understandings as they pay attention to how and what students think and learn.

Learning Labs

When we have been asked to demonstrate or model teach a thinking-routines-based lesson in schools, we have always declined. We think this sends a message that thinking routines are somewhat hard to pull off in the classroom and that there is some kind of magic in doing so. We always say that if there is any magic to routines, it is in the planning before and analysis afterward. We designed the Learning Labs to focus on this process. The Learning Lab occurs in three parts: the initial planning, the classroom teaching, and the follow-up discussion. Each takes roughly one class period, though the planning often benefits from slightly more time and the teaching itself a bit less. For the lab, a host teacher volunteers to carry out the lesson in his or her classroom with the help of a coach or co-facilitator. However, this is in no way to be considered a demonstration or model lesson. The host will be trying something new from which we all can learn and is not expected to put on a show. The lesson will be co-constructed by the team of teachers participating in the lab and thus will be "owned" by everyone. We think of the lesson as a prototype with all the messiness and false starts that entails and not as a polished performance.

During one recent Learning Lab, the host teacher shares the desire for students to go deeper into their exploration of the American Dream and is interested in potential source material that might be a good stimulus for doing so. The teacher then shares both an image and a poem that might provoke some thinking. The pros and cons of each are discussed in relation to the teacher's goals and the potential learning each affords.

The group decides the image is more provocative and begins to discuss optional routines that might facilitate students' engagement with it. The group tries to select a routine that will be new for the host teacher so that everyone can engage authentically in the planning process. *Beauty & Truth* page 124 and *The Story Routine* (page 117) are explored as possibilities, and the group decides they think that *The Story Routine* will allow students to examine ways that systemic barriers often impede access to the American Dream for marginalized groups.

The teachers next move to plan the logistics of carrying out the routine including discussions of: How will students work, in groups or as individuals? How will the learning be documented and why might that be useful versus another way? How will groups be formed? How should the learning task be introduced? What questions might be used to prompt students if they are struggling? The idea is that by the end of this planning, the group should "own" the lesson as a collaborative undertaking.

With a prototype lesson in hand, the group then goes into the classroom to observe the host and co-facilitator carry out the plan, paying attention primarily to the students, the lesson decisions the group has made, and the effects these are having on students' learning. While the host teacher has primary responsibility, the coach or co-facilitator supports efforts as needed. Other members of the group take advantage of the luxury of observation, focusing on what students are doing, how they are responding, what questions students ask each other, and how groups solve problems when a teacher isn't there to intervene.

In the post-observation discussion, the focus is on the students and the routine. Teachers do not give the host teacher feedback on performance but review the group's instructional decisions and how those played out. New possibilities emerge for how things could have been handled. This is not a critique of the teacher or even the lesson, however, just another possibility. Someone says, "We hadn't even discussed the possibility of first having students explore the audience for the painting before jumping into the routine, but now, having seen the routine, I'm thinking it might be useful and that is something I might try when I do this in my class." There is specific attention to students' thinking. Students' work is brought back so it can be more specially examined. Individuals share what they heard and noticed and raise new questions for further exploration. Finally, the group discusses how each individual is now thinking about how they might use this particular routine in his or her classroom, utilizing the group to do some quick pre-planning.

On one hand, Learning Labs provide an opportunity to learn new thinking routines – the toolset. However, the discussion, close observation, and analytic debrief allow teachers to develop the skill set of making thinking visible as well. Furthermore, a facilitator or coach can model the mindsets by having faith in students' ability to think and encouraging this belief in others. Time and time again, we find the biggest sticking point in co-constructing a new thinking-routines-based lesson is that teachers often want to over-scaffold tasks, reduce challenge and complexity, and guide students toward specific outcomes. We as facilitators need to express our confidence in students and discourage such overplanning even as we think of possible ways to support the thinking if needed.

The Looking At Student Thinking (LAST) Protocol

We developed the LAST protocol as part of the original Visible Thinking project and have found it a powerful tool for enriching efforts to make thinking visible. The protocol takes about 45–60 minutes to complete with each stage progressing through set times in a predetermined sequence. As with most protocols, the artificialness of structuring a conversation is weighed against the benefits of making sure the discussion is complete, all meaningfull issues are addressed, and all voices are heard. A video of a group of teachers from Bialik College engaging in the LAST protocol can be viewed at https://www.youtube.com/ThePowerOfMakingThinkingVisible. The protocol itself is provided in Figure 7.1.

Figure 7.1 Looking At Student Thinking (LAST) protocol.

<hr>

Presentation & Preparation

<hr>

Presenting the work (no more than 5 minutes)

Presenting teacher provides the context, goals, and requirements of the task. The group asks clarifying questions that will help them understand the work.

Reading the Work (as much time as needed though not to exceed 7 minutes)

Read the work silently. Take notes for later comment. Categorize your notes to fit in with the stages of the protocol.

<hr>

Discussion & Analysis

<hr>

NOTE: Presenting teacher does not talk during the discussion and analysis but takes notes or documents the group's conversation for later comment.

1. **Describing the Work** (5-7 minutes)

   What do you actually see in the work itself? The purpose is to raise one another's awareness of all the features of the work. Avoid interpretation and just point out what things can be seen.

2. **Speculating about the Students' Thinking** (5-7 minutes)

   Where in the work do you see thinking? What aspects of the work provide insights in students' thinking? Interpret the features of the work and make connections to different types and ways of thinking. The Understanding Map may be useful.

3. **Asking Questions about the Work** (5-7 minutes)

   What questions does this work raise for you? NOTE: These are questions about the thinking and understanding and not questions about the lesson itself. Frame questions to get at broad issues as well as specifics. Ask the question behind the question. Rather than, "How long did this take?" ask, "This raises questions for me about the time needed to do this kind of work."

4. **Discuss Implications for Teaching and Learning** (5-7 minutes)

   Where might this work go next to further extend and build on students' thinking? Suggest practical possibilities and alternatives for the presenting teacher. Raise general implications the work suggests for promoting students' thinking.

Debriefing the Conversation & Protocol

<hr>

Presenting Teacher Responds to the Discussion (maximum of 5 minutes)

What have you as presenting teacher gained from listening to the discussion? Highlight for the group what you found interesting in the discussion. Respond to those questions that you feel need addressing by you. Explain briefly where you think you might now go with the work.

Reflecting on the Protocol (5 minutes)

How did the process go and feel? Reflect general observations. Notice improvements and changes since the last time the group used the protocol. Make suggestions for next time.

Thank the Presenting Teacher and the Documenter

The group acknowledges everyone's contribution. Decide how the documentation will be shared, used, and archived or the group. Establish roles for the next meeting.

In a LAST Protocol discussion there is a presenting teacher who brings a collection of student work, usually from a thinking routine a facilitator, and three to six other participants. After the presenter briefly describes the work, the other group members read through it silently and take notes. The heart of the protocol moves through four phases: describing the work without judgment or evaluation, speculating about the thinking that is present, raising questions, and considering implications. The presenting teacher is silent throughout this discussion so that he or she does not exert undue influence over the group's analysis. It is quite easy to defer to a presenting teacher once he or she starts explaining the work, so this imposed silence serves an important purpose. We don't want the conversation to become a monologue focused on the teaching rather than on an analysis of student learning and thinking. Only once the group's analysis concludes does the presenting teacher come back into the conversation.

If the LAST was only about providing feedback and suggestions for the presenting teacher, we couldn't justify the time. It is a luxury and often hard to find a full class period to convene six to eight teachers to look at student work. Therefore, the benefit of the LAST Protocol must extend beyond the individual work that is being examined. Although teachers are likely to encounter a new routine and better understand its possibilities (the toolset) through their participation in a LAST protocol, teachers also develop skill at analyzing student work, recognizing thinking, raising questions about encouraging thinking and understanding, and planning responsive instruction.

The Protocol for Collaborative Analysis of Documentation

Another useful protocol is the *Protocol for Collaborative Analysis of Documentation* or CAD (see Figure 7.2) developed by our Project Zero colleagues Mara Krechevsky, Ben Mardell, Melissa Rivard, and Daniel Wilson (Krechevsky et al. 2013). As the name suggests, it focuses on analyzing a piece of documentation brought to the group. Rather than progressing through a specific series of prompts, this protocol takes the analysis, questioning, and considering of implications more as a free-flowing discussion – though some groups choose to take each question prompt in sequence. This protocol tends to be shorter than the LAST and can often be done in 25 minutes, allowing the possibility for two rounds of sharing and discussion in a typical class period.

As with the LAST, the CAD protocol asks teachers to ground their interpretations in the documentation itself. What can they actually see? What is there on the page? Teachers are encouraged to point out the specific elements that support the claims they make about students' learning and thinking. This often gives rise to debate and rich discussion.

Figure 7.2 Protocol for collaborative analysis of documentation.

<table>
<tr><td colspan="1" align="center">Presentation & Preparation</td></tr>
</table>

Presenting the work (no more than 5 minutes)

Presenting teacher provides brief context for documentation. Group asks presenter clarifying questions. Group looks at documentation in silence.

<table>
<tr><td align="center">Discussion & Analysis</td></tr>
</table>

NOTE: Presenting teacher does not talk during the discussion and analysis but takes notes or documents the group's conversation for later comment.

Group Responds to the Following Questions. Questions may be taken in sequence or be woven together in a free-flowing conversation (10-20 minutes)

➤ *What do you see or hear in the documentation? What strikes you? What are you noticing as important or meaningful aspects?* Explain what makes you say that.

➤ *What questions does the documentation raise?* Note: Presenter does not answer questions.

➤ *What are the implications for teaching and learning and next steps for the presenter?*

<table>
<tr><td align="center">Debriefing the Conversation & Protocol</td></tr>
</table>

Presenter Take-Aways. Presenter shares his or her take-aways.

Group Take-Aways. Group members jot down at least one idea to use in their classrooms and share their ideas with the group.

Debrief Protocol and Thank Presenter.

What may seem clear and obvious to one person is not to another. When we are challenged with alternative, evidence-grounded interpretations, it pushes us to reexamine our own interpretation. Often teachers will suggest questions that might be asked of students, additional evidence they would like to see, and ways a teacher might collect that evidence. Teachers become students of their students, inquirers into learning and thinking itself. These are the types of conversation that can propel real professional growth in making thinking visible.

Teacher Reflections

Often when we convene professional learning groups, we begin with general reflections on the enterprise of making thinking visible in our individual classrooms. The following question prompts can be useful. We ask teachers to select one or two prompts from the list and spend three to five minutes doing some reflective writing. We then share our reflections, either with a partner, group of three, or occasionally as a whole group.

1. What moment/s this week did you feel your students were most connected and engaged to their learning? Why was that?

2. What moment/s this week did you feel that your students were disconnected or disengaged from their learning, like they were just going through the motions? What might have led to that?

3. What is an example of student thinking that most took you by surprise and opened up new possibilities and avenues for exploration?

4. Of everything you did in your teaching to make thinking visible this week, what would you do differently if you had the chance to do it again?

5. What questions did you hear yourself asking this week that were most effective in revealing, pushing, or prompting students' thinking?

6. Where were there opportunities (taken advantage of or not) for documenting and capturing students' thinking this week?

7. Where and when did you notice yourself listening with vigorous intent? Where do you wish you could have a "do over" and go back and listen more intently?

Another way we have used these reflection prompts is as part of an ongoing reflection process in which teachers keep a reflection log or journal. Teachers keep the questions on hand, reflecting upon them on either a daily or weekly basis. The intent is not to address the entire set of question prompts, though some teachers do, but to use them as vehicles for prompting meaningful reflections on our teaching. Teachers may then bring their reflections to the professional learning group to share.

IN CONCLUSION

We began this chapter by discussing the challenging nature of teaching. Teaching is not simply a matter of content knowledge coupled with delivery skills. Teaching is complex because learning is complex. At the same time, teaching can be energizing, precisely because learning is energizing. Being in the presence of deeply engaged learners is incredibly motivating. There are few things better. When we end a class period in which students have been deeply engrossed, we don't feel depleted, we feel revitalized.

Some people think that teachers are charged with producing learning, but this is a misunderstanding of our role. As teachers we are charged with producing the conditions for learning. Herein lies the promise and power of making thinking visible: It offers a window into the learning process. By using the various tools presented in this book, questioning, listening, documentation, and the use of thinking routines specifically, educators can support the thinking of students and thus their learning. However, the strategies provided in this book are just tools and like any tool must be applied in the right context and in skilled hands to see their full potential. To learn to do so requires community. We need the community of the classroom in which we learn with and from our students, becoming students of our students. We also rely on the community of our school in which we learn with and from our colleagues as we seek not only to apply thinking routines but also to develop the skill set and mindsets needed to use them well. Finally, we benefit from and build on the broader professional community of educators worldwide in which we learn from the new perspectives, challenges, and insights of others.

For some readers, this book represents the continuation of a journey to make thinking visible and create a culture of thinking in their classrooms and schools. For others, it will be the beginnings of a new endeavor. In either case, we hope that you take inspiration from the stories of the teachers presented in this book. Although these are pictures of excellent practice, recognize that these teachers also once encountered these tools as new processes that needed to be tried out, reflected upon, and then retried. Allow yourself to make mistakes and to learn from, and with, your students. Find colleagues with whom you can share and discuss your efforts and ongoing learning. Each time you make your students' thinking visible, use it as the natural springboard for your next teaching move so that your teaching is a responsive act that meets learners where they are. In this way you will find yourself well on the way to realizing the power of making thinking visible.

REFERENCES

Allen, D. and Blythe, T. (2004). *The Facilitator's Book of Questions: Tools for Looking Together at Student and Teacher Work*. New York: Teachers College Press.

Black, P. and Wiliam, D. (2002). *Inside the Black Box: Raising Standards Through Classroom Assessment*. London: Department of Education & Professional Studies King's College London.

Boaler, J. and Brodie, K. (2004). *The Importance, Nature and Impact of Teacher Questions*. Toronto: Psychology of Mathematics Education North America.

Briggs, S. (2014). Improving working memory: How the science of retention can enhance all aspects of learning. http://www.opencolleges.edu.au/informed/features/how-to-improve-working-memory (accessed 24 November 2019).

Briggs, S. (2017). Why curiosity is essential to motivation. http://www.opencolleges .edu.au/informed/features/curiosity-essential-motivation (accessed 2 April 2019).

Brookfield, S.D. and Preskill, S. (2005). *Discussion as a Way of Teaching: Tools and Techniques for Democratic Classrooms*. San Francisco: Jossey-Bass.

Brown, J. (2016). "Fire," The Sea Accepts All Rivers & Other Poems. Bloomington: Trafford.

Brown, P.C., Roediger, H.L.,.I.I.I., and McDaniel, M.A. (2014). *Make It Stick: The Science of Successful Learning*. Cambridge, MA: Belknap Press.

City, E.A., Elmore, R.F., Fiarman, S.E., and Teitel, L. (2009). *Instructional Rounds in Education: A Network Approach to Improving Teaching and Learning*. Cambridge, MA: Harvard Educational Publishing Group.

Claxton, G., Chambers, M., Powell, G., and Lucas, B. (2011). *The Learning Powered School: Pioneering 21s Century Education*. Bristol: TLO Limited.

Cochran-Smith, M. and Lytle, S. (1999). Relationships of knowledge and practice: teacher learning in communities. *Review of Research in Education* 24: 249–305.

Collins, A., Brown, J.S., and Holum, A. (1991). Cognitive apprenticeship: making thinking visible. *American Educator* 15 (3): 6–11, 38–46.

Deslauriers, L., McCarty, L.S., Miller, K. et al. (2019). Measuring actual learning versus feeling of learning in response to being actively engaged in the classroom. *Proceedings of the National Academy of Sciences* 116 (39): 19251–19257.

Dweck, C. (2006). *Mindset: The New Psychology of Success*. New York: Ballantine Books.

English, A.R., Hintz, A., and Tyson, K. (2018). *Growing Your Listening Practice to Stupport Students' Learning (Handbook)*. Edinburgh, UK.

Giudici, C., Rinaldi, C., and Krechevsky, M. (eds.) (2001). *Making Learning Visible: Children as Individual and Group Learners*. Reggio Emilia, Italy: Reggio Children.

Given, H., Kuh, L., LeeKeenan, D. et al. (2010). Changing school culture: Using documentation to support collaborative inquiry. *Theory Into Practice* 49: 36–46.

Goodlad, J.I. (1983). *A Place Called School: Prospects for the Future*. New York: McGraw-Hill.

Hattie, J. (2009). *Visible Learning: A Synthesis of over 800 Meta-Analyses Relating to Achievement*. New York: Routledge.

Hattie, J. and Timperley, H. (2007). The power of feedback. *Review of Educational Research* 77 (1): 81–112.

Hewlett Foundation (2013). Deeper learning competencies. https://hewlett.org/wp-content/uploads/2016/08/Deeper_Learning_Defined__April_2013.pdf (accessed 20 November 2019).

Karpicke, J.D. (2012). Retrieval-based learning: Active retrieval promotes meaningful learning. *Current Directions in Psychological Science* 21 (3): 157–163.

Krechevsky, M., Mardell, B., Rivard, M., and Wilson, D. (2013). *Visible Learners: Promoting Reggio-Inspired Approaches in All Schools*. Hoboken, NJ: Wiley.

Leinhardt, G. and Steele, M.D. (2005). Seeing the complexity of standing to the side: Instructional dialogues. *Cognition and Instruction* 23 (1): 87–163.

Liljedahl, P. (2016). Building thinking classrooms: conditions for problem-solving. In: *Posing and Solving Mathematical Problems* (eds. P. Felmer, J. Kilpatrick and E. Pekhonen), 361–386. Cham: Springer.

Lyons, L. (2004). Most teens associate school with boredom, fatigue. http://www.gallup.com/poll/11893/most-teens-associate-school-boredom-fatigue.aspx (accessed 20 November 2019).

MacKenzie, T. and Bathurst-Hunt, R. (2019). *Inquiry Mindset*. Elevate Books Edu.

Mehta, J. and Fine, S. (2019). *In Search of Deeper Learning: The Quest to Remake the American High School*. Cambridge, MA: Harvard University Press.

Miller, G.A. (1956). The magical number seven, plus or minus two: Some limits on our capacity for processing information. *Psychological Review* 63 (2): 81–97.

Murdoch, K. (2015). *The Power of Inquiry*. Melbourne: Seastar Education.

Newmann, F.M., Wehlage, G.G., and Lamborn, S.D. (1992). The significance and sources of student engagement. In: *Student Engagement and Achievement in American Secondary Schools* (ed. F.M. Newmann), 11–39. New York: Teachers College Press.

Newmann, F.M., Marks, H.M., and Gamoran, A. (1996). Authentic pedagogy and student performance. *American Journal of Education* 104: 280–312.

Newmann, F.M., Bryk, A.S., and Nagaoka, J. (2001). *Authentic Intellectual Work and Standardized Tests: Conflict or Coexistence*. Chicago: Consortium on Chicago School Research.

Onosko, J.J. (1992). Exploring the thinking of thoughtful teachers. *Educational Leadership* 49 (7): 40–43.

Perez-Hernandez, D. (2014). Taking notes by hand benefits recall, researchers find. https://www.chronicle.com/blogs/wiredcampus/taking-notes-by-hand-benefits-recall-researchers-find/51411 (accessed 11 June 2019).

Perkins, D.N. (1992). *Smart Schools: From Training Memories to Educating Minds*. New York: The Free Press.

Perkins, D.N., Tishman, S., Ritchhart, R. et al. (2000). Intelligence in the wild: A dispositional view of intellectual traits. *Educational Psychology Review* 12 (3): 269–293.

Perkins, D.N. (2003). *King Arthur's Round Table: How Collaborative Conversations Create Smart Organizations*. Hoboken, NJ: Wiley.

Pianta, R.C., Belsky, J., Houts, R., and Morrison, F. (2007). Opportunities to learn in America's elementary classrooms. *Science* 315: 1795–1796.

Ritchhart, R. (2000). Developing intellectual character: A dispositional perspective on teaching and learning, PhD dissertation. Harvard University Graduate School of Education.

Ritchhart, R. (2002). *Intellectual Character: What It Is, Why It Matters, and How to Get It*. San Francisco: Jossey-Bass.

Ritchhart, R. (2015). *Creating Cultures of Thinking: The 8 Forces We Must Master to Truly Transform Our Schools*. San Francisco: Jossey-Bass.

Ritchhart, R., Turner, T., and Hadar, L. (2009). Uncovering students' thinking about thinking using concept maps. *Metacognition and Learning* 4 (2): 145–159.

Ritchhart, R., Church, M., and Morrison, K. (2011). *Making Thinking Visible: How to Promote Engagement, Understanding, and Independence for All Learners*. Jossey-Bass: San Francisco.

Rothstein, D. and Santana, L. (2011). *Make Just One Change: Teaching Students to Ask Their Own Questions*. Cambridge, MA: Harvard Education Press.

Schoenfeld, A.H. (1999). Models of the teaching process. *Journal of Mathematical Behavior* 18 (3): 243–261.

Schwartz, K. (2015). How memory, focus and good teaching can work together to help kids learn. KQED Mindshift. www.kqed.org/mindshift/2015/04/09/how-memory-focus-and-good-teaching-can-work-together-to-help-kids-learn (accessed 9 April 2015).

Schwartz, M.S., Sadler, P.M., Sonnert, G., and Tai, R.H. (2009). Depth versus breadth: How content coverage in high school science courses relates to later success in college science coursework. *Science Education* 93 (5): 798–826.

Sepulveda, Y. and Venegas-Muggli, J.I. (2019). Effects of using thinking routines on the academic results of business students at a Chilean tertiary education institution. *Decision Sciences Journal of Innovative Education* 17 (4): 405–417.

Shernoff, D.J. (2010). *The Experience of Student Engagement in High School Classrooms: Influences and Effects on Long-Term Outcomes*. Saarbruken: Lambert Academic.

Shernoff, D.J. (2013). *Optimal Learning Environments to Promote Student Engagement*. New York: Springer Science + Business Media.

Smith, M. and Y. Weinstein (2016). Learn how to study using . . . retrieval practice. http://www.learningscientists.org/blog/2016/6/23-1 (accessed 11 June 2019).

Thornburg, D.D. (2004). Campfires in cyberspace: Primordial metaphors for learning in the 21st century. *International Journal of Instructional Technology and Distance Learning* 1 (10): 3–10.

Tishman, S. (2017). *Slow Looking: The Art and of Practice Learning Through Observation*. New York: Routledge.

Vygotsky, L.S. (1978). *Mind in Society*. Cambridge, MA: Harvard University Press.

Wallace, T.L. and Sung, H.C. (2017). Student perceptions of autonomy-supportive instructional interactions in the middle grades. *Journal of Experimental Education* 83 (3): 425–449.

White, R.T. and Gunstone, R.F. (1992). *Probing Understanding*. London: Falmer Press.

Wiliam, D. (2014). Is the feedback you're giving students helping or hindering?. https://www.dylanwiliamcenter.com/is-the-feedback-you-are-giving-students-helping-or-hindering (accessed 25 April 2019).

Wiliam, D. (2016). The secret of effective Feedback. *Educational Leadership* 73 (7): 10–15.

Yinger, R.J. (1979). Routines in teacher planning. *Theory Into Practice* 18: 163–169.

Van Zee, E. and Minstrell, J. (1997). Using questioning to guide student thinking. *Journal of the Learning Sciences* 6 (2): 227–269.

INDEX

K

L

M

T

Take Note: for biology, 142; content for, 141; for engaging with ideas, 34, 97, 140–146; formative assessment for, 143–144; for history, 144–146; prompts in, 140, 141, 144; purpose of, 140–141; setup for, 141; sharing in, 141–142; steps of, 141–142; tips for, 144; uses and variations of, 142–143

Teachers: curiosity of, 11; curriculum and, 10; documentation for, 27; formative assessments by, 11–13; roles of, 9–11; thinking routines for, 9–10

Teaching for Understanding, 6

Ted Talk, for *The Story Routine: Main-Side-Hidden,* 121

Thampi, Tahireh, 100–101; on priming, 213

Thinking dispositions: MTV for, 17–18; planning for, 207, 210; priming for, 214; questions in, 25

Thinking routines, xx, 5, 6; behavior patterns and, 32–33; content and, 31–32; curriculum and, 220–221; in deep learning, 7; discussion in, 30, 33; for engagement with action, 35, 145–197; for engagement with ideas, 34, 95–146; for engagement with others, 34, 39–93; in formative assessment, 12–13; Learning Labs for, 235; maximum effect from, 201–221; organizing, 33–35; planning in, 203–210; for poetry, 12–13; positioning in, 204, 219–221; pressing in, 204, 215–218; priming in, 204, 211–214; in Project Zero, xix; prompts in, 28; responses to, 137; for scaffolding, 28; sequential aspect of, 30–31; standardized tests and, 13–17; as structures, 30–31; in student engagement, 7–9; for teachers, 9–10; for thinking dispositions, 18; as tools, 28–29. *See also specific routines*

Think-Puzzle-Explore, 96

Thompson-Grove, Gene, 174

Thornburg, David, 217

321 Bridge, 96

3 Y's, 25; content for, 182–183; for engaging with action, 35, 149, 182–189; formative assessment for, 186–187; *4 If's* and, 190, 191, 195; for growth mindset, 185, 186; for language, 187–189; for literacy, 184; purpose of, 182; setup for, 183; sharing in, 184, 188; for Spanish, 187–189; steps of, 183–184; tips for, 187; uses and variations of, 184–186

Timekeeper, for *Leaderless Discussion,* 61

Tishman, Shari, xviii

Truth. *See Beauty & Truth*

Tug-of-War, 195

Turner, Terri, 27

Tyson, K., 26–27

U

Understanding Map, 29–30; for connections, 229; for planning, 205–206; priming and, 211; *Question Sorts* and, 102; thinking dispositions and, 19; *What? So What? Now What?* and, 177

Universality, 183

Upton, Michael, 153–157

V

Venegas-Muggli, Juan I., 17

Verbs, in *NDA,* 135

Veres, Emily, 142–143, 144

Vermeulin, Nora, 53

Viewpoints: from *Beauty & Truth,* 124, 125; from *Peeling the Fruit,* 107; teacher roles and, 10; from thinking routines, 28

Vigors, Alice, 152

Visible Thinking, xviii; *ESP+1* in, 158; LAST in, 235; *Peeling the Fruit* in, 107; resistance to, 13; thinking routines in, 28

Visualization, in *NDA,* 133

Vocabulary: *Making Meaning* for, 80; *NDA* for, 132, 134, 137, 139

Voltaire, 25

Vyas, Hardevi, 7–8

Vygotsky, L. S., 24

W

Water quality, *PG&E* for, 152

Watson, Jeff, 7, 89, 217

Weber, Connie, 185–186

Weinstein, Yana, 86–87

What makes you say that? (WMYST), 25

What? So What? Now What?, 25; content for, 175; for engaging with action, 35, 149, 174–181; formative assessment for, 177; for jazz, 178–181; for music, 178–181; purpose of, 174; reflection in, 174, 176; setup for, 175; sharing in, 176; steps of, 175–176; tips for, 178; used and variations of, 176–177

Whitmore, Steven, 119–120

Why?. *See 3 Y's*

Williams, Caitlin, 195–197

Wilson, Daniel, 237

Winston, Sam, 184

WMYST. *See* What makes you say that?

Woodcock, Heather, 59

Word response, for *Making Meaning,* 78

Working memory, *NDA* and, 34, 132, 133, 137

Writing: *Ladder of Feedback* and, 56; *NDA* and, 134; standardized tests for, 16; *The Story Routine* and, 123; *3 Y's* and, 187

W9-DGX-562

The Master and Minerva

The Master and Minerva

Disputing Women in French Medieval Culture

HELEN SOLTERER

FRANKLIN PIERCE
COLLEGE LIBRARY
RINDGE, N.H. 03461

University of California Press

BERKELEY   LOS ANGELES   LONDON

University of California Press
Berkeley and Los Angeles, California

University of California Press, Ltd.
London, England

© 1995 by the Regents of the University of California

Library of Congress Cataloging-in-Publication Data

Solterer, Helen.
    The master and Minerva : disputing women in French medieval
culture / Helen Solterer.
        p.   cm.
    Includes bibliographical references and index.
    ISBN 0-520-08565-5 (alk. paper).—ISBN 0-520-08835-2 (alk. paper :
pbk.)
    1. French literature—To 1500—History and criticism.   2. Women—
France—History—Middle Ages, 500–1500.   3. France—History—
Medieval period, 987–1515.   4. Women and literature—France—
History.   5. Quarreling in literature.   6. Law and literature.
7. Rhetoric, Medieval.   8. Dialectic.   I. Title.
PQ155.W6S65   1995
840.9′ 352042′ 0902—dc20   93–47918

PQ
155
.W6
S65
1995

Printed in the United States of America
9   8   7   6   5   4   3   2   1

The paper used in this publication meets the minimum requirements of
American National Standard for Information Sciences—Permanence of
Paper for Printed Library Materials, ANSI Z39.48-1984.

For Josef Solterer

Contents

Illustrations

Acknowledgments

This book has already had many lives, and the one it now enjoys in print is thanks in large part to colleagues and friends. In the beginning, during my graduate school time in Toronto, I was guided by Frank Collins and encouraged steadily by Brian Stock and Leonard Boyle. Over the years in Durham, my project took shape with the North Carolina Research Group on Medieval and Early Modern Women. I count myself lucky to have found in this group and its spirited discussions an intellectual home. Jane Burns and Judith Bennett always spurred me to think further with questions at crucial moments. Ann Marie Rasmussen and Monica Green got me to see my argument as a whole. Even at a distance, Linda Lomperis and Bonnie Krueger made me realize how my work was already part of a collective venture. Along the way, there have been many people whose reactions and suggestions have made their mark on my writing, I trust for the better. For dialogue that led me in new and unexpected directions, I am grateful to: Anne Dooley, Ann Rigney, Ronald Witt, and Charity Cannon Willard; for brainstorming sessions, to Kristen Neuschel, Paula Higgins, Danielle Régnier-Bohler, Nancy Miller, and Sarah Kay; for thought-provoking conversation, to Karen Pratt, Kevin Brownlee, and Lesley Johnson; and for proverbial wit, to Seán ÓTuama. My book took final shape as a result of four challenging readings of the manuscript from Jody Enders, David Hult, Nancy Regalado, and Gabrielle Spiegel. Engaging with them made revision a creative process and showed me again what debate is all about. In the last stages, my book has benefited greatly from the linguistic savvy of Frank Collins, David Hult, John Magee, and Brian Merrilees, and the sleuthing of my student collaborators, Louis Vavrina and Jennifer Winslow. In the end, I could not have pulled it off without Elizabeth Waters, whose staying power during record-breaking heat made the difference.

It is a pleasure to acknowledge the American Council of Learned Societies and Duke University Research Council, who funded my research throughout. The aid of many librarians here and abroad, and of the ever-ready staff at the Institut de recherche et d'histoire des textes in Paris is here gratefully recorded. Jean-Jacques Thomas and the cohort at Duke University's Department of Romance Studies sustained me with true collegial support.

My special thanks go to three fellow adventurers: Elizabeth Curran Solterer for teasing me into coming out with this book, Stephanie Sieburth for urging me to pin it down, and Michael Menzinger (+ fritz) for helping me to produce it at long last.

I dedicate this book to my father, who did not live to see it completed. His own inimitable zest for debate runs through its pages. *Se non é vero é ben trovato.*

Toronto/Durham
July 1993

The Master and Minerva

1. The respondent and the master in *La Response au Bestiaire d'amour*. Vienna, Österreichische Nationalbibliothek, Cod. 2609, fol. 32. Courtesy of the Österreichische Nationalbibliothek.

Introduction

She is seated at a scriptorium desk, wielding the tools of writing (Figure 1). He stands back, his hands open-palmed as if to bear the imprint of her work. Reversing the conventional configuration found in many medieval vernacular manuscripts, this miniature depicts a woman who supplants a cleric at his customary post and assumes his function as guardian of textual culture. Further, as the rubric makes clear, this woman is busy composing her response to the master's text—"the response to the bestiary, which the lady made against the request made by master Richard de Fournival" (la response dou bestiaire que la dame fist contre la requeste que maistres richars de furnival fist). Her taking to writing gives her the chance to answer his *requeste* directly, in the same medium. As she writes, her eyes hold him with a challenging look: here it is a master who attends to the word of a literate woman.

This image forms the initial *H* for the first line of the narrative: "Hom qui sens a et discretion" (Man, who has sense and understanding). The woman's response is placed within the very letter beginning the word *Hom*. It is represented in a way that breaks apart the unitary, homogeneous character of mankind. In so doing, her response breaks open the discourse defining and figuring it. Her version of mankind is illustrated as a give-and-take between a particular woman and man. What would ordinarily be a subject for disputation among clerical masters such as Richard de Fournival is taken over here by a woman. At the beginning of the narrative, the confrontation between a master who disputes and a disputing woman engenders debate that, in the ensuing text, will be played out according to their two positions. Questioning the concept *mankind* and its constituent languages leads to a sustained interrogation of the learning of one exemplary master. Given that the opening sentence paraphrases the incipit of the

1

Metaphysics, this woman's response takes on a well-known treatise of the Master Philosopher, as Aristotle was called in the high Middle Ages.

I begin my study of the medieval dialectic between masterly writing and woman's response with this miniature from the *Response au Bestiaire d'amour* because it delineates vividly many of its key questions. First, the image poses a question concerning the figuration of women in medieval narrative. What does such figuration suggest a female figure writes in response to what she reads? That women are represented as quarrelsome interlocutors or even respondents was already an integral element of European literature by the twelfth century. Their part is inscribed in the numerous debate forms that characterize medieval lyric and narrative— the Provençal *tenso*, the Old French *requeste, complainte,* and dialogue poems, among others. Andreas Capellanus's mock dialogues in the *De amore (On Love)* project female voices that reply to and often foil the suits of male lovers. The epistolary tradition pairs the work of male writers with that of women who reply warily. Even in medieval versions of Ovid's *Heroïdes*, the letters attributed to female correspondents mark a type of interaction. Yet what happens when a woman is portrayed reacting negatively to a text already in circulation? What happens when her response, once coded and contained within love literature, breaks out and is established separately in the circuit of texts? What are the implications of a disputing female figure whose opposition operates within literate and even learned culture?

This illumination from the late-thirteenth-century *Response au Bestiaire d'amour* also raises the issue of how such figures of master and disputing woman register socially. It prompts us to consider the connection between figurative languages and conventions of reading and writing prevailing in medieval Europe. Such a connection needs to be gauged extremely carefully. We can neither reduce the figure to a symptom or effect of those conventions nor regard them critically as distinct phenomena. In this manner, the figure of the woman respondent occasions an inquiry into the practices of vernacular literate culture.

To embark on such an inquiry is to face straightaway a heritage of vying claims regarding the relation between medieval laywomen and the domain of written texts. The first investigations sought to establish such a relation empirically. In the early nineteenth century, critics set out to prove that medieval women were indeed literate. The French historian Jules Michelet exemplified this approach. His essay, "Fragments d'un mémoire sur l'éducation des femmes" (1838) established the standard for tracing the development of women's skills. "They [women] were deemed worthy of reading and writing . . . they became learned as well as pious."

Michelet's claim launched the argument for laywomen's entry into the world of letters.[1] In most subsequent efforts to survey the European Middle Ages, critics collected cases such as the *Bestiaire* respondent as evidence for women's participation in literate culture.[2] Whether those examples involved known individuals or textual personae, they were used to substantiate the argument for women's involvement with written texts. Such a quantitative way of proceeding laid the groundwork for the view that laywomen presided over the two principal poles of vernacular literary production—as patron and privileged reader. One of the first theorists of literacy, Herbert Grundmann, articulated this view best when he asserted: "By women and through them, vernacular poetry achieved a literate form and became 'literature.' "[3] Grundmann's formula typifies the habit of interpreting the numbers of medieval women linked with bookish culture as proof of their decisive activity.[4]

But because such literate women appeared prominently in a world mediated by a figurative language, their prominence has merited closer scrutiny. The presence of women readers in vernacular literature raises the question of their function. As Georges Duby has observed, the instance of women playing an authoritative role of patron and reader suggests a complex mechanism whereby their bookish superiority works to the advantage of their overlords.[5] Far from demonstrating women's influence over vernacular writing, it points to their likely function as go-betweens in a game of clerical control. The figures of "masterful" women readers show the signs of a certain autonomy: they exercise the skills of reading and writing associated with the clergy. Yet, at the same time, these figures bespeak the designs of a small, literate caste that presents women in this light so as to better discipline them. The long-standing link between women and the literary sphere is too fraught to allow for a one-to-one correspondence between textual figure and social role. Under the iconoclastic pressure of feminist analyses, the convention of the female reader has been effectively dismantled so as to reveal the fact that such images need not necessarily confirm laywomen's influential participation in literate culture.[6]

For all their differences, what these two interpretative positions share, paradoxically, is a very limited conception of women's relation to the domain of written texts. Women are restricted to first-degree literacy. While they are attributed the elementary skills of reading and writing, rarely, if ever, are they deemed to use them practically. Their involvement in letters is passive. Moreover, medieval laywomen in these accounts are missing the "literate" mentality by which one interprets and adjudicates the world textually. Such an understanding is discernible across much high-medieval vernacular literature. Women are commonly typed as literalists—unable to pass beyond the letter of a text. From the scores of inscribed female readers in romance to Dante's Francesca, they are presented as reading poorly, prone to misunderstanding.[7] And their poor reading record has everything to do with their inability to gain access to the symbolic: "The woman says: these things are too obscure for me, and your words are too allegorical; you will have to explain what you mean" (Mulier ait: hi mihi sunt nimis sermones obscuri nimisque verba reposita, nisi ipsa tua faciat interpretatio manifesta; *De amore*, book I).[8] Like one of Andreas Capellanus's personae in the *De amore*, women are represented as confused by any level of signification other than the literal. They appear beholden to their masterly interlocutors to make the symbolic comprehensible. Yet even with such instruction, it is unclear whether they are ever fully initiated into the symbolic mode (verba reposita).

By contrast, the cleric is singled out by his subtle and sophisticated figurative understanding.[9] Trained to extract the kernel of meaning from its various husks—as the exegetical trope describes the process—the clerk excels in working his texts symbolically. The *figura* is his characteristic property.[10] It is, of course, the master—the head of clerkly culture—who champions the symbolic register.[11] Like the cleric in the *Response au Bestiaire* miniature, the *magister* is meant to brandish the *figura*, and with it all the tools of text-based learning.

This typing of the woman vis-à-vis the master brings us to the basis of a literate mentality. As Brian Stock has argued, the difference between literal and symbolic makes sense only within the framework of literate culture. He writes: "Such a distinction [figure/truth, symbolic/literal], of course, was unthinkable without a resort to the intellectual structures of allegory, which were in turn a byproduct of the literate sensibility. For, to find an inner meaning, one first had to understand the notion of a text *ad litteram*."[12] In this sense, the idea of women's participation in the work of high-medieval literate culture looks compromised. Insofar as they are usually depicted laboring over a literal sense, they are not judged to be literate in the fullest possible measure. Women's second-degree literacy appears untenable. So too their capacity to operate within a world defined by texts. The masterful act of symbolic interpretation seems out of reach, with the result that women's engagement with such interpretation through writing looks an even more remote affair.

Is the *Bestiaire* respondent then just another in the long line of literalists represented by medieval narrative? When she takes stylus in hand to write against the master's *requeste*, does she concentrate only upon its literal sense? Early on in her text, she observes: "For truly I know that there is no beast who should be feared like a gentle word that comes deceiving. And I think it well that one can be a little on guard against it" (Car je sai vraiement qu'il n'est beste qui tant fache a douter comme douche parole qui vient en dechevant. Et si cuic[h] bien que contre li se puet on peu warder).[13] This respondent recognizes the power of the symbolic and begins to pick the master's bestiary metaphors apart adroitly. She analyzes the symbolic language they comprise as a form of damage to women. Yet in so doing, she is represented as capable of deploying the symbolic herself. In fact, her reading exploits the *figura* as fully as would any master's lesson. In the *Response*, it is no longer a question of whether a woman can interpret symbolically or not, but rather what her interpretation enables her to do.

I shall argue that the encounter between the master and the woman respondent changes the medieval type of the female literalist in significant ways. There we can discern how women respondents emerge as decoders of the symbols of masterly writing. More importantly, in such an encounter we can find them becoming critics of that writing. If the case of the *Bestiaire d'amour* respondent gives us any clue, women are seen to interpret negatively the symbolic language associated with the masters. Far from remaining at a superficial level, stumped by the letter of a text, the respondent comes to exercise her own skills in symbolic interpretation. With these skills, she is equipped to contest the sexualized representations of women—the various feminine metaphors of flora and fauna—that hold sway, and to challenge the very symbol system that defines the clerico-courtly discourse authoritatively.[14] Indeed, the respondent disputes what I call, after Pierre Bourdieu, the symbolic domination of a tradition of representing women in medieval letters.[15]

Once we begin to entertain such an argument, we should consider any medieval models of a woman's response. There are, in fact, many, though they have rarely been conceptualized as such.[16] The first, pervasive model is a rhetorical one. A variety of medieval topoi existed that associated woman's language with the format of response. Dante evokes them suggestively in the *De vulgari eloquentia* where he surmises: "But although in the Scriptures woman is found to have spoken first, it is nevertheless reasonable for us to believe that man spoke first. For it is incongruous to think that such an extraordinary act for humankind could have first flowed forth from a woman rather than from a man . . . man spoke first by way of response" (Sed quanquam mulier in scriptis prius inveniatur locuta, rationabile tamen est ut hominem prius locutum fuisse credamus: et inconvenienter putatur, tam egregium humani generis actum, vel prius quam a viro, a foemina profluisse . . . per viam responsionis primum fuisse locutum (book I, iv).[17] According to the standard topoi taken from the Bible, the first human speech act in Eden is attributed to Eve. Yet even when this is denied and reassigned to Adam, Eve's speech remains situated in the framework of response. If she did utter the originary word, she did so in reply to the Lord. If she did not, she is still described implicitly as responding to her human lord. This account of the first Edenic dialogue reiterates the scholastic belief in the secondary status of human language. And in its puzzlement over Eve, it accentuates the peculiar secondariness of her speech. Starting in paradise, women are allotted the role of respondent.[18]

In the high-medieval didactic work known as the *Miroir des bonnes femmes* we can see how the rhetoric of the woman's response is further reinforced.[19] Commenting upon the Biblical scenario in Eden, the *Miroir* focuses on Eve's response not to God or Adam but to the snake. The rubric reads: "The second stupidity of Eve was that she responded too frivolously" (la seconde sotie de eue fu en ce quele respondi trop liegierement). In this manual on noblewomen's comportment, Eve's responsiveness is introduced as a negative exemplum. It is a preeminent illustration of how not to behave. The passage continues: "I want you to know the story of the wise lady who responded to the mad knight and who spoke of [his] folly. She did not reply without her lord, but she would talk openly with him [her lord] about it. If she took the knight for mad, he took her for wise."[20] In this comparison between Eve and *la sage dame*, the first woman is one with a loose tongue who does not recognize the dangers of her responsiveness. The wise lady, however, refrains from the linguistic errors of her progenetrix. In an obvious courtly setting, the lady reacts circumspectly to the problem of answering men. She is seen to recognize the dangers of their "mad" language. With this exemplum, the *Miroir* promotes a lesson of a wary response. The wise lady rebuffs the advances of unreliable suitors who speak to her and follows instead the verbal lead of her lord. Whoever that lord might be, she is positioned to speak *after*, to take up his first utterance. The wise woman's response is defined by the moral "Don't speak until spoken to."

These two cases from the late Middle Ages testify to the rhetoric of women's propensity for response. There are many others. Found in fictional and didactic works alike, the topos of the woman respondent establishes the link between woman's language and the posture of replying to man's. This link could be constructed negatively or positively. As we have seen, once responsiveness is labeled a fault, a woman's response per se is colored pejoratively. And yet absolute silence being impossible, the form and substance of a woman's response were also addressed. In this sense the topos could be inflected positively, in keeping with the classical Latin etymology of the verb *respondere*—to reciprocate, to promise or pledge in return. As long as a woman's response conformed to the dictates of a man's verbal act, it could function usefully in the network of human communication.

These rhetorical characterizations undergird the second, generic model of woman's response. Again, the etymology of the word makes the point clearly: *response* is a Provençal, Old French neologism—a characteristically medieval form. Already apparent in the range of Provençal genres in the eleventh and twelfth centuries, it involves dialogue and debate poems that evolve between a female and a male speaker.[21] Of the various poetic genres that fit this definition, the most noteworthy is the *tenso*, one that, significantly enough, is well represented in the repertory of the *trobaritz*, the women troubadours.[22] According to Peter Dronke, all these "response" forms share "the spontaneous movement of poetic answering."[23] Without delving into the stereotypes that lead Dronke to associate spontaneity with putative female genres—something we have already found to be amply borne out rhetorically (compare spontaneous/*legere*)—I want to point out the key element of "answering." The Provençal *tenso* develops as a series of responses to a statement of love. The genre depicts adversarial male and female personae who dispute various aspects of love. Invariably the woman is in a position of resisting the man's onslaught. The *tenso* between Guillelma de Rosers and Lanfranc Cigala exemplifies this dynamic:

> Domna, poder ai eu et ardimen
> Non contra vos, qe.us vences en iazen,
> Per q'eu fui fols car ab vos pris conten,
> Mas vencut vueilh qe m'aiatz con qe sia.
>
> Lafranc, aitan vos autrei e.us consen
> Qe tant mi sen de cor e d'ardimen
> C'ab aital geing con domna si defen
> Mi defendri'al plus ardit qe sia.
> (lines 49–56)[24]

Lady, I have the strength and the daring not to oppose you since I could vanquish you lying down, for which reason I was crazy to have started disputing with you, but because I desire that you should vanquish me in whatever way possible. Lafranc, I grant and assure you that I feel such daring of heart that with the savvy with which a woman defends herself, I shall defend myself in the most brazen way possible.

These two final stanzas of the *tenso* reveal the twofold challenge of a woman's response. Guillelma is reckoning with the various maneuvers that typify Lanfranc's language—here, the characteristic claim that the man will prevail by being overcome by the woman. This paradoxical contention is coded in terms of men's force (poder) versus women's savvy (geing). Yet the woman interlocutor is confronting the designs of amorous discourse the personae articulate. The defense she must mount is also directed against the very tradition of speaking about love to women. Guillelma and Lanfranc's *tenso* dramatizes the formidable power of a prevailing symbolic language.

In the Old French repertory of *requeste/response*, the problem of contesting that symbolic power also comes to the fore. Take, for instance, an early-fourteenth-century case entitled *La Prière d'un clerc et la response d'une dame.*[25] The woman contends:

> Dites quanque voudrez, je vous escouterai,
> Mes ja, certes, pour cen plus tost n'ous amerai.
> Ja pour toutes vos truffles plus fole ne serai.
> Ausi com la cygoigne ne plus ne mainz ferai.
>
> La cygoigne mengüe le venim et l'ordure
> Ja ne li mesfera, quer c'est de sa nature.
> Mes non fera a moi, j'en sui toute seüre,
> Trestout vostre parler, quant je n'i met ma cure.
>
> (lines 181–88)

Say whatever you want to, I'll listen to you. But I will not love you, that is more than certain. For all your foolishnesses, I will not be so mad. Just like the stork, I'll do no more, no less. The stork ingests venom and dung so that they will not hurt it, for that is its nature. But so long as I take care, your talk will not do it [harm] to me, I'm sure of it.

Her response focuses on the question of the clerk's dangerous language. The trope of *truffles* (foolishnesses) captures the flavor of a language that is outlandish and at the same time disturbing. Further, it carries with it a foul intent (venim/ordure). The respondent thus deploys her own symbol of the stork not only to keep her distance but to expose the potential harm of the clerk's word. Implicitly she elaborates a critique. From within the conventions of amorous discourse, this woman's response signals a challenge to that discourse. However discreetly, the response raises the issue of the discourse's possible destructive effects.

There are also signs of such a challenge in the epistolary genres of Old French known as *saluts d'amour*. In the unusual instance of a late-thirteenth-century love letter attributed to a woman (*salus d'amours féminin*), the respondent takes her clerkly interlocutor to task linguistically:[26]

> Biaus amis, qui si me proiez,
> je ne cuit pas que vous soiez
> si destroiz por moi com vous dites,
> car trop de losenges petites
> savez por la gent decevoir.
> *Honis soit qui a dame dira*
> *qu'il l'aint, s'il ne dit voir.*
>
> (lines 1–7)

Dear friend who beseeches me, I don't think that you can be quite so distressed about me as you say, for you know too many of the little slanderous expressions [losenges] to deceive people. *"He who does not tell the truth when he says he loves a woman shall be shamed."*

The problem, once again, resides in the disturbing and fraudulent character of the clerk's language. "Losenges" is no external threat here. It does not refer to the paradigmatic slander of those outsiders called *lauzengiers* or *mesdisants* who play a stock role in medieval love poetry. Instead "losenges" is internalized. It comprises a danger intrinsic to the prevailing discourse invoked by a lover to address his lady. The notion of verbal destructiveness thus applies to its conventional figures. It is the woman respondent who begins to say as much.

Such a concept of verbal destructiveness was taken over by many medieval clerical writers to justify the model of the modest woman who speaks circumspectly. Witness the late-twelfth-century didactic text, *Le Chastoiement des dames* of Robert de Blois.[27] In a commentary on woman's social manners, Blois is concerned with instructing women how to decline *requestes* or offers of love. His concern has everything to do with the likely harmful quality of those offers. In Blois's account, declining means knowing how to avoid this harm by responding to the would-be lover in an unambiguously negative way. To this end, he sees fit to include a trial response for his women readers:

> Quant vos sa plainte oï avrez,
> Tot ensi se li respondez:
> "Beaux sire, certes a mon vuil
> N'avroiz vos jai de par moi duil,
> Et se vos por moi vos dolez,
> Saichiez bien que fol cuer avez....
> Ne sai qu'en moi veü avez,
> Mes bien pert que vos me tenez

> A la plus nice, a la plus fole,
> Quant dite m'avez tel parole.
> De tel beaulté ne suis je mie,
> Qu'ale face panser folie.
> Et certes se je tele estoie,
> Plus natemant me garderoie....
> Ne le dites pas en riant,
> Mes ausi con par mautalant.
> (lines 684–89, 714–21, 738–39)

When you have heard his complaint, respond in the following manner. "Dear sir, it is certainly not my wish that you have any sorrows, and if you are grieving on my account, you should know that you have a mad heart. . . . I don't know what you saw in me, but you are lost if you take me for the most gullible and naive when you speak to me with that language. I am hardly that beautiful; it would be madness to think so. And were I like that, I would be careful to be on guard. . . ." Don't tell him [the knight] this laughingly, but with a certain irritation.

Blois elaborates an unyielding "woman's response"; it exposes the fallacies of the knight's beguiling pretty talk, just as it queries its ulterior motives. Moreover, it is meant to be delivered sharply and judgmentally.

As the final recommendation in a comprehensive scheme to discipline women's conduct, Blois's set piece gives us some sense of the net of maneuver and manipulation in which a woman's response is caught. That Blois ordains what the response should say and how it should be spoken is symptomatic of the habit in high-medieval culture to prescribe women's voices. It is his prerogative as cleric to establish how the woman responds. Further, it points to the larger social value of training laywomen to be wary as far as men's advances are concerned. This is part of the clerical learning about women that I shall explore in part 1. Yet precisely this interest of Blois's in mandating a woman's response gives us a glimpse of the response's considerable strategic potential. His insistence on devising his own version bespeaks a concern for all that women could say in response to the dominant courtly and clerical discourse on them. Whereas Blois's response lets that discourse stand unscathed, there is always the possibility for others to take on that discourse critically.

Here we circle back to our argument regarding the woman's response. Throughout the high Middle Ages, the response increasingly became a field for challenging the dominant feminine symbols in poetic discourse. Rhetorically and generically, it provided a framework in which a critique of the standard figures could develop. And in this it corresponded strikingly with the scholastic ritual of the disputation. While the woman's response displayed a contestatory aspect typical of so much of medieval literature, it derived its particular force from the *disputatio*.[28] Moreover, it resembled the set role of the *responsio* (response) in these debates as they were conducted in the schools and the universities. This is the role of the student set the task of replying to the masters and disputing their propositions point for point. The *Bestiaire d'amour* respondent epitomizes such a student; in fact, the intense oppositional engagement of her response mimics the public sparring matches of the disputation that defined intellectual life in the high Middle Ages. This disputational character of the woman's response was further reinforced by a variety of social factors: the numbers of noble and bourgeois literate women during the fourteenth and fifteenth centuries were steady, the rudiments of education were placed in their hands, and opportunities for book learning were even available to them.[29] Socially, there were reasons supporting women's figurative affiliation with scholastic practices such as the *disputatio*. By the late Middle Ages, at the time of those heated debates known as the *Querelle des femmes*, the figure of the woman respondent/disputant no longer conformed to the many powerful courtly and clerical prototypes in the line of Blois.

But how could a woman's response intervene efficaciously in the domain of textual culture? Even when we account for the prestigious model of the *disputatio* informing it, the question of its specific challenge still remains. Faced with a discourse on women legitimated by clerkly scholarship, how precisely could the response dispute it? The cardinal criterion available to the woman's response, I shall argue, is the idea of injurious language: words in and of themselves can cause harm to the public. Such an idea proves especially elusive to us today. In a society where our sense of the power of language is so thoroughly attenuated by other media, where violence is linked more and more with audiovisual imagery, the possibility that words can enact harm is difficult to fathom. Were it not for the reemerging concern over hate speech and the idioms of "fighting words," the idea of verbal injury would seem remote, little more than a curious avatar of an earlier mentality.[30] Yet for much of medieval culture, injurious language was an article of faith. "Sometimes words cause more trouble than flogging" (aliquando plus turbant verba quam verbera). Gregory the Great's dictum, cited proverbially throughout the Middle Ages, exemplifies this sense of the damaging power of language. The echo "verba/verbera" gets at the heart of the analogy between words and physical blows. In a preprint society such as the medieval world, this link was acutely felt, and with it the fundamental connection between words and action. Simply put, words constituted action. Neither a substitute nor an alternative for action, they functioned as action. They were thus also actionable.

The signs for this medieval understanding of injurious language are legion. Inheriting the classical rhetorical conceptions of the languages of praise and blame, many thinkers from the twelfth century on were preoccupied with the good that words could incur and the harm that they could inflict.[31] Among the many treatises on the language arts, there were those that dealt specifically with disciplining the tongue. Take, for example, Albertano of Brescia's *Liber de doctrina loquendi et tacendi* (*Book on the Doctrine of Speaking and Being Silent*) and Hugh of Saint Cher's *De custodia linguae* (*Concerning the Care of Language*).[32] And there were those that focused on the problem of wayward language, such as Robert Grosseteste's *De detractione et eius malis* (*On Detraction and its Evil*).[33] Given this preoccupation, it is hardly surprising that catalogues of verbal transgression were drawn up. In the high Middle Ages, we can point to a significant number of clerical pastoral manuals that identified every possible transgressive speech act. Slander, perjury, rumor mongering, sarcasm, lying, invective, calumny, false praise: all these types were laid out and assessed according to motivation, defining features, and appropriate compensation.[34] In these analyses, the rhetorical categories of injurious language are approached practically. As a result, their occurrence in everyday speech and writing can be judged. Acts of verbal injury are subject to correction. Whether these particular pastoral manuals were ever used to condemn individuals and mete out punishment is a moot point. But what is clear is the governing mentality among the medieval clergy and society at large that evaluated any number of speech acts as punishable.[35] Indeed, such acts were criminalized. This is borne out amply by the inquisitional record of public beatings and mutilation of those convicted of various verbal sins. The person who spoke injuriously against ecclesiastical or political authority was to suffer the consequences physically: that person's words were turned back against the body itself.[36]

What was already a profound understanding of injurious language gained further technical weight during the later Middle Ages. This was due in no small part to the revival of Roman law.[37] The canonists' extensive commentary on Justinian's Code and other inherited precepts brought to the fore the Roman conception of *iniuria* as the code defined it.[38] "You can bring an action for injury in the usual way against those who are ascertained to have done anything for the purpose of reflecting upon your character" (quin immo adversus eos, quos minuendae opinionis tuae causa aliquid confecisse comperietur, more solito iniuriarum iudicio experiri potes).[39] This statute established a tort whereby any offense directed against an individual's or a group's reputation was subject to legal judgment. According to medieval canonists, it stigmatized any words intended to hurt a person's or group's public name.[40] The code's statute and its medieval interpretations thus served to reinforce the rhetorical and pastoral principle of injurious language. Over the course of the fourteenth century, this principle grew more and more prominent precisely because it was associated with the formidable apparatus of classical legal thought.[41] In this manner, it became a question of political discussion as much as a clerical, ecclesiastical concern. By the fifteenth century, the problem of verbal injury was focused in the public domain.[42]

I sketch this background so that we can recognize the context for the idea of verbal injury in the woman's response. Its use was by no means unique. In fact, it was symptomatic of the pervasive concern over *verba/verbera* animating high-medieval society. But it was nevertheless highly unusual for the woman's response to employ the concept of verbal injury as a powerful tool against the dominant symbolic discourse on women. Ordinarily, we are accustomed to attribute such a concept to the powers that be. It is the prerogative of the prevailing authorities, who invoke it as a way of securing the existing order. In periods of social unrest such as the later Middle Ages, the Church used it to brand the delinquent believer, or royalty employed it to single out the seditious language of citizens it suspected. With the charge of verbal injury, the heretic and the traitor were stigmatized, accused of the worst verbal infraction—blasphemy.[43] Yet in the case of the medieval woman's response, this charge was taken right to the center of a reigning poetic discourse. The criterion of injurious language was a spearhead directed against the most orthodox symbolic language about women, and thus against the most indisputable.[44] It was the driving principle of a developing critique of the prevailing feminine representation that passed for learning in vernacular medieval culture.

No work better stood for this learning than the *Roman de la rose*. Yet significantly, no French work more powerfully elicited the problem of verbal injury. Contained within Guillaume de Lorris's and Jean de Meun's text are both a stock of misogynous wisdom concerning women and an analysis of slander—all this in a narrative that closely resembles a university debate between masters and disciples. As many have remarked, the *Rose* is a *disputatio* gathering together various authorities who speak vehemently and often slanderously on the subject of loving women.[45] It is the female allegorical figure, Reason, who addresses explicitly the danger of such slanderous or injurious language:

> Tencier est venjance mauvese;
> et si doiz savoir que mesdire
> est encore venjance pire.
> Mout autrement m'en vengeraie,
> se venjance avoir en volaie;

> car se tu meffez ou mesdiz,
> ou par mes fez ou par mes diz
> secreement t'en puis reprendre
> por toi chastier et aprendre,
> sans blasme et sanz diffamement. . . .
> Je ne veill pas aus genz tancier,
> ne par mon dit desavancier
> ne diffamer nule persone,
> quele qu'ele soit, mauvese ou bone.
> (lines 6976–85, 6993–96)[46]

Quarreling is evil vengeance, and you should know that slander is even worse. If I wanted vengeance, I would avenge myself in quite another way. For if you misbehaved or spoke slanderously, I would secretly find a way through my actions and my words to chastise and instruct you without blame and without defaming you. . . . I do not wish to quarrel with people or to repel or defame anyone by my word, whomever he might be, good or bad.

Reason distinguishes her own teaching by the absence of any defamatory elements. It is, quite simply, blameless. Yet in making this distinction, Reason draws attention to the potential link between authoritative languages and slander. She suggests the possibility that those languages promoted as doctrine can prove injurious. Such a possibility inheres in the speeches of many of the allegorical personages in Jean de Meun's *Rose*. We have only to think of Genius, Ami, or *Male Bouche*, the emblematic bad-mouther. But in its largest terms, that possibility of slander implicates the narrative as a whole. The profound irony is that the text constituting the most encyclopedic medieval knowledge of women, as well as the most elaborate symbolic language representing them, raises the issue of its own injurious character.

This problematic of verbal injury was pursued specifically in relation to poetic texts by the fourteenth-century writer Guillaume de Machaut. His *Jugement dou Roy de Navarre* rehearses a dispute between a lady and Guillaume over the slander of women in his love poetry:

> Guillaume. . . .
> Se je le say, vous le savez,
> Car le fait devers vous avez
> En l'un de vos livres escript,
> Bien devisié et bien descript:
> Si resgardez dedens vos livres.
> Bien say que vous n'estes pas ivres,
> Quant vos fais amoureus ditez.
> (lines 862, 865–71)[47]

Guillaume. . . . If I know it, you know it, for the matter involving you is what you have written in one of your books and well described and depicted. So look in your books. I really know that you aren't drunk when you compose love poetry.

Here the charge of "mesdisance" (line 831) is levied against the writing of an individual poet. This disputant takes exception to one of his books, and by extension to all of his work. She is unwilling to accept the usual excuse of unruly behavior (*ivresse*) that is part and parcel of the lover-poet's identity in medieval amorous discourse. Of course we must not lose sight of the fact that her charge of verbal injury comes out of Machaut's own text. Like the *Rose*, the *Jugement* dramatizes the problematic. Indeed it goes so far as to represent Guillaume's desire for correction (line 911). Yet by dint of explicitly presenting the problem, the *Jugement* attempts to deflect it. Depicting the poet's own judgment and punishment is one way of defending him against the claim that his work is slanderous.

With the early-fifteenth-century *Querelle des femmes*, the problem of verbal injury gained particular momentum.[48] In this framework, it moved out of the context of poetic works and into that of public polemic. The first authoritative text targeted was, not surprisingly, the *Roman de la rose*. It was the professional writer Christine de Pizan who launched the charge of slander in an open debate with several Parisian humanists defending Maître Jean de Meun. This woman's charge exploited the issue of verbal injury in several innovative ways. To begin with, Christine's dispute with the *Rose* introduced a particular technical conception of defamation.[49] In her first letter addressed to Jean de Meun's humanist defenders, she asks:

En quel maniere puet estre vallable et a bonne fin ce que tant et si excessivement, impettueusement et tres nonveritablement il accuse, blasme et diffame femmes de pluseurs tres grans vices et leurs meurs tesmoingne estre plains de toute perversité?[50]

In what manner could it [the *Rose*] be valuable and directed toward a good end, that which accuses and blames women so excessively, impetuously and so untruthfully, which defames them by several enormous vices and finds their behavior full of all manner of perversity?

Christine's question draws attention to the effects of defamatory language. And it refines the general idea of words that do harm by reintroducing the classical notion that words can damage the fame (*fama*) of a person or group.[51] On a larger scale, Christine's critique of the *Rose* made visible the public reputation of women and its peculiar vulnerability to defamation.

Consequently, it planted the problem of texts defaming women squarely in the public domain. Her part in the *Querelle du Roman de la rose* made it an issue for the community as a whole. As Christine asserted in the same letter: "A work of no utility and out of the common good . . . is not praiseworthy" (oevre sans utilité et hors bien commun ou propre . . . ne fait a louer; Hicks, 21).

In this notion of "the common good" we can detect the second, far-reaching innovation of Christine's disputation. Putting the emphasis on the public implications of defamation enabled her to transform the *Querelle de la Rose* ethically. Ultimately Christine is concerned with the damaging effects a defamatory text can produce upon the public. What injures a particular social group injures that society at large—the body politic. Christine engaged with the *Rose* powerfully by gauging the social benefits or liabilities of this text and by holding it publicly responsible. Following her lead, we will examine this question of the value or end of medieval works representing women; our inquiry will bring us to consider their defamatory language from an ethical point of view.

However singular Christine's disputation may appear, its ethical point was by no means lost. Another debate in the fifteenth-century *Querelle des femmes* pushed it still further. With the controversy over the poem *La Belle Dame sans merci* by the well-known court poet Alain Chartier, the problem of the value of a work became a matter of public adjudication. In a response to Chartier's poem attributed to three women, "Jeanne, Katherine, and Marie," the notion of defamation against women was exploited in a fully legal sense. Such a juridical conception was already apparent in the *Querelle de la Rose*: when Christine lodges her complaint against Jean de Meun's text in the public forum, she speaks legalistically. Indeed there are many cases, such as Guillaume de Machaut's *Jugement* poems, where a legalistic force is brought to bear on literary language. The pattern reaches all the way back to the *Roman de la rose* and the teachings of Reason cited above, where she alludes to the right to plead the case of defamation before a judge (par pleindre, quant tens en seroit, au juige, qui droit m'en feroit; lines 6989–90).

What distinguishes the women's dispute with Chartier's *Belle Dame* is the move to charge an authoritative poetic text with a crime of defamation. Jeanne, Katherine, and Marie indict the poet for his "writings in which you defame us so greatly that we became infamous" (tes escrips, esquelz tu nous diffames Tant grandement que se fuissons infames; lines 12–13).[52] The women make the link between his defamatory writing and their infamy—their complete loss of fame or reputation legally speaking. Because the masterful writing of Chartier causes their name to become infamous, they seek amends. This fifteenth-century woman's response worked to make the language of an authoritative poem not only ethically responsible but legally actionable as well.

This move comes from figures not easily associated with the privilege of legal redress. In this late-medieval scene, the case of women disputants "suing" an established and well-regarded poet is eye-catching. Once again the roles are reversed, and women representing the public domain with the power of the law behind them dispute the defamatory language of a prominent poetic text: they take on a work of a master poet by recourse to the magistrate.

"In the search to injure another verbally, is there not, in effect, the idea of preventing the other from responding, of shutting the person up; is there not also this idea of combat in words—of jousting, so to speak—where the one who shuts up loses, and the art of responding is considered a type of self-mastery?"[53] Evelyne Larguèche's description echoes hauntingly with the problem and the promise of the medieval woman's response. The woman's response is bound by the dominant discourse on woman that promotes the model of the modest and wary woman. It is caught somewhere between discreet talk and silence, between reacting politely and, in Larguèche's terms, being shut up. Given the possibilities that such a discourse is injurious, such silence seems all the more likely. Yet the medieval woman's response allows for a challenge. More importantly it forges that challenge in the well-known but seemingly inapplicable terms of injurious language. Entering the combat of words that is the disputation, the woman's response reverses the usual dynamic of injurious language by naming it outright. As a result, the concept of verbal injury can be directed at the heart of the discourse on women relayed by clerical *magistri* and master vernacular poets. This concept can be attributed to the very powers that promulgate the notion and reserve it for stigmatizing outsiders. In the pages that follow, I shall track the various rhetorical, ethical, and legal ways the woman's response foregrounded the problem of the social controls of discourse. Tracing the response in late-medieval French culture will clarify what I take to be an important chapter in the history of the conception of verbal injury. Within the framework of the response, the conception is progressively shaped— from the general notion of insulting language to the technical understanding of defamation. The woman's disputational response attests to major developments in the view that language found to be damaging can be taken to public account. The polemical debates of late-medieval France offer a particularly rich site for establishing such language as actionable.

In order to study the dialectic between masterful writing and women's response, I have made this book a diptych, with one part for each position.

These positions are by no means fixed. I do not intend to reinforce two binary opposites pitting master against woman respondent. I derive these positions from the medieval disputation and use them pragmatically. My pragmatic choice is especially crucial when it comes to the position of the woman's response. By attributing a role from the disputation to female figures, I do not assign to them any particular definition of femininity. Nor do I assume them to be women. In this study, the medieval figure of a woman disputant is a role that can be played by anyone. This is already evident in the disputation, since its performative quality allows participants to take on a number of different roles. The disputational figure of a woman could be deployed by women or men. The *Bestiaire d'amour* respondent illustrates how difficult it is to know which is the case. But we do know that this figure was adopted by individual women, as the case of Christine de Pizan demonstrates clearly. I shall examine all these cases together because, in the end, it is not the gender of those who use the figure of the woman respondent that concerns me. Rather it is the functions and effects of the figure. What are the implications of this figure emerging in late medieval literate culture?

Pursuing such a question involves an enormous field of inquiry. This is particularly true because of the disputational character of so much of medieval literature. I have selected texts that explicitly stage the encounter between the figures of master and woman respondent. And I begin by studying the medieval institution of mastery so as to establish the context and the terms of the woman respondent's interventions. Part 1 traces the ritual practices of the clerical world of learning as they appear in high-medieval French narrative. Like their scholastic brethren, the vernacular figures of the master and disciple test their knowledge of women in the disputation. This testing process creates and reinforces a language about women that proves domineering. I will look first at the various ways the disputation over women functions as a binding agent between disciples, that trains them for the role of *magister*. But I will focus principally on a symbolic domination of women resulting from the language shared by master and disciple. Two models of mastery, the Ovidian and Aristotelian, will serve as test cases. Looking at a variety of debate poems that use these models will enable us to clarify how such a domination operates. In thirteenth-century and fourteenth-century narrative, however, there are signs that the intellectual mastery of women is no sure thing, and correspondingly, that the symbolic dominance it exerts does not hold. In chapters 2 and 3 of part 1, I shall trace the uneven legacy of this symbolic domination.

Part 2 investigates how the woman respondent came to dispute a dominant masterly discourse on women. By shifting from the figures of masters disputing the subject of women to the figures of women disputing, I sharpen the issue of a discourse's accountability to its audiences. In what ways did the woman's response press the problem of the social regulation of representation? There were already glimmerings of this problem within thirteenth-century and fourteenth-century narrative; the *Bestiaire d'amour* and the *Response au Bestiaire* illustrate this amply. Yet in the later Middle Ages the problem intensified. Not only did the woman's response indict existing texts, but in the case of Jean LeFèvre's *Livre de leesce* and the debate over the *Roman de la rose* it arraigned the canonical works of earlier generations. The woman's response reached back in textual time, extending its challenge of verbal damage to the literary tradition per se. In studying the later phenomenon of the *Querelle*, I wish, then, to draw connections between the critique of feminine representation internal to the masterly discourse and the critique coming from without, between a lover's "wounding, beautiful talk," as one respondent puts it, and the injurious character of the discourse as a whole.

1

PROFILES IN MASTERY

se meruelleit
tre · si enouret
tours romes
que keus por
ne montees
mur que p
li dragons si

uant li uarles entent si
le comande a dieu si sen
uait tant quil enuint
au castel · mais nus ne lui sot
tant demander de ceaus de fors
quil enuoille riens dire · fors
tant quil lor dist · cil qui le uol

2. The Master Philosopher meets a woman. Marginalia in a fourteenth-century *Roman d'Alexandre*. Paris, Bibliothèque Nationale, f.fr. 95, fol. 254. Photograph, Bibliothèque Nationale de France, Paris.

t parti de lor
e com il estoi
par maint
autre ariere
oit · Et pour
ent nouees

trouuer le peuilemes ·
el uenir entre nous fait li
ostes sans congie fu ce trop
grant folie · Ca ne le quit que
uous uous entrepentires ains q
uous empartes del tout · Et cil ne

3. Aristotle upended. Marginalia in a fourteenth-century *Roman d'Alexandre*. Paris, Bibliothèque Nationale, f.fr. 95, fol. 61 verso. Photograph, Bibliothèque Nationale de France, Paris.

1   Ovidian and Aristotelian Figures

> There are three things which Aristotle failed to explain: the toil of bees, the ebb and flow of the tides, and the mind of women.
>
> Irish proverb

With the thirteenth-century *Lai d'Aristote*, the medieval clergy offers us a parable of its relations with women. This is a "boy meets girl" tale involving no less than the Master Philosopher. He is depicted as a distracted intellectual, taken from his books, and she as a seductress who magnifies her alluring figure with a mirror (Figure 2). This encounter goes directly against Aristotle's recommendation to the emperor Alexander to keep away from women:

> Si vos porra on mener paistre
> Ausi com une best en pré!
> Trop avez le sense destempré,
> Quant por une pucele estrange
> Voz cuers si malement se change.
> (lines 166–70) [1]

One could thus put you out to pasture just like a beast in the field. When your heart changes so completely on account of a strange girl, you have destroyed your good sense.

The master fares no better than his "woman-crazy" student, for in the subsequent scenes of seduction, Aristotle is so attracted to this foreign creature that, as we see in the miniature, he allows her to ride him like an animal into Alexander's court (Figure 3). A woman thus consigns "the best clerk in the world" to bestiality (line 449), to the very place where his own teaching had relegated her. His book learning discredited and his mastery debased, Aristotle becomes the object of ridicule. As Cato's sentence sums it up: "It is disgraceful for the doctor when he convicts himself through his own fault" (Turpe est doctori cum culpa redarguit ipsum; line 521).

In its simplest terms, the *Lai d'Aristote* follows the proverbial wisdom: "Nature is worth more than nurture."[2] This lesson of a dominant nature runs implicitly along gender lines. With woman on top, in a position suggesting her sexual dominance, the natural is identified with the feminine (Figure 3). This coding of the nature/culture opposition suggests other feminine/masculine polarities. One maxim associated with the *Lai* reads: "Female cunning deceives even the most learned," and another: "Do not let woman's power trespass on your mind or enter into your spirit, or you shall be confounded."[3] Any intelligence ascribed to women (*astutia*) is defined *a contrario*, as a threat to men's. It rivals the trait distinguishing the clerk. According to these maxims, the *Lai* stresses the polarity between men's reason and women's nonrational intelligence. The "boy meets girl" plot is transformed into a meditation on the feminine rapport with intellectual authority and knowledge. Judging from the *Lai*'s widespread circulation and the iconography and commentary that it inspired, this meditation touched a nerve in the medieval clergy.[4] It provoked concern that—like these amusing marginalia—underlies their thinking.[5]

In its largest terms, then, the *Lai* raises questions about mastery. It thus rejoins a longstanding philosophical inquiry into the links between intellectual capital and authority—in Foucauldian terms, the power/knowledge nexus.[6] And it reformulates that inquiry specifically in terms of the feminine. When women are involved, what exactly does it mean to be masterful? Mastery refers first of all to a type of competence or expertise. For medieval clerks, as for us, it entails working through a particular body of material and gaining control over it. With mastery comes a certain assurance, since the masterful command of material itself comprises a mode of power. According to one Aristotelian axiom cited often in the late Middle Ages: "It would be strange if, when a man possesses knowledge, something else should overpower it and drag it about like a slave."[7] Already visible here is the related issue of domination. Mastery precisely evokes the struggle between people that leads some to dominate and others to submit. Understood sociologically as well as intellectually, it refers to the perpetual give-and-take between people. It exemplifies what Augustine called "the burning passion for domination." (*cupiditas ardens dominationis*).[8] From the first encounter between individuals or groups, each party attempts to gain the upper hand. The dynamic of dominance involves contending with the other person in the attempt to overcome his or her difference. In the Hegelian terms that color any contemporary analysis of mastery, it involves a sparring match whereby each tries to reduce the human qualities of the other and thus emerge master vis-à-vis a subordinate object.[9] The struggle is ongoing and the contradiction apparent, for each party depends on the need to be validated as a person by the antagonism or resistance of the other.

However separate and distinct these two senses of mastery are, the *Lai d'Aristote* brings to the fore their charged interrelations. With its scene of the master mastered, it discloses the clerical fear of losing intellectual control through women, and at the same time it reveals the pressures to maintain that control over them. By communicating the inverse scenario, the *Lai* suggests the impetus to command women effectively. It thus invites us to consider the ways masterful intellectual authority can become a form of domination. It focuses our attention on the process whereby what is valued positively, the production/possession of knowledge, can translate negatively into a mastery of women.

This process has occasioned various feminist reflections on mastery.[10] Given the potential for knowledge as an instrument of domination, there was reason to investigate how women were implicated. In Aristotelian terms, the question was: if women have been dispossessed of knowledge historically, does it follow that they could thus be dragged about like slaves?[11] Feminist theory began by analyzing mastery in its twofold sense as a normative system of relations elaborated and enacted principally by men. Such reasoning led some feminists to label both senses of mastery pejoratively. Mastery is deemed problematic because it represents a masculine way of leading an intellectual life. Correspondingly, women are seen to assume masterful intellectual authority reluctantly, since to do so brings with it the legacy of their subordination.[12]

By imputing to men the conversion of masterful expertise into domination, this critique runs into its own difficulties. The danger lies in confirming that conversion. While feminists have argued that intellectual authority can be used disadvantageously against women, by labeling it a "masculine" phenomenon they reinforce the pattern of disallowing women's intellectual mastery. "Just as the child's attempt to impose control and order on its world cannot be equated with exploitative domination," Toril Moi reminds us, "it is singularly unhelpful to see all forms of intellectual mastery simply as aggressive control and domination."[13] To do so is to run the risk of rejecting the potential for masterful expertise together with its abuse. Further, this critique is liable to confuse the instruments of mastery as domination with its causes.[14] The critical challenge lies instead in examining the logic undergirding the twofold notion of mastery. When Christine de Pizan calls her polemical participation in the *Querelle de la Rose* "nonhateful, a form of solace that outrages no one," she avoids an *ad hominem* critique and concentrates on the injurious language of the *Rose* itself.[15] In her study on the *Querelle des femmes*, Joan Kelly targets "not men, but misogyny and male bias in the literate culture," thereby echoing Christine's sentiment.[16] For medieval and contemporary critic alike, analyzing the ways authoritative traditions of knowledge work against women means critiquing the ideological system that individual masters represent.

In juxtaposing such feminist critiques of mastery with the *Lai*'s tale of Aristotle upended, I wish to situate the problem of the master in a specific context. My purpose is to introduce a historical framework for our theoretical discussion and thus to substantiate what Foucault has warned is notoriously insubstantial.[17] I shall argue that the medieval structures of mastery so tellingly displayed in the *Lai* provide a matrix for subsequent configurations. It was the scholastic institution of the master (*magister*), developed over the course of the twelfth century, that played a significant part in cultivating the affinities between mastery as intellectual authority and mastery as mode of domination. And it did so by casting the intellectual enterprise agonistically. As Martin Grabmann has taught us, the process of learning in the high Middle Ages was fundamentally defined by struggle.[18] Whether in a scholastic context or its vernacular counterpart, acceding to the station of master was, quite literally, a fight: "crude behavior, insults, threats, 'it came even to blows.'"[19] The very language of learning was imprinted with this aggressiveness. *Altercatio, conflictus, disputatio, querela*: many medieval pedagogical terms bespeak a potential for violence.[20]

This agonistic character of learning created the circumstances for converting intellectual authority into a mode of domination. Indeed, in Walter J. Ong's view it favored that conversion.[21] To what extent that particular conversion concerns women, however, is less clear. In the role-reversal game of the *Lai d'Aristote*, where are the signs of women's intellectual struggle? How does the dominating impulse that animates learning touch them? In order to answer these questions, we need first to study the dynamics between the medieval master and his disciple.

Learning to Dispute

Appearing with the twelfth-century schools, the *magister* occupied a prestigious position in the rarefied milieu of the literate clergy.[22] And with the foundation of the universities in the thirteenth century, he

grew to be an ever more prominent figure.[23] His official title distinguished him as an authoritative scholar who presided over the canonical texts. At the same time, the *licentia docendi* invested him with a specific pedagogical responsibility. The master was in charge of instructing
groups of student-disciples and of initiating them in a world of scholarship. This initiation staged a confrontation of wills that was to culminate
in the disciple bending to the master. According to the popular clerical
manual *De disciplina scholarium*: "He who has not learned that he is
subjugated [to the masters], could never come to know himself as master"
(qui se non novit subjici, non noscat se magistrari).[24] In vernacular descriptions as well, the master/disciple rapport develops out of a sense of
rivalry and respect. A late-thirteenth-century didactic work, the *Livre
d'Enanchet* portrays just how charged that rapport is:

> Et si-l doit metre ainz au boen meistre q'au mauvais, por ce que-u
> boens meistre est mout utel chose au deciple. Et il doit sorestier a la
> dotrine son maistre; por ce q'ausi com la grotere de l'aigue chaant
> [chaut] d'en haut cheive la piere dure, vance l'usage a savoir ce que-u
> cuers de l'ome ni voldroit maintes foiees. Mes il doit mult honorer son
> meistre, por qu'il est lo segond signe de science, et doit mult enquerir
> sa dotrine et noter ses paroles et son chastiemant.[25]

> And he should dedicate himself to a good master rather than to a bad
> one, since a good master is extremely useful to a disciple. And he should
> attend to the doctrine of his master, for just as a drop of water fallen
> from above pierces the hard rock, so too the use of knowledge hits a
> man's heart where it is oftentimes not receptive to it. But he should
> greatly honor his master, since he is the second sign of knowledge and
> he must seek energetically after his doctrine and take note of his words
> and teaching.

As "lo segond signe de science," the master embodies the world of learning
(*dotrine*), outfitting the disciple for an intellectual life. Yet that preparation involves yielding to the master's authority as well as to his knowledge. The *Livre d'Enanchet* shows the master handing down a *chastoiement*. This Old French term, echoing the Latin *castigare* found in the
Disciplina, combines the notions of instruction and latent strife: one goes
with the other. Imparting a doctrine entails a type of castigation or chas-
tisement. This castigation was directed toward both men and women; contemporaneous didactic texts such as *Le Chastoiement d'un père à son fils*
and *Le Chastoiement des dames* are built on one and the same model of
the master taking the student in hand.[26]

This sense of discipline discloses the tensions informing the master/ disciple relation. While the disciple struggles to attain the master's respect and wisdom, the master in turn castigates him. Contention fuels their exchanges and, paradoxically, binds the two figures together. If the surviving accounts give us any indication, such contentious relations ruled university life.[27] Even the latter-day humanist critic Vivès would describe the scene as all "that scholastic shadowboxing and contentious altercation" (scholasticasque illas umbratiles pugnas et contentiosas altercationes).[28] The medieval master inducted the disciple in an intellectual life whose characteristic methods were conflictual. The question-and-answer modes of instruction (*quaestiones*), the disputations (*disputationes*) that began the debates pitting masters against students (*quodlibeta*)—such standard dialectical methods trained the student to work against his master.[29] If the disciple was ever to assert himself, he had to proceed adversarially—in John of Salisbury's words, through "verbal conflict"—mounting challenges and refutations of what the master put forth.[30]

These challenges were never meant to jeopardize the institution of mastery. On the contrary, the entire agonistic process was geared to outfit the disciple for the master's role.[31] It distinguished those few disciples who would eventually assume the *magister* title from the many others who failed to meet the test. The sustained disputations sanctioned certain disciples as members of the scholastic elite. In the end, the *chastoiement* validated them as authorities able to discipline others. In this, the master/ disciple engagement resembles the sparring between knights, for there too the clash provides a mechanism for bonding that secures both men in the same courtly, chivalric roles.[32]

No more telling example of the disputational dynamic exists than the case history of Peter Abelard. The dialectical method of thought that he pioneered in his treatise the *Sic et Non* was illustrated uncannily in his own dealings with his peers: his unceremonious rejection of his master, Anselm of Laon, his attacks against a rival master, William of Champeaux, his sparring with his own followers. Abelard exemplifies the way the medieval system of intellectual mastery functioned by creating conflict so as to better establish control of intellectual problems. The difficulty in mastering a particular body of knowledge was played out through disputation. And far from dividing the masters and students definitively, their disputatiousness acted to consolidate their caste. The more bitterly they fought among themselves, the more tightly they closed ranks and cemented their control over intellectual matters. Abelard's reputation makes this clear. However he depicted himself as renegade and outcast, medieval posterity identified him as one of the masters' own.[33]

Abelard's case is also important because it reveals how the feminine begins to inform the disputatiousness of medieval masters and disciples. Intellectual traditions in Europe had long typed knowledge as a woman (*scientia*), and its highest form, wisdom, as a female deity (*sapientia*). Like many other masters straight on through the Renaissance, Abelard dedicated himself to the goddess of wisdom, Minerva. "I gave up completely the court of Mars so as to be brought up in the lap of Minerva. . . . I put the conflicts of the disputation over and above the trophies of combat."[34] Abelard's description of his entry into intellectual life gives us a telling sense of how the pursuit of knowledge is connected with the feminine. Embracing wisdom implies coming into contact with a woman. Yet this embrace is not incompatible with aggressive impulses. Although Abelard renounces the god of war, he does not relinquish the martial arts. For him, the bellicose and the feminine come together in the form of the disputation. Under the aegis of Minerva, verbal battles are to be waged. That Abelard chooses this goddess as mentor shows how the scholastic activity of disputing comes to be figured through women.

But if intellectual mastery is represented in part through the feminine, where do women figure in? We come back to the question of women's encounter with clerical intellectual life. Can they participate in the master/disciple disputation? Abelard's explosive experience with Héloïse hardly bears this out. His tutelage of her was short-lived, leading quickly to their sexual relation. In the vernacular domain, the picture is little different. In the *Livre d'Enanchet*, for instance, the master who debates with his disciple puts forth the following doctrine (*la dotrine dou clers*): "It is better to sit in a corner of the house that is not in the throughway; not like a woman who wags her tongue" (il est mieuz seoir en un angle de sa maison qe n'est en chiés comun. Ne com famme laengueice! Fiebig, 7).[35] This portrait of the model clerk distinguishes him from the woman who talks too much. And it spatializes his distinctive role. Whereas the woman plants herself in the middle, the clerk is recommended to place himself apart, in isolation. Such a scene, I would suggest, builds on the standard outline of the social hierarchy of roles in Andreas Capellanus's *De amore*: "In addition, among men we find one rank more than among women, since there is a man more noble than any of these, that is, the clerk" (Praeterea unum in masculis plus quam in feminis ordinem reperimus, quia quidam masculis nobilissimus invenitur ut puta clericus; II, 1; Parry, 36; Pagès, 10). The fact that the clerk inhabits a separate space underscores his unique position. Not only does he represent the "most noble" man, but he has no female equivalent. In the clerical schema of Capellanus or the *Enanchet*, there are few signs of women assuming the stance of disciple.

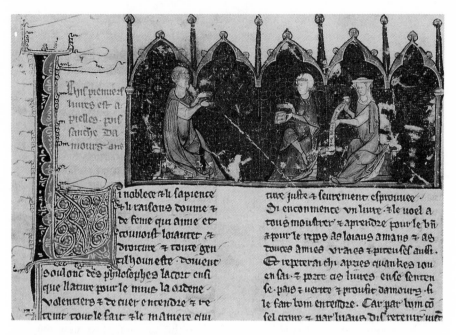

4.   The duke and duchess of Brabant and the master of the *Consaus d'amours*. Vienna, Österreichische Nationalbibliothek, Cod. 2621, fol. 1. Courtesy of the Österreichische Nationalbibliothek.

Such definitions of clerical life give us a first glimpse into the vexed position of women vis-à-vis intellectual mastery. They are at odds with the clerical role. Yet they are not completely evacuated from its domain. The inaugural miniature from the *Consaus d'amours,* a late-thirteenth-century didactic treatise, exemplifies this dilemma (Figure 4). The woman, the duchess of Brabant, sits side by side with her lord the duke—an apparent partner in the lessons the master pronounces.[36] But the text that follows relays a debate engaging the men alone. Designed implicitly as a master/disciple dialogue, it leaves little room for her. In fact, the insignia of the various figures in the miniature confirm this: while the book links the duke to the academic learning of the master, the scroll identifies the woman with the oral. The duchess appears ready to repeat the master's formulas but unable to engage with them fully and make them her own. The structure of the master/disciple dispute seems to both accommodate women and disqualify them.[37] While included theoretically as part of the proceedings, they are nonetheless blocked from participating in its work: mediums of the disputation, yes; real contestants, no.

A Clerkly Savoir Faire

This precarious position of women is established in Latin and vernacular literature in texts such as the Latin *Concilium Romarici montis* and the Old French *Jugement d'amour*.[38] These two related twelfth-century works offer a paradigm of women's circumscribed role in the world of intellectual mastery. The *Concilium* and the *Jugement* dramatize a disputation on love conducted exclusively by women. One side argues that the clerk is the best lover, and the other, the knight. Locked in an intractable quarrel, the female opponents bring their cases to be judged; in the *Concilium* before an assembly of women, and in the *Jugement* before the God of Love. Opinions are unanimously in favor of the clerk. Both these texts are obvious propaganda pieces for the clergy.[39] Yet the degree to which women advance its cause is surprising. Why this recourse to female surrogates? Why should clerical discourse articulate its own privileged claims by way of women?

From the outset of the debate, this surrogacy looks incomplete: "No one called a man is admitted to that place; nevertheless some were present who had come from faraway; they were not laymen, but respectable clerks" (nemo qui vir dicitur illuc intromittitur. Quidam inde aderant, qui de longe venerant, Non fuerant laici, sed honesti clerici; *Concilium*, 10–12). The androgynous clerks appear only on the sidelines. Yet such an appearance makes clear that while they do not speak their part, they are still directing it through a female agent. Women are deemed both capable and incapable of assuming the clerks' position. Later on in the narrative, the limits of their intermediary role are specified: "For the women, the art is in knowing the things of love, but they are ignorant of what a man should know how to do in practice" (Harum in noticia ars est amatoria; Sed ignorant, opere quid vir sciat facere, lines 34–35). The distinction here is between women's familiarity with the subject of love and "manly" clerks' ability to exploit it. One talks, the other acts on his knowledge. In effect, the women champion all those clerkly traits that the knight does not possess, especially knowledge: "I beseech you to love clerks above all, by whose wisdom everything is disposed" (Precor vos summopere clericos diligere, quorum sapientia disponuntur omnia; *Concilium*, lines 186–87). Or as the clerk's advocate, Blancheflor, argues in the *Jugement*: "The clerk *knows* more about courtliness, he ought to have a girlfriend more than anyone else, even more than the knight" (Ke clers *set* plus de courtoisie et ke mieus doit avoir amie ke autre gent ne chevalier; lines 249–51).

This clerkly brand of knowledge is presented in academic terms: recorded in writing, developed through commentary and disputation. Love is thus for the clerk less a physical affair than one of learning. Even the knight's advocate notes this: "When your lover is at the monastery, he pores over his psalter, he turns over and over again the parchment, and for you he makes no other play" (Quant vos amis est au moustier, torne et retorne son sautier, torne et retorne cele piel: por vous ne fait autre cembiel; *Jugement*, lines 115–17). From the opposing position, the clerk's commitment to written texts is also figured as powerful, if not all-engrossing.

Given the clerk's superior knowledge, what exactly is he alleged to know? While the image of the clerk with his psalter suggests theological learning, by the end of the *Concilium* he is associated with the secrets of women (*abdita*). The history of ideas in the West has long identified secrets as a choice intellectual category and typed them, like the Minervan myth of knowledge, invariably in feminine terms.[40] Whether we look to the Greek philosopher contemplating the mysteries of nature or the Renaissance man of science probing the material world, the quest for knowledge habitually seeks a feminine object. In medieval culture, this fascination with feminine secrets was widespread. Witness the pseudo-Aristotelian *Secretum secretorum* or the *Secres as philosophes*, two compendia of the most recondite items of scientific knowledge that maintain this feminine character.[41] Or the widely known thirteenth-century gynecological texts, *Secreta mulierum* (*The Secrets of Women*).[42] In contemporaneous vernacular literature as well, women's secrets were the quarry par excellence. Andreas Capellanus's *De amore*, for one, contends that the would-be lover should begin by tracking them: "Presently he begins to think about the fashioning of the woman and to differentiate her limbs, to think about what she does, and to pry into the secrets of her body" (Postmodum mulieris incipit cogitare facturas et eius distinguere membra suosque actus imaginari eiusque corporis secreta rimari; Parry, 29; Pagès, 3). This probing into secrets is also emphasized in Drouart La Vache's French version of the *De amore*:

> En son cuer recorde et ramenbre
> La faiture de chascun menbre,
> Les venues et les alees
> Et cerche les choses secrees.
> (*Li Livres d'amours*, lines 237–40)

In his heart he recalls and remembers the form of each member, its comings and goings, and he searches for their secrets.

The lover's fantasy about different members of the woman's body heightens the desire to get at her secrets. The greater the reflection on them, the greater their lure.

In the case of the *Concilium*, the women stake everything on the clerk's understanding of their secrets: "They strive to act on our affairs and take control of our cause, but thanks to them, even through their grace, our secrets will never be made known" (Causas nostras agere student atque regere, quantum possunt, etiam per eorum gratiam, nostra quedam abdita nunquam erunt cognita; lines 189–91). The inference is that the clerk knows how to keep women's secrets discreetly. Yet as vernacular love literature attests richly, the threat also exists that knowing such secrets invites their violation. Once they are thought, they will be made known. Through whatever party, they risk becoming common knowledge. The clerk's understanding of women's secrets carries a sexual charge insofar as those secrets are consistently associated with their bodies. If this understanding does not suggest "knowing" women in the sexual sense, it does involve a carnal knowledge of them. Since the pro-clerkly *Concilium* and *Jugement* both condemn the knight for having sex with women (lines 179–80), their claim on the secret knowledge of female sexuality is all the more important.

We can now begin to answer a number of our initial questions: if these texts include women in a version of the master/disciple disputation, they do so in a manner that ultimately counts them out. By projecting women as privileged mouthpieces of clerical wisdom, the *Concilium* and *Jugement* make them party to clerical claims on the knowledge of women. They enlist women complicitously: neither clerk nor master themselves, women are depicted enunciating the clerical right to possess women's own secrets. It is no surprise, then, that they are moved progressively out of the debate.

Once clerical disputation claims the topic of women, the risk emerges that mastering such knowledge means using it as a form of control. Just as the master/disciple dialogues stage a battle of sorts so as to secure their hold over a body of knowledge, so too the *Concilium* and *Jugement* battle over the clergy's prerogative to know women. The result is to reserve that knowledge for themselves and, concomitantly, to bar women from it. Both texts build the case implicitly for an exclusive clerical knowledge of women. In so doing, they represent that knowledge as potentially domineering.

The medieval clergy's appropriation of the topic of women's knowledge constitutes in and of itself a powerful order of symbolic domination. From the master/disciple configuration arguing over a feminine object to the story of women defending the clerk's superior knowledge, a discourse coercive to women is in the making. It is a masterful discourse in both the positive sense and the negative. Through the disputation, it represents and defends the clergy's special claim on women's knowledge. Their intellectual authority is seen to extend rightfully over it. Valorizing the clerks' prerogative to know women has the effect of disenfranchising them. In clerks' hands, such knowledge can become a way to dominate masterfully. We have here a discursive pattern that, as Pierre Bourdieu has shown us, can exert enormous power because of its social use.[43] It is a discourse attributed to the revered caste of the clergy. And it is elaborated didactically in a variety of texts called *enseignements* (teachings) that purport to relay a doctrine. Through such narratives, the model of masters disputing the "secrets" of women takes hold in French medieval culture, and with it the pattern of using the knowledge of women as a type of power over them.

Representations of the master/disciple debate create this symbolic domination by means of two models of mastery that recur in *enseignements*. The first, the Ovidian, is derived from habitual rereading of the *Ars amatoria* and the *Remedia amoris*.[44] In the thirteenth century, as much as in the twelfth-century "age of Ovid," these works formed an integral part of the school curriculum.[45] They were so well known that they laid the foundation for a particular model of mastery. With the second model, the Aristotelian, the picture is more complicated. This model took shape as a result of the thirteenth-century translation and assimilation of key works—the *Metaphysics*, *Politics*, and *Ethics*, as well as the biological treatises. In fact, the second model of mastery underwriting French narrative testifies to the turbulent reception of Aristotle's works at the University of Paris: the fitful recovery of the *Metaphysics*, the fragmentary understanding of the *Ethics*, the controversy over teaching the biological works.[46] As we shall see, the Aristotelian model of mastery typifies what Fernand van Steenberghen called the "eclectic Aristotelianism" of the period (126). It is thus based on the array of Greek and Arabic texts that were so frequently attributed erroneously to the Master Philosopher during the later Middle Ages.[47]

Studying the Ovidian and Aristotelian models of mastery together is important for several reasons. First, it will help identify the specifically Aristotelian terms of mastery. It will also bring into sharper relief the mark of the *magistri*'s learning in French medieval narrative. Yet by contrasting the Aristotelian model of mastery with the Ovidian, we can approach the problem of symbolic domination in a nuanced way. The differences between the two models will reveal the many, varied ways that dominance was expressed. This study will prepare the ground for considering the woman's response. It will set up our inquiry into how the response tackles the symbolic domination of women in masterly vernacular texts. Working through the models for such domination will enable us in part 2 to work the woman's response back the other way.

A Game of Prevarication

As an entry point into the Ovidian model of mastery, let us consider one of its most influential precepts:

> Posse capi: capies, tu modo tende plagas.
> uere prius uolucres taceant, aestate cicadae,
> Maenalius lepori det sua terga canis,
> femina quam iuueni blande temptata repugnet;
> haec quoque, quam poteris credere nolle, uolet.
> > (*Ars amatoria* I, 270–74)[48]

Women can always be caught: that's the first rule of the game.
Sooner would birds in the spring be silent or locusts in August,
sooner would hounds run away when the fierce rabbits pursue, than
would a woman well-wooed refuse to succumb to a lover; she'll
make you think she means No! while she is planning her Yes!

Relations between men and women are set up right away as a game, the object of which is to make women cede to their male lovers. This objective is described by a string of oxymorons. It would take a wholesale reversal of natural law—noise giving way to silence, prey turning into predators—to match the instance of women *not* succumbing to men. If we look closely, women's yielding is oxymoronic: it is expressed through a whole range of polarized oppositions.

Representing women as naysayers confirms the strategic value of this opposition. Whereas "No!" is a common initial response to any advance, here, as a rhetorical expression of difference, it blocks unanimity between men and women. It forestalls what is taken as inevitable. However briefly, the female "No!" suspends the sought-after conclusion of the man's game by swerving from automatic assent. Like the response of a hunted animal who, in a last desperate gesture, veers away, this "No!" is taken to seal the woman's fate. It is the signature trait of what I shall call feminine prevarication.[49] That the clerkly narrator takes it as a sign of the woman's compliance signals how in an Ovidian model of mastery a woman's opposition functions as the preface to her succumbing.

This oxymoronic quality of women's yielding is captured by another Ovidian maxim, this time from Andreas Capellanus's *De amore*: "For what greater thing can a woman give than to yield herself to the mastery of someone else?" (Quid enim mulier maius dare posset quam si suam personam alieno disponat arbitrio?; I, 3; Parry, 43; Pagès, 17). Capellanus's phrase is also based on the view that women are meant to give in. While the Latin does not specify the idea of mastery explicitly, the expression "disponere suam personam alieno arbitrio" conveys the sense that women are to bend to the will of another (that *alienum arbitrium* belonging, as a rule, to father, husband, confessor). In this manner, a single answer to Capellanus's question is projected: there *is* no greater thing for women to do than yield. Or is there? Because the maxim stands as a question, room is left for second thought. And because it occurred commonly in those scholastic anthologies of quotable quotes, the *florilegia*, readers were invited to speculate beyond the pat response: "No, women can give nothing greater."[50] But what alternative could there be? That women do have something greater to give, or that women are not meant to yield? Even if most medieval clerkly readers would work through the question dialectically to arrive at one answer, the fact that its syntax entertains others points to the pivotal role of opposition. The implicit structure of the masters' disputation makes this clear. Once again, we find how clerical discourse draws a close connection between opposition and yielding; in this instance, between women's opposition and their yielding to men.

The Ovidian model of mastery explores this connection through a playful dialogue between men and women. Orchestrated by a master-narrator, this dialogic format dramatizes the yes/no prevarication. It renders the opposition in the banter between male/female speakers; indeed, it intensifies that opposition through frequent impasses. All this is intended to set the stage for women ceding to the will of their male interlocutors. In order to show how this pattern of feminine prevarication functions for Ovidian mastery, I shall concentrate here on two dialogues from the *De amore*, the first because it includes the maxim "What greater thing can a woman give?" and the second because it offers the most complex piece.

Andreas's dialogue between a middle-class man and woman (*plebeius/ plebeia*) opens with a flourish of off-putting remarks. The woman responds to the man's praise of her beauty by accusing him of lying: "You seem to be telling fibs, since although I do not have a beautiful figure you extol me as beautiful beyond all other women and although I lack the ornament of wisdom you praise my good sense" (Tui videntur falsitatem continere sermones, quia, quum mihi non sit pulchritudinis forma decora, me quasi super omnes formosam mulieres extollis, et quum sim ornatu sapientiae destituta, me tanquam prudentem tua verba commendant; Parry, 37; Pagès, 11). Her challenge deflates his exaggerated claims in a manner that confirms women's putative modesty. The man is quick to come back, and chips away progressively at the woman's opposition. His rejoinders attack it by arguing a point both ways in the same breath. This strategy appears first in his assertion that she looks to be a noblewoman (Parry, 38). When she rebuffs his claim, the middle-class man is shown to take her response as both correct and mistaken: "Good character and good manners alone have given to you a more worthy kind of nobility . . . but since an excellent character makes noble not only women but men also, you are perhaps wrong in refusing me your love, since my manners, too, may illumine me with the virtue of nobility" (Parry, 38; Pagès, 12). Agreeing and disagreeing simultaneously with the woman enables the man to undermine her spurning remarks. Through such equivocal argumentation, the man makes it nearly impossible for her to reject his remarks out of hand because it is no longer evident what precisely is being rejected, or indeed to what end. The woman is meant to be baffled, with the result that she concedes the point and switches the subject abruptly: "You may deserve praise for your great excellence, but I am rather young, and I shudder at the thought of receiving solaces from old men" (Parry, 39; Pagès, 13). We find here a first-rate example of a dialectical method of reasoning whereby abandoning one's habitual stand and projecting other opinions provoke the same reaction in the interlocutor. As the master-narrator sets up the dialogue, the man's ruse of shifting his own adversarial stand aims to confuse the woman.

This strategy paves the way for the man's rhetorical gesture of his own yielding:

> Nonne maiori doctor est dignus honore vel laude, qui omnino discipulum imperitum sua facit doctrina prudentem, quam qui reddit doctum sua sapientia doctiorem? Noves ergo miles amoris ac in amore rudis te mihi peto magistram et tua doctrina plenius erudiri.
>
> (Pagès, 15)

> Doesn't a teacher who by his instruction makes a prudent man [disciple] out of one who has never had any instruction deserve more honor and praise than one who teaches more wisdom to a man who is already wise? That is why I, a new recruit in Love's service and awkward in love, ask you to be my teacher [master] and to train me more fully by your instruction.
>
> (Parry, 41)

In this description of the man's yielding, we find the key terms of mastery, terms that the French translator of the *De amore*, Drouart la Vache, expounds upon:

> .I. clers plus a loer feroit,
> Qui .i. disciple enseigneroit,
> en .i. art lui sage rendant,
> .que cil, qui .i. bien entendant
> rendroit plus saige par estude.
> (lines 1073–77)

A clerk would be more praiseworthy who would instruct one disciple, making him knowledgeable in one art, than a clerk who would make one already trained even wiser through further study.

Both Capellanus and Drouart cast the male/female relation as one between master and disciple. In this instance, the master role is allotted to a woman. After all the rhetorical maneuvering, the man rests his case by appearing to give her the intellectual upper hand: he names the woman *magistram*. Yet let us be careful in gauging this strategic naming. What is striking is the way the man acts out what he intends the woman to do.[51] To simulate assenting to the master is to contrive the woman doing the same thing. In the framework of the master/disciple debate, the master-narrator can use the man's apparent embracing of a subservient position to set up the woman's parallel action. Logically and rhetorically he works to move her into yielding: the more frequently she says "No," the more frequently it is interpreted in the opposite way. The more she is represented as an authority figure, the more she is identified as one to be bested. Here the man's obeisance correlates with the ultimate aim of the woman yielding.

This paradox is best understood in terms of the conventional give-and-take of power. In such a circumstance, it is those with authority who are able to give it up. Self-abnegation makes sense only when the person believes he is entitled. As Barbara Johnson puts it trenchantly: "It would seem that one has to be positioned in the place of power in order for one's self-resistance to be valued."[52] In the case of Ovidian narrative, the master-narrator capitalizes on just such a power: he redistributes the roles so as to overdetermine the woman's ceding to the man. Representing the man as temporarily submissive is meant to signify his ultimate dominance. The master-narrator's contention is this: to defer from a position of power can offer, paradoxically, a means of exerting it.

This projection of a *magistra* invites an oppositional reading on the part of the woman. Naming her "master" creates an opportunity for her resistance. In the ludic structure of Ovidian mastery, that projected name allows her to play the game differently. Instead of a simple role reversal, it implies reworking the very conception of mastery. As she states: "You say that you wish to submit to my instruction in this matter, but I absolutely refuse the task" (Sed dicis in hoc mea te velle disciplina doceri; hunc autem penitus recuso laborem"; Parry, 41; Pagès, 15). The woman can assume the *magistra* role without taking on its conventional task of disciplining disciples. If clerical representation legislates the incompatibility of women and mastery, then from her oppositional perspective, her play with mastery can signal something else—indeed, as she calls it, a type of wisdom (*sapientia*). Her intellectual authority can break out of the disputational dynamic of submission and domination.

Such is the potential of the *magistra*. Yet if we read the Ovidian model in context, the rhetorical projection of the *magistra* is used finally to elicit the woman's submission. This becomes all the more clear when we notice that it occurs in the discussion of the *gradus amoris*—the well-known ladder of love. Of the four steps, the lover dwells upon the last, defined as a "yielding of the whole person" (in totius personae concessione; Pagès, 16). Here is where the man poses the question "What greater thing can a woman give than to yield herself to the mastery of someone else?" The narrator moves from a scene persuading a woman to yield to a man's greater knowledge to one where she is encouraged to yield physically. The connection is telling: an act of intellectual mastery is associated with a physical act. By anticipating this end, sexual intercourse, the master-narrator argues that "woman can always be caught." Indeed, he attempts to prove his authoritative knowledge about them by projecting this image of their bodily submission. As it is, the woman's yielding is never fully represented; it is left in suspense. In her words: "If great things cannot be won without great labor, since what you are seeking is one of the greatest you will have to be exhausted by a great deal of labor before you get what you want" (Si absque gravi labore magna parari non possunt, quum id, quod postulas, sit de maioribus unum, multis te oportet laboribus fatigari, ut ad quaesita munera valeas pervenire"; Parry, 44; Pagès, 17). The dialogue thus reveals a decided gap between the cajoling words of the male lover and their physical effects. Correspondingly, in the framework of the master/disciple debate it shows up the discrepancy between the master's teaching and its being put into action by the disciple.

If we take this "plebeian" dialogue as a single unit of argumentation, then, all the exchanges show her opposition to the advances of the male lover. In the Ovidian scheme, a woman's prevarication is symptomatic of her fitful desire to defer to men's greater authority. And as such, it furnishes the master and disciple a reason to dictate to her. However, the fact that the woman is never seen to yield, that the lessons on women are never realized, offers a limit case for the Ovidian model of mastery.

In the second, aristocratic dialogue we shall examine, this game of feminine prevarication is extended as the banter between a man and woman is transposed allegorically. Both participants deploy a figurative language that culminates in the well-known story of the palace of love. Yet what happens exactly when the clerical argument for women's yielding is coded in the tropes of gates and castles of love (Parry, 69–70)?

From the outset, the woman shows the characteristic signs of prevarication. On the one hand, she admits to having granted the man favors: this is the "Yes!" element (Parry, 70). On the other, she asserts that he can never obtain what he is after: "For I am firmly resolved with all my heart never to subject myself to the servitude of Venus or endure the torments of lovers" (firmum etenim est et totius meae mentis propositum Veneris me nunquam supponere servituti nec amantium me poenis subiicere; Parry, 70; Pagès, 43). All these references to servitude and enduring pains (*poenas*) reveal the familiar dynamic of the woman fending off the man's rhetorical moves. If we accept Betsy Bowden's thesis of the double entendre of *poenas* (pains/penises), that dynamic is sexualized in a familiar way.[53] Here the woman prevaricates according to the Ovidian master's plan. Yet the woman's language also demonstrates her capacity to use allegory defensively. She turns the covert terms back against their author. Not only is she represented as understanding their veiled meaning, but she succeeds momentarily in deflecting them as well. This pattern builds when the woman introduces her own figure of French freedom:

> Malo igitur aere modico Franciae contenta adesse et liberum eundi, quo voluero, possidere arbitrium quam Ungarico quidem onusta argento alienae subiici potestati, quia tale multum habere est nihilum habere.
>
> (Pagès, 44)

> I would rather, therefore, stay in France and be content with a few coppers and have freedom to go where I would, than to be subject to a foreign power, even though I were loaded down with Hungarian silver, because to have so much is to have nothing.
>
> (Parry, 71–72)

Her trope contrasts freedom at home with submission to a foreign power. As we have seen in the previous dialogue, this "foreignness" is peculiarly charged. While it refers to the person and will of another, it casts that alterity, by way of the French/Hungarian comparison, adversarially. In the woman's configuration, she risks losing her free will and being dominated by an enemy with very little to show for it. This figure recalls the maxim with which I began. They both explore the question of yielding to another/foreign will (disponere suam personam alieno arbitrio). Furthermore, they both signal the Ovidian master's argument on the bending of women's will. But there the similarities end. In this case, the noblewoman speaks figuratively in self-defense. Whereas the clerical speaker of the maxim seems in the end to valorize yielding, the woman puts the highest premium on defending her freedom. She uses the trope to refuse to yield.

Her figurative efforts are nonetheless circumscribed. As Bowden aptly characterizes it, the nobleman's rhetoric gives the woman a false choice: have sex, or have sex (74). "If you choose to walk that path [of freedom], unbearable torments will follow you" (Si tali curaveritis via ambulare, intolerabilis vos poena sequetur; Parry, 72; Pagès, 45). In the act of acknowledging her freedom, the narrator threatens her with the double entendre of pain/penis. And it is this pun that sets the scene for the most ambitious allegory of the dialogue: the palace of love. Exploiting a classical tradition of sexualized allegory, the man represents a castle inhabited by "certain communities of ladies" (Parry, 73). It is a structure with many portals, some guarded by recalcitrant women, others by more welcoming types. The lover's goal involves finding a way in.

Constructing such an elaborate allegorical structure is a masterful ploy. As such, it distinguishes the lover as an authority on a near par with the clerk. This association is confirmed by the fact that the man mimics those teachings of a master found elsewhere in the *De amore*: "There are also other lesser precepts of love which it would not profit you to hear, since you can find them in the book written to Walter" (Sunt et alia amoris praecepta minora, quorum tibi non expediret auditus, quae etiam in libro ad Gualterium scripto reperies; Parry, 82; Pagès, 54). The man's allegory is a *mise en abyme* of the master-narrator's, indeed, of Capellanus's own. It is thereby legitimated. In this sense too, it is shown to surpass the woman's skills. As she confesses: "These things are too obscure for me, and your words are too allegorical; you will have to explain what you mean" (Hi mihi sunt nimis sermones obscuri nimisque verba reposita, nisi ipsa tua faciat interpretatio manifesta; Parry, 73; Pagès, 45). Like a subordinate, she is represented acquiescing in the end to the man's superior knowledge. While the exercise of mastering the woman intellectually works through a form of projection in the first dialogue, here it is established directly. The male speaker becomes a master vis-à-vis a female student by means of allegory.

As we saw in the first dialogue, this stance of intellectual mastery has a carnal dimension. And the woman brings it out: "But whether what you say is true or false, the story of these terrible punishments frightens me so that I do not wish to be a stranger to Love's service" (Sive igitur vera sint sive falsa, quae proponis, terribilium me deterret poenarum relatio, et ideo ab amoris nolo militia exsistere aliena, sed eius affecto consortio copulari; Parry, 83; Pagès, 55). The familiar language of pains/penises (*poenas*) is extended to include *copulare*. The objective of women yielding is described in obvious sexual terms. Allegorizing the game of feminine prevarication heightens the clerical move to represent women submitting in intercourse. Once again, we find a master-narrator who directs the male/female banter toward a sexual end, who privileges that end as a subject for clerical debate. As the *Roman de la rose* demonstrates all too well, the act of expounding allegorically about sex is a master's prerogative.

It is this very aspect of Ovidian mastery that may well have provoked the ecclesiastical condemnation of the *De amore* in 1277. Not only were methods of medieval schooling put to the service of disputing "women," but such disputations lent themselves to questions of sexuality. The value of intellectual authority was compromised by such ironic discussions of sexual relations with women. What's more, this compromise affected the domain of teaching. By using Ovidian mastery as a school subject, it gives it a certain credibility. As the article of condemnation puts it," "They presume to treat and dispute in the schools such ridiculous falsehoods." [54] This issue of falsehood clearly implicates master and disciple. Given the pedagogical exchange that frames the *De amore*, the danger lay in representing (falsely) the subject of mastering women as a reputable clerical concern.

In order to see how this Ovidian mastery is figured increasingly as a school subject—one of the medieval vernacular's "three Rs"—we need to turn to another text. Jacques d'Amiens's reworking of the *Ars amatoria* presents a series of dialogues.[55] But his *Art d'amors* uses them as set pieces of clerical analysis. "About entreating [women], I have well demonstrated my meaning and sense; I will now teach you what I think and know about [their] responses. They will respond to you in many different ways" (Or t'ai bien de proier moustre et mon sens et ma volenté, des responses t'enseignerai cou que i'en pens et que i'en sai. Diversement te respondront; lines 746–49). Separating out the men's *requestes* from the women's *responses*, it sets up an exegetical challenge. The masterly narrator is to test the disciple's knowledge about how to take charge of women verbally. In his commentary, the various women's responses become occasions for testing their hermeneutical skills. Five different *requestes*, followed by five hypothetical ripostes, provide a spectrum of *explications de texte*.

In keeping with the Ovidian model, each woman's response is by definition negative. In the case of the first woman, who rejects the lover because he defies her husband, the narrator's commentary revolves around the familiar figure of the master:

> Ha! douce dame debonnaire,
> aprendes, c'uns autres set faire;
> se un autre assayet avies,
> vostre baron mains priseries;
> par une escole et par un mestre
> ne puet nus hom bien sages estre;
> (lines 770–75)

Ah sweet, gentle lady, learn what another knows well how to do.
Had you tried another, you would appreciate your own lord more;
no one can be truly wise through just one master, at just one school.

The erotic relation is linked to the pedagogical. The master-narrator displays a woman ready to learn something new—a body of knowledge in another man's possession. He thus tries to manipulate her through her appetite for greater knowledge. Belittling her allegiance to a single master (her husband), he entreats her to embrace another. The inference is that her increasing knowledge involves her deference to an increasing number of masters. The process of learning is for her inextricably connected with a power dynamic, with being lorded over.

The second and third women's responses presented by the narrator dramatize opposition based on fear of treachery. For the third woman, this implies physical danger: "For you should well know the truth of the matter: for all that can befall me, I do not wish to lose my soul or to dishonor my body" (car bien sacies par verite: m'ame perdre et mon cors hounir ne voel, se miex ne m'en puet venir; lines 833–35). The woman's reference to sexual violence—"mon corps hounir"—prompts the narrator to intervene:

> Quant tu ces responses oras,
> en ton cuer ioie avoir devras,
> car celles qui ensi respondent
> lor corage molt bien espondent;
> puis c'a toi se veut desraisnier,
> il n'i a fors del embrachier
> et de parler bien sagement
> et si li respont doucement.
> (lines 836–43)

When you hear these responses, you should have joy in your heart, because those women who respond in this way are revealing their innermost thoughts. Since she wishes to debate with you, there is nothing to do but to embrace her, talk to her prudently, and respond gently.

The fact that the woman expresses her opposition in sexual terms is taken as a sure sign of her desirousness. That she explicitly says "No!" to sex signals her real interest. This analysis of the woman's prevarication is intended to embolden the lover and give him joy (*avoir en cuer ioie.*) For any medieval student of love, as for any critic of love literature, such *ioie* carries decided sexual implications.

This Ovidian pattern of divining the woman's likely assent in her most adamant objections intensifies with the fourth and fifth responses. Here the women protest too much. This excessive "No!" licenses the lover to proceed. As the master-narrator evaluates it, if the lover persists in stating his case, he should prevail over her fiercest resistance: "For the good sense, the courtesy, the valor and gallantry that she will discover will make her fall in love whether she wants to or not: this is no exaggeration" (car li sens et la cortoisie, la grans valors, la druerie k'elle i trueve, le fait amer, u voelle u non, tout sans fauser; lines 964–67). "Whether she wants to or not": the clerkly narrator is hardly concerned with the woman's desire. It has little bearing on the outcome because the man's authority insures that he will have ultimate sway.

With the final response, the narrator explicates the most facile conquest:

> . . . biaus sire ciers,
> Je ne sai nient de tes mestiers;
> por diu, sire, laissies me ester!
> je n'en quier plus oir parler,
> que ie ne sai, a coi ce monte. . . .
> ne voellies, que soie hounie;
> je ne sai mais voir, u ie sui,
> ce poise moi, c'ains vos connui,
> et nuit et iour, u que ie soie,
> me sanle, que adies vous voie.
>   (lines 986–90, 995–99)

Dear sir, I know nothing of your needs; for god's sake, sir, let me be. I don't want at all to hear talk about what I don't know, what's the point? . . . You should not wish that I be humiliated. Since I have known you, I don't even know where I am—that bothers me! And night and day, it seems to me that I see you wherever I am.

This time the woman's negativity is represented as self-negation, and her lack of confidence gives the lover grounds for taking her in hand. By emphasizing the woman's ignorance, the masterly narrator reinforces the idea that it is in her best interests to be seduced (lines 996–97). Clerical analysis recommends that the male lover save her from herself.

> Celle qui te respont ensi,
> elle est vencue, ie te di,
> il n'i a fors de l'embracier,
> de li acoler et baissier,
> elle est entree el decevoir:
> avoir en pues tout ton valoir [voloir].
> (lines 1000–1005)

I tell you, the woman who responds in this manner is won over. You have only to embrace her, hug and kiss her, she has entered into the deception; you can have everything you want.

In this scheme of things, a woman's limited knowledge serves the master's purposes twice over. It justifies the clerkly narrator's interest in knowing women. Since women are deemed to possess minimal self-knowledge, the subject falls appropriately into the clerkly domain. Furthermore, the task of mastering such a subject promises to be delightful for the disciple. The master's commentary makes clear that working through the range of women's responses yields a certain pleasure—one that is also colored sexually (ton valoir/voloir, line 1005).

This link between the pleasure in knowing women and the vicarious sexual pleasure is made explicit in Jacques d'Amiens's *Art d'amors*. The master reflects at length on women's yielding in sex. In thematic terms, this reflection builds on the standard Ovidian recommendation that forced sex is always in order with women (*Ars amatoria*, I, lines 673–76). Yet what is particularly telling is the placement of the master-narrator's commentary. That it follows directly after the women's *responses* shows yet again the clerical insistence on debating women's sexual yielding:

> La, u elle se desfendra
> et fera samblant de courcier,
> si le dois tu voir esforcier;
> la, u elle s'estordera,
> l'enforcement molt amera;
> honteuses sunt del otroier,
> por cou les doit on efforcier,
> seul a seul puis c'o toi s'enbat,

> outree veut soit sans debat,
> et telle i a qui de son gre
> t'otroiera sa volente,
> que faire vaura cortoisie
> ne force faire n'aime mie,
> mais durement se desfendroit,
> c'outre son gre l'en forceroit:
> se de tel afaire le vois,
> sa volente atendre dois
> et li pries molt doucement,
> que souffrir voelle ton talent.
> (lines 1203–21)

There where she defends herself and pretends to be angry, you should look to take her by force. There where she tries to escape, she really loves force. Women are too shy to grant it themselves: that's why one must force them. If she struggles with you, one on one, she really wants to be conquered without any further discussion. And there is the woman who willingly gives in to you in her own way and, with all respect to courtliness, does not like to be forced and defends herself fiercely, if one tries to force her beyond her desires. If you see such a situation, you should wait for her to yield; beg her very gently so that she is willing to submit to your desire.

The master-narrator considers every possible female reaction to sex, and no matter what the woman's attitude, his analysis attempts to justify force.[56] If she is obstreperous or insecure, pugnacious or obliging, the narrator has reasons to recommend that the man should take control. Such an analysis pushes the postulate of feminine prevarication to the limit. The woman's most strenuous self-defense is interpreted as an invitation for the man's force and as her incapacity to speak her own desires. Both female "No!" and female "Yes!" are read to mean much the same thing: the range of difference so meticulously recorded and commented upon in the *responses* is streamlined—reduced to a uniform representation of woman's yielding sexually to the man.[57]

In the debate between a masterly narrator and his student, the game of male/female dialogue is thus used to explore the pattern of feminine prevarication. The analysis of these *requestes/responses* charts the changing fortunes of women's negativity. There is enormous latitude for play here: the Ovidian predilection for teasing out that negativity comes through in the numerous variations in representing women's reactions. Yet the presiding master aims, finally, to telescope this rich variation in an image of women's yielding. Whether constructed literally or allegorically, this image becomes central. In fact, it comes increasingly to function as an incitement. The masterly transaction in knowledge about women recommends further action. As the narrator in Drouart la Vache's translation of the *De amore* describes it:

> Quant li amans sera venus
> A cogitation pleniere
> Des secres, en tele maniere
> Puisqu'il pensera as secrez,
> Si il estoit maistres de decrez
> Ne se savra il maintenir
> Aincois le convendra venir
> Tantost au fait, comment qu'il aille.
>   (lines 246–53)

When the lover will have thoroughly contemplated her secrets, thinking about those secrets much as would a master of decrees, he will not know what to do next. Thus it will behoove him to act as quickly as possible, however best he can.

The driving logic behind such didactic texts is to convert a newly gained intellectual power into a physical act. To what extent such an incitement was realized is, of course, impossible to gauge. We find ourselves here in the tricky realm of discourse's impact on action. Yet if we cannot establish that the Ovidian model of mastery led to physical violence against women, we can say that the climactic call to action substantiates that violence symbolically.[58] Ovidian knowledge is so powerful that it can inflict a form of verbal damage. Furthermore, this recommendation to exploit "the secrets" of women affects not only women but all those who come under the sway of this discourse. It indoctrinates those in the role of disciple into mastering a misogynist knowledge of women. For these reasons, it constitutes one of the principle sites of symbolic domination in Ovidian writing.

This type of symbolic domination of women gains another significant dimension in the vernacular with the influx of so-called Aristotelian learning.[59] Those works, debated vigorously at the University of Paris, also impinged upon late-thirteenth-century and fourteenth-century French narrative. They made a particular mark on a little-known cluster of texts: *La Poissance d'amours, Li Consaus d'amours* and *Li Houneurs et li vertus des dames*.[60] All three claim to dispute the learning of Aristotle.[61] All three also deploy a variety of material from Galen, Albert the Great, and Arabic commentary under his name. With this material they bring biological and political terms to the Ovidian argument for woman's yielding. These

French texts argue the topic of woman by interrogating her physical construction, what the *Houneurs* narrator calls "the natural strength of her power" (le natural vertu de se poissance; Zimmermann, 382). They also explore the political dimensions of the question found in many clerical works: "What is this thing woman, and what is she worth?" (quels cose feme est et kelle vaut; *Li Consaus,* Vienna 2621, fol. 2 verso)[62]

In this respect, the *Poissance, Consaus,* and *Houneurs* develop an Aristotelian model of mastery of enormous intellectual pretension. Imitating the disputations of the Parisian faculties, they are at once pugnacious and pedantic. The master-narrators problematize the question of women dialectically, and in order to master it they complicate it still further. In contrast with Ovidian narrators, they aspire to a comprehensive kind of knowledge. The *Consaus* narrator boasts: "I have said and shown how it could happen that a man could know everything about love."[63] While the Aristotelian narrator begins at degree zero, his dialectical reasoning is meant to lead him in the end to produce a whole and complete body of knowledge. This sense of totality implies a system, a set of categories according to which love and women should ultimately be defined.

With the *Poissance, Consaus* and *Houneurs,* this systematic approach of Aristotelian mastery reinforces the symbolic domination of women.[64] These late-thirteenth-century and early-fourteenth-century texts provide a field in which we can study the increasing abstraction of women, from a speaker, to a type of text in Ovidian dialogue (the *response*), to "this thing."

An Academic Matter

As vernacular texts assimilated scholastic learning, their analysis of woman began with her physical composition. In the *Poissance d'amours,* the master-narrator tells his disciple: "It is fitting that you learn first about the character and composition of woman; I will teach you about this in a way that is understandable to both clerics and lay people" (Il couvient que tu saces premierement connoistre le talent et le complexion de femme: si le vous aprenderai aukes, en maniere que li clerc et li lai me porront bien entendre; Speroni, 37).

This philosophical term *complexion* evokes the characteristic process of breaking down every object into an assembly of parts—the particles and quarks of scholastic thought. From person to *complexion* to body parts: the *Poissance* narrator reduces "woman" progressively to ever more manageable units—so manageable, in fact, that the master-narrator considers his analysis accessible to the laity.

Given the way these three narratives analyze a critical female object, we may expect their progressive breakdown to lead to some sort of biological essence. The very question "What is this thing?" seems to be heading toward a proposition "*This* is what woman is." On the contrary, treated dialectically the "woman" question gives rise to still more complex anatomical and biological issues. The *Poissance* version reads:

> Au conmencier, pour miex ataindre le verité de me matere, je di que femme a .vij. lius ou enfant puent recevoir noureture et vie, et sont li quatre liu proprement as enfans marles, et li autre troi liu proprement pour les femmes; dont il puet avenir et avient que uns enfes marles sera nouris ou propre liu de femme, et li femme ou propre liu de l'omme. De coi il avient que, quant femme a esté nourie ou ventre se mere en autre liu ke u sien propre, ele a d'aucune cose samblance d'omme; et se li hom a esté nouris ou ventre se mere en liu de femme, il sera en aucune cose femenins. Et bien saciés que femme ki n'est droite femmenine, c'est pour chou que ele n'a mie esté nourie ou ventre se mere en sen propre liu; et del homme qui est femenins ensement.
>
> (Speroni, 37–38)

> To begin with so as to better reach the truth of my subject matter, let me say that a woman has seven places where children may receive sustenance and life, and four of them are properly for males and the other three properly for females. And it can happen that a male child nurses at a place proper for the female, and a female at one proper for the male. And so it happens when a woman was nursed at her mother's breast at a place other than is proper for herself, she has a certain male semblance. And if a man was nursed at his mother's breast at the female place, he will be feminine. And you should know that a woman who is not truly feminine is so because she was not nursed at the proper place at her mother's breast, and conversely, for an effeminate man as well.

In this first attempt to reckon with woman's composition, the master-narrator considers those persons who contain within themselves both "feminine" and "masculine" elements. By invoking the popular pseudo-Galenic theory of the seven-celled uterus, he presents a picture of various hybrid creatures whose sex is highly ambiguous.[65] Far from locating a distinct female property, he grapples with outstanding variability, whereby the beings of women and men are shown to belie various combinations of femininity and masculinity.[66] Apparent here is a central crux for the biological inquiry: no matter what effort is made to pin down the female, to identify her by isolating and dissecting her intrinsic parts, this thing splinters into myriad other elements. As Sylviane Agacinski has argued in reference to Aristotle's *On the Generation of Animals*, this female object jeopardizes the strict logic of sexual difference that it has been used to define.[67] In this medieval "Aristotelian" text, by focusing on the origin of these hybrid creatures the *Poissance* master argues that the woman, as reproductive machine, bodies forth a womanly man and a manly woman. In other words, while the man may bear the effects of such a sexual mix, it is the woman who is the first cause. Described in biological terms, it is the woman's body that contains the necessary ingredients resulting in bisexual individuals. Even if the hybrids are represented as types of mistaken identity, the man having nursed at the female "place" on the mother's body and the woman at the male "place," the woman also possesses the capacity of determining sexual form. In this scheme of things, she is the exemplar of an all-inclusive difference. By this I mean she is an object that can be broken down into an indefinite number of paired oppositions and at the same time embrace them all.

While the *Poissance* explores this all-inclusive difference biologically, in the *Consaus* it becomes a metaphysical problem as well. Indeed, the one implies the other. Evaluating woman as a primal shaper of sexual being is thus to study her as a primal being per se:

> Car feme proprement est li matere dou monde qui les houneurs fait croistre et montepliier. Car les hautes proeches darmes et de cevaleries sont pour elles et par elles faites et alevees et maintenues en viertu. Feme est a un mot tout et feme vaut tout.
>
> (Vienna 2621, fol. 3)
>
> For woman is really the matter of the earth that makes all honors grow and multiply. For the greatest feats of chivalric and military prowess are accomplished for them and are elevated and maintained forcefully through them. Woman, in a word, is everything and is infinitely worthy.

With the expression "li matere dou monde," the master-narrator takes up the standard Platonic/Aristotelian formulation identifying the substratum of the world with the feminine, indeed, with the most elemental form— her menstrual flux.[68] Yet he goes on to align women's reproductive power with their social creativeness, their material value with their value as catalysts of men's prowess. As this masterly narrator designs it, women's generative capacity is comparable to their ability to generate action in others. Through this line of reasoning, he advances the proposition that women's worth is all-inclusive. Physically synthetic, linguistically complete, and metaphysically coherent, the female thing appears here as the sum of all differences. This simple tautological phrase—"feme est a un mot tout"— testifies strikingly to the habit of linking biological and metaphysical all-inclusiveness in women. The *Consaus* narrator extends the biological notion of women containing all manner of sexual difference to an ontological one of utter plenitude. In this, his argument resonates with the thirteenth-century Aristotelian commentaries that understand metaphysics as a type of natural philosophy.[69]

The *Houneurs* narrator makes much the same claims when he asserts:

> Je proeuue le vertu de femme ensi, que ie di que, se toutes les douceurs de toutes les riens du monde estoient d'une partie, et femme seule fust de l'autre part, ne porroit cuers ne cors d'oume tant de douceur sentir ne trouuer en riens qui soit, com il porroit en femme; car nule douceurs n'est apartenans a le douceur de femme.
>
> (Zimmermann, 382)
>
> I prove the specific female strengths of women in this manner: I say that if the gifts of everything in the world were placed on one side, and woman alone on the other side, neither man's heart nor body could find a better gentleness to experience than he can in woman, for no gentleness approaches that of woman.

By separating out woman and her qualities, this master asserts the completeness of the female part. For him, it stands apart in all senses. Whether that part is defined socially, physically, or ontologically, these three works all posit it as something greater, more comprehensive than any one definition of woman might first indicate. Such a proposition may seem at odds with the Aristotelian definition of woman as incomplete so dear to medieval commentators.[70] But I argue along Agacinski's lines that female lack also involves, in the Aristotelian dialectical structure, a form of surplus (120–21). If woman is defined dialectically as the lesser half, she is also the material foundation that sustains all those differences. Her incompleteness is symmetrically balanced by her capacity to exceed every formal limit. In this paradoxical sense these Aristotelian narrators postulate a female totality.

Such a *complexion* of woman complicates the initial question of these three narratives considerably. Rather than any one homogeneous concept, their masterful interrogation brings to the fore a multiple, superabundant female entity. And such an entity tests the intellectual authority of the Aristotelian master in these narratives. Or one might say it takes that authority to the limit. If for argument's sake the master is willing to entertain this superabundant female biology, one that escapes his grasp with each new category introduced, his intellectual command is challenged. It is not clear whether he can exert control over his knowledge of women by establishing a stable definition or whether instead he has let his object get out of hand. Under such circumstances, the narrator reframes the problematic female object politically. Having converted women into things to analyze and having found them to defy easy categorization, these Aristotelian narrators redefine the problem as the political issue of sovereignty: how to rule women.[71] As a way to test their working definition of an all-inclusive woman, they work through principles in Aristotle's *Politics* that lead to the conclusion that in household and public government, the male is by nature better fitted to command than the female (I, v., 1–2).[72]

The *Poissance* articulates this analysis most cogently:

> Je di ensi au conmencement: que li principes deseure toutes les coses du monde c'est hom, qui tout gouverne, et qui tout ajue a estre maintenu et demené juskes au definement du cors de toute cose. . . . Saciés que je di que hom a sour femme le pooir principaument, mais il ne l'a pas parfaitement, saciés le vraiement.
>
> (Speroni, 31)

> And so I say at the beginning that the principle reigning over all things in the world is man who governs everything and does so so that everything will be maintained until the physical end of all things. . . . You should know that I say man has the principal power over women, but he does not have it completely. You should also know this well.

The master-narrator represents man's governance of women as imperfect in the Old French sense of *parfaire* (to accomplish), incomplete.[73] No matter how well he states the principle of sovereignty, in the same breath he must also admit the conditions women place upon it. The sheer force of his masterful assertion (saciés que je di) cannot satisfy them: there is a cautionary hint of women's separate political position.

This recognition of the limits of men's political authority over women is but another version of the problematical biological definition. In both cases, the narrator is laboring at the conundrum of women not fitting into, or rather surpassing, his set categories. Just as the female entity did not conform exactly to the conventional lineaments of sexual identity, so too she breaks through the grid of men's governance.

But why exactly does a woman not fit politically? The *Poissance* master pushes the problem further, hypothesizing the female faculties:

Et pour chou k'ele fust a homme droite compaigne, plaine de douceur, mist Diex en femme, par gentil courtoisie, parole et vertu de counoistre et d'entendre raison. Et pour chou ke femme connoist et entent raison, ele se set et doit savoir garder d'omme. Par coi on voit souvent avenir ke, quant hom prie une femme k'ele soit acline a se volenté, li memoire et li raisons de cheli ne s'i acordera mie.

(Speroni, 32)

And so that she could be a fitting companion to man, full of gentleness, God placed in woman, in all kind courtesy, speech and the power to know and to understand reason. And since she has knowledge and understands rationally, she knows how to guard herself from man. Thus it is that often it happens that when a man bids a woman to yield to his will, her memory and reason do not agree.

The key factor is woman's rational capacity. Although she possesses it by dint of being man's partner, her rationality can serve to separate her from him. Reasoning is a mode of woman's self-assertion. In the master's hypothetical scenario, it is precisely her rational faculties and memory that explain why a woman does not consistently bend to the will of her men as she is ordained to do. That a woman thinks and remembers accounts for the breaks and so-called discord that underlie the imperfections of man's polity. In these breaks, of course, lies an enormous potential for a woman's distinct social and political capabilities.

In the master's formula describing woman's faculties of "speech and the power to know," the linchpin turns out to be linguistic. By speaking she exercises her knowledge and, in turn, by speaking she is to uphold the sociopolitical code of *courtoisie*. Without language, no matter how vigorous a person's rationality it cannot be brought to bear on a pattern of social conduct. As the Aristotelian master-narrators underscore time and time again, the linguistic element provides the indispensable medium through which modes of behavior are formulated and advanced:

Car parolle commence le droit d'amors, parolle le conduist et maintient, parolle fait amors durant et ferme et remuant. Parolle en fait venir le ioie et le soulas. Parolle droitement est li droite signourie qui toute amor gouverne et maintient en droite disne noblecche.

(*Li Consaus;* Vienna 2621, fol. 13 verso)

For the word is the fitting beginning of love, it cultivates and sustains love; the word makes it strong and lasting and ardent. The word brings joy and solace. The word is the just rule which governs all love and maintains properly its dignified nobility.

> Parole sert et confite le plus principal de l'oume, c'est le raison et le
> sapience; car parlers par nature est li principes desseure toutes coses
> faire auoir par droit goust d'entendement.
>
> (*Li Houneurs*; Zimmermann, 387)

> Language serves and confirms the principal [faculties] of man; that is,
> reason and wisdom. Because language is by nature the principle above
> all else by which one gets a taste for reasoning.

In light of the masters' analytic precedents, the problem then becomes: can woman's speech throw the reigning discourse of courtliness into disarray? Just as woman's generative capacity disrupts the master's biological paradigm, just as her action destabilizes his political structure, so too her language risks exploding the entire apparatus he is assembling. As a divinely accorded principle, it cannot easily be discounted.

The prospect of woman's verbal power turns out to be a tantalizing subject that generates enormous concern.[74] It represents the limit case of the Aristotelian order of intellectual mastery. Insofar as the language constitutes rationality and knowledge, insofar as it realizes "the just rule," women's *parole* is itself a sovereign form. As such, it calls into question the assertion of men's sovereignty. A potential instrument of "that rule," it contests the fact that sovereignty has been conceptualized exclusively as men's affair. In this manner, women's language also challenges the masters' authority. Rationally grounded, her *parole* can then rival the masters' and disciples' language deployed to justify men's sovereignty over women. There is an implicit conflict between the unaccountable verbal power of women and the masters' standard.

That is why these master-narrators put great store in training their disciples how to discipline women's speech:

> Saciés, biaus dous fieus, il i a deffense, si le vous aprenderai. Il est ensi
> que, par raison et par droiture, li poissance et li vertus et li sapience
> d'oume puet bien toutes les raisons que femme puet dire fraindre et
> apetier, tout par nature. Contre ces soutiues paroles que femme ara dit,
> hom doit dire ensi, et reprendre le sentense de tout ce que ele ara dit.
>
> (*La Poissance*; Speroni, 55)

> You should know, my fine dear son, that there are defenses—I will
> teach them to you. It is thus right and fitting that the power, strength,
> and wisdom of man can discipline and control all the arguments that
> woman can put forward, all through nature. Against the subtle words
> that woman will speak, man must first speak in this fashion, taking up
> the gist of all that she will have said.

Having conceded a measure of linguistic independence in women, the master must at all costs reimpose man's authority over it. Appealing once again to reason as man's prerogative (par raison et par droiture), he represents his "natural" superiority reasserting itself. This representation, we should note, combines power (poissance) with knowledge or wisdom (sapience). In other words, where women are concerned, wisdom will be used as a mode of power. It substantiates a formidable authority that can exert the type of symbolic domination we have been investigating. A masterful discourse that depicts women's language as requiring discipline is itself domineering.

As if to stress the urgency of regaining control over women's language, the Aristotelian master also directs this imperative toward women themselves. In an exceptional address to them, he states:

> Parole sert et donne sustance et entendement a tout le boin de l'oume, c'est sapience, et a toutes raisonnables meurs; car parole est conmencemens et gouvernemens de toutes coses mener a cief. Et si voel bien que dames sacent certainement que riens ne plaist tant a ami n'a nul houme conme biaus parlers et sagement.
>
> (*La Poissance*; Speroni, 71)

The word is enabling and gives substance and meaning to all men's efforts. It is wisdom and is fitting behavior. Because language is the origin and structure leading all things to their conclusion. And I really want ladies to know for certain that nothing is more pleasing to their male friends or to men in general than beautiful, wise talk.

> Et bien voel ke dames sacent qu'il n'est nus hom tant soit de diuerse vie ne de mauvaise, qui naime, qui ne crieme et qui ne honneure douce personne de femme droite feminine, de bele conuersation.
>
> (*Li Houneurs*; Zimmermann, 385)

And I deeply wish that ladies know that there is no man, whatever his social rank, who does not love the woman, who does not honor and respect the gentle, properly feminine woman of exquisite conversation.

The key to this disciplining strategy involves the notion of women's beautiful talk (*biaus parler/bele conversation*). And this beauty is amplified and intensified to a superlative degree. The woman's voice epitomizes "the *most* gentle," "the *most* powerful."[75] This beauty is perfected by the master and signals his manipulative rhetoric working to control woman's language. Lavish praise functions as a way to legislate a woman's speech and conduct. In fact, in the extreme it is used to determine her social identity; in this case, what it means to be properly feminine (personne de femme droite feminine). The fact that the masters dwell so much on woman's exquisite talk reveals their attempt to commit her to the sociolinguistic code of courtliness under their jurisdiction. Praising her language means trying to straitjacket it in a rhetoric that denies her *parole*'s putative sovereignty. The masters' impetus to praise should give us a sense of just how crucial the disciplining of women's language is. For not only does the men's "courtly" sovereignty over women ride upon it, but the masters' authority does so as well. Persuading women to conform to courtly language that captures them "beautifully" comprises another cardinal instance of the narrators exerting intellectual mastery over them.

Lest there be any ambiguity about the masterly design of vaunting woman's "beautiful language," let us look at the *Houneurs* narrator's parting shot. In a string of tautological compliments of women, he contends: "And everyone should know that no one can speak badly of women who does not say it about himself" (si sace cascuns que nus ne puet dire mal de femme quil ne le die de lui meismes; Zimmermann, 387). The defamation of women rebounds back on the male speaker. Indeed, it is defined as a critique of the male self. This narrator shows little recognition of the difference between the sexes. What exactly distinguishes women from men is largely blurred. As a consequence, the slandering of women cannot be interpreted as the hatred of alterity but only as a form of self-loathing—of self-destructiveness in a self that is inflected in masculine terms.

Femme/lui meismes: this equation of presumed equivalence bespeaks the tendency to convert intellectual mastery into a form of domination. The danger for the master-narrators of these texts is that their debates can lead to subjugating the other so thoroughly as to imperil its independent self-consciousness. Total control implies that the other may cease to exist, with the result that what is being mastered is little more than an inert, unresponsive object. With formulations such as these, the *Houneurs* makes apparent how easily Aristotelian intellectual mastery can be headed toward this dead end of domination. In the very lauding of woman's language, among other traits, lies the masters' desire for her total objectification. For all the discriminations introduced by their process of dialectical reasoning, the overriding aim has been to maneuver women critically into this position.

Once the masterful discourse on women betrays this domineering tendency, the question of sex is not far behind. Each of these three Aristotelian narratives concludes with references to taking women sexually at will. This recommendation is cast in the euphemistic language of *sourplus*. At the *Houneurs* master's prompting, the disciple aspires to "taste what the surplus of the [woman's] body contains" (gouster chou que li sourplus dou cors comprent; Zimmermann, 386). The *Consaus* recommends that he "do with the surplus what you think is reasonable" (del sourplus faites selonc le raison que vous i quidies; Vienna 2621, fol. 9 verso). And in the most suggestive rendition, the *Poissance* narrator contends:

> Car saciés que femme est si noble et si gentius que trop aroit grant honte de dire a son ami: "Faites de mi vo volenté"; et pour l'abomination que ses cuers aroit de ce dire, doit hom se compaignie conquerre aussi con par force.
>
> (Speroni, 68)
>
> For you should know that woman is so noble and gentle that she is too ashamed to say to her lover: do with me what you will. And since she cannot bring herself to utter this abomination, the man should thus conquer his companion by force.

A female surfeit, a surplus that had always exceeded the bounds of Aristotelian categories, is in these configurations finally mastered. In recommending that women be overpowered sexually, the Aristotelian masters use the very term that had up to this point typified their intellectual analyses of women. Rather than name coitus outright, they render it abstractly through an expression that signals their formidable intellectual authority. The double entendre of *sourplus* suggests how mastering the knowledge of women can itself become a form of domination—represented in physical terms and realized symbolically.

In the shape of these three works, the Aristotelian order of mastery comes into focus. Just like their doubles at the University, these master-narrators dispute a variety of properties of a female critical object, the most challenging being the linguistic. Whereas the Ovidian master gives voice to women, ventriloquizing them playfully in *responses*, the Aristotelian figures consider only the idea of their *parole*. This proves the crux that obliges them to muster all their analytic powers. As a medium of knowledge, woman's *parole* exemplifies the greatest threat to their own intellectual enterprise. It is no surprise, then, that the debate over woman's language hints at the drift from an intellectual control of women toward a physical mastery of them.

In the Aristotelian order of mastery there is virtually no place for a female public. Unlike the Ovidian model that grants a role to women in its dialogue and includes a doctrine for them, it admits women unwillingly. With an occasional aside in their direction, it is directed more and more toward the disciple. The result of this evacuation of women from the scene of disputation is a far more forbidding complex of mastery. In high-medieval vernacular literary culture, the Ovidian master was increasingly flanked by a figure of daunting intellectual acumen and professional pretension. What once was an artful game became an exercise in high-tech ratiocination. The Aristotelian model set a rigorous standard for representing the mastery of the idea of woman as a significant form of knowledge. In this, it strengthened the symbolic domination of women that the Ovidian model introduced in much French writing of the later Middle Ages.

Mastery Confounded

Did this Ovidian and Aristotelian pattern of symbolic domination prevail? For all the savvy and force of masterful disputation, the sense remains that these texts cannot insure this pattern absolutely. We have only to recall the notions of woman's biological surfeit, political unruliness, and linguistic independence to discern the rifts in this pattern. These breaks are never completely resolved. However imposing the masters' authority, it is not always translated into a didactic discourse that exercises full dominance. The *Consaus*'s final reflection on the dangers in ruling women is revealing in this respect. Quoting the Master Philosopher, the *Consaus* narrator introduces again the problem of women's will to surmount all manner of opposition:

> Et homs de se viertu et de sen sens doit ces humeurs de feme cou-noistre par quoi il se tiengne a raison et de point ferm et fier contre feme. . . . Car qui set feme tenir a tout famine de volente tant que volentes durra sera del amors sires. . . . Et dist aristotes damor qui de lui veut goir tant ken ce cas lui gouverner plus atempreement ken nul autre fait. Car raisons et atemprance est li medechine qui a folle amors apertient. Et sapielle aristotes folle amor lamor qui sourmonte le sens et le raison del home.
>
> (Vienna 2621, fol. 12 verso)

> And in his strength and understanding man should know woman's humors so that he can hold firm and fast in his reason against woman. . . . He who knows how to keep woman from exercising her will, for as long as his will lasts, he will be the lord of love. . . . And Aristotle says of love that he who wishes to enjoy it will govern over it temperately

like no other. For reason and temperance are the medicine that pertain to wild love. And Aristotle calls wild love the love that overcomes the sense and reason of man.

With these figures of woman overcoming man's reason and man one-upping her, we come full circle. We return to the issues the *Lai d'Aristote* raises about woman's relations to masterful knowledge. More importantly, we return to the premise that masterly discourse does not succeed in controlling those relations. Insofar as the *Consaus* stresses the lesson of "holding firm and fast against women," the dominance of its discourse is by no means sure. The need to repeat such lessons betrays the difficulty of realizing them.

If we read the *Lai d'Aristote* in relation to the Ovidian and Aristotelian masterly narratives, this difficulty is brought into sharp relief. Not only do they all endeavor to slot women into a well-articulated system of categories, but they disclose the sense that this is finally impossible. They project scenarios in which women challenge those epistemological and social categories proposed by their narrators. In the *Lai*, this takes the form of a burlesque "let's imagine," while in the didactic narratives it is a dialectical hypothetical. The effect is much the same: they all suggest how precarious their symbolic domination of women really is. They all express an unease over maintaining control over the knowledge of women.

So telling was this unease that it continued to disrupt the enormous late-medieval literature mounted in attack and defense of women. From the widely read misogynist tract the *Lamentations of Matheolus* straight through to the numerous fifteenth-century panegyrics, it breaks through:[76]

> Que proufita a Aristote
> Peryarmenias, Elenches,
> Devisées en pluseurs branches,
> Priores, Posteres, logique
> Ne science mathematique?
> Car la femme tout seurmonta
> Alors que par dessus monta
> Et vainqui des methes le maistre.
> Ou chief luy mist frain et chevestre.
> Mené fu a soloëcisme,
> A barbastome, a barbarisme;
> Son cheval en fist la barnesse
> Et le poignoit comme une asnesse. . . .
> Le gouverneur fu gouverné
> Et le gendre fu alterné.
> Elle est agent et il souffroit;

A hennir sous elle s'offroit.
La fu l'ordre preposteré,
Ce dessoubs dessus alteré
Et confondu; car mal s'accorde
Psalterion au decacorde.
Certes, ceste chevaucheüre
Fu incongrue, mal seüre.
En ce fu grammaire traïe
Et logique moult esbahïe.
(book I, lines 1080–92, 1095–1106)[77]

Of what good to Aristotle is the *Peri Hermeneias* and *Elenchi* in all their various parts? Of what value, the *Prior* and *Posterior Analytics*, the *Logic*, and the science of mathematics? For woman surmounted everything and rode on top, vanquishing the master and placing upon his head both bit and bridle. And so he was led to solecisms, barbarisms of all sorts. The baroness made him into her mount, kicking him about like an ass. . . . The governor was governed and gender was altered. She is the agent and he was suffering for it, left only to whinny and neigh under her. In this way all order was blown apart. The underling changed and confounded the one above. For the psalterion and harp do not go well together. Such riding was certainly incongruous, unsafe. In this, grammar was betrayed and logic rendered useless.

Matheolus's fulminations focus upon a figure of women who systematically demolishes the edifice of Aristotelian learning.[78] *The Logic*, (lines 1083, 1106), the *Analytics*, (line 1083): tract by tract, the edifice is broken down. In one of the most bitter reworkings of the *Lai*, the narrator casts the subjection of the philosopher as a wholesale destruction of his thought. The result of all this is devastating: "The governor was governed and gender was completely altered" (lines 1095–96). Not only is the masterful paradigm of knowledge as power completely blown apart, but the classificatory system of humankind—the genus, its gender—is altered unimaginably. The clerical idea of women does more than challenge existing knowledge; it represents a questioning of its very character, one that goes so far as to explode the understanding of human nature itself.

2 The Trials of Discipleship

Le Roman de la poire
and *Le Dit de la panthère d'amours*

It is because things are remote from you, filtered through books and hearsay, that you feel you have to dress them up, make metaphors . . . you have renounced the flesh, but you do not renounce the *thought* of the flesh and, since you are a man of words, you enjoy it more avidly at second hand.

Julia O'Faolain, *Women in the Wall*

In an intellectual and literary world so strongly shaped by the dynamics of mastery, the disciple emerges as the focus of particular attention. However visible the master is in French medieval culture, he remains an exceptional figure. He is part of an elite. Within the clerical caste, the university community, or the lay milieu of the thirteenth-century and fourteenth-century didactic narrative we have studied, he represents a minority.[1] The disciple, by contrast, is a popular persona. His story of immature, well-intentioned efforts is accessible and generalizable in a way his mentor's is not. His trajectory is meant to be Everyman's, one that illustrates the travails of becoming a masterful man. Moreover, it is through him that mastery in its two senses is transacted. Behind every *magister* in vernacular narrative stands an untested disciple. In fact, given the custom of calling a poet *maistres*, there is a way in which many narratives modeled on the *Roman de la rose* dramatize the career of the master and the process by which the disciple grows into the *magister* role occupied by the author. The fascination with the operations of mastery is thus cultivated by narrating again and again the story of the novice.

As numerous allegories recount that story, it involves student-narrators who apply the lessons of the master, this time the *magister amoris* (the

61

master of love.) Youthful and hardworking, these disciple figures are engaged in a characteristic twofold struggle: the need to debate with the master so as to prove their own competence and the challenge of reproducing his authoritative knowledge about women. From didactic to allegorical narrative, the shift is from representations of a doctrine to those of a discipline, from the laying out of precepts concerning "a woman's nature" to the practice of that learning. The disciple's goal of mastering such knowledge remains structured by the scholastic disputation. In the standard configuration, the bachelor took the role of the *respondens* or *responsalis* (respondent) and debated with the master as well as with the *opponens*, the opposing figure.[2] From the position of respondent, the disciple could articulate his version of the master's knowledge and establish his intellectual prowess. Ideally, such prowess would also signal his autonomy. His performance in a disputation was meant to sanction his eventual rise to mastery. The paradox was that his own mastery was by no means assured. The act of disputing disclosed the disciple's difficulties in making the master's role his own—difficulties often represented in terms of the disciple's inherent weakness. As the *Roman de la rose* describes the disciple's predicament, "The master wastes all his effort when the disciple who listens to him does not put his heart into retaining all that he should remember" (Li mestres pert sa poine toute quant li deciples qui escoute ne met son cuer el retenir si qu'il l'en puise sovenir; lines 2051–54).

This image of the faltering disciple comes into clearer focus when we recall the specifically submissive quality of his relations with the master. In the scholastic domain, submissiveness was the necessary rite of passage leading to the practice of mastery, but it carried with it the danger of indefinite subordination. It suggested the possibility that the disciple might never graduate to the powerful role of *magister*, lingering instead in a limbo of lost opportunity and underachievement. In a vernacular context where the disciple's search for mastery was directed toward women, this possibility was all the more apparent. No matter how vigorous his efforts to translate his submissiveness to a lady into ultimate command over her, this masterly goal might never be realized. Projecting a lady as *magistra* did not systematically insure the disciple's ultimate authority as Andreas Capellanus had intended. Like the figure in this miniature from the *Roman de la poire*, he might be caught in a posture of obeisance, unable to exercise his control, incapable of approaching a woman any other way (Figure 5).[3]

The role of discipleship points up deficiencies in the structure of masterful relations. As we saw in chapter 1, masters can be depicted as precarious figures; the faltering disciple adds one more blow to an already

5.   The writer in training offers his book to the lady. *Le Roman de la poire*. Paris, Bibliothèque Nationale, f.fr. 2186, fol. 10 verso. Photograph, Bibliothèque Nationale de France, Paris.

shaky structure of authority. His characteristic insecurity—"his not taking heart"—is further evidence of the instability of the system of mastery as a whole. Moreover, through the faltering disciple figure we can detect the uneven pattern of symbolic domination laid down by the discourses of mastery. His story calls into question the logic of mastering the subject of women and it does this at the very heart of the masterly system. The figure of the disciple under duress represents an implicit interrogation of that system from within.

In order to see what that interrogation entails, I shall concentrate here *à titre d'exemple* on two allegories exemplifying the disciple's predicament. The late-thirteenth-century *Roman de la poire* and the early-fourteenth-century *Dit de la panthère d'amours* depict the initiation of the disciple through letter writing.[4] Both texts build on the *Roman de la rose* by combining the disputational model with the common pedagogical genre of the *ars dictaminis* (the art of correspondence).[5] Their account of the disciple's efforts to compose a letter for a woman is thus designed as a school exercise. This exercise turns out to be an ordeal for the disciple. It is so fraught with problems that it provokes a condition in him far worse than the ill-preparedness of the *Rose* narrator. Fear, paranoia, a full-fledged panic attack: all these allegorical "states of mind" reveal a disciple on trial. By tracing out these various trials one by one, we shall discern more clearly the limits of discipleship.

A Trying Discipline

Like all neophytes in the clerical milieu, these two disciple-narrators begin from a position of real insecurity. Without the instructions of the master, they are tentative about their assignment of addressing a woman. Such uncertainty is the first symptom of the disciples' trouble in putting the master's knowledge about women into action. And it takes two forms. On the one hand, it highlights the difficulty they have with the art of writing that forms part of the master's craft. On the other, it shows how that difficulty increases significantly when their writing is directed toward women. That disciples cannot write easily is proof of their youthful inexperience; that they cannot write to women illustrates the charged relation the clerical domain has posited between women and textualized learning.

In the *Poire*, the disciple tackles his difficulty in writing alphabetically. Reciting his ABCs provides one reassuring starting point: "Amors qui par *A* se commence" (line 1). The *Poire* uses the favorite medieval ploy of an acrostic as a way to regulate the disciple's unease. It represents the disciple beginning to make sense of his writing exercise by working with its mechanics—by practicing the individual letters *B, C,* and so on. This letter game becomes, in effect, a field in which the disciple tests his developing skills.[6] It is a medium of his potential mastery. Yet if this acrostic promises a type of intellectual mastery in relation to the woman correspondent, at the same time it shows just how far the disciple-narrator must go to achieve it. It continues to reveal his trouble. His ongoing difficulty comes through in the extended letter game that follows—a narrative ABC of exemplary lovers telling their stories. This sequence spells out how the disciple-narrator should proceed. Cligés, Tristan, and Paris, in the role of master, all instruct him in their individual lessons. Through their examples the disciple is brought to articulate his own story:

> Ge, qui m'en entremet, en sui bien assenez.
> Cuer et pensee i met, et tant me sui penez
> que s'amor me pramet ma dame, buer fui nez!
> (lines 82–84)

I, who undertake this, am well supported. I put both heart and mind into this, and took such pains that I am promised the love of my lady. I am born lucky!

Wedged in between the testimonials of famous lovers is the account of the disciple's birth. He is represented narrating how he becomes an amorous subject. This narration evokes the process by which the disciple strives to establish his separateness vis-à-vis the master. Saying "I" is a crucial step in this process, because it moves beyond mere recitation of the master's words. It marks a major attempt at controlling his chronic insecurity and adapting the master's lessons himself. What has still to come, though, is the disciple's birth as a writing subject: will he be able to write masterfully about love to his woman reader?

That is why his difficulty over beginning persists. Through a second acrostic starting with the letter *A*, the *Poire* disciple speculates about the purpose of his writing exercise. And his speculation gets to the core of his relation to a master. As we have seen in those didactic narratives called *enseignements*, a chief goal of the disciple's disputation with the master is knowledge about women. Yet the *Poire* disciple admits his ignorance: "I am in no way learned" (ge ne sui mie gramment sages; line 368). Untrained, inexperienced, he appears unfit to write authoritatively. Out of this ignorance, however, the disciple forges another "obscure way" toward knowledge and autonomy (lines 342, 366).[7] As in Lorris's *Rose*, subjective experience comes to play a role in the disciple's formation. However unreliable that experiential way, it ranks with any textual knowledge the master can transmit to him. This comparison is, of course, misleading insofar as the notion of subjective experience is never pure or free of outside influences. No disciple can ever begin as a solo agent. Nor will he ever be rid of his masters. His subjective experience is always a cumulative affair—the sum of his interaction with others. The second acrostic makes this clear: it heralds another beginning of the *Poire* with a well-known lyric quotation.[8] In other words, the disciple conceives of his own knowledge through the voice of others. His coming into learning involves a variety of masterful material, all filtered through his experience. In doing battle with his uncertainties, the disciple is thus shown to articulate what are echoes of the master's authoritative voice.

While the disciple's insecurity complex about women makes a zigzag of the *Poire*'s beginning, in the *Panthère* it disrupts the narrative as a whole. The trope of *not daring* prevails. From the outset, when "he does not dare to write the name of his lady," the narrator is struck dumb (cilz qui son dous nom n'ose ecrire; line 3). The courtly topos of discretion is exaggerated to the extreme. This fearfulness correlates with the disciple's fundamental instability. His first thought is one of incapacity; instead of aspiring to action he broods over the little he can do at all. The structure of the *Panthère* foregrounds this problem of the resourceless disciple. By duplicating the stock device of the dream, it shows him to be doubly desperate for the understanding an allegorical vision should offer. Because he cannot fathom the fantastical bestiary landscape of the first dream, another is required. And the second dream imaging the lady is built into the first. This Chinese-box effect accentuates the helplessness of the *Panthère* disciple-narrator. The closer he draws to seeing the woman, the more disjointed his dreams appear. There is little sign of the disciple having learned anything. On the level of textual construction, this resourcelessness creates an aimless quality to the *Panthère*. We have the impression of reading a work that turns in on itself with no objective clearly in view. Such narrative disarray betrays the disciple's profound malaise over writing masterfully.

In keeping with the *Panthère*'s *mise en abyme* style, the only element that can dispel the disciple's malaise is the *dit* itself. Enclosed within the *Dit de la panthère* are what we can call drafts of *dits*—rough versions:

> Que je par amors lor deïsse
> Ma volenté, et descouvrisse
> Se de riens estoit ma pensee
> En loiaus amors assenee.
> Je leur dis c'un dit fait avoie,
> Ou ma volenté demonstroie,
> Si commençai le dit a dire
> Si com vous poez oïr lire.
> (lines 817–24)

Out of love, I owe it to them [various allegorical figures] to share my will and reveal that my thought has been all taken over by loyal love. I say to them that had I made a *dit*, I would show my desire. So I'll begin to speak the *dit* as you can hear it read.

However haltingly, the *Panthère* disciple gives voice to his doubts. Such an admission allows him to open up. It triggers a kind of self-reflection. As Jacqueline Cerquiglini-Toulet has argued persuasively, the *dit* involves an internalized debate based on subjective experience.[9] And such a debate provides not only a means of self-disclosure but also of a progressive steadying of the self. His *dit* is replete with phrases such as *ouvrir, descouvrir, dire apertement*, expressions that accentuate the effort to become articulate. At this early stage, the disciple is working to come into his own.

In this internalized debate we should recognize a version of the disputation. What is habitually conducted in a public forum is, in these two narratives, moved within the figure of the disciple himself. Yet this move does not entail leaving the master behind. He remains implicitly present. As we have already seen, his knowledge is refracted through the multiple voices the disciple assumes. The master's disputation is thus integrated into the flow of the disciple's inner musings. The familiar pattern of the master talking through the disciple intensifies.

The prospect of actually approaching the woman brings this disputatiousness out. Faced with a woman reader, the disciple experiences a type of clerical psychomachia whereby he disputes with various authoritative voices. In the *Poire*, this debate begins just as he broaches the subject of women. An unidentified interlocutor intervenes, and the ensuing dialogue takes the well-known pedagogical form of question and answer (quaestio et responsio; line 372). For every point the *Poire* disciple narrator advances, he is challenged by an opposing one. Nothing is left uncontested, especially his claim that love is an oxymoron:

> Max et biens, ce sunt .II. contraire,
> et vos lé metez en commun
> autresin con s'il fussent un!
> Ce n'est pas reison ne droiture;
> qui les juge selonc nature,
> ge n'i voi point d'acordement.
> Vos nos devez dire comment
> s'acorde l'une et l'autre part.
> (lines 507–14)

Bad and good, these are two contraries and you put them together as if they were one! This doesn't make sense; it isn't right. If you judge them according to their nature, I don't see any compatibility at all. You ought to tell us how one is compatible with the other.

This mock disputation invokes the criteria of contraries that shape so much of medieval logical thinking.[10] Can the disciple work through the contrary, defined in logic by its very difference and irreconcilability?[11] Can

he account for the irreconcilable? On the face of things, he and the masterly figure dispute love as it is emblematized by the bittersweet pear
of the narrative's title. But in the context of the narrative, that pear is
doubtless a cipher for women: master and disciple are in fact arguing over
the contrariness of women.[12] Poised on the threshold of addressing one
woman reader, the disciple is pressed to explain what it is the general class
of women represents for him. And his explanation is structured in the
characteristic terms of masterful knowledge. Such a debate over "contraries" is part of a scholastic epistemological model that abstracts women.
It plots them on a grid that defines them—this time—according to their
oppositional difference.[13] In arguing along these lines, the *Poire* disciple-
narrator begins to prove his competence in conventional scholastic reasoning. Yet by the same token, the disciple's disputing of women as contraries
suggests his difficulty in making sense of them. Insofar as contraries represent what is different or irreconcilable, "contrary" women exemplify the
disciple's trial in approaching the one woman reader. There is a critical discrepancy between his understanding and her existence. No matter how
thoroughly the disputation with the master analyzes this discrepancy, it is
never completely resolved. The idea of contrary women remains a persis-
tent conundrum—a sign of the disciple's limited understanding.

Those limits are more sharply delineated in the *Panthère*, where the
timorous narrator cannot even rise to the challenge of a disputation. Representing an earlier, green phase in development, this disciple "does not
dare" to argue with so many masterly voices, but seeks instead their
instruction:

> Si fu en grant merancolie,
> Comment aucun trouver porroie
> Qui de ce que veü avoie
> Me deïst la significance. . . .
>
> Car j'avoie grant apetit
> Et grant desirrier de savoir
> Se par l'un d'eulz porroie avoir
> La droite interpretation.
>   (lines 148–51, 200–203)

So I was in a deep melancholy. How was I to find someone who
would give me the significance of what I had seen? . . . For I have an
enormous appetite and great desire to know, if I could have the right
interpretation by one of them [a company that he sees].

Melancholia is the mark of the absent master. And the only way to cure it
involves having "the right interpretation" of women. Notice the distinc-

tion here: this is not the usual masterly drive to know, or even the disciple's penchant for debating as a way to test his new-found knowledge. Instead, the *Panthère* narrator searches for a set rule by which all phenomena can be interpreted correctly. The disputational process is reduced to an elementary and largely passive ritual whereby the disciple need only assimilate the various precepts concerning women that a master hands down to him. There are many. Following the example of Jean de Meun, the narrative sets out an encyclopedic variety recapitulating much contemporaneous literature. Allusions to the *Roman de la rose* and to Drouart La Vache's translation of the *De amore*, invocations of the poet Adam de la Halle's songs, long passages from lapidaries: all this represents the essential curriculum that a master passes on to a needy disciple.

Given such a program of instruction, the *Panthère* takes on the character of a clerical lecture (*lectio*), with its many participants.[14] The figures of the God of Love and Venus are certainly familiar from the *Rose*, yet in the *Panthère* they are not rival authorities. Venus is a complementary instructor who picks up the instruction of the disciple where the *magister amoris* leaves off:

> Bien sai que as esté tardis
> Et coars: or soies hardis
> D'ore en avant et corageus,
> Sans estre vilain n'outrageus.
> (lines 1049–52)

I well know that you have been timid and cowardly. So be brave from now on and courageous without being a fool or outrageous.

Halfway through the narrative, the disciple's uncertainty continues to be represented through the sheer number of authorities he requires.

What is the effect of this masterful lecture, or in the *Poire*, of the mock disputation? Far from securing the disciple in his knowledge about women, they create further setbacks. The workout with the master sends the disciple into a tailspin—the very antithesis of masterly control. Both narrators seem as far from the exercise of their discipline as they did at the outset. We find here another zigzag in the pattern of the disciple's story. For each promising step the disciple takes toward practicing his knowledge about women there is another that turns him away from her. His progress is erratic, his attention divided. It is customary to explain this irregular pattern in terms of erotic desire. Its cycle is seen to generate obstacles that cause the man to lose track, thus intensifying his desire. Yet in the disciple's case, his zigzagging suggests the pattern of casting the woman herself as an obstacle. Insofar as the clerical world of mastery creates a strong disjunction between the class of women and learning, one individual woman represents a perennial threat to that learning. She inspires misgivings about its command. Each time the aspiring disciple approaches his woman reader in order to test his learning, his confidence is necessarily undercut.

In the *Poire*, this loss of control is figured by the trope *ravir*. The disciple complains of being dispossessed progressively of his faculties:

> Mes or les sant, car un essoine
> si grant com de perde la vie
> m'a del tot ma pense ravie.
> —Ta pense?—Voire.—En quel maniere?
> N'a tu ta penssee premiere
> e ton savoir et ta vertu?
>
> (lines 631–36)

But I feel them [the pains of love], for a worry as serious as the loss of life has seized my entire thought.—Your thought?—Right.—In what way? Isn't your first thought with your knowledge and your power?

At stake are the very qualities that distinguish a rational man according to scholastic thought. Not only is the disciple distracted, but the defining traits of the master—his *savoir* and *vertu*—are severely compromised. He too suffers the predicament endured by Aristotle in the *Lai*: he is overwhelmed by a woman. His is a state of enthrallment. Let us not forget that this same term *ravir* evokes the ravishment or overwhelming of women. This is how Helen's abduction is described in the portraits of exemplary lovers at the beginning of the *Poire* (line 221). The echo is telling, for it reveals how the disciple's state is associated with women's conventional helplessness.[15] Granted, in the narrator's case the act of being carried off physically is transposed figuratively and refers to a loss of rational functions. Yet to link the two *ravissements* implicitly signals just how far the disciple is from the stance of intellectual mastery.

In the *Panthère* the disciple's vulnerability is underscored further. Whereas the *Poire* narrator's *ravissement* suggests an initial composure and expertise that is subsequently diminished, the *Panthère* narrator is already on the brink of collapse. Even the lecture on vernacular learning cannot steady him. In the face of actually addressing a woman, he is reduced to a subhuman state, emblematized in the following image:

> Car paor lors si te court seure
> Et si t'atorne en petit d'eure
> Que ne pues nis la bouche ouvrir
> Por ta pensee descouvrir,

> Si come .i. ymage entaillie,
> Qui n'a vois, ne sens, ne oÿe.
> (lines 1120–25)[16]

For fear has surely dogged you and turned you around in no time at
all so that you can't even open your mouth to reveal your thought,
just like a sculpted figure that has no voice, or sense, or hearing.

No Pygmalion, this *Panthère* disciple is, in fact, likened to his female creation—"a deaf and dumb image" as the *Roman de la rose* describes her
(une ymage sourde et mue; line 20821). Instead of the artist who tries to
create a woman, he is the created object—inert and struck dumb by his in-
capacities. This inanimate state represents the narrator's nadir point. And
it is bound up tightly with the single instance of the woman's reported
speech. Her voice rings condescendingly:

> N'aiez en moi nule atendance,
> Car sachiez que nule baance
> N'ai d'amer, ne point de corage,
> Si n'y avrez point d'avantage. . . .
> De moi si tost s'esloigna donques,
> Que respondre ne li poi onques.
> (lines 1456–59, 1464–65)

"Don't have any hope in me. For you should know that I have no
desire to love, nor indeed any will. Thus there is absolutely no gain
for you." . . . She took her distance from me right away so that I
could not respond to her in any way.

Such a curt rejection sends him to the lowest point yet, the dead center of
the narrative.

If this state of paralysis poses questions as to the disciple's ultimate mastery, it also recalls the paradoxical strategy of taking a submissive stance toward another as a way of acquiring power. Like the middle-class lover in
Andreas Capellanus's *De amore*, the disciple adopts a position of weakness
before a *magistra* in order to gain the upper hand. Describing himself *in ex-
tremis* is meant to project her into the same place. Will she too be *ravie*?
This state of enthrallment thus bespeaks both the ambitions and the limits
of that intellectual mastery sought by the disciple. It discloses ambitions
because the figure of ravishment communicates subliminally his aim of
taking charge of the woman reader. Faced with the prospect of losing control, the disciple attempts to convert that loss to his advantage by transferring it onto the woman. However, in light of his trials of uncertainty up to
this point, there are few assurances that such a design can work. And here
is where the limits of mastery are discernible. No matter how well tutored

the *Poire* and *Panthère* narrators are, their learning brings them no closer to exercising an intellectual authority over women. Working earnestly to command his woman reader, the disciple is never sure that he will succeed in doing so. The impetus to achieve mastery over the woman reader is broken by the suspicion that it is no sure thing.

Learning to Write

This uncertainty increases the pressure to practice the masterly craft of writing. As the *Poire* and the *Panthère* represent it, one chief way to regain the hope of intellectual mastery vis-à-vis women is to concentrate on perfecting textual skills. At the point of the disciples' greatest weakness, both texts begin to narrate the formation of a writer. The inference is that the exercise of composition could bring them some greater success than their other clerical training: writing may yet make them masters.

In the case of the *Poire*, once again, an acrostic reveals the real challenge of the disciple's writing. The disciple's loss of control is enunciated in the very place where the woman's name takes shape. With each letter of A.N.N.E.S., the disciple's "ravishment" is accentuated:

> *A.* et se te vels vers lui deffendre,
> il te vendra a force prendre.
> > (ll. 864–65)

> *N.* ge le vos di, bien vos gardez:
> vos n'i avroiz ne pes ne trive,
> ainz vos prendra a force vive.
> > (lines 993–95)

> *E.* lors vint Amors qui me menace,
> si ge ne me rent tot a lui.
> > (lines 1160–61)

A. And if you want to defend yourself against him [Love], he'll take you by force.

N. I'll tell you, be on your guard: You'll have neither rest nor respite, for he'll take you by great force.

E. So Love came who threatens me if I don't offer myself up completely to him.

Yet, by the same token, describing his own loss of control in the process of constructing a woman's name is a mode of self-discipline. Moreover, it is a gesture of power, for it evokes the originary and divine act of creating a person by composing her name. It mimics Adam's naming of the animals that established his sovereignty. Here the *Poire* disciple's naming of A.N.N.E.S. is tantamount to an imperative. Not only does it bring her into being textually speaking, commanding her *to be* for the purposes of his text, it also uses her nominal being to communicate a single message: follow my example—offer yourself up. She exists insofar as she is meant to duplicate the disciple's own condition of "être pris à force vive." Because the woman is understood primarily as his textual creation, her being is inextricably caught up with the transferable message of ravishment.

That writing enables the disciple to reestablish a modicum of control is made even clearer by the woman's appearance. In contrast to the *Rose* and many other narratives with inscribed women readers, the *Poire* represents "A.N.N.E.S." entering into the discourse: she speaks. And this speaking entrance signals her ravishment. As soon as the woman promises herself to the disciple, he observes: "Love carried my lady away for me, and took her there where it pleased him." (Amors m'ot ma dame ravie et l'en mena la ou li plot; lines 2300–2301). The sheer repetition of the *ravir* trope over the course of her name culminates in the woman's seduction: she is represented "ravie" (line 2300).

The disciple's transfer of loss of control seems to work—so well, in fact, that the woman is also figured naming the disciple acrostically. T.I.B.A.U.T. marks the textual space where the woman articulates her desire for him. These letters, however, detail aspects of the disciple's position rather than her own. They relay further canonical advice about how to win the woman over: the importance of gifts, of dialogue, of taking swift action (lines 2466–78, 2537–61, 2623–28). Her naming of him is thus conjoined to his experience. Far from a sovereign act of nomination, it is a ventriloquistic stunt: she is calling to him through his writing. Let us not forget that when the disciple's acrostic has her saying "Friend, you will have sovereignty over me," we have another textual figure for the woman's yielding. (*Vos avroiz la seignorie amis, sur moi*; lines 2568–69).

At this point we can see how crucial the letter games are for the disciple's potential mastery. The clerkly exercise in writing enables him to simulate control over his woman reader. In fact, the acrostic proves to be the site of the disciple's vicarious experience of mastering her.[17] There—in the most elementary, alphabetic way—he can spell out her reactions and legislate her desire. And this he does without ever representing an actual encounter or extended dialogue between them. Like so many "men of words," the disciple exploits the clerkly practices of writing as a way of figuring his control. Granted, this acrostic control is predicated on the idea of a fully literate woman reader. It presupposes a persona able to decipher the most sophisticated textual forms. Her literacy is the foil necessary for the disciple to project a semblance of dominance. Yet within the terms of the *ars dictaminis*, it matters less whether the receiver of the disciple's letter conforms to his representations of her or not. What counts is the power the clerks' written medium affords him in creating the guise of his own mastery.

When we turn to the *Panthère*, this recourse to the powers of writing is no less in evidence. The key trope is that of *oeuvrer*:

> . . . Tu te doutes
> Por noient, gette jus les doutes;
> Amans doit toujours esperer
> Que son desir puist averer,
> Encores n'en soit il pas dignes;
> Car c'est de bien amer .i. signes.
> Et s'ainsi estoit que tu fusses
> Refusez, et bien le sceüsses,
> Si ne t'en dois tu pas retraire
> De bien dire ne de bien faire.
> *Oeuvre* par sens, et si t'avise;
> Car se tu selonc ma devise
> Veus ouvrer, moult grans avantages
> T'en vendra, et as amans sages
> Par ce faire te comparras.
>   (lines 1502–16, emphasis mine)

You are a doubter for nothing, cast away your doubts. A lover should always hope that his desire will be realized, otherwise he would not be worthy of it. For this is one sign of loving well. And if indeed you were refused, and well you know it, you don't try to speak and act well. Act [*oeuvre*] sensibly, that is what I advise you; for if you wish to work according to my precept, you will gain a great advantage, and in the doing you will be compared to wise lovers.

For the disciple to realize both his erotic and intellectual desire, Venus tells him, he must commit himself to hard labor: work is required. This trope should remind us first of the travails the disciple endured early on in the narrative. There he was represented struggling to no avail—completely overextended (lines 685–736). At the same time, Venus's work order suggests a type of productivity that goes beyond the hackneyed labor of love. In the allegorical terms of the disciple's training, it also involves a hermeneutical labor. The task is for him to decode the various allegorical signs, including that of the lady-panther. His industry should yield interpretations of the many significances of his world. What had first seemed undecipherable—including the woman—becomes gradually comprehensible.

This hermeneutical dimension of the *Panthère*'s trope brings to the fore an important implication as far as the disciple's mastery is concerned. While he labors away, his love letter is materializing. In fact, the end result of his endeavors, his "ouvre" (line 1514) is his "salut," his "oevre" (lines 8, 2599).[18] The culmination of his personal travail is nothing less than his text. That the trope registers in this double way is made clear by the many scenes of composing in the second part of the narrative. The first sign of this creativity is the disciple singing himself. In the place of his various instructors, he speaks through the songs of Adam de la Halle. Admittedly, his composition works by way of a *vox prius facta*—an oft-quoted external voice of authority.[19] Yet as we have seen, such a mixed voice can demonstrate the disciple's capacity to incorporate the materials of vernacular learning. Adam de la Halle's authoritative voice is now assimilated, used as an integral part of the disciple's own writing project.

This emphasis on the disciple's textual work increases with the final recommendations of the God of Love:

> Et quant un poi la pues veoir,
> Si pren en ton cuer hardement,
> Et li di tout apertement
> Comment por li vis a martire.
> Après ce li porras escrire.
> (lines 1733–37)

And when you can see her [the lady-panther] for a little while, then take her in your heart confidently, and tell her openly how you live a martyr's life for her. After that you will be able to write her.

The disciple looks more and more like Pygmalion—creative, confident, able to create a woman for himself out of nothing. The clerical practice of letter writing is no longer a tortuous ordeal for the disciple but has become his very livelihood. All the effort in textual study played out in the course of the dreams can be put to good use. In fact, the principal lesson from the dream experience—always work away loyally—is so fully assimilated that the disciple begins to compose his own *oeuvre*: the dream labor is transformed into his own "collected works"—the all-encompassing *Dit de la panthère*. The entire cycle of his insecurity and disastrous first approach to the woman is now recounted confidently in a textual sequence of his own making. And through that sequence his intellectual mastery is posited.

In this case, the disciple's increasingly masterful writing does not project a woman reader's response. Because he represents a far more insecure persona than his *Poire* confrere, the commitment to textual work is all-absorbing. There is little space for figuring the woman; no simulated dialogue between them ensues. In contrast to the *Poire*, the *Panthère* foregrounds a failed encounter. Yet that very failure proves the mainspring of the disciple's creativity. Having hit bottom, he rises to the clerical task of writing as a way to secure the self. In other words, writing is pursued in order to turn the disciple into a master. We might even say that writing is pursued for its own sake. As it turns out, the God of Love's recommendation to direct his text toward the woman is rhetorical.

Intransitive Lessons

Does all this textual labor work? Does the disciple become the woman reader's master through writing? If we recall the clerical pedagogical model outlined in chapter 1, the cardinal factor is dialogue. It is the give-and-take, the heated exchanges between *magister* and disciple in a disputation, that prime the disciple for assuming authority. By expending his adversarial energy dialogically, the disciple accedes to the master's role. Both of these narratives rehearse these sorts of exchanges: the disciple shadow-boxes with a masterly persona represented by disparate voices. Yet the crux lies in the problem of recasting that hypothetical dialogue to include the woman reader. Only then could the disciple be shown to exercise mastery fully.

In the *Poire*, the makings of such dialogue are visible. As we have seen, not only does the woman speak the disciple's name but the two are represented speaking to each other. The third and final acrostic is a duet with the disciple and woman taking turns composing the word A.M.O.R.S. Their voices are intertwined in the act of producing a text together.[20] Yet does this common text substantiate dialogue? To be sure, it caps a sequence of acrostics that serve to juxtapose the disciple's and the woman's words. What was first a matter of literal juxtaposition develops into a type of interaction. The *Poire* climaxes with an exchange—disciple to woman and vice versa. But if we consider this represented exchange in terms of the disciple's letter writing, it is by no means clear whether it is transferable to the woman reader. The ideal scenario of their union is certainly intended to convince her to respond favorably to the letter. However in the end, the narrative cannot establish that. Whereas it posits an obvious synchrony between A.N.N.E.S. and the inscribed woman reader, one meant to determine an identical positive reaction to the disciple, that reader's interest in dialogue cannot in the end be represented. It remains the moot point in the narrative.

In this sense the disciple's prospects for gaining authority over women through dialogue are deeply ambiguous. Because the woman reader is never depicted responding one way or the other, his authority is never validated. It is as if the dialogue he has projected remains intransitive.[21] Given the woman reader's silence, the disciple is in a hiatus. All his training and textual exertions have brought him to this: a position where his hopes for intellectual mastery of women are held in abeyance. The privilege of acquiring the master's doctrine about them does not translate automatically into practice.

This pattern of intransitivity is even more pronounced in the *Panthère*. As we have seen, the shock value of a woman is so enormous for this disciple that most of his energy is expended on gaining control of the self through writing. The disciple's work is complete when it describes his subjective condition (de tout mon estat descrire; line 2629), and not his understanding of women. Exchange with the woman reader thus looks hypothetical at best. "Were you willing to say this rondel. . . . If I would hear this from you": the *Panthère* represents the one scrap of dialogue conditionally (Que vous veilliez cest rondel dire. . . . Et se de vous oÿ l'avoie; lines 2512, 2527). The disciple imagines what it would be like were the woman to sing a rondeau in answer to his. Unlike the *Poire*, which goes so far as to project a woman's response, this narrative casts it as an as yet to be realized speech act. The woman's direct discourse is manifestly beyond the disciple's limits. Even within the freer dream space of the text, he cannot entertain interaction with the woman. In the *Panthère*, an intransitive relation exists with the allegorical lady-panther as well.

Such intransitivity provides a key to discipleship as it is represented by allegorical narrative. It extends far beyond the syntactical issue of dialogue and epitomizes the narrator's dilemma over failing to realize the master's lessons regarding women. This dilemma is anticipated from the beginning of the disciple's initiation. He undergoes increasing trials in order to prove his intellectual credentials. The process is protracted, pushed beyond the extreme model of the *Rose*. Yet with this extended initiation comes no greater certainty that he can apply his learning on specific women. The disciple's authority does not carry beyond his own solipsistic writing. While he enjoys avidly at second hand the representation of the woman's acquiescence, the clerical practicum of letter writing insures no follow-through.

In this gap between the master's doctrine of women and the disciple's discipline we can detect what Bourdieu calls the double-edged privilege of domination.[22] In both these narratives, the disciple is motivated by the desire to prove his mastery through his letter. Yet insofar as that writing can never guarantee domination of the one persona that eludes him—his woman reader—he as much as she risks being dominated. The paradox lies in the disciple's stubborn determination to prevail. By trying over and over again to put the master's lessons about women into textual use, the disciple becomes spellbound, caught in the grip of a desire that is never fully satisfied. As a consequence, he too is subject to the immense pressure of a discursive system that can turn intellectual authority into a form of domination. He too can be imposed upon.

In recognizing this paradoxical position of discipleship, we should not discount the fact that the disciple remains a prominent and respected figure in French medieval narrative. The story of his trials contributes indispensably to the notion that women can be known and that some disciples can indeed graduate to the station of *magister*. But to the degree that the disciple is represented as so overwrought, his writing bears the signs of mastery's limits. To the degree that his authority over women is never confirmed, the symbolic dominance that his writing should put into place is, in the end, a doubtful affair.

3   The Master at Work
Richard de Fournival's *Bestiaire d'amour*

Aestho-autogamy with one unknown quantity on the male side
has long been a commonplace. For fully five centuries in all parts
of the world epileptic slavies have been pleading it in extenuation
of uncalled-for fecundity. It is a very familiar phenomenon in
literature.

Flann O'Brien, At Swim-Two-Birds

If the disciple wavers indefinitely when faced with women interlocutors,
what then of his superior, the master? At the apex of the scholastic institution of mastery, the *magister* appears in a nearly invincible position. In
Thomas Aquinas's own portrait, "Like the mountains, the masters are elevated above the earth and thus first illuminated by the rays of the sun."[1]
On ground level, the master presides over a network of pedagogical and
intellectual relations. He is its guarantor, as the miniature from the *Bestiaire d'amour* depicts it, orchestrating the labor of writing and supervising
his disciples (Figure 6). He is thus responsible for the continuity of mastery. In Aristotelian terms (as indeed in Flann O'Brien's playful ones), the
master's charge involves a type of reproduction: replicating the masterly
persona and his system through his own work.[2]

In the literature of the *magistri*, any extended dealings with women
were represented as a threat to this process of replication. In fact, so threatening did this appear that the idea of dialogue with women—of *colloquium
mulierum*—was classified as a sin.[3] In pastoral manuals and treatises on
linguistic arts, this sin was numbered together with cursing or bad language (*turpiloquium*) and buffoonery (*scurrilitas*). All three were considered to express a desire for the filthy and foul; a desire, if we translate literally, to disfigure (*ex insolentia feditatis*). This conception of disfigurement
gets to the heart of the problem of any dealings between clerkly figures
and women interlocutors. First of all, by dint of speaking with them the

clergy risks defiling their privileged languages of learning. When their words are directed toward personae identified by scholastic thought in base, material terms, the words themselves are debased; so too the subjects under discussion. It is as if all that clerks represent through their exchanges with women could be befouled. The world of learning itself could be disfigured.

Such a conception of the *colloquium mulierum* may well have been ritualistic—a sin in name only. Its definition in these thirteenth-century treatises smacks of the clerical habit of creating fantastical categories for the sake of analysis. Yet the fact that it was formulated at all and recurred in scholastic writing signals just how problematic the dialogue between clergy and women was taken to be. For the powerful figurehead of the clergy, the *magister*, it posed the gravest problems of all.

Nowhere is this threat more clearly dramatized than in the *Lamentations of Matheolus*. Not only does the masterly protagonist brave the interdiction against *colloquium mulierum*, but he consorts with a woman as a bigamist. The consequences for his identity are devastating: "I used to be a master" (Iamque eram magister).[4] From the opening line, the *Lamentations* traces a story of degradation. It narrates what is another expulsion from Eden: a clerical fall from grace. This time a woman is shown to cause an exile from the mountains of masterly dominion. The so-called lamentations that follow are in fact a powerful diatribe against women. Because of the demoted master's desire to disfigure, he is reduced to speaking nothing but a disfiguring language: slander, blasphemy, expletives.

Matheolus is the alter ego—the dark shadow—of the master. As such, he provides the counterexample against which we can best study how the master undertakes dialogue with a woman. Matheolus's disgrace represents the position the reputable master figure must avoid at all costs. Although they both break the taboo of *colloquium mulierum*, the reputable master must find a way of maintaining his formidable authority while pursuing dialogue with women interlocutors. My test case will be Maître Richard de Fournival's *Bestiaire d'amour*.[5] This thirteenth-century text is exemplary on two counts. In the framework of a master's address to a woman interlocutor, it casts the narrator in the double role of pedagogue and lover. While he is more intelligent than the disciple figure, he approaches the woman in a similarly amorous way. And this combination of roles raises the question of his masterly control, a question that becomes all the more charged because it is associated with the signature of "Maistre Richard de Fournival." A celebrated polymath of the high Middle Ages, Fournival exemplifies the *magister*'s intellectual command.[6] Indeed, his far-ranging philosophical, literary, and scientific learning suggests the model

6. The master's work in progress: from writing to book production. Oxford, Bodleian Library, Douce 308, fol. 90 verso. By permission of the Bodleian Library, Oxford.

of Aristotelian mastery coalescing in Parisian university circles during the mid-thirteenth century.[7]

These two aspects of Fournival's *Bestiaire*, structural and biographical, will focus our inquiry on the master's relations with women. Examining how the Fournival master's intellectual authority is established will help chart the dynamic of mastery—what it is that separates and does not separate Richard's master from his alter ego Matheolus. It will also lead to the overarching issue of the symbolic domination of women created by the master's discourse.

Laying the Groundwork

The *Bestiaire* master allies himself straightaway with the intellectual leaders of the day through the Aristotelian language he invokes.[8] His subject is a favorite of scholastic disputation and commentary. Beginning with the incipit, he teases out the principal concepts of Aristotle's *Metaphysics*:

> All men desire to know. An indication of this is the delight we take in our senses; for even apart from their usefulness they are loved for themselves; and above all others the sense of sight.

> By nature animals are born with the faculty of sensation, and from sensation memory is produced in some of them, though not in others. And therefore the former are more intelligent and apt at learning than those which cannot remember.

> The animals other than man live by appearances and memories, and have but little of connected experience; but the human race lives also by art and reasonings.[9]

Rationality, knowledge, memory: the *Bestiaire* master works through the very traits that distinguish men and women from animals, and more importantly, that explain men's rule over all.[10] In his address to the inscribed woman reader, he uses these Aristotelian terms to suggest his rule over her. This rule the alter ego Matheolus squanders. Whereas the *Bestiaire* narrator works to secure his rule through such formidable scholastic reasoning, Matheolus bewails the loss through invective: one goal, two counterbalancing rhetorics.

The *Metaphysics* subtext also raises the issues of irrationality and knowledge based on the senses. As the corresponding opposites of the ruling traits, they are implicitly aligned, in the master's schema, with "woman."[11] If he claims the powers of rational knowledge, she, then, is allotted all that is irrational and purely sensory.[12] In the most extreme terms, woman is thus limited to an animalistic existence. Such a theorem is crucial for the *Bestiaire*'s composition of a series of bestiary exempla. The master's letter to a woman reader involves various lessons concerning animals that, given this implicit conception of woman, are meant to be adopted easily by her.[13] The presumption is that one beast should recognize another.[14] By reading the master's commentary on the hedgehog or the crocodile, she should identify so completely with these animals that she should defer immediately to his erudition. As a result, not only is he meant to gain control over her, but his theorem on women's animalistic nature should be reinforced as well. In this, the *Bestiaire* master's attitude differs little from his alter ego's. It is a matter of degree. Since his authority is completely shaken, Matheolus figures a woman in the most terrifying bestial terms. Woman becomes "a hermaphroditic monster and shows herself to be a chimera" (Femme est hermafrodite monstre et pour chimere se desmonstre; *Lamentations*, II, lines 4127, 158) Out of his control, she turns into a wild, sexually ambiguous beast (and, we might add, into pure illusion).

This series of associations—the animalistic/the feminine/the deference to man's rule—brings us to the issue of mastery's dynamic. Our question then becomes: how is the *Bestiaire* narrator to command the favor of his woman reader? The sequence of bestiary exempla derived from an authoritative Aristotelian tradition is used to create a dynamic of domination and subordination between the master and his female correspondent. Given his erudition, the master starts off from a dominant position. And his disputational commentary on the exempla exaggerates that dynamic. For one thing, his account of human erotics shifts between bestiary exempla for different types of aggression or servility. It moves back and forth between figures for predatory and passive behavior, between, for instance, the viper who attacks the unsuspecting, and the careless monkey captured at once. Furthermore, the gender coding of the master's exempla fluctuates. Far from using exempla systematically to assert the case of masculine dominance, the master comments upon types for masculine passivity, as indeed for feminine aggressiveness. The viper signifies for the *Bestiaire* narrator a feminine tendency to lash out at the lover, while the monkey is a lover too easily beguiled by women. This alternation of gender types maps the master's effort to prescribe the woman reader's reaction. Each time he shifts from an exemplum detailing masculine traits to one exemplifying those that are feminine, we glimpse the master-narrator working to ordain the woman's response. If he can use his gendered learning to dictate to her, then his intellectual mastery will be confirmed in the process.

This strategy is hardly implemented without a hitch. The more the *Bestiaire* master alternates between masculine and feminine exempla, the more complicated his goal of commanding the woman becomes. This alternating pattern signals the master's difficulty in projecting relations of pliancy onto her. And that uneasiness comes through in a second pattern. The *Bestiaire* narrator is liable to change the gendered lessons of the exempla. An animal conventionally read as masculine can metamorphose in the space of the master's commentary into a feminine one and vice versa. Such semantic mobility, coupled with a structural one, suggests how checkered his campaign to induce the woman's yielding is. His tendency to revise the gendered sense of his own material is symptomatic of the larger problem of the master's intellectual authority. To understand this trouble in relation to the woman reader, it is as important to trace the sequence of change in bestiary exempla as it is to examine what each exemplum entails.

Take the case of the tiger exemplum. Introduced to describe the master's seduction, it signifies a creature mesmerized by its own image in a mirror. Medieval bestiaries conventionally treat the tigress and not the male of the species.[15] In the framework of the master's teaching, this animal should lend itself "naturally" to interpreting the woman's behavior. It conveys perfectly notions of feminine vanity and self-absorption. In the master's rendition, however, its conventionalized gender is recast to represent his predicament:

> Oïl, miex fu je pris par mon veoir ke tigres n'est al mireoir, ke ja tant ne sera corchie de ses faons, s'on li emble, ke s'ele encontre un mireoir qu'il ne li covingne ses iels aerdre. Et se delite tant a regarder la grant beauté de sa bone taille, k'ele oblie a cachier chiax ki li ont emblé ses faons, et s'areste illuec comme prise.
>
> (Segre, 40–41)

Yes, I was better seized through my sense of sight than the tiger in the mirror. For however enraged she is when one has stolen her cubs from her, if she encounters a mirror, she has to fix her eyes upon it. And she delights so much in looking at the great beauty of her good form that she forgets to hunt those men who stole her cubs. She stands there as if seized.

What of this subtle shift, where the master assumes the feminine position himself? On one level, the masculine and feminine coding of his exempla appear interchangeable.[16] Little does it seem to matter whether an animal is typed by one gender or another, since the master's erudition empowers him to manipulate the interpretation as he sees fit. On a still deeper level, however, such a switch should alert us to just how tricky it proves for the master to wield his authority over his woman correspondent. The fact that he identifies subjectively with the tigress betrays a certain narcissism. Like the Freudian subject fascinated with women depicted as "beasts of prey," the master-narrator exhibits his own feminine weakness; his attraction is an expression of his feminized narcissistic impulses.[17] Drawn toward what he is trying desperately to overcome, the *Bestiaire* narrator exemplifies the male subject enthralled and repulsed by the self-absorbed, indifferent woman.

Herein lie the initial signs of the master's difficulty in imposing his intellectual authority on the woman reader. At the very juncture where the *Bestiaire* could use the tigress exemplum to set up the woman's obliging response to him, instead it collapses so-called feminine experience and the master's together. The bestiary commentary becomes a mode of autoreflection (or in Flann O'Brien's terms, of aestho-autogamy, of replicating the male self via a feminine persona). Furthermore, it comprises the place where the master scrutinizes himself obsessively via the woman. Not only is she the screen for his reveries, but she is supposed to be titillated by them. His learning becomes more and more self-engrossed.

This narcissism informs the narrator's revision of a number of exempla. The wolf, described as a timorous creature paralyzed by a man's gaze, is introduced to represent the first phases of attraction. Following bestiary tradition, the master considers the animal feminine, thus highlighting her silence: "She then lost the courage to refuse [him]" (elle a puis perdu le hardement d'escondire; Segre, 11). Yet once again the master applies the exemplum to his own predicament:

> Mais pour chu ke jou ne me puc[h] tenir ne souffrir de vous dire men corage avant ke je seüse riens del vostre, m'aveis vous eschivé. Che vous ai oï dire aucune fois. Et puis ke je sui primerains veüs, selonc le nature del leu j'en doi bien perdre le vois.
>
> (Segre, 11–12)

> But since I cannot bear and fail to tell you my intimate feelings before I know of yours, you have rejected me. I have heard you say this once. And since I am the first one spotted, according to the nature of the wolf, it is fitting that I lose my voice.

Claiming a feminine type of speechlessness for himself can be a self-serving gesture. The master is quick to assume "feminine" silence insofar as it contributes to his own self-reflection. By adopting the weaker, feminine position, the master also tries to persuade the woman to follow suit. Yet at the same time, playing the she-wolf is a gamble for the master. His conversion of a "feminine" trait into a "masculine" one unsteadies his authority. The fact that the master is suspended by such specular moments suggests that his own control is weakening. At times the game of feminizing the self is more fascinating to the master than the task of taking charge of the woman reader. He is caught also by a self-canceling gesture.

When this play with the gendered significance of an exemplum accompanies a change in the sequence of masculine and feminine types, the tensions over the master's command intensify. The case of the wolf is particularly interesting in this respect because it marks the transition from portraits of a suffering lover to those of a self-defensive and, of course, predatory woman. In other words, it is reintroduced at a point where the narrator endeavors to project the woman reader's response:

> Et ne vous mervelliés mie se j'ai l'amor de feme comparé a le nature del leu. . . . Et selonc le tierce nature si est ke s'elle va si avant de parolle ke li homme se perchoive k'ele l'aint, tout ausi ke li leus se vaingne par sa bouce de son pié, si set elle trop bien par force de paroles recovrir et ramanteler chu k'ele a trop avant alei. Car volentiers voet savor d'autrui chu k'ele ne veut mie c'on sache de lui, et d'omme k'elle quide k'il l'aint se set elle tres fermement garder. Ausi comme li wivre.
>
> (Segre, 15–17)

> And you should not wonder that I have compared woman's love to the nature of the wolf. . . . And according to its third nature, if the woman

goes so far with her words that the man realizes she loves him, just like the wolf who avenges herself biting the foot with her mouth, so too the woman knows how to recover and retrieve herself through her word when she has gone too far. For she wishes greatly to know of another what she never wants known of herself, and she knows how to protect herself stoutly against a man whom she believes to love her, like the viper.

In returning to the feminine gender of the wolf, the master focuses on a type of self-protective aggressiveness in the woman. No matter how authoritatively he comments on this trait, his commentary reveals his fear, for it raises the specter of women's vengeance. All the bestiary portraits here accentuate a violence in women that is cause for his alarm. The pattern is becoming clearer: the master-narrator first shows signs of weakness when he identifies narcissistically with the feminine; that weakness emerges full-blown when he complains of the destructiveness of women.

If we look closer at this pattern, the master's anxiety over control and his concern over a feminine violence are both linked to the woman's desire to know. "For she wishes greatly to know of another what she never wants known of herself, and she knows how to protect herself securely against a man whom she believes to love her, like the viper": a woman's appetite for knowledge is assessed as dangerous. And given the snake image, it can be fatally dangerous. By extension, the reader is figured as one who seeks knowledge in a savage manner. She is deemed wily and obstructionist because she aspires to her own self-knowledge. To portray women's "wish to know" in this negative light betrays the narrator's nervousness about its effects. The animus behind such a portrait is his urge to consider any knowledge acquired by women as a threat to his own. His desire involves limiting their knowledge. The aggressiveness he imputes to women thus increases in proportion to his fear over his ultimate sovereignty. The image of feminine harmfulness is commensurate with his own dread.

The Aristotelian character of the *Bestiaire* commentary suggests one further aspect of women's desire to know, namely, their rational potential. With the wolf/viper exemplum the master ruefully admits such a potential. In so doing, the distinctions between the Aristotelian metaphysical and biological understanding of rationality are brought to the fore. The incipit with which the master begins does not differentiate between women's and men's capacities. It defines the appetite for knowledge as a common human venture. By contrast, the biological theories informing the *Bestiaire* mark those differences. The distinctions between a rational man and a sensate woman imply that while she may possess the faculties, she is incapable of developing them.[18] Biologically speaking, women's possibility of knowing is an exclusively sensory affair. This Aristotelian discrepancy runs straight through the *Bestiaire*. And the tensions it generates place the master's power over controlling the woman reader in jeopardy. That is why the biological learning, with all its exempla, must override the metaphysical. That is also why his admission of women's rational potential is the place where he must labor to prove his authority. In this sense, the master's formula— "For she wishes greatly to know of another what she never wants known of herself"—refers as easily to himself. The affirmation of his authority entails barring women from the practice of knowledge, just as it targets them as its privileged object. The *Bestiaire* master subscribes, in effect, to Capellanus's elimination of a female clergy. One of the conditions for exercising intellectual mastery in clerical discourse is canceling out its female counterpart—a move displaced onto the woman herself.

It is worth underlining the crucial link between the shifting gendered valence of the bestiary exempla and the narrator's concern over his intellectual mastery. The extent to which he revises the significance of his material through gender intimates his increasing struggle in securing his dominant position. At times this struggle is configured narcissistically: the master grapples with the woman's resistance by filtering it through myriad self-reflections. At times the full brunt of the struggle is acted out and displaced through various representations of the predatory woman. Whichever, the anxiety over his authority grows steadily until in the second part of the *Bestiaire* it reaches a crisis point:

> Dont sui je mors, c'est voirs. Et ki m'a mort? Jou ne sai, ou vous ou jou, fors ke ambedoi i avons coupes. Ausi com de celi cui le seraine ocist, quant elle l'a endormi par son chant.... Si me samble ke le seraine i a grans coupes quant elle l'ocist en traïson, et li hom grans coupes quant il s'i croit. Et si je sui mors par itel ockoison, et vous et jou i avons coupes. Mais je ne vous ose susmetre traïson, si n'en metrai les coupes se sour moi non, et dirai ke je mismes me sui mors.
>
> (Segre, 29–31)

> So I am dead, it's true. And who has killed me? I don't know, either you or I, we are both guilty. Just as when the siren killed the man whom she has lulled to sleep by her song. . . . It seems to me that the siren is culpable for killing the man treacherously, and he as well for having been so trusting. And if I am dead through such a murder, both you and I are guilty. But I do not dare to put the treason on your account, so I shall assume the guilt myself and I'll say that I have killed myself.

With the trope of the lover's death, the master's dread over the limits of his authority is transformed into dread of his failure to maintain control. This fatal lapse is figured by none other than the siren. Half woman, half beast, such a hybrid being displays a human capacity of reasoning together with the most powerful senses. This combination places the *Bestiaire* master's control in the severest jeopardy.[19]

The siren is the only bestiary exemplum in the entire narrative identified explicitly as a human female. Herein lies her double importance: at a pivotal point in seducing the woman reader, the siren emblematizes the master's endeavor to convert his dread into an instrument of control. The identification of the siren with a woman enables him to reinforce biologically the link between the feminine and the noxious. It thereby creates the circumstances for blaming the woman reader. With the usual strategy of taking the weaker position, the *Bestiaire* narrator is shown to shift the burden of culpability (read: fear) away from himself, toward the woman. And this transfer involves another measure of narcissism. No sooner does he confess a joint guilt than he pretends to take it all upon himself. In an extravagantly servile gesture, he claims to have killed himself. So enormous is the anxiety of losing control that clerical discourse depicts man, narcissistically, as woman's willing victim. In the Aristotelian terms of the *Bestiaire*, not only is woman typed a nefarious creature, but man is represented succumbing to her animalistic and sensorial impulses.

This process of converting anxiety into a form of control culminates with the exemplum that represents splitting open the female body.

> Si m'en avés ochis de tel mort com Amours apartient. Mais se vous voliés vostre douc[h] costé ouvrir, tant que vous m'eussiés arousé de vostre bone volenté, et douné le biau douc[h] cuer desirré qui dedens le costé gist, vous m'ariés resuscité. Quar c'est la sovrainne medechine de moi aidier que de vostre cuer avoir.
>
> (Segre, 56–57)

> Thus you have killed me with the kind of death belonging to Love. But if you wanted to open your gentle side so that you sprinkled me with your good will and gave me the beautiful, gentle, and desired heart that lies in your side, you would have resuscitated me. For the sovereign medicine to help me is to have your heart.

The figure of the lover's death is countermanded here by that of a woman's bodily sacrifice. Having complained at such great length about feminine violence toward him, the master transfers that danger onto a female body, depicting how *she* suffers division. What's more, that division is figured as freely chosen. In the master's scenario, it is the woman who offers herself up physically to the lover. Like the pelican who feeds others with its own flesh, the woman is to submit to vivisection as proof of her desire to save the lover. As a rule, this pelican exemplum was interpreted theologically. Its image of breaking the body for others and of resuscitation was linked to Christ's sacrifice.[20] And yet as this exemplum is deployed in the master's scheme of things there is nothing charitable or life-giving about it. On the contrary, it signifies the most acute malaise over surrendering physically to women. Moreover, it signals the effort to displace the threat of scission onto her. In order to avoid his death, the master endeavors to persuade his woman reader to undergo it willingly herself.

Danielle Régnier-Bohler has argued that the figure of the dissected female body demonstrates the power it exerts upon the imagination of medieval clerisy.[21] Confronted with it, a clerkly persona such as the *Bestiaire* master proceeds to divide and conquer. By portraying the division and even dismemberment of the female body, he attempts to reestablish authority over it: he dehumanizes it as a brute form. Few images could better reveal the clerical determination to control his woman reader than that of the broken female body with its heart extracted.

It is worth noting that all three animals used to illustrate woman's necessary self-sacrifice are identified as male. "The father lion resuscitates his young"; "The father pelican pierces his side and sprinkles the young with the blood of his side" (Segre, 54, 55–56). With the third beast, the masculine identification is especially glaring: "You should give me your heart to be freed from my torment, as the beaver does. This is an animal with a member containing medicine . . . well it knows it is being hunted only for that member, so it sets upon it with its teeth, tears it off and drops it in the middle of the path (Segre, 57–58). What would be the effect of this figure of castration?[22] If we cannot fathom the medieval receptions of such a figure, particularly by women, at the very least we can acknowledge the masterly reflex to dictate women's behavior according to male types. The pressure brought to bear here is not only gendered, but fundamentally sexualized. That the image of torn male genitalia is the high point of the *Bestiaire*'s commentary bespeaks the depths of clerical insecurities. It also conveys this master's willful insistence to overcome them by imagining a woman's physical submission.

Lest there be any doubt about this aim, we need only look at a passage toward the end of the text:

> Et pour c[h]ou dist Ovides que amours et segnourie ne puent demourer ensanlle en une caiere. Et li poitevins qui en sievi Ovide si dist: "Non pot l'orgueill od l'amour remanoir"; et li autres qui redist: "Non pos poiar s'el non descen," il le dist pour c[h]ou que puis qu'ele estoit plus

haute et il plus bas, que a c[h]ou que il fuissent ouni il couvenoit que
ele descendist et il montast. Et la raisons de ceste iveleté si est prise de
c[h]ou que c[h]ou est un meïsmes chemins qui va de Saint Denis a Paris
et qui vient de Paris a Saint Denise.

(Segre, 88–89)

Wherefore also Ovid said that love and mastery cannot remain together on a single throne; and the Poitevin who followed Ovid in this,
said, "Pride cannot coexist with love." And that other for his part said,
"I cannot ascend if she does not descend" meant that, since she was
higher and he lower, she must descend and he ascend to be one. The
reason for this equality is to be found in the fact that the same path
goes from St. Denis to Paris as from Paris to St. Denis.

(Beer, 31)

In the proverbial formulation "I cannot ascend if she does not descend,"
the *Bestiaire* master discloses the unspoken constant of much medieval
vernacular literature. While the majority of personae and poets proceed on
this basis, they invert the roles and simulate a woman in ascendancy, with
the lover, correspondingly, down and—often—out. By sharp contrast, our
narrator acknowledges the dialectic animating representations of the infe-
rior male persona. In order to insure the master's authority, the *dame*
must be brought down. The image of the master/lover on the rise confirms
the objective of his ultimate dominance.

Nevertheless, this precept is phrased in the diplomatic terms of parity.
Quoting no less than the *magister amoris*, Ovid, the *Bestiaire* narrator maintains that erotic relations between men and women are not compatible with the idea of sovereignty—a phrase Jeanette Beer translates in
terms of mastery. Her choice is well founded, for if we continue to the end
of the passage, an Aristotelian order of intellectual mastery reasserts itself.
Equality means establishing each persona in his/her rightful station. It involves a hierarchy that necessarily places the woman in a lesser and beholden relation to the master.

Following directly after this analysis of equality/mastery is the one and
only first person plural of the text: "And so I say that if you desire that we
love each other . . ." (ausi di jou ke se vous voliés ke nous nos entra-
missiesmes; Segre, 89). That the master presumes the woman's longing
for their love demonstrates just how this equality is to be understood. This
is a virtual prescription. The woman is represented in a position in which
she is not to interpret her equality as she so desires but rather according to
the master's design of their common purpose. His speaking for her illustrates the desired outcome of the master's work—that his intellectual
mastery hold the ultimate power over the woman's reactions.

As it is, the *Bestiaire* does not substantiate that power. Such masterly narratives do not, in the end, yield any sign of the woman reader's compliance. The course of the master's learned commentary leads to a hiatus. No matter how subtle or comprehensive his analysis, the impetus to realize his authority through the woman's action is interrupted. His massive advantage in learning does not enable the master to bring every subject and every interlocutor under his control. When it comes to women interlocutors, the vernacular master is not ready to make a *determinatio* (determination)—that concluding stage in scholastic disputation where every question is finally resolved and every interlocutor falls into line behind the *magister*. Ironically, he is situated in much the same unsettling position as the disciple. The difference is that the disciple internalizes his insecurity while the master externalizes his. The first traces of the master's anxiety appear in the vacillating gender types of his bestiary lessons. It breaks through explicitly in the expression of his own death. Faced with this unnerving picture, the master struggles with his sense of loss of control by projecting it onto the woman interlocutor.[23] The image of her fractured body offers a spectacular instance of his externalized fears.

Forcing the Issue of Women

If the idea of mastering women intellectually is left hanging in the balance, masterly narratives such as the *Bestiaire* continue to force the issue. As a whole, they suppress the problems of achieving such mastery by persisting in the attempt to do so. Even in the most precarious moments, the master resorts to shows of intellectual force—to attempting to overpower a subject such as women when it threatens to defeat him. While the *Bestiaire* does not explicitly represent such force, there are other, related didactic narratives that give us a clear sense of what it might involve. The *Commens d'amour*, often attributed to Richard de Fournival, offers the following account as part of a master's commentary on man's erotic life:

> Si avint une fois ke, par nuit, il entra el gardin de la chambre ou s'amie gisoit, et attendi tant k'ele issi hors pour li deporter; dont fist il tant par carnins et par enchantemens, dont il savoit assés, qu'il le fist endormir emmi liu del gardin. Et chil qui desirans estoit et escauffés, jut a li carnelment pour chou ke se volentés fust acomplie; et puis si fist .I. petit d'escrit, et en cel escrit estoient escrit teil mot: "Chis chastiaus qui lonc tamps a esté assegiés par grant force d'engien, a hui esté brisiés"; et puis prist .I. petit de sa robe a enseignes et le mist avoec l'escript, et

mist l'escript deseure le cose qui tant avoit esté desiree, et le laissa toute
descouverte dusques a le poitrine, et s'en parti. Et quant li carnins fu
passés, et ele s'esvilla, et se trouva ensi descouverte et trouva l'escript
mis desus le fleur de ses membres, si le liut, et vit bien ke chils i avoit
esté a sa volenté; adont dist ele: "En .VII. ans vient aighe a son caneil;
tant cache on le cerf ke on le prent; et j'ai esté prise, et chils a eu le
merchi qu'il queroit, ne mie par mon gré ne par ma volenté; et de ceste
premiere merchi ne me seit il gré si a droit, et de la seconde, s'il l'avoit
par ma volenté, il m'en saroit gré; dont li couvient il avoir."[24]

And so it happened one time that at night, he entered the garden of the
room where his lady was lying, and he waited for her to come out to
enjoy herself. Through various charms and spells, about which he knew
a great deal, he put her to sleep in the middle of the garden. And he,
who was most desirous and excited, took carnal pleasure in her until he
accomplished his will. And then he made a little text and in his writing
were written the words: "This castle that was so long under siege by
great force of cunning was finally broken." And then he took a small
bit of her dress as a sign and placed it with the writing and he put the
writing on the very thing so long desired. Leaving her uncovered up to
the chest, he departed. And when the spell broke and she awoke to discover herself nude and with the written note placed on the flower of
her body, she read it and saw that he had had his way with her. So she
said: "In seven years, water finds its channel; the stag is chased for so
long that he is finally taken. I have been taken and he who had the
favor he sought, had it neither with my pleasure nor consent. Of the
first favor, if he had the right, he is not grateful to me for it; of the second, if he had it with my consent, he would have been grateful to me
for it; so it is fitting for him to have it."

That the lover is figured as having sex with his unwitting female partner is
the least surprising element of this scene. Though veiled by dreams, the
commonplace of a woman's sexual yielding is barely occulted. The narration sets it up as something inevitable, even banal. What *is* out of the ordinary here is the conjunction of the violated female body and the lover's
writing. Her sexual anatomy is entwined with his textualization of it: "and
he put the writing on the very thing for so long desired." The inscription
of sex gains a carnal dimension, so much so that the commentary of the
masterful lover seems to rival the act itself. Moreover, what is written represents a quintessential allegorical formulation. The lover's message is cast
in those familiar Ovidian terms of an assault on love's castle. As such it
epitomizes a widely used clerical discourse on women, one that is the particular privilege of the elite *magistri*.

Is this not a masterful show of force—this time depicted physically?

Unlike the *Bestiaire* master, the *Commens* persona exercises his control over the woman carnally and then, as if to confirm it definitively, he leaves a written trace. The outstanding sign of his authority is the ability to textualize his experience, to turn it into learning. The work mentioned by the *Bestiaire* narrator at the end of his letter—"but if you had kept me in your service, I would show you through my work" (mais se vous m'avies retenue, je vous monsteroie bien per ovre; Segre, 102)—is doubly achieved here. The *Commens* masterly figure enjoys the fruits of his labor both physically and intellectually.

I single out the *Commens* scene for two reasons. First of all, it offers an emblem for the clerical tendency to transform intellectual mastery over women into a form of domination. Indeed, it makes clear how such a dominance is represented invariably in carnal terms. The man's allegorical writing affixed to the woman's sex illustrates the way in which masterful exegesis can slip into the domination of women by representing their physical submission. Learning is proven masterful insofar as it considers the issue of women's sexual yielding. Such scenes reveal how closely the clerical practices of disputation and writing are bound up with figures of subordinating woman. To dispute is to argue the case for women's necessary and proper deference. And what passes for textual knowledge is a wealth of material on women as carnal entities. In fact, if we look back over the various didactic narratives we have surveyed, they all promote a final lesson of disputing and commenting authoritatively on women's bodies. From didactic texts to allegories, the task of entering the masters' ranks involves knowing women in a physical sense. Although such knowledge does not comprise carnal knowledge strictly speaking, it is no less powerful. Therein lies the potential for symbolic domination. Representing masters and disciples disputing the subject of sex with women can be a domineering form of discourse. Whether this domination is consistent throughout medieval vernacular narrative is unclear. The *Bestiaire*, as well as the narratives of discipleship, would suggest otherwise. But the principal aim underlying the spectrum of didactic works is nonetheless to establish such symbolic domination.

The *Commens* scene is telling for a second reason. By representing the woman's reaction to her rape, it introduces the issue of a woman's response in general. Within the narrative, the woman's reaction is largely complicitous. Speaking a proverbial language of popular wisdom, she confirms the master's allegorical *sententia*: it is fitting that women be taken. While this woman is figured regretting her unaccounted-for pleasure, at the same time she envisages her likely consent and the man's gratitude. In this master's rendition, the woman comes around to acknowledging how her consent ratifies the fait accompli of a man's will.

Beyond the narrative, however, this issue of a woman's response raises questions about the impact of the master's authoritative learning about women. No matter how uniformly such learning is relayed through the didactic and allegorical narratives we have been studying, the very idea of women responding challenges it. From an oppositional position—even according to the master's criteria—the woman's response implicitly disputes the sexualized learning about women. The woman's response thus raises a still larger question about the symbolic domination created by the vernacular discourse of mastery. How extensive is this pattern of domination in high medieval French narrative? If we begin to think in terms of responses not as individual speech acts, but as distinct texts, that pattern may not persist uncontested. Conceptualizing the discourse of mastery from the point of view of respondents other than the male disciple may open up a different picture.

2

PROLIFERATING RESPONSES

4   Contrary to What Is Said

The *Response au Bestiaire d'amour*
and the Case for a Woman's Response

What kind of beast would turn its life into words?
Adrienne Rich

I should not seem to be teaching Minerva herself.
Héloïse

As the medieval clergy conceived of it, the "response" (*responsio*) was pivotal to the workings of intellectual mastery.[1] In the structure of disputation, it provided a way for the disciple to assume an authoritative role and argue the master's knowledge in his stead.[2] It was the occasion for establishing his position. This process reveals a paradox inherent to the response, and examining its paradoxical character brings us straight to the problem posed by a woman's response. On the one hand, the numerous works designated responses appear repetitive, reiterating the terms established by the master's work. Precisely because the response follows that lead, it is caught in the circuit of the always already said. While it may elaborate upon the masterly prototype, the response serves to reproduce that type, with the result that the respondent is a mimic, cast in the role of yes-man. On the other hand, the response represents a virtual space for difference. Rather than conforming to the contours of the master's earlier work, the response can diverge from its dictates. Point for point, the response can answer in opposition and thereby create a type of counterbalancing resistance. Far from confirming a redundant structure, the response jeopardizes it. Dissembling and combative, in this sense it breaks ranks.

True to its disputational spirit, clerical writing during the high Middle Ages cultivated the paradoxical response form because it could vent various agonistic impulses and in the end resolve them. This is particularly evident in the didactic narratives called *enseignements* that we studied in chapter 1.

As we saw, the master/disciple rapport was highly charged: both figures were drawn together and polarized by a drive for intellectual control that worked itself out within the framework of their disputation. In fact, it was the very process of working this drive through—of responding in contestatory *and* iterative fashion—that prepared certain disciples to become master. Far from countermanding each other, the affirming and the oppositional aspects of the response served to secure the same end: the master's dominance and the disciple's eventual graduation to that position.

The thirteenth-century *Dialogues de Salemon et Marcoul* offers a case in point. In the exchanges between an exemplary wise man and his protégé, Marcoul represents an implicit challenge to Salemon's wisdom.[3] Yet the fact that the lesser Marcoul comes each time to reformulate that wisdom insures the continuity of Salemon's authority:

> Dame otroie a ami
> Cors et cuers autresi,
> Ce dit Salemons;
> Fax amanz sanz merci
> On meint beax cors trahi,
> Marcol li respont.
> (stanza 12)

When a lady pledges herself to her lover, she pledges him heart and body; so says Salemon. False lovers are without mercy and have betrayed many beautiful bodies, Marcoul responds to him.

In this kernel of debate between master and student over women, Marcoul's response makes him complicitous with the system of mastery. While it qualifies the master's definition of women, the response still commits Marcoul to the system. So it is with many contemporaneous sapiential narratives; their staging of debates between *magister* figures such as Aristotle and the inscribed audience of initiates revolves around the dual quality of the initiate's response.[4] By responding to the master's pronouncements, the inscribed audience also undergoes the rite of passage of disputation. Their paradoxical response seals the legitimacy of both the knowledge they are disputing and the system in which it functions. The mechanism of responses works not only to reinforce the complementary positions of dominance and subordination, as Hans-Robert Jauss has argued, but also to authenticate the master's authoritative knowledge by means of the respondent.[5] Rising to respond thus involves participating in the ongoing consolidation of the hierarchical order of mastery.[6]

This reinforcing function is so powerful that it even informs narratives structured only implicitly as responses. Take the example of the *Livre*

7. Responding in writing. *La Response au Bestiaire d'amour.*
Vienna, Österreichische Nationalbibliothek Cod. 2609, fol. 32.
Courtesy of the Österreichische Nationalbibliothek.

d'Enanchet or the contemporaneous *Chastoiement d'un père à son fils.*
They present their sententious material within the framework of a
father/son or elder/disciple debate. Through the animated give-and-take
of both parties, the father/elder's teachings are finally imparted. The disciple's responsiveness is similarly pivotal insofar as it supplies some
obstacle internal to the system of mastery while upholding its logic.
Combining a deep-seated sense of respect with a measure of insubordina-
tion, these implicit responses constitute the site where the master figure
confirms the operations and apparatus of clerical learning.

By delineating the paradoxical aspects of the clerical response form, we
can begin to see the problem posed by a woman's response (Figure 7). If
the facets of contentiousness and iteration that define a response apply

easily to texts attributed to women, their net result does not. While we have little trouble cataloguing myriad representations in vernacular narrative of women replying oppositionally or iteratively to their male interlocutors, rarely does such narrative yield the profile of a woman master. While the two sides of the response are the veritable prerequisites for the male student entering the system of mastery, in the case of the woman respondent they suggest the limits of her access. They seem to furnish the reasons for her exclusion and progressive objectification by that same system. According to the Ovidian and Aristotelian orders of mastery, the paradoxical response generates, in the case of women, a non sequitur: a female disciple cannot enter the ranks of *magistri*.

This inquiry into responses attributed to women enables us to break through to the other side of this clerical model of representation. To begin with, doing so involves recognizing the pervasiveness of the tenacious clerical topoi about women during the Middle Ages. It also means reckoning with the tenacious influence they exert over critical discourse today. Across the range of didactic literature, it was the figure of women saying "Yes" and "No," of women responding both iteratively and antagonistically, that pointed to their disqualification from any type of intellectual mastery. The conventional scholastic analysis of feminine responsiveness justified taking women in hand. Indeed the recommendation became an integral element of vernacular clerical learning. In the case of the *Bestiaire d'amour*, the choice of merging the master and lover personae intensifies the clerical desire to formulate a woman's response as a tacit invitation to ravishment. The *Bestiaire* narrator's mastery is bound up with the assumption that she would be his yes-woman or that, prevaricating as ever, her contestatory response would signal her eventual capitulation—a far cry from her ever joining his ranks.

Both these designs for the woman's response dramatize the most widely held patriarchal presumptions about female speech. In the case of the iterative response, as we have seen, the issue of redundancy is particularly exaggerated with women interlocutors. Because the medieval clergy interpreted the figure of Eve in such a way as to assert the "natural" repetitiveness of female speech, the woman's response was logically deemed excessive and derivative. Even when this redundancy is cast pejoratively, and Eve is represented as overeager in her responsiveness to the devil, her aptitude for being a yes-woman is underscored. "Original sin" is a consequence of the first woman being too quick to answer. With the oppositional response as well, we find corroborating evidence of a longstanding clerical attempt to conceptualize negativity as feminine. The Ovidian pattern of representing women interlocutors as obstreperous enables the narrators to exacerbate antagonism usefully so as to validate the operations of mastery.

From a clerical perspective, characterizing a response as adversarial and as the work of women amounts to much the same thing; they offer similar ploys in securing the master's authority. This is a ploy that can be used by critics today. When Alexandre Leupin describes the *Bestiaire* respondent as "a lady who functions as the text's point of refraction, abstention, opposition," he restates a postulate perfectly consonant with those of medieval masterly personae.[7] The woman's response is understood to be negative insofar as it provides the tension necessary to the functioning of mastery. This it does without ever seriously menacing such mastery and without ever including women. In critiquing clerical compositions of the feminine, the danger lies, then, in duplicating or assimilating them to a significant degree.

That the woman's response exemplifies the paradoxical character of the clerical genre, that it accommodates the putative conundrum of women's language: all these signs should alert us to the task of rethinking this category. Further, given the tendency of modern critics to recapitulate the medieval terms of the woman's response in their own work, it is all the more pressing to envisage different models. Are there different ways to contemplate the response inflected as feminine? How do we approach the woman's response in a way that acknowledges the determining influence of its clerical frame without discounting other valences? Such questions call for another critical point of departure. At the very least, they suggest the possibility that the woman's response can be conceptualized differently by modern-day critics. To do so opens up debate over the monolithic character of medieval clerical culture in the vernacular and its central claim of reproducing intellectual mastery unerringly. And these questions chart territory cut by fault lines in the monopoly of magisterial learning—fault lines that betray the disturbances caused by women's involvement uncovered in chapter 1.

The category of the woman's response thus becomes a key site for interrogating the structures of intellectual mastery and critiquing its symbolic domination. This critique builds on the disciple's discourse, which already brings to the surface some of the inherent weaknesses of mastery. The inscribed woman respondent occupies a disputational position similar to the disciple's. But because its critique focuses on the effects of mastery, the woman's response goes beyond the disciple's to contest the problem of the symbolic domination of masterly writing. This contesting, let me emphasize, does not involve women alone. I use the term "woman's response" to describe an attribution. The woman's response can refer to clerical forms within the world of mastery that are merely voiced by women. But the fact that such attributions were made helped create the occasion for actual women to rise to the challenge of responding. With the advances in lay literacy during the later Middle Ages, the clerical version of a woman's response inside the masterly domain invited women outside to forge their own.

I wish to broaden the issue of the woman's response considerably— beyond that of the speech act. The response also represents a genre of text in action. As such, it is linked progressively with a variety of textual registers, with philosophical as well as amorous discourse. Such an inquiry leads to pondering the implications of individual response texts, for they signal reactions to the predominant textual practices of the clerisy. By working outward through concentric interpretative circles, my exploration of the woman's response will then move in turn from discursive strategies to specific episodes of public debate over clerical textual practices. As I suggested in the introduction, the largest, most ambitious interpretative circle will thus examine the woman's response as a social movement that calls to account clerical conceptions and figurations of women.

Because the notion of woman's response is relatively unfamiliar, I shall begin with the simplest concerns: how to respond? why respond? who is responding? The *Response au Bestiaire d'amour* serves as a test case for exploring these questions.[8] Not only does this late-thirteenth-century narrative constitute one of the earliest replies to a master's text already in circulation, but it responds with remarkable erudition to the style and substance of that text. Engaging with the master, the *Response* begins by commenting on the creation of women. It takes up the master's eroticized exegesis of bestiary exempla point for point so as to question his interpretations and their underlying intentions. This questioning results in a meditation on the public force of language. For these reasons, the *Response au Bestiaire* will also serve as a fulcrum text: as I hope will become clear over the next four chapters, it structures my thought on the phenomenon of the woman's response per se.

How to Respond?

The woman answering the *Bestiaire* master grounds her response in what I shall call a principle of contrariety:

> Tout autel vous puis je dire que puis que je seroie contraire a vostre volenté et vous a le moie, et que nous nous descorderiens d'abit et de volenté, je ne me porroie acorder a vostre volenté comment que vous vous acordissiés a moi.
>
> (Segre, 113)[9]

8. In the heat of debate. *La Response au Bestiaire d'amour.* Vienna, Österreichische Nationalbibliothek, Cod. 2609, fol. 34. Courtesy of the Österreichische Nationalbibliothek.

> Likewise, I could tell you that since I would be contrary to your will and you to mine, and we would disagree both in habit and in will, I could not agree with your will however much you might agree with me.

This is no mere disagreement (Figure 8). From the outset, the respondent introduces a logical structure that establishes a principle of contrariety and sets it in relation to contradiction. Whereas contradictory objects are mutually exclusive, thus canceling each other out logically, contraries constitute coexisting differences. That is, they are defined oppositionally to each other in a way that admits the separate distinctiveness of each other. Contrary pairs can stand side by side despite their evident opposite properties.

This logical distinction between contrariety and contradiction is often muddied today. The result is that they are conflated, understood to signify a single, amorphous type of negation. But in their original Aristotelian formulation in the square of oppositions, the distinction was rigorously maintained.[10] If we recall the preponderant Aristotelian substratum for

most high-medieval masterly works, especially for Richard de Fournival's
Bestiaire, the woman respondent's choice of this logic is noteworthy. On
one level, this contrary logic places her writing on a par with her interlocutor's: she is represented as his intellectual match. On another, her use
of the terms of contrariety sets her at complete odds with several of the
Master Philosopher's most formidable theories. It transforms the notion
of contrariety to women's advantage.[11] In effect, the *Bestiaire* respondent
works *a contrario* so as to argue against the Aristotelian postulate of the
incomplete woman and its corollary of her irrationality. That the respondent retrieves one element of Aristotle's thought in order to contest
another means turning the entire corpus of Aristotelian learning against
itself. This iconoclastic brand of argumentation undergirds her contrary
choice of how to respond.

Questions of knowledge offer the first arena in which the issue of
contrariety is tested in the *Response*. In the prologue, the respondent acknowledges that any transaction in knowledge operates differently according to gender. Furthermore, given the relations established by the *Bestiaire*,
a woman recipient of the master's teaching risks being adversely affected.
But here this sort of scholastic discrimination prompts her to espouse a
knowledge specific to women:

> Et pour che, biaus maistres, vous proi je que selonc che que vous m'avés
> dit ne tenés mie a vilenie se je m'aïe de vostre sens, selonc che que je en
> ai retenu. Car encore ne puisse je savoir tout che que vous savés, si sai je
> aucune chose que vous ne savés mie. Dont il m'est bien mestiers que
> je m'en aïe selonc che que li besoins en est grans a moi, qui feme sui.
>
> (Segre, 106)

> Dear master, I ask you in accordance with what you have told me, not
> to take it badly if I avail myself of your meaning insofar as I have
> understood it. For although I cannot know all that you know, I do know
> something which you do not know at all. So it behooves me to take ad-
> vantage of it, since I, as a woman, have great need of it.

This respondent maps out her own intellectual province. The *Bestiaire*
master's erudition notwithstanding, she reserves for herself something
inaccessible to him. Her distinct and separate knowledge is fundamentally
allied with the subjective enunciation: "je... qui feme sui." Not only does
she recognize gender's part in the production of knowledge, but she asserts her intellectual power on that basis. The claim to her epistemological
field is made on the strength of her subjective identity: one gesture follows from the other. Together they suggest this respondent's very different approach to learning. Instead of meeting the master's erudition

head-on, in the habitual agonistic stance, the woman respondent defers rhetorically. She bows and scrapes in a familiar posture of humility. Yet this self-deprecating manner, which Hélène Cixous has dubbed wittily the rhetoric of *sexecuser*, is the very means whereby she can move past the stark, mutually reinforcing confrontations between antagonists.[12] A semblance of acquiescence can point the way out of a magisterial system of controlling conflict. By configuring difference in nonexclusive, nonadversarial terms, the *Bestiaire* response posits a woman's knowledge that is not defined in contradiction to the master's. It advances an oppositional epistemology. From the very beginning, this respondent argues for a specifically feminized relation of contrariety with the world of clerical learning.

In this context, she sets into play an alternate account of female generation. Having distinguished the particular terms of her knowledge, the respondent proposes a different model of creation. Her version recoups the theory of dual creation from Genesis 2, a theory discounted by orthodox Christianity and yet widely circulating in apocryphal form in Talmudic exegesis and elsewhere.[13] In other words, the female persona deploys a reading at complete odds with the canonical account of Adam's rib. Its deviance is twofold; for not only does it describe the woman's birth as simultaneous and independent of the man's, but it relates how he murders her:

> Dont il avint que quant dex eut doune lun et lautre vie et cascun forme et doune a cascun sens naturel, il lor conmanda sa volente a faire. Et ne demora mie longues apries quant adans ochist sa feme por aucun courouc dont ie ne doi ci faire mention. Dont saparut nostre sires a adan et li demanda pour coi il avoit ce fait. Il respondi ele ne m'estoit rien, et pour cou ne la pooie iou amer.
>
> (Vienna 2609, fol. 32 verso; Segre, 107)

> Then it happened that when God had given to one and the other life, form, and natural intelligence, He commanded them to do his will. And it was not long after that Adam killed his woman out of anger, which I shall not discuss here. Our Lord then appeared to Adam and asked him why he had done this, and Adam replied, "She meant nothing to me and so I could not love her."

Through such a scene of murderous violence, the woman's response develops its contrariety in two further ways. First of all, it confronts the preeminent topos of a nefarious woman apt to kill the lover. If the *Bestiaire* lover complains of the siren's lure, here, the respondent points out, the first woman is killed without provocation. Her answer to the master's symbolic death is to match it and deflect it with her own. Moreover, her rendition of Adam's crime offers a parable of man's enormous difficulty in entertaining any contrary element, for he is represented killing out of sheer ambivalence toward Eve's existence: "ele ne m'estoit rien." His reflexive reaction is to strike out her being; even in Eden, man's antipathy toward a potential female rival generates violence against her.

Despite its violent and misogynistic terms, the lesson of this parable is far from grim. By reviving an alternative account of woman's genesis, the respondent comes to argue for a superior female composition. This is an argument concerning matter well known by the late thirteenth century: "Adam was made from the mud of the earth while Eve was made from Adam's rib" (de materia qui Adam factus de limo terre, Eva de costa Ade).[14] The respondent bolsters this argument with the language of Aristotelian materialism and contends that the first woman's murder occasions a new female creation of more suitable material, "de mains soufissant matere."[15] Made from peerless ingredients and still further refined, the species of woman is a handiwork apart. Since God continues to work over the matter of the first man, he produces in the woman a better artifact— "une matiere amendee" (fol. 34). The second, female object builds on the original, enhancing it. No mere pejorative sign of derivation, the respondent's Eve exemplifies a perfectible human being. Such an account is confounding insofar as Eve's origin in the male body does not prove her inferiority, as Aristotelian wisdom and countless medieval commentaries would have it. On the contrary, it proves her greater integrity.[16] While the respondent retains the shell of this well-known scholastic argument, she changes its very matter to discomfiting effect.

I play with this pun on "matter" here because it is in perfect keeping with the respondent's tactics. Her experiment with the term "matter" salvages it from its usual disenfranchising Aristotelian context and casts it anew. This she accomplishes by parodying the concept of sufficient matter (*souffisant matieres*), usually reserved for the concept "man" to the detriment of "insufficient woman." By forging the notion of "improved matter," the respondent can place a woman in a category apart. Her recuperation of Aristotelian formulae turns the criterion of matter to women's advantage, for it refers to both the raw materials of creation and those of writing. The two "matters" are often combined so that the respondent's text reads like a multilevel commentary on this primordial issue. Again and again she returns to it, developing the links between the creation of the first woman and the fashioning of her text. What matter makes up her writing? In the wake of her anti-Aristotelian meditation on matter, the respondent envisages a female matter relatively free of disabling connotations.[17]

This notion of matter as writing material sets up her exploration of the master's characteristic figurative language. In exegetical style, she approaches tropes as the building blocks of clerical composition. And the figure singled out epitomizes the clerical project to render women figuratively. In the respondent's terms, it is "the castle that is woman." This figure of the female body as military fortification is so endemic that most medieval works assess it from the outside alone—as a facade to scale, a construction to besiege and overwhelm. The only perspective is that of the aggressor. Remarkably, this woman's response places us within the castle wall:

> Et por cou qe chastiaus de feme si est souent pourement porueus solonc cou que dex si ne douna mie si ferme pooir a la feme come il fist al home: mest il mestiers de meillor garde auoir qe il ne feroit uous qi hom estes solonc cou que deuant est traitie. Et uoel uenir a cou que com il soit ensi que dex uous ait done plus ferme pooir: ne fu il pas si uileins que il ne nos donast noble entendement de nous garder tant come nous nos uorrons metre a deffense. Et por cou que iou ai oi dire que il nest plus de faintisses que de soi recroire tant come force puist durer. Iou ai mestier que ie gietie de mes engiens au deuant et face drecier perieres et mangouniaus ars atour et arbalestres a cest chastel deffendre que iou uoi que uous auez asailli.
>
> (Segre, 105)

> The castle that is woman is so poorly protected because God gave much less firm power to woman than he did to man. It is necessary for me to be on close guard against you who are a man as was mentioned before. And so I wish to come to this point: since God gave to you this greater power, it would have been wicked if God had not given us noble intelligence so that we can protect and defend ourselves properly. And so I have heard it said that it is hardly cowardly to renounce the fight so long as force prevails. It is crucial that I employ my shrewdness, that I know how to deploy my weaponry in order to defend this castle, which I see you have already assailed.

The response makes over the castle so that the audience can observe the trope working from a contrary position—from inside the female body. There is no impetus to dismantle the predominant figurative structure. Rather, the move is to open it up and examine it ironically from the inside out. The castle still stands, but in disarming fashion it is represented subjectively, as feminine. From this rarely adopted vantage point the respondent converts the standard elements of the erotic trope according to an explicitly defensive vision.

Central to this problem of defense in the *Bestiaire Response* is a conception of power that contrasts the physical force of man with the intelligence of woman. Such a conception redresses the usual balance of power whereby the cognitive belongs exclusively to a man on the attack. Here, by contrast, the woman is credited with rational faculties and her putative physical vulnerability acts as a cover for them. As Elizabeth Janeway has elucidated, the patriarchal presumption of feminine weakness can translate for women into a show of improbable strength.[18] By protesting her limitations, the respondent, in fact, musters her own intellectual resources. What's more, she exercises them in her defense. The flourish of naming weaponry, "perieres et mangouniaus ars atour et arbalestres," identifies a woman's resources in the very figurative idiom that is, as a rule, marked off-limits to her. Unlike the women in Capellanus's *De amore*, this respondent is adept at allegorical discourse and uses it to construct her rhetorical defense. Not only does the *Response* disclose the destructive motives behind a hallmark clerical symbol such as the castle, but it represents a woman wielding the master's figurative language to her own ends.

Such a strategy is conceived in terms of the recurring issue of matter:

> Premierement iou uoel qe uous sacies de qoi iou me uoel deffendre contre le premier assaut de cest arriere ban que uous auez amene sor mi. Iou qui principaus sui de la guerre ameintenir vous fac sauoir qe se uous fussies auises dune chose dont iou me sent forte et garnie que molt le doit on tenir a merueilleuse folie. Et ne tenes mie a mencoigne la raisson tele come ie le uous dirai solonc cou qe iou lai oie. Il est uoirs qe souent auient que li fors sil ceurt sus le foible por ce que il ne sait pooir de deffendre. Et por cou que uos cuidies que ie meusse pooir de deffendre mauez uos del premier enuaie. Or uous semble qe uous ne seres ia recreus. tant come alaine uous dure. Et iou mestres si me deffenc de ce que iou daussi soffissant matere sui engenree et faite come uous iestes qui seure me coures et le uous uoel prouuer ensi.
>
> (Segre, 105–6)

> First of all, I want you to know, I can defend myself against the first assault that your writing has directed toward me. I, who am the principal defender in the war, must advise you that I feel strong and well guarded, so much so that some might take it as wild folly. Don't take lightly the reasons that I am telling you according to what I have heard. True, there are those who secure their strength on the weak since they do not know how to defend themselves; so you may think that I do not have the power to defend myself and that you have me at the first shot. It may seem to you that you will never be vanquished so long as you have breath. But I, master, defend myself because I was engendered from just such sufficient matter as you who are secure, and I want to prove it to you in this manner.

The feminized trope of the castle constitutes an inviolable defense because of its makeup. Since the first woman is distinguished from Adam on the basis of her material, so too are the respondent's figures. The bedrock of a contrary female substance transforms the significance of her symbolic structures. Engendered from a different, yet equally suitable matter, she is depicted as one who takes the initiative in conceptualizing her body anew and defending it rhetorically. Thereby she is shown to gain a masterful position. This last point may appear dubious. The epithet, *maistres*, slips in subtly, like so many gestures of respect. We are accustomed to read it in terms of the clerkly interlocutor. But the phrasing is unlike any other in the text. It can qualify her subjective stance. This possibility of it referring to the female subject—*iou mestres*—inflects it otherwise. For the woman respondent to articulate her subjective power in a reformed symbolic language implies a mode of mastery.

The chance of her assuming this title calls into question the relations governing the *Bestiaire* and its *Response*. The figure of a female master reverses the conventional dynamic between an irreproachable *magister* and his pusillanimous female pupil. This reversal is all the more apparent in a woman's response that puts on the mantle of scholastic authority with such ease. Her text reads as a scholastic set piece comparable to the *Bestiaire* and far surpassing most contemporaneous Old French texts. Small wonder then that the *Response* pushes still further the connection between female matter and symbolic language.

The respondent's next argumentative move is paradoxical, for it reaffirms the orthodox hierarchy "in which the woman should obey the man, and man the earth, and the earth the Lord Creator who rules over all creatures" (dont doit la feme obeir al home et li hom a la terre et la terre a diu ki creeres fu et souverains de toute creature; fol. 34). The respondent can afford to reiterate the quintessential scholastic view of world order because a woman's domain has already been staked out. At the heart of this divinely ordained system there is a designated material site at complete odds with it. Yet situating womankind in this different matrix does not necessitate destroying the superstructure. Beyond any mere iconoclasm, the respondent's debate with the master bespeaks the desire to design a rhetorical and epistemological space for women. This is a space both contiguous with and outside the bounds of man's dominion. While located within the conventional superstructure, it is also disengaged from it. At the very moment of taking on the master, the narrative lays out this contrary space as a legitimizing ground for a woman's response.

I have teased out the prologue of the *Response au Bestiaire* line by line because it clearly articulates the axiom of woman's contrariety. Beginning with beginnings, this narrative posits a distinctive female matter, and with it a different epistemology. On these twin bases, the respondent can answer the master efficaciously. For she is positioned right away in a contrary relation to the master's erudition and can thus dispute his propositions. Having forged a way to respond, the narrative moves on to confront the problem of a dominant figurative language. It tackles the question: why? If the prologue lays the groundwork for a woman's response, then the main narrative shows why it is crucial for her to answer the master. The *Response* builds on the incipit alluding to the potential damage of linguistic constructions: "Nothing should be said or done to hurt a person" (a cose nule dire ne faire par coi nus ne nule soit empiries; Segre, 105). The focus is on gauging the effects of clerical composition.

Why Respond?

Faced with the master's bestiary figures, the respondent makes the following observation:

> Car je sai vraiement qu'il n'est beste qui tant fache a douter comme douche parole qui vient en dechevant. . . . Car vos paroles ont mains et piés, et sanle vraiement que nule raison ne doi avoir de vous escondire cose que vous voeilliés.
>
> (Segre, 118)
>
> For truly I know that there is no beast who should be feared like a gentle word that comes deceiving. . . . For your words have hands and feet, and it truly seems that I can have no reason to refuse you anything that you want.

In her hands, the habitual figurative equation breaks down. The bestiary metaphor no longer refers to an aspect of human erotics but to language, specifically the master's "gentle deceptive word."[19] The respondent's analysis goes on to demonstrate the treacherous character of his bestiary formula. It is not the woman who is dangerous like a siren or vulture, but rather the master's discourse, which transforms her symbolically into such a creature. The "beasts" to watch out for are those figures describing women in consistently noxious terms.

The respondent's metaphorical equation is doubly ironic. Rending the veil of the master's metaphors, it unmasks the manipulative design behind the prevailing symbolic language. Since her metaphor identifies the master's "soft word" as an instrument of deception, it implies that all those sinister, threatening, female personae in the master's *Bestiaire* are a form of

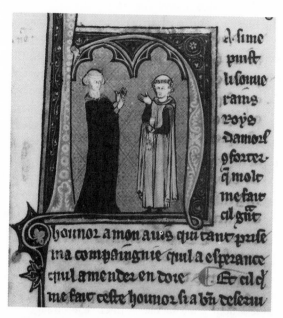

9. Further disputation. *La Response au Bestiaire
d'amour*. Vienna, Österreichische Nationalbibliothek,
Cod. 2609, fol. 44. Courtesy of the Österreichische
Nationalbibliothek.

displaced animus, an expression of the misogyny informing medieval vernacular writing. This ironic finding is itself cast metaphorically. The respondent does not relinquish the privilege of figuration even in the act of
criticizing its conventional uses. As in the prologue, her dispute with the
master's language is played out on the same level (Figure 9). It works
through a recuperated and transformed figurative idiom. But of what kind?
Presented as a subjective truth claim (car je sai vraiement), the respondent
can appraise magisterial symbolic language differently, in a language particular to a woman. Anchored in this "I" (*je . . . qui feme sui*), her critique
deploys a figurative register that is by definition contrary to the master's.

We come here to a crux in the *Bestiaire Response*. If this narrative
breaks down the magisterial symbolic language, why does the female persona persist in analyzing the various bestiary exempla? Part of an answer
involves the principle of gender contrariety undergirding this narrative.
With each new bestiary metaphor, the *Response* pushes the difference
further between a woman's analysis of the symbolic and the master's. Her
explications de texte operate according to a different logic that necessitates a distinct language. Precisely because the respondent is represented

contesting the master's entire repertory of bestiary images, the principle of feminine contrariety is systematically developed—linguistically, as well as epistemologically and materially.

The reason for developing it systematically (and here we get to the other part of the answer) is the respondent's thesis that the master's discourse is deceitful. If the *Response* is to demonstrate "what she knows to be true" (line 1), that is, the profound deceitfulness of such language toward its intended female audience, then it must do so on a comprehensive scale. For anything less would serve only to reinforce the master's discourse. In order to prove how it works to the detriment of its female public, the *Response* mounts an exemplum-by-exemplum critique.

Consider, *à titre d'exemple*, the *Response*'s undoing of the wolf exemplum:

> Je doi bien dire que je fui premierement veüe de vous, que je doi par cesti raison apeler leu. Car je puis mauvaisement dire cose qui puist contrester a vous. Et pour che puis je bien dire que je de vous ai esté veüe premiers: dont je me doi bien warder, se je sui sage.
>
> (Segre, 110–11)

> I must well say that I was seen first by you, who I must for this reason call the wolf. For I can only poorly say anything that could counter you. And for this reason I can well say that I was first seen by you, and I must be on guard if I am prudent/wise [*sage*].

We remember the master's ploy of feminizing the wolf and taking it upon himself; here the respondent is quick to thwart the maneuver. She catches the master acting the helpless woman. Her analysis reveals the transfer mechanism of his feminine figures and their potentially detrimental effect. In turn, the respondent reverses the transfer. She makes the wolf signify again a predatory animal, and by inference, the master. This reversal is couched in the self-deprecating terms typical of the prologue: the *sexecuser* rhetoric prevails. But as we have seen, this rhetoric can belie an improbable flourish of knowledge, in this instance a pun on *sagesse*. Referring to both prudence and wisdom, this play of words highlights the fundamental connection between wisdom and self-protection. Whereas the master's *sagesse* suggests an outward, aggressive motion, the woman respondent's, by contrast, entails an inner consolidation. In this sense, her interpretation of the master's predatory figure does not launch a comparably predatory language.

Using the master's tropes for seduction, the *Response* extends its exposé of their harmful effects. Take her reading of the tiger:

Car je voi bien et sai que tout aussi que on giete les miroirs devant le
tigre pour lui aherdre, tout aussi faites vous pour mi vos beles paroles
qui plus delitaules sont a oïr que tigres a veoir, si comme deseure
est dit. Et bien sai que il ne vous caurroit qui i perdrist, mais que
vo volentés fust faite.

(Segre, 117)

For I clearly see and know that just as one casts mirrors in front of the
tiger to catch it, so you make for me your beautiful words. They are
more delectable to hear than the tiger is to see, as has been said above,
and I know well that it would not concern you who perished by them
as long as your will be done.

The *Response* returns to the traditional bestiary typing of the female
tiger—a revision that, at first glance, appears to reinforce the clerical commonplace of the narcissistic woman. Yet if we look closer, the comparison
between the beauty of the tiger and the more beautiful words of the master shifts attention away from the putative issue of female narcissism and
toward the damaging function of the mirror. The problem is less one of
a woman enthralled by her self-image than of the mesmerizing quality
of the master's words. The respondent's contrary metaphorical formula
equates the master's comely discourse with the fatal attractions of the mirror. It also makes explicit the dialectical terms of power so characteristic of
the master's reasoning: "And I know well that it would not concern you
who perished as long as your will be done" (Et bien sai que il ne vous caurroit qui i perdrist, mais que vo volentés fust faite). Uncovering the master's show of will (vo volentés) gives the respondent more reasons why she
should argue against him.

If the *Response* exposes the malicious tropes for seduction, it also
challenges their various symbolic associations with death. Hence the
elimination of all the master's figures for resuscitation and resurrection.
In the woman's schema, there is no place for the pelican, lion, and beaver
exempla for the simple reason that once seduction is interpreted as a
form of death for a woman, it is absolute. As the respondent describes
it: "For who loses his honor is truly dead. Indisputably it is true: whoever is dead is unlikely to recover" (Car qui s'onneur pert, il est bien
mors. Certes c'est voirs; qui mors est, pau i puet avoir de recouvrier;
Segre, 121).

A figure unique to the *Response* equates such "death" with a threat of
sexual violence:

Tout aussi comme li cas qui a ore mout simple chiere, et du poil au de-
fors est il mout soues et mout dous. Mais estraingniés li le keue: il
getera ses ongles fors de ses .iiij. piés, et vous desquirra les mains se

vous tost ne le laissiés aler. Par Dieu, je cuit aussi que teus se fait ore
mout dous, et dist paroles de coi il vauroit estre creüs et avoir se volenté, que se il en estoit au deseure et on ne li faisoit du tout se volenté,
qui pis feroit que li cas ne puist faire.

(Segre, 123)

Just like the cat who has the straightest face, and the softest, gentlest fur
outside, is very sweet and gentle. But were you to pull its tail, then it will
stick out its claws on all four paws and rip your hands to pieces until you
let go. By God, I believe there is that type of man who is all gentleness
and who speaks words to convince you and to get his way, and yet he is
capable of far worse, were he on top and not getting his way.

The cat exemplum dramatizes the nexus in the master's amorous discourse of elegance, malicious intent, and force. The effects are graphically
portrayed: what passes for love talk is a language of physical blows. There
is little mistaking the image of the cat on top for the type of sexual force
described in the Aristotelian didactic treatises considered in chapter 1.
The respondent's original trope underscores the link between the master's
exquisite figurative language and its domineering impetus expressed in
sexual terms.

At these junctures, where the *Response* supplants the master's figures
with its own, the full import of its contrariety comes into focus. Dismantling the *Bestiaire*'s metaphors, stroke for stroke, exposes the detrimental
power of the master's language. It shows the harmful aftereffects of that
language on the public of women. In short, the *Response* formulates the
problem of verbal injury. There is no quibbling or self-belittling rhetoric
here: it disputes the amorous discourse of the *Bestiaire* on the grounds of
its injuriousness.

The linchpin of this indictment occurs in a mock dialogue between
lovers:

Mais che seroit bien parlers a rebours se je disoie a aucun cose dont il
me vausist traire en cause et mener maistrie seur moi. Car mout se
moustrent bien amours ou eles sont, si que li parlers et li descouvrirs
amie a son ami, ne ami a s'amie, n'est fors parlers a rebours. Jou ne di
mie que bien n'ait raisson de dire amie a son ami: "Il me plaist bien que
toute li honneurs et li biens que vous poés faire soit en mon non"; et
chil a l'autre lés dira: "Dame, ou damoisele, je sui du tout sans contre-
faire a vostre volenté." Mais dire: "Amie, je me doeil, ou muir, pour
vous; se vous ne me secourés je sui traïs et me morrai," ja, par Dieu,
puis qu'il se descouverra ensi, je n'i arai point de fianche; anchois me
sanle que teus paroles sont mengiers a rebours.

(Segre, 129–30)

But that would be "speaking at cross purposes" if I were to say something that he could use against me and thereby master me. For love truly shows that talk and secrets shared between lovers, whether woman to man or man to woman, is nothing more than "speaking at cross purposes." I am not saying that it is not right for a woman to say to her lover: "It is pleasing to me that all the honor and good that you accomplish is done in my name" or that a man says to her: "Lady, I am completely at your service." But to say: "Lady, I'm tormented, I'm dying for you; if you do not save me, I am betrayed and shall die." My Lord, whosoever reveals himself in that manner is not trustworthy. Such a talk, it seems to me, is "eating [speaking] at cross purposes."

All the key elements of the respondent's analysis converge in the term "parlers a rebours" (speaking at cross purposes). First: the issue of figurative language. The risk of speaking at cross purposes arises from the metaphors specific to amorous discourse. This is especially the case with the paradigmatic figure of lovesickness, *li maux d'amour*. By resorting to such metaphors, both men and women run this risk. Second: the drive to dominate. At the core of such a figurative *parlers a rebours* is the desire for domination, flagged by the vocabulary of will (*volenté*) and mastery (*maistrie*). Once we recognize the connection between figuration and domination, the differences between so-called masculine and feminine *rebours* are patent, and those differences are bound up with the desired effect on the interlocutor. Whereas the respondent evaluates a man's speech act— the infamous death threat—as manipulative, she introduces no female analogue. In fact, the woman's speech act may result in her being mastered herself (se je disoie a aucun chose dont il me vausist traire en cause et mener maistrie seur moi). This scene is set up hypothetically (che seroit . . . se je disoie). As if for argument's sake, the respondent considers the possibility of a woman speaking *a rebours*, but it remains pure conjecture. On two scores, then, the *Response* argues that it is virtually impossible for a woman to speak in this manner. Since her own figurative language reveals no dominating impulse, it does not impose the respondent's will on her audience. And since her male interlocutor is incapable of understanding the recourse to figurative language otherwise, he is likely to exploit hers as an opportunity for his own mastery (et mener maistrie seur moi).

Through this notion of *parlers a rebours*, the *Response* brings pressure to bear on that proposition linking figurative language to domination. It calls to account the process whereby the figurative speech act inflicts harm, a process so utterly conventionalized through the configurations of vernacular writing that it appears unremarkable—except, according to the *Response*, in the case of women speakers. Precisely because their language shows no signs of injuriousness, because the male interlocutor interprets it instead as an invitation to overpower, that proposition breaks down. What is *rebours*, then, is not a woman's negativity, as the master's paradigm would have it, but rather the potential destructiveness of the reigning figurative language. *Parlers a rebours* exemplifies the system of mastery operative in vernacular love narratives insofar as it reveals how its founding theorem—using the figurative → achieving dominance—is invalid for a woman. She is represented as neither able to achieve a dominant position through the figurative nor desirous of it. For a female persona, such a proposition does not hold.

Having explicated the domineering function of men's *parlers a rebours*, the *Response* pins it explicitly on the clerical caste:

> [C]he sont chil clerc qui si s'afaitent en courtoisie et en leur beles paroles, qu'il n'est dame ne demoisele qui devant aus puist durer qu'il ne veullent prendre. Et sans faille bien m'i acort, car en eus est toute courtoisie, si que j'ai entendu. Et en aprés sont li plus bel, de coi on fait clers, et sont li plus soutil en malisse, et sousprendent les non sachans. Pour che les apele je oisiaus de proie, et bon feroit estre garnie contre aus.
>
> (Segre, 133)

> These are clerks so expert in courtesy and fine talk that if they are after women, there is no one, neither lady nor young girl, who can withstand them. And I can well understand, for these men are impeccably courteous, according to what I've heard. And moreover they are among the most handsome which is why they are made clerics, and most subtle in their malice, and they outwit the untrained. For this reason, I call them birds of prey, and it would do well to guard oneself against them.

This is no standard outburst of anticlericalism. Instead of attacking clerks for what they are lacking, as in the long line of *clerc/chevalier* debates, the *Response* focuses on their outstanding talents. The clerical skill in formulating intellectual problems, *subtilitas*, transmutes into a form of malice. It signals a perverse desire to use those skills to the detriment of others. Whence the relevance of the birds of prey exemplum: the nefarious "beles paroles" of the clergy resemble so many snares for the unsuspecting. Rather than use this exemplum to describe the animalistic quality of erotic relations, the respondent works it back the other way, portraying how bestial the clerical representations of those relations are, which she describes elsewhere as "wounding, beautiful talk" (si trenchans cose n'est comme de bel parler; Segre, 118).

Just as the respondent disputes clerical figuration per se, she defends women in general. Increasingly, she speaks on behalf of "all those women who need persevere in love" (toutes celles qui en amor vauront perseverer; fol. 33). These inclusive gestures function both negatively and positively. Negatively, they function as a caveat, because the respondent depicts those gullible women who "thrill to hear the clerks' words" as an antitype (celes qui s'aerdent a escouter leur paroles; Segre, 134–35). She uses them to designate the female type targeted by clerkly amorous discourse. In fact, the *Response* goes so far as to show the way deceived women often reproduce their own deception among other women (Segre, 132–33). At the same time, the *Response* projects a positive female type, an image around which women can rally so as to avoid complicitous self-deception.

> Tout aussi vaurroie je vraiement que toutes se vardassent . . . que quant .j. venroit qui si feroit le destravé, et puis si li deïst on une cose que il feroit le plus a envis et dont mains de damages seroit.
>
> (Segre, 130–31)
>
> I would truly like all women to watch out for themselves . . . so that when a man comes along and acts desperately, he would then be told something that he would do most begrudgingly, and from which the least damage would ensue.

In a gesture of solidarity, the respondent envisages those women who could deflect the advances of a feigning male interlocutor. She hypothesizes a general guardedness in women. What is most striking about this projection is the aim of avoiding all destructiveness. In this scenario, the woman's response to the feigning male speaker incurs little or no damage (dont mains de damages seroit). Unlike clerkly amorous discourse, a woman's speech act has no backlash on its intended audience. The destructive character of a man's *requeste* is not met in kind.

To the question why respond? then, the *Bestiaire Response* replies not only "Because," as the response form dictates, or "Because a woman should," as the gendered logic of contrariety has it, but most importantly, "Because clerical discourse should answer to a woman's charge of injuriousness." Herein lies the innovation of this text. Rarely did French narrative of the twelfth and thirteenth centuries represent the act of bringing an accusation against a discourse. However self-conscious this culture was about literary composition, it was preoccupied for the most part with the process of writing. Even when it broached the problem of a writing's effect on its audiences, this did not implicate its own practices. At the time of the *Bestiaire Response*, Old French literary culture seldom pursued the possibility that it could commit acts of verbal injury so abundantly in evidence in other contexts. Like the clerical catalogues detailing various verbal infractions, narratives in the line of the *Roman de la rose* addressed the problem only to locate elsewhere. To be sure, this culture was concerned with slander and calumny and all malicious language meant to harm. Such are the habitual complaints about *mesdisants* (gossips, slanderers).[20] Yet the concern over *mesdisance* involves a threat coming from outside the domain of amorous discourse. Never is *mesdisance* associated with or deemed representative of a normative discourse.

Bringing the charge of verbal injury against the prevailing masterly discourse makes the *Bestiaire Response* singular in another way. It locates all problems of textual representation in the social domain. Its attention to the effects of figuration places that figuration in relation to a community. In turn, the *Response* suggests that group's chance of regulating it. The case of one respondent does not constitute a community, especially when she is part of the intricate configurations of erotic/didactic narrative. Yet the fact that the *Bestiaire* respondent evaluates the ways textual representation can injure a public raises in a powerful manner the idea of social controls. The fact that a female persona raises the idea of verbal injury in terms of a female public bespeaks a critical connection in late medieval culture between women and the social accountability of clerical discourse. I shall return to this point again and again.

Naming Names

Surprisingly, in one instance we are able to see how the *Response*'s charge against clerical discourse resonated for some of its audiences. In one manuscript, the *Bestiaire* and *Response* are followed by yet another woman's response (hereafter referred to as *Response 2*).[21] Someone saw fit to extend the exchange between master and respondent and to pursue the problem of injurious language. At the center of this second *Response* is the question of fame or reputation.

By taking up the topic of reputation, this text builds on the question of a discourse's effects posed in the first. It considers the object of such discursive damage: women's names. To broach this topic represents another effort to dispute the masterly discourses. In the largest scheme of things, it suggests other ways of naming women.

Response 2 introduces the notion of a name as a symbolic value established publicly. In contrast to proper names such as Marie or Blanchefleur, the name it considers refers to the sum of properties that a person/persona represents for a particular community.[22] As the woman respondent stresses, it is constituted primarily by those discourses in public circulation:

Et dautre part sens et valours si sunt ausi comme ensemble quant il
sunt sans loenge, ne mis ne doit savoir quil soit larges et boins sil na
autre tiesmoingnage que lui li quel lensiucent et sacent que cou soit
voirs par le conversation quil ait entre eaus.

(Vienna 2609, fol. 46)

And on the other hand, if the intelligence and reputation [of a person]
are also together when they are without praise, it is impossible to
know, and indeed one should not know, whether they are widespread
and good unless there are other witnesses that follow from it and know
it to be true from the conversation that there was between them.

Everything hinges on the ways a person is represented before the public.
However deserving an individual, his or her good name depends on the
witness of others. Reputation is contingent on the prevailing public discourse. It follows, then, that the process of gaining a reputable name is
necessarily subject to what the respondent calls "conversation . . . between them" (le conversation quil ait entre eaus; fol. 46). Caught in the
web of such discourses, a name cannot escape their terms. On the one
hand, there is the model of panegyric (*loenge*, fol. 46), an excessive, ide-
alizing discourse that Leo Braudy has associated with the "frenzy of
renown." And on the other, there are multiple negative forms—damning praise (*fausse loenge*, fol. 46), "name-calling," outright denunciation. Common to both these discursive modes is the threat of falsehood.
In the public domain where the recourse to witnesses and the criterion of
verifiability do not hold uniformly, the status of names becomes increasingly difficult to evaluate. How to account for the discursive involvement of others in shaping a name? If a person/persona can exist publicly
in name only, how exactly is that name created and regulated?[23]

The *Response* reformulates these questions subjectively: "Oh God,
what is it to me that the witness of others attest to my intelligence and
reputation since I know it to be true that he would be openly lying?" (Ha!
Dex, que me vaut tiesmoignage de gens a moi essaucier pour quel raison
iaie sens et valor puis que ie sai de voir quil mentiroit tout a plain; Vienna
2609, fol. 46). We have here the nub of the problem of reputation making:
the difference between a subjective articulation of a "good name" and a
public construction of it. By comparing the two, the respondent accentuates the process of making a name and the dominant discourses governing
that process. She questions the legitimacy of reputations based solely on
the "tiesmoignage de gens" (the witness of others). In her own case, the
discursive constructions of others are exposed as patently fraudulent: "ie
sai de voir quil mentiroit tout a plain." Yet the respondent's critique still
takes the form of a question: how much *is* the witness of others worth?—
a rhetorical question, perhaps, but one that conveys the importance of

reckoning with that *tiesmoignage*. The fact remains that a person's reputation, such as the respondent's, hangs invariably in the balance of the predominant public discourses.

This balance is all the more precarious when it comes to women's names. As the first *Response* argues, they are a frequent target of an injurious clerical amorous discourse. For the second *Response*, this circumstance underscores the importance of reclaiming their names. Where one text identifies the problem of verbal injury, the other attempts to alleviate such injury by taking over the function of making a woman's name. Early on in the text, the respondent states:

> Pour coi ie di que dex et nature a bien moustre que li hom est la plus dingne coze que il onques feist. Et quant ie noume home, jou entent a noumer home et feme ausi comme il avient.
>
> (Vienna 2609, fol. 44 verso)

> For this I say that both God and nature well demonstrate that man is the most noble thing that he ever made. And when I name man, I mean to name man and woman as it is fitting.

The respondent returns to the Genesis scene. In so doing, she assumes nothing less than the divine prerogative of naming. She denominates woman along with man, thereby guaranteeing the distinct and particular existence of both parties.[24] By adopting the Genesis formula to create woman herself, the respondent claims responsibility for the female name. From the determining space of Eden, she attempts to secure women's reputations for a wider social domain.

As a result, the second *Response* challenges implicitly the public construction of women's names.[25] The respondent's gesture throws into question the multiple arbitrary versions of women's reputations fashioned by the predominant discourses. By calling forth the name of woman, this narrative disputes the validity of the existing ones. And it does so not only by echoing the irreproachable divine voice, but by speaking through it subjectively: "I mean to name man and woman" (iou entent a noumer home et feme). If only in the discrete space of the second *Response*, a woman's name is also ordained by a woman subject. Having transformed the process of naming into a divinely inspired, female, subjective affair, the second *Response* impeaches the public and conventional standard of women's reputations.

This problem of women's names pushes still further the first *Response*'s concern with injurious language. Together the two responses specify the circumstances whereby a woman's name is held hostage by the predominant discourses and made vulnerable to their vagaries. A woman's name is both authorized product of such discourses and its most common casualty. As both respondents intimate, if a woman does not participate in the normative discursive system, she cannot exercise control over her public name. Such a person is subject to existing in name only—a name as malleable as putty. To quote a contemporaneous poem, the villein can have thirty different names, each more abusive than the last.[26] A woman may leave a similarly long trail of misshapen, distorted reputations.

Nevertheless, the second woman's response does represent a woman who articulates women's names anew. It signals some attempt to break up the discursive stronghold. The effort is admittedly small-scale, the opening little more than a crack. But the very fact that the respondent dwells on the question posed by women's names foregrounds the cardinal issue of verbal injury. Both *Responses* focus attention on how clerical discourse on women can operate damagingly, and how to reckon with that pattern. Their dispute involves making it a public issue—a strategy that would be exploited dramatically several generations later.

Who Is Responding?

Who is responsible for such a critique of masterly figuration? This final question concerning the phenomenon of the woman's response has elicited conflicting views. Insofar as the two *Responses* are cast in a subjective voice, the issue of the respondent's identity rears its head tantalizingly (Figure 10). Or should I say heads? With the pair of narratives, the initial respondent transmutes into another, multiplying progressively by dint of "variant authors and scribal variance."[27] In the plural or singular, the respondent figure nonetheless spurs critics to pin her down. There are those who attempt to identify her personally: her full name, her whereabouts, her biography.[28] Their detective work endeavors to link the *Bestiaire* respondent with a distinct individual, akin to Héloïse or, a century earlier, Constance, the learned respondent to the clerical writer from the school of the Loire, Baudri de Bourgueil.[29] There are others who, espousing the ludic character of medieval narrative, regard the subjective profile of the *Bestiaire* respondent as fundamentally and delightfully suspect.[30] Far from providing a lead to a historical personage, her subjectivity functions parodically, its very fictiveness mocking the critic's desire to secure provenance. As Alexandre Leupin puts it, "she" involves nothing more than a figure of speech (165–66). In fact, that a scholarly woman respondent emerges as a subject corroborates the wide range of personae in medieval vernacular narrative.

10. Another rejoinder. *La Response au Bestiaire d'amour.* Paris, Bibliothèque Nationale, f.fr. 412, fol. 236. Photograph, Bibliothèque Nationale de France, Paris.

Caught between these two poles—individual mystery woman and textual ruse—analysis of the *Bestiaire* respondent's identity runs quickly aground. Reading "her" is restricted either to an indefinite search for one learned woman, now as ever unidentified, or an exercise in deciphering textual conundrums. The *Response* thus appears an isolated, extraordinary example of opposition voiced by a woman or, at the other extreme, a quintessential game-playing narrative that confirms Ovid's ploy of using feminine and masculine pronouns interchangeably to fool the public.

Are these the only possibilities? By way of proposing a different answer, I suggest listening to Christine de Pizan, who several generations later ruminated on the conventions of creating female personae. In the course of the early-fifteenth-century *Querelle* over the *Roman de la rose*, she asked:

Qui sont fames? Qui sont elles? Sont ce serpens, loups, lyons, dragons, guievres ou bestes ravissables devourans et ennemies a nature humainne, qu'il conviengne fere art a les decepvoir et prandre? Lisés donc l'*Art*: aprenés a fere engins! Prenés les fort! Decevés les! Vituperés les! Assallés ce chastel! Gardés que nulles n'eschappent entre vous, hommes, et que tout soit livré a honte! Et par Dieu, si sont elles vos meres, vos suers, vos filles, vos fammes et vos amies; elles sont vous mesmes et vous meesmes elles.

(Hicks, 139)

Who are women? Who are they? Are they serpents, wolves, lions, dragons, vipers, or ravenous predatory beasts and enemies of human nature whom one must plot against to deceive and capture? Read the *Art of Love* then: learn how to be ruseful! Take them by force! Trick them! Malign them! Assault the castle! Take care that none of the women escape from you men, and that all is accomplished shamefully! And by God, if they are your mothers, sisters, and daughters, your wives and friends, they are you, and you yourselves are these women.

As Christine reminds us, the question of identity in complex figurative texts like the *Rose* is ultimately a misleading one. Whether it involves depictions of women characters, the bestiary/bestial portrait, or in our case, the profile of a female subject, identity looks problematical. For when it comes to figuration in such texts, no relation of equivalence pertains, no one-way correspondence between character and author. Instead these texts involve a chiasmus: "if they are your mothers . . . they are you, and you yourselves are these women." A crossover occurs, one that in the wake of Ovidian models operates easily across gender lines. Through the mechanisms of subjective figuration and personification, a poet assumes a variety of personae that at the same time display characteristics of that poet's writing culture.[31] Not only does a poet use the subjective figure as a mask, but that mask relays cardinal features of conventional textual composition.

This distinction of chiasmus is all the more crucial when it comes to the creation of female personae. The pressure to identify those personae with the values of a male author and audience is enormous. And presuming that a female subject can only be their projection serves to obliterate her female character. In this sense, Christine's phrase "if . . . they are you, and you yourselves are these women" recalls hauntingly the *Houneurs des dames* formula, "*femme/lui meismes*," that we considered in chapter 1. Yet there is one significant difference. The *Houneurs* phrase bridges the chiasmus, merging *femme* with *lui meismes* in order to extinguish the difference between them. The result is to see them in identical terms. By contrast, Christine's phrase maintains the chiasmus in order to underline the correspondences between the bestiary/bestial *femme* and *lui meismes*.

It thus emphasizes the discrepancies between mothers, sisters, daughters, and *lui meismes*. Christine recognizes the way clerical figuration of women reveals more about the writers and their views than it does about the women they claim to depict. Taking stock of the chiasmus enables Christine to separate out persona, person, and poet. As a consequence, it points to the social circumstances shaping all three.

This chiasmic character of female subjective identity thus leads us to consider it in relation to specific social situations. Rather than limit analysis to the fact that certain female figures constitute masks—an *idée fixe* for many critics—I wish to investigate how such figures are disposed. In Christine's example, associating the female personae of dragons and predatory beasts with "you men," that is, with her masterly interlocutors, marks only the first step. The critique widens to include evaluating how the masters' social situation supports such a "beastly" portraiture of women. The crossover works both ways. To answer questions like "who are women?" or "who is this woman?" means exploring the degree to which a woman's identity could be imputed to a particular social group. It involves turning the female figure around so as to gauge its social matrix. Just as Christine links the animalistic female personae to works such as Capellanus's *De amore* and their clerkly milieu, we can hypothesize a connection between the *Bestiaire* respondent and a particular setting. As Toril Moi has argued, what matters is not so much whether a particular work is formulated by a woman or a man, but whether its effects can be characterized as sexist or feminist in a given situation.[32] Even if we could attribute the *Response* to an individual woman, the respondent figure's social context remains crucially important. Conversely, even if we deem her identity a textual cipher, it is still embedded in a specific social matrix. Our interpretative challenge lies in assessing that context. My aim, then, is to study the respondent herself as a constituent part of a certain social logic.[33]

The *Bestiaire* responses afford us an unusual chance to pursue the question of a female persona's social circumstances. Because the first *Response* occurs in a small number of manuscripts, each with localizable features, and *Response 2* in only one, these narratives can be more precisely situated in a particular milieu than many Old French works.[34] The consensus has long been that these various texts belong to the Artois and Hainaut in the north of France and in the Brabant in modern-day Belgium.[35] Compared with the *Bestiaire* that circulated widely in Europe in several vernaculars, the *Responses* seem principally linked to this northern Francophone setting.[36] What has not been acknowledged, however, is the link between the one manuscript containing both *Bestiaire* responses (Vienna 2609) and the mid-fourteenth-century gathering containing the *Consaus d'amours* (Vienna 2621).[37] As we mentioned in chapter 1, this manuscript's provenance can be established by its dedicatory address to the duke and duchess of Brabant. Identified explicitly as Brabantine property, it was likely commissioned by the circle of Jean III and Marie d'Evreux and read first in the major Brabantine centers of Brussels and Louvain. If we consider these two manuscripts together, we find striking similarities. Layout, scribal hand, dialect, iconography, thematic coherence: their many common features suggest not only a homogeneous pattern of poetic composition but the stamp of similar circumstances of production. Both manuscripts can be associated with the same workshop. They appear to share the same context. Without claiming that the *Response* and the *Consaus* were grouped together in a single codex, we can posit a Brabantine court setting for both.

To situate the *Responses* in mid-fourteenth-century Brabant involves placing the respondent persona in a notoriously charged social landscape. Virtually every account of medieval Brabantine culture begins by underscoring the perennial strife that troubled its social relations.[38] "The Brabant has as many quarrels as France has vineyards."[39] This thirteenth-century proverb sums up multiple conflicts. The local nobility was struggling with an encroaching royal Capetian power. But they were also at loggerheads with their own citizens over the government of the towns. Clerical communities were deeply divided as well. They were caught between their long-standing alliance with the seigneurial caste and their growing involvement in bourgeois affairs. Their aristocratic loyalties conflicted with their support for the class of nouveau riche. This turmoil has been interpreted largely in economic terms, the result of the ascending bourgeoisie in cities across Brabant and neighboring Flanders, Hainaut, and Artois.[40] In these terms, the story of the Brabantine Communes is one of urban emancipation based on the growing mercantile influence and autonomy of the middle classes.[41] Yet another aspect of this characteristic climate of contention in the Brabant became discernible in the arena of what we might call cultural politics. While the balance of power in matters economic and political was being sharply contested between the local duchy and the bourgeoisie, such fractiousness also impinged on intellectual life. It affected the commerce and use of texts. The authority over learning was no longer exclusively regulated by the nobility and clergy. As the bourgeoisie fought for greater municipal control, they also sought greater involvement in the world of letters and learning.

Nowhere was this more apparent than in the issue of schooling.[42] In Brussels, Ghent, Cambrai, and across Picardy, the late thirteenth and fourteenth centuries witnessed an important social struggle over lay education.[43] Custom granted the privilege of establishing schools and selecting schoolmasters to the local nobility—one that, in practice, depended upon the close collaboration with the clergy. Yet there is much evidence that many municipalities across the north agitated for the right to administer their own schools independently of the nobility. Such a struggle often gave way to an outright split between the bourgeoisie and the court, between the city and the *Cité*—the ducal residence. Local ordinances drawn up during this period confirm the common maneuver among the urban bourgeoisie of abandoning the schools designated by the court and founding their own with clerks and masters of their own choosing.[44] Action was taken to wrest control over education from the nobility and thereby to intervene strategically in the arena themselves. At the time of the Brabantine *Responses*, the bourgeois was challenging the clerk and the duke for the management of rudimentary lay literacy. Behind their representations of a laywoman debating with a master, then, we might well divine a controversy between these various factions arising from the bourgeoisie's mounting activism in the world of letters.[45]

Where does the woman respondent figure in this picture? In most surveys of lay literacy, the claim has been repeated ritually that the spread of Aristotelianism and scholastic culture proved disadvantageous for women.[46] Put another way, the high-medieval practices of intellectual mastery and women's learning were not easily compatible. In the case of Brabant, where Aristotelian treatises were in vogue at the ducal court, the climate seemed hardly favorable to the development of women's intellectual life.[47] We have only to recall the miniature from the *Consaus* manuscript depicting the duchess of Brabant (Figure 4). Side by side with the duke, she is still not portrayed as an equal participant in the dialogue with the master. While the duke holds a book, the marker of his involvement in the master's erudition, the duchess has a scroll inscribed with a love song (*amour amoureces*). Associated with amorous refrains alone, she has limited access to their debate. She is effectively left out of the duke and master's rarefied academic discourse.

Yet let us not forget that out of the same milieu comes the image of the respondent equipped with the tools of textual culture (Figure 7). Not only do we find the commonplace repressive image of the woman who approaches the master only in a diversionary way, but also the surprising one of the actively engaged literate woman. The fact that these manuscripts present both images is telling. Indeed, the fact that their Brabantine communities could accommodate them together leads me to suggest that our respondent persona exemplifies the tensions concerning lay learning in general and the training of laywomen in particular. Far from confirming an existing situation or intensifying a fantasy, the respondent persona galvanizes the conflicting attitudes prevailing in fourteenth-century Brabant. She recapitulates the differences—promising and limiting—that made up the dispute over the regulation of lay instruction and the laity's access to texts.

What has often been overlooked is the way the controversy over education—itself the consequence of considerable social turbulence—changed the prospects of laywomen's training. Bourgeois militancy tested the established categories that reserved the practices of writing and debating for the clerisy and the male nobility. The campaign to diversify pedagogical opportunities across social lines could also translate into changed opportunities for women across classes. With the laicization allied to the rise of urban culture, a space opened up for noble and bourgeois women that was not as tightly surveyed as the hermetic enclosure of courtly society.[48] And the moral necessity to discipline women's reading to pietistic works was conspicuously absent in the heady context of fourteenth-century Brabant. We find no prescription comparable to those issued in the Capetian court.[49]

Several points are in order here. If we take a cross section of the urban landscape in northern France and Brabant at the time of the *Bestiaire Response*, we find that a primary school for girls was commonly established at the same time as one for boys. In Brussels, one seat of the Brabantine duchy, a statute survives that details the foundation of a girl's school (Stallaert, 101). This school made provisions for upper-level instruction. Not only could laywomen learn to read and write, but they were able to pursue studies beyond the rudiments of Donatus's ABCs, notably in *ars dictaminis* (the art of composition). Whereas these skills hardly point to the sophisticated labor of scholastic commentary, they nonetheless do associate a wider group of laywomen with a textual practice beyond that of mere passive reading and recitation.

That such an opportunity existed is borne out by the incidence of city women who owned books. During the fourteenth and fifteenth centuries, there are cases of those who possessed a basic collection of romances and religious works—a pattern that surely contributes to the early-modern reputation of Flemish *bourgeoises* as linguists and bibliophiles.[50] One exemplary case, several generations earlier than the *Response*, involves a certain Maroie Payene of Tournai who in 1246 willed to her children grammar books, a Marian devotional manual, and a copy of the *Roman du chevalier du cygne*.[51] Her testament makes clear the range of texts in her possession and their importance to her. The fact that she transmitted them legally, together with her property and jewelry, emphasizes just how committed she was to her personal library.

If we can account for laywomen as students and as bookworms, it is hardly surprising to discover that in this context they were also emerging as teachers. Side by side with *clerici*, we find laywomen who instructed children in basic skills.[52] Whereas it could be argued that they assumed this responsibility as part of their domestic work of overseeing the young, it is well worth noting that they were identified publicly in this capacity. In censuses and other city rolls during the fourteenth century, their names are often inscribed as schoolmistresses (Derville, 771). Paris provides an analogous case, for in proceedings of the city council dated 1380, the names of twenty-two *magistrae* are listed on the rolls.[53] The epithet, *magistra*, resonates strongly. By no means does it convey the same status or authority as the *magister*. Nonetheless, the woman teacher was recognized officially as a member of a profession. As such, she took her place in the ranks that descend from *magister in artibus* (master of arts), *dominus* (lord), *baccalareus* (bachelor), to the lay *magistra*.

These glimpses of a *magistra* should remind us of the beguines, those contemporaneous communities of religious laywomen. Of all the signs of changing pedagogical opportunities for laywomen in northern Europe during the high Middle Ages, the most influential by far was the beguinage.[54] These residences, located in the midst of numerous Brabantine, Flemish, and French towns, functioned as nerve centers for women's training and study.[55] Beguines occupied themselves with the schooling of the laity, particularly young girls. But their tutelage did not stop there. They created a milieu in which the exegesis of canonical Latin texts was pursued together with the reading of contemporary vernacular literature. The beguines were conversant with and equally disposed toward the two traditions, as a Francophone beguine rule entitled "La rigle des fins amans" demonstrates well.[56] And their commitment to a culture of women's learning ushered in a notable phase of women's writing—as notable for its sophistication as for its bulk. Late-medieval Church history bears this out amply. The fact that the beguines so systematically cultivated women's intellectual talents outside clerical jurisdiction branded them as suspect if not heretical communities.

Beguinage, *magistrae*, girls' elementary training: such are the social features that work chiasmically through the *Bestiaire* respondent. This persona is richly traced with the controversies that mobilized so many groups in Brabant over lay instruction. And the disputational dynamic of her text is animated by the disputes over learning in general. However strong the correspondences between diversifying pedagogical/intellectual opportunities for laywomen and our woman respondent, I do not want to claim they make for a causal argument. I do not claim that the occurrence of this persona is a result of advances in northern European lay literacy, nor do I wish to draw a direct connection between one distinct textual community and the respondent figure. That critical tack would lead into the tangled skein of noble/bourgeois relations—a question that the *Response* manuscript as such cannot substantiate. Whether the respondent is labeled noble or even bourgeoise would always remain a moot point. Instead, I am outlining the principal controversies polarizing Brabantine literate communities that the respondent figure recapitulates. In this manner, the reciprocal influence between the Brabantine quarrels over intellectual life and the master/woman respondent disputation comes to the fore.[57]

Several key features of the "woman's response" phenomenon emerge from the case of the *Bestiaire*. First of all, against all odds, there is indeed a logic of the woman's response. The gendered principle of contrariety provides a means whereby the woman respondent can enter into debate with the master figure on her own terms without being caught in a vicious disputational circle. In this respect, she is fundamentally distinguished from the disciple figure. She escapes his characteristic quandary of never being good enough. Since her language is conjugated as separate and distinct from the master's language, she can exit the trap of reiterating or quibbling with his. Furthermore, the different material ground of her language substantiates another mode of argumentation. Her mode dispenses with the tit-for-tat exchanges that define the master's dealings with his disciples. As the second respondent puts it, "and expressly the one who respects himself must take care not to dispute with anyone. For . . . one who disputes with either wise or foolish resembles the one who fights with his shadow; that is to say, who fights with somebody who doesn't exist."[58] The woman's response breaks with the disputational dynamic that prolongs indefinitely the volleys of contradictory charges and countercharges. "Fighting with his shadow": the respondent's image gets right to the heart of the master's tactics that assimilate his interlocutor to the point of obliterating their differences. As the humanist Vivès would repeat centuries later, the magisterial disputation amounts to little more than shadowboxing. By working in a contrary manner, however, the woman's response avoids the danger of absorption and obliteration. It thereby insures its coexistence with the master's writing. Even within a disputational framework, it does not entail a shadowy projection of the master's text, for it possesses its own epistemological and linguistic density.

It is the response's logic of contrariety that creates the conditions for its critique of the clerical figuration of women. As we have seen, this critique evolves in very specific reference to Richard de Fournival's *Bestiaire d'amour*. Every metaphor is picked apart in order to expose its general malicious design and damaging effect. The respondent's analysis thus conceptualizes a link in clerical discourse between textual figures and the will to dominate. It foregrounds the way that figuring women in certain "bestial," sexualized ways can prove deleterious to its audiences. In its largest terms, the two responses pose the key question of verbal injury.

For this reason alone, the *Bestiaire Response* invites us to extrapolate from its critique of one particular example of clerical writing. Such a critique can be generalized to implicate a vein of discourse running across various genres from the late thirteenth century onward. What we discovered in the specific case history of these Brabantine texts raises the issue of other cases. The pitch of these responses' critique deepens significantly in an environment where access to and regulation of textual practices were hotly debated. Are there signs of analogous cases? If we consider the *Bestiaire* responses retrospectively, its reflection on verbal injury appears anomalous. Yet if we read it in relation to various literary quarrels in the late fourteenth and fifteenth centuries, it contributes a crucial, formative piece to an ongoing critique of the clerical figuration of women.

5   Defamation and the *Livre de leesce*
The Problem of a Sycophantic Response

I strayed abhorrent, blazing with my Self.
    John Berryman, *Delusions, Etc.*

Running through much of later medieval literature written for and against women is the couplet *feme/diffame* (woman/defamation). It appears like a refrain in the paradigmatic misogynistic treatise, the *Lamentations of Matheolus*, and recurs persistently in the many works written in women's defense. At first glance, *feme/diffame* entails a damning slogan that harangues women as garrulous and contentious: women as defamers. This is one of the central claims advanced by the *Lamentations* and perpetuated by much clerical learning. By casting women as slanderous speakers, such texts slander them. Their representations turn women into objects of defamatory discourse, making them the target. So widespread is this pattern that it has given rise to an axiom of much current criticism; medieval writing is animated by a calumny of women. Consider in this light Howard Bloch's recent definition of misogyny as a speech act.[1]

But what happens if we turn this refrain around and begin with the concept of defamation? In another way, *feme/diffame* suggests the peculiar link between women and a language that proves damaging to its public. It underscores the way so much medieval literature is concerned with the harmful power of words directed toward women. In fact, it heightens the concept of verbal injury that we have been exploring thus far in the context of the woman's response.

This heightening is first apparent within the sphere of masterly writing. In Jean de Meun's *Roman de la rose*, the master narrator ponders the problem of defamatory language:

> Si vos pri toutes, vaillanz fames,
> soiez damoiseles ou dames,
> amoureuses ou sanz amis,
> que se moz i trouvez ja mis
> qui samblent mordant et chenins
> ancontre les meurs femenins,
> que ne m'an voilliez pas blamer
> ne m'escriture diffamer,
> qui toute est por anseignement;
> (lines 15165–73)

So I beg all upstanding women, whether they be ladies or young girls, in love or without lovers, that if you find words placed here [in this book] that seem biting and offensive to feminine behavior, that you would not wish to blame me, or defame my writing, that is throughout a form of teaching.

The clerical learning relayed by the *Rose* risks injuring the very female public inscribed in the text. Much as the allegorical figure Reason had suggested, the master figure has to admit the injurious potential of his words. Yet the form that admission takes deflects any responsibility for defamation away from the master. It shifts the responsibility onto the women themselves. By warning them against defaming the master's writing, the *Rose* displaces the problem of defamation and brings us straight back to the stereotype of contentious women. This displacement reveals the narrator's complicity with the world of magisterial learning. Because he is so invested in maintaining and reproducing its learning about women, any criticism he offers of it is necessarily compromised. The insider's concern over verbal injury thus comes out as an excuse. Such a denial is perfectly consonant with the well-known claim of de Meun's narrator that he is only reciting the words of earlier masters, "je n'i faz riens fors reciter" (line 15204). In one of its earliest vernacular formulations, the issue of defaming women is bound up with the masterly writing that is under dispute.

Nowhere is this complicity more evident than in the late-fourteenth-century *Livre de leesce* attributed to Jean LeFèvre.[2] The *Leesce* is, first of all, a response to the *Lamentations*. As its common alternate titles make clear, *Le Rebours de Matheole* or *Le Contraire de Matheole* was conceived as a direct riposte to that paragon of medieval misogynistic reasoning. Like so many gynocentric treatises of the later Middle Ages, the *Leesce* attempts to nullify all Matheolus's defamatory premises.[3] But consider carefully its circumstances: LeFèvre is also identified as the principal vernacular translator of the *Lamentations*.[4] He is largely responsible for its popularization during the later Middle Ages. At the same time, he is the

11. The master in his book-lined cell. *Le Champion des dames*. Grenoble, Bibliothèque Municipale, BM Rés. 352, fol. 355. Courtesy of the Bibliothèque de Grenoble, France.

first clerkly critic to dispute the *Lamentations* systematically. Furthermore, LeFèvre's work as a lawyer at the Parlement de Paris may offer additional evidence of his reaction against misogynistic thinking. If we put any stock in the fact that he pleaded most of his cases on behalf of female clients, his involvement in representing women emerges all the more clearly.[5] Here is an exemplary complicitous respondent. Having implicitly promoted the founding misogynistic text for vernacular culture, Maître LeFèvre turns against it, responding with a profoundly conflicted "advocacy" of women.[6] The *Leesce* thus comprises a response twice over: to the original Latin text and to his own translation and investment in it.

LeFèvre's complicity is manifest in his translation of the expression "defamation." LeFèvre was faced with the problem of rendering the Latin word *diffamare* recurring throughout Matheolus's text. The vernacular equivalent, *diffamer*, thus similarly patterns his French version. Yet in the *Leesce*, *diffamer* takes on the character of a verbal tic. Repeated ever more frequently, it vibrates with anxiety, especially when it appears in the refrain that has no Latin equivalent—*feme/diffame*.[7] LeFèvre's rhyme hints at his growing sense of responsibility for the ongoing defamation of women. The fact that he speaks *feme/diffame* over and over again suggests the degree to which he is torn over his own discourse. Is the translator fatally committed to relaying a defamatory language?

This dilemma is accentuated further by two intermediary roles that LeFèvre's narrator plays in the *Leesce*. He begins by mediating between the master figure, Matheolus, and the clergy in general. At the outset of the *Leesce* he adopts the role of the faithful translator. Yet this posture traps him, and he appears unable to shake free from absolute allegiance to his confreres. By dint of summarizing sections of the *Lamentations* so as to better dispute them, he shows just how deeply enmeshed he is in their learning. He too emerges as a first-class defamer of women. Yet the narrator experiences a turnaround that aligns him increasingly with virtuous women. This orientation places him in a second configuration. In this he moves back and forth between Leesce, a female deity representing joy, and the "dames de Paris," his inscribed audience. Throughout the latter part of the text, his mediation between these women is intended to supplant his earlier alignment with *magistri*. Furthermore, it is allied with a progressive transformation in his language. The translator-narrator claims to purge from his work all that is defamatory toward women, expressing something joyful about them instead.

But is the masterly habit of defamation so easy to shed? If we take account of the overall shape of the narrative, there is something fundamentally erratic about it. The *Leesce* charts the shift in language away from men, whom the narrator calls initially "nous, hommes" (line 517), and toward women, with whom he tries to say, "vous, masles" (line 3648). It traces a change in the translator that begins with his complicity and proceeds toward his defense of women. This movement gives us a glimpse into the disturbance internal to the advocacy of women in late-medieval masterly writing. The very pattern of vacillation is symptomatic of the unease coloring many gynocentric works attributed to clerkly figures such as LeFèvre. It is an unease akin to that voiced by certain male critics who grapple with feminist issues today.[8] That unease has everything to do with recognizing deficiencies within the reigning system of discourse they have espoused. Indeed as one feminist critic has suggested, it can become a defense against the imperfections of that system.[9] The swing toward defending "good" women marks the concerted effort to avoid reckoning with the limitations of masterly writing as a whole. With LeFèvre's *Leesce*, this swing brings out the further concern over the damaging or defamatory character of that writing.

What could the *Leesce*'s anxiety over defamation contribute to the critique of medieval masterly writing about women? As a text planted squarely in the clerkly domain, this narrative seems an unlikely candidate for disputing its conventions of representing women. The *Leesce* narrator's "defense" of women appears more like a self-defense. In much the same way as the contemporaneous clerkly narrator of the *Champion des dames*, he offers a model of utter self-absorption that commits the clerk ever more deeply to the world of his masters (see Figure 11). His work seems hopelessly caught up with the discursive standards it claims to indict. Moreover, this clerkly text is not voiced by a woman. What could it add to the category of the woman's response and its particular dispute with the symbolic domination of so much of masterly medieval writing? Let me emphasize again that I do not reserve the term "woman's response" for one gender. The category is available to men and women alike, anyone who seeks an oppositional position from which to dispute the dominant representation of women. My purpose in reading this clerkly woman's response involves investigating the effects of the *Leesce*'s concern with defamation. As we discovered in studying the *Bestiaire* response, much is to be learned by examining the way a response registers in a particular environment. I wish to track the aftereffects of this translator's response to defamatory language on those controversies called the *Querelle des femmes*.

Pre-curseher

LeFèvre's sense of complicity with masterly misogynistic writing breaks through first in his translation of the *Lamentations*. The initial sign is, paradoxically, silence. Before disputing the conventions of representing women, the translator withdraws quietly:

> Combien que Mahieu, en son livre,
> En ait assés versifié,

> Et leurs meurs diversifié.
> Si fist maistre Jehan de Meun;
> Tous les reproucha un et un,
> Ou chapitre de Faulx Semblant.
> Je m'en tais, si m'en vois amblant
> Le chemin que j'ay commencié.
> Je pourray bien estre tencié
> Ou mauldit par inadvertence.
> Je n'en puis mais se l'on me tence;
> C'est pour bien quanque j'en diray;
> Cy après m'en escondiray.
>   (book 2, lines 1794–1806)

Just as Mahieu [Matheolus] composed sufficient verses about them [women] in his book and made diverse comments about their habits, so did Master Jean de Meun; one by one he reproached them all in his chapter on *Faulx Semblant*. I'll shut up, for if I continue on down the road I've started, I'll get into a quarrel or be bad-mouthed inadvertently. If someone picks a fight with me, I don't want any part of it; it will be on account of what I shall say. Hereafter I shall refuse all this.

This retreat into reticence betrays a double misgiving. The narrator is anxious not only about the matter he is translating but about the fact that he is now the mouthpiece for it. There is no apparent safety in numbers; neither Matheolus's authority nor Jean de Meun's masterly stature allays his fears. On the contrary, Jean de Meun's rationale of recitation is called implicitly into question.[10] It can no longer easily clear the translator as an accomplice. The risk lies in his translations provoking *tencons*. LeFèvre's translation of Cato's proverbial wisdom highlights this: "After disagreements, do not pass by litigation: always stay away when people quarrel, for the quarrel [*tencon*] is the enemy of peace. It falls to evildoers to slander, and those who are moved by anger speak lies."[11] In the case of the *Lamentations*, then, if the translator continues to represent women as slanderers and quarrelmongers according to the letter of Matheolus's text, he could be the butt of slander himself. At first sight, such a qualm seems to justify the stereotype of contentious women. Were the *Leesce* narrator bad-mouthed, named a *poète maudit*, the message of his translation would be confirmed. Why then desist? By withdrawing into silence, he tries to break out of the circuit that defines women's language as "naturally" slanderous. He attempts to abdicate from the ongoing repetition of misogynistic clichés. And such a gesture implies that verbal malice is not purely a women's problem.[12]

These scruples pave the way for a show of remorse:

> Excuser me vueil en mes dis
> Que des bonnes point ne mesdis

Ne n'ay voulenté de mesdire.
J'ameroye mieulx moy desdire
Qu'estre haï pour fol langage. . . .

Se je ment, je vueil qu'en me bate.
Il convient, puis que je translate,
Que je die ou que je me taise.
Pour ce suppli qu'il ne desplaise,
S'en cest dittié suy recordans
Aucuns mos qui soient mordans.
Car de moy ne procede mie.
(book 2, lines 1541–45, 1559–65)

I wish to apologize for my verse, for I am in no way slandering any good women, nor do I have any wish to do so. I would much prefer to denounce myself than to be despised for outrageous language. . . .

If I am lying, I wish to be beaten. When I am translating, it is appropriate that I speak up or shut up. For this reason I pray it not be displeasing to anyone when I recall in this tract any word that might be biting. For it never comes from me.

The narrator moves through apology and denial to self-repudiation. It is a sequence that leads, finally, to a form of violence. His desire to be beaten represents the most extreme version of his musing on the problem of *mesdire* (slander). He takes on the conventional position of the beaten wife. And because the move functions subjectively, it suggests a self-inflicted beating. In his reflection on verbal harm, the narrator goes so far as to embrace this harm himself—to internalize it.

The problem of *mesdire* is nothing new to a discourse on women or to medieval amorous discourse in general. As we have already seen, the fear over *mesdisants/lauzengiers* pervades numerous lyrics and romances. It is a paradigmatic fear, for the status of the lover and his lady is established in opposition to it. What distinguishes the translator's reflection on *mesdire* is its internal quality. Whereas the threat of slander is exported from most lyrics and romances, and is seen to lie somewhere outside their bounds, in LeFèvre's translation of the *Lamentations* it is beginning to be conceptualized as a constituent element of the discourse. The suspicion is that the narrator's language, like the writing he is translating, is intrinsically slanderous. Furthermore, there is a hint this inherent slander is directed toward one particular group. The class of women appears a special target, hence the narrator's urgent claim that it is better to repudiate his work and take a beating himself than be implicated in such *mesdisance*.

There is a telling symmetry here between admitting the slanderous character of masterly writing on women and punishing the self. This symmetry signals an important stage in the history of disputing the calumny of women. It leads to identifying the infraction of injurious language, "parole injurieuse" (I, 1572). The *Leesce*'s own term strengthens the notion of wounding, beautiful talk (trenchans bel parler) in the *Bestiaire* response with a more technical meaning. As a whole, the narrator's self-punishing reflection on *mesdisance* marks an important turn in that history of calumny because the problem is acknowledged within the sphere of clerical writing. Here is a clerkly persona who finds the problem of verbal injury critiqued by generations of scholastic commentaries lodged in his own work. Granted, his reflection is a minor lapse in an enormous tract. The narrator soldiers on to translate four thousand more lines. Further, his self-deprecating tone betrays a certain manipulative quality. Disparaging himself offers the narrator a means of displacing the problem he faces. Nevertheless, such a reflection makes possible the translator's ultimate response to the misogynistic *Lamentations*. It provides the mainspring. The impetus to respond negatively to the problem of *mesdisance* defines the *Livre de leesce*.

Cutting Off His Nose to Spite His Face

The makeup of the *Leesce* shows just how difficult it is for a clerical narrator like LeFèvre's persona to break with the masterly tradition of representing women. Over two-thirds of the text rehashes the first book of the *Lamentations*. It is a hodgepodge of the narrator's own translation of Matheolus. By rehearsing his version again, he attempts to exorcize from his writing the traces of his indebtedness to his masters. The *Leesce* reads like an exercise in purging the clerkly self. All those claims to repudiation made in the *Lamentations* are played out in the *Leesce*. This process has a decidedly painful side to it. Autocitation serves here as a goad of sorts. Far from authorizing the narrator's current writing, it functions instead to disparage it.[13] With each subsequent quotation, he further condemns his part in the misogynistic fulminations of Matheolus. At the same time, this pattern of self-condemnation through rewriting is a painful process for his readers to endure. While it is supposed to show him suffering with the women targeted by the *Lamentations*, from the readers' perspective it confirms his ongoing complicity. The more the narrator repeats himself, the more he mires himself in the masters' slander. Ironically, the attempt of ridding himself of its most offensive elements underscores his connection to them.

This self-condemning / self-incriminating dynamic runs through the

Leesce. It is particularly exacerbated by the imbalance between those sections rehashing Matheolus's text and those responding negatively to it. At the places where the narrator could best demonstrate his opposition to the clichés of demonic women and so on, he holds back. While he presents the misogynistic position in detail, he gives his own critical response short shrift. One example will make the point. In treating the subject of women's insatiable curiosity, the narrator lifts whole passages from his translated *Lamentations.* He repeats all those anecdotes that dramatize the impossible trust between husband and wife (lines 1805–90). There follows "a rather brief response" of three sentences (la response en est assez brieve; line 1891). So brief is the narrator's rejoinder that it does little to contest the type of the "busybody" woman. In fact, by recommending that men learn not to share their secrets with women, the narrator actually reinforces the type. The balance between repeating and disputing Matheolus is thus skewed in Matheolus's favor: the misogynistic tradition of representing women is effectively valorized. What is more, the *Leesce* makes a mockery of the need to respond at all. As the narrator says aptly, "When the fart is out, it's too late to restrain oneself." (tart main a cul, quant pet est hors; line 161) With this unrestrained proverbial wisdom he admits that once misogynistic language is unleashed—language as objectionable and gratuitous as a fart—there is little point in protesting it after the fact. Put another way, if injurious language is rehearsed ad nauseam, any attempt to dispute it is seriously compromised.

To meet this risk, the *Leesce* deploys a strategy that is familiar to us from the *Response au Bestiaire.* Its argument against the verbal injury of the *Lamentations* is structured according to contrariety:

> Il n'est riens qui n'ait son contraire,
> Qui en voulroit les preuves traire
> Et penser justement aux choses. . . .
>
> Qu'ay fait cest livre, pour complaire
> Par argument de sens contraire,
> Pour vous excuser loyaument
> Et monstrer especiaument
> Que nul ne doit femmes blasmer;
>   (lines 21–23, 33–37)

There is nothing that does not have its contrary, for whoever wants to extract the proofs and think correctly of things. . . . I have done this book in order to complete the argument with a contrary sense, so as to apologize loyally to you and especially to show that no one should blame women.

If there is any way to exit from the vicious circle of complicity with masterly writing, it will depend on arguing through contraries. In its simplest terms, such argumentation begins by asserting the opposite of the various derogatory epithets for women. *Rioteuse, noiseuse, jangleresse*: each element is turned back on itself. The *Leesce* maintains that misogynistic writing is "riotous," "*noiseuse*," and so on.[14] Because the *Lamentations'* propositions stand untested by the standard techniques of reversal and negation, they are vulnerable. The *Leesce* has only to apply these techniques to expose the faultiness of the *Lamentations*. Furthermore, the contrary propositions of the *Leesce* function to contradict those of the *Lamentations*.[15] They cancel them out. Without any gesture toward the evidence of empirical reality, the *Leesce* refutes its chief tenets concerning women.

In its extended terms, such argumentation through contraries questions the logic of misogynistic thought.[16] The *Leesce* tries to show the spurious reasoning of the *Lamentations*: "It doesn't follow truthfully; in logic, it is quite the opposite, provided that he speak the truth" (il ne s'ensuit pas vrayement; en logique est tout autrement, posé qu'il deïst verité; lines 803–5). As the *Leesce* analyzes the *Lamentations*, this illogic characterizes both the individual proposition and the work as a whole. By demonstrating the bad logic operative at the micro level, the *Leesce* thus seeks to expose the entire work as a set of faulty syllogisms—in short, as an exercise in sophism.

Yet given the outstanding problem of the narrator's self-incrimination, there is something insufficient about the claim of bad logic. Coming from a figure whose own writing is enmeshed in sophistic syllogisms, how could this claim offer an adequate explanation? This narrator is, by definition, complicitous. Because of his complicity, his argumentation through contraries diverges from that of the *Response au Bestiaire*. While the structure of the *Leesce's* argument appears the same, it is put to a very different use. This narrator employs it in a way that still confirms the most orthodox of scholastic practices. Precisely because he is not a neutral party and his argument still functions like the masters', his response to the verbal injury of women in the *Lamentations* must go still further. It reaches beyond questions of logic to those of desires:

> Il y a envie de bien
> Et envie qui ne vault rien.
> Homme ou femme qui estudie
> A bien faire, c'est bonne envie;
> Ainsi le doit on raconter.
> Qui puet les autres surmonter,

> Soit en armes ou en science
> Et avoir bonne conscience,
> C'est bonne envie, ce me semble,
> De pouoir et savoir ensemble.
> Mais qui d'autruy mal s'esleesce
> Et qui d'autruy bien a tristesce,
> C'est envie faulse et mauvaise.
> Cuer envieus n'est pas a aise,
> Car il prent tout en desplaisance
> Et ne puet avoir souffisance.
> C'est maufait d'autruy a tort mordre,
> Car en toutes choses a ordre;
> Le philosophe le tesmoingne.
>
> (lines 2253–71)

There is good desire and desire that is worth nothing at all. A man or a woman who strives to do good, that is good desire. So one should talk about it. The one who surpasses others, whether in military or intellectual matters, who has a good conscience, that, it seems to me, is good desire, of power and knowledge together. But the one who takes pleasure in the misfortunes of others, who enjoys their sadness, that is false and bad desire. An envious heart is not at ease, for it takes everything disagreeably and can have no satisfaction. It is criminal to cruelly mistreat others, for in all things there is an order. So says the Philosopher.

This reflection on desire is an attempt to get at the root causes of a masterly misogynistic writing. Evoking a pseudo-Aristotelian theory, it describes a "bad desire" as one that throws off the balance between knowledge and power. The result is a destructive, even sadistic discourse. Were a "good desire" to maintain the balance, however, the occasions for slander would not arise. In the *Leesce*'s analysis, as long as the incipient impulse to dominate (*seurmonter*) is grounded by this balance, the domineering language of *mesdire* cannot occur.

That the *Leesce* narrator analyzes "bad desire" in this manner does not discredit masterful misogynistic writing. It merely explains that writing, or I would say, explains it away. For all the distinctions made to promote "good desire" and the socially valuable knowledge associated with it, the narrator's explanation does not, finally, grapple with the "bad." While it may account for the mechanisms of bad desires, it does not dispute them. Grasping power at the level of desires does not necessarily lead to critiquing its many expressions.[17] Furthermore, such an analysis overlooks the possibility that the practices of knowledge can be damaging. Since the *Leesce* concentrates on the disequilibrium of knowledge and power caused by "bad desire," it does not reckon with the way such knowledge can constitute a symbolic practice of domination. In this respect, the *Leesce* avoids considering how bad desire and knowledge can be used injuriously against groups such as women.

What this paradigm of desire does provide is a clue to the dyad *leesce/ire* (joy/anger) governing this narrative. As an obvious expression of "good desire," *leesce* must be understood in opposition to the "bad," angry desire that rankles the *Lamentations*. The power of joy is to offset all those dark, corrosive emotions that can burst forth in the form of invective against women. That LeFèvre's text introduces the female figure Leesce as his mentor and names his work after her are the strongest signs that joy is to cure the injuriousness of misogynistic writing. It does not take much to see the gender coding of this dyad: wrathful and resentful emotions are allied with the masculine and delightful, calming ones with the feminine. What with the narrator's increasing allegiance to the cause of women, it is clear that any positive attribute is to be inflected as feminine. The *Leesce* is elaborating another pair of gendered contraries that operate, this time, at the primordial level of desire.

If we pursue the *Leesce*'s theory of gendered desires to its conclusion, we come to the source of the narrator's self-condemning / self-incriminating dynamic. As an embittered, masculine type, his translating is caught up in the cycle of slandering women. Animated by a "bad" desire, it is fated to attack them. His anger gives rise to a language that can inflict damage.[18] Yet such preordained attacks—and here we reach the *Leesce*'s source—are nothing but an assault on the self:

> Fols est qui soy meïsme blasme
> Et le lieu dont il naist diffame.
> Uns proverbes nous est donnés;
> C'est que cil qui coupe son nés
> Trop laidement sa face empire.
> Aussi ne puet homme mesdire
> De femme qu'il ne se mesface;
> Fols est donc qui coupe sa face.
> (lines 1029–36)

He is mad who blames himself and defames the place where he is born. A proverb is given to us: it is that he who cuts his nose, injures his face too hideously. No man can slander a woman without also disfiguring himself. So it is that he who cuts his face is mad.

The *Leesce* equates the desire to lash out against others with self-blame. Given the gendered contraries at play in this text, we need to read this formula as equating the desire to lash out against women as the Other with the tendency to blame the self as masculine.[19] Bad-mouthing women is a form of self-torture that can be understood only in terms of a masculine self. Blaming *her* damages *him*.

The comparison with the *Lamentations* is striking. In that text, any threatening difference found in the masculine self is isolated and ostracized in the character of women. The *Leesce*, by contrast, endeavors to draw woman's character back into the masculine self. It thus corrals her in a conception of ontological sameness. By interpreting any speech act slanderous to women as a byproduct of a man's bad blood, it subsumes women into a single homogeneous being. In this sense, the *Leesce*'s view that bad-mouthing women is ruinous to the self presupposes a uniform, unified body politic. The real threat of disfigurement, then, is that of an all-embracing masculine being.

In the *Leesce*'s view, we find another version of the *Houneurs des dames* expression *femme/lui meismes* discussed in chapter 1. This time it is cloaked in the terms of nature. As the *Leesce* narrator describes it, "sinners (slanderers) are estranged, for out of the womb they are changed and have erred against nature" (les pecheeurs sont estrangiés, Car hors du ventre sont changiés et ont erré contre nature; lines 1023–25). Slander is an antinatural form. It comes from those who are estranged not only from the masculine self but from their natural origins. Notice that this conception brings us back to the maternal matrix where the *Leesce* narrator must reckon with his origins in female matter. Slandering women transgresses nature because it vilifies the masculine self generated from women. Once again, the emphasis is put on the predicament of the male speaker rather than on the damaging effects of his slander. The *Leesce* dwells on the alienation of those men and the way slander jeopardizes "their nature," not women's.

This connection between masculine self-blame, the antinatural, and defamatory writing about women is emblematized by the case of Ovid:

> Car on raconte en verité
> Qu'on lui coupa ambdeux les couilles. . . .
> Que, haïneus et tout plain d'ire,
> Femmes après ce fait blasma
> N'oncques depuis ne les ama. . . .
> Ovides fu mal enfrenés
> Quant sa bouche femmes blasmoit;
> Il meïsmes se diffamoit
> Par courroux et par felonie;
> Sur soy en soit la vilenie.
> (lines 2710–11, 2720–22, 2778–82)

> For the story is told truthfully that both his balls were cut off. . . .
> After this happened, he was so full of anger and hatred that he
> railed against women. Since then, he could love them no more. . . .
> When he spoke out against women, Ovid was badly distempered;
> out of rage and maliciousness, he even defamed himself; on him be
> heaped the villainy.

Castration lies at the base of defamation. Because the Roman poet's sex is no longer "naturally" clear, he vents his anger on the other sex.[20] As the *Leesce* appraises it, Ovid's misogynistic corpus exists in direct relation to his disfigurement: one is not possible without the other. Therein lies the poignant charge of this exemplum for the *Leesce*. And it stands out all the more when we take into account LeFèvre's translation of the Ovidian text *De vetula*, where the *castrato* is portrayed at length.[21] While the castrated poet is reviled, in Ovid's case he also inspires sympathy. For this poet succeeds in writing by means of his mutilation. His (self-) mutilation is the very signature of his work.[22] However strongly the *Leesce* denounces Ovid, it too is spellbound by his example. Although it invokes the castrated poet as a negative exemplum, it betrays a deep affinity with him. The *Leesce* narrator is haunted by a bond in writing that makes them once, as always, intellectual brothers.

Here is where we can best gauge a second crucial implication of the *Leesce*'s equation between masculine bad desire and self-blame. To repeat the key phrase: "He is mad who blames himself and defames the place where he is born" (lines 1029–30). By describing defamation in these terms, the *Leesce* narrator identifies himself implicitly as a first-class defamer in league with Ovid. Having expended most of his own response excoriating himself, he reveals his own consummate participation in the defamation of women so characteristic of medieval masterly writing. The theory of the origins of slandering women never works so well as when it implicates the narrator.

An Imperfect Conversion

This definition of slandering women as self-blame would seem to condemn the narrative outright. What defense is left to a writer who convicts himself? Given the destructive character of his own words, any dispute he might have with the dominant codes of representing women seems utterly untenable. Yet the definition of defamation is precisely what is intended to salvage the *Leesce*. It sets the stage for the narrator's transformation—for nothing less than a conversion experience. As we have seen, the narrator's self-scrutiny has a progressively estranging effect. This, coupled with the

realization of his defamatory work, brings him to the threshold of renewal: "Whosoever would look into the self, would cease slandering" (Qui
dedens soy regarderoit De mesdire se cesseroit; lines 2769–70).

Such a model of conversion works in two powerful ways. Theologically,
it offers a familiar strategy for reviving the *Leesce* narrator.[23] He can be
represented as a lost and hapless persona about to be saved. Through a new
self-knowledge, he is liberated from bad desire, released from all past
anger and remorse and thus ready to be converted. Textually speaking,
this conversion bears even more important consequences. It provides a
way to rehabilitate the narrator's writing. As Susan Stewart has argued,
the notion of conversion appears as a remedy for crimes of writing.[24] Such
a transformation can remove all traces of past verbal damage and make his
language new. In the case of the *Leesce* narrator, it saves him from his
record of defamation. Ultimately, his language can be converted to salu-
tary ends—to advancing rather than destroying women's names.[25] Conversion can usher in a gynocentric writing.

This reversal is marked by a clear switch in stylistic register. The narrator composes his own *balade*, invoking for the first time the amorous discourse typical of court poets such as Guillaume de Machaut and Eustache
Deschamps:[26]

> Je forgeray toute ma vie
> Pour plaire a ma dame Leesce,
> Et en soustenant sa partie
> Blasmeray courroux et tristesce.
> Des dames et de leur haultesce
> Diray bons mos clers et luisans,
> Pour confondre les mesdisans.
> (lines 3447–53)

I will work away all my life to please my lady Leesce, and in supporting her cause, I shall decry anger and sadness. I shall speak a
clear and bright language about ladies and their dignity so as confound the slanderers.

Here is a form of autocitation that registers powerfully. After goading
himself with the degraded quotes of his own translation, the narrator is capable of speaking anew.[27] His new language continues to be defined by the
Leesce's gender code. Insofar as it is dedicated to women's causes, it is
"joy-ful." His language becomes feminized. In the remaining part of the
Leesce, where various arguments advocating women are presented, this
converted, feminized language is supposed to prevail.

Yet does this conversion process work? Does it really "confound the
slanderers" (pour confondre les mesdisans), as the ballad refrain claims?

On one level, the *Leesce's* argumentation through contraries does indeed dispute the precepts advanced by so many medieval masters writing on women. It brings them to naught, exposing the illogic of stereotyping women's "nature." In this way it challenges the defamatory character of such writing. On a deeper level, however, it continues to be bound up with that illogical, defamatory tradition of representing women. Listening to the double entendre of this refrain, I would say that the *Leesce* remains confused (*confondre*) with the most influential model of representing women. The plight of the divided, masculine self is not so easily resolved by the scenario of conversion. Nor is his language fully reformed. The turn to peaceful lyrics is insufficient. So profound is the narrator's plight that it makes its mark on this transformed text when least expected, contaminating its clear, bright, feminized language. In the process of articulating a new self and responding against the symbolic domination of women, his complicity with masterly writing reasserts itself.

Such is the problem of what I call the sycophantic response. The sycophant is a classic insider/informer. He is known to espouse different positions so as curry favor. His reputation rides on his ability to assume allegiances deceptively. He is also known for an excessive, flattering language. His flattery is dangerous precisely because it belies its slanderous potential. The sycophant is an archetypal calumniator. In stressing both the changeable and the calumniating character of the sycophant, I am playing with the simplest understanding of the term. But I do so in order to clarify the character of the *Leesce*. By exaggerating its support of the very subjects it habitually reviles, the *Leesce* displays a fundamental sycophancy. It conveys a two-timing discourse: neither of its positions is convincing— neither condemnation nor adulation of women. And the switch from one to the other makes the sycophantic deceptiveness of the *Leesce* all the more apparent. While the conversionary model may turn the narrator into an advocate of women, it does not completely transform his purpose. Given his chronic sycophantic tendencies, his choice to praise women remains tainted with the concerns of misogynistic masterful writers. It is a servile gesture.

Nowhere is the issue of sycophancy more evident than in the final part of the *Leesce* where the converted narrator espouses a number of theorems in support of women. The question arises: to what end could such arguments be put? All of the theorems taken up belong to the standard gynocentric repertory of the later Middle Ages: the argument for women's superior material composition (lines 3724–26), the notion that women alone were created in paradise (lines 3728–35), the catalogue of exemplary martial and intellectual women (lines 3531–3679), even the view that many women surpass men in the sheer range of their achievements (lines 3499–3502). Some of these, we will recall, are employed by the *Response au Bestiaire*. Still others are invoked by LeFèvre's contemporary, Christine de Pizan.[28] And all of them together are recapitulated in the paradigmatic sycophantic response, Martin LeFranc's *Champion des dames*, written several generations later.[29] In other words, the same arguments are deployed by responses of diverse character. Here is where the question of ends comes in. For what different reasons could the same arguments be used? Insofar as these various texts deploy a single repertory of arguments, it is only by examining the function of the argument that we can distinguish those responses that confirm the existing symbolic domination of women from those that envisage some change. If responses such as the *Response au Bestiaire* or the *Leesce* look similar rhetorically, they can still be set apart by the ways they exploit gynocentric theorems.

The *Leesce* uses such theorems to the conventional, limiting ends of so much masterly writing. In the final part of the narrative, the idea of women's sexualized identity rules. All the arguments marshaled for women are shot through with the *masle/femelle* lexicon. One example will make the point:

> Les masles aiment pillerie
> Et larrecin et roberie,
> Occision et convoitise
> Et tout ce qui a mal atise.
> Les femelles sont debonnaires
> En tous cas et en tous affaires.
> (lines 3688–93)

Males like pillage, larceny, and theft, murder, and lust, and everything that is maliciously incited. Females are gentle in every instance and under all circumstances.

In these male/female polarities lie the terms that define women's existence sexually.[30] While the depiction of the perfect woman can be read superficially as laudatory, the logic informing that praise bases it upon "femaleness," that is, upon woman's sexuality. The same is true of the portraits of exemplary women such as Sappho and Cassandra (lines 3646, 3666). They continue to predicate their achievements on their sexual identity. Individual women may be poetesses or inventors of writing, but they are still to be regarded first and foremost as "female." Far from disputing clerical representations of women, such praise reinforces them all the more strongly. As Denise Riley has rightly observed, the sexualized definition of woman used by many such gynocentric texts further constrains the subjects they claim to champion.[31] In this context the very privileging of *leesce* (joy) and the penultimate claim that women are men's joy (line 3982) make the whole work sound like a sycophantic praise poem of female sexuality—of *jouissance* we might say—as long as it ensures the continuity of the patriarchal line.

With the return of the most conventional definitions of female nature, there can be little doubt about the *Leesce's* ultimate use of arguments in support of women. Far from figuring any significant change in the representation of women, it conforms to the principal masterly models.[32] It bodies forth a feminine type—genteel, fertile, and above all easy to handle. The irony is that the gallery of exceptional women is also presented to promote their voluntary and responsible acceptance of existing authority. Even Minerva's wisdom is invoked to communicate the importance of deference—for the good of the body politic and of the learning that has for so long survived in the hands of the clergy (lines 3650–54). In elaborating its final refutation of misogynistic arguments, the *Leesce* projects figures of women who are not only not argumentative but who lend themselves to being mastered, women "whose husbands have the mastery through true love and common agreement" (dont leurs maris ont la maistrie par vraye amour et par concorde; lines 380–81). The *Leesce* comes eerily full circle, espousing a view with which its clerkly adversaries would not disagree— yet with which the *Bestiaire* respondent most certainly would.

But lest we forget, such are the recommendations of a sycophant. And precisely this sycophancy should alert us to other possible inferences. Since this persona has switched sides, flip-flopped, the discerning critic is licensed to read the text in spite of itself. The conflicted aspects of such a sycophantic work are liable to let slip issues at odds with its general character. In the long term, I believe, the *Leesce* did contribute an important element to the ongoing dispute with masterful misogynistic writing. Against itself, it added to the critique of the dominant sexualized representations of women by exploring further the issue of injurious language. Here I am circling back to LeFèvre's translation anxiety over the *feme/ diffame* refrain with which I began. Through a language deeply divided and arguments deployed to repressive ends, this clerkly response helped to foreground a concept of defamation. Paradoxically, it advanced the idea of identifying an established text as slanderous.

On the face of it, there is nothing new about such ideas. In the later Middle Ages defamation was commonly understood as the language abusive to a person's name (*contumeliosa verba*).[33] Such language was deemed dangerous enough to merit physical punishment. As the principal digest of medieval legal opinion, Gratian's *Decretum*, assessed it, (and as LeFèvre's case corroborated): "Whosoever devises in public words or writing insulting to another's reputation and once having been discovered does not defend the writings, should be beaten" (qui in alterius famam publice scripturam aut verba contumeliosa confinxerit, et repertus scripta non probauerit, flagelletur).[34] This understanding, we recall, derived from Roman views concerning reputation (*fama*) and loss of reputation (*infamia/diffamatio*).[35] It was based on an overarching conception of injury that included physical gestures, words, and texts (*iniuria*).[36] These views were well known to medieval audiences through various commentaries, notably Augustine's meditations on the issues of the good name.[37] Yet LeFèvre's text moves beyond these general understandings of defamation and changes their frame of reference. The *Leesce*'s reflection on the origin of defamation begins to situate it in a context that emphasizes its relation to women. It picks up on the specific connection between verbal injury and women's names that was already apparent in Justinian's Code. Furthermore, its *feme/diffame* refrain hints at an entirely different way that relation could be understood. In this way, LeFèvre's expression is symptomatic of the *Leesce*'s sycophancy because it communicates at cross purposes. It dramatizes the fact that women are the perennial object of defamatory writing. By a simple reversal of terms, it also points to the concept of unjust verbal damage done to women. Speaking against itself, the *Leesce* brings to the fore an important and more technical way of naming and disputing injurious language.

It is in this sense that the refrain resonates in the latter parts of the *Leesce*. When the narrative uses it to identify defamation as a "crime" (line 3201) and a "sin" (line 3419), it points to a nascent understanding of symbolic damage inflicted textually on women. It focuses on what Susan Stewart has dubbed suggestively "*a crime of writing.*" When it reviews the work of clerkly authors, it even goes so far as to suggest that defamation may apply to an entire literary tradition:

> en leurs libelles ne leurs fables
> N'en leurs fais qui sont mal prouvables,
> Ou il alleguent poësies
> Et merveilleuses frenesies,
> Desquelles il ne font a croire.
> (lines 3806–10)

[I]n their little books, fables and ill-founded works, where they put forward poetries and marvelous madnesses that should not be believed.

While the term defamation does not occur here, the connection made between unbelievable poetry and madness implies the problem of injurious language. As the *Leesce* has shown all too well, the angry frenzy of poets (*frenesie*) frequently takes a defamatory form.

This is the sense too in which Christine de Pizan and other late-medieval writers exploit the idea of defamation. In fact, it is tempting to hear LeFèvre's *feme/diffame* refrain reverberating within Christine's public accusation of clerical writing about women.[38] It would take many more developments on political, legal, and intellectual fronts before defamation could be wielded as a charge by women. It would require still others for defamation to be brought to bear on the status of *poësie* and the question of a written text's liability. Such was the labor of various fifteenth-century respondents we shall examine. Yet LeFèvre's conflicted understanding plays no small part in this process.

Beyond its response to the *Lamentations of Matheolus*, the *Leesce's* sycophantic play with the *feme/diffame* dyad fosters thinking about the impact of masterly writing on women in an increasingly judgmental manner. Like a jingle, it works its way into the prevailing system of discourse, triggering different perceptions about the convention of defaming women, occasioning as yet untested strategies for bringing it to task. While this late-fourteenth-century work did not capitalize on any such perceptions and strategies, it helped to make them possible. Therein lies its most unorthodox long-term effect.

6   Christine's Way

The *Querelle du Roman de la rose* and the Ethics of a Political Response

Your stylus is dipped in corrosive sublimate,
How can you scratch out
Indelible ink of the palimpsest
Of past misadventure?
                    H.D., *The Walls Do Not Fall*

Of all those who take on the problem of defamation in late-medieval literature, it is the poet and professional writer Christine de Pizan who disputes it most vigorously. In her allegorical poem the *Epistre au dieu
d'amours* (*Letter to the God of Love*), Christine lodges her first complaint
of defamation against women:

> Pour ce conclus en diffinicion
> Que des mauvais soit fait punicion
> Qui les blasment, diffament et accusent
> Et qui de faulz desloiaulz semblans usent
> Pour decepvoir elles.[1]
>
> (lines 775–79)

> For this reason I conclude with the definition that the wrongdoers be
> punished, those who blame, accuse, and defame women and those who
> employ false and treacherous appearances in order to deceive them.

In Cupid's Court of Love, she charges both courtly and clerical writers
with speaking and writing injuriously about women in general. Unlike
Jean LeFèvre, she exploits a particularly prestigious literary medium to
launch her critique. By resorting to allegory, she implicates the very tradition of writing she aims to dispute.

As if a poetic charge of defamation does not register sufficiently, Christine turns it into a polemical one. Her accusation against defamatory literary
language is the fuse that ignites one of France's first major literary controversies, known as the *Querelle du Roman de la rose*.[2] This turn toward
polemics is critical, for it transforms a verbal action into an event.[3] It

151

arraigns Jean de Meun's *Rose* before the general public, requiring its response in turn. Polemically, Christine's accusation of defamation creates a happening that her Parisian milieu is pressed to acknowledge.[4] It calls upon the representative powers in early-fifteenth-century Paris: royal administrators and lawyers, city officials, and the Queen Regent, Isabeau of Bavaria. Christine's initiation of the *Querelle* mobilizes the entire community, with the result that her words raise a spectacular public challenge.

Such a move signals another stage in the medieval dispute with magisterial representations of women. It constitutes an especially vociferous case that surpasses the standard clerical *disputatio*. While Christine's polemic shares a disputational form with many of the works we have been examining, it ups the ante by targeting an even wider public. It breaks the academic stronghold of many disputations and situates its challenge in the midst of the city. It involves the usual clerical community, in this instance a circle of humanists prominent in Parisian intellectual life at the beginning of the fifteenth century. But it also summons the citizenry. The force of a *querelle* (quarrel) engages everybody.[5] In this respect, Christine's polemic critiques the masterly textual tradition in the very social space it claims to monopolize. Indeed, it occupies that space.

In this polemical context we can begin to gauge Christine's particular charge of defamation: Jean de Meun's *Rose* as a "public defamer" (diffameur publique; Hicks, 22). Such an accusation may first call up the image of a person ranting and raving on the street corner. It conjures up a disturbing scene, but hardly one involving a public offense. In a late-medieval setting, however, the problem of defamation was placed necessarily in the public domain. If any invective was to work, it had to register out in the open, before the people in their implicit role as witnesses. Insofar as an individual or group reputation (*fama*) rides on the words of others—on public opinion—it could be damaged in this context alone. Created publicly, it can be devalued only *in choro publico*. This circle of public adulation and damnation was all the more vicious where women's reputations were concerned.[6] As the index of family and societal honor over and above their own personal honor they were peculiarly susceptible to attack. In Claude Gauvard's suggestive phrase, in medieval and early-modern society, a woman's name was condemned to be defamed.[7]

Yet Christine's charge does more than clarify the setting of defamation. It also identifies a celebrated literary work as defamatory of the public. That is, it finds the depiction of women in Jean de Meun's *Rose* to be injurious to the community as a whole. While this charge represents an individual grievance, something that Christine's first-person address makes clear, at the same time it speaks for women as a constituent element of the public. It represents the class of women as part of the community. It thereby enlarges the frame of reference for the dispute over masterly writing about women. It brings into view its destructive social impact. The defamation of women becomes a matter of civic concern because it jeopardizes the very languages that help to define a particular community.

Christine's charge of the *Rose* as a public defamer capitalizes on a Roman model for regulating language on behalf of the people (comme anciennement les Rommains triumphans; Hicks, 21). This model appraises defamatory language as a potential threat to the commonweal. As it was outlined to medieval audiences by Augustine, the Roman model interprets the individual speech act or text functionally: it ties the speech act to the welfare of the community.[8] In fact, so tightly are they bound together that the defamer is seen as one whose transgressive language assaults the integrity of the group. Slandering any single member violates the polis. Consequently, there is enormous pressure to isolate the defamer and stigmatize him publicly. In the extreme, this leads even to exile, as Ovid's well-known case underscores.[9] Against the menace of public defamation, then, the forces of government and its laws are marshaled. This means criminalizing the defamer. In the terms of Cicero, the Roman authority hovering over the *Querelle*:[10]

[I]n his hanc quoque sanciendam putaverunt, si quis occentavisset sive carmen condidisset, quod infamiam faceret flagitiumve alteri. praeclare; iudiciis enim magistratuum, disceptationibus legitimis propositam vitam, non poetarum ingeniis, habere debemus nec probrum audire nisi ea lege, ut respondere liceat et iudicio defendere.

(*De re publica*, IV, x, 12)[11]

Though they provided the death penalty for only a few crimes, [our Twelve Tables] did provide it for any person who sang or composed a song which contained a slander or insult to anyone else. This was an excellent rule; for our mode of life ought to be liable to judgment by the magistrates and the courts of law, but not by clever poets; nor ought we to be subject to disgrace unless we have an opportunity to answer and defend ourselves in a court of law.

The crime of defamation is inflected poetically. Implicit here is the rivalry between the poetic and the legal—the right to "figure" freely and the duty to do so in keeping with the polis. This is a fundamental opposition to which I shall return. For now, suffice it to remark the irony of the Roman model for the *Querelle de la Rose*. Christine holds both the role of the defamer and the one stigmatizing the defamer. Let us not forget that for the Parisian humanist intelligentsia, her polemical maneuvering would confirm the time-honored stereotype of woman as defamer. At the same time, by issuing the charge Christine aligns herself with the civic and legal authorities. The lawbreaker breaks into the law. The putative defamer becomes the judge, and this reversal sends her to the very center of the polis.

Such a rhetorical move brings home the fact that there is nothing natural about the categories "defamer" and "judge" and the social boundaries that distinguish them. Nor are the linguistic norms that mark off defamation from socially acceptable language absolute. Protocols specific to a social milieu designate certain locutions as slanderous, and such protocols are themselves subject to change. Christine's initiation of the *Querelle* involves a role reversal that sets just such a change into motion. By assuming the stance of judge before the public, she places her critique at the center of the public sphere. From this position, Christine can question the logic that continues to identify her rhetorically as a defamer. More importantly, she challenges the way that defamation has been conceptualized in relation to women: how it is that such defamation appears, for the most part, perfectly licit. This is something that LeFèvre's writing could not accomplish, since as a quintessential insider's work it was always already aligned with the law.

But what sort of public territory does Christine intend to take over? Given the reactions of her interlocutors, Christine appears, at first sight, to enter into the realm of humanist debate. An entry into this public realm is labeled straightaway a form of trespass. One disputant, Gontier Col, attacks her charge of defamation for its "outrageous presumptuousness" (presumpcion oultrageuse; Hicks, 100).[12] Another, Jean de Montreuil, associates Christine with a proverbial range of outcasts—heretics and Jews newly banished from Paris.[13] Both attacks suggest a deep insecurity. Col and Montreuil speak from a threatened, even precarious position. And the fact that all of Christine's interlocutors interpret her critique of Maistre Jean de Meun's writing as a transgression from without suggests just how defensive they are about their own clerico-humanist domain—what Grover Furr has called "the group-exclusive" preserve of humanism.[14] Their dealings with Christine make no allowances for her entry into that public sphere. Far from it: Montreuil's description of the weapons of speech, writing, and physical force marks the *Querelle* as a serious battle over that sphere (Hicks, 30).

To encroach upon the territory of humanist intellectuals, however, involves breaking into an even more prestigious and extensive public space. Christine aspires to nothing less than the *res publica*—the space of the commonwealth:

> Et comme anciennement les Rommains triumphans n'atribuassent
> louenge aucune ne honneur a chose quelconques se elle n'estoit a l'util-

ité de la chose publique, regardons a leur exemplaire se nous pourons couronner cestuy rommant.

(Hicks, 21)

And as in ancient times when the triumphant Romans would not accord praise or the slightest honor to anything if it were not to the utility of the commonwealth [*la chose publique*], let us look to their example to see whether we can crown this romance.

By establishing what are Ciceronian coordinates for the civic domain, she situates the problem of defamation toward women at its very center. Correspondingly, she becomes the chief guardian of that domain. She assumes the persona of a Roman *censor*. From the outset of the *Querelle*, this implicit configuration invests her with the role of evaluating utility, bestowing honor, praise, and blame. That is, she is empowered with the censorious functions of the adjudicator of public welfare.[15] As this Roman model was understood in the fifteenth century, the censor stood for the common good.[16] He surveyed the citizenry's language and behavior that might jeopardize the social equilibrium. In this sense the censor figure exemplifies public authority—the power acting on behalf of the people.[17] In this sense too, we can qualify Christine's position in the *Querelle*. Having traversed the greatest possible rhetorical distance from no-man's-land to the center point of public authority, her persona pronounces the charge of defamation against women censoriously. While Christine's charge does not involve the specific terms of censure, it carries that weight. And as we have seen, it registers strategically as well as rhetorically. Christine's pronouncement operates within the Parisian commonwealth; it realizes the Roman rhetorical figure. Her entrance into a humanists' disputation thus opens up the civic space and invests her with the task of adjudicating the public issue of defaming women.

The notion of public, civic space, in the *Querelle de la Rose*—"la chose publique"—directs our attention once again toward the effects of texts defamatory to women. It resembles the *Bestiaire Response*'s effort to dispute a category of masterly writing on behalf of all women. It builds on the *Leesce*'s conflicted attempt to conceptualize the injurious character of so many clerical figures of women. This it did in the peculiarly charged social environment of late-medieval Paris, where disputes were the rule, not the exception.[18] As a result, Christine's polemic asks us to examine how defamatory writing affects not only the individual parties represented but the social group of which they were a part.

Following Christine's lead, I shall pursue this question pragmatically. My analysis will thus concentrate less on Christine's polemical reading of the *Rose* than on the bearing it has on the public. Within the common-wealth, how are representations of women identified as injurious and how then are they judged? This way of proceeding may seem to take us on a detour, beyond the *Querelle* to another of Christine's allegories, the *Chemin de long estude* (*The Way of Lengthy Study*). But by taking this route, we will be better able to discern the implications of Christine's dispute with the conventions of masterly writing about women.

From Insult to Injury

We can begin with no more telling instance of Christine's pragmatics than her objection to Reason's naming of genitalia in the *Rose*. This argument has been understood habitually as one of nominalism versus empiricism.[19] Gontier Col and Jean de Montreuil are seen to defend the use of any name, no matter what its significance. Christine, by contrast, is seen to be concerned (and shocked) by the sexual significance. Consequently, Christine appears to occupy the moral high ground while the humanists aim for a more sophisticated level where names are unencumbered by morality and signification is a purely linguistic affair. With such a view, it is hardly surprising that the humanists emerge as the discerning critics and Christine as the easily offended prude.

Yet if we pay close attention to the way Christine formulates the issue of naming genitalia, her position looks anything but empiricist. For her, a name must be gauged according to its function in social intercourse. Anything named—*la chose nommée*—is inextricably bound up in the common-wealth—*la chose publique*. Moving away from a purely formalist problem of signification, Christine is concerned with the way significance is determined socially. What a name is taken to signify is a matter of social consensus. In attending to the circumstances of names such as *vis* (dick) or *couilles* (balls), Christine is interested in their conventional social efficacy. She focuses on their effects in the body politic:

> Et que honte doye estre deboutee en parlant en publique des choses
> dont nature mesmes se hontoye, je dis que, sauve la reverence de l'aut-
> teur et la vostre, grant tort commectéz contre la noble vertu de honte,
> qui de sa nature reffraint les goliardises et deshonnestetés en dis et fais;
> et que ce soit grant vice et hors ordre de pollicie honneste et de bonnes
> meurs appert en mains lieux de l'Escripture saincte.

> (Hicks, 14)

> And whether shame/modesty should be insulted in speaking publicly
> of things about which even nature itself is ashamed, let me say that ex-
> cept for your reverence, and the author's, you commit a great wrong

against the noble virtue of shame/modesty, which naturally restrains dishonesty and bad behavior in word and deed, and the fact that it is a serious vice beyond the order of honest government and good behavior is made apparent in several places of Holy Scripture.

Speaking the words for genitalia is not shameful. Rather, what is shameful is the fact that their articulation in this particular society can realize a symbolic form of violence against women. More often than not, these words signify damagingly for them. Furthermore, this pattern of signification is linked to irresponsible and harmful behavior, "goliardises et deshonnestetés." Unleashing such language publicly can act as a trigger mechanism for abusive conduct. The use of such words in what are habitual, sexualized slurs about women can often culminate in physical aggression. Under these circumstances, female shame is less symptomatic of excessive modesty than it is of the anxiety about verbal violence—about defamation—and its carnal counterpart. Aristotle's *Ethics*, translated by one of Christine's favorite authorities, the philosopher/translator Nicole Oresme, defines shame in just these terms. Oresme's version reads: "Fear of infamy; that is to say, fear to suffer confusion, dishonor, blame" (Vercunde est paour de ingloriacion; c'est a dire, paour de avoir confusion, deshonneur ou vitupere).[20] That women blush while reading the *Rose* indicates that they recognize the defamatory way the words of sex can signify for them in courtly society (Hicks, 20). It is a measure of this language's potentially harmful consequences.[21] Such consequences are borne by individual and group alike. In Christine's view, a determining link exists between the injury defamation inflicts on a woman and on her community—the "ordre de pollicie" as a whole.

This issue of social ramifications is pivotal to her conception of defamation. Insofar as defamatory language is part of a social code governing the public place, she insists on analyzing it in relation to that place. Consider the following cameo scene from the *Mutacion de Fortune*, another allegory Christine was composing at the time of the *Querelle*:

> Sont ilz courtois ou gent honnie
> Ceulx, qui tant dient villenie
> A femme, comme pourroit dire
> Le plus ort villain de l'Empire? . . .
> Tesmoing d'un, que je ne cognoiz,
> Mais il bati, n'a pas .III. mois,
> Une femme, dessus le pont
> De Paris, dont il meprist moult;
> Et si est homme de renom,
> Ce dist on, je ne sçay son nom.

> La son saoul la bati d'un aulne,
> Devant chacun, et de la paume,
> Pour ce que elle ne vouloit,
> Pour lui, faire ce qu'il ne loit
> Faire a quelconques preude femme,
> Et si n'a renom de diffame.
> (lines 5353–56, 5359–70)[22]

Are those who speak maliciously of women courtly or despicable people, as they might say, the most ignoble villain in the Empire? . . . I attest to one whom I do not know, but on top of the bridge in Paris, he beat a woman, not three months ago, and in so doing acted wrongly. And he is a man of a certain reputation, as they say, though I do not know his name. There he beat her to his satisfaction with a stick before everyone, and with his bare palm, because she did not want to do for him what is not fitting for any upstanding woman to do, and he still has no reputation for defamation.

The connection here between slander and violence toward a woman is immediate and direct. So too is the involvement of "everyone" in the city. The scene is set up in such a manner that every citizen, including Christine, the eyewitness, is implicated. But how are they complicitous? Because they observe firsthand the passage from defamation to brutal abuse? Christine's analysis foregrounds the public arbitration of reputation and thereby accentuates the public's unavoidable involvement in its effects. Here is a reputable man who is seen to turn his verbal abuse into blows and a woman who in the attempt to avoid defamation is assaulted. To the degree that the public maintains the man's good name, they are his accomplices. And to the degree that they tolerate his defamation or do not perceive it as such, they are responsible for his conduct. The defamer/assaulter is not the only guilty party. Once set in the public theater, the infractions of defamation become the commonwealth's affair.

That is why one principal criterion in Christine's dispute with the *Rose* is utility. How does a work contribute to the common good? Or, as Christine puts it early on in the *Querelle*: "To what advantage or profit is it to the listeners?" (et a quel utilité ne a quoy prouffite aux oyans; Hicks, 15). This notion of utility can provide an antidote to defamation of women. Pragmatically it is its very opposite: useful speech or writing works to the public's benefit. Christine's critique of the *Rose* as a "useless" text pushes this opposition further. Not only does the *Rose* accomplish nothing, a work that does no work, but as a form of idleness (*oisiveté*) it fosters destructive action.[23] In this sense, the ultimate danger of a useless text lies in the way it can wreak havoc in the very public it is meant to serve.

Because the *Querelle* works polemically, Christine's principle of utility is never taken up. It is matched instead by a competing one: the autonomy of poetic form. As many critics have noted, this principle is introduced into the debate by way of the new humanist theories of poetry circulating in fifteenth-century Paris:[24]

> Aussi en ce pas la y faingny poetiquemant, et aux poetes et paintres a tousjours esté licence pareille de tout faindre, comme dit Orace.
>
> (Hicks, 93)
>
> At this point he also feigns poetically; and to poets and painters there has always been such a license to feign everything, as Horace says.

> Aussy veult monstrer Meung qu'il estoit naturel et crestien en parlant de Nature, et sy estoit poete, come j'ay dit, par quoy li laissoit de tout parler par ficcion.
>
> (Hicks, 98)
>
> Meun also wishes to show that it is natural and Christian to talk about Nature, and in this manner he was a poet, as I have said, by which he was permitted to talk about everything through fiction.

Pierre Col advances an early-modern "Notes Toward a Supreme Fiction." At its center lies the notion of *licence*: an unconditional liberty to speak. Whether coded in figurative or fictional terms, it constitutes an utter freedom: the poet says anything and everything (tout faindre, tout parler). Yet by its own definition, this freedom is double-edged. It legislates its own law. It is, etymologically speaking, licit. Conversely, it breaks with the established public law. Poetic license also goes beyond the bounds, and borders on excess. It is licentious, prone to disregard the accepted rules. Included, then, within this single pivotal locution are the warring aspects of lawfulness and lawlessness, judicious and dangerous freedom. Paradoxically, the very articulation of absolute poetic freedom contains within it the signs of its own danger. It carries with it the potential for violence. As we have already discovered in the Ciceronian configuration, this is the paradox that sets the irrepressible poetic at loggerheads with the public law. There is a perennial tension between the unfettered poetic word and its injurious potential. In the case of the *Rose*, this tension is directed for the most part against women. Licentious *poetria*, inflected as a feminine form, threatens being visited upon them.

By espousing the principle of poetry's licentious license, Col invests Jean de Meun's *Rose* with an omnipotence as form. As a consequence, the question of utility is never addressed. In our terms, this means that a poetic form whose omnipotence is expressed through the feminine is kept strictly divorced from its pragmatic results. However strongly humanist understandings of poetry are based on its social value, Col and Montreuil do not entertain this aspect of humanist doctrine in the *Querelle*. Their interest lies in vindicating the formal autonomy of the *Rose* without acknowledging its defining feminine figure and without regard to its effect on its female audiences.

This formalist position is corroborated by a belief in the sacredness of the poetic text: "The gravities of mysteries and the mysteries of gravities" (misteriorum pondera ponderumque misteria; Hicks, 28). As Pierre-Yves Badel has pointed out, Montreuil's phrase conjures up the "holy of holies" of the biblical text, a writing so magnificent that only the elect can fathom its meaning (419). Through such an analogy between romance fiction and the Bible, the poetic is subsumed into the hieratic. Its mysterious character distinguishes it from all other verbal types, rendering it sublime. This sublimation of form is further borne out by the theorem regarding speech *par personnages*. According to this theorem, the words of Jean de Meun's allegorical characters are the touchstone of poetic license. And their total impunity is applicable to other cases:

> "Se ung se nomme adversaires du roy de France (ce dit dame Eloquance), et soubz ce non il li fait guerre . . . se en la persone d'ung Sarrazin . . . ung home seme erreurs en la foy, en sera il excusé?" Et d'autres pareilles, qui tant soit pou ne sont a propos. Je li demande: pour tant, se Salluste recite la conjuracion de Catiline encontre la chose publique de Romme, en est il pour ce coulpable? pour tant, se Aristote recite les oppinions des anciens philozophes contenans erreurs en philozophie, est il semeur d'erreurs en icelle?
>
> (Hicks, 101–2)

> "If someone names himself an enemy of the king of France (so says Lady Eloquence), and under this name he wages war against him . . . if in the persona of a Sarrasin, a man sows errors in the faith, will he be excused for it?" And other similar cases that are not really relevant. I ask her: nevertheless, if Sallust recites Catiline's conspiracy against the commonwealth of Rome, is he himself guilty? Further, if Aristotle recites the opinions of the ancient philosophers containing philosophical errors, is he thereby propagating errors in this?

Col extends full liberties to any figurative formulation, even in political and philosophical discourse. He argues for the philosopher's right to enunciate errors. Exploiting de Meun's term *reciter*—the very one used in the *Rose* to rebuff the complaint of misogynistic defamation—Col champions the autonomy of any speech act enunciated hypothetically or through an assumed persona. And he does so, tongue in cheek, by means of the projected speech of such a persona, Lady Eloquence. As long as the speech act occurs under these conditions, anything goes—including the dreaded word of sedition. We have here the most radical elaboration of a notion of speech that tolerates no limitation. And this is most clearly evidenced in the political arena, where curses and verbal plots against the commonwealth abound. The statesman reserves the right to entertain or repeat injurious statements by virtue of his protected speech. By introducing such an example, Col takes up Christine's concern with the public domain only to deride it—or, one might say, to dismiss it knowingly. By focusing on the nature and the exercise of such a privileged and autonomous speech, Col disregards the question of utility. His commentary deflects the question of a text's pragmatic relation to the body politic—a question that certainly plays a central role in the humanist enterprise. Consequently, he blocks the charge of defamation of women before it can ever take hold. If injurious language is sanctioned absolutely by a principle of verbal autonomy even when it is entertained against the polis, then the idea of defaming women has no bearing. This is for two reasons. Not only does defamation per se make no sense under such conditions, but the specific case of defamation against women is inconceivable. When the criterion of utility does not pertain, even the simplest understanding of verbal injury cannot take shape.

We come here to the core of the *Querelle*: the confrontation of set positions that pits the humanists' sacrosanct poetic form against Christine's notion of a socially profitable language. The only possible change is one of rhetorical degree. Over the course of the *Querelle*, a language of absolutist power develops: orthodoxy versus apostasy, legitimacy versus criminality. Such oppositions conjure up scenes of interrogation and punishment in the public square, even of exile and book burning. As Christine invokes this language, she takes it to the extremes of heresy and treason:

> Mais je te demende se quant yceulx ou autres, ou la sainte Escripture recite telz choses, se il y a devant ou aprés personnages ou aultre propos qui conforte et afferme par molles parolles et attrayans que l'en trahisse ou que l'en soit herite, et ainssy des autres maulx: tu sces bien que nennil.

> (Hicks, 133–34)

But I ask you whether when these or others, or the holy Scripture recite such things either before or after characters or other speeches, that

through soft and attractive words encourage and spur people to treason, heresy, or other evils? You know very well that it is not the case.

Naming the *Rose* a heretical and treasonous text escalates the problem of
verbal injury to the greatest possible degree. It turns the injury into a civic
threat. Theologically and politically, it codes defamation as the gravest
crime.

That Christine resorts to this language has a decided iconoclastic punch
to it. We must remember that her persona begins as the classic defamer—
the deviant whose reversed charge of defamation propels her toward a central seat of power. Speaking in this absolutist idiom is for her, then, a sub-
versive act. It represents her ultimate challenge, her final effort to bring
the textual problem of defaming women into view. At the same time, it
points to her success in appropriating the public arena. Her claim to expel
Jean de Meun's *Rose* from the city demonstrates her skill at making a text
injurious to women publicly accountable.

However troubling Christine's absolutist language may appear to readers today, it provides the best measure of her own disputational project.
Like the *Bestiaire* respondent before her, she is working to make the general principle of injurious language relevant and applicable to the canonical
representation of women. Their common aim is to make public the relation between verbal figuration and domination. Yet Christine goes further.
By situating this relation in the space of the commonwealth, her response
to defamatory masterly writing pioneers the grounds of the social responsibility of that writing. In a fashion virtually unprecedented in European
vernacular culture, it explores the idea that an authoritative poetic discourse can be rendered answerable to its publics; specifically, that *the* authoritative discourse on women can be taken to task. Critical attention
long has been riveted on the *Querelle* as either an expression of medieval
culture's characteristic misogyny or an emancipatory credo for poetry.
What has gone largely unremarked is the confrontation between the humanistic notion of a "supreme fiction" and Christine's Roman notion of its
public accountability. It is the representation of women that brings this
confrontation to a climactic point. A textual model of pure form clashes
with one of social pragmatics. This clash has had enormous cultural
ramifications. Over the centuries following the *Querelle,* the debate over
the responsibility of the poetic text to its community is rehearsed again
and again.[25] The balance is continually renegotiated, sometimes in favor of
the public, sometimes in favor of poetry. But in one of its earliest vernacular formulations, this debate hinges on the defamatory representation of
women as it is disputed by a woman.

An Ethical Turn

The logic of polemics leaves the *Querelle de la Rose* at a standoff. There is a sense in which its polarized disputation leads nowhere. The particular argument over defamation does not evolve, nor do the positions of the disputants change significantly. Without the final determination (*determinatio*) of a master figure, this *querelle* finds no definitive and satisfying conclusion. Christine's alchemical analogy captures this sense of stasis in the *Querelle de la Rose*. The huffing and puffing of alchemists that she describes accentuates the illusory production of the dispute: "And they blow hard, and for a tiny bit of sublimate or residue that seems marvelous to them" (et soufflent fort, et pour ung petit de sulimacion ou congyeil qui leur appere merveillable; Hicks, 126).[26]

At the same time, Christine's description highlights the specific limits of her position as respondent:

> Ainssy est il de toy et de moy et de plusseurs: tu l'entens et le prens d'une maniere, et moy tout au rebours; tu recites, je replique. Et quant nous avons fait et fait, tout ne vault riens; car la matiere en est tres deshonneste, ainssy come aucuns arguemistes qui cuident fere de fiens or.

> (Hicks, 126)

> So it is with you and me and many others. You understand it [the book] and take it in one way, and I, at cross purposes. You recite, I respond. And when we have worked and worked, it all comes to naught; for the matter is very dishonest, just like alchemists who think they can make gold out of dung.

All the elements that we have linked to the dispute with masterly writing about women converge in this passage. *A rebours*: like the *Bestiaire* respondent, Christine finds that the disputational dynamic places her "at cross purposes" with her interlocutors. She too is brought to argue counterproductively. She is unable to exit from the *Querelle* with the clear conviction that her response to Jean de Meun's *Rose* has registered effectively. Why? *Recitation/Response*: the familiar terms of masterly debate reassert themselves. Jean de Montreuil and Gontier Col, like Jean de Meun before them, continue reciting the positions of earlier masters. Recitation permits them to deny all commitment and responsibility for what they have been saying about women. Correspondingly, Christine risks being trapped in the reiterative form of response—a type of echo chamber that may bring her argument against the prevailing masterly representation of women "to naught."

Lest this alchemical trope give the impression that Christine abandons the problem of the defamation of women, leaving it unresolved, it is important to look beyond the *Querelle de la Rose*. Indeed, it is worthwhile thinking through the *Querelle* in an entirely different way. In this respect, we can do no better than to follow the lead of Christine's authorities, Nicole Oresme and Aristotle, who state in the *Ethics*: "Accusations, quarrels and complaints occur only, or rather primarily, out of friendship, that is, for the sake of utility. This is a reasonable thing."[27] According to this standard, a disputation can at times prove socially useful or productive.

The key to this rethinking is to be found in the conjunction of the *Querelle* with the allegory Christine composed immediately thereafter. The *Chemin de long estude* narrates Christine's intellectual development as a journey across the earth and the heavens.[28] It culminates with her return from heaven and her mandate to instruct rulers. The last part of the *Chemin* reads like an exemplary portrait of the prince. In the passage from the *Querelle* to the *Chemin* we can detect the makings of Christine's most ambitious response to the defamatory character of magisterial writing about women.[29] The key is this: if a polemical mode cannot succeed in countering the public defamation of women, then she will oppose it in another mode. Put another way, if Christine's rhetorical occupation of the public sphere does not rid it of defamatory, socially destructive language, then she will forge another language to do so. The *Chemin* marks her first major experiment in working ethically and politically. In this turn, Christine appropriates and refashions the Boethian case.[30] But what exactly is the connection Boethius offers between the concerns of the *Querelle de la Rose* and the *Chemin*? As she interprets his dilemma, it represents the fate of a public servant falsely slandered: "What greater evil or displeasure or what greater reason for impatience could besmirch the innocent than to hear oneself defamed without cause, as is apparent in the accounts of Boethius in his book of consolation?" (quel plus grant mal et desplaisir peust sourdre a linnocent ne plus grant cause de impacience que de soy oir diffamer sanz cause comme il appert par les rapors de boece en son livre de consolacion).[31] Like Boethius, Christine personally confronts the dangers of defamation. And like him, she reacts by addressing those dangers in a different, ethical framework. Unlike him, however, her ethical experiment in the *Chemin* also transforms her into a political advocate. More than a censor of the public language about women, more than its ethical defender, she becomes the author of a political discourse beneficial to all citizens.

12. Christine and the Sibyl before the five heavenly deities, *Chevalerie, Noblece, Richece, Sagece,* and *Raison.* Paris, Bibliothèque Nationale, f.fr. 836, fol. 19. Photograph, Bibliothèque Nationale de France, Paris.

Visionary Advice

How to become a credible spokesperson for a discourse that represents the entire city's interests? In order to meet this challenge, the *Chemin* cultivates what I shall call a prophetic mode. Such a mode is by no means foreign to Christine's strategies in the *Querelle*. Her polemic is forward-looking insofar as it works to establish a useful language about women for the future. Yet the *Chemin* pushes the prophetic even further. It forges a language for the polis that covers both past and future representations of the people. This all-inclusive dimension distinguishes prophetic language and gives it a predictive force.

The first agent of the *Chemin*'s prophetic mode is the Cumaean Sibyl—the *grande dame* of prophecy for medieval culture.[32] Existing solely as voice, this female figure epitomizes the elusive power of the prophet.[33] She seems to come from nowhere, and yet because she oversees all that is known and will be known, she is everywhere. Her vision spans the world. In this manner, the Sibyl represents a fitting companion guiding Christine's persona through the *Chemin*'s lengthy allegorical journey: across the known world, its marvelous fringes, and all the way to the heavens, where the figures of *Noblece* (Nobility), *Richece* (Wealth), *Chevalerie* (Chivalry), and *Sagece* (Wisdom) preside (Figure 12). The Sibyl's guidance is also crucial because her prophetic powers are linked expressly to governance. She stands in a long line of vatic women whose inspired words pronounce on city rule, indeed, whose words determine the fates of cities:

> Et a cel homme [Aeneas]
> Dis la fondacion de Romme,
> Dont il meismes seroit la souche.
> Ce lui prophetisay de bouche. . . .
> Portay a Romme neuf volumes
> De livres de lois et coustumes
> Et des secrez de Romme, ou temps
> Que la gouvernoit par bon sens
> Tarquinius Priscus.
> (lines 609–12, 621–25)

And to this man, I spoke about Rome's foundation of which he himself would be the stock. I offered him prophesies from my lips; I carried to Rome nine tomes of the laws, customs, and secrets of Rome of the time when it was governed sensibly by Tarquinius Priscus.

The Cumaean Sibyl embodies the source of law and custom, of all that is most sacred about the originary city. She is responsible for its foundation, and by inference for its ongoing development. Her example thus underscores the critical degree to which the prophetic is bound up with the city's welfare: its language is committed to its equitable rule.

That the *Chemin* begins with the Cumaean prophetess reveals Christine's particular interest in the prophetic. Invoking the Sibylline example creates an implicit comparison with Vergil's model in the *Aeneid*. Christine does not miss the opportunity to contrast her prophetic mode to that of Latinity's first civic poet. This is clear in the passage where the Sibyl is represented leaving Aeneas to his city-building task and turning her attention to Christine's persona:

> Or me suis je manifestee
> A toy que je voy apprestee
> A concevoir, s'en toy ne tient
> Ce que grant estude contient,
> Et pour ce me suis apparue
> Cy endroit.
>
> (lines 635–40)

Thus I came to you, whom I see ready to conceive of such things; even if all that great study contains does not take in you. And for this reason I have appeared in this place.

Christine's transition from Vergil's account to her own is direct and self-legitimizing. Furthermore, given the echo with Dante's *Inferno*, this rite of passage signals her complementary ambition to imitate the prophetic example of Italy's first civic poet.[34] The implication is that her work (*estude*) will benefit from the examples of both masters. It will create a language befitting an equitable city—a goal that neither Vergil nor Dante finally accomplished.

Let us not forget, however, that at the outset of the *Chemin* Christine's persona does not recognize the Sibyl. This misapprehension is the surest indication of the distance she must travel before gaining the power of prophecy. Unable to see or speak clearly at first, she will grow in assurance through the course of the narrative (*Chemin*). And the aim of this development is to combine the prophetic and the wise—the two discursive categories that prove indispensable to the city according to Christine's Greek and Roman authorities. The fact that Christine's persona mistakes the Sibyl for Minerva, the goddess of wisdom, implies that the defining traits of these two discourses are as yet missing in her. Yet it sets the standard for their coming together. Christine's misprision suggests that the vatic and the sapiential will ultimately converge to sanction her discourse.

The second agent of the *Chemin*'s prophetic mode is its heavenly vector. The narrative traces Christine's ascent along Dantian lines. It maps out what she calls elsewhere "la Voye de Paradis" (the route to Paradise).[35] With its intense heat and blinding light, this way points Christine's persona unmistakably toward another realm that demands an enhanced vision:

> Mais tant oz desir de savoir
> Et congnoistre et appercevoir
> Toutes les choses de cel estre,
> Que bien voulsisse, s'il peust estre,
> Que tous mes membres fussent yeux
> Devenus, pour regarder mieux
> Les belles choses que veoir
> Povoie.

(lines 1805–12)

But I had such a great desire to learn, know, and perceive everything of this being that I really would have wished, if it were possible, that my entire body could become eyes so as to inspect more fully the beautiful things that I was able to see.

The fantasy of being transformed into all eyes epitomizes the limitless vision associated with Paradise. This is the same vision that sanctions prophecy and makes for omniscience. As Dante conceives of it, this heavenly vision involves the desire to pass into another dimension, indeed, to push beyond the limits of mundane representation.[36] Here is the paragon of "pure poetry" as form, what would doubtless be *the* fiction of mysteries and *the* mystery of fictions for Montreuil, Col, and their humanist brethren. In Christine's case, however, such a heavenly vision serves a more pragmatic purpose. Its power can be put to the use of the commonwealth. Once fathomed, it can be redirected toward a social end. It can be relayed through the salvific language Christine seeks to establish. So it is that her persona comes back from Paradise. This is no descent in a pejorative sense. Rather it constitutes a return and progressive reintegration of the seer and her transformed vision/language into the body politic. Whereas Dante's persona rises higher and higher to a point of no return, Christine's returns earthward with the gifts of prophecy, ever mindful of her social responsibility. The language of the *Chemin* remains bright with "the great festival of flashing lights"—the fluorescent trace elements of an all-seeing, all-knowing perspective (*Paradiso*, XX, 84). But in the end, it is grounded in a worldly, specifically civic enterprise.[37]

This return is cast as a feminist move of sorts. If we recall the theories of women's origin rehearsed by many gynocentric respondents such as LeFèvre, woman alone is born in Paradise. That is, woman issues from the terrestrial paradise. In Christine's description: "Ancient, true stories from the Bible that cannot lie, tell us that woman was first formed in terrestrial paradise, not man."[38] This is the predominant landscape in the *Chemin*. Having achieved the summit of Paradise, Christine's persona returns to earth by way of the terrestrial paradise (lines 2055–56). In fact, it is the setting for the *Chemin*'s lengthy debate over the ideal character of the prince and the citizenry. This stands to reason because in Christine's thinking the earthly paradise represents the best link between the heavens and the city. It is a perfect mediating site. As one associated with women, it provides an ideal place for her transformation into a prophetess. It stages her new political role as mediator between the heavens and the commonwealth.

This mediating character brings us to the third element of the *Chemin*'s prophetic mode. Astrology entails for Christine an authoritative discourse, indeed, a popular or secular prophetic form:

> Astrologien est parfait,
> Par science scet quanqu'on fait,
> Des planetes congnoist le cours
> Et des estoilles tous les tours,
> Tout le compas du firmament
> Et toutes scet entierement
> Les choses qui sont a venir;
> Comment elles doivent venir
> Scet il tout par sa grant science.
> Brief, en lui est, je vous fiance,
> Toute philosophie entiere.
>   (lines 3399–3409)

> The astrologer is perfect because he knows scientifically whatever happens; he knows the orbits of the planets and the cycles of the stars, he knows the compass of the firmament, as well as everything about the future; he knows through his great learning how it will all transpire; in short, I swear to you, in him is gathered all of philosophy.

Christine's panegyric accentuates the important alliance between astronomy and good governance. Insofar as the astrologer comes as close as is humanly possible to possessing total knowledge—"en lui est toute philosophie entiere"—he represents the ideal public counselor. Following Plato, Aristotle, and even Cicero, she places the astrologer beside the ruler. She enlists him as a public servant and makes his star-gazing civic business. It is important to remember, however, that this configuration was under attack during this period. Not only was astronomical science challenging the prophetic claims of astrology, but Christine's authority, Nicole Oresme, argued against astrology's political value.[39] The fact that Christine continues to speak astrologically in the face of such opposition reveals how personally committed she is to its prophetic language. Her father, Tommaso de Pisano, was the court astrologer for Charles V. Astrology represents a powerful

legacy for Christine, so powerful that it underwrites her advocacy of politicized astrology.[40] Christine's transformation into an ethical/political writer
depends on her exploiting her astrological patrimony.

Yet is the preoccupation with this particular prophetic mode merely a
family affair? We have a clue, I believe, in the term, *aviser*, which recurs in
the latter part of the *Chemin*. *Aviser* combines the closely connected
senses of seeing ahead and advising. The word reveals the critical ligature
between vision and counsel, between a vatic faculty and a political role. Intervening in the debate over the ideal character of the prince, Christine's
persona says:

> Puis qu'il vous plaist, diray le voir
> De mon avis sus l'ordenance
> De la mondaine gouvernance.
>   (lines 3080–82)

> Since it is pleasing to you, I'll tell you the truth of my view [*mon
> avis*] on the ordinance of earthly governance.

The truth she claims is predicated on prophetic insight. No matter of opinion, it constitutes an otherworldly order of knowledge—akin to the perceptions of a Boethian "pure discerning mind." (IV, vi, 1) This turn of
phrase, "diray le voir De mon avis," is worth dwelling on for a moment.
Read in the context of the *Chemin*, it exemplifies Christine's ethico-
political ambitions. It identifies her as the ideal civic counselor. When read
in the larger context of Christine's work, it highlights a further element in
her ongoing dispute with masterly writing. "Le voir de mon avis" offers
the perfect corrective to the humanists' slogan in the *Querelle*: "tout parler par ficcion" (saying everything by fiction). As Joël Blanchard has argued convincingly, one of the most pressing challenges facing the poet in
early-fifteenth-century Paris involved *véridiction*—the capacity to speak
the truth fully.[41] As Christine takes up this challenge, she roots her
"truth" in so many layers of prophetic language that it appears, at least
rhetorically, incontestable. Furthermore, her *avis* is properly dedicated to
the polis. Vision/counsel versus fiction, truth-telling versus autonomous
speech: Christine's juxtapositions reveal the impoverishment of Col's
"fictive" autonomy. What is missing in Col is precisely the ethico-political
dimension. Christine's *avis* possesses this dimension because it both serves
and contributes efficaciously to the community. With its overarching perspective, it claims to represent the interests of the entire group in a truth-
bearing language beneficial to all. This is not to say that free speech cannot
be exercised ethically. Nor is it to suggest that an ethical fiction does not
exist. On the contrary: Christine's writing from this stage on is the proof

of that. Rather it is to say that where the humanists fail in vindicating "fictive" autonomy, Christine succeeds in articulating a socially responsive one. Where they fail in defending the *Rose* ethically, the *Chemin* proves exemplary.

Towards the Sapiential

With this order of "visionary advice," then, Christine's persona is ready to represent a type of civic ethics. And the emblem for this ethics, as classical thought defined it, is nothing less than *sapientia* or wisdom. Having authorized itself prophetically, the *Chemin* experiments with what I shall call sapiential writing. Inspired and learned, forward-looking and yet committed to the present, this narrative pursues a way of speaking and writing about wisdom as a necessary civic virtue. In so doing, it embodies wisdom itself. The *Chemin* realizes the virtue in the process of advocating it for the polis. Such a course is startling on several accounts. That a female persona practices wisdom moves beyond the passive identification of wisdom with the feminine that Minerva represents for so much of medieval clerical writing. Christine's persona disputes the exclusive claims on wisdom made by the male clergy—a claim so well-defended, according to Michèle LeDoeuff, that a woman cannot easily contest it.[42] This was particularly the case in Christine's milieu, where intellectual life was still tightly controlled by the clergy. Her sapiential writing thus raises the question of a woman humanist.[43] Furthermore, it explores the conflicted position of "wise women" in the polis. To what degree can their actions constitute a critical part of a community's deliberations? Christine seems intent on envisaging a more active role for them than her Greek and Roman models posited.[44] Indeed, her sapiential writing projects a determining ethical/political role for women. I shall return to these two startling questions again.

In the simplest terms, Christine's sapiential writing is defined by its erudition. The debate over the ideal qualities of the citizenry in the second half of the narrative marshals a remarkable array of citation and commentary, the so-called *dits d'auteurs*. It turns the *Chemin* into a model *florilegium* that could rival any clerical anthology of the day.[45] Here is a work that delights in the stuff of learning, amassing disparate material and displaying it in ever more inventive ways. It communicates the thrill of acquiring bookish knowledge.[46] Yet Christine's obviously pleasurable erudition is no self-engrossing affair. It develops in accordance with its social utility. In this sense, it realizes one of Aristotle's ethical principles as the philosopher/translator Nicole Oresme renders it: "The study of all books engenders, fosters, and cultivates in the hearts of those who listen to them an affection and love for the commonwealth, which is the best quality to be found in a prince and his counselors after the love of God (L'estude de tous livres engenre et embat ou acroist es cuers de ceuls qui y entendent, affeccion et amour au bien publique, qui est la meilleur qui puisse estre en prince et en ses conseilliers aprés l'amour de Dieu; *Livre de Ethiques*, Prologue, 1d [Menut, 99]). For Christine, the study of all books is a measure of her ethical and political responsibilities. The process of working through such learning equips her for a civic role. In fact, it commits her to that role all the more strongly. As her writing gains intellectually, it rises to the challenge of overseeing the affairs of the polis. In this sense, her sapiential writing comprises a practice as well. It realizes the same ethical conduct that it recommends for the benefit of the prince and his people. It participates in the essential functioning of the commonwealth.

When we approach Christine's sapiential writing as a practice, we can begin to detect the important ethico-political role it devises for women. Her portrait of the prince among his people depends in large part on their intervention. Whereas most humanist versions of this portrait do not make room for any female political activism, Christine's, by contrast, highlights it. Two examples will make the point clear. In the first, Christine details the case of a woman unjustly accused of a crime. She is condemned by a drunken monarch gone out of control. The rule of the kingdom looks in jeopardy. Yet the woman's pleas remind us that wisdom is not merely the personal trademark of the ruler, but in the best of circumstances a trait informing the entire body politic. She challenges the prince's judgment, thus appealing to another standard: "So after his drunkenness, he went to listen to her and revoked the sentence he had given that was so badly ordained" (Dont apres l'ivrece vaca A elle oir, et revoca La sentence qu'il ot donnee, Qui moult estoit mal ordenee; lines 5567–70). In Christine's example, the proverbial victim becomes a decisive agent of wise justice. The woman calls the errant prince back to good rule. By playing the role of the fully empowered citizen, she insures not only that justice is rendered her personally but also that the community's welfare is respected. Her voice is the ethical one, and it speaks responsibly for the polis as a whole.

In the second case, that female ethical voice is further strengthened. It belongs to a widow who turns to the delinquent prince seeking justice for her murdered son:

> Tu es, dist elle, mon debteur.
> Que te vauldra, s'autre me paie;
> Tenus es de faire la paie.

Et lors l'empereur, esmeu
Des paroles, si a veu
Le cas, et du cheval descent,
Et a celle femme en present
Fist droit et satisfacion.
Dont fu grant approbacion
Qu'il estoit parfait justicier
Sanz prolongnier ne delaissier.
                    (lines 5790–5800)

You are, she said, my debtor. What will it be worth to you, if another pays me; you are bound to keep the bargain. Whereupon the emperor, moved by these words, and having seen the case, got down from his horse and made good on the spot with this woman, giving her satisfaction. Thus there was great approval that he was a perfect judge without hesitation or procrastination.

The woman articulates a classical definition of justice: speak the truth and pay your debts. She is the mouthpiece for an ethical principle meant to sustain the commonwealth. Furthermore, her exchange with the prince secures his reputation: were she not to require justice from him, his good name would be diminished. Through a woman's intervention, the prince's necessary fame as judge is vindicated and his judgment is perfected.

These scenes capture the essence of Christine's sapiential writing. Like the intervention of the two women, her work is to function ethically on behalf of the people, but it must do so in the face of irresponsible discourse and delinquent governance. Because the appointed representatives of justice—rulers and philosophers alike—have failed, the *Chemin* claims the task of pronouncing ethically. Women take over the duty of protecting the citizen's name and thereby of defending the integrity of the group. Against all philosophical precedent, it is women's work that sets the ethico/political standard. Against most literary conventions, it is a woman's writing that exemplifies it.

What is the connection between this ethical stance and Christine's writing as a whole? What bearing could her ethics possibly have on her dispute with Jean de Meun's *Rose*? With these questions, my argument comes full circle. Christine's ultimate response to the *Querelle de la Rose*, emerges through the practice of sapiential writing in the *Chemin*. Such an ethical textual practice responds to the general problem of defamation. In the most efficacious way, it disputes the particular problem of defamatory masterly texts about women. If defamatory writing is defined by its injuriousness, then the sapiential is defined by its beneficence. Where the former wreaks symbolic violence, the latter makes amends. In fact, sapiential writing seeks to counteract past symbolic violence. Because of its commitment to the polis, it rehabilitates earlier damaging writing and endeavors to reorient it ethically to the society's benefit.

These distinctions make Christine's sapiential writing her most potent reply to the defamatory *Rose*. But they also empower her critique of its humanist defenders. Her ethical textual practice calls into question their practice, one linked specifically in the *Querelle* to *Dame Eloquence* (Hicks, 92–112.) Although Christine can hardly challenge the eloquence of Col and Montreuil, she can point up the absence of any accompanying wisdom. Christine's own sapiential writing serves, in effect, to indict retroactively the *Rose*'s humanist defenders for their lack of wisdom. And this in turn impugns their dedication to the commonwealth. According to the Roman authority so beloved by the humanists and Christine herself: "But if you have eloquence without wisdom, then Cicero teaches you that such eloquence is pernicious to the state and the commonwealth."[47] Judged by this standard the humanists' contribution to the *Querelle* is devoid of the very quality that defines the ethico-political. Christine argues implicitly that the humanists' eloquence is pernicious or defamatory itself. Under such circumstances, her own sapiential writing in the *Chemin* (and thereafter) functions doubly. Its principal aim is to compensate for the verbal injury of women in a masterly text such as the *Rose*. But in so doing, it surpasses the humanists' discourse ethically and politically. Christine's work is distinguished by the same civic virtues they claim for their own.

This strategy did not go unnoticed. A contemporaneous pedagogical treatise composed by a noblewoman for her sons gives us a glimpse of the effects of Christine's writing:

> Cristine de pisay a si bien et honnestement parle, faisant dictiers et
> livres a l'ensaignement de nobles femmes et aultres, que trop seroit
> mon esperit failly et surpris voulloir emprendre de plus en dire. Car
> quant j'auroie la science de Palas ou l'eloquence de Cicero, et que, par la
> main de Promoteus, fusse femme nouvelle, sy ne porrose je parvenir ne
> attaindre a sy bien dire comme elle a faict.
>
> (*Enseignemens que une dame laisse a ses filz en forme
> de testament*, B.N. f.fr. 19919, fol. 27)[48]

Christine de Pizan has spoken so well and so honestly, composing treatises and books concerning the instruction of noblewomen and others, that my spirit would surely be surprised and overwhelmed in trying to say anything more. For even when I had the learning of Minerva or the eloquence of Cicero and were I, by the hand of Prometheus, to become a new woman, even then I could still not reach her level nor attain speaking as well as she has done.

We have here the virtues that distinguish Christine's way: Minervan wisdom and Roman eloquence define her writing as a powerful ethico-political medium for women and men in the community. As the very antithesis of the defamatory, it offers a socially responsible discourse. Her eloquent sapiential writing dismantles the symbolic domination of women maintained so effectively by the masterly clerical tradition. In its place, it devises a language that represents women's interests equitably. If such a language cannot change social relations between women and men, it *can* name them differently.[49] It can thus safeguard the welfare of all citizens, the making of "new women and men." All Christine's subsequent writing pioneers just such a socially enriching idiom, of which one sign might well be the locution—*femme/fame/sapience*—of defamed women made newly famous by their wisdom.

7 A Libelous Affair

The *Querelle de la Belle Dame sans merci* and the Prospects for a Legal Response

Her voice—of all her admirables the admirablest, the very pitch
and timber of *La Belle Lettre sans merci*.

John Barth, *Letters*

In late-medieval France, the *feme/diffame* problem took another important turn legally. What had prompted Jean LeFèvre's conversion and
Christine de Pizan's ethical critique of Jean de Meun's *Rose* could also occasion juridical accusations. The problem of damaging women's names,
indeed one might say of "de-naturing" them (*di-ffame*), became a matter
of litigation and public redress. Writers and poets could be charged according to a legal definition of defamation.

Formulating the problem of defamation in legal terms taps into an im-
mense body of speculation that extends all the way back to Justinian's
Code and Roman law. The canonical conception described defamation as an
unjust harming of another's reputation (*injusta alienae famae laesio*).[1]
This harm could take many forms and occur in many places. As Justinian's
Code outlined it:

> Si quis famosum libellum sive domi sive in publico vel quocumque
> loco ignarus reppererit, aut corrumpat, priusquam alter inveniat, aut
> nulli confiteatur inventum. Sin vero non statim easdem chartulas vel
> corruperit vel igni consumpserit, sed vim earum manifestaverit, sciat
> se quasi auctorem huiusmodi delicti capitali sententia subiugandum.[2]

> If anyone should find defamatory material in a house, in a public place,
> or anywhere else, without knowing who placed it there, he must either
> tear it up before anyone else finds it or not mention to anyone that he
> has done so. If, however, he should not immediately tear up or burn

the paper, but should show it to others, he is notified that he will be liable to the punishment of death as the author.

Defamation involves an attack on a person enacted symbolically. The fact that it targets the symbolic entity of a reputation and not a body does little to diminish its seriousness. In such a world, where words were not yet sundered from deeds, defamation was tantamount to physical assault. Hence the defamer or the one who collaborates in defamation is subject to corporal punishment—even death. As medieval canon and customary law continued to propound Justinian's statute, its stringent force varied little: in Gratian's rendition, defamation was a verbal infraction and the defamer, a criminal who must take a beating.[3]

When it comes to the cause of a poet, this prevailing medieval conception of verbal injury poses a variety of questions: in what way is a speaker or writer accountable to the public?; are texts actionable?; if so, how are they rendered liable for damages? It also raises key issues concerning the social parameters of discourse and the controls developed to enforce them. At stake is that charged rapport between language and action—the relay between verbal representation, its effects, and the public regulation of both. For jurists and poets of the late Middle Ages, defamation offered a crucial model for reckoning with the power of discourse. Since it attempts to account for the influence of linguistic forms on its audiences and the public domain as a whole, defamation charts the boundaries of responsibility: the place where a party assumes, in legal terms, liability.

Nowhere is the juridical problem of defamation of women more clearly articulated than in the controversy provoked by Alain Chartier's *Belle Dame sans merci.*[4] The title of this fifteenth-century courtly poem hints at the *Querelle* that ensued. Portraying the lady as merciless prompted immediate and vehement reactions. In fact, Chartier's *Belle Dame* seems to have polarized the court of Charles VII, where it first circulated in 1424. It touched off a far more acrimonious debate than the *Querelle de la Rose* a generation earlier. This is hardly surprising, given the state of civil war in France at the time: internecine rivalries between Armagnac and Burgundian factions divided the royal court where Chartier served as secretary. A group of anonymous courtiers lodged the first complaint, objecting to the way the poem acts to "disrupt the quest of humble servants, and snatch from you [women] the happy name of mercy" (rompre la queste des humbles servans et à vous tolir l'eureux nom de pitié; Laidlaw, 362). Chartier answered with his own *Excusacioun aus dames*, patterned after Jean de Meun (*Rose*, lines 15129–212). It was the second work that sparked a woman's response. And *La Response des dames faicte a maistre Alain*, attributed to "Jeanne, Katherine, and Marie," launched an indictment of defamation.[5] The confrontation between Chartier's *Belle Dame / Excusacioun* and the *Response des dames* brought out the legal problem of the text's public accountability. It is difficult to ascertain if and how this confrontation was ever adjudicated. The *Querelle de la Belle Dame* continued to be played out in the years thereafter; a flurry of poems were composed in defense of Chartier's poem. Yet despite its inconclusiveness, the affair retained its legalistic tenor.

With its legal conception of defamation, this little-known *Querelle* pushes our investigation into the symbolic domination of masterly writing about women still further. We should first recognize it as another disputational encounter between a well-known courtly text and a woman's response, this time involving a poet in his prime. Yet the recourse to legal models in the woman's response to Chartier's *Belle Dame* changes the very terms of such a disputation. Invoking the law of defamation adds a novel and powerful criterion to the medieval critique of masterly representations of women.

At the same time, the *Querelle de la Belle Dame* highlights the considerable difficulties in interpreting the woman's response in any disputation. The major pitfall, as ever, is the stereotype of the defaming woman.[6] In the reception of the *Querelle de la Belle Dame*, this stereotype comes through in the efforts to identify the respondents with the *damoiselles d'honneur* so frequently depicted in contemporaneous manuscripts (Figure 13).[7] While there are favorable images of a close-knit circle of loyal women— such is the case of the *Champion des dames* miniature—there are also unfavorable images. The identification of "Jeanne, Katherine, and Marie" with such *damoiselles* reproduces the negative portrayal of them found throughout chronicle literature of the early fifteenth century.[8] It stigmatizes them with the clichéd reputation of *damoiselles d'honneur* as gossips and bad-mouthers. The modern critical tendency to name the respondents as such women of the court reconfirms unwittingly the favorite clerical exemplum of *damoiselles* for calumny.[9]

Secondly, the reading of the *Querelle de la Belle Dame* as a politicized literary game elides the specific character of the woman's response.[10] It is based on the premise that the respondents are figures caught up in the intrigues of courtly ritual. It takes them to be pawns in the hands of more powerful political players.[11] Whether the respondents are allied with the Armagnac or Burgundian camp, whether they are deemed actual women or figurative ploys manipulated by these camps, the result is much the

13. A circle of *dames* and *damoiselles d'honneur*. *Le Champion des dames*. Grenoble, Bibliothèque Municipale, BM Rés. 352, fol. 384 verso. Courtesy of the Bibliothèque de Grenoble, France.

same. Jeanne, Katherine, and Marie are seen as formidable opponents to Chartier when women are linked deterministically to defamation. This dismissive reading of the *Querelle de la Belle Dame* rides on the cliché that women are exemplary defamers.

If our analysis of the woman's response has demonstrated anything, it is the imperative of breaking out of the vicious circle that defines women's language pejoratively. In the case of the *Querelle de la Belle Dame*, this means shifting the focus away from the respondents as women—ergo, as defaming women. Such a focus has reinforced commonplace medieval views of the feminine and obscured the innovation that is the *Querelle*'s central strategy: pursuing a defamatory text legally. By moving attention away from the gender typecasting, we can better gauge the effects of the woman's response in this *Querelle*. Whether "Jeanne," "Katherine," and "Marie" represent women or men is not the determining issue. What matters more is the consequence of their interventions. If we attend to what I have called the chiasmic link between respondent figures and their context, we are in a better position to discern the implications of their legal charge of defamation.

The Sting of Verbal Injury

The medieval law of defamation hinges first and foremost on the concept of injury (*laesio/iniuria*).[12] The *Response des dames* to Maître Alain's *Belle Dame* involves testing such a principle of verbal injury on a particular figuration of women. It attempts to assess the connection between the representation of something hurtful and hurtful representation. The *Response des dames* does not object to the portrait of the pitiless lady but to the transfer of such a portrait from a specific female persona to other women. It questions how the poet gets from the figure of a merciless lady (dame est sans mercy, line 4) to representing existing women as cruel (nous sommes crüelles, line 19).

On closer inspection, we discover that the contested figure is an *unattached* woman:

> Je suis france et france vueil estre,
> Sans moy de mon cuer dessaisir
> Pour en faire un autre le maistre.
> (lines 286–88)

I am free and wish to remain free, without relinquishing my heart to make another its master.

Repeated obsessively throughout the *Querelle*, Chartier's version of a woman's liberty gets to the core of medieval representations that code female separateness as merciless.[13] When read conventionally, it converts women's freedom into an instrument of torture for men. That woman speaks her freedom wounds her male interlocutor; that she speaks a desire to have no master is liable to kill him. The *Belle Dame*'s claim brings out the tortuous impulses informing so much of medieval amorous discourse. Yet read another way, her claim also stands as the credo of a free agent. It suggests a noncommittal stance, one that identifies the woman on her own terms, in relation to no one else. The crux lies in the fact that Chartier's poem allows for both readings. It showcases a woman able to claim her *franchise*, yet it reprimands her for her liberty's cruel ends—the lover's death.[14] It should not be forgotten that this "free woman" is also set up as a negative exemplum to Chartier's audience:

> Et vous, dames et damoiselles
> En qui Honneur naist et asemble,
> Ne soyés mie si crüelles,
> Chascune ne toutes ensemble.
> (lines 793–96)

And you, ladies and young women, in whom honor is born and re-sides, never be so cruel, not one of you, nor all of you together.

According to the *Response*, what risks being defamatory is the depiction of a woman's freedom as nefarious. It is this perverse figure of her independence that appears objectionable. This finding is highly ironic. As any reader of medieval love poetry knows, there could be no more banal portrayal. Before Chartier, there was a good two-century run of the merciless female type. Yet it is the one element distinguishing Chartier's variation on a hackneyed image that changes the picture. A female persona who is both liberated and a murderer brings to a head the problem of injurious representation. She epitomizes the cause of verbal injury.

I should mention that such a contested figure of *la femme france* may well carry another political charge. Chartier's figure also conjures up the female personification, *La France*. During this period of foreign occupation and deep civil unrest, her freedom was most certainly under attack. As Chartier portrayed her in the *Quadrilogue invectif*, she was the butt of considerable verbal abuse.[15]

By singling out Chartier's negative characterization of a woman's *franchise*, the *Response* points to a transfer mechanism whereby the exasperation of men is displaced onto women. In the poetic economy of the *Belle Dame*, such a mechanism dictates the fate of the lover and his final denunciation of the woman. Yet as the *Response des dames* maintains, it also applies to the condition of the poet: "don't assign your madness to women" (ne charge point ta frenesie aux femmes, line 15). Chartier's "madness" is the corollary of the lover's characteristic malaise. To put it another way, this "male malady" is an animus driving the text of the *Belle Dame* as much as it drives the lover's hostile speech acts toward the free-standing woman. It functions as the motor of the poem. By identifying *frenesie* as an animus of Chartier's work, the *Response des dames* takes the allegation of defamation one step further. Not only does it field the threat of verbal injury, but it attempts to explain its processes. It offers a reason why a language defamatory toward women occurs.

Here we can discern the fundamental difference separating the *Response des dames* from the courtiers' complaint against the *Belle Dame sans merci*. Whereas the *Response* tackles the issue of verbal injury legalistically, the complaint is concerned only with the ways Chartier's persona threatens the courtiers' poetic models and social role. The terms of their objection quoted above make this clear. "The quest of humble servants" takes precedence over "the woman's happy name of mercy." The rituals of courtly life, as men perform them, outweigh the value of a woman's reputation. Or to invoke another expression of the *galants*, "the damage to and estrangement of the humble servants" caused by the *Belle Dame* is more serious than "the diminishing of the women's power" (dommage et esloingnement aux humbles servans et amandrissement de voustre pouoir, 362). For all the anguish experienced on behalf of women, the courtiers' challenge to Chartier's work comprises a self-absorbed lament. Caught in this narcissistic bind, it can never address the problem of injurious language. While its rhetoric may imply it, its argument never pursues it.

Emblematic of the *Response*'s focus on verbal injury is the scorpion image:

> Tu es ainsy comme l'escorpion.
> Tu oingz, tu poins, tu flattes, tu offens,
> Tu honnoures, tu fais bien, tu le casses,
> Tu t'acuses et puis tu t'en deffens,
> Tu dis le bien, tu l'escrips, tu l'effaces.
>
> (lines 24–28)

You are thus like the scorpion. You speak unctuously, you sting; you flatter, you attack; you honor, you do good, you destroy it; you accuse yourself and then you defend yourself; you say the right thing, you write it, you erase it.

This figure captures the menace of words; indeed, it is a canonical image used to describe slander.[16] In keeping with medieval bestiary lore, the scorpion illustrates a type of poisonous harm: its sting could be fatal. With one deft metaphoric stroke, then, the *Response des dames* turns Chartier's persona of the murderous *Belle Dame* back on itself. It shows its baleful influence to register not on lovers and courtiers but on the public of women. At the same time, the *Response*'s scorpion image is seen to injure discreetly and deceptively. Unlike the animalistic images that assault the *Bestiaire* respondent, it attacks under cover. This aspect of the image gives us a clue to the resistance the *Response* faces. It implies Chartier's denial of the very notion of verbal injury. Let us not forget, the women's text responds to the *Excusacioun* as well as to the *Belle Dame*, and it is Chartier's second text that elaborates strategies for outmaneuvering the *Response*'s subsequent charge of defamation. The scorpion's flailing motions, the swift turnabouts in position, suggest the evasiveness of the *Excusacioun*. One example will make the point. In the God of Love's interrogation of the besieged poet, Cupid asserts:

> Tu fais et escriz et envoyes
> Nouveaulx livres contre mes droiz.
> Es tu foul, hors du sens ou yvre,
> Ou veulx contre moy guerre prendre,
> Qui as fait le maleureux livre,
> Dont chascun te devroit reprendre,
> Pour enseigner et pour aprendre
> Les dames a geter au loing
> Pitié la debonnaire et tendre,
> De qui tout le monde a besoing?
> (*Excusacioun*, lines 23–32)

You compose, write, and send off new books against my laws. Are you mad, out of your mind, or drunk? Or do you want to wage war against me? Who has composed this accursed book from which each person must gain from you how to teach and instruct ladies to banish that elegant and tender Pity, of which everyone is in need?

To which the writer of "this accursed book" replies:

> Leur serviteur vueil demourer
> Et en leur service mourray,
> Et ne les puis trop honnourer
> N'autrement ja ne le vourray;
> Ains, tant qu'en vie demourray,
> A garder l'onneur qui leur touche
> Employeray ou je pourray
> Corps, cuer, sens, langue, plume et bouche.
> (lines 145–152)

I wish to remain their servant and die in their service [of women]. And I could not honor them any more, nor vow to it in any other way. So, for as long as I shall remain living, I shall use as I can, body, heart, senses, tongue, pen, and mouth to guard their honor from whatever concerns them.

By placing this critique in the mouth of the God of Love, Chartier shifts the burden of responsibility. Indeed, by representing the writer as apologetic to Cupid alone, he makes the writer subject to a mythic authority. Chartier and his poem will stand corrected only before the supreme literary arbiter of the law. With such a scene, Chartier tries to neutralize the courtiers' complaint and the *Response des dames*. Yet in the terms of the *Response's* scorpion image, the shifts between admitting the damaging quality of the *Belle Dame* and protesting the poet's honorable service of women accentuate the injuriousness of Chartier's writing. They substantiate the injury. The fact that the *Excusacioun* accommodates both the flattery and the attack, the acknowledgement of guilt and the implicit disavowal of it, epitomizes its continuing harmfulness. Moreover, this vacillation applies to the relation between the *Belle Dame* and the *Excusacioun* as well. By entertaining the problem of harmful representation only to leave it in suspense, the second text aggravates the danger of the first. Read together, Chartier's poems exacerbate the injury.

A Literary Disclaimer

We come here to a key stage in our inquiry into the effects of the women's legal charge of defamation. In the confrontation between the *Response* and the *Excusacioun*, we can detect signs of the struggle over the criterion of verbal injury. These two texts signal changes in the conceptualization and social uses of defamation in French late-medieval culture. On the one hand, the *Response's* extremist language signals the power invested in the legal principle of verbal injury. On the other, the *Excusacioun's* evasiveness intimates the strategies being developed to block it. If the *Response* is legitimated by long-standing juridical and philosophical conceptions of defamation, it also faces tactics designed to deflect the allegation of injurious language, tactics that have everything to do with the status of literary discourse.

In order to clarify changes in the concept and use of defamation, compare the various medieval terms that I have introduced over the last three chapters. Justinian's formulation in the code inherited by the Middle Ages leaves considerable latitude as to the form defamation takes. It can involve spoken language (*verba*), written material (*scriptura*), even pictures (*imagines*). The Ciceronian description, well known in late-medieval France, concentrates specifically on the song (*carmen*). As we discussed in chapter 6, the abusive language (*flagitium*) of the song is attributed to the particular talents of poets (*ingenium poetarum*). Defamation thus enters into the province of the literary arts. Augustine's commentary on Cicero underscores this link between the defamatory and the literary even further. In the *City of God* passage read widely in the late Middle Ages, the defamatory work of the poets is characterized specifically in fictive terms (*conficta a poetis*). What is potentially defamatory is poetic confabulation—fiction.

It is not at all clear that medieval commentators capitalized on these various distinctions. Yet the continuing repetition of distinctions made in high-medieval commentaries signals a new preoccupation with classical arguments over the accountability of poetry. The fact that they dwell on the defamatory *cantilenus* (song) and *libellus* (little book, pamphlet) points to their concern with the opposition between the autonomy of poetic/fictive forms and the regulatory mechanisms of the law.[17] The claim for the inviolability of literary language is already visible in these terms.[18] Equally discernible, however, is the opportunity for legal recourse against defamation committed by poets.

The two poles of this argument may well remind us of today's controversy over what constitutes "free speech."[19] While such a notion is certainly foreign to the Middle Ages, there is a way in which the confrontation between Chartier's *Excusacioun* and the *Response* raises the question of what is "free" language and what is actionable, injurious language. Both debates, the contemporary and the medieval, revolve around the principle of words as harmful. And in the process, they both come up against that most hallowed version of free speech: literature. The problem lies in establishing whether the particular character of the literary or the fictive renders it inviolable and safe from any public action. In one version of the contemporary debate, the feminist legal theorist Catharine A. MacKinnon has argued for the need to elaborate anew the principle of verbal injury in relation to various sacrosanct categories of "free speech."[20] To do so offers one way to establish legal grounds that would enable women to sue the "free speech" of others that proves offensive to them. The fierce opposition mounted against MacKinnon's argument gives us an indication of just how entrenched the notion of an inviolable language is in contemporary jurisprudence. In the debate as the *Querelle de la Belle Dame* rehearses it, such a notion is only beginning to take shape. The *Response* runs up against an early version of the argument for making certain types of language free from legal action. It contends with a nascent defense of literary language as legally unactionable. In spite of their differences, when these two debates are placed side by side, they set into relief the enormous stakes involved in establishing the damage of words and proving legal liability.

As the *Response* lays claim to these stakes, it accentuates the problematic status of the literary. This is already evident in the scorpion image when the women remark Chartier's habit of speaking well, writing, and effacing: "tu dis le bien, tu l'escrips, tu l'effaces" (line 28). Their turn of phrase sums up the poet's self-serving vacillation. Yet there is something further disclosed by the link between writing and effacement. In fact, if we look to one of Chartier's cameo portraits of the writing process, writing appears to constitute a form of effacement:

> Et s'enfermë en chambre ou en retrait
> Pour escripre plus a l'aise et a trait,
> Et met une heure a faire un tout seul trait
> De lettre close.
> Un peu escript, puis songe et se repose,
> Puis efface pour mettre une autre chose.
> *Le Débat des deux fortunés d'amours* (lines 322–27)

And he shuts himself up in a room or in isolation so as to write more easily and at leisure. And it takes him an hour to do a single stroke of a private letter. He writes a little, then dreams and relaxes. Then he erases so to put something else.

What is on one level an astute description of the rhythms of revision points on another to the way writing can efface what it represents. The visible and the invisible, the assertion of a point and the denial: writing accommodates both these possibilities in its own characteristic white space. In critiquing the *Belle Dame* and the *Excusacioun* together, the *Response* is alert to this prospect. It recognizes in the notion of writing that effaces a strategy for dodging responsibility for the injuriousness of its language. If writing is capable of erasing what it represents, how can one determine verbal injury? Or to put it in terms introduced by the *Response*, how can anyone pinpoint defamatory writing when it relays "a double language" (line 63)?

The *Response*'s criteria of effacement and doubleness become all the more telling when we look at the structure of Chartier's *Excusacioun*. His apology is set up as an "if" clause:

> Se vous ne lisez et voyez
> Tout le livret premierement. . . .
> (lines 123–24)

If you do not first read or look at the whole book. . . .

> S'en doit tout le monde amasser
> Contre moy a tort et en vain. . . .
> (lines 213–14)

If everyone should gather against me wrongfully and in vain. . . .

> S'ilz en ont rien dit ou escript
> Par quoy je puisse estre repris. . . .
> (lines 222–23)

If they have said or written anything by which I could have been accused. . . .

The *Excusacioun* reads like a series of conditionals culminating in one particularly audacious one: "If I dared to say or imagine that any lady was merciless, I would be a false liar, and my word injurious" (Se j'osoye dire ou songier Qu'onques dame fust despiteuse, Je seroye faulx mensongier Et ma parole injurïeuse; lines 177–180). Such an "if clause" enables the narrator to protect himself by appearing to assume the blame. Admitting to the crime of slander within brackets that stay firmly closed is his way of exonerating himself of the charge. And the form that self-exoneration takes—the "if" condition—is the classic paradigm for literary discourse. From Aristotle straight through to Wittgenstein, the literary is distinguished by its framework of double meaning, one that aligns it structurally (although not functionally) with the lie and the dream.[21] In Chartier's case, the *Excusacioun* attempts to defend the *Belle Dame* on the grounds not only that the figure of the cruel woman is mendacious, but also, implicitly, that as a literary object it is tenable. The heuristic parentheses of literature seek to render the *Response*'s accusation of defamation irrelevant, and they do so in the same terms as a dream.[22] By opening up an oneiric space between truth and falsehood where his writing becomes double, Chartier's *Excusacioun* tries to vindicate the *Belle Dame* as a literary form that cannot, by definition, defame women.

This strategy recalls Pierre Col's argument in the *Querelle de la Rose* concerning the distinction between poet and persona.[23] There too a space is opened up in which characters as objectionable as *la Vieille* are legitimized and at the same time disassociated from Jean de Meun. The hypothetical status of the persona defended by Col is another version of the "if" clause exploited by Chartier, and the rationale behind these two positions is similar: to liberate the writer from liability. While the Parisian humanists, like Chartier, understand language to carry with it the power to injure, they award poets a special dispensation from it. Such is poetic license.

Chartier, however, pushes this privilege further. He maintains:

> Quant un amant est si estraint,
> Comme en resverie mortelle,
> Que force de mal le contraint
> D'appeller sa dame crüelle,
> Doit on penser qu'elle soit telle?
> (lines 201–5)

When a lover is so anguished as in a fatal reverie, when the force of malaise constrains him to call his lady cruel, why should one believe she is so?

Here the emphasis has already shifted from the relation between the poet and his figures to the figures' believability. At first glance, such a standard of believability suggests the common criticism of reading *à la lettre*. Once again, it appears, women are deemed incapable of deciphering the figurative, let alone of detecting its presence. Chartier's respondents join the long line from Andreas Capellanus's women through Christine de Pizan who are typed as crude and naive readers. Yet by the early fifteenth century, "believability" referred less to the opposition between the letter and the figure, and hence to women readers' difficulty in navigating it, than to the idea of verisimilitude.[24] It signaled that revived classical notion central to the humanists' apologies for poetry.[25] Chartier's question, "why should one believe she is cruel?" lies somewhere on the cusp between theories of figurative writing and theories of the literary as a distinct type of writing.[26]

This transition distinguishes Chartier's part in the *Querelle de la Belle Dame*. The fixation on *figura*, invariably linked to a clerical disapprobation of fables, was subsiding. Rising in its place were the various classical theories that charted a separate and autonomous terrain for the literary. Such an orientation is not surprising. We have only to recall the early-fifteenth-century French vogue of Boccaccio's writings on "the fervent and exquisite invention of poetry," or the Petrarchan formula of *velamen figmentorum* (veil of fictions).[27] As we have discovered, the *Querelle de la Rose* was already significantly indebted to all these new articulations of the power of poetry.[28] Yet in the *Querelle de la Belle Dame*, these various articulations are exploited in such a way as to assert the distinct ontological status of Chartier's poems. Moreover, this assertion serves as the ultimate legal disclaimer. Informed by the impressive repertory of apologies for poetry, Chartier aims to exculpate his writing ontologically from all liability.

Liable for Libel

This point is not lost on the *Response des dames*. If the women's text engages first with Chartier on the score of verbal injury, it goes on to attack the ultimate defense that his poems are only literary compositions. In other words, it takes on directly the thorny problem of their ontological status:

> Tu dis moult bien, que on ne doit pas croire,
> Pour cuidier toy et ton livre excuser,
> Et que l'effort d'amours t'a fait recroire
> De bien parler et de bon sens user.
>
> (lines 73–76)

> You say well that in order to trust you and pardon your book, one
> shouldn't believe it, and that the force of love made you give up on
> speaking well and using your good sense.

The fundamental critique is this: how can Chartier query the believability
of the cruel woman persona by bracketing it literarily and make his own
defense believable? Put another way, what is the difference ontologically
between the *Excusacioun* and the *Belle Dame*? Why should his readers
believe in one any more than the other? Having chided them for their
interpretative naïveté, how can he expect them to give credence to his
Excusacioun written in an identical mode? In effect, the *Response* catches
Chartier at the game implicit in all literary discourse. To use the women's
turn of phrase, the literary "doubleness" enabling him to admit the
"falsity" of his female representations in one poem need not destabilize
his writing per se. Literature's double standard authorizes him to denounce his writing as duplicitous by the same means that it equips him to
defend it. The paradox is that it can change ontological footing, entertaining empirical truth claims together with literary ones. Yet here is where
we need to be most conscious of our own conceptions of literary discourse, as well as of our aptitude to interpret the *Querelle de la Belle
Dame* accordingly. Whereas most readers today take such a game for
granted, it was by no means a given in the early fifteenth century. Indeed,
the *Response des dames* would not credit such an understanding, block-
ing the logic that allows for the *Excusacioun* to be "true" and the *Belle
Dame* "false." Their text refuses to accord ontological autonomy to Chartier's texts as literary objects—under certain circumstances. More precisely, it rejects the notion of literary autonomy as grounds for the writer's
evasion of accountability. This is not to say that the idea of the autonomous literary work escapes the *Response des dames*; such a position
would reinforce the common, condescending identification of women
readers as literalists.[29] On the contrary, while the *Response* grants the
particular ontology of the literary text, it repudiates it as a means of deny-
ing public, legal responsibility. According to the *Response des dames*,
"literariness" is not a valid disclaimer, nor can it be invoked so as to have
one text render null and void another. Chartier's writing is still accountable before its audiences. This is all the more so in light of the prestige of
the written text and its wide public circulation.[30]

That the *Response* rejects the ontological argument underscores the
force of its defamation charge. It is a power we can best gauge in two ways.
First of all, the *Response des dames* meets the challenge of the *Excusacioun*
by criminalizing the charge of defamation. It changes radically the legal
process by which language injurious to women can be held accountable.

Such an action gains another dimension when we contrast it to other actions taken at the Châtelet court in Paris during this period. The causes concerning *paroles injurieuses* abounded.[31] They involved women and men, bourgeois and noble alike. Even corporate entities such as the University served as plaintiffs.[32] No social group in the city was excluded from this trend. Yet no matter how notoriously litigious fifteenth-century French society is taken to be, it is remarkable to consider that an expletive spoken in public could be common and sufficient grounds for legal complaint.[33] Expressions such as *putain, maquerelle* (slut, whore) or *maquereau, ruffien* (pimp, lush) could bring a defendant into court.[34] While the legal theory of defamation interpreted by canonists hinges on a far graver verbal assault, on the false imputation of a crime, the surviving record leaves open the possibility for many forms of verbal abuse.[35] So deep-seated was the understanding that abusive language is actionable that any number of citizens rose swiftly to the challenge of a slur. This phenomenon built stronger and stronger momentum, occasioning by the early sixteenth century a veritable explosion in litigation.[36] Defamation was an exemplary late-medieval cause.

Women were no strangers to this spirited legal scene. As coplaintiffs and defendants, they were as engaged as any other group in pursuing their defamers and seeking public redress.[37] And given the frequency with which the crime of defamation was accompanied by the threat of physical attack, their taking action was not uncommon. As Christine de Pizan and the three *Belle Dame* respondents noted, when injurious language is hurled at women, it frequently involves a violent follow-through. In the causes that come down to us, *la femme diffamée* also risks bodily abuse. Such instances by no means offer an equivalent to the charge of "Jeanne, Katherine, and Marie." Nor indeed should we be looking for one. Whether a replica of the respondents' case is visible or not is irrelevant for our argument. What is significant is the surrounding circumstances that confirm the idea of citizens suing on the basis of defamation. That such an act involves a crime marks an important correlation between the *Response des dames* and the Parisian legal record. That it involves a crime of writing sued for by women signals the novelty of the *Response*, and the second powerful influence that it exercises: libel.

The *Response* to Alain Chartier introduces a case of defamation that we recognize today as peculiar to written and pictorial texts. And it does so in a manner that plays adroitly with the multiple, fluid meanings of the medieval term *libelle*. Put another way, the women's text spans a rich, semantic complex whereby *libelle*, that simple, all-purpose word for book, refers to writing as artifact, type of infraction, and formidable legal instrument. Exploiting this full range of meaning, it focalizes the legal encounter between a text deemed defamatory and its aggrieved female public. Furthermore, it addresses its two chief aspects—the occurrence of defamation and the legal process for pursuing it. To elucidate the many different ways the *Response* realizes the term *libelle*, let me tease out here its various implications.[38]

One common meaning in the late-medieval context appears in the juridical expression *libelle diffamatoire* (defamatory writing). A straight-forward translation of the Roman term *libellus famosus*, it denotes those instances of defamation committed in written form. And as such, it stig-matizes them as illegal.[39] This term hangs thick in the various *Querelles* we have considered thus far. Indeed, it was part of the juridical jargon and apparatus that stamp the writings of almost every Parisian intellectual at the time.[40] A few examples are in order. In Jean LeFèvre's *Livre de leesce,* the narrator converted to the cause of women labels all clerical texts after Matheolus "libelles diffamatoires" (line 3522). In the controversy over Jean de Meun's *Roman de la rose,* Jean Gerson inveighs similarly against such works:

> Aucun escripra libelles diffamatoires d'une personne, soit de petit estat ou non—soit neis mauvaise—, et soit par personnaige: les drois jugent ung tel estre a pugnir et infame. Et donques que doivent dire les lois et vous, dame Justice, non pas d'ung libelle, mais d'ung grant livre plain de toutes infamacions, non pas seulement contre homes, mais contre Dieu et tous sains et saintes qui ainment vertus?

> (Hicks, 72, xxiii)

> Anyone who writes defamatory books of a person, whether of mean es-tate or not, whether not at all bad, whether through another character: the laws judge such a person infamous and worthy of punishment. And thus, what should the laws, and you, lady Justice, say about not just a small book [*libelle*], but a huge book full of all sorts of vituperations, directed not only against men, but against God and all saintly men and women who love virtue?

And in the statutes of the *Cour Amoureuse,* that stylized Parisian Court of Love devised by Parisian courtiers, the following article is included: "All that is said is, whatever accursed delinquent who will have composed per-sonally defamatory books or have had them made by one or others will be under pain of having his arms stripped" (Tout ce que dit est, sur peine de effacier les armes de tel maleureux delinquant qui telz libelles diffama-toires aroit fait en sa personne ou fait faire par autres, .I. ou pluseurs).[41] All three examples use the expression *libelles diffamatoires* as a way of point-ing the finger at works judged abusive of women. Whether they situate those works in a clerical or courtly context, whether they denounce them as a type of intellectual fantasm, in the case of LeFèvre, or as a debasement of chivalric ideals, in the *Cour*, or even as a threat to religious orthodoxy, in Gerson, the understanding of injurious writing remains much the same. Naming works *libelles diffamatoires* serves as a convenient derogatory label. It identifies them as publicly unacceptable and actionable within a classical and medieval rhetoric of liability. And because Gerson sets up an allegory of a court of justice, the specifically legal dimensions of the term are accentuated.

So far the *Response des dames* appears to abide by a common understanding of *libelle*. It is structurally consistent with LeFèvre's and Gerson's use, for it too singles out the existence of such damaging, misogynistic writing to condemn it. Functionally, however, in a text voiced by three women there is a profound difference distinguishing the *Response*'s naming of *libelles diffamatoires*. The *Response des dames* breaks out of the vicious circle of idolatry that fetishizes a female reputation the better to control it. It suggests other modus operandi that bespeak an alliance between women and the law. It moves beyond stigmatizing the defamatory writing ritualistically in a manner that has no bearing on the parties involved. For "Jeanne, Katherine, and Marie" to identify such *libelles* is to represent a legal inquiry initiated by the women personally affected.

Here is where a second, major inference of the medieval term *libelle* enters in. It is important to remember that the Latin word for *book* was adapted during the earliest phases of Western jurisprudence to designate the writ publicizing an allegation.[42] It is the brief bearing a charge that would ultimately serve as an indictment. By definition a public document, the *libelle* brought an infraction out into the open and through the intervention of a magistrate gave it technical weight. Such is the predominant sense of the word as it emerges in the juridical lexicon of Old French. In the thirteenth-century *Coutumes de Beauvaisis*, Philippe de Beaumanoir offers this account:

> Et pour ce, de ce qui plus souvent est dit en la court laie et dont plus grans mestiers est, nous traiterons en cest chapitre en tel maniere que li lai le puissent entendre. C'est assavoir des demandes qui sont fetes et que l'en puet et doit fere en court laie, lesqueus demandes li clerc apelent *libelles*; et autant vaut demande comme libelle.[43]

> And for this reason, we will discuss in this chapter, in such a way that laymen can understand it, what is most often said in secular courts and what is most needful. This is concerning complaints which are made and which you can and should make in secular courts, which complaints are called by the clerks *libelles*; and a complaint is the same as a brief.[44]

Such a usage carries over into late-medieval parlance. So widely accepted is this connotation that it occurs even in satires of legal process. In the fifteenth-century *Farce du maître Pathelin*, the lawyer's blusterings make this clear: "How the tricky man toils long and hard over presenting his complaint!" (Comme le meschant homme forge de loing, pour fournir son libelle!" lines 1273–74).

The *Response des dames* thus delivers a *libelle* (legal brief) against the *libelle diffamatoire* (defamatory writing) of Chartier. It throws the book at the *Belle Dame*. Having challenged the writing formally, it realizes the next, crucial step whereby the women as plaintiffs accuse it legally—on their own account—of libel. The *Response* works to establish the liability of Chartier's poem and binds it to the legal requirement of ensuing investigation. Once a brief is lodged, the chances for evasions are severely restricted. Whether that brief is eventually upheld or dismissed, it has defined the crime of writing against which all further proceeding must be measured.

As a *libelle*, a little legal book, the women's *Response* also circulates oppositionally in the space of the city. Where Matheolus sends off the misogynistic *Lamentations* with an Ovidian envoi—"va t'en, petit livre, va t'en en la cité"—here the respondents are quick to launch their own *libelle* publicly. They promulgate it as a court order against another defamatory text in the civic domain that it appears to dominate.[45] The *Response* thereby claims its own place in the public square, just as it does in the civic discourse so prized by fifteenth-century clerical writers and humanists.

Libel, legal brief, little book: I have followed all the resonances of the medieval term *libelle*, including echoes with the English word "libel." These are echoes, let me emphasize, that hold neither in Old nor modern French. *Libelle* is not used, strictly speaking, to juridically designate a crime. But I have entertained this word play because it enables us to reach the heart of the *Response des dames'* challenge. The *libelle* represented by this work recapitulates a wide and revealing semantic range that covers the literal meaning of written material, the extended meaning of defamatory writing, as well as the stiff, technical sense of a legal writ. The singular action this narrative takes capitalizes on the malleable and charged concept of defamation in the late Middle Ages, and it does so in a manner suggesting its particular advantage for women. Articulated in their voice, *libelle*—in all its senses—is not invoked lightly or hypothetically. It is performed by female personae who are not proxies but are themselves the plaintiffs. It becomes their legal instrument.

The *Response des dames's libelle* is shot through with a lurid language. There are notable allusions to hanging and burning, references to recanting and the public disgrace of infamy (lines 6–8, 45–48).[46] The *Response* even types Chartier a heretic, much as Christine did with Matheolus and Jean de Meun (line 78).[47] Such a rhetoric resonates with the turbulence reigning in early-fifteenth-century Paris. Given the charged political tensions, the threats concerning heresy proliferated, and in an ecclesiastical context these could result in the rituals of book burning and execution.[48] The profound belief in verbal injury coupled with a fear of social chaos frequently sanctioned a violent end for the heretic and his works.[49] Mimicking details of these rituals, the *Response* participates in the inflammatory atmosphere of the times.

By the same token, this extremist language is a defining element of polemical logic. As we discovered with the *Querelle de la Rose*, it is the gesture of challenge and disputation. No point is made neutrally, nor are its consequences underplayed. In the case of the *Response*, this language full of menace also points to the particular force of its polemic. It underscores the seriousness of its legal charge. Here again is the idiom of absolutist power, which enables women respondents to exert rhetorical influence they would not otherwise possess.

But it does not convey the spirit of the public redress the *Response des dames* seeks. For one thing, it does not presume to ban Chartier's writing. In delivering the brief, the respondents maintain: "For you write as you shall want to write" (Or escrips ce que escripre vouldras, line 80). At some level, they acknowledge the incorrigible continuity of poetic composition, its boundlessness. Insofar as the *Response* makes no claim to prohibit Chartier from writing, its *libelle* motion does not carry with it any program of enforcing textual conformity. After all, it challenges a text that, however politically precarious, remains the paragon of poetic orthodoxy. Its ambition is to explode such orthodoxy. Its chief concern lies in the harmful consequences of a dominant mode of representation. It seeks to adjudicate those consequences to the satisfaction of the aggrieved parties involved without eliminating the writing outright.

So it is that the *Response* accentuates the open-endedness of its litigation. Any *libelle* is caught in the rounds of charge and countercharge, and the *Response* is no exception. It anticipates a later stage, where Chartier would be confronted with the respondents' advocates (lines 101–4).[50] In its conclusion it promises an ongoing exchange between the women plaintiffs and the poet. Such an exchange would entail not only negotiation but further writing. To issue a *libelle* against a crime of writing, let me repeat again, occasions more and more text, a prospect in perfect keeping with the *Response*'s purposes. In the attempt to reconcile injurious textual representation and offended parties, the prerogative to write is by no means destroyed. Nevertheless, the *libelle* for libel still stands. The peculiar, novel power of the women's *Response* resides in its legal action that confronts a writer with his public.

A Matter of Fiction and Treason

That the *Querelle* continued after the *Response des dames* suggests the strong impact of its *libelle*. In the decade following the *Belle Dame*, five other works appeared that sought to undo the charge of defamatory libel levied against Chartier.[51] At the center of these works is an interrogation of the *Belle Dame* persona. She is put on trial—over and over again. Such a scene enables these works to answer the *Response*'s *libelle*: it makes the literary character and not the writer accountable. Yet it also discloses the ongoing struggle with the defining issues of the *Querelle*: the writer's liability for verbal injury and the ontological standing of his book. As we shall see in the two following examples, the poets in Chartier's circle experimented obsessively with deflecting the charge of defamation. This experimentation hints at the tensions remaining over the writer's responsibility and the sovereignty of his literary text. It discloses frustration over the fact that these questions are unresolved or unresolvable. To what degree this exasperation is vented on the women respondents should become clear.

In the trial of the *Belle Dame* mounted by the poem *La Cruelle Femme d'amour*, the issue of Chartier's liability is met head-on. When the allegorical figure Truth is called as a witness to vouch for the woman, she balks, stating:

> Celle qui se mist en mon nom
> Pour ceste cause soustenir
> Ne fu aultre que Fiction:
> Poeterie la fist venir
> Et ma semblable devenir;
> Et se transmua Faulseté
> Pour sa trahison parfurnir
> En la semblance Leauté.
> (lines 329–36)

The one who took my name to support this cause was none other than Fiction. Poetry made her come and become like me. And Falsehood changed herself into a semblance of Loyalty to accomplish her treason.

The *Cruelle Femme* supplies the missing component that hovers over the entire *Querelle*: Fiction. On first glance, Fiction appears to be the stand-in for Truth, and a fraudulent one at that. The chief alliance thus unites Fiction, Falsehood, and the *Belle Dame*. Yet given the *Cruelle Femme*'s intricate allegory, which sets the courtroom scene within several dream frames, we must interpret this configuration carefully. Although the humanist understanding of poetry is invoked pejoratively here—that is, to distinguish a false portrait of a woman from a true one—it serves to valorize Chartier's text. Fiction functions here in her tantalizing duality: as falsehood and as distinct discursive mode. She recoups the standard clerical disapproval of deceptive fiction together with the emancipatory concept of fiction as the highest exaltation of truth. Indeed, she plays one off against the other. Consequently, the *Cruelle Femme* can accommodate the charge of defamatory representation, appearing to appease the women respondents in the very act of marking out a separate sphere for the fictive. By admitting that Chartier's *Belle Dame* is cruel and not even a lady, *La Cruelle Femme en amour* appears to credit the *Response*'s charge. It entertains the poet's liability. Yet by making that admission through Fiction, transformed now into a positive, potent term, it checks that liability from ever being established legally. What we most commonly think of as an early modern concept of fictionality is introduced here as a means of making the *Belle Dame* legally inviolable. The *Cruelle Femme* defends Chartier's poem on ontological grounds.

We have here the most explicit and technical reply to the claims of verbal injury in the *Response des dames*. The *Cruelle Femme* explicitly names a principle already apparent in the *Querelle de la Rose* and prominent in Chartier's *Excusacioun*. The double epithet it thus introduces—Poetry/Fiction—places the notion of a literary ontology squarely in the technical vocabulary of a philosophical debate that is more or less foreign to Chartier's own work.[52] Furthermore, the pronounced legal frame brings out the often-overlooked fact that Fiction also represents a juristic formula.[53] *Fictio figura veritatis* was at the center of several canon legal debates during the late Middle Ages.[54] As a concept in the *Cruelle Femme*, then, Fiction commands particular influence, benefiting from a specifically legal meaning as well as from a poetico-philosophical one.

Reinforced doubly, the ontological vindication of fiction would appear to win the day. In a shrewd move, one legal premise of *fictio figura veritatis* blocks another—the *Response*'s claim of *laesio/iniuria*. Yet if we note the subsequent development in the *Cruelle Femme*, this is far from the case.[55] No matter how strongly the case for fiction's sovereignty has been propounded, there lingers the suspicion that it does not completely nullify the *Response*'s legal claims. In some fundamental way, the criterion of an autonomous literary object fails to dispense with the issue of accountability for damages. This failure has less to do with the irregular currency of the Poetry/Fiction theory in fifteenth-century France than it does with the uneasy fit between the theory and the legal doctrine of defamatory writing. Once again we discern the irreconcilability of literature and libel at this particular historical moment. It prompts still more exaggerated defenses of Chartier.

In the wake of Fiction's mock denunciation of the *Belle Dame* persona, the *Cruelle Femme* represents her as convicted of the most heinous crime. The God of Love pronounces that she has committed lèse-majesté—an infraction for which she is to lose her own proper name (lines 747–52). To find the *Belle Dame* guilty of treason is to throw one last sop in the direction of the women respondents. Condemning the literary persona is meant ultimately to appease them. Yet this "condemnation" also signals the frustration of Chartier's defenders over the sheer intractability of the liability question. The more numerous the arguments for the fictive text's unaccountability, the more unavoidable a text's responsibility to its community appears. The more sophisticated those arguments, including even the "Fiction as Poetry" theorem, the more unyielding the question of verbal injury remains. Let us not forget that the crime of treason, "lèse-majesté," is itself formulated as a wounding (*lèse*) perpetrated through words: "de sa bouche a arresté."[56] The final recourse left to Chartier's defenders involves recasting the charge of verbal injury and foisting it back onto those who raised it.

Here is where we can detect that the ultimate object of the *Cruelle Femme*'s accusation of treason is "Jeanne, Katherine, and Marie." According to this poem, the *Response des dames* dared to attack the work of a royal poet. As many critics have suggested, late-medieval intellectuals were deeply preoccupied with treason and the damage done to sovereignty—so preoccupied, in fact, that the problem was easily transferable.[57] Any number of social phenomena were associated with treason. It is in this sense that Jean de Montreuil attempts first to interpret Christine de Pizan's critique of the *Rose* as an attack on the integrity of the master.[58] And it is in this sense too, that Chartier's defenders use the charge of treason to accuse the respondents implicitly of another form of injuriousness. By introducing the crime of lèse-majesté, they turn the tables on the *Response des dames* and thereby try to exit the intractable *Querelle* over liability with the law on their side.

Such a gesture should be familiar by now. Targeting "Jeanne, Katherine, and Marie" in this manner reconfirms the stereotype of women as defamers. To characterize them as treasonous is another way of defining their own language as inherently damaging and dangerous. Indeed, it casts their language as nothing less than demonic.[59] As *Le Jugement du povre triste amant banny*, another poem in Chartier's defense, appraises it, women's defamation holds dire consequences for the entire body politic: "For when they want to attempt to be hurtful, everyone is devastated" (Car quant vouldroient tascher a nuyre, / Tout le monde seroit gasté; lines 831–32).

This ploy of labeling the women treasonous and by implication defamatory was intended to shift the focus of the *Querelle* away from the outstanding problem of the poet's legal liability for his writing. Rhetorically, it may well have worked. The controversy seems to have trailed off at this stage. Yet that it comes to the point of invoking the gravest crime against women is revealing, for it suggests the disturbing power the *Response des dames* as *libelle* could have exercised.

What, then, are the consequences of the *Response des dames*? The inconclusiveness of the *Querelle* around Alain Chartier's writing should not fool us into concluding that there were none or that the consequences were ineffectual. However short-lived the incident, it represents an important step toward legal recourse. In fact, it appropriates legal recourse as a mechanism with which to combat the symbolic domination of women through a masterly poetic discourse. It manipulates the prevailing laws of defamation in such a way as to stigmatize the individual writer involved and to put his writing—symbolically—in the dock. Given how influential the legal regulation and rhetoric of defamation was in fifteenth-century France, the *Response*'s deft play with the law proves all the more provocative. It is, let me underline, first and foremost a form of play. It does not substantiate a case of three women plaintiffs suing for damages. But exploiting ludically the legal apparatus concerning defamation does elicit other strategies for challenging publicly the dominant representation of women. This, as the *Response* suggests in jest, is in the unlikely event that their words will come to blows: "For it will never happen that woman will fight you" (Car point n'affiert que femme t'en combatte; line 88).

To play with the power of the law was by no means the principal strategy available to the woman's response. As we have seen in the previous chapter with Christine de Pizan, there was always the possibility of assuming the symbolic register of the masterly poetic discourse on women and thereby disputing the problem of its domination on its own grounds. The woman's response could generate its own brand of symbolic structures, sometimes in notably learned form. In the terms of the *Querelle de la Belle Dame*, it can co-opt the fictive for its own purposes. This is something that Christine de Pizan also demonstrates ably when she claims: "I shall say, through fiction, the fact of this transformation, how it was I became a man from a woman."[60] But what distinguishes this *Response des dames* is its complementary choice of exploring a legal option. In the wake of the experiments legitimated by the *Querelle de la Rose*, the *Response* confronts fiction with the law. To mimic filing a *libelle* for defamation provides another formidable means of disputing the symbolic domination of women. For it charts a space between the absolute, unqualified freedom of discourse and arbitrary censorship, between bearing no responsibility whatsoever to the public and being utterly beholden to the prevailing authority. In this sense, it pioneers a middle ground made possible through litigation, a ground where the underrepresented can render public the time-honored recurrence of verbal injury to women and seek compensation. In the most far-reaching sense, such compensation would not comprise an empirical computation of damages. Rather, it promises the practice of changing the masterly discourse on women. It involves forging another discourse, shaping other images of women that would not prove so confining. To make over Chartier's own expression, it would launch a freer figuration of women. I risk this formulation on the basis of an image in the *Response des dames*:

> Tu trouveras et le verras au fort
> Que leaulté, doulceur, bonté, franchise,
> Portent la clef du chastel ferme et fort
> Ou honneur a nostre pitié soubzmise.
> (lines 53–56)

You will find and you will see well that loyalty, gentleness, goodness, freedom, carry the key to the strong and stout castle where honor yields to our mercy.

Always in the terms of the prevailing symbolic language, the *Response* forecasts a moment when *franchise* (freedom) would typify women. And this would provide "the key to the castle"; that is, according to the trope of woman as castle, it would legitimize a different code of representing women, unlocking them from the decorous yet tyrannical one that holds them. Such a key has no single owner. This passage can be read as referring to Chartier and the existing cadre of court poets or to women as purveyors of discourse. Whichever the case, the discursive stronghold can be broken through, replaced by a discursive model that figures women more freely. Such a figurative prospect is still framed here by other symbolic structures that are less than favorable to women: the catalogue of feminine virtues, the code of honor, and the posture of the idol. But that is why it is projected in the future tense; that is also why it is couched in an enigma— *la clef*—a common password for outmaneuvering hostile readers.[61] If a freer figuration of women is presented so enigmatically, it is because it is far from being realized. If it is alluded to at all, it is because in this highly divisive, highly sophisticated milieu of fifteenth-century Paris, it is nonetheless conceivable.

14. Héloïse instructing courtiers in Capellanus's lessons on love. London, British Museum, Royal 16.F.11, fol. 137. By permission of the British Library.

Coda

Clotilde de Surville and the Latter-Day History of the Woman's Response

Across a spectrum of late-medieval French culture, the figure of the woman respondent stands out. Side by side with the better-known master figure, she takes her part in the ritual of disputation. Her role displaces that of the disciple. Or rather she makes over that role insofar as she mounts a sustained challenge to the discourses on women belonging to clerical *magistri* and master-poets. Woman's disputing centers on the problem of injurious language, how it is that conventional models of representation can be damaging to their various audiences. This critique turns into a public call for accountability, and such a move places the woman respondent increasingly in the fractious context of *Querelles*. Misogynistic invective is matched by accusation, defamation by polemic. If the symbolic dominance of language injurious to women is to be broken, it requires the counterbalancing rhetoric of correction and judgment. The woman's response is rarely presented as an individualistic act in the framework of disputation; rather, it is proposed in the name of women in general. With the public controversies of the later Middle Ages, the response is made on behalf of the community at large. Its dispute with the masters over verbal injury becomes an ethical and political concern. In this it prepares the ground for the woman respondent's own mastery. While the scholastic monopoly of intellectual life still pertained in late-medieval vernacular culture, there was nonetheless a prospect of representing woman as a protomaster. Humanists continued to represent the scholarly life as a cult of Minerva, but the woman respondent also became a Minerva figure, invested with the prerogatives of learning, if not with the official title.[1] By the mid-fifteenth century, the respondent's learning may even register authoritatively. Consider this miniature illustrating a version of Capellanus's *De amore* attributed, this time, to Héloïse (Figure 14).[2] A magisterial woman such as Héloïse holds the position of scholar/counselor. Her teaching can set a standard, as this image depicts it, not only for a community of women but also for courtiers and by extension for the public as a whole.

My study of the dialectic between masterful writing and woman's response has tried to establish the importance of the respondent's profile.
But I should better say: it has tried to *re*establish its importance. There is,
in fact, nothing new about this figure. She already has a modern history.
However unfamiliar she may first have appeared to us, she was known
throughout the nineteenth century in France, where she was the subject of
considerable scrutiny and debate. I am referring to the case of the
fifteenth-century figure Clotilde de Surville. In the course of my research,
I came across Clotilde and recognized in her another instance of what I
have chosen to call a medieval woman respondent. Indeed, as I shall
show, her case brings to the fore the category of respondent itself. It illustrates the various different ways the woman respondent has been
viewed in the past. Her case thus reminds us that whether we recognize it
or not, any medieval object we examine already carries with it a legacy of
interpretation. Furthermore, the animated debate that she provoked
raises the question of the relation between critic and object. It discloses
one telling example of the presuppositions at play in establishing or rejecting the category of respondent. The nineteenth-century affair of
Clotilde dramatizes the problem of how critics approach the medieval
woman respondent. I wish to tell her latter-day story for several reasons.
First of all, it fills in a little-known backdrop for my study, and it reveals
why it has proven so difficult to discern the respondent figure. It goes a
long way in explaining her absence from our interpretative map of the
later Middle Ages. But Clotilde's story is revealing in larger terms as
well. Telling it will help, in the end, to clarify the terms of our own critical engagement with the medieval woman's response.

Correcting the Master

In 1803, the works of Marguerite-Eléonore Clotilde de Vallon de Surville
were published in Paris.[3] These included epic poetry, epistolary verse in the
manner of Ovid's Heroïdes, debate pieces, *chansons d'amour*, and various
ballades and *rondeaux*. Attributed to this fifteenth-century woman was a
poetic range that could put her in the company of any contemporaneous
poet. Clotilde's biography was just as eye-catching as her writing. She was
introduced as a provincial prodigy—a woman who imitated the verses of
Petrarch and *trouvères* with the same ease.[4] Her talent was developed
through an extensive literary education: Clotilde resembled a humanistic
bibliophile. This training brought her into contact with the Parisian court.
Yet her creative efforts were equally dedicated to a group of young women
gathered around her. Clotilde's biography accentuates the image of a
woman writer schooling her own circle.

The lyric poetry attributed to Clotilde includes several *rondeaux* directed to "Maistre Alain Chartier." Addressing a leading poet of the day, they mark her public entry onto the literary scene: they are challenges. They correspond to the longstanding pattern of women figures debating with master-poets. Like many of the respondents we have considered, Clotilde takes on her interlocutor to demonstrate her poetic prowess, but more significantly, to question the terms of his.[5] That questioning revolves first around the character of Chartier's language. Her *rondeau*, "Le feu d'enfer," makes this ambition clear:

> Le feu d'enfer, sans notoire hablerie,
> Contez bien long comme lui[ct], maistre Alain,
> Sanz esclayrer: point n'est sorcellerie;
> Dante cogneust, quaz'en ung tour de main,
> Tous les secrets d'icelle diablerie.
>
> Sur ce grand faict, plus on ne contrarie
> Ne vous ne luy, se treuvoit le proschain,
> Comme en ses vers, dans vostre parlerie,
> Du feu.
>
> Au demourant, bien est la resverie
> En cour; beau livre onc ne fist tant de train:
> Quand va vous veoir Apollo, je parie
> Vous bayzera; de quoy moult serez vain,
> Mais quant l'oyra, grand peur ay que s'escrie:
> Au feu.
>
> (1825 edition, 70)[6]

You describe the fire of hell at length, master Alain, with no notable skill, as he did, without clarifying anything. This is no sorcery. Dante knew well all the secrets of this devilry with sleight of hand. On this point, one bothers neither you nor him anymore, if the next one were to find, in his verse, as in your way of talking, fire. In the meanwhile, there is great dreaming at court. A good book never caused such a fuss. When Apollo comes to see you, I bet that he'll kiss you; but when he hears it, I greatly fear that he'll cry out: into the fire!

In its simplest terms, Clotilde's piece plays with the master's writing. Not only does it mimic Alain's *rondeau* of the same name, but it echoes Dante's *Inferno* as well.[7] It sets one authoritative poet against the other. In disputing the trope of being on fire, her *rondeau* juxtaposes Alain's exclusively erotic significance with Dante's eschatological one. This play thus signals a learned critique of master Alain, exposing his use of the trope as limited, even hackneyed, in comparison with the Italian's. Clotilde's *rondeau* delivers this critique in a petulant tone. It is teasing, if not taunting. Implicitly it charges Alain and his famous rhetoric with incompetence. Moreover, because that rhetoric is evoked to celebrate his name, Clotilde's critique targets the poet's reputation. To make this point provocatively, the *rondeau* introduces a third sense of fire. Alain's writing is consigned to nothing less than the censorious flames of hell. The scene would be familiar to anyone acquainted with the two *Querelles* of the *Rose* and of the *Belle Dame*. It evokes a mock judgment and public condemnation of a book; it mimics an act of censorship not untypical in fifteenth-century Paris. While Clotilde's *rondeau* transposes this scene mythically, locating it in Apollo's court, its defining turn of phrase, "au feu," yields a forceful twofold critique of Alain. The word play on fire corrects his rhetoric and his public reputation as well. Clotilde's own composition is intended as the beneficiary.

The woman's debate with Alain extends further, to the issue of a poet's status. Such is the aim of Clotilde's *rondeau*, "l'air de la cour":

> L'air de la cour, vous le diray-je? enteste,
> Chier maistre Alain; c'est ung dogme receu
> Despuys le jour que vous cuydez poëste,
> En cheveulx gris, et qu'on s'est apperceu
> Que d'Hélicon projectiez la conqueste.
>
> Ainz comme offriez vos oeuvres pour requeste
> Au blond Phoebus, devinez veoir ung peu
> Ce qu'y treuva, quand en eust faict l'enqueste?
> De l'air.
>
> S'en esbayoit; à bien rire estoit preste
> Tout sa cour; quand moult fort entendeu
> Phesycien, lors présent à la feste
> Dict: N'en gabez, ung jour de lune indeu,
> Par fascheux cas, il s'endormist nud-teste
> A l'air.

>   (1825 edition, 54)

An air of courtliness—will I say to you? Oh my dear willful master Alain, that's a received dogma around since the day you thought yourself a white-haired poet, and since it became clear that you aimed to conquer Helicon. Having offered your works as a petition to blond Phoebus, did you try to see a bit of what one found there, when the inquiry was done? Something of that air? He was dumbfounded. All the court was on the verge of laughter. When the doctor, who was there at the festivities, understood perfectly and said:

don't fool yourself. One night, by bad luck, he fell asleep bare-
headed in the open air.

Clotilde's poem chides Alain over the concept of courtliness. It challenges
the slavish adoption of convention that Alain sees as authorizing his talent and Clotilde recognizes—on the contrary—as having nothing to do
with creativity. The woman writer outside the Parisian court disputes the
insider's criteria. And the implicit term of her dispute is a humanistic idea
of the poet. In effect, the *rondeau* contrasts the age-old courtly model of
poetry with a "new," increasingly prestigious model. It challenges Alain's
style as retro. He is represented as behind the times—a somewhat pa-
thetic figure who merits gentle mockery. His outmodishness is all the
more striking in Apollo's court, a humanistic framework of poetic composition. By playing with the referent for court and placing Alain before the
classical god of poetry, Clotilde's *rondeau* sharpens her critique. Her writing deploys an alternative, humanistic poetic model unknown to Chartier.
It thus establishes its own claims to a new poetic courtliness in the act of
discrediting the courtly doctrine of the master.

This attack on the qualifications of the master-poet is generalized in a
rondeau composed about Chartier. Instead of a direct address to the poet, it
opens out to the public at large. It implicates them in the ongoing critique.
In the piece "Le monde est sot qu'admire ung sot ouvrage," Clotilde's
rhetoric borders on the polemical.[8] By charging the master-poet with bad
writing, it sets up the opposition between *sottise* and rationality, between
a writer's vainglory and his/her courage. "They only have one life,"
Clotilde's persona says of good writing, "but the works produced by reason survive their own age" (Ils n'ont qu'ung temps; mais les oeuvres pro-
duicts par la rayson survivent à leur aage; lines 10–11). The claim is that
Chartier's writing enjoys popularity because of court support. What
Clotilde finds missing is a rational ground for this view. On this score she
privileges her own poetry and sees it as ultimately surpassing his.

Still, Clotilde's writing does not relinquish the chance of beating the
court poet at his own game, as the piece "Epistre à Marguerite d'Écosse"
makes clear.[9] This poem does not mount the same sort of polemic as the
other poems we have considered. But by approaching Chartier's influential
patron, it continues to target Chartier's work. The strategy this time involves reading him in relation to a gamut of other medieval poets: Jean de
Meun, Charles d'Orléans, François Villon, even Christine de Pizan. As
Clotilde represents it, Alain's poetic reputation looks safe if his work is set
against an empty backdrop. But once the works of rival poets are filled in,
his masterful status is by no means clear cut.

However pointed Clotilde's critique of Alain is, its social influence
remains unclear. Can it stick? Toward the end of the letter, her persona
acknowledges the difficulty:

> Mais que t'en prend, Clotilde, à censurer
> Ung qui desjà s'ose aux roys mesurer?...
> Car bien appriz que n'est oncques d'usage,
> Par bons adviz et touschantes rayzons,
> De corriger ceux-là qu'applaudissons.
>
> (1825 edition, 120–21)

But what moves you, Clotilde, to censor one who already dares to compare himself to kings? . . . For you well know that it is hardly customary according to good advice and touching reasons to correct those whom we applaud.

The trouble lies in pinning down an established poet like Chartier and in holding his writing accountable. No matter how justified her dispute with Chartier, its likely effect is minimal. Given Chartier's preeminent reputation and her own precarious one, her correction of his poetry occupies a tricky position. Censure works for the most part against the underrepresented, securing the dominance of those already in control. Here the Clotilde figure is trying to work it back the other way. Yet insofar as the problem is inscribed in Clotilde's *rondeaux* and the "Epistre à Marguerite d'Écosse," the move is not impossible. The letter keeps attention focused on the challenge of putting poetic representation to the test. By alluding to a censure that would condemn the reigning dogma, it raises the question of how poetic or figurative norms can be contested effectively from without.

These three texts comprise a small part of Clotilde's attributed oeuvre. But examining the rondeaux and epistle together brings out uncanny correspondences with the woman's response we have studied. Chief among these is the impetus to break with a mode of symbolic domination prevailing in high-medieval letters. Clotilde's poems resemble the work of the *Bestiaire* respondent in their deft dismantling of the master's figures. Both respondents analyze figurative language in order to expose its limitations. By making such analysis a public issue, Clotilde's poems also recall Christine de Pizan's polemic with Jean de Meun. For both respondents, disputing the master's writing is an affair of public concern. Yet Clotilde's astringent challenge to the living poet, Alain Chartier, approximates even more closely the text of "Jeanne, Katherine, and Marie." There is a haunting parallel between the two bouts of sparring with this major fifteenth-century poet.

In their general shape, then, Clotilde's *rondeaux* mirror the woman's response as we found it in late-medieval French culture. They do not match the substance of the *Bestiaire's* or Christine's critique. What is missing is the particular focus on the figuration of women in masterly writing. Absent too is the argument over the injurious quality of such figuration. Yet while they do not share the particular detail of the woman's disputation with the master-poets, they do display the same profile. They all exploit the disputational structure as a way to render masterly writing answerable to its public.

Correcting the Woman's Response

For Clotilde's earliest readers in the nineteenth century, it was this disputational profile that touched off extreme reactions. To begin with, the instance of a woman poet debating with Alain Chartier was received enthusiastically. As the eminent critic Sainte-Beuve reported it: "The first success of Clotilde was enormous, the discussions spirited; there still remains a great attraction and curiosity for poetic spirits."[10] The Romantic poet Lamartine was characteristically ecstatic:

> Yesterday I came across a volume entitled *The Poetry of Clotilde de Surville:* these are the Gallic poems of a woman up until now unknown, whose manuscripts have just been brought to light. I won't talk to you about all this coolly, with a level head, because I was transported. . . . [H]ow is it that in a time of the deepest ignorance, a woman who never left her Gothic castle could have written such things that, in my opinion, are worthy of Tibullus, of any poet, whosoever he is?[11]

Lamartine's zeal was shared by the general public. Over the first half of the nineteenth century its steady interest occasioned several editions of Clotilde's work.[12]

At the same time, the profile of such a woman poet aroused concern. The fact that Clotilde sparred with Alain Chartier and yet remained unknown gave rise to suspicions. She did not fit easily into any recognizable record of late-medieval French culture. Further, the circumstances of Clotilde's modern emergence were mysterious. Clotilde's late-eighteenth-century descendent, the Marquis de Surville, claimed to have retrieved her poetry from the family archives. This labor was threatened by the Reign of Terror. The Marquis was forced to relay his version of Clotilde's poetry clandestinely to a certain Charles Vanderbourg, a German bookseller, who became her first official publisher. Such cloak-and-dagger aspects of Clotilde's publication posed the question of her veracity. This was a notorious era for literary forgeries: the scandals of Macpherson's Ossian and Chatterton's late-medieval monk, among others, were still piquing the public's curiosity.[13] In fact, Vanderbourg was pressed to acknowledge these concerns in later editions of Clotilde's poetry: "If certain well-informed journalists have raised doubts as to the veritable authors of these poems, all men of letters are in unanimous agreement to recognize her authorship."[14] Lines were drawn between the literati inclined to take her seriously and those new classes of professional skeptic—journalists and academic critics—who were not. Where was the material proof of her sizable corpus? Why were there no obvious medieval references to her? Questions of this sort culminated in an accusation of fraud. The conflict between advocates and opponents of Clotilde was best exemplified by the writer Charles Nodier, who managed to take both sides. As an advocate, he contributed significantly to the fracas by republishing the most contested element of Clotilde's corpus, a set of critical notices on medieval women poets.[15] "Clotilde's reputation reigns above all in the hearts of women. It is to them that we offer some of her poetry. It is up to them to defend the glory of her sex against the disdainful science of men."[16] Nodier lent Clotilde his imprimatur. As an opponent, however, in his guise as professional critic, Nodier adopted a "scientific" position. Several years after publishing the notices on women poets, he exposed Clotilde's writing as imposture: "The verdict is now in on the veritable author of these interesting works. I don't believe that one can doubt that it was the Marquis de Surville himself."[17] Nodier's reversal was symptomatic of the two principal critical attitudes that were coalescing by the mid-nineteenth century. There were literati who appreciated the genius of a woman poet and polemicist from the distant past and there were others who for the professional reasons of criticism and scholarship could not credit it. As these attitudes hardened over the course of the next generations, cases for and against Clotilde's writing were put forward. Indeed, so heated was the debate that by the 1870s it was still a matter of public concern.

Clotilde's work was challenged first on linguistic grounds. Was her language in fact the idiom of fifteenth-century Burgundy? The syntax, the vocabulary, the rhetorical coloring: all these elements seemed to suggest a later form of French. Further, the versification did not accord with what was known of fifteenth-century court poetry. Nor did the genres correspond; they matched those of eighteenth-century fashions as well as those in any medieval period. In short, the various codes shaping Clotilde's language were all suspect.

The force of this critique was to identify her language as modernized. Under the veneer of an antique language, what Sainte-Beuve described as "the air of the good old days," a forger was at work (492). By studying the extant medieval relics, say the writings of Jean de Meun or Alain Chartier, such a forger could have cobbled together poems that simulated them linguistically. With a public both fascinated with and ignorant of the medieval past, this artificial age-old language could pass for legitimate. For a scientific critic such as Sainte-Beuve, however, there was always a tell-tale trace that gave the modern forger away. A neologism or a Latinate word reintroduced into French in the sixteenth century could signal the modern research effort that informed Clotilde's language. As the study of Old and Middle French became more sophisticated, the list of such traces grew exponentially.

This objection about Clotilde's faked medieval tongue did not go unnoticed. There were advocates of Clotilde who openly acknowledged the extent to which it had been reworked. As one critic remarked: "Four authors have declared having undertaken revisions of the original work of Marguerite-Clotilde de Surville."[18] The problem resided in the character of this revision process. Or to put it in still more probing terms, it resided in the nature of editorial intervention. For those inclined to give credence to the medieval provenance of Clotilde's writing, such intervention was inescapable. It would be foolhardy to claim that texts from an age before printing could arrive in modern hands directly, without any mediation. Yet such a fact need not pose a threat to its authenticity. The act of copying and modifying a medieval "original" does not impugn in and of itself that original's existence. It merely updates it. It is the explicit mark of its reception and interpretation by a later period. In the case of Clotilde, this meant a complex layering effect involving the eighteenth-century editing of the Marquis de Surville and the seventeenth-century editing of yet another descendant, Jeanne de Vallon, reaching all the way back to Clotilde's own time. As another critic stressed, this fifteenth-century woman poet was herself represented as correcting and emending the writing of others. In her humanistic role, Clotilde was seen to revise Héloïse in an effort to bring Héloïse's language into line with the linguistic and stylistic mores of the later Middle Ages.[19] Clotilde's writing thus underwent the same sort of modification she insisted on imposing on others.

This debate over medieval language hints at the very crux that continues to underwrite today's editions of medieval texts. Where does the medieval "original" end and the modern editing begin? In Clotilde's case, this question was all the more vexing since the editions of her work appeared at the time when the philological sciences were beginning to claim that they could establish texts objectively and definitively. Given the knowledge of medieval languages during the nineteenth century, the claim was audacious. But as research into medieval languages progressed, it gained greater authority, so that by the end of the century it looked irrefutable. By that time, critics could self-righteously scoff at Vanderbourg's Clotilde, for they did indeed know a great deal more about the structure and style of fifteenth-century French. What they would not acknowledge, however, was the degree to which their own critical work still resembled Vanderbourg's. Their belief in a perfectly unmediated rendering of a fifteenth-century text was at the same time a denial of their own editorial practices.[20] If Clotilde's language was exposed as an eighteenth-century fake, could later editions of any medieval text not be called nineteenth-century versions thereof?

Together with the objections concerning language came the related one concerning thematic anachronism. In the same way that philologists picked out linguistic tics, others found elements that did not fit with the prevailing understanding of late-medieval literature. While the overall subject matter looked plausible, the details often did not. There were references to planets unknown in the fifteenth century, to classical authors still untranslated into the vernacular, and to events yet to transpire.[21] Critics were quick to note a network of allusion that linked Clotilde's writing to a literary culture of the Enlightenment. Such allusions betrayed the forger's own affiliations, so the argument went, affiliations so strong that they slid imperceptibly into the texture of the writing. Supporters of Clotilde had no real answer to these charges. The list of thematic discrepancies stood. Yet if there was no way to account for these discrepancies, there was still the problem of the critics' own familiarity with fifteenth-century letters. Did they know the period of Clotilde and Chartier through and through? The inconsistencies they attributed to Clotilde could also, conceivably, reflect gaps in their own erudition.

When we take these issues of thematics together with questions of language, we find that what was most disconcerting about Clotilde's writing was its apparent lack of context. To her critics, it was as if she appeared *ex nihilo*, one of a kind. Given the absence of any verifiable mention of her work during the fifteenth century and thereafter, Clotilde was a freefloating figure, shorn of any historical circumstance. In the evolutionary terms typifying critical parlance of the day, this was patently impossible. According to the often-quoted motto of the lexicographer Littré: "Nothing in history can be born except through filiation, from an ancestor to a succeeding generation."[22] Because there was no evidence of a poetic line for Clotilde, no forerunners, no school following thereafter, her writing could not be historically validated. It was an aberration—a literary parthenogenesis. The Romantic theory of genius notwithstanding, her existence seemed little more than modern conjecture.

This concern over a lack of filiation was, in fact, symptomatic of a far greater fear. As another of Clotilde's critics expressed it, the controversy was ultimately about "the origin and veritable paternity of these poems."[23] In this phrase lies one major preconception about the status of poetry: in the beginning was the Father. Somehow, the notion of a feminine poetic origin is beyond reason, and with it the notion that medieval poetry could be attributed in part to women disputational poets. Insofar as the medieval period was considered a point of origin by many literati, the emergence of Clotilde risked feminizing it—a prospect that seemed untenable to the growing numbers of historical and philological critics. In their view, "The history of women poets was so fantastical that it would be better not to talk about it at all."[24]

Under these circumstances, the case of Clotilde's writing became a catalyst for the argument over women's creative potential per se. It opened up a question of literary talent that extended far beyond Clotilde's own putative medieval situation. "We are of the opinion that this author [Clotilde] was a man, for once it is acknowledged that the work involves a pastiche, it seems to us that a man alone could have given it this perfection."[25] The irony in this critic's assessment is doubly strong. Not only does he consider the possibility of a medieval woman poet a matter of pastiche, but in doing so he commends a man for devising such an ingenious one. In other words, the suppression of female literary talent signifies man's greater one. Discrediting her gifts vindicates his.

That Clotilde's poetry was discredited so vehemently is due in no small part to the acclaim it received as the work of a woman. In the preface of the first two editions, the editor Vanderbourg made much of the fact:

> Que vous importe le siècle où vécut Clotilde, et les corrections que ses ouvrages ont pu subir? Lisez-les, et si vous y trouvez une mère tendre, une épouse embrasée de tous les feux de l'amour, poète par sentiment bien plus que par le désir de la gloire, demandez à votre coeur si un froid imitateur d'une langue surannée a pu écrire ces morceaux pleins de chaleurs et de vérité; si un homme a pu composer ces poésies, où le cachet du sexe le plus tendre et le plus désintéressé dans ses affections est si fortement empreint?

> (1825 edition, x)

> What does it matter to you the century in which Clotilde lived and the corrections her works have undergone? Read them, and if you find in them a tender mother, a wife inflamed with all the fires of love, a poet by virtue of her emotions much more than of any desire for glory, ask your heart whether a cold imitator of an outmoded language could have written these pieces so full of warmth and truth. Ask yourself whether a man could have composed these poems where the mark of her sex, the most tender and the most innocent in her affections, is so strongly imprinted.

Vanderbourg tried to fend off misgivings about Clotilde's work through a Romantic definition of femininity. The cardinal traits are obvious: Clotilde's passion versus a man's coolness, her tenderness versus his rigid, mechanical ways, her disinterested search for truth versus his vainglory. In the face of all opposition, then, the value of the work is predicated on its gender. In fact, the genuineness of the work is wagered upon it. This wager was pushed still further by subsequent editors. Nodier, in his advocate phase, turned it into an imperative. He challenged all women writers who knew of Clotilde to use her example as a witness. Her disputational writing was to represent the determining evidence that women, in his slogan, "created French poetry."[26]

One is prompted to speculate about such an insistent championing of Clotilde's cause. What was the special appeal of a medieval woman poet for early-nineteenth-century Europe? Why were several poets spurred to adopt her as a figurehead of sorts? Put another way, why would anyone want to assume her persona? Readers of Lamartine or Keats, Goethe or Chateaubriand, have long remarked on the common desire to feminize.[27] In the obsessive search for an original purity, there was much to be gained by playing with a feminine persona, since it appeared to offer all that was antirational, unfettered emotionally, and passionately subjective.[28] Paradoxically, then, the feminine could serve as both the means and the end of such a search. Clotilde's writing could represent both a conduit toward and a figure for the origin of what constituted a Romantic poetics.

Once we hit upon this Romantic involvement in Clotilde's writing, we can begin to recognize a spectrum of ideological issues that govern the way it is evaluated, for and against. Her case reveals not only how the existence of a late-medieval woman poet is assessed, but under what conditions that assessment proceeds. Far from existing atemporally and inviolably, these conditions themselves are products of mentalities that vary from generation to generation. In the case of Clotilde, the controversy brings together various conceptions that preoccupied a French public throughout the nineteenth century as much as it does evidence for the reality or fakery of a medieval woman poet. To state it baldly: Clotilde became a battleground between the Romantics and the professional men of criticism, between the poets and the philologists. Along this line of confrontation, we can mark out other related polarities: the royalist Clotilde, steeped in a nostalgic, ancien régime patriotism versus the thoroughly revolutionary Clotilde,[29] the Clotilde belonging to a Middle Ages of Viollet le Duc and Mérimée versus the Clotilde belonging to academicians, a genius of the medieval past versus a specimen of that past, the maternal Clotilde versus the virile fantasm, and of course the "genuine" woman versus the manly fake.

It took nearly a century for these polarities to be exhausted fully. By the 1880s, the debate over Clotilde's writing had more or less run its course. Yet over this same period, the positivist model of historical criticism began to prevail.[30] In fact, it was progressively institutionalized, and given such a model the figure of Clotilde was "an odd man out." So too was the idea of a woman writer who disputed with her literary peers, because it had no place in the picture of medieval vernacular letters as the philologists were composing it. In this respect, it is not surprising that Clotilde was effectively eliminated, expunged from what was becoming the official medieval record. When the doyen of philology, Gaston Paris, handed down his opinion on her, it was absolutely condemning: "The content of Clotilde's poems is just as impossible in the fifteenth-century as its form; the ideas, sentiments, subjects, knowledge, vocabulary, grammar, versification are all inconceivable."[31] There was no space left for even entertaining the disputational figure of a medieval woman writer, for the full force of revolutionary, misogynistic science came down upon her.

A Question of Identification

In teasing out the history of the Clotilde affair, I do not pretend to resolve the issues it poses once and for all. We are faced here, I suspect, with what one curator has called "the intractable conundrum of authenticity."[32] On the one hand, the irregular surviving evidence of Clotilde's work offers an ambiguous picture. The character of some of her verse and the context of its rediscovery do not consistently support the case for a medieval poet. On the other hand, what survives of Clotilde does bear striking resemblances to the woman's response that we have identified in late-medieval France. As Charity Cannon Willard remarked a number of years ago, Clotilde and Christine de Pizan are so similar that they appear cousins— literary replicas, one of the other.[33] It is just this double-edged resemblance that proves the crux. Faced with this picture, we may never be able to answer with certainty the query: was Clotilde a medieval disputational writer or wasn't she?

Yet, in telling her story, my chief interest lies less in closing the puta- tive case of fraud than it does in showing what that case tells us about the category of the woman respondent. This controversy had effects extending far beyond the individual Clotilde. In the formative years of medievalism, it played a part in discounting the figure we have been studying. The philological repudiation of Clotilde that eventually won out over the Ro- mantic campaign for her helped to preclude the idea of the woman respon- dent. In exposing a single counterfeit, the medievalist establishment sought to dispense with the general premise that in the later Middle Ages there were female figures who responded to and engaged with masterful writing. It foreclosed prematurely the question of women's own disputa- tional writing. I put the emphasis on women's engagement because, as ever, I mean to signal the notion of active participation. The figures at stake are not those in *chambres des dames,* the commonly represented cir- cles of laywomen who read to be disciplined. As it turned out, this image was perfectly viable for many philological critics. Refuting Clotilde meant refuting the category of engaged women who wrote in response to what they read. Although the aim of late-nineteenth-century historical criti- cism was to reveal Clotilde's persona as nothing more than a fanciful ci- pher, one of its ramifications was to prevent the hypothesis of medieval women respondents from ever being fully explored. In this, Clotilde's case set the stage for the many subsequent debates over the authenticity of me- dieval women writers that continue into our own day.[34]

With this argument, I do not wish merely to chastise an earlier gener- ation of medievalist in a self-congratulatory manner. Such a gesture would be far too easy. *Mutatis mutandis*: my own critical view is subject to the same perennial process of revision. Instead I wish to push this argument further. Examining nineteenth-century criticism's relation to Clotilde brings us to consider our own rapport with the medieval woman respondent. If we are to take full advantage of her case, we should turn the problem of involvement with a critical object in our own direction. If we take nineteenth-century critics such as Sainte-Beuve and Gaston Paris to task for discounting the category of the respondent that even a "fake" Clotilde might mirror accurately, what can we say of our project to promote it?

One strong impetus behind many feminist inquiries involves a search for positive, validating models for women in the past. In an attempt to reclaim that past as something other than unrelievedly oppressive, there is a tendency to focus upon what look like ideal if not idealized figures. Such an impetus is animated in part by a desire to identify. In investigating figures of the past, feminist critics are as liable as any other critics to visit upon them their revisionist ambitions. They apprehend those figures through the lens of their own critical concerns, with the result that those medieval figures are imported into the present day. Identifying with them means making them an integral part of current feminist debates over social and discursive change.

As this process is played out in medieval studies, Christine de Pizan has come to occupy pride of place. She fast became a heroine, championed as a spokeswoman for feminist thought.[35] The sharpness of her critiques of Jean de Meun and the sheer breadth of her own writing made her a powerful vehicle for critical identification. Both within the field and without, Christine elicited a sense of solidarity and a sense that medieval culture could be recast critically à la femme.

The figure of the woman respondent represents an equally obvious candidate for such identification. She does so on several scores. Visible through several centuries of medieval vernacular culture, this figure traverses a considerable historical span. She creates a semblance of continuity. From the heyday of scholastic intellectual life to the earliest phase of humanism in fifteenth-century France, her disputatiousness seems part of a pattern that invites a predisposed critic to extrapolate into modern times. Secondly, her disputational stance offers an auspicious structure for identification. It corresponds with the agonistic position struck deliberately by numerous feminist critics.[36] In fact, a telling parallel appears between the medieval woman respondent's entry into the fray of masterly disputation and the reflection on the importance of conflict in feminist thought: out of the very clash of rhetorical confrontation could come an insight into gender representation.[37] Yet perhaps the most compelling aspect of the woman respondent is the criterion of verbal injury that she forged, because it fits well into a brand of feminist ethics being formulated today. Raising the issue of defamation and launching the charge of libel are moves that are consonant with contemporary projects of making gender representation and all our discourses socially responsible. As Drucilla Cornell puts it aptly: "Without an ethical affirmation of the feminine which involves a different way of envisioning political struggle itself, we cannot slip beyond the replication of hierarchy inherent in the master/ slave dialectic."[38]

I have thought through a chapter in medieval cultural history by identifying the category of the woman's response. On the face of things, this is an utterly conventional category. The genre of the *responsio* and the posture of the respondent are fixtures in medieval intellectual life as scholasticism defined it, and even as it evolved with the advent of humanism. Yet the simple action of inflecting that genre and posture according to gender yields a very different picture of the standard medieval disputation. It is this feminized picture, I hope to have shown, that contributes a cardinal element to the history of defamation and libel.

Undoubtedly, my thinking has been colored by my affinity with the figure of the woman respondent. It shows none of the studied indifference with which nineteenth-century academic critics claimed to analyze Clotilde and dispense with her kind. Yet neither does my thinking involve the opposite (Romantic) extreme of total investment. And here I am circling back to the question of identification. My project is tempered by the conviction that the category of the woman respondent is not automatically transferable to today's concerns. However tantalizing the analogies between her case and the terms of various feminist debates today, there is good reason to keep their particular differences in mind. We have only to think of the case of censorship and its death sentence to recognize the differences in mentality and practice separating the Middle Ages from most of today's world. Such mindfulness has everything to do with attending to the circumstances particular to each historical moment. In this sense, identifying the category of the medieval woman respondent does not mean identifying with her completely.[39]

This distinction comes into clearer focus if we pay heed to the medieval term *identificare* as it functioned in scholastic Latin and Middle French, indeed, as it came into the vernacular through Nicole Oresme's translation of Aristotle's *Nicomachean Ethics*.[40] "To identify" refers to the process of determining the various integral properties that make up a phenomenon. Such was my inquiry into the who?, how?, and why? of the woman respondent. Yet *identificare* also refers to the act of entertaining those properties, taking them upon the self and experiencing their similarities or sameness (*idem*). Such is the activity of identification, even of identity formation. This medieval usage thus clarifies the fundamental links between these two activities of identifying. Yet it also accommodates the nuances distinguishing them. It maintains them separately.

In identifying the woman respondent as a key disputational figure in French medieval culture, my work has entertained her various properties: her contrariness, her increasingly confrontational rhetoric, her charge of slander, her appeal to the public sphere.[41] But in so doing, it aims for two complementary but different ends: understanding how medieval debates over the injurious power of representation were articulated through gender, and pondering in our own distinct ways how representation continues to be ethically shaped.

Notes

1. Jules Michelet, *Oeuvres complètes*, 21 vols., ed. Paul Viallaneix (Paris: Flammarion, 1971), 3:888. Michelet's interest in the relation between women and clerical learning would be drastically revised later as a result of his anti-clericalism.

2. The classic survey was Charles Jourdain's *L'Education des femmes au moyen âge* (Paris: Firmin-Didot, 1871). Jourdain typified the tendency of treating the case of religious women separately. Because these women inhabited the world of the Church, Jourdain and others saw them as benefitting more easily from its bookish learning.

3. Herbert Grundmann,"Die Frauen und die Literatur im Mittelalter: Ein Beitrag zur Frage nach der Entstehung des Schriftums in der Volksprache," *Archiv für Kulturgeschichte* 26 (1936): 133.

4. Emblematic of this approach is Susan Groag Bell's fastidious accounting of women bibliophiles; see her "Medieval Women Book Owners: Arbiters of Lay Piety and Ambassadors of Culture," *Signs: Journal of Women in Culture and Society* 7, no. 4 (summer 1982): 742–68.

5. Georges Duby, *Que sait-on de l'amour en France au XIIᵉ siècle?* (Oxford: Clarendon Press, 1983), 16.

6. Roberta L. Krueger puts forward this argument powerfully in *Women Readers and The Ideology of Gender in Old French Verse Romance* (Cambridge: Cambridge University Press, 1993), 1–14. For a comparable analysis in relation to English texts, see Susan Schibanoff, "Taking the Gold out of Egypt: The Art of Reading as a Woman," in *Gender and Reading: Essays on Readers, Texts, and Contexts*, ed. Elizabeth A. Flynn and Patrocinio P. Schweickart (Baltimore: Johns Hopkins University Press, 1986), 100.

7. My characterization of the woman reader limited to a literal sense finds a certain parallel with Susan Noakes' discussion of the stereotype of the "bad" woman reader who stays on the surface of a text; see her "On the Superficiality

of Women," in *The Comparative Perspective on Literature: Approaches to Theory and Practice*, ed. Clayton Koelb and Susan Noakes (Ithaca, N.Y.: Cornell University Press, 1988), 340–42.

8. *Andreae Capellani regii Francorum De amore libri tres*, ed. Amadeo Pagès (Madrid: Castellon de la Plana, 1929), 45; *The Art of Courtly Love*, trans. John Jay Parry (New York: Norton, 1969), 73. While Parry's choice to translate the expression *verba reposita* as "too allegorical" may not work completely, it does get at the polarity between literal and symbolic modes that underlies this sentence.

9. Here I am deliberately echoing the choice term *soutilité* (*subtilitas*) linked by Jacqueline Cerquiglini-Toulet with the emergent class of professional clerkly writer in the high Middle Ages. See *"Un Engin si soutil": Guillaume de Machaut et l'écriture au XIVe siècle* (Paris: H. Champion, 1985), 7–9.

10. Eric Auerbach best outlined the prestige of *figura*; see "Figura," *Scenes from the Drama of European Literature*, trans. Ralph Mannheim (New York: Meridien Books, 1959), 11–78.

11. On the master (*magister*) as figurehead, see Émile Durkheim, *L'Évolution pédagogique en France* (1938; Paris: Presses Universitaires de France, 1990), 96–103.

12. Brian Stock, *The Implications of Literacy: Written Language and Models of Interpretation in the Eleventh and Twelfth Centuries* (Princeton: Princeton University Press, 1983), 91.

13. *Li Bestiaires d'amour di Maistre Richart de Fournival e li Response du Bestiaire*, ed. Cesare Segre, Documenti di Filologica 2 (Milan: Riccardo Ricciardi, 1957), 118. All translations from the Old French are mine.

14. Gerda Lerner reminds us that it was "men's hegemony over symbol systems which most decisively disadvantaged women, for it deprived women of the act of making their own definitions." *The Creation of Patriarchy* (Oxford: Oxford University Press, 1986), 219.

15. Pierre Bourdieu, *Ce que parler veut dire: L'Économie des échanges linguistiques* (Paris: Fayard, 1982), 35–36. In making this assertion, I am taking up Bourdieu's question, "Qu'adviendrait-il en effet de la vie littéraire si l'on en venait à disputer non de ce que vaut le style de tel ou tel auteur, mais de ce que valent les disputes sur le style?" (47). But my answer is somewhat different from his, for I shall argue that the woman's disputation is not necessarily absorbed back into the literary system it critiques.

16. Daniel Poirion makes passing reference to "le genre des réponses que les dames envoient à leurs amants et dans toutes les circonstances où un personnage féminin prend la parole." *Le Poète et le prince: L'Évolution du lyrisme courtois de Guillaume de Machaut à Charles d'Orléans* (Paris: Presses Universitaires de France, 1965), 253.

17. On this passage, see Danielle Régnier-Bohler's remarks in "Voix littéraires, voix mystiques," *Histoire des femmes en Occident*, vol. 2, *Le Moyen Age*, ed. Christiane Klapisch-Zuber (Paris: Plon, 1991), 2:443–44.

18. On this point of secondariness, see R. Howard Bloch, *Medieval Misog-*

yny and the Invention of Western Romantic Love (Chicago: University of Chicago Press, 1991), 24–25.

19. This late-thirteenth-century text, of which there are three known copies, remains unedited. For a résumé and lengthy description, see John L. Grigsby, "Miroir des bonnes femmes," *Romania* 82, no. 4 (1961): 458–81; 83, no. 1 (1962): 30–51.

20. "Jeo uodroie que uous seussiez le conte de la sage dame que respondi a fol chiualer et qui parloit de folie quele ne respondroit pas sans son seigneur mes ele en parleroit uolontiers a li. si se tint pour fol et la tint pour sage." Paris, Bibliothèque de l'Arsenal 2156, fol. 4 verso. The rubric cited above is found on fol. 4.

21. On this pivotal structure of debate, see R. Howard Bloch, *French Medieval Literature and Law* (Berkeley; University of California Press, 1977), 167–89, and Laura Kendrick, *The Game of Love: Troubadour Word Play* (Berkeley: University of California Press, 1988), esp. 184.

22. See Matilda Tomaryn Bruckner, "Fictions of the Female Voice: The Women Troubadours," *Speculum* 67, no. 4 (October 1992): 873.

23. Peter Dronke, *Women Writers of the Middle Ages: A Critical Study from Perpetua (203) to Marguerite Porete (1310)* (Cambridge: Cambridge University Press, 1984), 106.

24. *Il Canzoniere di Lanfranco Cigala*, ed. Francesco Branciforti (Florence: Leo S. Olschki, 1954), 175–76.

25. "Le Débat du clerc et de la damoiselle: Poème inédit du XIVᵉ siècle," ed. A. Jeanroy, *Romania* 43 (1914): 1–17.

26. "Ein ungedruckter *Salu d'amors* nebst Antwort," ed. O. Schultz-Gora, *Zeitschrift für romanische philologie* 24 (1900): 358–69.

27. *Robert de Blois: Son oeuvre didactique et narrative*, ed. John Howard Fox, (Paris: Nizet, 1950), 153–54. Roberta L. Krueger argues that "the moralist who so essentializes feminine difference also inscribes the response and resistance of female readers." "Constructing Sexual Identities in the High Middle Ages: the Didactic Poetry of Robert de Blois," *Paragraph* 13, no. 2 (July 1990): 10–11. The woman's response composed by Blois is marked off in manuscript by the rubric "li response contre l'amant." Paris, Bibliothèque de l'Arsenal 5201, fol. 9 verso.

28. R. Howard Bloch demonstrated this contestatory character of medieval literature, which he calls the "verbalization of trial," in *Medieval French Literature and Law*, 139–147. The classic analyses of the medieval disputation are Martin Grabmann, *Die Geschichte der scholastischen Methode: Nach den gedruckten und ungedruckten Quellen dargestellt*, 2 vols. (1909–11; Darmstadt: Wissenschaftliche Buchgesellschaft, 1957), and Palémon Glorieux, *La Littérature quodlibétique de 1260–1320*, 2 vols. (Le Saulchoir: Kain, 1925; Paris: Vrin, 1935).

29. On these questions of women's schooling and literate practices, see Joan Ferrante, "The Education of Women in the Middle Ages in Theory, Fact, and Fantasy," in *Beyond Their Sex: Learned Women of the European Past*, ed. Patricia Labalme (New York: New York University Press, 1980), 9–42, and Alain

Derville, "L'Alphabétisation du peuple à la fin du moyen âge," *Revue du Nord* 66 (April–September 1984): 761–77.

30. Emblematic of the Critical Legal Studies movement's exploration of this concept is Richard Delgado's, "Words That Wound: A Tort Action for Racial Insults, Epithets, and Name-Calling," *Harvard Civil Rights–Civil Liberties Law Review* 17, no. 1 (spring 1982): 133–81. Catharine A. MacKinnon focuses on the specific relation between verbal injury and women in *Only Words* (Cambridge, Mass.: Harvard University Press, 1993). MacKinnon argues for making the law concerned with what speech does, not with what it says (29).

31. Aristotle maintains "In epideictic speeches, the sources of the exordia are praise and blame." *The "Art" of Rhetoric*, ed. and trans. John Henry Freese (London: William Heinemann, 1926), III, xiv, 5–7. On *laus* and *vituperatio*, see also Cicero, *De inventione*, II, in *"De inventione" and "Topica,"* ed. and trans. H. M. Hubbell (Cambridge, Mass.: Harvard University Press, 1949), 173–78, and Quintilian, *Institutio oratoria*, 4 vols., ed. and trans. Harold E. Butler (London: W. Heinemann, 1920–22), III, 4, 2, and III, 7. For an account that typifies the scholastic and humanist understanding of *louenge* and *vitupere* in the French Middle Ages, see Jacques Legrand, *Archiloge Sophie: Livre de bonnes meurs*, ed. Evencio Beltran (Geneva: Slatkine, 1986), 88–95.

32. Albertano's text is translated in *Dei Trattati Morali di Albertano da Brescia*, ed. Andrea Da Grosseto (Bologne: Gaetano Romagnoli, 1873), 1–174, esp. 141–143 on *iniuria*. Hugh's text is edited by G. Hendrix in *Recherches de théologie ancienne et médiévale* 48 (1981): 172–97.

33. This text exists only in a seventeenth-century edition; see Carla Casagrande and Silvana Vecchio, *Les Péchés de la langue: Discipline et éthique de la parole médiévale*, trans. Philippe Baillet (Paris: Cerf, 1991), 240. The original Italian edition is *I Peccati Della Lingua: Disciplina ed Ethica della Parola nella Cultura Medievale* (Rome: Istituto della Enciclopedia Italiana, 1987).

34. Casagrande and Vecchio review all of these categories meticulously, and many more; see ibid., 187–212, 223–29, 239–52, 275–89, 303–12.

35. For ample evidence of this mentality, one has only to consult the *Bullaire de l'Inquisition française au XIVe siècle et jusqu'à la fin du grand schisme*, ed. J.-M. Vidal (Paris: Letouzey et Ané, 1913), 475–76, 492–94.

36. See R. I. Moore, *The Formation of a Persecuting Society: Power and Deviance in Western Europe, 950–1250* (Oxford: Basil Blackwell, 1987), 132–33, and Edward Peters, *Inquisition* (New York: Free Press, 1988), 48–52. Both Moore and Peters underscore the point that heretics were commonly accused of slandering the ecclesiastical authority, for which they were often subject to torture.

37. The influence of the law, P. S. Lewis reminds us, "haunts any investigation of later medieval society," *Later Medieval France: The Polity* (London: Macmillan, 1968), 10.

38. *Corpus iuris civilis: Codex Iustinianis*, 2 vols., ed. Paul Krueger (Berlin: Weidmann, 1928), book 9, xxxvi; 2:387. On the Roman and medieval canonical study of *iniuria*, see the entry in the *Enciclopedia del Diritto* (Rome: Giuffre, 1964), s.v. *iniuria*.

39. *The Civil Law, Including the 12 Tables, the Institutes of Gaius, the Rules of Ulpian, the Opinions of Paulus, the Enactments of Justinian, and the Constitutions of Leo*, 17 vols., trans. Samuel P. Scott (Cincinnati: The Central Trust Co., 1932), 15:60. For the Latin text, see *Corpus iuris civilis: Codex Iustinianus*, book 9, xxxv, 2:386–87. It is interesting to note that this earliest legal formulation of *iniuria* is accompanied by another statute involving the specific cases of women's names: "The action of injury will lie in your favor for two reasons: first, because a husband is understood to have some regard for his wife's reputation for chastity; and second, because a father is considered to sustain damage when the character of his daughter is assailed." *The Civil Law* 15:59. (Iniuriarum actio tibi duplici ex causa competit, cum et maritus in uxoris pudore et pater in existimatione filiorum propriam iniuriam pati intelleguntur. *Corpus iuris civilis: Codex Iustinianus* book 9, xxxv, 2:386.) Consider, however, that women's names are linked here to injury not on their own individual terms, but as a function of their family's reputations.

40. The thirteenth-century canonist Hostiensis (Henry de Segusio) provides a characteristic commentary on Justinian's statute. See his *Summa aurea*, ed. Oreste Vighetti (Turin: Bottega d'Erasmo, 1963), book 5, 1720–24.

41. See Claude Gauvard, *"De Grace especial": Crime, état, et société en France à la fin du moyen âge*, 2 vols., Publications de la Sorbonne Histoire ancienne et médiévale, no. 24 (Paris: Éditions du C.N.R.S., 1991) 1:111–43, 2:719–52. Gauvard pays particular attention to the ways in which the principle of verbal injury is explored in terms of honor.

42. See Gauvard's extensive discussion of verbal injury and questions of political crime, notably treason, 2:832–49.

43. On the notion of blasphemy, see David Lawton, *Blasphemy* (Philadelphia: University of Pennsylvania Press, 1993), 85–96; *Injures et blasphèmes*, ed. Jean Delumeau (Paris: Imago, 1989); and *Paroles d'outrage, Ethnologie française* 22, no. 3 (July–September 1992), especially the commentary of Gérard Lenclud and Jacques Cheyronnaud, 262–64.

44. There is, of course, room for great experimentation in any poetic tradition. In this sense, the tradition appears to be continually disputed. Yet once the dispute involves the damaging power of its language, it surpasses any notion of poetic play.

45. Alan M. F. Gunn puts it well when he argues: "The pilgrim-student becomes the audience and the target of an archetypal symposium—one having the particular form of a university *disputatio* as conducted by the masters of rival lecture halls. "Teacher and Student in the *Roman de la Rose*: A Study in Archetypal Figures and Patterns," *Esprit Créateur* 2, no. 3 (fall 1962): 133.

46. Guillaume de Lorris and Jean de Meun, *Le Roman de la rose*, 3 vols., ed. Félix Lecoy (Paris: H. Champion, 1973).

47. *Oeuvres de Guillaume de Machaut*, 3 vols., ed. Ernest Hoepffner (Paris: Firmin-Didot, 1908), vol. 1.

48. Alice Jardine rightly identifies this *Querelle* as a pivotal moment in the history of the relation women/representation: *Gynesis: Configurations of*

Women and Modernity (Ithaca, N.Y.: Cornell University Press, 1985), 96. However, as I hope to show, the various debates that make up the *Querelle* do not appear out of the blue.

49. Thomas Aquinas's assessment is representative of the definition of defamation prevailing in the high and late Middle Ages: "Insofar as words are signs representing something to the attention of others, they are able to inflict much damage; one way a man can be damaged in this manner is the detriment of either his honor or respect that is shown to him by others. If anyone will say anything disparaging about him in front of many others; this therefore is a major form of defamation (*contumelia*)" (Inquantum vero [verba] sunt signa repraesentia aliquid in notitiam aliorum, sic possunt damna multa inferre; inter quae unum est quod homo damnificatur quantum ad detrimentum honoris sui vel reverentiae sibi ab aliis exhibendae. Et ideo major est contumelia, si aliquis alicui defectum suum dicat coram multis). *Summa Theologica*, ed. Fathers of the English Dominican Province (London: Burns, Oates and Washbourne, 1914), 2a2ae, q. 72. We should note the frequent variation in translating the Latin terms *contumelia* and *detractio*. I am translating *contumelia* as defamation and *detractio* as detraction or slander. For an overview of the classical and medieval understanding of defamation, see T. Ortolan, s.v. *diffamation*, in *Dictionnaire de théologie catholique, contenant l'exposé des doctrines de la théologie catholique, leurs preuves, et leur histoire*, 15 vols., ed. Alfred Vacant and Eugène Mangenot (Paris: Letouzey et Ané, 1930–1950). For a review of the Roman conception on which the medieval understanding was based, see Arrigo Diego Manfredini, *La Diffamazione verbale nel diritto romano* (Milan: A. Giuffre, 1979).

50. *Le Débat sur le roman de la rose*, ed. Eric Hicks (Paris: H. Champion, 1977), p. 16.

51. "Slander is the belittling of the glory and fame of another person through biting and envious words" (Detractio est alienae gloriae et famae mordax et invida per verba, aut diminutio). Vincent de Beauvais's definition exemplifies this classical notion as it was received by medieval thinkers. *Speculum doctrinale* (Venice: Hermannus Liechtenstein, 1494), IV, c. 169.

52. In *"La Belle Dame sans mercy* et ses imitations," ed. Arthur Piaget, *Romania* 30 (1901): 28–35.

53. "N'y a-t-il pas en effet dans la recherche d'une injure l'idée d'empêcher l'autre de répliquer, de lui 'clouer le bec'? N'y a-t-il pas aussi cette idée de combat oratoire—de joûte, dit-on parfois—ou perd celui qui se tait et dans lequel l'art de répliquer est considéré comme une maîtrise de soi?" Evelyne Larguèche, *L'Effet injure: De la pragmatique à la psychanalyse* (Paris: Presses Universitaires de France, 1983), 7.

ONE: OVIDIAN AND ARISTOTELIAN FIGURES

1. *Li Lai d'Aristote d'Henri d'Andeli*, ed. Maurice Delbouille (Paris: Belles Lettres, 1951).

2. At a key moment in Aristotle's seduction, this proverb is introduced by way of the story of the cat and the candle. One popular version goes as follows:

L'en puet bien par usage
Faire le chat si sage
Qu'il tient chandoile ardant
Ja n'iert si bien apris
Se il voit la souris
Qu'il n'i aut maintenant.
Mieux vaut nature que nourreture.

                    (no. 262, 107)

Through training one can make the cat so smart that he holds a burning candle. But he will never be so well trained that when he sees a mouse he won't have it right away: nature is worth more than nurture.

Li Proverbe au vilain, die Sprichwörter des gemeinen Mannes, Altfranzö-sische Dichtung nach den bisher bekannten Handschriften, ed. Adolf Tobler (Leipzig: S. Hirzel, 1895).

3. "Mulierum astutia decepit sapientissimos." "Ne de mulieri potestatem animae tua, ne ingreditur in virtute tu et confundaris." (These are written in the characteristic cribbed Latin of the schools.) See Joachim Storost's discussion of the various thirteenth-century and fourteenth-century maxims, "Femme chevalchat Aristotte," *Zeitschrift für französische Sprache und Lite-ratur* 66 (1956): 189–90.

4. The *Lai* figured in several influential clerical manuals, including the *Disciplina clericalis* of Jacques de Vitry; see Delbouille in *Li Lai d'Aristote*, 39–40. It is interesting to contrast this with a woman's reading. The late-thirteenth-century mystic Marguerite Porete turned the *Lai* into a theological exemplum on the limits of human love. "But the young girl was at such a distance from the great lord in whom she had placed her love that she could neither see nor have him. For this reason she was often troubled, because no love other than this was satisfying to her. And when she saw that this faraway love that seemed so close and so much a part of her was so removed from her, she thought that she could assuage her malaise through imagining some figure of the lover who had pierced her heart (Mais si loing estoit ceste damoiselle de ce grant seigneur, ou quel elle avoit mis son amour d'elle mesmes, car veoir ne avoir ne le povoit; par quoy en elle mesmes souvent estoit desconforter, car nulle amour fors que ceste cy ne luy souffisoit. Et quant elle vit que ceste amour loingtaigne, qui luy estoit si prouchaine ou dedans d'ele, estoit si loing dehors, elle se pens que elle conforteroit sa malaise par imaginacion d'aucune figure de son amy, dont elle estoit au cueur navree). "Il 'Miroir des simples âmes' di Margherita Porete," ed. Romana Guarnieri, *Archivio italiano per la storia della pietà* 4 (1965): 521.

5. For a survey of *Lai d'Aristote* iconography, see Pietro Marsilli, "Réception et diffusion iconographique du conte 'de Aristote et Phillis' en Europe depuis le moyen âge," in *Amour, mariage, et transgressions au moyen âge,* ed. Danielle Buschinger and André Crépin (Göppingen: Kümmerle, 1984), 239–70, and Susan L. Smith, "The Power of Women Topos on a Fourteenth-Century Embroidery," *Viator* 21 (1990): 228. Natalie Zemon Davis comments on the sixteenth-century legacy of the narrative in "Women on Top," in *Society and*

Culture in Early Modern France (Stanford, Calif.: Stanford University Press, 1975), 135–36.

6. "Power is strong because, as we are beginning to realize, it produces effects at the level of desire—and also at the level of knowledge. Far from preventing knowledge, power produces it." Michel Foucault, *Power/Knowledge: Selected Interviews and Other Writings, 1972–77,* ed. and trans. Colin Gordon (New York: Pantheon, 1980), 59.

7. Aristotle, *Nicomachean Ethics,* book 7, chap. 2, in *The Complete Works of Aristotle: The Revised Oxford Translation,* 2 vols., ed. Jonathan Barnes (Princeton: Princeton University Press, 1984).

8. Augustine, *De civitate Dei,* 2 vols., ed. Bernhard Dombart (Leipzig: Teubner, 1909), book 5, chap. 19.

9. It is hardly anachronistic to evoke Hegel's model of the master/slave dialectic here. While most readers tend to understand this model in the subjective terms of desire as Hegel outlined it in the *Phenomenology of the Spirit,* chapter 4, it is crucial to recall that he also analyzed it in objective, historical terms. In the *Philosophy of History,* Hegel studied the dynamic between mastery (*Herrschaft*) and slavery or servitude (*Knechtschaft*) as it appeared during the European Middle Ages. His study focused on two phenomena: feudal rule and intellectual life in the universities. Both the relation between the feudal lord and vassal and the university master and student offered him important examples of the historical manifestation of the master/slave dialectic. He dwelled particularly on the case of intellectual life: "Just as all Europe performed the spectacle of knightly warfare, feuding, and tournaments, so also was speculation a tournament scene" (Wie Europa allgemein das Schauspiel von Ritterkämpfen, Fehden und Turnieren darbiet, so war es jetzt auch der Schauplatz des Turnierens der Gedanken). Georg Wilhelm Friedrich Hegel, *Philosophie der Geschichte,* in *Sämtliche Werke,* 22 vols., ed. Hermann Glockner (Stuttgart: Frommanns, 1949), 11:503.

10. I mention here two exemplary studies. Sandra Lee Bartky pursues the philosophical investigation of oppression and women in *Femininity and Domination: Studies in the Phenomenology of Oppression* (New York: Routledge, 1990), 22–33. In a psychosocial context, Jessica Benjamin considers the problem of sexual domination by concentrating on "the desires of the dominated": *The Bonds of Love: Psychoanalysis, Feminism, and the Problem of Domination* (New York: Pantheon, 1988), 52–68.

11. In the Hegelian master/slave model, the dialectic suggested male/female terms too. As Genevieve Lloyd has argued, this dialectic posited implicitly the role of dominant men in opposition to subservient women; see *The Man of Reason: "Male" and "Female" in Western Philosophy* (Minneapolis: University of Minnesota Press, 1984), 91–92.

12. Hélène Cixous put forward this premise clearly in "A Woman Mistress": "It is a discourse agreeing more with masculinity than with femininity . . . woman doesn't enjoy herself in it, I never said she was incapable of it." See Hélène Cixous and Catherine Clément, *The Newly Born Woman,* trans. Betsy Wing (Minneapolis: University of Minnesota Press, 1986), 146.

13. Toril Moi, "Patriarchal Thought and the Drive for Knowledge," in *Between Feminism and Psychoanalysis*, ed. Teresa Brennan (London: Routledge, 1989), 192.

14. Consider in this light Joan Cocks's observation: "The self-identity and self-understanding of the population assigned the position of the masculine Master are generated out of the regime rather than the other way around, so that men can think, speak, and write the terms of masculine/feminine, and decorate, refine, and extend them, without being their true author or first heretic at all." *The Oppositional Imagination: Feminism, Critique, and Political Theory* (New York: Routledge, 1989), 186–87.

15. "Si feray fin mon dittié du debat non hayneux commencié, continué et finé par maniere de soulas sans indignacion a personne." *Le Débat sur le roman de la rose*, 150.

16. Joan Kelly, "Early Feminist Theory and the *Querelle des femmes*, 1400–1789," *Signs* 8, no. 1 (autumn 1982): 19.

17. Foucault speaks of "the insubstantiability of the notion of the master, an empty form haunted only by the various phantoms of the master and his slave, the master and his disciple, the master and his workman, the master who pronounces law and speaks the truth, the master who censors and forbids." *Power/Knowledge*, 139.

18. In his now standard survey of the teaching methods of the master in the twelfth and thirteenth centuries, Martin Grabmann identifies the disputation (*disputatio*) as a form of combat. Grabmann, *Geschichte der scholastichen Methode*, 2:16–21.

19. The description is Durkheim's, *L'Évolution pédagogique en France*, 166. See his discussion of the pedagogical process as a whole (164–87).

20. Hans Walther, *Das Streitgedicht in der lateinischen Literatur des Mittelalters* (Munich: Beck, 1920), 3.

21. Walter J. Ong, *Rhetoric, Romance, and Technology: Studies in the Interaction of Expression and Culture* (Ithaca, N.Y.: Cornell University Press, 1971), 113–41, examines this medieval pattern. Ong goes on to make the case that this drift toward domination is still apparent in today's pedagogy: see *Fighting for Life: Contest, Sexuality, and Consciousness* (Ithaca, N.Y.: Cornell University Press, 1981), 20–25. Janice Moulton traces the full legacy of this pattern in "A Paradigm of Philosophy: The Adversary Method," in *Discovering Reality: Feminist Perspectives on Epistemology, Metaphysics, Methodology, and Philosophy of Science*, ed. Sandra Harding and Merrill B. Hintikka (Dordrecht: D. Reidel, 1983), 149–64.

22. See the following portraits of the master: Jacques LeGoff, *Les Intellectuels au moyen âge* (Paris: Seuil, 1957), 80–89, and John W. Baldwin, "Masters at Paris from 1179 to 1215: A Social Perspective," in *Renaissance and Renewal in the Twelfth Century*, ed. Robert L. Benson and Giles Constable (Cambridge, Mass.: Harvard University Press, 1986), 143–53.

23. See Hastings Rashdall, *The Universities of Europe in the Middle Ages*, 2 vols. (Oxford: Clarendon Press, 1895), 1:21–22, and Gordon Leff, *Paris and*

Oxford Universities in the Thirteenth and Fourteenth Centuries (New York: John Wiley and Sons, 1968), 167–73.

24. *De disciplina scholarium* (Pseudo-Boethius), ed. Olga Weijers (Leiden: E. J. Brill, 1976), 99. The potential explosiveness of this pattern of subjection and mastery is brought out in the following warning: "Let the disciple never be violent toward his master" (ne sit autem discipulus violentus erga magistrum; 99).

25. *Das "Livre d'Enanchet" nach der einzigen Handschrift 2585 der Wiener Nationalbibliothek*, ed. Werner Fiebig (Jena : Wilhelm Gronau, 1938), 5–6.

26. *Le Chastoiement d'un père à son fils*, ed. Edward D. Montgomery, Jr. (Chapel Hill: University of North Carolina Press, 1971), *Robert de Blois*, 133–55.

27. For many such accounts, see the *Chartularium Universitatis Parisiensis*, ed. Henricus Denifle and Aemilio Chatelain (Paris: Delalain, 1891). As Jody Enders has suggested recently, the controversies and brawls recorded there create the picture of "an intellectual battlefield." *Rhetoric and the Origins of Medieval Drama* (Ithaca, N.Y.: Cornell University Press, 1992), 93–94. On this picture, see Enders's full discussion (92–98), and John W. Baldwin, *The Scholastic Culture of the Middle Ages, 1000–1300* (Lexington, Mass.: Heath, 1971), 60–65.

28. Juan Luis Vivès, *In Pseudodialecticos: A Critical Edition*, ed. Charles Fantazzi (Leiden: E. J. Brill, 1979), 82–83.

29. Palémon Glorieux calls the quodlibet "the magisterial act par excellence," stressing the "hostility" that frequently enlivened the form. *La littérature quodlibétique* 1:14, 28. Glorieux outlines the medieval master's pedagogy as a whole in "L'Enseignement au moyen âge: Techniques et méthodes en usage à la faculté de théologie de Paris au XIIIᵉ siècle," *Archives d'histoire doctrinale et littéraire au moyen âge* 35 (1968): 65–186, esp. 106–11, 123–24. See also Leonard E. Boyle's commentary on the quodlibet as a "free-for-all": *Pastoral Care, Clerical Education, and Canon Law, 1200–1400* (London: Variorum Reprints, 1981), 52–56, Bernardo C. Bazan, John W. Wippel, Gerard Frauden, and Danielle Jacquart, *Les Questions disputées et les questions quodlibétiques dans les facultés de théologie, de droit, et de medicine*. Typologie des sources du moyen âge occidental, 44–45. (Turnhout: Brepols, 1985), 35–48, and Jody Enders, "The Theater of Scholastic Erudition," *Comparative Drama* 27, no. 3 (fall 1993): 341–63.

30. *The Metalogicon of John of Salisbury*, trans. Daniel McGarry (Berkeley: University of California Press, 1955), 190.

31. Alexander Murray's discussion of the "latent or open combativeness" of intellectuals makes this process clear: *Reason and Society in the Middle Ages* (Oxford: Oxford University Press, 1978), chap. 10, esp. 234–35.

32. On this parallelism, see my discussion in "Figures of Female Militancy in Medieval France," *Signs* 16, no. 3 (spring 1991): 526–29.

33. For all of Abelard's bad press, as David E. Luscombe reminds us he was also admired throughout the Middle Ages and named a doctor in the same league as Thomas Aquinas. See *The School of Peter Abelard: The Influence of*

Abelard's Thought in the Early Scholastic Period (Cambridge: Cambridge University Press, 1969), 12–13. As far as his letter writing goes, Abelard gained a new following among early-fifteenth-century Parisian humanists such as Jean de Montreuil and Gontier Col; see Carla Bozzolo, "L'Humaniste Gontier Col et la traduction française des *Lettres* d'Abélard et Héloïse," *Romania* 95, no. 2–3 (1974): 212.

34. "Martis curie penitus abdicarem ut Minerve gremio educarer; et quoniam dialecticarum rationum armaturam omnibus philosophie documentis pretuli, his armis alia commutavi et tropheis bellorum conflictus pretuli disputationum." Peter Abelard, *Historia calamitatum*, ed. J. Monfrin (Paris: J. Vrin, 1967), lines 24–28, 63–64. It is worthwhile comparing Abelard's twelfth-century portrait of the relation between the master and Minerva with a fifteenth-century one; see Jacques Legrand's commentary on "the fiction of Minerva as the mother of wisdom" [la ficcion Minerva est appellee mere de Sophie], *Archiloge Sophie*, 27.

35. This expression, *famme laengueice*, is intriguing. If we accept the rendering in Godefroy as one who chatters and gossips, then we can recognize it as the topos of the garrulous witless woman. Frédéric Godefroy, *Dictionnaire de l'ancienne langue française et de tous ses dialectes du IXe au XVe siècle*, 10 vols. (Paris: F. Vieweg, 1885), s.v. *langoieur*.

36. The identification of these figures with the duke and duchess of Brabant is made in the prologue on the same folio as the illumination.

37. Michèle Gally investigates the structure of the disputation as it occurs in many of the same texts, but without attending to the figuration of women: "Le Huitième Art: Les clercs du XIIIe siècle, nouveaux maîtres du discours amoureux," *Poétique* 75 (September 1988): 279–95.

38. For the *Concilium*, see *Les Débats du clerc et du chevalier dans la littérature poétique du moyen âge*, ed. Charles Oulmont (1911; Geneva: Slatkine Reprints, 1974), 93–110; for the *Jugement*, also known as *Florence et Blancheflor*, see Edmond Faral, *Recherches sur les sources latines des contes et romans courtois du moyen âge* (Paris: E. Champion, 1913), 251–69.

39. See Sylvia Huot's remarks on the representations of the clerk-poet in contemporaneous manuscripts: *From Song to Book: The Poetics of Writing in Old French Lyric and Lyrical Narrative Poetry* (Ithaca, N.Y.: Cornell University Press, 1987), 59–64.

40. Evelyn Fox Keller has traced the metaphorical language of secrets prevailing in science and the predominant trope of wresting the secrets away from a feminized nature: "Making Gender Visible in the Pursuit of Nature's Secrets," in *Feminist Studies/Critical Studies*, ed. Teresa de Lauretis (Bloomington: Indiana University Press, 1986), 69. See also her most recent remarks in *Secrets of Life, Secrets of Death: Essays on Language, Gender, and Science* (New York: Routledge, 1992), 40.

41. See Jacques Monfrin, "La Place du *Secret des Secrets* dans la littérature française médiévale," in *Pseudo-Aristotle, "The Secret of Secrets": Sources and Influences*, Warburg Institute Surveys, no. 9 (London: Warburg Institute,

1982), 73–113; *Placides et Timéo ou Li secrés as philosophes*, ed. Claude Alexandre Thomasset (Geneva: Droz, 1980), and Claude Alexandre Thomasset, *Commentaire du dialogue de Placides et Timéo: Une Vision à la fin du XIIIᵉ siècle* (Geneva: Droz, 1982), and Steven J. Williams, "The Scholarly Career of the Pseudo-Aristotelian 'Secretum Secretorum' in the Thirteenth and Early Fourteenth Century" (Ph.D. diss., Northwestern University, 1991).

42. See Martin Levey and Safwat S. Souryal, "Galen's *On the Secrets of Women and on the Secrets of Men*: A Contribution to the History of Arabic Pharmacology," *Janus* 55, no. 2–3 (1968): 208–19, "Pseudo–Albertus Magnus: *Secreta mulierum cum commento*, Deutsch. Critical Text and Commentary," ed. Margaret Schleissner (Ph.D. diss., Princeton, 1987), and *Women's Secrets: A Translation of Pseudo–Albertus Magnus' "De secreta mulierum" with Commentaries*, trans. Helen Rodnite Lemay (Albany: State University of New York Press, 1992). My colleague Monica Green's ongoing research on vernacular translations of the *Secreta mulierum* and the other important gynecological text, the *Trotula*, leads her to argue that the term "secrets" gained a new significance scientifically throughout the thirteenth century. I am grateful to her for sharing with me "Slander and the Secrets of Women," a chapter from a current book manuscript tentatively entitled *Women and Literate Medicine in Medieval Europe: Trota and the "Trotula."*

43. Bourdieu, *Ce que parler veut dire*, 103–5.

44. For a general review of the so-called *aetas Ovidiana*, see Birgen Munk Olsen, "Ovide au moyen âge (du XIᵉ au XIIᵉ siècle)," in *Le Strade del testo: Studi di tradizione manoscritta*, ed. Guglielmo Cavello (Bari: Adriatica Editrice, 1987), 67–96. Peter L. Allen examines the Ovidian legacy in French medieval literature: *The Art of Love: Amatory Fiction from Ovid to the Romance of the Rose* (Philadelphia: University of Pennsylvania Press, 1992), 38–58.

45. On this point, see Ralph J. Hexter, *Ovid and Medieval Schooling: Studies in Medieval School Commentaries on Ovid's "Ars amatoria," "Epistulae ex Ponto," and "Epistulae Heroidum"* (Munich: Arbeo Gesellschaft, 1986).

46. *The Cambridge History of Later Medieval Philosophy: From the Rediscovery of Aristotle to the Disintegration of Scholasticism*, ed. Norman Kretzmann, Anthony Kenny, and Jan Pinborg (Cambridge: Cambridge University Press, 1982) lays out the various waves of translation and commentary on Aristotle. The *Metaphysics* was translated in stages, and was not completely known and commented on before 1220. So too with the *Ethics*. The *Politics* was recovered ca. 1260. Since the biological works were censored from the Parisian faculties, they were also not fully available until that time (74–79). Fernand van Steenberghen proposes much the same scenario in *Aristote en occident: Les origines de l'aristotélisme parisien* (Louvain: Éditions de l'Institut supérieur de philosophie, 1946), 60–61, 91, 96–97.

47. In this chapter, my Aristotelian rubric reflects this medieval tendency to associate any number of learned classical texts with the name of Aristotle. As the editors of the *Cambridge History of Later Medieval Philosophy* remind us: "An examination of the medieval Latin Aristotle cannot consider only the

genuine works of Aristotle, but must also deal with works credited to Aristotle in the Middle Ages although now believed to be spurious" (45). The same holds true for Aristotelianism in vernacular works. My rubric is a citational marker signifying great authority, and may not always refer to the works of the Greek thinker.

48. Ovid, *Ars amatoria P. Ovidi Nasonis*, ed. E. J. Kenney (Oxford: Oxford University Press, 1961); *The Art of Love*, trans. Rolfe Humphries (Bloomington: Indiana University Press, 1957), 113.

49. We find this same expression describing women's behavior in that paradigmatic text of misogyny, the *Lamentations of Matheolus*, here cited in Jean LeFèvre's translation: "Woman leads man to his limit. It is fitting that I give you an example of their prevarication" (La femme maine l'omme a methe. Droit est qu'exemple vous en mette De leur prevarication; I, lines 845–47).

50. Judging from those *florilegia* that included material from the *De amore*, this sentence was particularly important; see Alfred Karnein, *"De amore" in volkssprachlicher literatur: Untersuchungen zur Andreas-Capellanus-Rezeption in Mittelalter und Renaissance* (Heidelberg: Carl Winter Universitätsverlag, 1985), 297.

51. Toril Moi reads the lover's claim on the subordinate role as a sign of "a certain sadistic dominance": "Desire in Language: Andreas Capellanus and the Controversy of Courtly Love," in *Medieval Literature: Criticism, Ideology, and History*, ed. David Aers (New York: St. Martin's, 1986), 24. Compare this with Joan Ferrante's reading: "Male Fantasy and Female Reality in Courtly Literature," *Women's Studies* 11 (1984): 78–84.

52. See Barbara Johnson, *A World of Difference* (Baltimore: Johns Hopkins University Press, 1987), 45.

53. Betsy Bowden, "The Art of Courtly Copulation," *Medievalia et Humanistica* 9 (1979): 81–82.

54. The key phrase in the condemnation was: "In the schools they presume to treat and to dispute these ludicrous falsehoods" (insanias falsas in scolis tractare et disputare presument); quoted by Alex J. Denomy in "The *De amore* of Andreas Capellanus and the Condemnation of 1277," *Mediaeval Studies* 8 (1946): 107.

55. *L'Art d'amors und Li Remedes d'amors: Zwei altfranzösische Lehrgedichte von Jacques d'Amiens*, ed. Gustav Korting (Geneva: Slatkine Reprints, 1976).

56. On this issue of force, see Kathryn Gravdal's discussion of *esforcier*, the term used to designate sexual violence: *Ravishing Maidens: Writing Rape in Old French Literature and Law* (Philadelphia: University of Pennsylvania Press, 1991), 4–6.

57. Consider the cynical step-by-step account laid out by the contemporaneous *Art d'amour* of Guiart: "And so she'll cry out when she feels your hand, 'Get away from me, I certainly don't love you!' The more she will say that to you, the more you should tighten your grip. Press yourself upon her body-to-body and you will have your fill, since you will have had her virginity" (Et se ele s'escrie, quant sentira ta main: "Fuyez vos deseur moi certes pas ne vous

aim!" Com plus le te dira, et tu plus la destrain Join toi pres nu a nu, si en feras ton plain Puis qu'auras eu part dedanz son pucelage). See *Artes amandi: Da Maître Elie ad Andrea Cappellano,* ed. A. M. Finoli (Milan: Istituto Editoriale Cisalpino, 1969), lines 93–102, 233. Compare this with the *Clef d'amours:* "And as much as you resort to force, such force is very pleasing to young girls. Don't let them do what can best be done to them. A woman would never dare to say out loud what she desires greatly" (Et combien que forche l'appeles, tel forche plest mout as puceles: ne lesse mie por lor fet a fere cen qui bien lor fet. James feme n'oseroit dire de bouche cen que tant desire"). *La Clef d'amours,* ed. Auguste Doutrepont (Geneva: Slatkine Reprints, 1975), lines 1137–42).

58. Pierre Bourdieu identifies such symbolic violence as not only a dimension of all domination but as essential to the phenomenon of masculine domination: "La domination masculine," *Actes de la Recherche en sciences sociales* 84 (September 1990): 11.

59. One of the few critics to study this influx as far as French literature is concerned is Tony Hunt. But he concentrates on Chrétien de Troyes. See "Aristotle, Dialectic, and Courtly Literature," *Viator* 10 (1979): 95–129.

60. See *La Poissance damours dello Pseudo–Richard de Fournival,* ed. Gian Battista Speroni, Pubblicazioni dell Facoltà di Lettere e Filosophia dell'Università di Pavia 21 (Florence: La Nuova Italia, 1975), and "Li Houneurs et li vertus des dames par Jehan Petit d'Arras," ed. Rudolf Zimmermann, *Archiv für das Studium der neueren Sprachen und Literaturen* 108 (1902): 380–88. The version of *Li Consaus d'amours* that I am working with here is as yet unedited. My study is based on the manuscript text found in Vienna, Österreichische Nationalbibliothek 2621, fols. 1–17 verso. This text is not to be confused with another related didactic text called *Li Consaus* attributed to Richard de Fournival: "Li Consaus d'amors," ed. Gian Battista Speroni, *Medioevo Romanzo* 1 (1974): 217–278. Similarly, it should be noted that in the description of the manuscript, Hermann Julius Hermann misnames it *La puissance d'amour,* after a rubric, thereby overriding the name as it is also found on fol. 1. *Die westeuropäischen Handschriften und Inkunabeln der Gothik und der Renaissance mit Ausnahme der niederländerischen Handschriften,* 2 vols. (Leipzig: Karl W. Hiersemann, 1935–36), 2:62.

61. I cite passages from the beginning of these works that indicate their Aristotelian allegiance: "So that we might come to this [understanding], our master Aristotle instructs us for our advantage and profit, and he says in this way that . . ." (Arristotes nostre maistres pour a cou venir nous enseigne pour no proufitable avantage et dist en tel maniere . . .); *Li Consaus,* Österreichische Nationalbibliothek 2621, fol. 1. "Dear son, our master Aristotle demonstrates to us by reason that man's heart which would desire woman cannot speak badly or dishonestly of it; I will show you how" (Biaus fieus, aristotes nos maistres nous moustre par raison que cuers d'oume qui femme conuisteroit, n'en puet dire mal ne deshouneste; si vous mousterrai coument); "Li Houneurs,", ed. Zimmermann, lines 8–10, 382. "Thus all should know that whatever will be said hereafter will be confirmed by the fitting evidence of na-

ture, firm and true, and spoken from the mouth of the Philosopher, established truthfully" (si sacent tout que cankes ci aprés sera dit sera fermé par droite proeve de nature, ferme et veritaule, dite de bouce de philosophe esprouvé de verité); *La Poissance*, ed. Speroni, 30.

62. This question exists separately in numerous *florilegia* of the late Middle Ages: *quid mulier sit*. See Bruno Roy, "A la recherche des lecteurs médiévaux du *De amore* d'André le Chapelain," *Revue de l'Université d'Ottawa / University of Ottawa Quarterly* 55, no. 1 (January–March 1985), 56.

63. *Li Consaus d'amours*, Vienna 2621, fol. 1 verso: "iou ai dit et pour moustrer comment il puist avenir que uns hom puist damours dou tout savoir."

64. These three Aristotelian narratives are also found with several other key narratives; *Le Jugement d'amour, Art d'amours*, as well as *Le Bestiaire d'amour* and *La Response au Bestiaire* that I shall consider later. Because they are grouped together, these works beg to be read in relation to each other. For details on their manuscript settings, see Sylvia Huot, *From Song to Book*, 66–74 (for *Li Houneurs*, Paris, Bibliothèque Nationale 25566), and 152–6 (for *La Poissance*, Dijon, Bibliothèque Municipale 526), and Ferdinand Wolf, "Über einige altfranzösische Doctrinen und Allegorien von der Minne," *Denkschriften der Kaiserlichen Akademie der Wissenschaften in Wien* (Philosophische-Historische Klasse) 13 (1864): 135–92, (for *Li Consaus*, Vienna, Österreichische Nationalbibliothek 2609, 2621).

65. This theory posits the cooler cells on the left side of the uterus as the matrix for females and those on the warmer right as the matrix for males. Any fetus developing in the middle cells would, of course, be hermaphroditic. On this theory, see Robert Reisert, *Der siebenkammerige Uterus: Studien zur mittelalterlichen Wirkungsgeschichte und Entfaltung eines embryologischen Gebarmuttermodells* (Pattensen: Horst Wellm Verlag, 1986). I am grateful to Monica Green for drawing my attention to this work. Joan Cadden remarks on the way this theory became a virtual doctrine for medieval authors, often being associated with other classical and late ancient (including Aristotelian) views that operated according to binary oppositions. "The strings of associations, right-warm-male and left-cool-female, return us also to the gender implications of medieval views of sex difference," *Meanings of Sex Difference in the Middle Ages: Medicine, Science, and Culture* (Cambridge: Cambridge University Press, 1993), 198.

66. On the Greek background of this "outstanding variability" see Maud W. Gleason, "The Semiotics of Gender: Physiognomy and Self-Fashioning in the Second Century C.E.," in *Before Sexuality: The Construction of Erotic Experience in the Ancient Greek World*, ed. David M. Halperin, John J. Winkler, and Froma I. Zeitlin (Princeton: Princeton University Press, 1990): 389–416.

67. Sylviane Agacinski, "Le tout premier écart," in *Les Fins de l'homme: À partir du travail de Jacques Derrida*, ed. Philippe Lacoue-Labarthe and Jean-Luc Nancy (Paris: Galilée, 1981), 120.

68. See E. Jane Burns's commentary on Aristotle's "messy matter," *Bodytalk: When Women Speak in Old French Literature* (Philadelphia:

University of Pennsylvania Press, 1993), 89–91. See also Thomas Laqueur's remarks on the way this feminine matter functions within a metaphysically ordered hierarchy: *Making Sex: Body and Gender from the Greeks to Freud* (Cambridge, Mass.: Harvard University Press, 1990), 61–62. Lynda Lange critiques this formulation in "Woman Is not a Rational Animal: On Aristotle's Biology of Reproduction," in *Discovering Reality*, 1–16.

69. Prudence Allen discusses how the Aristotelian biological understanding of "woman" and the metaphysical frequently come together; see *The Concept of Woman: The Aristotelian Revolution, 750 B.C.–A.D. 1250* (Montreal: Eden Press, 1985), esp. 83–126, 252–467.

70. See the version of this definition in the late-thirteenth-century didactic dialogue *Placides et Timéo*: "And Aristotle in his book on Nature [the *Metaphysics*] agrees with this, and he says that woman is an incomplete man; that is to say, a failed, imperfect one" (Et a ce s'accorde Aristote en ses Natures et dit que femme est homme achoisonne, ce est a dire faillis et non mie parfet; *Placides et Timéo*, 150–51).

71. According to Walter Ullmann, one of the effects of the medieval reception of Aristotle's *Politics*, *Ethics*, and *Physics* is the problem of the seat of ultimate sovereignty: *Principles of Government and Politics in the Middle Ages* (London: Methuen, 1961), 233.

72. Since the *Politics* was translated into Latin ca. 1260, it is possible that the authors of these texts knew these principles in Aristotle, and not only through commentaries and other indirect sources. On the contemporaneous tradition of commentary, see Martin Grabmann, "Die mittelalterlichen Kommentare zur *Politik* des Aristoteles," *Sitzungsberichte der Bayerischen Akademie der Wissenschaften*, Philos.-hist. Abteilung 2, no. 10 (1941).

73. Alfred Karnein discusses this idea of imperfection in terms of Aristotle's metaphysical lexicon: specifically, his distinction between perfect and principal attributes. *"Wie Feuer und Holz*: Aspekte der Ausgrenzung von Frauen beim Thema Liebe im 13. Jahrhundert," *Zeitschrift für Literaturwissenschaft und Linguistik* 19 (1989): 101.

74. On this point, see Sharon Farmer on the way women's speech is figured in contemporaneous sermon literature: "Persuasive Voices: Clerical Images of Medieval Wives," *Speculum* 61, no. 3 (July 1986): 517–43.

75. "So the lady's voice is the most gentle that ever was, the most powerful for all time" (Dont est vois de dame ki est li plus douce vois ki soit, li principaus poissance dou siecle); *Li Houneurs*, Zimmermann 387. "The most powerful thing in love is woman's comely language" (Li cose ki de li a plus de pooir en amor com bielle parolle [de feme]); *Li Consaus d'amours*, fol. 3.

76. Consider also the version appearing in Martin LeFranc's fifteenth-century *Champion des dames*: "Aristotle barely understood the secrets of nature. I don't know if you believe it, but it is said that woman outwitted him and taught him to act as a horse does. When she had undertaken to do this, she stuck her spurs into him" (Aristote tous les secrez de nature a paine comprit. Je ne scay pas se vous ce crez, mais l'en dit que femme le prit a son engin, et lui

aprit comme le chevalet feroit qui quant a ce faire entreprit, elle des talons le feroit; lines 6089–96). Martin LeFranc, *Champion des dames*, ed. Arthur Piaget, Mémoires et documents publiés par la société d'histoire de la suisse romane, 3rd series, 8, (Lausanne: Payot, 1968), 194.

77. *Les Lamentations de Matheolus et le Livre de leesce de Jehan LeFèvre, de Resson*, 2 vols., ed. Anton Gérard van Hamel (Paris: Emile Bouillon, 1892–1905), 1:33–34.

78. For another reading of this passage, see Bloch, *Medieval Misogyny*, 52.

TWO: THE TRIALS OF DISCIPLESHIP

1. Jacques LeGoff alludes to the small monopoly of *magistri* in Paris during this period and to the dangers of an "intellectual technocracy" that they posed: *Les Intellectuels au moyen âge*, 132.

2. This configuration was well established by the early thirteenth century: the *magister* who presided and made the final determination (*determinatio*), the *opponens* who raised the problems and posed the questions, and the *respondens*, the disciple or bachelor who explicated and clarified the problems. See Bazan et al., *Les Questions disputées*, 42.

3. This miniature also represents the standard presentation portrait of an author to his patron. But by placing the lady in the patron position, it accentuates the disciple's precarious role all the more. Through this configuration we can catch glimpses of the disciple's particular dilemma as fledgling writer approaching his patroness.

4. *"Le Roman de la poire" par Tibaut*, ed. Christiane Marchello-Nizia (Paris: A. & J. Picard, 1984); *Le Dit de la panthère d'amours par Nicole de Margival*, ed. Henry A. Todd (Paris: Firmin-Didot, 1883).

5. Ernstpeter Ruhe elucidates the importance of the love letter, or as it is called in Old French, the *salut d'amour*, for teaching the *ars dictaminis*; see *De Amasio ad amasium: Zur Gattungsgeschichte des mittelalterlichen Liebesbriefes*, Beiträge zur romanischen Philologie des Mittelalters, vol. 10 (Munich: Wilhelm Fink, 1975), 215–69.

6. For details on how this letter game forms part of an elaborate audiovisual design in manuscript, see Sylvia Huot, *From Song to Book*, 177–84.

7. On this trope of obscurity, see Douglas Kelly, "Obscurity and Memory: Sources for Invention in Medieval French Literature," *Studies in Medieval Culture* 16 (1984): 33–56.

8. Marchello-Nizia outlines this pattern of lyric refrains; see *Le Roman de la poire*, xxxiv–xlviii.

9. Jacqueline Cerquiglini-Toulet, "Le Clerc et l'écriture: Le 'Voir-dit' de Guillaume de Machaut et la définition du 'dit,'" in *Literatur in der Gesellschaft des Spätmittelalters*, ed. Hans-Ulrich Gumbrecht (Heidelberg: Carl Winter Universitätsverlag, 1980), 151–68.

10. On this criterion of contraries in scholastic argumentation as it is adapted by vernacular narrative, see Gérard Paré, *Les Idées et les lettres au*

XIIIe siècle: "Le Roman de la rose" (Montréal: Centre de psychologie et de pédagogie, 1947), 31–32.

11. G. E. R. Lloyd outlines the Aristotelian category of contraries that made such an impact on medieval logic. See *Polarity and Analogy: Two Types of Argumentation in Early Greek Thought* (Cambridge: Cambridge University Press, 1966), 86–89.

12. Nancy Freeman Regalado underscores the connection between *contraires choses* and the erotic: "Une fois de plus 'les contraires choses,' les *exempla*, fournissent à Jean de Meun le vocabulaire nécessaire pour parler littéralement de la partie de l'expérience humaine qui échappe au langage, l'expérience érotique." " 'Des contraires choses': La fonction poétique de la citation et des *exempla* dans le *Roman de la Rose* de Jean de Meun," *Littérature* 41 (February 1981): 77. I would argue that in the case of the *Roman de la rose* as in the *Poire*, the erotic must be inflected in terms of women.

13. On the definition of "the contrary woman" in medieval Aristotelian thought, see Allen, *The Concept of Woman*, 468–69.

14. It is just this feature of the "multiplicity of actors" that Palémon Glorieux finds characteristic of masters' debates: "L'Enseignement au moyen âge," 123.

15. As Kathryn Gravdal points out, there is an important semantic shift when *"ravir"* signifying "to carry away by force" in the twelfth century evolves to mean "being carried away" by the later Middle Ages. *Ravishing Maidens*, 4–5.

16. See the comparable representation in the *Poire*: "Then I lose all speech and I seemed like a figure struck dumb who does not move or react and cannot sound a word" (Adont pert la parole tote et m'estoit com ymage mue que ne se muet ne se remue ne que ne puet soner un mot"; lines 2182–85).

17. It should not be surprising, then, to find in the acrostic allusions to the question of physical force: "Woman prefers that one force her to accomplish her will rather than that she authorizes it; thus she refuses her desire" (fame aime mielx qu'en la forçoit d'acomplir son bon qu'el l'otroit, si que son desirier refuse"; lines 2674–76).

18. This synchrony of the two *oeuvres* is made explicit at one point: "And Love, who takes charge of the actions of lovers and of their work, does not labor out of kindness for me" (et Amors, qui enprent Les fais des amans et lor oevre, Par sa bonté por moy n'i oevre; lines 1817–19). This phonic pun between *oeuvrer* and *ouvrer* runs through the *Panthère*.

19. I borrow this musicological term from Jacques Chailley, "La nature musicale du *Jeu de Robin et Marion*," in *Mélanges d'histoire du théâtre du moyen âge et de la Renaissance offerts à Gustave Cohen* (Paris: Nizet, 1950), 115.

20. As Sylvia Huot puts it, "lover and lady literally 'make love.'" *From Song to Book*, 190.

21. Christiane Marchello-Nizia coined this expression for amorous discourse in general: "L'Invention du dialogue amoureux: Le masque d'une différence," in *Masques et déguisements dans la littérature médiévale*, ed. Marie-

Louise Ollier (Montréal: Presses de l'Université de Montréal, 1988), 227.

22. Pierre Bourdieu, "La Domination masculine," 23.

THREE: THE MASTER AT WORK

1. "And similarly the consecrated masters first receive the brilliance of the intellect" (Et similiter sacri doctores mentium splendorem primo recipiunt. Sicut montes enim doctores primitus radiis divinae sapientiae illuminantur). From *Breve principium de commendatione sacrae scripturae*, in *Opuscula theologica*, 2 vols., ed. Raymond A. Verardo (Rome: Marietti, 1954), 1:442; quoted in *The Cambridge History of Medieval Philosophy*, 81. For a fuller consideration of the master figure in Aquinas, structured as a question and response, see the *Quaestiones disputatae*, XI, and *Summa theologica*, 1, q. 117, a. 1: *Über den Lehrer, de magistro*, ed. and trans. G. Jüssen, G. Krieger, and J. H. J. Schneider (Hamburg: Felix Meiner, 1988).

2. "Each thing is perfect in its activity when it can produce another thing similar to itself." This notion of reproduction was the subject of considerable contemporaneous speculation; see Thomas Aquinas's *Commentary on the Metaphysics of Aristotle*, 2 vols., trans. John P. Rowan, (Chicago: Henry Regnery, 1961), 1:15.

3. This classification occurs in a thirteenth-century Aristotelian treatise *De lingua*, that outlines various sins of language. On this classificatory scheme, see Casagrande and Vecchio, *Les Péchés de la langue*, 129; *I Peccati Della Lingua*, 159–60.

4. This is the commonest *incipit*; see "Matheus von Boulogne: *Lamentationes Matheoluli*," ed. Albert Schmitt (Ph.D. diss., Rheinischen Friedrich-Wilhelms-Universität, Bonn, 1974), 44. In the version translated by Jean LeFèvre, it comes after the Ovidian preface: "Je fus jadis maistre clames"; see van Hamel's edition, *Les Lamentations de Matheolus et le Livre de leesce*, 1:3.

5. For the Italian picture, in addition to the Segre edition, see *Il Bestiario d'Amore e la Riposta al Bestiario*, ed. Francesco Zambon (Parma: Pratiche Editrice, 1987), and *Una Versione Pisana Inedita del "Bestiaire d'Amours,"* ed. Roberto Crespo (Leiden: Leiden University Press, 1972); also Jeanette Beer's fine translation, *Master Richard's Bestiary of Love and Response* (Berkeley: University of California Press, 1986). All translations are mine, except where I refer specifically to Beer and cite hers.

6. For details of Fournival's biography, see *L'Oeuvre lyrique de Richard de Fournival*, ed. Yvan G. LePage (Ottawa: Éditions de l'Université d'Ottawa, 1981), 9–12. Christopher Lucken is in the process of publishing his thesis, which represents the most comprehensive study of Fournival's writing to date. See "Les Portes de la mémoire: Richard de Fournival et l'"ariereban' de l'amour," (Ph.D. diss., University of Geneva, 1994).

7. Richard H. Rouse surveys his exceptional library in "Manuscripts Belonging to Richard de Fournival," *Revue d'histoire des textes* 3 (1973): 253–69. Of particular interest are Fournival's Aristotelian holdings, which in-

cluded the *De animalibus* and Avicennan versions of the *Physica*, *De caelo et mundo*, and the *De anima* (263–64).

8. Both Beer and Alexandre Leupin mention the connection with Aristotelianism but do not explore its full dimensions: Beer, *Master Richard's Bestiary of Love*, xv, and Alexandre Leupin, *Barbarolexis: Medieval Writing and Sexuality* (Cambridge, Mass.: Harvard University Press, 1989), 147.

9. *The Complete Works of Aristotle*, book I, 980a–b, 2:1552. For a medieval Latin version, see *Metaphysica Aristotelis: Translatio anonyma sive "media"*, ed. Gudrun Vuillemin-Diem (Leiden: E. J. Brill, 1976), 7.

10. On Fournival's use of memory, see Mary Carruthers, *The Book of Memory: A Study of Memory in Medieval Culture* (Cambridge: Cambridge University Press, 1990), 223–24; see also Huot, *From Song to Book*, 141–47.

11. Elizabeth V. Spelman critiques this problem of women's sensory character and their potential for rationality in "Aristotle and the Politicization of the Soul," in *Discovering Reality*, 27.

12. I explore these distinctions further in "Seeing, Hearing, Tasting Woman: The Senses of Medieval Reading," *Comparative Literature* 46, no. 2 (spring 1994): 129–45.

13. On the *Bestiaire* in the context of the *ars dictaminis*, see Ruhe's remarks in *De amasio ad amasium*, 254–55. On the Aristotelian animal lore that the *Bestiaire* exploits, see Miguel J. C. de Asúa, "The Organization of Discourse on Animals in the Thirteenth Century: Peter of Spain, Albert the Great, and the Commentaries on the *De animalibus*" (Ph.D. diss., University of Notre Dame, 1991).

14. I have studied this pattern of recognition in "Letter-Writing and Picture-Reading: The *Bestiaire d'amour* and Medieval Textuality," *Word and Image* 5, no. 1 (1989): 131–47.

15. See Florence McCulloch, "Le Tigre au miroir: La vie d'une image de Pline à Pierre Gringore," *Revue des sciences humaines* 130 (April–June 1968): 149–60.

16. Ignacio Malaxecheverria's reading of the bestiary genre touches upon this issue of ambivalence; see *Le Bestiaire médiéval et l'archétype de la féminité* (Paris: Lettres modernes, 1982), 9.

17. I invoke here Sarah Kofman's rich commentary on the inferences of the Freudian equation—narcissistic woman = beast of prey (*Raubtiere*) found in the *Essay on Narcissism*; see *L'Enigme de la femme: La femme dans les textes de Freud* (Paris: Galilée, 1980), 63–64.

18. Sarah Kay shows how these distinctions can yield a curious set of associations in clerical analysis: "if women are to body as man is to mind, and the body is a necessary source of knowledge, then women are a necessary source of knowledge." As Kay rightly points out, "this is not serious philosophy, but an elaborate joke." See "Women's Body of Knowledge: Epistemology and Misogyny in the *Romance of the Rose*," in *Framing Medieval Bodies*, ed. Sarah Kay and Miri Rubin (Manchester: Manchester University Press, 1994): 211–35. I am grateful to her for sharing her essay with me.

19. That this combination continues to be fascinating is borne out by Giuseppe Tomasi di Lampedusa's novella, *The Professor and the Siren* (Milan: Feltrinelli, 1961), itself a fantasy on the rapport between the master figure and the bestial woman.

20. Beryl Rowland touches on the Christological implications in "The Art of Memory and the Bestiary," in *Beasts and Birds of the Middle Ages: The Bestiary and Its Legacy*, ed. Willene B. Clark and Meradith T. McMunn (Philadelphia: University of Pennsylvania Press, 1989), 13.

21. Danielle Régnier-Bohler, "Femme/Faute/Fantasme," in *La Condicion de la mujer en la Edad Media*, ed. Yves-René Fonquerne and Alfonso Esteban (Madrid: Universidad Complutense, 1986), 486–87.

22. Leupin reads the lady as a symbol of castration; see *Barbarolexis*, 160.

23. On this issue of loss, see Christopher Lucken, "Du ban du coq à l'*Ari-ereban* de l'âne (A propos du *Bestiaire d'amour* de Richard de Fournival)," *Reinardus* 5 (1992): 123–24.

24. "Li Commens d'amour," ed. Antoinette Saly, *Travaux de linguistique et de littérature* 10 (1972): 49. This text is commonly attributed to Richard de Fournival because it occurs in manuscript with the *Bestiaire* and the *Poissance d'amours*.

FOUR: CONTRARY TO WHAT IS SAID

1. An excellent index of the importance of the *responsio* is the thirteenth-century commentary on the art of responding. See, for instance, the popular treatise attributed to Albert the Great, *Die Mittelalterlichen Traktate De modo opponendi et respondendi: Einleitung und Ausgabe der einschlagigen Texte*, ed. Lambert Marie de Rijk, Beiträge zur Geschichte der Philosophie und Theologie des Mittelalters, vol. 17 (Munster: Aschendorff, 1980).

2. P. Mandonnet offers the following description: "La dispute se tenait sous la direction du maître; mais ce n'était pas lui, à proprement parler, qui disputait. C'était son bachelier qui assumait l'office de répondant et commençait ainsi son apprentissage de ces exercices." Quoted by LeGoff, *Les Intellectuels au moyen âge*, 102. See also the discussions of the *responsio* and the respondent role by Glorieux, *La Littérature quodlibétique*, 1:31–32, J. F. Wippel, "The Quodlibetal Question as a Discursive Literary Genre," in *Les Genres littéraires dans les sources théologiques et philosophiques médiévales: Définition, critique, et exploitation*, Actes du Colloque international de Louvain-la-Neuve, May 25–27 1981. (Louvain-la-Neuve: Institut d'études médiévales de l'Université Catholique de Louvain, 1982), 68, and Boyle, *Pastoral Care*, 53–54.

3. *Li Proverbes au vilain: Untersuchungen zur romanischen Spruchdichtung des Mittelalters*, ed. Eckhard Rattunde, Studia Romanica 11 (Heidelberg: Carl Winter, 1966), 135.

4. I am thinking of works such as *Les Diz et proverbes des sages*, ed. Joseph Morawski, Bibliothèque de la Faculté des Lettres Université de Paris, 2nd series, 2 (Paris: Presses Universitaires de France, 1924), and the "Enseignements

d'Aristote et d'Alixandre," of which Hermann Kunst gives a partial edition in *Mitteilungen aus dem Eskurial,* Bibliothek des Literarischen Vereins in Stuttgart 141 (1879).

5. According to Jauss, "Le droit de questionner est une prérogative qui reste du côté des seigneurs; devoir répondre et ne pouvoir parler que lorsqu'on est interrogé est le sort de l'assujetti." Hans-Robert Jauss,"Adam Interrogateur (pour une histoire des fonctions du modèle question/réponse)," *Texte* 3 (1984): 160–61.

6. On this double bind of the "good student" in relation to the master's infallibility, see Pierre Bourdieu and Jean-Claude Passeron, *La Reproduction: Eléments pour une théorie du système d'enseignement* (Paris: Minuit, 1970), 136–38.

7. Leupin, *Barbarolexis,* 158.

8. Segre, *Li Bestiaires d'amour,* 105–36. See also Beer's translation, *Master Richard's Bestiary of Love and Response,* 41–58.

9. All citations and translations are based on Segre's edition and my reading of the manuscript, Vienna, Österreichische Nationalbibliothek 2609, fols. 32–53 verso.

10. On the Aristotelian paradigm, see Lloyd, *Polarity and Analogy,* 86–89. See also Ian Maclean's commentary on the paradigm in early modern scholastic thought, *The Renaissance Notion of Woman: A Study in the Fortunes of Scholasticism and Medical Science in European Intellectual Life* (Cambridge: Cambridge University Press, 1980), 2–3.

11. In this formulation, I am improvising with Elizabeth Berg's notion of the "third woman"—the figure who plays fast and loose with the master's precepts in order to push beyond the dominant representations of her; see "The Third Woman," *Diacritics* 12, no. 2 (summer 1982): 14, 16.

12. Hélène Cixous, Madeleine Gagnon, and Annie Leclerc, *La Venue à l'écriture* (Paris: Union générale d'éditions, 1977), 41.

13. Jeanette Beer has placed the respondent's version in the context of latemedieval Judaic exegesis: "Richard de Fournival's Anonymous Lady: The Character of the Response to the *Bestiaire d'amour,*" *Romance Philology* 42, no. 3 (November 1989): 272. Mieke Bal argues that such a version calls into question "man's priority and domination." See *Femmes imaginaires: L'Ancien testament au risque d'une narratologie critique* (Paris: Nizet, 1986), 216.

14. For the canonical catologue of these arguments as they circulated in Latin and the vernacular in the high Middle Ages, see Paul Meyer, "Les Manuscrits français de Cambridge," *Romania* 15 (1886): 321.

15. Like Thomas Aquinas and numerous other thirteenth-century exegetes, the respondent glosses Aristotle's exposition on matter: *Metaphysics,* book 8. See *Commentary on the Metaphysics of Aristotle,* 2:619–50.

16. By far the best-known medieval commentary on the creation of woman in the Aristotelian mode is that of Aquinas in *Summa theologica,* 1, q. 92 ("The Production of Women), 93 ("The End or Term of the Production of Man"), 99 ("Of the Condition of the Offspring as to the Body"), and 102 ("Of Man's Abode,

Which is Paradise"). *Summa theologica,* 4:274–304, 4:350–54, 4:364–72.

17. It is important to remember here that matter and essence are not synonymous in Aristotelian terms and hence even less so in the respondent's revisionist argumentation. As Diana Fuss rightly observes, debating the problem of matter, and notably matter as body, does not infer that matter has an essence. See *Essentially Speaking: Feminism, Nature, and Difference* (New York: Routledge, 1989), 50–51.

18. Elizabeth Janeway, "On the Power of the Weak," *Signs* 1, no. 1 (autumn 1975): 103–9.

19. Nancy Freeman Regalado speculates on this point in *"Vos Paroles ont mains et piés*: Woman's Wary Voice in the *Response au Bestiaire d'amors de Maître Richard de Fournival."* I am grateful to Prof. Regalado for sharing with me this unpublished paper presented at the Kentucky Romance Languages conference, 1986.

20. Roger Dragonetti argues that they "symbolisent les réactions sociales malveillantes." See his sketch of *lauzengiers/mesdisants* and their function in courtly discourse in *La Technique poétique des trouvères dans la chanson courtoise* (Geneva: Slatkine Reprints, 1979), 272–78.

21. Vienna, Österreichische Nationalbibliothek 2609, fols. 43 verso–53 verso. For details of this text in manuscript see Hermann, ed., *Die westeuropäischen Handschriften,* 2:62–66; Segre, *Li Bestiaires d'amour,* lxiii–lxiv.

22. Derrida, following Lévi-Strauss, meditates on what it means to lose a proper name and what it means to have all names socially obliterated. Jacques Derrida, *Of Grammatology,* trans. Gayatri Chakravorty Spivak (Baltimore: Johns Hopkins University Press, 1980), 107–18.

23. It is worthwhile recalling here that the lure of a woman's reputation was the trigger mechanism for the master's *Bestiaire.* As the first respondent observes: "For there are so many people who have dealings with you and you with them that you first heard talk of me through hearsay. For this reason I listen gladly to the talk and I see readily those who know how to speak and behave well. That is the reason why, I believe, that you came here first to find out who I was, and whether anything about me might please you" (Car tant de gent ont a vous a faire et vous a eux. Que par oir dire aves aucun de moi oit parler por cou que ieu oi volentiers parler et voi volentiers ceaus qui sevent parler et iestre. Et par cesti raison cuic iou que vous premiers venissies ca et savoir qui iou estoie ne se aucune coze qui en moi fust vous poroit neint plaire; fol. 41; Segre, 136).

24. This gesture repeats the qualifier running through the first *Response:* "je qui feme sui." It also recapitulates what the opening miniatures of the two *Responses* illustrate: together and apart, the woman respondent and master exist within the overarching H of HOM (Man).

25. In this sense, the second *Response* echoes tellingly with Denise Riley's aim of querying the "substantial realms of discursive historical formation." *"Am I That Name?": Feminism and the Category of "Women" in History* (Minneapolis: University of Minnesota Press, 1988), 5.

26. See "Des Vilains ou des xxii manieires de vilains," ed. Edmond Faral, *Romania* 48 (1922): 243–64.

27. The phrase is Bernard Cerquiglini's: "Variantes d'auteur et variance de copiste," in *La Naissance du texte*, ed. Louis Hay (Paris: José Corti, 1989), 105.

28. Jeanette Beer exemplifies this critical search; see "Richard de Fournival's Anonymous Lady," 267–73.

29. Peter Dronke comments on the vexed historicity of Héloïse and Constance: *Women Writers of the Middle Ages*, 84–90, 140–43.

30. Behind the woman respondent, Cesare Segre discerns a "uomo di certa cultura religiosa, turbato dalla gioiosa mondanità del *Bestiaire*" (xxviii); Ernst-peter Ruhe concurs, putting the *Bestiaire/Response* in the context of elaborate epistolary games typical of high medieval clerics: "La Peur de la transgression: À propos du *Livre d'Enanchet* et du *Bestiaire d'amour*," in *Amour, mariage, et transgressions au moyen âge*, ed. Danielle Buschinger and André Crépin (Göppingen: Kümmerle, 1984), 320–22.

31. Gerald A. Bond makes a similar point in "Composing Yourself: Ovid's Heroïdes, Baudri of Bourgueil, and the Problem of Persona," *Medievalia* 13 (1989 [for 1987]): 84.

32. Toril Moi, "Feminist, Female, Feminine," in *The Feminist Reader: Essays in Gender and the Politics of Literary Criticism*, ed. Catherine Belsey and Jane Moore (New York: Blackwell, 1989), 120.

33. Gabrielle Spiegel's discussion of social logic is helpful here: "Sites of linguistic usage, as lived events, are essentially local in origin and therefore possess a determinate social logic of much greater density and particularity than can be extended from totalizing constructs like 'language' and 'society.'" "History, Historicism, and the Social Logic of the Text in the Middle Ages," *Speculum* 65, no. 1 (January 1990): 77.

34. As Roger Chartier recommends, there is much to be gained by attending to "particularity"—to studying materials within precise, local, and specific contexts." See *The Culture of Print: Power and the Uses of Print in Early Modern Europe* (Princeton: Princeton University Press, 1989), 3; French edition, *Les Usages de l'imprimé (XVᵉ–XIXᵉ siècle)* (Paris: Fayard, 1987), 10.

35. For details of the manuscripts, see Segre, *Li Bestiaire d'amour*, xxxii–lxv, Huot, *From Song to Book*, 148–49, and Hermann, *Die westeuropäischen Handschriften*, 2:53–62.

36. This northern Francophone provenance is a function of our current understanding of the *Response*'s manuscript transmission. Ongoing codicological research may lead us in additional directions. By all accounts, the *Bestiaire* was copied and read in fourteenth-century Flanders, Britain, and Italy. This variegated reception history suggests that it fanned out rapidly over Europe. Its earliest copies, however, link it to the Parisian court and northern France. For the *status quaestionis* of *Bestiaire* manuscripts, see the appendix to Christopher Lucken's dissertation, "Les Portes de la mémoire."

37. Vienna 2609 includes the *Medecines d'amour*, *Bestiaire d'amour*, and *Response au Bestiaire d'amour*; Vienna 2621 includes *La Poissance d'amours*,

which I call, after the name given in the text, *Li Consaus d'amours, Li Prison d'amour,* and *L'Art d'amour.* See the discussion in chapter 1. See also Hermann, *Die westeuropäischen Handschriften,* 2:62–66. Hermann proposes a limited affiliation between the two codices; that is, between 2609 and the folios of 2621 containing *Li Prison d'amours* of Baudouin de Condé.

38. For the thirteenth-century and fourteenth-century versions, see *Chronica noblissimorum ducum Lotharingiae et Brabantiae ac regum Francorum, auctore magistro Edmundo de Dynter,* ed. J. Wauquelin (Brussels: M. Hayez, 1854–57) and *Chroniques de Brabant et de Flandre,* 4 vols., ed. Charles Piot, (Brussels: F. Hayez, 1879), vol. 4. Among modern historiographical accounts, see Henri Pirenne, *Les Anciennes Démocraties des Pays-Bas,* Bibliothèque de philosophie scientifique (Paris: Ernest Flammarion, 1910), 157–94, and for the analogous Flemish case, David M. Nicholas, *Town and Countryside: Social, Economic and Political Tensions in Fourteenth-Century Flanders* (Bruges: de Tempel, 1971). Martha C. Howell makes a similar case in feminist terms in *Women, Production, and Patriarchy in Late Medieval Cities* (Chicago: University of Chicago Press, 1986).

39. "Francia quot vites, tot habet Brabantia lites." Quoted by Alphonse Wauters in *Les Libertés communales: Essai sur l'origine et leurs premiers développements en Belgique, dans le nord de la France, et sur les bords du Rhin,* (Brussels: A. N. Lebègue, 1878), 643.

40. Pirenne, *Les Anciennes Démocraties,* 95–135, esp. 126–29.

41. On the history of the Communes, it is interesting to juxtapose a nineteenth-century liberal assessment with a contemporary socialist one; see Alphonse Wauters, *Les Libertés communales,* and Michel Mollat and Philippe Wolff, *Ongles bleus: Jacques et Ciompi, les révolutions populaires en Europe aux XIVᵉ et XVᵉ siècles* (Paris: Calmann-Levy, 1970).

42. In histories of Brabantine, Flemish, and Artesian town life, as in literary surveys, it is commonplace to postulate the significant degree of literacy among the bourgeoisie, as well as their intervention in questions of education. See André Uyttebrouck, *Le Gouvernement du duché de Brabant au bas moyen âge (1355–1430),* (Brussels: Éditions de l'Université de Bruxelles, 1975), 26–28; Henri Pirenne, *Histoire de Belgique,* 7 vols. (Brussels: Maurice Lamertin, 1929–32), 1:350.

43. See Charles Stallaert and Philippe van der Haeghen, *De L'Instruction publique au moyen âge du VIIIᵉ au XVIᵉ siècle,* Mémoires couronnés et mémoires des savants étrangers publiés par l'Académie royale des sciences, des lettres, et des beaux-arts de Belgique 23 (Brussels: Académie royale, 1850); Alphonse Wauters, *Les libertés communales,* 619–20. For an analogous French example, see Gustave Carré, *L'Enseignement secondaire à Troyes du moyen âge à la Révolution* (Paris: Hachette, 1888), 1–26. Henri Pirenne, L'Instruction des marchands au moyen âge," *Annales d'histoire économique et sociale* 1 (1929): 13–28, and Lynn Thorndike, "Elementary and Secondary Education in the Middle Ages," *Speculum* 15, no. 4 (October 1940): 400–408, cover similar ground. Much of the trenchwork in digging up source materials

was undertaken in the second half of the nineteenth century as a result of the twofold interest in the Middle Ages and pedagogical reform.

44. Stallaert and van der Haeghen,"De L'Instruction publique," 100–102.

45. This is a process that Adam de la Halle's late thirteenth-century *jeus* had already attested to ironically. Consider the *Jeu de la Feuillée*, where Adam, the Artesian tradesman, attempts to cast off his business life for the life of a cleric, only to fail miserably:

> Seigneur, savés pour coi j'ai men abit cangiét?
> J'ai esté avoec feme, or revois au clergiét. . . .
> Or ne pourront pas dire aucun ke j'ai antés
> Ke d'aler a Paris soie nient vantés. . . .
> Par Dieu! sire, je n'irai hui.
> (lines 1–2, 5–6, 958)

> Lords, do you know why I've changed my habit? I was with a woman, now I'm returning to the clergy. Those whom I've frequented will not be able to say that I have only bragged about going to Paris. . . . My God, sir, I won't be going today.

46. Joan Ferrante's discussion illustrates this tendency well: "The Education of Women in the Middle Ages," 12. See also James Westfall Thompson, *The Literacy of the Laity in the Middle Ages*, University of California Publications in Education, vol. 9 (Berkeley: University of California Press, 1939), and Léopold Delisle, "Études historiques: De l'instruction littéraire de la noblesse française au moyen âge," *Le Correspondant* 36 (1855): 444–50.

47. See Pirenne, *Les Anciennes Démocraties*, 154–55.

48. Paul Rousselot is one of the very few who acknowledges the discrepancy; see *Histoire de l'éducation des femmes en France*, 1883; rpt., Research and Source Works Series, History of Education, vol. 8 (New York: Burt Franklin, 1971), 44–98. David M. Nicholas acknowledges the likely parity between schooling for boys and girls in *The Domestic Life of a Medieval City: Women, Children, and the Family in Fourteenth-Century Ghent* (Lincoln: University of Nebraska Press, 1985), 127–29. See also Erika Vitz's comments to this effect: *Women in the Medieval Town*, trans. Sheila Marnie (London: Barrie and Jenkins, 1990), 71–72, 97–98. In this respect the figure of Catherine of Alexandria in a saint's life from thirteenth-century Picardy is telling. She is represented as a highly literate woman, impeccably schooled and well able to dispute with the kingdom's best orators.

> Ainc ne fu feme mix lettree
> Ne des .vii. ars mix escolee. . . .
> Pour une femme a disputer
> A fait l'empereres mander . . .
> .L. maistres orateurs
> (lines 73–74, 307–10)

> Never was a woman more literate, or as well schooled in the seven arts. . . .
> The emperor commanded such a woman to dispute with fifty master orators.

"De Sainte Katherine": An Anonymous Picard Version of the Life of St. Catherine of Alexandria, ed. William McBain (Fairfax, Va.: George Mason University Press, 1987). This portrait of the woman disputant seems to suggest contemporaneous pedagogical opportunities for women in this region.

49. Philippe de Navarre's recommendation went as follows: "A fame ne doit on apanre letres ne escrire, se ce n'est especiaument por estre nonnain; car par lire et escrire de fame sont maint mal avenu" (One should instruct women neither in writing nor reading, unless it is especially for nuns; for women's reading and writing come to a bad end). See *Les Quatre Ages de l'homme: Traité moral de Philippe de Navarre,* ed. Marcel de Fréville (Paris: Firmin-Didot, 1888), 16.

50. See extracts of a sixteenth-century chronicle quoted by Myriam Greilshammer in *L'Envers du tableau: Mariage et maternité en Flandre médiévale* (Paris: Armand Colin, 1990), 13.

51. Charles Jourdain brought this remarkable case to light; *L'Education des femmes au moyen âge,* 10. See Maroie's will, Paris, Bibliothèque Nationale, Collection de Flandre, Tournai, no. 8.

52. See Derville, "L'Alphabétisation du peuple," 765.

53. See Philippe Philibert Pompée, *Rapport historique sur les écoles primaires de la ville de Paris* (Paris: Imprimerie Royale, 1839), 24–25. The proceedings are reproduced on 156–61.

54. For a review of beguine culture in northern Europe, see Herbert Grundmann, *Religiöse Bewegungen im Mittelalter* (1939), rpt. in *Ausgewählte Aufsätze,* 3 vols., vol. 1 (Stuttgart: Hiersemann, 1976), Ernest W. McDonnell, *The Beguines and Beghards in Medieval Culture, with Special Emphasis on the Belgian Scene* (New Brunswick, N.J.: Rutgers University Press, 1954), 365–87, Walter Simons, "The Beguines in the Southern Low Countries: A Reassessment," *Bulletin de l'Institut Historique Belge de Rome* 59 (1989): 63–105, and Carol Neel, "The Origins of the Beguines," *Signs* 14, no. 2 (winter 1989): 321–41. Alphonse Wauters attests to the importance of beguinages in the Brabant, *Le Duc Jean Ier et le Brabant sous le règne de ce prince (1267–1294),* in Mémoires couronnés et autres mémoires publiés par l'Académie royale des sciences, des lettres, et des beaux-arts de Belgique 13 (Brussels: Académie royale, 1862): 378–79, 424, 432; Bernard Delmaire explores the communities in the Franco-Flemish arena we are considering: "Les Béguines dans le nord de la France au premier siècle de leur histoire (vers 1230–1350)," in *Les Religieuses en France au XIIIe siècle,* ed. Michel Parisse (Nancy: Presses Universitaires, 1985), 121–62. Jean-Claude Schmitt charts the analogous case of German communities in *Mort d'une hérésie: L'Église et les clercs face aux béguines et aux beghards du Rhin supérieur du XIVe au XVe siècles* (Paris: Mouton, 1978).

55. Caroline Walker Bynum makes the point that thirteenth-century beguines came from the "new bourgeoisie" and other townspeople: *Holy Feast and Holy Fast: The Religious Significance of Food to Medieval Women* (Berkeley: University of California Press, 1987), 18.

56. "La Règle des fins amans: Eine Begininregel aus dem Ende des XIII. Jahrhunderts," ed. Karl Christ, in *Philologische Studien aus dem Romanische-Germanischen Kulturkreise*, ed. B. Schädel and W. Mulert (Halle: M. Niemeyer, 1927), 192–213.

57. As Brian Stock has pointed out, contexts are less functionally supportive of a text than they are interactive with it in both reinforcing and disruptive ways: see *Listening for the Text: On the Uses of the Past* (Baltimore: Johns Hopkins University Press, 1990), 34–35.

58. The entire passage from which this comes is well worth quoting: "Et noumeement li hom qui saime se doit garder de tencier a nului. Car bien se wart quiconques tence a sen parel si est fourconsellies. Et qui tence a plus haut de lui si est foursenerie. Et qui tence a plus bas de lui si est une vuites. Et dautre part sil tence a un sage home il ne puet avoir nul droit. Car nous savons bien ke nus sages ne desiert com tence a lui. Et dautre part qui tence a fol ne a sage si resamble celui qui se combat encontre son ombre. cest a dire a celui qui nest mie" (And truly the man with self-respect must keep from disputing with everyone. For the one well guarded knows that whosoever disputes with peers is badly advised. And who disputes with superiors is crafty. And who disputes with subordinates is a base person. And on the other hand, who disputes with a wise man has no right. For we well know that no wise person deserves to be disputed with. Furthermore, he who disputes with the fool as with the wise man resembles the one who fights with his shadow, that is to say, with somebody who doesn't exist at all; Vienna 2609, fol. 49). Interestingly enough, this proverbial expression, *se combattre encontre son ombre*, crops up repeatedly in the *Querelle des femmes*. On this point, see Geneviève Hasenohr, "La Locution verbale figurée dans l'oeuvre de Jean LeFèvre," *Le Moyen Français* 14–15 (1984): 247.

FIVE: DEFAMATION AND THE *LIVRE DE LEESCE*

1. Bloch, *Medieval Misogyny*, 4.

2. Jean LeFèvre, *Les Lamentations de Matheolus et le Livre de leesce*, vol. 2.

3. I am referring here to works such as Boccaccio's *De claribus mulieribus* (1350s), Martin LeFranc's *Champion des dames* (1450s), Jean Marot's *Vray-Disante advocate des dames* (1480s), and even Henri Corneille Agrippa's *Traité de l'excellence de la femme* (1509). As Marc Angenot has argued, all these texts can be read as one discursive register with a single ideological function. See his *Les Champions des femmes: Examen du discours sur la supério-rité des femmes 1400–1800* (Montréal: Presses de l'Université de Québec, 1977), 159–61.

4. Geneviève Hasenohr-Esnos surveys the principle works in LeFèvre's translating career, beginning with the *Lamentations* and including the pseudo-Ovidian *De vetula* and the *Distiques Caton*, Cato's proverbial wisdom. See the introduction to her edition of *Le Respit de la mort de Jehan LeFèvre* (Paris: A. & J. Picard, 1969), xviii–lv.

5. Hasenohr-Esnos cites three such cases in *Le Respit de la mort*, xiii–xiv: these are Paris, Archives Nationales, X^{ic} 14, no. 62 (LeFèvre defending Marie de Basentin, dame de Flary, in 1364), X^{ic} 19B, no. 173 (Jeanne de Fay in 1368), and X^{ic} 24A, no.130 (Marie Aucoch in 1372).

6. Ironically, a critic such as Italo Siciliano finds the move to recant even more unacceptable than the rehearsal of misogynistic learning. "LeFèvre, aterré par le remords d'avoir traduit les *Lamentationes* du clerc bigame, crut effacer ce crime par un crime bien plus déplorable en composant le "Rebours de Matheolus." *François Villon et les thèmes poétiques du moyen âge* (Paris: Armand Colin, 1934), 363–64.

7. I give here only a sampling of its occurrences in the *Leesce*: lines 281–82, 328–29, 801–2, 893–94, 2139–40, 2231–32, 3193–94, 3933–34. Jacqueline Cerquiglini-Toulet remarks the homology *fame* (*woman*), *fama* (*fame*) in medieval writing and underscores the fact that the pronunciation of the two terms, and often their spelling, was identical. *La Couleur de la mélancholie: La Fréquentation des livres au XIVe siècle 1300–1415* (Paris: Hatier, 1993), 142.

8. Stephen Heath epitomizes this critical unease when he asks: "If I take it [feminism] up into me, into my life, calling into question the assumptions of the position of myself . . . how do I develop a reflection on it, how do I think and talk and write about—*with*—feminism without falling back into the male argument, without producing another version of the object feminism up for grabs, 'the stakes'?" "Male Feminism," in *Men in Feminism*, ed. Alice Jardine and Paul Smith (New York: Methuen, 1987), 2.

9. Toril Moi, "Patriarchal Thought and the Drive for Knowledge," 195.

10. "Honorable ladies, if, on the other hand, it seems to you that I am telling stories, don't take me for a liar, but take it up with the authors who have written down in their books the words that I have spoken and those which I will speak; if wise men who composed books long ago did not lie, I will not lie in any manner . . . I have done nothing but recite" (D'autre part, dames honorables, s'il vos samble que je di fables, por manteür ne m'an tenez, mes aus aucteurs vos an prenez qui an leur livres ont escrites les paroles que g'en ai dites, et ceus avec que g'en dirai; ne ja de riens n'an mentirai, se li preudome n'en mentirent qui les anciens livres firent . . . je n'i faz riens fors reciter). *Roman de la rose*, lines 15185–94, 15204.

11. " '*Litis preterire noli, Post inimicias*': Se gens tancent, ne le repelles mie Car la tancon est de paix ennemie Il appartient au mauvais de mesdire Et ceulz mentent qui sont meuz en yre." See J. Ulrich, ed., "Die Übersetzung der Distichen des Pseudo-Cato von Jean de Paris," *Romanische Forschungen* 15 (1904): 86–87. LeFèvre cites another similar proverb in the *Leesce*: "Lest the horror of strife/litigation resound, a wild tongue should be restrained" (linguam refrenans temperet Ne litis horror insonet; lines 1579–80).

12. This abdication is highly ironic since the subject he refrains from translating, elderly women, has already been treated at great and scurrilous length in his translation of the Ovidian *De vetula*: Jean LeFèvre, *La Vieille ou les derniers amours d'Ovide: Poème français du XIVe siècle traduit du latin de*

Richard de Fournival par Jean LeFèvre, ed. Hippolyte Cocheris (Paris: Auguste Aubry, 1861), book 2, lines 2829–3042.

13. While this pattern illustrates Antoine Compagnon's notion of quotation as the defining labor of a text, it also is crucial to see it as a working out of the writer's past textual habits: *La Seconde Main: Ou, le travail de la citation* (Paris: Seuil, 1979), 36.

14. Renate Blumenfeld-Kosinski makes the case that in LeFèvre's argument the term "riote" applies equally powerfully to the discourse of men. I am grateful to her for sharing with me an early version of her essay "Jean LeFèvre's *Livre de Leesce*: Praise or Blame of Women?" *Speculum* 69, no. 3 (July 1994): 705–25.

15. In this sense, LeFèvre makes R. Howard Bloch's contention that "you are not only wrong, you also contradict yourself." *Medieval Misogyny*, 4.

16. Karen Pratt has argued similarly that the *Leesce* puts logic in the service of exploding the spurious analogies elaborated by the *Lamentations*. Many thanks for sharing with me her paper "Analogy or Logic, Authority or Experience? Rhetorical and Dialectical Strategies for and against Women."

17. In this, the *Leesce* corresponds well to Foucault's own analysis of power and desire. See *Power/Knowledge*, 59.

18. Such an analysis dovetails with commentaries in contemporaneous pastoral manuals extending all the way back to Gregory the Great's analysis that diagnose *mesdire* in terms of anger. See Casagrande and Vecchio, *Les Péchés de la langue*, 29, 224–45.

19. This is, of course, one of the main tenets of Luce Irigaray's critique of patriarchal reasoning: "toute théorie du 'sujet' aura toujours été appropriée au 'masculin.'" See Luce Irigaray, *Speculum de l'autre femme* (Paris: Minuit, 1974), 165.

20. The story of castration is a crucial but rare incident in medieval versions of Ovid's life; see Fausto Ghisalberti, "Medieval Biographies of Ovid," *Journal of the Warburg and Courthauld Institutes* 9 (1946): 32.

21. LeFèvre, *La Vieille*, book 2, 2087–2556. LeFèvre's translation of this biographical version of the *De vetula* never names Ovid's castration outright, but refers to it obliquely as *sa mutacioun* (7). It does expound at length on the biology and social status of the *castrato*. In an Aristotelian scientific language typical of the didactic treatises considered in chapter 1, it stigmatizes him as sexually indeterminate. In other words, it wields the conventional criteria that identify him as a natural abomination. On this figure, see Marie-Christine Pouchelle, "L'Hybride," *Nouvelle revue de psychanalyse* 7 (1973): 49–61. Given the incident of Ovid's own castration, LeFèvre's translation too bears all the traces of a poetics of self-blame.

22. Much ink has been spilled on the question of castration in medieval texts. Leupin calls it "the originary loss that is the primordial instance of metaphor." *Barbarolexis*, 95. R. Howard Bloch sees it linked paradoxically to the problems and potencies of language; *Etymologies and Genealogies: A*

Literary Anthropology of the French Middle Ages (Chicago: University of Chicago Press, 1983), 139–40. My interest here is to point out the way this myth about fear of women is deployed to excuse, if not to legitimate, a slanderous writing about them.

23. See John Freccero's discussion of the predominant Augustinian model of conversion; *Dante: The Poetics of Conversion,* ed. Rachel Jacoff (Cambridge, Mass.: Harvard University Press, 1986), 4–5.

24. Stewart goes on to make the case that the conversions posed, of the plagiarist or the forger, are "re-forms not of writing, but of authorial subjectivity." Susan Stewart, *Crimes of Writing: Problems in the Containment of Representation* (New York: Oxford University Press, 1991), 23.

25. "To everything he [Matheolus] can say about it, I respond without grief and without anger, thanks to the counsel of Leesce" (A tout quanqu'il en pourra dire Je respon sans dueil et sans ire, tout par le conseil de Leesce; lines 2319–21).

26. In fact, "Guillaume"'s sentence in the *Jugement dou Roy de Navarre* for having spoken badly of women is nothing less than to write "un lay . . . sans tenson," "une chanson," and "une balade" (lines 4182–83, 4184, 4189).

27. It is interesting to note that this formulation also displays the *engin* that is LeFèvre's typical signature: *forgier.* In other words, the site of the narrator's conversion is also the place where the author chooses to sign his own name. On this signature, see Hasenohr-Esnos, *Le Respit de la mort,* xv–xvi.

28. Christine considers the theory of female matter and of woman's creation in paradise in *Livre de la Cité des dames.* See Christine de Pizan, "The *Livre de la Cité des dames* of Christine de Pizan: A Critical Edition," 2 vols., ed. Maureen Lois Cheney Curnow (Ph.D. diss., Vanderbilt University, 1975), 1:651–53 (part 1, chap. 9). Like LeFèvre, she includes in her account of exemplary women: Semiramis (1:677–81; chap. 15), Panthisilea (1:694–701; chap. 19), Lambethe (1:682–83; chap. 16), Camilla (1:716–17; chap. 24), Carmen (1:747–49; chaps. 37–38), Medea (1:732–34; chap. 31), Sappho (1:728–30; chap. 30), Minerva (1:739–43; chap 34), the Sibyls (2:786–94; part 2, chaps. 1–3), and Cassandra (2:798–99; chap. 5).

29. I consider Martin LeFranc's work the paradigm (if not parody) of the sycophantic response because it claims to gather all the arguments in support of women circulating in the fourteenth and fifteenth centuries. Across five books, it narrates allegorically an academic disputation on women. It pits *Malebouche* (a *clerc/magister* figure) against a knightly *Champion,* creating a *clerc/chevalier* debate in reverse. It summarizes arguments on the composition of the female body (book 2), includes a critique of Jean de Meun's *Rose* (book 3) and a catalogue of virtuous women (book 4), and concludes with the crowning of the *Champion* as the victor (book 5). So encyclopedic is this tract that it was rarely read in full; such is the claim of the "Complainte du livre du Champion des Dames de maistre Martin LeFranc," ed. Gaston Paris, *Romania* 16 (1887): 383–437. For very much the same reasons, one suspects, the same

could be said today. The text remains unedited in its entirety. As Simone de Beauvoir suggested, the *Champion* is difficult to take in. *Le Deuxième Sexe*, 2 vols. (Paris: Gallimard, 1949), 1: 171. Only the first two books are available in *Le Champion des Dames*, ed. Piaget.

30. For other instances of this sexual definition of woman, see lines 3530–32, 3660, 3736–40, 3837–39, 3902–5.

31. Riley, *"Am I That Name?"* 10–13.

32. Jill Mann makes a similar point when she states: "Jehan LeFèvre's two works confirm the view that writing against women and then apologising for it is as often as not just a convenient way of manufacturing a literary subject; neither activity is evidence of a seriously held view of women." *Apologies to Women* (Cambridge: Cambridge University Press, 1991), 25.

33. On this formula as it was cited by numerous medieval commentators, see the exemplary discussion of the thirteenth-century canonist Hostiensis, *de iniurias et damno dato*, book 5, in his *Summa aurea*. See also R. H. Helmholz, *Select Cases on Defamation to 1600*, Publications of the Selden Society, 101 (London: The Selden Society, 1985), xix. For a discussion of the discursive problem posed by defamation, see Ann Rigney, "Fame and Defamation: Toward a Socio-pragmatics," *Semiotica* 99, no 1–2 (1994): 53–65.

34. *Corpus iuris canonici*, 2 vols., ed. A. Richter and A. Friedburg, (1879; Graz: Akademische Druck und Verlagsanstalt, 1959), 1: C. 5, q. 1, c. 1. There is a telling echo here between this punishment for defamation and LeFèvre's desire to be beaten (line 1559).

35. The catchphrase of this understanding was "reputation is personal dignity" (fama autem dignitas est). On this understanding, see Francesco Migliorino, *Fama e Infamia: Problemi della società medievale nel pensiero giuridico nei secoli XII e XIII* (Catania: Giannotta, 1985), 75.

36. "And whosoever says or does anything in order to diminish the reputation of another is considered to have done injury" (et quicumque causa minuendae opinionis alicuius aliquid fecerit vel dixerit; iniuriam tenetur). "In what way does injury happen: in three ways, by a thing, by words, and by letters [texts]" (Quot modis fiat iniuria. Trib. re, verbis, et litteris). Hostiensis, *Summa aurea*, 1717.

37. One telling index of this concern is the considerable space given the subject in contemporaneous *florilegia*. See, for instance, the dozens of citations concerning *fama* in the popular anthology circulating in fourteenth-century and fifteenth-century France, Thomas Hibernicus's *Manipulus florum*. See a later incunabulum version, (Piacenza: Jacobus de Tyela, 1483), fols. 64–64 verso. Among the authorities cited, Augustine is preeminent. See, for instance, his discussion of different Roman and Greek attitudes toward *fama* in literary or theatrical contexts: "For they [the Greeks] saw that their gods approved and enjoyed scurrilous language in plays, not only of men, but of the gods themselves, whether the infamous actions imputed to them were the fictions of poets or were their own iniquities commemorated and acted in the theaters" (cum viderent dis suis accepta et grata esse obprobria non tantum hominum, verum et ip-

sorum deorum in scaenicis fabulis, sive a poetis essent illa conficta, sive flagitia eorum vera commemorarentur et agerentur in theatris.) Augustine, *City of God*, book 2, chap. 9. Compare this with his discussion of the search for a good reputation (book 5, chap. 19) Significantly enough, this is a search that Augustine links explicitly with the passion for domination (*cupiditas dominationis*).

38. Thelma S. Fenster and Mary Carpenter Erler propose LeFèvre as a source for Christine's work: *Poems of Cupid, God of Love: Christine de Pizan's "Epistre au dieu d'amours" and "Dit de la rose," Thomas Hoccleve's "The Letter of Cupid"* (Leiden: E. J. Brill, 1990), 114–15. Rather than concern ourselves with the vexed problem of the origins of ideas, I would prefer to direct critical attention to the different ways LeFèvre and Christine capitalized on similar conceptions.

SIX: CHRISTINE'S WAY

1. *L'Epistre*, in *Oeuvres poétiques de Christine de Pisan*, 3 vols., ed. Maurice Roy (Paris: Firmin-Didot, 1886–96), 2:25.

2. *Le Débat sur le roman de la rose*, ed. Hicks. All references will be to this edition; all translations are mine. A complete English translation can be found in Joseph L. Baird and John R. Kane, *La Querelle de la Rose: Letters and Documents* North Carolina Studies in the Romance Languages and Literatures no. 199 (Chapel Hill: University of North Carolina Press, 1978).

3. See Marc Angenot's remarks on the structure of polemic: *La Parole pamphlétaire: Contribution à la typologie des discours modernes* (Paris: Payot, 1982), 38–39.

4. Kevin Brownlee distinguishes carefully between Christine's participation in the *Querelle* as a whole and her polemical transformation of it into a book. "Discourses of the Self: Christine de Pizan and the *Romance of the Rose*," *Romanic Review* 79, no. 1 (1988): 213–14. By "polemics" I mean to refer to both, insofar as one could not exist without the other.

5. The language of disputation runs straight through the letters of Christine and her various interlocutors, Jean de Montreuil, Gontier, and Pierre Col (Hicks, 7, 30). In modern discussions, this language has been effectively replaced by that of *querelle* (quarrel) or debate. For reasons of convenience, I adopt this more familiar term while reminding my readers that the *Querelle du Roman de la rose* fits into the categories of disputational forms I am investigating.

6. Jean-Claude Carron describes this circle aptly: "Nous ne sortons pas du champs de la parole . . . médisance, diffamation, injure ou louange: nom, renom, honneur, ou diffamation; dire, médire, dédire, interdire ou bénir." "Les Noms de l'honneur féminin à la Renaissance: Le nom tu et le non dit," *Poétique* 67 (September 1986): 273.

7. "Ce sont les hommes qui dénoncent l'honorabilité des filles et qui, par l'injure sexuelle, les condamnent à être 'diffamées.'" Gauvard, *"De Grace especial,"* 1:320.

8. See *City of God* book 2, chap. 9. For a discussion of the ways this Roman model was understood by medieval commentators, see Migliorino, *Fama e Infamia*, 148–49. On the model itself, see Peter Garnsey, *Social Status and Legal Privilege in the Roman Empire* (Oxford: Oxford University Press, 1970), 191–93. Paul Veyne offers a good analysis of the public regulation of defamation in "Le Folklore à Rome et les droits de la conscience publique sur la conduite individuelle," *Latomus* 42, no. 1 (January–March 1983): 3–30. I am grateful to Philippe Roussin for bringing this essay to my attention.

9. Fausto Ghisalberti, "Medieval Biographies of Ovid," 32.

10. In the late-medieval intellectual milieu of the *Querelle*, Cicero emerges alongside Aristotle as a key figure. In Étienne Gilson's description, "Dans les oeuvres de type scholastique, le nom propre de l'auteur le plus frequémment cité est celui d'Aristote; c'est encore l'*aetas aristoteliana*; dans celles du type que nous nommerons "humaniste," le nom qui revient sans cesse est celui de Cicéron: c'est déjà l'*aetas ciceroniana*." "Le Message de l'humanisme," in *Culture et politique en France à l'époque de l'humanisme et de la Renaissance*, ed. Franco Simone (Turin: Accademia delle Scienze, 1974), 4.

11. *Cicero: "De re publica," "De legibus,"* trans. Clinton Walker Keyes (Cambridge: Harvard University Press, 1948), 240–41; Cicero's fourth book was not known in the Middle Ages, although this particular passage was well known through Augustine's citation and commentary on it in the *City of God*, book 2, chap. 9. I quote it because it gets to the heart of the legal problem posed by defamatory poetry as medieval respondents would reckon with it. It is interesting to note that another translator renders the passage "si quis occentavisset sive carmen condidisset, quod infamiam faceret flagitiumve alteri" explicitly in terms of defamation: "the offense of making a pasquinade or composing a song which was defamatory or libelous." *Cicero: On the Commonwealth*, trans. George Holland Sabine and Stanley Barney Smith (New York: Bobbs Merrill, 1960), 240.

12. The whole passage reads: "But you say 'I do not condemn the author in all parts of the said book . . .' as if you wanted to say that you condemn him in what you take from it [the book], and make yourself judge after you have spoken by opinion and outrageous presumption" (Mais, fais tu, 'je ne condampne pas l'aucteur en toutes pars du dit livre . . .'; comme se tu voulsisses dire que tu le condampnes en ce en quoy tu le reprens, et te fais juge, aprés ce que tu as parlé par oppinion ou presumpcion oultrageuse; Hicks, 99–100).

13. "Therefore they act up, as Lactantius said, and they cut in so as not to hear: 'They close their eyes lest they would see the light that we bring,' observing the customs of the Jews against Our Savior, according to which enemies are made judges" (Obstrepunt igitur, ut ait Lactantius, et intercidunt ne audiunt: 'oculos suos opprimunt ne lumen videant quod offerimus,' morem Judeorum adversus Salvatorum Nostrum observantes, penes quem inimici facti sunt judices"; Hicks, 34). This startling comparison between Christine and the Jews as heretics shows one powerful technique of stigmatizing her work. Nadia Margolis reviews Christine's very different characterization of

the Jews in "Christine de Pizan and the Jews: Political and Poetic Implications," in *Politics, Gender, and Genre: The Political Thought of Christine de Pizan* (Boulder: University of Colorado Press, 1992), 53–73.

14. Grover Carr Furr III, "The Quarrel of the *Roman de la Rose* and Fourteenth-Century Humanism" (Ph.D. diss., Princeton University, 1979), 227. Furr puts forward the case for the inevitable professional defensiveness of the French humanists endeavoring to carve out a space for themselves in the legal and notorial circles of the Parisian court. "Their solidarity," he writes, "is reflected in a desire for reconciliation even in serious disputes, an attempt to keep all disagreements within the group" (167). That Col and Montreuil escalated the *Querelle de la Rose* offers another sign of their refusal to consider Christine's entry into their circle.

15. On this model, see Emile Benveniste, *Le Vocabulaire des institutions indo-européennes*, 2 vols. (Paris: Minuit, 1969), 2:143–51. See also Georges Dumézil's analysis of the mythology undergirding the Roman censor in *Servius et la fortune: Essai sur la fonction sociale de louange et de blâme et sur les éléments indo-européens du cens romain* (Paris: Gallimard, 1943), 173–76.

16. The censor's power derived, of course, from Roman law, which according to medieval commentators represented "the holiest civil wisdom" (*res sanctissima civilis sapientia*). On this formula in medieval commentary, see Pierre Legendre, *L'Amour du censeur: Essai sur l'ordre dogmatique* (Paris: Seuil, 1974), 103.

17. Benveniste reminds us that "il est une notion complémentaire de *censor*, qui s'y trouve constamment associée dans les emplois latins, et que notre définition implique: c'est celle d'autorité'; *censeo* est très souvent employé avec *auctor* et *auctoritas*. . . . On qualifie de *auctor*, dans tous les domaines, celui qui 'promeut,' qui prend une initiative, qui est le premier à produire une activité, celui qui fonde, celui qui garantit, et finalement 'l'auteur.'" *Le Vocabulaire*, 148, 150.

18. I am referring here to the internecine political rivalries dividing Paris between the Armagnacs, the Burgundians, and the royal faction. On the horizon as well, there is the specter of the papal schism and the prospect of an English occupation. In this climate, a polemic like the *Querelle de la Rose* flourishes particularly well.

19. Daniel Poirion's view is emblematic here; see "Les Mots et les choses selon Jean de Meun," *L'Information littéraire* 26 (January–February 1974): 9.

20. The passage continues: "And shame comes about and is visible in a similar way as does fear when a person is in danger. For those who feel shame blush, and those who feel fearful of death go pale" (Et vercunde se parfait and se monstre semblablement comme fait la paour que l'en a en perilz. Car ceulz qui ont vercunde rougissent, et ceulz qui ont paour de mort palissent). *Maistre Nicole Oresme: Le Livre de Ethiques d'Aristote*, ed. Alfred Douglas Menut (New York: G. E. Stechert, 1940), 273. The terms *honte* and *vercunde* have slightly different significances, but in this context they both refer to that innate feeling of modesty.

21. In Sandra Lee Bartky's analysis of shame, it functions as the mark of women's "pervasive affective attunement to the social environment." While this is often interpreted as the sign of women's subordination in that environment, it can also signal their critical understanding of the conventions ruling it: *Femininity and Domination*, 85.

22. Christine de Pizan, *Le Livre de la Mutacion de Fortune par Christine de Pisan*, 4 vols., ed. Suzanne Solente (Paris: A. & J. Picard, 1959), 2:38. It is striking to notice that the *Mutacion* includes many such reflections on the problem of defamation; see, for instance, lines 5301–52, 5388–91, 5770–5802, 6975–88.

23. "This said work could better be called idleness than a useful work in my judgment" (celle dicte euvre, qui mieulx puet estre appellee droicte oysiveté que oevre utile, à mon jugement; Hicks, 12).

24. Pierre-Yves Badel exhaustively reviews the indebtedness of Jean de Montreuil and the Col brothers to humanist figures such as Boccaccio, Petrarch, and Coluccio Salutati. See *"Le Roman de la rose" au XIVᵉ siècle: Étude de la réception de l'oeuvre* (Geneva: Droz, 1980), 420–26. See also A. Coville, *Gontier et Pierre Col et l'humanisme en France au temps de Charles VI* (Paris: Droz, 1934), 147.

25. On this debate, see Marc Fumaroli, *L'Age de l'éloquence: Rhétorique et "res litteraria" de la Renaissance au seuil de l'époque classique* (Geneva: Droz, 1980). Fumaroli emphasizes how the argument for the civic responsibility of eloquence is consistently advanced as an *imitatio ciceroniana* (110–13).

26. This trope also represents Christine's parting shot about the humanists' belief in the uplifting, transformative power of poetry. The sublime, in this case, is a tradition of defamatory feminine representation made over falsely.

27. "Mais accusacions, quereles, et complaintes sont faites seulement ou mesmement et principalement en amistie qui est pour utilite. Et c'est chose raysonnable." *Maistre Nicole Oresme: Le Livre de Ethiques*, 446. While Jean de Montreuil seems to share much the same view when he claims that truth is born of a dispute, "like gold from a furnace" (Hicks, 30), as we have seen, Christine sees this gold as little more than dung.

28. This conjunction is underscored by the dates Christine incorporates in the two works: 2 October 1402 for the *Querelle* (Hicks, 150) and 5 October 1402 (Christine de Pizan, *Le Livre du chemin de long estude*, ed. Robert Püschel [Berlin: Damköhler, 1881], 8). Charity Cannon Willard maintains that the *Chemin* was begun immediately after Christine finished her most vehement rebuttal of Col: *Christine de Pizan: Her Life and Her Works* (New York: Persea Books, 1984), 105–6. All references to the *Chemin de long estude* will be to Robert Püschel's edition. Andrea Tarnowski's edition with Lettres gothiques is forthcoming.

29. Several critics have commented on this shift. Joël Blanchard, for instance, considers the *Querelle* as "un détournement d'intérêt": "Compilation et légitimation au XVᵉ siècle," *Poétique* 74 (April 1988): 141. And he recognizes the way Christine's *Mutacion de Fortune*, *Chemin de long estude*, and

Lavision-Christine represent a new intellectual and poetic departure: "Christine de Pizan: Les raisons de l'histoire," *Le Moyen Age* 92, no. 3–4 (1986): 417. Nadia Margolis comments on the turning point of moral concerns: "Christine de Pizan: The Poetess as Historian," *Journal of the History of Ideas* 47, no. 3 (July–September 1986): 366. So too does Charity Cannon Willard, *Christine de Pizan*, 73, 100. Our challenge lies in interpreting the affinities between the *Querelle* and Christine's subsequent efforts that make such a shift possible.

30. Glynis M. Cropp surveys the extent of their affinities in "Boèce et Christine de Pizan," *Le Moyen Age* 87, no. 3–4 (1981): 387–418.

31. Christine de Pizan, *Lavision-Christine: Introduction and Text*, ed. Sister Mary Louis Towner (Washington, D.C.: Catholic University of America, 1932), 157, lines 19–22. It is clear from the subsequent passages the extent to which Christine identifies with the unjustly defamed Boethius: "Wasn't it said of me all across town that I was in love . . . for so it is that such reputations become common knowledge, and often erroneously, through the great contact and commerce between people together, and by conjecture and what seems true" (ne fut il pas dit de moy par toute la ville que ie amoye par amours . . . car comme telz renommees communement vienent et souvent a tort par grant accointance et frequentacion les personnes ensemble et par coniectures et couleurs voir semblables; lines 22–27). Christine Reno and Liliane Dulac are currently preparing a new edition of *Lavision-Christine*.

32. The phrase is Bernard McGinn's: *"Teste David cum Sibylla*: The Significance of the Sibylline Tradition in the Middle Ages," in *Women of the Medieval World: Essays in Honor of John Hine Mundy*, ed. Julius Kirshner and Suzanne F. Wemple (Oxford: Oxford University Press, 1985), 17. See also Josiane Haffen, *Contribution à l'étude de la Sibylle médiévale* (Paris: Belles Lettres, 1984), 13–20, and Maureen Quilligan's discussion of the Sibylline example in other works of Christine, *The Allegory of Female Authority: Christine de Pizan's "Cité des Dames"* (Ithaca, N.Y.: Cornell University Press, 1991), 105.

33. "I am known by my voice alone; my voice the Fates will leave me" (Voce tamen noscar; vocemque mihi fata relinquent; Ovid, *Metamorphoses*, 2 vols., trans. Frank Justus Miller (London: Heinemann, 1916), 2:14, 153).

34. On Christine's double bind of indebtedness and rivalry with Dante, see Kevin Brownlee, *Discourses of the Self: Autobiography and Literary Models in Christine de Pizan*, forthcoming.

35. Un autre chemin plus perfaict
 Y a, qui des mains Dieu fu fait. . . .
 Qu'il maine cellui qui le passe
 Si hault qu'il voit Dieu face a face.
 C'est la Voye de Paradis.
  Mutacion de Fortune, lines 3243–44,
    3251–52, 3273

There is another more perfect way, made by the hands of God . . . that leads the one who takes it so high that he sees God face to face. It is the route to Paradise.

36. John Freccero puts it best when he observes: "By attempting to represent poetically that which is by definition beyond representation, this *cantica* achieves what had scarcely seemed possible before (even for the poet of the *Inferno* and the *Purgatorio*) and has remained the ultimate aspiration of poets ever since." *Dante*, 209–10.

37. This movement away from the public space of the commonwealth and then back toward its center is analogous to the movement in the *Querelle*. Whereas Christine's defamer begins from a negative position outside and makes her way to the central position of the *censor* in the polis, in the *Chemin* she reaches the positive position outside, Paradise, and makes her way back to the polis. This pattern also resembles the movement in Boethius's *Consolatio* between the ethereal reaches of theoretical philosophy and the ground level of practical philosophy. Boethius, "*Tractates*," "*De consolatione philosophiae*," ed. and trans. H. F. Stewart, E. K. Rand, and S. J. Tester (Cambridge, Mass: Harvard University Press, 1973), I, i, 19–22.

38. Et les vrayes hystoires anciennes de la Bible,

> qui ne puet mençonge estre,
>
> Nous racontent qu'en Paradis terrestre
>
> Fu formée femme premierement
>
> Non pas l'omme.
>
> *L'Epistre au dieu d'amours*, lines 604–8

39. It is interesting to note that Oresme's treatise, *Le Livre de divinacions*, critiques this notion of judicial astrology on the grounds that it risks harming the body politic: "Such a thing is more dangerous for persons of this estate, such as princes and lords, to whom belong public governance" (telle chose est plus perilleuse a personnes d'estat comme sont princes et seigneurs auxquels appartient le gouvernement publique). G. W. Coopland, *Nicole Oresme and the Astrologers: A Study of His Livre de Divinacions*, (Cambridge, Mass.: Harvard University Press, 1952), 50.

40. See Charity Cannon Willard, "Christine de Pizan: The Astrologer's Daughter," in *Mélanges à la mémoire de Franco Simone: France et Italie dans la culture européenne* (Geneva: Slatkine, 1980), 95–111.

41. What counts is "ce passage de qualification au cours duquel le poète se constitue comme sujet disant la vérité en évoquant le plus souvent l'autorité qu'il detient et qui lui confère une pré-eminence pour parler." Joël Blanchard, "L'Entrée du poète dans le champ politique au XVe siècle," *Annales E.S.C.* 41, no. 1 (January–February 1986): 47–48. Here Blanchard is evidently drawing on a Foucauldian notion of *le franc-parler*: the truth-speaking claim.

42. Michèle LeDoeuff, "Women, Reason, Etc.," *Differences* 2, no. 3 (fall 1990): 6. In light of LeDoeuff's point that women involved in learning pay a price, it is interesting to consider Christine's becoming a man in the *Mutacion de Fortune* (lines 149–53). That the representation of her own gender oscillates in her writing at just the time when Christine is beginning to wrestle with philosophical discourse suggests how difficult a task it is.

43. On this problem see Susan Groag Bell, "Christine de Pizan: Humanism and the Problem of a Studious Woman," *Feminist Studies* 3, no. 3–4 (1976): 174, and Anthony Grafton and Lisa Jardine, *From Humanism to the Humanities: Education and the Liberal Arts in Fifteenth- and Sixteenth-Century Europe* (Cambridge, Mass.: Harvard University Press, 1986), 441.

44. In this respect, Christine's texts confront the Aristotelian conundrum as Elizabeth Spelman describes it: "Without their work, the polis could not exist, but they [women] do not participate in the activities of the polis." *Inessential Woman: Problems of Exclusion in Feminist Thought* (Boston: Beacon Press, 1988), 38.

45. The *florilegium* model is, of course, the epitome of the clerical method of compilation that Joël Blanchard describes, in Christine's hands, as "à la fois une appropriation et un affrontement. C'est interventionniste." "Compilation et légitimation au XVe siècle," 153.

46. Jacqueline Cerquiglini-Toulet describes this pleasure in learning in another way as "ce rapport boulimique, anthropophagique au savoir." "L'Etrangère," *Revue des langues romanes* 92, no. 2 (1988): 243. See also her reflections on this pleasure in *La Couleur de la mélancholie*, 67, 73–80.

47. "Si vero sine sapientia habes, docet te Tullius talem eloquentiam civitatibus ac rebus publicis esse pernitiosam." I am quoting here the version of Nicolas de Clamanges, an Avignon humanist, considered by many, including the Parisians, to be the exemplary humanist. Cicero, *Opera omnia*, ed. Johannes Lydius (Lugdini Butavorum, 1613), 356.

48. The text is found on fols. 1–27. This passage is quoted and mistranscribed by Mathilde Laigle, *Le Livre des trois vertus de Christine de Pisan et son milieu historique et littéraire* (Paris: H. Champion, 1912), 39.

49. As Pierre Bourdieu puts it: "Il n'est pas d'agent social qui ne prétende, dans la mesure de ses moyens, à ce pouvoir de nommer et de faire le monde en le nommant: ragots, calomnies, médisances, insultes, éloges, accusations, critiques, polémiques, louanges ne sont que la petite monnaie quotidienne des actes solennels et collectifs de nomination, célébrations ou condemnations, qui incombent aux autorités universellement reconnues." *Ce que parler veut dire*, 99.

SEVEN: A LIBELOUS AFFAIR

1. This conception of harm (*laesio*) inflicted by words was divided into two subcategories: slander, the unjust revelation of a hidden charge (*detractio est revelatio injusta criminis occulti*) and calumny, the revelation of a false accusation (*calumnia est revelatio criminis falsi*). For a résumé of these medieval canon legal formulations, see *Dictionnaire de droit canonique*, 7 vols., ed. R. Naz (Paris: Letouzey et Ané, 1949), s.v. *diffamation*, and Helmholz, *Select Cases on Defamation to 1600*, xvi–xxvi.

2. *Corpus iuris civilis: Codex Iustinianus*, book 9, xxxvi; 2:387. The translation that follows is taken from *The Civil Law*, 15:61–62.

3. Justinian's article appears verbatim in Gratian's *Decretum*, C. 5, q. 1, c. 3; *Corpus iuris canonici*, 1:545. The rubrics for the *causae* read: "He who neglects to pronounce good on the reputation of another in writing shall be beaten" ([F]lagelletur qui scripta in alterius famam probare neglexerit) and "Those who place defamatory material in a church shall be anathematized" (Anathematizentur qui famosos libellos in ecclesia ponunt).

4. For Chartier's texts, as well as the first letters in the *Querelle*, see *The Poetical Works of Alain Chartier*, ed. James C. Laidlaw (Cambridge: Cambridge University Press, 1974), 328–78. References are to this edition; all translations are mine.

5. See Piaget, *"La Belle Dame sans merci* et ses imitations," Romania 30 (1901): 28–35.

6. Piaget's reaction is paradigmatic: "Faut-il prendre au sérieux cette querelle ridicule? Les courtisanes ont-elles réellement monté une cabale contre le secrétaire du roi?" *"La Belle Dame sans merci* et ses imitations," 35.

7. Pierre Champion inaugurated this critical tack by naming the three *Belle Dame* respondents as Jeanne Louvet (Mme de Bothéon), Marie Louvet (Mme de Vaubonnais) and Catherine de l'Isle-Bouchard; see his *Histoire poétique du quinzième siècle*, 2 vols. (Paris: H. Champion, 1923), 1:71.

8. One telling example involves the account of several *damoiselles* attending Isabeau of Bavaria who were imprisoned for slander. See *Chronique du religieux de Saint-Denys contenant le règne de Charles VI, de 1380 à 1422*, 6 vols., ed. and trans. Louis François Bellaguet and Amable-Guillaume-Prosper Brugière, baron de Barante, (Paris: Crapelet, 1839–52), 3:268–73. For another contemporaneous version of this exemplum, see Michel Félibien and D. Guy-Alexis Lobineau, *Histoire de la ville de Paris*, 5 vols. (Paris: G. Desprez & J. Desessartz, 1725), 2:765.

9. Yann Grandeau outlines this exemplum as it is propounded by Jacques Legrand and Jean Juvenal des Ursins, "De Quelques Dames qui ont servi la reine Isabeau de Bavière," *Bulletin philologique et historique (jusqu'à 1610) du Comité des travaux historiques et scientifiques* (1975): 159–62. It is this exemplum that Christine de Pizan seeks to overturn with her recommendations to women at court concerning the dangers of *mesdire*: "So with this it is said similarly that women at court should be on their guard not to blame or defame one another because of the sin and other causes that can result from it. Further, whosoever defames another deserves to be defamed himself" (Avec ce, les femmes de court se doivent garder, semblablement que dit est, de ne blasmer ne diffamer l'une l'autre, tant pour le pechié et aultres causes ja assignees comme aussi que qui diffame autre, dessert que lui meismes soit diffaméz. *Le Livre des trois vertus*, ed. Charity Cannon Willard with Eric Hicks (Paris: H. Champion, 1989), 146.

10. I take exception with Leonard W. Johnson's view that it involves "a literary game not to be taken too seriously, except in a literary context." *Poets as Players: Theme and Variation in Late Medieval French Poetry* (Stanford, Calif.: Stanford University Press, 1990), 143–44.

11. *Poèmes d'Alain Chartier,* ed. James Laidlaw (Paris: Union générale d'éditions, 1987), 25.

12. From the Justinian Code to Gratian, through most every medieval legal commentator, defamation falls under the heading *de iniuriis*; see *Corpus iuris civilis,* book 9, xxv–xxxvi, and *Corpus iuris canonici* C. v, q. 1, c. 1–3.

13. As William W. Kibler remarks, this separatedness has been the interpretative key, taken by some critics in the past as the sign of her bourgeois identity and by others as the sign of her modernity: "The Narrator as Key to Alain Chartier's *La Belle Dame sans mercy,*" *The French Review* 52, no. 5 (April 1979): 716.

14. We should be careful to note the semantic evolution of the term *franchise*. In much love literature of the high Middle Ages it signifies the courtly virtue of nobility of spirit, as in the *Roman de la rose* (line 942). But by the later Middle Ages it increasingly means liberty or independence. In this sense, *franchise* can be specifically linked to the *damoiselles d'honneur* with whom the respondents are associated. At the time of the *Querelle de la Belle Dame* they were seeking *franchise* as employees of the court; Charles VI had issued decrees in 1411–12 offering to "the officers, servants, and relations, noble and nonnoble, all the liberties, exemptions, and freedom [*franchise*] which ours enjoy and employ" (les officiers, serviteurs, et familiers nobles et non nobles toutes les libertez, exempcions et franchise dont les nostres joïssent et usent). On this point, see Yann Grandeau, "De Quelques Dames," 145.

15. Only two years earlier, ca. 1421–22, Chartier depicted *la France* in this manner: "a lady who maintains her dignified bearing and nobility that signified her excellent pedigree. But she was in such suffering and so disconsolate that she seemed like a lady fallen from a state of high honor, given what her condition showed. And in her appearance she was severely distressed and troubled by a great misfortune and pain to come" (une dame dont le hault port et seigneury maintien signifioit sa tresexcellente extraction, mais tant fut dolente et esplouree que bien sembloit dame decheue de plus hault honneur que pour lors son estat ne demonstroit. Et bien apparissoit a son semblant que forment feust espoventee et doubteuse de plus grant maleurté et douleur advenir). Alain Chartier, *Le Quadrilogue invectif,* ed. Eugénie Droz (Paris: H. Champion, 1923), 6. Given the desperate political stakes at the time, it is hardly far-fetched to discern in the homology *la femme france* another sign of the fight over who and how to represent France. On this development, see Colette Beaune's analysis, *The Birth of an Ideology: Myths and Symbols of Nation in Late-Medieval France,* trans. Susan Ross Huston, ed. Fredric L. Cheyette (Berkeley: University of California Press, 1991), 289–92.

16. For another instance of this canonical figure, see Alan of Lille's twelfth-century account: "The slanderer resembles a scorpion in that a scorpion approaches the face of a virgin and consequently emits a sting and inflicts stinging injury from above. So too the slanderer. He offers favorable words face to face with men and then on the sly he concludes with the sting of a slanderer. And as if wounding them from above, he disparages the better

ones" (Detractor scorpionis gerit imaginem, quia sicut scorpio praefert virginis vultum, et consequenter emittit aculeum, et a superiori vulnus infert acuatum; sic detractor in facie hominum verba favorabilia proponit, et in occulto aculeum detractionis concludit, et quasi a superiori vulnerans, melioribus detrahit). Alan of Lille, *Summa de arte praedicatoria*, printed in *PL* 210: 166B–C.

17. The discussion of the thirteenth-century canonist William of Drogheda will serve as a representative example of the high-medieval focus on these terms: "I lodge a complaint against N., who has committed an injury against me; namely, by calling me a prostitute's son, or thief or robber or farmer's son, he has written a defamatory pamphlet about me, or composed a defamatory song, or sung an abusive ditty about me; such an injury I would not want spread about. Since he had said or sung or written injuriously about me for a hundred pounds of silver, I seek to be given those hundred pounds, or I seek this injury to be made manifest through the action of *iniuria*; and I take civil action . . . out of this same injury criminal action can be taken" (Conqueror de N., qui talem iniuriam [mihi intulit], scilicet vocando me filium meretricis vel furem vel latronem vel filium rustici vel scripsit de me famosum libellum vel composuit carmen famosum vel cantavit de me malum cantilenum quam iniuriam [vulgari] nollem, quod mihi dixisset vel cantasset vel scripsisset pro centum libris argenti, quas peto dari vel praestari actione iniuriaram; et ago civiliter. . . . Potest etiam agi criminaliter ex eadem iniuria). See Ludwig Wahrmund, *Quellen zur Geschichte des Römisch-Kanonischen Processes im Mittelalter*, 2 vols. (Innsbruck: Wagner, 1913), 2:2, 2:219.

18. My point here fits well with Kathy Eden's contention that the "influence of Greco-Roman legal theory on Christian ethics, generally, and on Augustinian ethics, in particular . . . bears significantly on the development of Christian literary theory." *Poetic and Legal Fictions in the Aristotelian Tradition* (Princeton: Princeton University Press, 1986), 138.

19. For a characteristically trenchant and witty assessment of this debate, see Stanley Fish, *There's No Such Thing as Free Speech and It's a Good Thing Too* (New York: Oxford University Press, 1994), 102–119.

20. She argues that "to reassert atomistic linear causality as a sine qua non of injury . . . is to refuse to respond to the true nature of this specific kind of harm." Catharine A. MacKinnon, *Feminism Unmodified: Discourses on Life and Law* (Cambridge: Harvard University Press, 1987), 157. It is interesting to note that MacKinnon's most recent arguments concerning the legal actionability of pornography explore the concept of verbal injury in the specific terms of defamation: "Pornography as Defamation and Discrimination," *Boston University Law Review* 71, no. 5 (November 1991): 793–815.

21. On this point see Wolfgang Iser, "Fictionalizing: The Anthropological Dimension of Literary Fictions," *New Literary History* 21, no. 4 (autumn 1990): 940–41.

22. The *Excusacioun* begins as a direct address to women:

Mes dames et mes damoiselles,
Se Dieu vous doint joye prouchaine,
Escoutés les durez nouvelles
Que j'ouÿ le jour de l'estraine.

(lines 1–4)

My ladies and young women, If God grants you joy soon again, Listen to the difficult news I heard on New Year's day.

But it quickly establishes the requisite dream frame:

Ce jour m'avint en sommeillant,
Actendant le soleil levant,
Moitié dormant, moitié veillant.

(lines 9–11)

That day it happened that I was drowsy, waiting for the sun to rise, half asleep, half awake.

23. "And I say that master Jean de Meun introduced characters in his book and makes each character speak in a manner that befits him; this is known, *le jaloux* like a jealous man, *la vieille* like an old woman, and so on with the others. And it is too wrongheaded to say that the author finds evil in woman as the jealous man claims, in keeping with his character" ([E]t dy que maistre Jehan de Meung en son livre introduisy personnaiges, et fait chascun personnaige parler selonc qui luy appartient: c'est assavoir le Jaloux comme jaloux, la Vielle come la Vielle, et pareillement des autres. Et est trop mal pris de dire que l'aucteur tiengne les maulx estre en fame que le Jalous, en faisant son personnaige, propose; Hicks, 100).

24. Christine de Pizan hints at this shift in her critique of the *Rose* when she maintains: "Since human understanding can barely reach to the heights of a clear knowledge of earthly truths and understand hidden things . . . so it happens that one determines imagined things more believable through opinion rather than through sure science" (Pour ce que entendement humain ne puet estre eslevé jusques a haultesse de clere cognoissance d'enterine veritey entendre des choses occultes . . . convient par oppinion plus que de certainne science determiner des choses ymaginees plus voirsemblables; Hicks, 115).

25. On this revival see Gilbert Ouy, "Paris: L'un des principaux foyers de l'humanisme en Europe au début du XVe siècle," *Bulletin de la société d'histoire de Paris et de l'Ile de France* 94–95 (1967–68): 95, Eden, *Poetic and Legal Fictions*, 5, and Fumaroli, *L'Age de l'éloquence*, 18–19.

26. It is important to stress the difference between the issue of figurative speech and that of literary discourse. On this point see John Searle, "The Logical Status of Fictional Discourse," *New Literary History* 6, no. 2 (winter 1975), 320–21.

27. Boccaccio, *Genealogie deorum gentilium*, ed. Vincenzo Romano (Bari: Laterza, 1951), book 14; Petrarch, *Collatio Laureationis*, chap. 9. Stephanie H. Judd makes the compelling argument that such humanistic formulae and the distinctiveness of "literary" writing that they establish keep us from acknowledging the violence underwriting many humanistic narratives as well as "the judicial origins of our own practice of literary criticism." *Chaste Thinking: The Rape of Lucretia and the Birth of Humanism* (Bloomington: Indiana University Press, 1989), 2.

28. See Pierre-Yves Badel, *"Le Roman de la rose" au XIVᵉ siècle*, 419–23.

29. Daniel Poirion's remark exemplifies this pattern of identification: "Elles [Jeanne, Katherine, Marie] demandent que l'auteur fasse amende honorable. *L'Excusacioun* ne les a pas satisfaites; mais elles l'ont mal lue." "Lectures de la *Belle Dame sans mercy*," *Mélanges de langue et de littérature médiévales offerts à Pierre Le Gentil* (Paris: S.E.D.E.S., 1973), 693.

30. Let us not forget that the *Belle Dame* was by far the most popular of Chartier's works across Europe, being rapidly translated into English, Italian, and Catalan; See Piaget *"La Belle Dame sans mercy* et ses imitations," 25–26.

31. Louis Douët d'Arcq transcribes a variety of statements from the Châtelet registers in *Choix de pièces inédites relatives au règne de Charles VI*, 2 vols. (Paris: Jules Renouard, 1863–64), esp. 2:51, 2:131–32, 2:180–81, 2:185–87, 2:237–38, 2:270–72.

32. One remarkable case involves the rector of the University of Paris in the company of various *magistri* who sought justice at court on 19 July 1404 "for the abuse that is alleged to have been done last Monday past to the said University" (sur l'injure que on dit avoir este faicte lundi derrenier passe à ladicte Université; Douët d'Arcq, *Choix de pièces inédites*, 1:261–64).

33. In Peter Shervey Lewis's view, during Charles VI's reign, "litigation was incessant." *Later Medieval France*, 142. On this pattern of litigiousness, see Bernard Guenée, *Tribunaux et gens de justice dans le bailliage de Senlis à la fin du moyen âge (vers 1300–vers 1550)*, Publications de la Faculté des lettres de l'Université de Strasbourg no. 144 (Paris: Belles Lettres, 1963).

34. Douët d'Arcq, *Choix de pièces inédites*, 2:131, 2:190. This pattern suggests the growing importance of questions of personal honor that would dominate early-modern Europe. On this phenomenon, see Kristen B. Neuschel, *Word of Honor: Interpreting Noble Culture in Sixteenth-Century France* (Ithaca, N.Y.: Cornell University Press, 1989), 93–101.

35. Helmholz, *Select Cases on Defamation to 1600*, xiv.

36. Alfred Soman, "Press, Pulpit, and Censorship in France Before Richelieu," *Proceedings of the American Philosophical Society* 120, no. 6 (December 1976): 445. England offers an analogous picture according to J. A. Sharpe, *Defamation and Sexual Slander in Early Modern England: The Church Courts at York* (York: University of York, Borthwick Institute of Historical Research, 1980), 3.

37. In the surviving record, there are no individual women who bring complaints on their own, although by this period, we should remember, the

requirement of a man's intervention had been, for all intents and purposes, superseded. That men and women sued together was often a matter of formality. See Annick Porteau-Bitker, "Criminalité et délinquance féminines dans le droit pénal des XIIIᵉ et XIVᵉ siècles," *Revue historique de droit français et étranger* 58, no. 1 (January–March 1980): 24.

38. For a general etymological survey of *libelle* see Marc Angenot, *La Parole pamphlétaire*, 379–80.

39. This expression from the *Corpus iuris civilis* (book 9, xxxvi, *de famosis libellis*) occurs in Gratian's *Decretum* (C. v, q. 1, c. 3) from whence it passes into every medieval legal commentary.

40. Jean de Montreuil's usage epitomizes this pattern: "I would like my error, which they would consider not a vice, but a sin and heresy (and this I cannot fail to have uttered), to be amended and corrected by you and in letters from you and the same lord and father, lest my error ever be related to my correctors and yours too, I might add, by vicious and vain rumor, and they construct from it charges of defamation (*libellos diffamatorios*)" (Meum tamen errorem, qui non vicium putarent, sed peccatum et heresim (et illum non eructasse non possum), emendari et corrigi tuis et eiusdem domini mei et patris in litteris a te velim, ne, si vento aut aura levissima ad hos usque correctores meos—et tuos, dico—relatum si[t], libellos diffamatorios inde struant). Jean de Montreuil, *Opera*, 2 vols., ed. Ezio Ornato (Turin: G. Giappichelli, 1963), 1:39.

41. Carla Bozzolo and Hélène Loyau, *La Cour amoureuse, dite de Charles VI: Étude et édition critique des sources manuscrites*, 3 vols. (Paris: Léopard d'Or, 1982–92), 1:42.

42. For a brief description of this meaning, see *Dictionnaire de droit canonique*, s.v. *libelle*. For a history of the initial step in legal procedure it represents, see Artur Steinwenter, "Die Anfänge des Libellprozesses," *Studia et documenta historiae et juris* 1 (1935): 32–52.

43. Philippe de Beaumanoir, *Philippe de Remi, de Beaumanoir: Coûtumes de Beauvaisis*, 2 vols., ed. Amédée Salmon (Paris: A. Picard et fils, 1899–1900), 1:98.

44. Philippe de Beaumanoir, *The Coûtumes de Beauvaisis of Philippe de Beaumanoir*, trans. F. R. P. Akehurst (Philadelphia: University of Pennsylvania Press, 1992), 76.

45. "Liber, ibis in urbem," (Go, little book, go into the city); *Lamentations*, line 1; LeFèvre's translation, lines 83–84. Whereas this turn of phrase begins Ovid's work in exile, the *Tristia*, its invocation here has as much to do with the crucial place and function of texts in the civic sector as many late-fourteenth-century writers understood it. This becomes clear in a subsequent passage that LeFèvre inserts in Matheolus's text:

> La grant doleur dont je labeure,
> (Je ne suis a repos nulle heure)
> Afin que, quant ils orront dire,
> Ils ne se puissent escondire
> Ne excuser par ignorance.

Fay publier par toute France
Que nul, s'il n'a ou corps la rage,
Plus ne se mette en mariage,
Et mesmement par bigamie.
                    (lines 95–103)

I labor under considerable pain—finding repose at no hour—so that when they'll hear speak of it, they will not be able to avoid it, or excuse themselves through ignorance. I am having it publicized through all of France, that no one, no matter what his bodily lusts, should engage in marriage, or similarly, in bigamy.

46. Invoking *infamia* is no idle rhetorical gesture, since by the mid-thirteenth century there could be no greater penalty. For the development of the doctrine of infamy, see Edward Peters, *Torture* (Oxford: Basil Blackwell, 1985), 45–53.

47. Christine de Pizan, *Le Livre de la Cité des dames*, ed. Curnow, 1:624.

48. For contemporaneous incidents of book burning, see Paul Lacroix, *Histoire de l'imprimerie et des arts qui se rattachent à la typographie* (Geneva: Slatkine Reprints, 1971), 26, and Félibien and Lobineau, *Histoire de la ville de Paris*, 4:563.

49. R. I. Moore considers the social manipulation that went into identifying the heretic: *The Formation of a Persecuting Society*, 144–47.

50. The naming of "our advocates Dessarteaulx and Chastel" has been the subject of much speculation since "Chastel" was the name of Christine de Pizan's son, who served as a lawyer and notary in the Parisian court as well as at the Dauphin's court at Bourges. But just as we must be wary of identifying "Jeanne, Katherine, and Marie" as individual *damoiselles d'honneur*, we must take care in identifying M. Chastel. This is all the more important in light of the symbolic charge of the name "chastel" and its use as a figure for women.

51. The earliest, the *Parlement d'amour* of Baudet Harenc remains unedited. Of the ten known manuscripts, I consulted Paris, B.N. f. fr. 1727, fols. 136–44 verso. Arthur Piaget comments on the *Parlement*: "*La Belle Dame sans mercy* et ses imitations," *Romania* 30 (1901) 317–20. The rest of the poems are edited by him in the ongoing series of articles of the same name: "La Dame leale en amours," *Romania* 30 (1901): 323–51; "La Cruelle Femme en amour" *Romania* 31 (1902): 322–49; "Les Erreurs du jugement de la Belle Dame sans mercy," *Romania* 33 (1904): 183–99; and "Le Jugement du povre triste amant banny," *Romania* 34 (1905): 379–416.

52. This is a debate that Wesley Trimpi surveys exhaustively in "The Ancient Hypothesis of Fiction: An Essay on the Origins of Literary Theory," *Traditio* 27 (1971), 1–78, and "The Quality of Fiction: The Rhetorical Transmission of Literary Theory," *Traditio* 30 (1974), 1–118; esp. 108–18.

53. In Ernst H. Kantorowicz's commentary on this formula, he surmises "the jurists not only fell in with the literary and artistic theories, but may have had even the function of pathfinders, since they embarked on that theory—derived from the Roman laws of adoption—much earlier than

others." *The King's Two Bodies: A Study in Medieval Political Theology* (Princeton: Princeton University Press, 1957), 302–12, esp. 307.

54. Pierre Legendre goes even so far as to insist on "fiction figuring truth" as a pivotal problematic for late-medieval legal thought, a telling theorem in light of today's Critical Legal Studies movement: *Ecrits juridiques du moyen âge occidental* (London: Variorum Reprints, 1988), XI, 514.

55. This strategy also governs another of Chartier's defenses, the "Erreurs du jugement de la Belle Dame sans mercy"; see lines 44–48.

56. On the emergence of the concept of lèse-majesté in this period, See S. H. Cuttler, *The Law of Treason and Treason Trials in Later Medieval France*, Cambridge Studies in Medieval Life and Thought, 3rd series, vol. 16 (Cambridge: Cambridge University Press, 1981), 14–21.

57. Walter Ullman sees the late-fourteenth-century pattern of kings, popes, and their legal counsels debating *crimen laesae majestatis* as an effort to pin down the idea of sovereignty: *Law and Jurisdiction in the Middle Ages*, ed. George Garnett (London: Variorum Reprints, 1988), VII, 24. P. S. Lewis advances much the same view in *Later Medieval France*, 82–87. What is of particular interest to us, however, is the way this problem is generalized to refer to myriad infractions. As Jacques Chiffoleau analyzes it: "Il faut attendre le XVᵉ siècle pour observer chez les juristes une extension importante, une dilatation progressive des qualifications du *crime de majesté* qui finit par absorber une quantité de crimes communs." "Dire l'indicible: Remarques sur la catégorie du *nefandum* du XIIᵉ au XVᵉ siècle," *Annales E.S.C.* 45, no. 2 (March–April 1990): 294.

58. "[S]o that I, who don't forsake my masters and benefactors without giving my all to the very last, at least as far as I will be able—do not allow their honor to be attacked either" (ut qui magistros et benefactores meos ad extremum usque singultum non desero, aut suo in honore—quoad potero—[non] sinam ledi). Hicks, 30. The key word, again, is *laedere*.

59. Et semble que tel chose infame,
> Scelon ce que d'elle est escript,
> Ne soit pas comme une aultre fame,
> Mais soit quelque maulvais esprit
> Qui ymaige de feme prit.
> Pour mettre a mort vrai ammoreux
> (*Cruelle Femme*, lines 681–86)

> And it appears that such an infamous thing, according to what is written of her, could not be like any other woman, but like some evil spirit that took the form of a woman to put to death the true lover.

60. "Mais, je diray, par ficcion, le fait de la mutacion comment de femme devins homme." Christine de Pizan, *La Mutacion de Fortune*, lines 150–53.

61. On this phrase, "the key to" as an index of the concern over censorship, see Annabel Patterson, *Censorship and Interpretation: The Conditions of Reading and Writing in Early Modern England* (Madison: University of Wisconsin Press, 1984), 7–8.

CODA

1. Jacques Legrand, the early-fifteenth-century Parisian humanist, gives a telling image of this cult in his description of the disciple dedicating himself to philosophy: "And I, Philo, have mustered my power to seek a way to gain the love of Sophie. . . . She came from an especially noble lineage; Minerva, beloved in Athens, was her mother and Ulysses who spent his entire life chivalrously—unlike Hercules—was her father. And so I began to speak with my lady and friend in a place secreted away where there was not a soul. I began pondering her body, her eyes, and her appearance as a whole and straightaway it seemed to me that any other love would be miserable" (Sy ay fait mon pouoir, je Philo, de querir Maniere pour l'amour de Sophie acquerir. . . . Elle aussy estoit de tres noble ligniee; Minerve fu sa mere en Athene aouree, Et son pere Ulixes qui de chevalerie Contre Hercules gaigna toute sa vie. Sy me prins a parler a m'amie et dame En un lieu moult secret ou quel n'y avoit ame; En avisant son corps, ses yeux et son viaire, Et tantost me sembla toute autre amour misere; lines 12–13, 30–37). *Archiloge Sophie*, 26. The life of learning, as ever, is cast as a love affair, an image that the woman respondent as Minerva recasts significantly.

2. On this little-known narrative, see L. Brook, "Un 'Art d'amour' inédit de la fin du moyen âge: Son cadre et ses métaphores," in *Courtly Literature*, ed. Keith Busby and Erik Kooper (Amsterdam: Brepols, 1989), 49–60.

3. *Poésies de Marguerite-Eléonore de Vallon-Chalys depuis Madame de Surville, poëte français du XVᵉ siècle*, published by Charles Vanderbourg (Paris: Heinrichs, 1803).

4. For all details, see Vanderbourg's introduction, xlvi–lii.

5. Another relevant analogue involves Jacqueline de Hacqueville and the case of *damoiselles d'honneur* at the Parisian court in the fifteenth century who composed *rondeaux* and *ballades*. See Paula Higgins, "Parisian Nobles, A Scottish Princess, and the Woman's Voice in Late Medieval Song," *Early Music History* 10 (1991): 161–72.

6. All citations are from the later edition, *Poésies de Clotilde de Surville, poëte français du XVᵉ siècle*, new edition published by Charles Vanderbourg (Paris: Nepveu, 1825). All translations are mine.

7. See Alain's *rondeau* "Au feu," *The Poetical Works of Alain Chartier*, XIX, 383–84.

8. *Poésies* (1825 edition), 62.

9. Ibid., 113–21.

10. "Le premier succès de Clotilde fut grand, la discussion animée, et il en resta un long attrait de curiosité aux esprits poétiques." Charles Sainte-Beuve, *Tableau historique et critique de la poésie française et du théâtre français au XVIᵉ siècle* (Paris: Charpentier, 1843), 497.

11. Quoted by Auguste LeSourd in *Autour de Clotilde de Surville: Lettres inédites de Vanderbourg et du Marquis de Surville* (Aubenas: Clovis Habuzit, 1928), 10–11.

12. *Poésies* (1825 edition), *Poésies Inédites de Marguerite-Eléonore Clotilde de Vallon et Chalys, depuis Madame de Surville, poète français du XVᵉ siècle*, published by Madame de Roujoux et Charles Nodier (Paris: Nepveu, 1826).

13. Susan Stewart sees this fashion for fakes "in light of a larger eighteenth-century crisis in authenticity." See *Crimes of Writing*, 35.

14. "Si des journalistes très instruits ont élevé des doutes sur le véritable auteur de ces poésies, tous les hommes de lettres se sont unanimément accordés à y reconnaître." 1825 edition, x.

15. I am currently completing an essay on the problem of writing the history of medieval women's poetry that considers these notices.

16. "Clotilde règne surtout dans le coeur des femmes. C'est à elles que nous offrons quelques'unes de ses poésies. C'est à elles à défendre la gloire du sexe contre toute la science orgueilleuse des hommes." *Poésies inédites*, xv.

17. Charles Nodier, *Questions de littérature légale: Du plagiat, de la supposition d'auteurs, des supercheries qui ont rapport aux livres*, 2 vols. (Paris: Crapelet, 1828), 1:83–84.

18. The whole quote reads "Quatre auteurs ont déclaré avoir fait subir des remaniements à une oeuvre première due, selon eux, à Marguerite-Clotilde de Surville: ce sont Jean de Surville, Jeanne de Vallon, Étienne de Surville, et Brazais." Eugène Villedieu, "Marguerite de Surville: Sa vie, ses oeuvres, ses descendants devant la critique moderne," *Bulletin de la Société des sciences naturelles et historiques de l'Ardèche* 7 (1873): 141.

19. Antoine Macé, *Un Procès d'histoire littéraire: Les poésies de Clotilde de Surville* (Grenoble: Prudhomme, 1870), 23.

20. Bernard Cerquiglini makes this point even more powerfully: "Dans l'authenticité généralisée de l'oeuvre médiévale, la philologie n'a vu qu'une authenticité perdue. La philologie médiévale est le deuil d'un Texte, le patient travail de ce deuil. Quête d'une perfection toujours antérieure et révolue du moment unique où la voix de l'auteur, que l'on suppose, se noua à la main du premier scribe, dictant la version authentique, première et originelle, que va désagréger la multitude et l'insouciance des individus copiant une littérature vulgaire." *Eloge de la variante: Histoire critique de la philologie* (Paris: Seuil, 1989), 58.

21. Nodier made a catalogue of just such inconsistencies; *Questions de littérature légale*, 82.

22. "Rien en histoire ne peut naître que par filiation d'antécedent à conséquent." Quoted by Anatole Loquin, "Réponse à M. Antoine Macé: Les poésies de Clotilde de Surville," *Actes de l'Académie des Sciences, Belles Lettres, et Arts de Bordeaux* (1873): 158.

23. "L'origine et la véritable paternité de ces poésies," ibid., 10.

24. Ibid., 30.

25. "Nous sommes de l'avis que cet auteur était un homme. Car dès qu'il est admis que l'oeuvre est un pastiche, il nous semble qu'un homme seul a pu lui donner cette perfection." A. Mazon, *Marguerite de Chalis et la légende de Clotilde de Surville* (Paris: Lemère, 1873), 58.

26. "Il appartient aux femmes poètes de persuader à tous les hommes de goût que les femmes ont crée la poésie française." *Poésies inédites*, xvii.

27. Margaret Waller makes the point that writers in this period "treat the traditional subject of sentiment—woman—as object of a feminized man's desire." "*Cherchez la femme*: Male Malady and Narrative Politics in the French Romantic Novel," *PMLA* 104, no. 2 (1989): 148. Waller makes the point in reference to Chateaubriand, but I would argue that it is equally relevant to the fascination with and defense of Clotilde.

28. Charles Maurras puts it forthrightly: "Le romantisme a fait efféminer les âmes; l'imagination fut féminine." *Romantisme et révolution: L'Avenir de l'intelligence* (Paris: Nouvelle librairie nationale, 1922), 218. Whereas we have to take this in the context of Maurras's reactionary rejection of such effeminacy, the observation is still telling.

29. Vanderbourg highlights the revolutionary/royalist opposition with the following description in the introduction: "Les révolutionnaires de France ont détruit les oeuvres de Clotilde; tous les papiers de la famille fut la proie des flammes." *Poésies* (1825 edition), xvi.

30. R. Howard Bloch traces some of the key implications of this model as far as medieval literary studies are concerned. See "'Mieux vaut jamais que tard': Romance, Philology, and Old French Letters," *Representations* 36 (fall 1991): 64–86.

31. "Mais le fond des poésies de Clotilde est tout aussi impossible au XVe siècle que la forme; les idées, sentiments, sujets, connaissances, vocabulaire, grammaire, syntaxe, versification sont invraisemblables." Gaston Paris,"Un procès d'histoire littéraire," *Revue critique*, 1 March 1873, 138.

32. Mark Jones, introduction, *Fake? The Art of Deception*, ed. Mark Jones, with Paul Craddock and Nicholas Barker (London: British Museum Publications, 1990), 17.

33. Charity Cannon Willard, "The Remarkable Case of Clotilde de Surville," *L'Esprit Créateur* 6, no. 2 (summer 1966): 112. See also her discussion in *Christine de Pizan*, 221.

34. The most obvious recent example involves John Benton's assertion that Héloïse was not the author of her letters. Barbara Newman analyzes these debates, summing them up with the statement: "Embarrassing as it it to expose these unwarranted, often misogynist assumptions, it is essential to do so. In some quarters, there still lingers a nineteenth-century bias against the very idea that medieval women wrote." "Authority, Authenticity, and the Repression of Héloïse," *Journal of Medieval and Renaissance Studies* 22, no. 2 (spring 1992): 128.

35. On this role of Christine, see Judith Bennett, "Feminism and History," *Gender and History* 1, no. 3 (autumn 1989): 251–52.

36. On this position see B. Honig, "Toward an Agonistic Feminism: Hannah Arendt and the Politics of Identity," in *Feminists Theorize the Political*, ed. Judith Butler and Joan W. Scott (New York: Routledge, 1992), 215–35, esp. 232.

37. Feminists have long acknowledged and explored this issue; see *Conflicts in Feminism*, ed. Marianne Hirsch and Evelyn Fox Keller (New York: Routledge, 1990).

38. Drucilla Cornell, *Beyond Accommodation: Ethical Feminism, Deconstruction, and the Law* (New York: Routledge, 1991), 132.

39. With this point, I concur with Kathleen Biddick's remarks about "the collapse of historian, reader, and historical subject" in medieval studies. See "Genders, Bodies, Borders: Technologies of the Visible," *Speculum* 68, no. 2 (April 1993): 416–17. On the general issue of the critic's relation to figures and texts of the medieval past, see Jeff Rider, "Other Voices: Historicism and the Interpretation of Medieval Texts," *Exemplaria* 1, no. 2 (fall 1989): 293–312, and "Whence? Whither?" *Exemplaria* 3, no. 1 (spring 1991): 243–66.

40. *Medieval Latin Word-List*, prepared by R. E. Latham (London: Oxford University Press, 1965), s.v. *identificare, Glossarium Mediae et Infimae Latinitatis Regni Hungariae*, ed. Antonius Bartal (Hildesheim: Georg Olms, 1970), s.v. *idem*. Nicole Oresme's definition goes as follows: "Car le identité ou unité que ilz ont a leur parens les fait estre ensemble come uns meïsme" (For the identity or unity they have with their relations makes them exist together as one and the same). *Le Livre de Ethique d'Aristote*, 172b, 442. Littré cites this as the first appearance of the term *identité* in the vernacular: *Dictionnaire de la langue française*, s.v. *identité*, as does the *Oxford English Dictionary*, s.v. *identity*.

41. Joan W. Scott's observation is germane here: "Treating the emergence of a new identity as a discourse event [in our case, the emergence of the woman respondent] is not to introduce a new form of linguistic determinism, nor to deprive subjects of agency. It is to refuse a separation between 'experience' and language and to insist instead on the productive quality of discourse." "Experience," in *Feminists Theorize the Political*, 34.

Bibliography

PRIMARY TEXTS

Abelard, Peter. "Abelard's Letter of Consolation to a Friend (*Historia Calamitatum*)." Ed. J. T. Muckle. *Mediaeval Studies* 12 (1950): 163–213.

———. *Historia calamitatum*. Ed. Jacques Monfrin. Paris: J. Vrin, 1967.

Adam de la Halle. *Le Jeu de la Feuillée*. Ed. Ernest Langlois. Paris: H. Champion, 1923.

Agrippa, Henri Corneille. *De nobilitate et praecellentia foeminei sexus*. Paris: Coloniae, 1567.

Alan of Lille. *Summa de arte praedicatoria*. Printed in *PL* 210, 111–98.

Alard de Cambrai. *Le Livre de philosophie et de moralité d'Alard de Cambrai*. Ed. Jean-Charles Payen. Paris: Klincksieck, 1970.

[Albert the Great?]. *Die Mittelalterlichen Traktate De modo opponendi et respondendi: Einleitung und Ausgabe der einschlagigen Texte*. Ed. Lambert Marie de Rijk. Beiträge zur Geschichte der Philosophie und Theologie des Mittelalters, vol. 17. Munster: Aschendorff, 1980.

Albertano of Brescia. *Dei Trattati Morali di Albertano da Brescia*. Ed. Andrea Da Grosseto. Bologna: Gaetano Romagnoli, 1873.

Andreas Capellanus. *Andreae Capellani regii Francorum De amore libri tres*. Ed. Amadeo Pagès. Madrid: Castellon de la Plana, 1929.

———. *The Art of Courtly Love*. Trans. with introduction by John Jay Parry. New York: Norton, 1969.

Aquinas, Thomas. *Commentary on the Metaphysics of Aristotle*. 2 vols. Trans. John P. Rowan. Chicago: Henry Regnery, 1961.

———. *Opuscula theologica*. 2 vols. Ed. Raymond A. Verardo. Rome: Marietti, 1954.

———. *Summa theologica*. Ed. and trans. Fathers of the English Dominican Province. London: Burns, Oates and Washbourne, 1914–38.

———. *Über den Lehrer, de magistro*. Ed. and trans. G. Jüssen, G. Krieger, and J. H. J. Schneider. Hamburg: Felix Meiner, 1988.

Aristotle. *The "Art" of Rhetoric*. Ed. and trans. John Henry Freese. London: William Heinemann, 1926.

————. *The Complete Works of Aristotle: The Revised Oxford Translation.* 2 vols. Ed. Jonathan Barnes. Princeton: Princeton University Press, 1984.

————. *Introduction to Aristotle.* Ed. Richard McKeon. New York: Random House, 1947.

————. *Metaphysica Aristotelis: Translatio anonyma sive "media."* Ed. Gudrun Vuillemin-Diem. Leiden: E. J. Brill, 1976.

Artes amandi: Da Maître Elie ad Andrea Cappellano. Ed. Anna Maria Finoli. Milan: Istituto Editoriale Cisalpino, 1969.

Augustine. *City of God.* Trans. Henry Bettenson. Harmondsworth: Penguin, 1972.

————. *De civitate Dei.* 2 vols. Ed. Bernhard Dombart. Leipzig: Teubner, 1909.

————. *De magistro.* Ed. W. B. Green. Corpus Christianorum series Latina, vol. 29. Turholt: Brepols, 1970: 155–203.

Boccaccio, Giovanni. *Boccaccio on Poetry.* Ed. and trans. Charles G. Osgood. Princeton: Princeton University Press, 1930.

————. *Concerning Famous Women by Giovanni Boccaccio.* Trans. Guido A. Guarino. New Brunswick, N.J.: Rutgers University Press, 1963.

————. *Genealogie deorum gentilium.* 2 vols. Ed. Vincenzo Romano. Bari: Laterza, 1951.

Boethius. *Boethius: "Tractates," "De consolatione philosophiae."* Ed. and trans. H. F. Stewart, E. K. Rand, and S. J. Tester. Cambridge, Mass.: Harvard University Press, 1973.

Bonet, Honoré. *L'Apparicion Maistre Jehan de Meun et le somnium super materia scismatis d'Honoré Bonet.* Ed. Ivor Arnold. Paris: Belles Lettres, 1926.

Brunetto Latini. *Li Livres dou Tresor de Brunetto Latini.* Ed. Francis J. Carmody. Berkeley: University of California Press, 1948.

Bullaire de l'Inquisition française au XIVᵉ siècle et jusqu'à la fin du grand scisme. Ed. J.-M. Vidal. Paris: Letouzey et Ané, 1913.

Il Canzoniere di Lanfranco Cigala. Ed. Francesco Branciforti. Florence: Leo S. Olschki, 1954.

Chartier, Alain. *Les Oeuvres latines d'Alain Chartier.* Ed. Pascale Bourgain-Hemeryck. Paris: Éditions du C.N.R.S., 1977.

————. *Poèmes par Alain Chartier.* Ed. James Laidlaw. Paris: Union générale d'éditions, 1988.

————. *The Poetical Works of Alain Chartier.* Ed. James C. Laidlaw. Cambridge: Cambridge University Press, 1974.

————. *Le Quadrilogue invectif.* Ed. Eugénie Droz. Paris: H. Champion, 1923.

Chartularium Universitatis Parisiensis. Ed. Henricus Denifle and Aemilio Chatelain. Paris: Delalain, 1891.

Le Chastoiement d'un père à son fils. Ed. Edward D. Montgomery, Jr. Chapel Hill: University of North Carolina Press, 1971.

Choix de pièces inédites relatives au règne de Charles VI. 2 vols. Ed. Louis Douët d'Arcq. Paris: J. Renouard, 1863–64.

Christine de Pizan. *Lavision-Christine: Introduction and Text.* Ed. Sister Mary Louis Towner. Washington, D.C.: Catholic University of America, 1932.

————. "The *Livre de la Cité des dames* of Christine de Pizan: A Critical Edition." 2 vols. Ed. Maureen Lois Cheney Curnow. Ph.D. diss., Vanderbilt University, 1975.

————. *Le Livre de la Mutacion de Fortune par Christine de Pisan.* 4 vols. Ed. Suzanne Solente. Paris: A. & J. Picard, 1959–66.

―――. *Le Livre des fais et bonnes meurs du sage roy Charles V.* Ed. Suzanne Solente. Paris: H. Champion, 1936–41.

―――. *Le Livre des trois vertus de Christine de Pizan.* Ed. Charity Cannon Willard with Eric Hicks. Paris: H. Champion, 1989.

―――. *Le Livre du chemin de long estude.* Ed. Robert Püschel. Berlin: Damköhler, 1881.

―――. *Le Livre du corps de policie de Christine de Pisan.* Ed. Robert H. Lucas. Geneva: Droz, 1967.

―――. *Oeuvres poétiques de Christine de Pisan.* 3 vols. Ed. Maurice Roy. Paris: Firmin-Didot, 1886–96.

―――. *Poems of Cupid, God of Love: Christine de Pizan's "Epistre au dieu d'amours" and "Dit de la rose," Thomas Hoccleve's "The Letter of Cupid."* Ed. and trans. Thelma S. Fenster and Mary Carpenter Erler. Leiden: E. J. Brill, 1990.

Chronica noblissimorum ducum Lotharingiae et Brabantiae ac regum Francorum, auctore magistro Edmundo de Dynter. Ed. J. Wauquelin. Brussels: M. Hayez, 1854–57.

Chronique du religieux de Saint-Denys contenant le règne de Charles VI de 1380 à 1422. 6 vols. Ed. and trans. Louis François Bellaguet and Amable-Guillaume-Prosper Brugière, baron de Barante. Paris: Crapelet, 1839–52.

Chroniques de Brabant et de Flandre. 4 vols. Ed. Charles Piot. Brussels: F. Hayez, 1879.

Cicero. *Cicero: "De re publica," "De legibus."* Trans. Clinton Walker Keyes. Cambridge: Cambridge University Press, 1948.

―――. *Cicero: On the Commonwealth.* Trans. George Holland Sabine and Stanley Barney Smith. New York: Bobbs Merrill, 1960.

―――. *"De inventione" and "Topica."* Ed. and trans. H. M. Hubbell. Cambridge, Mass.: Harvard University Press, 1949.

―――. *Opera omnia.* Ed. Johannes Lydius. Lugdini Butavorum, 1613.

The Civil Law, Including the 12 Tables, the Institutes of Gaius, the Rules of Ulpian, the Opinions of Paulus, the Enactments of Justinian, and the Constitutions of Leo. 17 vols. Trans. Samuel P. Scott. Cincinnati: The Central Trust Co., 1932.

La Clef d'amours. Ed. Auguste Doutrepont. Geneva: Slatkine Reprints, 1975.

"Li Commens d'amour." Ed. Antoinette Saly. *Travaux de linguistique et de littérature* 10 (1972): 21–55.

"Complainte du livre du Champion des Dames de maistre Martin LeFranc." Ed. Gaston Paris. *Romania* 16 (1887): 383–437.

Corpus iuris canonici. 2 vols. Ed. A. Richter and A. Friedburg. Leipzig, 1879. Graz: Akademische Druck und Verlagsanstalt, 1959.

Corpus iuris civilis: Codex Iustinianus. 2 vols. Ed. Paul Krueger. Berlin: Weidmann, 1928.

"La Cruelle Femme en amour." Ed. Arthur Piaget. In *"La Belle Dame sans mercy et ses imitations," Romania* 31 (1902): 322–49.

"La Dame leale en amours." Ed. Arthur Piaget. In *"La Belle Dame sans mercy et ses imitations," Romania* 30 (1901): 323–51.

Dante Alighieri. *De vulgari eloquentia.* Ed. Pier Vincenzo Mengaldo. Padua: Antenore, 1968.

―――. *The Divine Comedy.* 3 vols. Trans. with a commentary by Charles S. Singleton. Princeton: Princeton University Press, 1975.

De disciplina scholarium (Pseudo-Boethius). Ed. Olga Weijers. Leiden: E. J. Brill, 1976.

"De Sainte Katherine": An Anonymous Picard Version of the Life of St. Catherine of Alexandria. Ed. William McBain. Fairfax, Va.: George Mason University Press, 1977.

"Le Débat du clerc et de la damoiselle: Poème inédit du XIVe siècle." Ed. A. Jeanroy. *Romania* 43 (1914): 1–17.

Le Débat sur le roman de la rose. Ed. Eric Hicks. Paris: H. Champion, 1977.

Les Débats du clerc et du chevalier dans la littérature poétique du moyen âge. Ed. Charles Oulmont. 1911; Geneva: Slatkine Reprints, 1974.

"Des Vilains ou des xxii manieres de vilains." Ed. Edmond Faral. *Romania* 48 (1922): 243–64.

"Deux Traités sur l'amour tirés du manuscrit 2200 de la bibliothèque Ste. Geneviève." Ed. A. Langfors. *Romania* 56 (1930): 361–88.

The "Disciplina clericalis" of Petrus Alfonsi. Ed. Eberhard Hermes. Trans. P. R. Quarrie. Berkeley: University of California Press, 1977.

Les Diz et proverbes des sages. Ed. Joseph Morawski. Bibliothèque de la Faculté des Lettres Université de Paris, 2nd series, 2 (Paris: Presses Universitaires de France, 1924).

Drouart la Vache. *Li Livres d'amours de Drouart la Vache.* Ed. Robert Bossuat. Paris: H. Champion, 1926.

"Ein ungedruckter *Salu d'amors* nebst Antwort." Ed. O. Schultz-Gora. *Zeitschrift für romanische philologie* 24 (1900): 358–69.

Eine mittelniederfrankische übertragung des Bestiaire d'amour. Ed. John Holmberg. Uppsala: Almqvist & Wiksells, 1925.

"Enseignements d'Aristote et d'Alixandre." Ed. Hermann Kunst. In *Mitteilungen aus dem Eskurial.* Bibliothek des Literarischen Vereins in Stuttgart 141 (1879).

"Les Erreurs du jugement de la Belle Dame sans mercy." Ed. Arthur Piaget. In *"La Belle Dame sans mercy* et ses imitations," *Romania* 33 (1904): 183–99.

Gerard de Nevers. *Le Roman de la violette ou de Gerart de Nevers.* Ed. Douglas Labaree Buffum. Paris: H. Champion, 1928.

Guillaume de Conches. *Das Moralium Dogma Philosophorum des Guillaume de Conches.* Ed. John Holmberg. Uppsala: Almqvist & Wiksells, 1929.

Guillaume de Lorris and Jean de Meun. *Le Roman de la rose.* 3 vols. Ed. Félix Lecoy. Paris: H. Champion, 1973.

Guillaume de Machaut. *Oeuvres.* 3 vols. Ed. Ernest Hoepffner. Paris: Firmin-Didot, 1908.

Henri d'Andeli. *The Battle of the Seven Arts: A French Poem.* Ed. Louis John Paetow. Berkeley: University of California Press, 1914.

———. *Li Lai d'Aristote d'Henri d'Andeli.* Ed. Maurice Delbouille. Paris: Belles Lettres, 1951.

Henry de Segusio (Hostiensis). *Summa aurea.* Ed. Oreste Vighetti. Turin: Bottega d'Erasmo, 1963.

Hibernicus, Thomas. *Manipulus florum, seu Sententiae patrum.* Piacenza: Jacobus de Tyela, 1483.

Hugh of Saint Cher. "De custodia linguae." Ed. G. Hendrix. *Recherches de théologie ancienne et médiévale* 48 (1981): 172–97.

Jacques d'Amiens. *L'Art d'amors und Li Remèdes d'amors: Zwei altfranzösische*

Lehrgedichte von Jacques d'Amiens. Ed. Gustav Korting. Geneva: Slatkine Reprints, 1976.

Le Jardin de plaisance et fleur de rethorique. 2 vols. Ed. Eugénie Droz and Arthur Piaget. Paris: Firmin-Didot, 1910–25.

Jean de Montreuil. *Opera*. 2 vols. Ed. Ezio Ornato. Turin: G. Giappichelli, 1963.

Jean LeFèvre. *Le Respit de la mort de Jehan LeFèvre*. Ed. Geneviève Hasenohr-Esnos. Paris: A. & J. Picard, 1969.

———. *Les Lamentations de Matheolus et le Livre de leesce de Jehan LeFèvre, de Resson*. 2 vols. Ed. Anton Gérard van Hamel. Paris: Emile Bouillon, 1892–1905.

———. "Die Übersetzung der Distichen des Pseudo-Cato von Jean de Paris." Ed. J. Ulrich. *Romanische Forschungen* 15 (1904): 41–149.

———. *La Vieille ou les derniers amours d'Ovide: Poème français du XIVᵉ siècle traduit du latin de Richard de Fournival par Jean LeFèvre*. Ed. Hippolyte Cocheris. Paris: Auguste Aubry, 1861.

Jehan Petit d'Arras. "Li Houneurs et li vertus des dames par Jehan Petit d'Arras." Ed. Rudolf Zimmermann. *Archiv für das Studium der neueren Sprachen und Literaturen* 108 (1902): 380–88.

John of Salisbury. *The Metalogicon of John of Salisbury*. Trans. Daniel D. McGarry. Berkeley: University of California Press, 1955.

"Le Jugement du povre triste amant banny." Ed. Arthur Piaget. In *"La Belle Dame sans mercy" et ses imitations," Romania* 34 (1905): 379–416.

LeFranc, Martin. *Le Champion des dames*. Ed. Arthur Piaget. Mémoires et documents publiés par la société d'histoire de la suisse romane, 3rd series, 8. Lausanne: Payot, 1968.

Legrand, Jacques. *Archiloge Sophie: Livre de bonnes meurs*. Ed. Evencio Beltran. Geneva: Slatkine: 1986.

Das "Livre d'Enanchet" nach der einzigen Handschrift 2585 der Wiener National-bibliothek. Ed. Werner Fiebig. Jena : Wilhelm Gronau, 1938.

Le Livre des Manières. Ed. Josef Kremer. Marburg: N. G. Elwert, 1887.

Li Livres des Mestiers de Bruges et ses dérives: Quatre anciens manuels de conversation. Ed. Jean Gessler. Bruges: Maîtres Imprimeurs Brugeois, 1931.

Maistre Pierre Pathelin: Farce du XVᵉ siècle. Ed. Richard T. Holbrook. Paris: H. Champion, 1937.

Maître Elie's Überarbeitung der altesten französischen Übertragung von Ovid's Ars Amatoria. Ed. H. Kuhne and E. Stengel. Marburg: N. G. Elwert, 1886.

Margaret of Porete. "Il Miroir des simples âmes di Margherita Porete." Ed. Romana Guarnieri. *Archivio italiano per la storia della pietà* 4 (1965): 501–708.

Marot, Jean. *Oeuvres*. Geneva: Slatkine Reprints, 1970.

Martial d'Auvergne. *Les Arrêts d'amour de Martial d'Auvergne*. Ed. Jean Rychner. Paris: A. & J. Picard, 1951.

"Matheus von Boulogne: Lamentationes Matheoluli." Ed. Albert Schmitt. Ph.D. diss., Rheinischen Friedrich-Wilhelms-Universität, Bonn, 1974.

Michault, Pierre. "Le 'Procès d'honneur féminin' de Pierre Michault." Ed. Barbara Folkart. *Le Moyen Français* 2 (1977): 1–133.

Nicole de Margival. *Le Dit de la panthère d'amours par Nicole de Margival*. Ed. Henry A. Todd. Paris: Firmin-Didot, 1883.

Oresme, Nicole. *Maistre Nicole Oresme: Le Livre de Ethiques d'Aristote*. Ed. Albert Douglas Menut. New York: G. E. Stechert, 1940.

————. *Maistre Nicole Oresme: Le Livre de Politiques d'Aristote.* Ed. Albert Douglas Menut. Philadelphia: Transactions of the American Philosophical Society 60, part 6 (1970).

Ovid. *Ars amatoria P. Ovidi Nasonis.* Ed. E. J. Kenney. Oxford: Oxford University Press, 1961.

————. *L'Art d'amours: Traduction et commentaire de "l'Ars amatoria" d'Ovide.* Ed. Bruno Roy. Leiden: E. J. Brill, 1974.

————. *The Art of Love.* Trans. Rolfe Humphries. Bloomington: Indiana University Press, 1957.

————. *Metamorphoses.* 2 vols. Trans. Frank Justus Miller. London: Heinemann, 1916.

Petrarch, Francis. *Opera latine di Francesco Petrarca.* 2 vols. Ed. Antonietta Bufano. Turin: Unione tipografico-editrice torinese, 1975.

Philippe de Beaumanoir. *Coûtumes de Beauvaisis.* 2 vols. Ed. Amédée Salmon. Paris: A. Picard et fils, 1899–1900.

————. *The Coûtumes de Beauvaisis of Philippe de Beaumanoir.* Trans. F. R. P. Akehurst. Philadelphia: University of Pennsylvania Press, 1992.

Philippe de Navarre. *Les Quatre Ages de l'homme: Traité moral de Philippe de Navarre.* Ed. Marcel de Fréville. Paris: Firmin-Didot, 1888.

Placides et Timéo ou Li secrés as philosophes. Ed. Claude Alexandre Thomasset. Geneva: Droz, 1980.

Poésies de Clotilde de Surville, poëte français du XVe siècle. New edition published by Charles Vanderbourg. Paris: Nepveu, 1825.

Poésies de Marguerite-Eléonore de Vallon-Chalys depuis Madame de Surville, poëte français du XVe siècle. Published by Charles Vanderbourg. Paris: Heinrichs, 1803.

Poésies inédites de Marguerite-Eléonore Clotilde de Vallon et Chalys, depuis Madame de Surville, poète français du XVe siècle. Published by Madame de Roujoux et Charles Nodier. Paris: Nepveu, 1826.

La Poissance damours dello Pseudo–Richard de Fournival. Ed. Gian Battista Speroni. Pubblicazioni dell Facoltà di Lettere e Filosofia dell'Università di Pavia 21. Florence: La Nuova Italia, 1975.

Li Proverbe au vilain, die Sprichwörter des gemeinen Mannes, Altfranzösische Dichtung nach den bisher bekannten Handschriften. Ed. Adolf Tobler. Leipzig: S. Hirzel, 1895.

Li Proverbes au vilain: Untersuchungen zur romanischen Spruchdichtung des Mittelalters. Ed. Eckhard Rattunde. Studia Romanica 11. Heidelberg: Carl Winter Universitätsverlag, 1966.

Proverbes et dictons populaires. Ed. G. A. Crapelet. Paris: Imprimerie de Crapelet, 1831.

Pseudo–Albertus Magnus. "Pseudo–Albertus Magnus: *Secreta mulierum cum commento,* Deutsch. Critical Text and Commentary." Ed. Margaret Schleissner. Ph.D. diss, Princeton University, 1987.

————. *Women's Secrets: A Translation of Pseudo–Albertus Magnus' "De secreta mulierum" with Commentaries.* Trans. Helen Rodnite Lemay. Albany: State University of New York Press, 1992.

Quintilian. *Institutio oratoria.* 4 vols. Ed. and trans. Harold E. Butler. London: W. Heinemann, 1920–22.

"La Règle des fins amans: Eine Begininregel aus dem Ende des XIII. Jahrhunderts." Ed. Karl Christ. In *Philologische Studien aus dem Romanische-Germanischen Kulturkreisen*. Ed. B. Schädel and W. Mulert. Halle: M. Niemeyer, 1927: 192–213.

"La Response des dames faicte a maistre Alain." Ed. Arthur Piaget. In *"La Belle Dame sans mercy et ses imitations," Romania* 30 (1901): 28–35.

Richard de Fournival. *Li Bestiaires d'amours di Maistre Richart de Fornival e li Response du Bestiaire*. Ed. Cesare Segre. Documenti di Filologica 2. Milan: Riccardo Ricciardi, 1957.

——. *Il Bestiario d'Amore e la Riposta al Bestiario*. Ed. Francesco Zambon. Parma: Pratiche Editrice, 1987.

——. *"Li Consaus d'amors."* Ed. Gian Battista Speroni. *Medioevo Romanzo* 1 (1974): 217–278.

——. *Master Richard's Bestiary of Love and Response*. Trans. Jeanette Beer. Berkeley: University of California Press, 1986.

——. *L'Oeuvre lyrique de Richard de Fournival*. Ed. Yvan G. Lepage. Ottawa: Éditions de l'Université d'Ottawa, 1981.

——. *Una Versione Pisana Inedita del "Bestiaire d'Amours."* Ed. Roberto Crespo. Leiden: Leiden University Press, 1972.

Robert de Blois. *Robert de Blois: Son oeuvre didactique et narrative*. Ed. John Howard Fox. Paris: Nizet, 1950.

Tibaut. *"Le Roman de la poire" par Tibaut*. Ed. Christiane Marchello-Nizia. Paris: A. & J. Picard, 1984.

Villon, François. *Le Testament Villon*. Ed. Jean Rychner and Albert Henry. Geneva: Droz, 1974.

Vincent de Beauvais. *Speculum doctrinale*. Venice: Hermannus Liechtenstein, 1494.

Vivès, Juan Luis. *In Pseudodialecticos: A Critical Edition*. Ed. Charles Fantazzi. Leiden: E. J. Brill, 1979.

STUDIES

Agacinski, Sylviane. "Le tout premier écart," in *Les Fins de l'homme: à partir du travail de Jacques Derrida*, ed. Philippe Lacoue-Labarthe and Jean-Luc Nancy. Paris: Galilée, 1981: 117–32.

Allen, Peter L. *The Art of Love: Amatory Fiction from Ovid to the Romance of the Rose*. Philadelphia: University of Pennsylvania Press, 1992.

Allen, Prudence. *The Concept of Woman: The Aristotelian Revolution, 750 B.C.–A.D. 1250*. Montreal: Eden Press, 1985.

d'Alverny, Marie-Thérèse. "Comment les théologiens et les philosophes voient la femme." *Cahiers de civilisation médiévale* 20 (1977): 105–29.

Angenot, Marc. *Les Champions des femmes: Examen du discours sur la supériorité des femmes 1400–1800*. Montréal: Presses de l'Université de Québec, 1977.

——. *La Parole pamphlétaire: Contribution à la typologie des discours modernes*. Paris: Payot, 1982.

Auerbach, Eric. "Figura." *Scenes from the Drama of European Literature*. Trans. Ralph Mannheim. New York: Meridien Books, 1959: 11–78.

Badel, Pierre-Yves. *"Le Roman de la rose" au XIVe siècle: Étude de la réception de l'oeuvre*. Geneva: Droz, 1980.

Baird, Joseph L., and John R. Kane. *La Querelle de la Rose: Letters and Documents.* North Carolina Studies in the Romance Languages and Literatures no. 199. Chapel Hill: University of North Carolina Press, 1978.

Bal, Mieke. *Femmes imaginaires: L'Ancien testament au risque d'une narratologie critique.* Paris: Nizet, 1986.

Baldwin, John W. *The Language of Sex: Five Voices from Northern France Around 1200.* Chicago: University of Chicago Press, 1994.

———. "Masters at Paris from 1179 to 1215: A Social Perspective," in *Renaissance and Renewal in the Twelfth Century*, ed. Robert L. Benson and Giles Constable. Cambridge, Mass: Harvard University Press, 1986: 143–53.

———. *The Scholastic Culture of the Middle Ages, 1000–1300.* Lexington, Mass.: Heath, 1971.

Barbey, Leon. *Martin LeFranc: Prévôt de Lausanne, avocat de l'amour et de la femme au XVᵉ siècle.* Fribourg: Éditions universitaires, 1985.

Barendt. Eric. *Freedom of Speech.* Oxford: Clarendon Press, 1985.

Barfield, Owen. "Poetic Diction and Legal Fiction," in *Essays Presented to Charles Williams*, ed. C. S. Lewis. London: Oxford University Press, 1947: 106–27.

Bartky, Sandra Lee. *Femininity and Domination: Studies in the Phenomenology of Oppression.* New York: Routledge, 1990.

Bazan, Bernardo C., John W. Wippel, Gerard Frauden, and Danielle Jacquart. *Les Questions disputées et les questions quodlibétiques dans les facultés de théologie, de droit, et de medicine.* Typologie des sources du moyen âge occidental 44–45. Turnhout: Brepols, 1985.

Beaune, Colette. *The Birth of an Ideology: Myths and Symbols of Nation in Late-Medieval France.* Trans. Susan Ross Huston. Ed. Fredric L. Cheyette. Berkeley: University of California Press, 1991.

Beauvoir, Simone de. *Le Deuxième Sexe.* 2 vols. Paris: Gallimard, 1949.

Beer, Jeanette. "Duel of Bestiaires," in *Beasts and Birds of the Middle Ages: The Bestiary and Its Legacy*, ed. Willene B. Clark and Meradith T. McMunn. Philadephia: University of Pennsylvania Press, 1989: 96–105.

———. "Richard de Fournival's Anonymous Lady: The Character of the Response to the *Bestiaire d'amour.*" *Romance Philology* 42, no 3 (November 1989): 267–73.

Bell, Susan Groag. "Christine de Pizan (1364–1430): Humanism and the Problem of a Studious Woman." *Feminist Studies* 3, no. 3–4 (1976): 173–84.

———. "Medieval Women Book Owners: Arbiters of Lay Piety and Ambassadors of Culture." *Signs: Journal of Women in Culture and Society* 7, no. 4 (summer 1982): 742–68.

Beltran, Evencio. *L'Idéal de la sagesse d'après Jacques Legrand.* Paris: Études augustiniennes, 1989.

Benjamin, Jessica. *The Bonds of Love: Psychoanalysis, Feminism, and the Problem of Domination.* New York: Pantheon, 1988.

Benjamin, Walter. *Illuminations: Essays and Reflections.* Ed. with an introduction by Hannah Arendt. Trans. Harry Zohn. New York: Schocken Books, 1969.

Bennett, Judith. "Feminism and History." *Gender and History* 1, no. 3 (autumn 1989): 251–72.

Benveniste, Emile. *Le Vocabulaire des institutions indo-européennes.* 2 vols. Paris: Minuit, 1969.

Berg, Elizabeth. "The Third Woman." *Diacritics* 12, no. 2 (summer 1982): 11–21.

Biddick, Kathleen. "Genders, Bodies, Borders: Technologies of the Visible." *Speculum* 68, no. 2 (April 1993): 389–418.

Blamires, Alcuin, ed., with Karen Pratt and C. W. Marx. *Woman Defamed and Woman Defended: An Anthology of Medieval Texts.* Oxford: Clarendon Press, 1992.

Blanchard, Joël. "Artéfact littéraire et problématisation morale au XVe siècle." *Le Moyen Français* 17 (1985): 7–47.

———. "Christine de Pizan: Les raisons de l'histoire." *Le Moyen Age* 92, no. 3–4 (1986): 417–36.

———. "Christine de Pizan: Tradition, expérience, et traduction." *Romania* 111 (1990): 200–35.

———. "Compilation et légitimation au XVe siècle." *Poétique* 74 (April 1988): 139–57.

———. "L'Entrée du poète dans le champ politique au XVe siècle." *Annales E.S.C.* 41, no. 1 (January–February 1986): 43–61.

Bloch, R. Howard. *Etymologies and Genealogies: A Literary Anthropology of the French Middle Ages.* Chicago: University of Chicago Press, 1983.

———. *French Medieval Literature and Law.* Berkeley: University of California Press, 1977.

———. *Medieval Misogyny and the Invention of Western Romantic Love.* Chicago: University of Chicago Press, 1991.

———. "'Mieux vaut jamais que tard': Romance, Philology, and Old French Letters." *Representations* 36 (fall 1991): 64–86.

Blumenfeld-Kosinski, Renate. "Christine de Pizan and the Misogynistic Tradition." *Romanic Review* 81, no. 3 (May 1990): 279–92.

———. "Jean LeFèvre's *Livre de Leesce*: Praise or Blame of Women?" *Speculum* 69, no. 3 (July 1994): 705–25.

Bond, Gerald A. "Composing Yourself: Ovid's Heroïdes, Baudri of Bourgueil, and the Problem of Persona." *Medievalia* 13 (1989 [for 1987]): 83–117.

Bossuat, Robert. *Drouart la Vache: Traducteur d'André le Chapelain.* Paris: H. Champion, 1926.

Bossy, Michel-André. "Woman's Plain Talk in *Le Débat de l'Omme et de la Femme* by Guillaume Alexis." *Fifteenth-Century Studies* 16 (1990): 23–41.

Bourdieu, Pierre. *Ce que parler veut dire: L'Économie des échanges linguistiques.* Paris: Fayard, 1982.

———. "La Domination masculine." *Actes de la Recherche en sciences sociales* 84 (September 1990): 2–31.

Bourdieu, Pierre and Jean-Claude Passeron. *La Reproduction: Éléments pour une théorie du système d'enseignement.* Paris: Minuit, 1970.

Boureau, Alain. *La Papesse Jeanne.* Paris: Aubier, 1988.

Bowden, Betsy. "The Art of Courtly Copulation." *Medievalia et Humanistica* 9 (1979): 67–86.

Boyle, Leonard E. *Pastoral Care, Clerical Education, and Canon Law, 1200–1400.* London: Variorum Reprints, 1981.

Bozzolo, Carla. "L'Humaniste Gontier Col et la traduction française des *Lettres* d'Abélard et Héloïse." *Romania* 95, no. 2–3 (1974): 199–214.

Bozzolo, Carla and Hélène Loyau. *La Cour amoureuse, dite de Charles VI: Étude et édition critique des sources manuscrites.* 3 vols. Paris: Léopard d'Or, 1982–1992.

Bozzolo, Carla and Ezio Ornato. *Préludes à la Renaissance: Aspects de la vie intellectuelle en France au XVᵉ siècle.* Paris: Éditions du C.N.R.S., 1992.

Braudy, Leo. *The Frenzy of Renown: Fame and Its History.* New York: Oxford University Press, 1986.

Brook, L. "Un 'Art d'amour' inédit de la fin du moyen âge: Son cadre et ses métaphores," in *Courtly Literature,* ed. Keith Busby and Erik Kooper. Amsterdam: Brepols: 49–60.

Brownlee, Kevin. *Discourses of the Self: Autobiography and Literary Models in Christine de Pizan.* Forthcoming.

——. "Discourses of the Self: Christine de Pizan and the *Romance of the Rose.*" *Romanic Review* 79, no, 1 (1988): 199–221.

——. "Structures of Authority in Christine de Pizan's *Ditié de Jehanne d'Arc,*" in *Discourses of Authority in Medieval and Renaissance Literature,* ed. Kevin Brownlee and Walter Stephens. Hanover, N.H.: University Press of New England, 1989: 131–50.

Bruckner, Mathilda Tomaryn. "Fictions of the Female Voice: The Women Troubadours." *Speculum* 67, no. 4 (October 1992): 865–91.

——. "Na Castelloza, *Trobairitz,* and Troubadour Lyric." *Romance Notes* 25, no. 3 (spring 1985): 239–53.

Brundage, James A. *Law, Sex, and Christian Society in Medieval Europe.* Chicago: University of Chicago Press, 1987.

Burke, Peter, and Roy Porter, eds. *Language, Self, and Society: A Social History of Language.* Cambridge: Polity, 1991.

Burns, E. Jane. *Bodytalk: When Women Speak in Old French Literature.* Philadelphia: University of Pennsylvania Press, 1993.

Burns, E. Jane et al. "Feminism and the Discipline of Old French Studies: '*Une Bele Disjointure,*'" in *Medievalism in a Modernist Temper: The Discipline of Medieval Studies,* ed. R. Howard Bloch and Stephen G. Nichols. Baltimore: Johns Hopkins University Press, forthcoming.

Bynum, Caroline Walker. *Holy Feast and Holy Fast: The Religious Significance of Food to Medieval Women.* Berkeley: University of California Press, 1987.

Cadden, Joan. *Meanings of Sex Difference in the Middle Ages: Medicine, Science, and Culture.* Cambridge: Cambridge University Press, 1993.

The Cambridge History of Later Medieval Philosophy: From the Rediscovery of Aristotle to the Disintegration of Scholasticism. Ed. Norman Kretzmann, Anthony Kenny, and Jan Pinborg. Cambridge: Cambridge University Press, 1982.

Carré, Gustave. *L'Enseignement secondaire à Troyes du moyen âge à la Révolution.* Paris: Hachette, 1888.

Carron, Jean-Claude. "Les Noms de l'honneur féminin à la Renaissance: Le nom tu et le non dit." *Poétique* 67 (September 1986): 269–80.

Carruthers, Mary. *The Book of Memory: A Study of Memory in Medieval Culture.* Cambridge: Cambridge University Press, 1990.

Casagrande, Carla, and Silvana Vecchio. *I Peccati della lingua: Disciplina ed Etica della Parola nella Cultura Medievale.* Rome: Istituto della Enciclopedia Italiana, 1987.

——. *Les Péchés de la langue: Discipline et éthique de la parole dans la culture médiévale.* Trans. Philippe Baillet. Paris: Cerf, 1991.

Cecchetti, Dario. *Il Primo umanismo francese.* Turin: Albert Meynier, 1987.

Cerquiglini, Bernard. *Eloge de la variante: Histoire critique de la philologie.* Paris: Seuil, 1989.

———. "Variantes d'auteur et variance de copiste," in *La naissance du texte,* ed. Louis Hay. Paris: José Corti, 1989: 105–19.

Cerquiglini-Toulet, Jacqueline. "Le Clerc et l'écriture: Le 'Voir-dit' de Guillaume de Machaut et la définition du 'dit,'" in *Literatur in der Gesellschaft des Spätmittelalters,* ed. Hans-Ulrich Gumbrecht. Heidelberg: Carl Winter Universitätsverlag, 1980: 151–68.

———. *La Couleur de la mélancholie: La Fréquentation des livres au XIVᵉ siècle, 1300–1415.* Paris: Hatier, 1993.

———. "L'Etrangère." *Revue des langues romanes* 92, no. 2 (1988): 239–51.

———. *"Un Engin si soutil": Guillaume de Machaut et l'écriture au XIVᵉ siècle.* Paris: H. Champion, 1985.

Chailley, Jacques. "La Nature musicale du *Jeu de Robin et Marion,*" in *Mélanges d'histoire du théâtre du moyen âge et de la Renaissance offerts à Gustave Cohen.* Paris: Nizet, 1950: 111–17.

Champion, Pierre. *Histoire poétique du quinzième siècle.* 2 vols. Paris: H. Champion, 1923.

Chartier, Roger. *The Culture of Print: Power and the Uses of Print in Early Modern Europe.* Princeton: Princeton University Press, 1989.

———, ed. *Les Usages de l'imprimé (XVᵉ–XIXᵉ siècle).* Paris: Fayard, 1987.

Chiffoleau, Jacques. "Dire l'indicible: Remarques sur la catégorie du *nefandum* du XIIᵉ au XVᵉ siècle." *Annales E.S.C.* 45, no. 2 (March–April 1990): 289–324.

Cixous, Hélène, and Catherine Clément. *The Newly Born Woman.* Trans. Betsy Wing. Minneapolis: University of Minnesota Press, 1986.

———. Madeleine Gagnon, and Annie LeClerc. *La Venue à l'écriture.* Paris: Union générale d'éditions, 1977.

Cocks, Joan. *The Oppositional Imagination: Feminism, Critique, and Political Theory.* New York: Routledge, 1989.

Cohen, Esther. "'To Die a Criminal for the Public Good': The Execution Ritual in Late Medieval Paris," in *Law, Custom, and the Social Fabric in Medieval Europe: Essays in Honor of Bruce Lyon,* ed. Bernard S. Bachrach and David Nicholas. Studies in Medieval Culture 28. Kalamazoo, Mich.: Medieval Institute Publications, 1990: 285–304.

Compagnon, Antoine. *La seconde main: Ou, le travail de la citation.* Paris: Seuil, 1979.

Coopland, G. W. *Nicole Oresme and the Astrologers: A Study of his "Livre de Divinacions."* Cambridge, Mass.: Harvard University Press, 1952.

Cornell, Drucilla. *Beyond Accommodation: Ethical Feminism, Deconstruction, and the Law.* New York: Routledge, 1991.

Cosquin, Emmanuel. "Le Conte du chat et de la chandelle dans l'Europe du moyen âge et en Orient." *Romania* 40 (1911): 371–430.

Coville, A. *Gontier et Pierre Col et l'humanisme en France au temps de Charles VI.* Paris: Droz, 1934.

Cropp, Glynis M. "Boèce et Christine de Pizan." *Le Moyen Age* 87, no. 3–4, (1981): 387–418.

Cuttler, S. H. *The Law of Treason and Treason Trials in Later Medieval France.*

Cambridge Studies in Medieval Life and Thought, 3rd series, vol. 16. Cambridge: Cambridge University Press, 1981.

Davis, Natalie Zemon. *Society and Culture in Early Modern France.* Stanford, Calif.: Stanford University Press, 1975.

de Asúa, Miguel J. C. "The Organization of Discourse on Animals in the Thirteenth Century: Peter of Spain, Albert the Great, and the Commentaries on the *De animalibus.*" Ph.D. diss., University of Notre Dame, 1991.

Delgado, Richard. "Words that Wound: A Tort Action for Racial Insults, Epithets, and Name-Calling." *Harvard Civil Rights–Civil Liberties Law Review* 17, no. 1 (spring 1982): 133–81.

Delisle, Léopold. "Études historiques: De l'instruction littéraire de la noblesse française au moyen âge." *Le Correspondant* 36 (1855): 444–50.

Delmaire, Bernard. "Les Béguines dans le nord de la France au premier siècle de leur histoire (vers 1230–1350)," in *Les Religieuses en France au XIIIᵉ siècle*, ed. Michel Parisse. Nancy: Presses Universitaires de Nancy, 1985: 121–62.

Delumeau, Jean, ed. *Injures et blasphèmes.* Paris: Imago, 1989.

Denomy, Alex J. "The *De amore* of Andreas Capellanus and the Condemnation of 1277." *Mediaeval Studies* 8 (1946): 107–49.

Derrida, Jacques. *Of Grammatology.* Trans. Gayatri Chakravorty Spivak. Baltimore: Johns Hopkins University Press, 1980.

Derville, Alain. "L'Alphabétisation du peuple à la fin du moyen âge." *Revue du Nord* 66 (April–September 1984): 761–77.

Dictionnaire de droit canonique. 7 vols. Ed. R. Naz. Paris: Letouzey et Ané, 1935–65.

Dictionnaire de théologie catholique, contenant l'exposé des doctrines de la théologie catholique, leurs preuves, et leur histoire. 15 vols. Ed. Alfred Vacant and Eugène Mangenot. Paris: Letouzey et Ané, 1930–1950.

Dollimore, Jonathan. *Sexual Dissidence: Augustine to Wilde, Freud to Foucault.* New York: Oxford University Press, 1991.

Douglas, Mary. *Risk and Blame: Essays in Cultural Theory.* London: Routledge, 1992.

Dow, Blanche Hinman. *The Varying Attitude toward Women in French Literature of the Fifteenth Century: The Opening Years.* New York: Institute of French Studies, 1936.

Dragonetti, Roger. *La Technique poétique des trouvères dans la chanson courtoise.* Geneva: Slatkine Reprints, 1979.

Dronke, Peter. *Women Writers of the Middle Ages: A Critical Study of Texts from Perpetua (203) to Marguerite Porete (1310).* Cambridge: Cambridge University Press, 1984.

Duby, Georges. *Le Chevalier, la femme et le prêtre: Le mariage dans la France féodale.* Paris: Hachette, 1981.

———. *Mâle moyen âge: De l'amour et autres essais.* Paris: Flammarion, 1988.

———. *Que sait-on de l'amour en France au XIIᵉ siècle?* Oxford: Clarendon Press, 1983.

Dumézil, Georges. *Servius et la fortune: Essai sur la fonction sociale de louange et de blâme et sur les éléments indo-européens du cens romain.* Paris: Gallimard, 1943.

Durkheim, Émile. *L'Évolution pédagogique en France.* 1938; Paris: Presses Universitaires de France, 1990.

Eden, Kathy. *Poetic and Legal Fictions in the Aristotelian Tradition.* Princeton: Princeton University Press, 1986.

Enciclopedia del Diritto. Rome: Giuffre, 1964, vol. 12.

Enders, Jody. *Rhetoric and the Origins of Medieval Drama.* Ithaca, N.Y.: Cornell University Press, 1992.

———. "The Theater of Scholastic Erudition." *Comparative Drama* 27, no. 3 (fall 1993): 341–63.

Evans, Ruth, and Lesley Johnson. "*The Assembly of Ladies*: A Maze of Feminist Sign Reading," in *Feminist Theory and Practice*, ed. Susan Sellers. London: Simon and Schuster, 1991: 171–96.

Fake? The Art of Deception. Ed. Mark Jones, with Paul Craddock and Nicholas Barker. London: British Museum Publications, 1990.

Faral, Edmond. *Recherches sur les sources latines des contes et romans courtois du moyen âge.* Paris: E. Champion, 1913.

Farmer, Sharon. "Persuasive Voices: Clerical Images of Medieval Wives." *Speculum* 61, no. 3 (July 1986): 517–43.

Félibien, Michel, and D. Guy-Alexis Lobineau. *Histoire de la ville de Paris.* 5 vols. Paris: G. Desprez & J. Desessartz, 1725.

Ferrante, Joan. "The Education of Women in the Middle Ages in Theory, Fact, and Fantasy," in *Beyond their Sex: Learned Women of the European Past*, ed. Patricia Labalme. New York: New York University Press, 1980: 9–42.

———. "Male Fantasy and Female Reality in Courtly Literature." *Women's Studies* 11 (1984): 67–97.

Fish, Stanley. *There's No Such Thing as Free Speech and It's a Good Thing Too.* New York: Oxford University Press, 1994.

Foucault, Michel. *Power/Knowledge: Selected Interviews and Other Writings, 1972–1977.* Ed. and trans. Colin Gordon. New York: Pantheon, 1980.

Freccero, John. *Dante: The Poetics of Conversion.* Ed. Rachel Jacoff. Cambridge, Mass.: Harvard University Press, 1986.

Fumaroli, Marc. *L'Age de l'éloquence: Rhétorique et "res litteraria" de la Renaissance au seuil de l'époque classique.* Geneva: Droz, 1980.

Furr, Grover Carr III. "The Quarrel of the *Roman de la Rose* and Fourteenth-Century Humanism." Ph.D. diss., Princeton University, 1979.

Fuss, Diana. *Essentially Speaking: Feminism, Nature, and Difference.* New York: Routledge, 1989.

Gally, Michèle. "Le Huitième Art: Les clercs du XIIIe siècle, nouveaux maîtres du discours amoureux." *Poétique* 75 (September 1988): 279–95.

Garnsey, Peter. *Social Status and Legal Privilege in the Roman Empire.* Oxford: Oxford University Press, 1970.

Gauvard, Claude. *"De Grace especial": Crime, état, et société en France à la fin du moyen âge.* 2 vols. Publications de la Sorbonne. Histoire ancienne et médiévale, no. 24. Paris: Éditions du C.N.R.S., 1991.

Ghisalberti, Fausto. "Medieval Biographies of Ovid." *Journal of the Warburg and Courthauld Institutes* 9 (1946): 10–59.

Gilson, Etienne. "Le Message de l'humanisme," in *Culture et politique en France à l'époque de l'humanisme et de la Renaissance*, ed. Franco Simone. Turin: Accademia delle Scienze, 1974: 3–9.

Gleason, Maud W. "The Semiotics of Gender: Physiognomy and Self-Fashioning in the Second Century C.E.," in *Before Sexuality: The Construction of Erotic*

Experience in the Ancient Greek World, ed. David M. Halperin, John J. Winkler, and Froma I. Zeitlin. Princeton: Princeton University Press, 1990: 389–416.

Glorieux, Palémon. "L'Enseignement au moyen âge: Techniques et méthodes en usage à la faculté de théologie de Paris au XIIIᵉ siècle." *Archives d'histoire doctrinale et littéraire au moyen âge* 35 (1968): 65–186.

———. *La littérature quodlibétique de 1260–1320.* 2 vols. Le Saulchoir: Kain, 1925; Paris: J. Vrin, 1935.

Glossarium Mediae et Infimae Latinitatis Regni Hungariae. Ed. Antonius Bartal. Hildesheim: Georg Olms, 1970.

Godefroy, Frédéric. *Dictionnaire de l'ancienne langue française et de tous ses dialectes du IXᵉ au XVᵉ siècle.* 10 vols. Paris: F. Vieweg, 1885.

Grabmann, Martin. *Die Geschichte der scholastischen Methode: Nach den gedruckten und ungedruckten Quellen dargestellt.* 2 vols. 1909–11; Darmstadt: Wissenschaftliche Buchgesellschaft, 1957.

———. "Die mittelalterlichen Kommentare zur *Politik* des Aristoteles." *Sitzungsberichte der Bayerischen Akademie der Wissenschaften.* Philos.-hist. Abteilung 2, no. 10 (1941).

Grafton, Anthony, and Lisa Jardine. *From Humanism to the Humanities: Education and the Liberal Arts in Fifteenth- and Sixteenth-Century Europe.* Cambridge, Mass.: Harvard University Press, 1986.

Grandeau, Yann. "De Quelques Dames qui ont servi la reine Isabeau de Bavière." *Bulletin philologique et historique (jusqu'à 1610) du Comité des travaux historiques et scientifiques* (1975): 129–238.

———. *Jeanne insultée: Procès en diffamation.* Paris: Albin Michel, 1973.

Gravdal, Kathryn. *Ravishing Maidens: Writing Rape in Medieval French Literature and Law.* Philadelphia: University of Pennsylvania Press, 1991.

Green, Monica H. *Women and Literate Medicine in Medieval Europe: Trota and the "Trotula."* Forthcoming.

Greilshammer, Myriam. *L'Envers du tableau: Mariage et maternité en Flandre médiévale* Paris: Armand Colin, 1990.

Grévy-Pons, Nicole. *Célibat et nature: Une controverse médiévale, à propos d'un traité du début du XVᵉ siècle.* Paris: Éditions du C.N.R.S., 1975.

———. "L'Honneur de la couronne de France": Quatre libelles contre les Anglais, vers 1418–vers 1429.* Paris: Klincksieck, 1990.

Grigsby, John L. "Miroir des bonnes femmes." *Romania* 82, no. 4 (1961): 458–81; and *Romania* 83, no. 1 (1962): 30–51.

Grosse, Max. *Das Buch im Roman: Studien zu Buchverweis und Autoritätszitat in altfranzösischen Texten.* Munich: Wilhelm Fink, 1994.

Grundmann, Herbert. *Ausgewählte Aufsätze.* 3 vols. Stuttgart: Hiersemann, 1976–78.

———. "Die Frauen und die Literatur im Mittelalter: Ein Beitrag zur Frage nach der Entstehung des Schrifttums in der Volkssprache." *Archiv für Kulturgeschichte* 26 (1936): 129–61.

Guenée, Bernard. *Tribunaux et gens de justice dans le bailliage de Senlis à la fin du moyen âge (vers 1380–vers 1550).* Publications de la Faculté des lettres de l'Université de Strasbourg no. 144. Paris: Belles Lettres, 1963.

Gunn, Alan M. F. "Teacher and Student in the *Roman de la rose*: A Study in Archetypal Figures and Patterns." *L'Esprit Créateur* 2, no. 3 (fall 1962): 126–34.

Haffen, Josiane. *Contribution à l'étude de la Sibylle médiévale.* Paris: Belles Lettres, 1984.

Hasenohr, Geneviève. "La Locution verbale figurée dans l'oeuvre de Jean LeFèvre." *Le Moyen Français* 14–15 (1984): 229–81.

———. "La vie quotidienne de la femme vue par l'église: L'Enseignement des 'journées chrétiennes' de la fin du moyen âge," in *Frau und spätmittelalterlichen Alltag.* Ed. M. Heinrich Appelt. Vienna: Verlag der Österreichischen Akademie der Wissenschaften, 1986: 19–101.

Heath, Stephen. "Male Feminism," in *Men in Feminism,* ed. Alice Jardine and Paul Smith. New York: Methuen, 1987: 1–32.

Hegel, Georg Wilhelm Friedrich. *Phenomenology of Spirit.* Trans A. V. Miller. Oxford: Clarendon Press, 1977.

———. *Philosophie der Geschichte. Sämtliche Werke.* 22 vols. Ed. Hermann Glockner (Stuttgart: Frommanns, 1949).

Helmholz, R. H. *Select Cases on Defamation to 1600.* Publications of the Selden Society, 101. London: The Selden Society, 1985.

Hermann, Hermann Julius, ed. *Die westeuropäischen Handschriften und Inkunabeln der Gothik und der Renaissance, mit Ausnahme der niederländischen Handschriften.* 2 vols. Leipzig: Karl W. Hiersemann, 1935–36.

Hexter, Ralph J. *Ovid and Medieval Schooling: Studies in Medieval School Commentaries on Ovid's "Ars amatoria," "Epistulae ex Ponto," and "Epistulae Heroidum."* Munich: Arbeo Gesellschaft, 1986.

Hicks, Eric, and E. Ornato. "Jean de Montreuil et le débat sur le *Roman de la rose.*" *Romania* 98, no. 1 (1977): 34–64 and *Romania* 98, no. 2 (1977): 186–219.

Higgins, Paula. "Parisian Nobles, A Scottish Princess, and the Woman's Voice in Late Medieval Song." *Early Music History* 10 (1991): 145–200.

Hillgarth, J. N. *Readers and Books in Majorca 1229–1550.* Paris: Éditions du C.N.R.S., 1991.

Histoire des femmes en Occident. Vol. 2, *Le Moyen Age.* Ed. Christiane Klapisch-Zuber. Paris: Plon, 1991.

Hirsch, Marianne, and Evelyn Fox Keller, eds. *Conflicts in Feminism.* New York: Routledge, 1990.

Honig, B. "Toward an Agonistic Feminism: Hannah Arendt and the Politics of Identity," in *Feminists Theorize the Political,* ed. Judith Butler and Joan W. Scott. New York: Routledge, 1992: 215–38.

Howell, Martha C. *Women, Production, and Patriarchy in Late Medieval Cities.* Chicago: University of Chicago Press, 1986.

Hult, David. *Self-Fulfilling Prophecies: Readership and Authority in the First "Roman de la rose."* Cambridge: Cambridge University Press, 1986.

Hunt, Tony. "Aristotle, Dialectic, and Courtly Literature." *Viator* 10 (1979): 95–129.

Huot, Sylvia. *From Song to Book: The Poetics of Writing in Old French Lyric and Lyrical Narrative Poetry.* Ithaca, N.Y.: Cornell University Press, 1987.

———. *"The Romance of the Rose" and its Medieval Readers: Interpretation, Reception, Manuscript Transmission.* Cambridge: Cambridge University Press, 1993.

———. "Seduction and Sublimation: Christine de Pizan, Jean de Meun and Dante." *Romance Notes* 25, no. 3 (spring 1985): 361–73.

Irigaray, Luce. *Ce sexe qui n'en est pas un.* Paris: Minuit, 1977.

————. "Equal to Whom?" Trans. Robert L. Mazzola. *Differences* 1, no. 2 (summer 1989): 59–76.

————. *Speculum de l'autre femme*. Paris: Minuit, 1974.

Iser, Wolfgang. "Fictionalizing: The Anthropological Dimension of Literary Fictions." *New Literary History* 21, no. 4 (autumn 1990): 939–55.

Janeway, Elizabeth. "On the Power of the Weak." *Signs* 1, no. 1 (autumn 1975): 103–9.

Jardine, Alice. *Gynesis: Configurations of Woman and Modernity*. Ithaca, N.Y.: Cornell University Press, 1985.

Jauss, Hans-Robert. "Adam Interrogateur (pour une histoire des fonctions du modèle question/réponse)." *Texte* 3 (1984): 159–78.

Johnson, Barbara. *A World of Difference*. Baltimore: Johns Hopkins University Press, 1987.

Johnson, Leonard W. *Poets as Players: Theme and Variation in Late Medieval French Poetry*. Stanford, Calif.: Stanford University Press, 1990.

Jones, Kathleen B. "The Trouble with Authority." *Differences* 3, no. 1 (spring 1991): 104–27.

Jordan, Constance. "Feminism and the Humanists: the Case of Sir Thomas Elyot's Defence of Good Women." *Renaissance Quarterly* 36, no. 2 (summer 1983): 181–201.

Jourdain, Charles. *L'Education des femmes au moyen âge*. Paris: Firmin-Didot, 1871.

Judd, Stephanie H. *Chaste Thinking: The Rape of Lucretia and the Birth of Humanism*. Bloomington: Indiana University Press, 1989.

Kantorowicz, Ernst H. *The King's Two Bodies: A Study in Mediaeval Political Theology*. Princeton: Princeton University Press, 1957.

Karl, Louis. "L'Art d'amour de Guiart: Ovide poète de l'amour au moyen âge." *Zeitschrift für romanische philologie* 44 (1924): 66–80.

Karnein, Alfred. *"De amore" in volkssprachlicher literatur: Untersuchungen zur Andreas-Capellanus-Rezeption in Mittelalter und Renaissance*. Heidelberg: Carl Winter Universitätsverlag, 1985.

————. *"Wie Feuer und Holz*: Aspekte der Ausgrenzung von Frauen beim Thema Liebe im 13. Jahrhundert." *Zeitschrift für Literaturwissenschaft und Linguistik* 19 (1989): 93–115.

Kay, Sarah. "Women's Body of Knowledge: Epistemology and Misogyny in the *Romance of the Rose*," in *Framing Medieval Bodies*, ed. Sarah Kay and Miri Rubin. Manchester: Manchester University Press, 1994: 211–35.

Keller, Evelyn Fox. "Making Gender Visible in the Pursuit of Nature's Secrets," in *Feminist Studies/Critical Studies*, ed. Teresa de Lauretis. Bloomington: Indiana University Press, 1986: 67–77.

————. *Secrets of Life, Secrets of Death: Essays on Language, Gender, and Science*. New York: Routledge, 1992.

Kelly, Douglas. "Obscurity and Memory: Sources for Invention in Medieval French Literature." *Studies in Medieval Culture* 16 (1984): 33–56.

Kelly, Joan. "Early Feminist Theory and the *Querelle des femmes*, 1400–1789." *Signs* 8, no. 1 (autumn 1982): 4–28.

Kendrick, Laura. *The Game of Love: Troubadour Word Play*. Berkeley: University of California Press, 1988.

Kibler, William W. "The Narrator as Key to Alain Chartier's *La Belle Dame sans mercy.*" *The French Review* 52, no. 5 (April 1979): 714–23.

Kofman, Sarah. *L'Énigme de la femme: La femme dans les textes de Freud.* Paris: Galilée, 1980.

Krueger, Roberta L. "Constructing Sexual Identities in the High Middle Ages: The Didactic Poetry of Robert de Blois." *Paragraph* 13, no. 2 (July 1990): 10–31.

———. "Desire, Meaning, and the Female Reader in *Le Chevalier de la Charrete,*" in *The Passing of Arthur: New Essays in Arthurian Tradition,* ed. Christopher Baswell and William Sharpe. New York: Garland, 1988: 31–51.

———. "Double Jeopardy: The Appropriation of the Heroine in Four Old French Romances of the 'Cycle de la Gageure,'" in *Seeking the Woman in Late Medieval and Renaissance Writings: Essays in Feminist Contextual Criticism,* ed. Sheila Fisher and Janet E. Halley. Knoxville: The University of Tennessee Press, 1989: 21–50.

———. "Misogyny, Manipulation, and the Female Reader in Hue de Rotelande's *Ipomedon,*" in *Courtly Literature: Culture and Context,* ed. Keith Busby and Erik Kooper. Amsterdam: Benjamins, 1990: 394–409.

———. *Women Readers and the Ideology of Gender in Old French Verse Romance.* Cambridge: Cambridge University Press, 1993.

Lacroix, Paul. *Histoire de l'imprimerie et des arts qui se rattachent à la typographie.* Geneva: Slatkine Reprints, 1971.

Laigle, Mathilde. *Le Livre des trois vertus de Christine de Pisan et son milieu historique et littéraire.* Paris: H. Champion, 1912.

Lange, Lynda. "Woman is Not a Rational Animal: On Aristotle's Biology of Reproduction," in *Discovering Reality: Feminist Perspectives on Epistemology, Metaphysics, Methodology, and Philosophy of Science,* ed. Sandra Harding and Merrill B. Hintikka. Dordrecht: D. Reidel, 1983: 1–16.

Laqueur, Thomas. *Making Sex: Body and Gender from the Greeks to Freud.* Cambridge, Mass.: Harvard University Press, 1990.

Larguèche, Evelyne. *L'Effet injure: De la pragmatique à la psychanalyse.* Paris: Presses Universitaires de France, 1983.

Lawton, David. *Blasphemy.* Philadelphia: University of Pennsylvania Press, 1993.

LeDoeuff, Michèle. *L'Étude et le rouet.* Paris: Seuil, 1989.

———. "Women, Reason, Etc." *Differences* 2, no. 3 (fall 1990): 1–13.

Leff, Gordon. *Paris and Oxford Universities in the Thirteenth and Fourteenth Centuries.* New York: John Wiley and Sons, 1968.

Legendre, Pierre. *L'Amour du censeur: Essai sur l'ordre dogmatique.* Paris: Seuil, 1974.

———. *Écrits juridiques du moyen âge occidental.* London: Variorum Reprints, 1988.

LeGoff, Jacques. *Les Intellectuels au moyen âge.* Paris: Seuil, 1957.

Lerner, Gerda. *The Creation of Patriarchy.* New York: Oxford University Press, 1986.

LeSourd, Auguste. *Autour de Clotilde de Surville: Lettres inédites de Vanderbourg et du Marquis de Surville.* Aubenas: Clovis Habuzit, 1928.

Leupin, Alexandre. *Barbarolexis: Medieval Writing and Sexuality.* Cambridge, Mass.: Harvard University Press, 1989.

Levey, Martin, and Safwat S. Souryal. "Galen's *On the Secrets of Women and on*

the Secrets of Men: A Contribution to the History of Arabic Pharmacology."
Janus 55, no. 2–3 (1968): 208–19.

Lewis, Peter Shervey. *Later Medieval France: The Polity*. London: Macmillan, 1968.

Little, Lester K. *Benedictine Maledictions: Liturgical Cursing in Romanesque France*. Ithaca, N.Y.: Cornell University Press, 1993.

Lloyd, G. E. R. *Polarity and Analogy: Two Types of Argumentation in Early Greek Thought*. Cambridge: Cambridge University Press, 1966.

Lloyd, Genevieve. *The Man of Reason: "Male" and "Female" in Western Philosophy*. Minneapolis: University of Minnesota Press, 1984.

Loquin, Anatole. "Réponse à M. Antoine Macé: Les poésies de Clotilde de Surville." *Actes de l'Académie des Sciences, Belles Lettres, et Arts de Bordeaux* (1873).

Lucken, Christopher. "Du ban du coq à *l'Ariereban* de l'âne (A propos du *Bestiaire d'amour* de Richard de Fournival)." *Reinardus* 5 (1992): 109–24.

———. "Les Portes de la mémoire: Richard de Fournival et l'"ariereban' de l'amour." Ph.D. diss., University of Geneva, 1994.

Luscombe, David E. *The School of Peter Abelard: The Influence of Abelard's Thought in the Early Scholastic Period*. Cambridge: Cambridge University Press, 1969.

MacCormack, Carol P., and Marilyn Strathern, eds. *Nature, Culture, and Gender*. Cambridge: Cambridge University Press, 1980.

Macé, Antoine. *Un Procès d'histoire littéraire: Les poésies de Clotilde de Surville*. Grenoble: Prudhomme, 1870.

MacKinnon, Catharine A. *Feminism Unmodified: Discourses on Life and Law*. Cambridge: Harvard University Press, 1987.

———. *Only Words*. Cambridge, Mass.: Harvard University Press, 1993.

———. "Pornography as Defamation and Discrimination." *Boston University Law Review* 71, no. 5 (November 1991): 793–815.

Maclean, Ian. *The Renaissance Notion of Woman: A Study in The Fortunes of Scholasticism and Medical Science in European Intellectual Life*. Cambridge: Cambridge University Press, 1980.

Malaxecheverria, Ignacio. *Le Bestiaire médiéval et l'archétype de la féminité*. Paris: Lettres modernes, 1982.

Manfredini, Arrigo Diego. *La Diffamazione verbale nel diritto romano*. Milan: A. Giuffre, 1979.

Mann, Jill. *Apologies to Women*. Cambridge: Cambridge University Press, 1991.

Marchello-Nizia, Christiane. "L'Invention du dialogue amoureux: Le masque d'une différence," in *Masques et déguisements dans la littérature médiévale*, ed. Marie-Louise Ollier. Montréal: Presses de l'Université de Montréal, 1988: 223–32.

Margolis, Nadia. "Christine de Pizan and the Jews: Political and Poetic Implications," in *Politics, Gender, and Genre: The Political Thought of Christine de Pizan*. Boulder: University of Colorado Press, 1992: 53–73.

———. "Christine de Pizan: The Poetess as Historian." *The Journal of the History of Ideas* 47, no. 3 (July–September 1986): 361–75.

Marsilli, Pietro. "Réception et diffusion iconographique du conte 'Aristote et Phillis' en Europe depuis le moyen âge," in *Amour, mariage, et transgressions au moyen âge,* ed. Danielle Buschinger and André Crépin. Göppingen: Kümmerle, 1984: 239–70.

Maurras, Charles. *Romantisme et révolution: L'Avenir de l'intelligence.* Paris: Nouvelle librairie nationale, 1922.

Mazon, A. *Marguerite de Chalis et la légende de Clotilde de Surville.* Paris: Lemère, 1873.

McCulloch, Florence. "Le Tigre au miroir: La vie d'une image de Pline à Pierre Gringore." *Revue des sciences humaines* 130 (April–June 1968): 149–60.

McDonnell, Ernest W. *The Beguines and Beghards in Medieval Culture, with Special Emphasis on the Belgian Scene.* New Brunswick, N.J.: Rutgers University Press, 1954.

McGinn, Bernard. "*Teste David cum Sibylla*: The Significance of the Sibylline Tradition in the Middle Ages," in *Women of the Medieval World: Essays in Honor of John Hine Mundy,* ed. Julius Kirschner and Suzanne F. Wemple. Oxford: Oxford University Press, 1985.

Medieval Latin Word-List. Prepared by R. E. Latham. London: Oxford University Press, 1965.

Meyer, Paul. "Les Manuscrits français de Cambridge." *Romania* 15 (1886): 236–357.

Michelet, Jules. *Oeuvres complètes.* Vol. 3. Ed. Paul Viallaneix. Paris: Flammarion, 1971.

Migliorino, Francesco. *Fama e infamia: Problemi della società medievale nel pensiero giuridico nei secoli XII e XIII.* Catania: Giannotta, 1985.

Miller, Nancy K. *Subject to Change: Reading Feminist Writing.* New York: Columbia University Press, 1988.

Moi, Toril. "Appropriating Bourdieu: Feminist Theory and Pierre Bourdieu's Sociology of Culture." *New Literary History* 22, no. 4 (autumn 1991): 1017–49.

———. "Desire in Language: Andreas Capellanus and the Controversy of Courtly Love," in *Medieval Literature: Criticism, Ideology, and History,* ed. David Aers. New York: St. Martin's, 1986: 11–33.

———. "Feminist, Female, Feminine," in *The Feminist Reader: Essays in Gender and the Politics of Literary Criticism,* ed. Catherine Belsey and Jane Moore. New York: Blackwell, 1989: 117–32.

———. "Patriarchal Thought and the Drive for Knowledge," in *Between Feminism and Psychoanalysis,* ed. Teresa Brennan. London: Routledge, 1989: 189–205.

Mollat, Michel, and Phillippe Wolff. *Ongles bleus: Jacques et Ciompi, les révolutions populaires en Europe aux XIVe et XVe siècles.* Paris: Calmann-Levy, 1970.

Monfrin, Jacques. "La Place du *Secret des Secrets* dans la littérature française médiévale," in *Pseudo-Aristotle, "The Secret of Secrets": Sources and Influences.* Warburg Institute Surveys, no. 9. London: Warburg Institute, 1982: 73–113.

Moore, R. I. *The Formation of a Persecuting Society: Power and Deviance in Western Europe, 950–1250.* New York: Blackwell, 1987.

Morel, Maurice. *L'Excommunication et le pouvoir civil en France du droit canonique au commencement du XVe siècle.* Paris: Rousseau, 1926.

Moulton, Janice. "A Paradigm of Philosophy: The Adversary Method," in *Discovering Reality: Feminist Perspectives on Epistemology, Metaphysics, Methodology, and Philosophy of Science,* ed. Sandra Harding and Merrill B. Hintikka. Dordrecht: D. Reidel, 1983: 149–64.

Murray, Alexander. *Reason and Society in the Middle Ages*. Oxford: Oxford University Press, 1978.

Neel, Carol. "The Origins of the Beguines," *Signs* 14, no. 2 (winter 1989): 321–41.

Neuschel, Kristen B. *Word of Honor: Interpreting Noble Culture in Sixteenth-Century France*. Ithaca, N.Y.: Cornell University Press, 1989.

Newman, Barbara. "Authority, Authenticity, and the Repression of Héloïse." *Journal of Medieval and Renaissance Studies* 22, no. 2 (spring 1992): 121–57.

———. *Sister of Wisdom: St. Hildegard's Theology of the Feminine*. Berkeley: University of California Press, 1987.

Nicholas, David M. *The Domestic Life of a Medieval City: Women, Children, and the Family in Fourteenth-Century Ghent*. Lincoln: University of Nebraska Press, 1985.

———. *Town and Countryside: Social, Economic, and Political Tensions in Fourteenth-Century Flanders*. Bruges: de Tempel, 1971.

Nichols, Stephen G. "Medieval Women Writers: Aisthesis and the Powers of Marginality." *Yale French Studies* 75 (1988): 77–94.

Nicholson, Linda J. *Gender and History: The Limits of Social Theory in the Age of the Family*. New York: Columbia University Press, 1986.

Noakes, Susan. "On the Superficiality of Women," in *The Comparative Perspective on Literature: Approaches to Theory and Practice*, ed. Clayton Koelb and Susan Noakes. Ithaca, N.Y.: Cornell University Press, 1988: 339–55.

Nodier, Charles. *Questions de littérature légale: Du plagiat, de la supposition d'auteurs, des supercheries qui ont rapport aux livres*. 2 vols. Paris: Crapelet, 1828.

Olivier-Martin, François. *Histoire de la coutume de la prévôté et vicomté de Paris*. 2 vols. Paris: E. Leroux, 1922–30.

Olsen, Birgen Munk. "Ovide au moyen âge (du XIᵉ au XIIᵉ siècle)," in *Le Strade del testo: Studi di tradizione manoscritta*, ed. Guglielmo Cavello. Bari: Adriatica Editrice, 1987.

Ong, Walter J. *Fighting for Life: Contest, Sexuality, and Consciousness*. Ithaca, N.Y.: Cornell University Press, 1980.

———. *Rhetoric, Romance, and Technology: Studies in the Interaction of Expression and Culture*. Ithaca, N.Y.: Cornell University Press, 1971.

Ornato, E. *Jean Muret et ses amis Nicolas de Clamanges et Jean de Montreuil: Contribution à l'étude des rapports entre les humanistes de Paris et ceux d'Avignon 1394–1420*. Paris: Droz, 1969.

Ouy, Gilbert. "Paris: L'un des principaux foyers de l'humanisme en Europe au début du XVᵉ siècle." *Bulletin de la société d'histoire de Paris et de l'Ile de France* 94–95 (1967–68): 71–98.

Paré, Gérard. *Les Idées et les lettres au XIIIᵉ siècle: "Le Roman de la Rose."* Montréal: Centre de psychologie et de pédagogie, 1947.

Paré, Gérard Marie, Adrien Marie Brunet, and Pierre Tremblay. *La Renaissance du XIIᵉ siècle: Les écoles et l'enseignement*. Publications de l'Institut d'études médiévales d'Ottawa. Paris: J. Vrin, 1933.

Paris, Gaston. "Un procès d'histoire littéraire." *Revue Critique*, 1 March 1873, 133–40.

Paroles d'outrage. Ethnologie française 22, no. 3 (July–September 1992).

Patterson, Annabel. *Censorship and Interpretation: The Conditions of Writing and*

Reading in Early Modern England. Madison: University of Wisconsin Press, 1984.

Patterson, Lee. *Negotiating the Past: The Historical Understanding of Medieval Literature.* Madison: University of Wisconsin Press, 1987.

Paupert, Anne. *Les Fileuses et le clerc: Une étude des Evangiles des Quenouilles.* Paris: H. Champion, 1990.

Peignot, Gabriel. *Essai historique sur la liberté d'écrire chez les anciens et au moyen âge.* Paris: Crapelet, 1832.

Peters, Edward. *Inquisition.* New York: Free Press, 1988.

———. *Torture.* Oxford: Basil Blackwell, 1985.

Piaget, Arthur. "Un Manuscrit de la cour amoureuse de Charles VI." *Romania* 20 (1891): 417–54.

Pirenne, Henri. *Les Anciennes Démocraties des Pays-Bas.* Bibliothèque de philosophie scientifique. Paris: Ernest Flammarion, 1910.

———. *Early Democracies in the Low Countries: Urban Society and Political Conflict in the Middle Ages and the Renaissance.* New York: Harper and Row, 1963.

———. *Histoire de Belgique.* 7 vols. Brussels: Maurice Lamertin, 1929–32.

———. "L'Instruction des marchands au moyen âge." *Annales d'histoire économique et sociale* 1 (1929): 13–28.

Poirion, Daniel. "Lectures de la *Belle Dame sans mercy.*" *Mélanges de langue et de littérature médiévales offerts à Pierre Le Gentil.* Paris: S.E.D.E.S, 1973: 691–706.

———. *Milieux universitaires et mentalité urbaine au moyen âge.* Paris: Presses de l'Université de Paris–Sorbonne, 1987.

———. "Les Mots et les choses selon Jean de Meun." *L'Information littéraire* 26 (January–February 1974): 7–11.

———. *Le Poète et le prince: L'Évolution du lyrisme courtois de Guillaume de Machaut à Charles d'Orléans.* Paris: Presses Universitaires de France, 1965.

Pompée, Pierre Philibert. *Rapport historique sur les écoles primaires de la ville de Paris.* Paris: Imprimerie royale, 1839.

Porteau-Bitker, Annick. "Criminalité et délinquance féminine dans le droit pénal des XIIIᵉ et XIVᵉ siècles." *Revue historique de droit français et étranger* 58, no. 1 (January–March 1980): 13–56.

Posner, Richard A. *Law and Literature: A Misunderstood Relation.* Cambridge, Mass.: Harvard University Press, 1988.

Pouchelle, Marie-Christine. "L'Hybride." *Nouvelle revue de psychanalyse* 7 (1973): 49–61.

Pratt, Karen. "Analogy or Logic, Authority or Experience? Rhetorical and Dialectical Strategies for and against Women." Forthcoming.

Quilligan, Maureen. *The Allegory of Female Authority: Christine de Pizan's "Cité des Dames."* Ithaca, N.Y.: Cornell University Press, 1991.

Rashdall, Hastings. *The Universities of Europe in the Middle Ages.* 2 vols. Oxford: Clarendon Press, 1895.

Regalado, Nancy Freeman. " 'Des Contraires choses': La fonction poétique de la citation et des *exempla* dans le *Roman de la Rose* de Jean de Meun." *Littérature* 41 (February 1981): 62–81.

———. "*Vos Paroles ont mains et piés*: Woman's Wary Voice in the *Response au Bestiaire d'amors de Maître Richard de Fournival.*" Unpublished paper.

Régnier-Bohler, Danielle. "Femme/Faute/Fantasme," in *La Condicion de la mujer en la Edad Media*, ed. Yves-René Fonquerne and Alfonso Esteban. Madrid: Universidad Complutense, 1986: 475–99.

———. "Voix littéraires, voix mystiques," in *Histoire des femmes en Occident*. Vol. 2. *Le Moyen Age*. Ed. Christiane Klapisch-Zuber. Paris: Plon, 1991: 443–500.

Reinterpreting Christine de Pizan. Ed. Earl Jeffrey Richards. Athens: University of Georgia Press, 1992.

Reisert, Robert. *Der siebenkammerige Uterus: Studien zur mittelalterlichen Wirkungsgeschichte und Entfaltung eines embryologischen Gebarmuttermodells*. Pattensen: Horst Wellm Verlag, 1986.

Richardson, Lula McDowell. *The Forerunners of Feminism in French Literature of the Renaissance: From Christine of Pisa to Marie de Gournay*. Baltimore: Johns Hopkins University Press, 1929.

Rider, Jeff. "Other Voices: Historicism and the Interpretation of Medieval Texts." *Exemplaria* 1, no. 2 (fall 1989): 293–312.

———. "Whence? Whither?" *Exemplaria* 3, no. 1 (spring 1991): 243–66.

Rigney, Ann. "Fame and Defamation: Toward a Socio-Pragmatics." *Semiotica* 99, no 1–2 (1994): 53–65 .

Riley, Denise. *"Am I That Name?": Feminism and the Category of "Women" in History*. Minneapolis: University of Minnesota Press, 1988.

Rouse, Richard H. "Manuscripts Belonging to Richard de Fournival." *Revue d'histoire des textes* 3 (1973): 253–69.

Rousselot, Paul. *Histoire de l'éducation des femmes en France*. 1883. Reprint, Research and Source Works Series, History of Education, vol. 8. New York: Burt Franklin, 1971.

Rowland, Beryl. "The Art of Memory and the Bestiary," in *Beasts and Birds of the Middle Ages: The Bestiary and Its Legacy*, ed. Willene B. Clark and Meradith T. McMunn. Philadelphia: University of Pennsylvania Press, 1989: 12–25.

Roy, Bruno. "A la recherche des lecteurs médiévaux du *De amore* d'André le Chapelain." *Revue de l'Université d'Ottawa / University of Ottawa* 55, no. 1 (January–March 1985): 45–73.

Ruhe, Ernstpeter. *De amasio ad amasium: Zur Gattungsgeschichte des mittelalterlichen Liebesbriefes*. Beiträge zur romanischen Philologie des Mittelalters, vol. 10. Munich: Wilhelm Fink, 1975.

———. "La Peur de la transgression: à propos du *Livre d'Enanchet* et du *Bestiaire d'amour*," in *Amour, mariage, et transgressions au moyen âge*, ed. Danielle Buschinger and André Crépin. Göppingen: Kümmerle, 1984: 317–24.

Sainte-Beuve, Charles. *Tableau historique et critique de la poésie française et du théâtre français au XVIe siècle*. Paris: Charpentier, 1843.

Schibanoff, Susan. "Taking the Gold out of Egypt: The Art of Reading as a Woman," in *Gender and Reading: Essays on Readers, Texts and Contexts*, ed. Elizabeth A. Flynn and Patrocinio P. Schweickart. Baltimore: Johns Hopkins University Press, 1986: 83–106.

Schmitt, Jean-Claude. *Mort d'une hérésie: L'Église et les clercs face aux béghines et aux béghards du Rhin supérieur du XIVe au XVe siècle*. Paris: Mouton, 1978.

Schor, Naomi. *Reading in Detail: Aesthetics and the Feminine*. New York: Methuen, 1987.

Scott, Joan W. "Experience," in *Feminists Theorize the Political*, ed. Judith Butler and Joan W. Scott. New York: Routledge, 1992: 22–40.

Searle, John R. "The Logical Status of Fictional Discourse." *New Literary History* 6, no. 2 (winter 1975): 319–32.

Sharpe, J. A. *Defamation and Sexual Slander in Early Modern England: The Church Courts at York.* York: University of York, Borthwick Institute of Historical Research, 1980.

Siciliano, Italo. *François Villon et les thèmes poétiques du moyen âge.* Paris: Armand Colin, 1934.

Simons, Walter. "The Beguines in the Southern Low Countries: A Reassessment." *Bulletin de l'Institut Historique Belge de Rome* 59 (1989): 63–105.

Smith, Susan L. "The Power of Women Topos on a Fourteenth-Century Embroidery." *Viator* 21 (1990): 203–28.

Solterer, Helen. "Figures of Female Militancy in Medieval France." *Signs* 16, no. 3 (spring 1991): 522–49.

———. "Letter-Writing and Picture-Reading: the *Bestiaire d'amour* and Medieval Textuality." *Word and Image* 5, no. 1 (1989): 131–47.

———. "Seeing, Hearing, Tasting Woman: The Senses of Medieval Reading." *Comparative Literature* 46, no. 2 (spring 1994): 129–45.

Soman, Alfred. "Press, Pulpit, and Censorship in France Before Richelieu." *Proceedings of the American Philosophical Society* 120, no. 6 (December 1976): 439–63.

Spelman, Elizabeth V. "Aristotle and the Politicization of the Soul," in *Discovering Reality: Feminist Perspectives on Epistemology, Metaphysics, Methodology, and Philosophy of Science*, ed. Sandra Harding and Merrill B. Hintikka. Dordrecht: D. Reidel, 1983: 17–30.

———. *Inessential Woman: Problems of Exclusion in Feminist Thought.* Boston: Beacon Press, 1988.

Spiegel, Gabrielle M. "History, Historicism, and the Social Logic of the Text in the Middle Ages." *Speculum* 65, no. 1 (January 1990): 59–86.

Stallaert, Charles, and Philippe van der Haeghen. *De L'Instruction publique au moyen âge du VIIIᵉ au XVIᵉ siècle.* Mémoires couronnés et mémoires des savants étrangers publiés par l'Académie royale des sciences, des lettres, et des beaux-arts de Belgique 23 (Brussels: Académie royale, 1850).

Steenberghen, Fernand van. *Aristote en occident: Les origines de l'aristotélisme parisien.* Louvain: Éditions de l'Institut supérieur de philosophie, 1946.

Steinwenter, Arthur. "Die Anfänge des Libellprozesses." *Studia et documenta historiae et juris* 1 (1935): 32–52.

Stewart, Susan. *Crimes of Writing: Problems in the Containment of Representation.* New York: Oxford University Press, 1991.

Stock, Brian. *The Implications of Literacy: Written Language and Models of Interpretation in the Eleventh and Twelfth Centuries.* Princeton: Princeton University Press, 1983.

———. "Lecture, intériorité, et modèles de comportement dans l'Europe des XIᵉ–XIIᵉ siècles." *Cahiers de civilisation médiévale* 33, no. 2 (1990): 103–12.

———. *Listening for the Text: On the Uses of the Past.* Baltimore: Johns Hopkins University Press, 1990.

Storost, Joachim. "Femme chevalchat Aristotte." *Zeitschrift für französische Sprache und Literatur* 66 (1956): 186–201.

Telle, Emile Villemeur. *L'Oeuvre de Marguerite d'Angoulême, reine de Navarre, et la Querelle des femmes*. Toulouse: Imprimerie Toulousain Lion et fils, 1937.

Thomasset, Claude Alexandre. *Commentaire du dialogue de Placides et Timéo: Une Vision à la fin du XIIIe siècle*. Geneva: Droz, 1982.

Thomassy, Raymond. *Essai sur les écrits politiques de Christine de Pisan*. Paris, Debécourt, 1838.

Thompson, James Westfall. *The Literacy of the Laity in the Middle Ages*. University of California Publications in Education vol. 9. Berkeley: University of California Press, 1939.

Thorndike, Lynn. "Elementary and Secondary Education in the Middle Ages." *Speculum* 15, no. 4 (October 1940): 400–408.

———. *University Records and Life in the Middle Ages*. New York: Columbia University Press, 1944.

Trexler, Richard C. "*Correre La Terra*: Collective Insults in the Late Middle Ages." *Mélanges de l'école française de Rome* 96, no. 2 (1984): 845–902.

Trimpi, Wesley. "The Ancient Hypothesis of Fiction: An Essay on the Origins of Literary Theory." *Traditio* 27 (1971): 1–78.

———. "The Quality of Fiction: The Rhetorical Transmission of Literary Theory." *Traditio* 30 (1974): 1–118.

Ullmann, Walter. *Law and Jurisdiction in the Middle Ages*. Ed. George Garnett. London: Variorum Reprints, 1988.

———. *Principles of Government and Politics in the Middle Ages*. London: Methuen, 1961.

Uyttebrouck, André. *Le Gouvernement du duché de Brabant au bas moyen âge (1355–1430)*. Brussels: Éditions de l'Université de Bruxelles, 1975.

Vance, Eugene. *From Topic to Tale: Logic and Narrativity in the Middle Ages*. Minneapolis: University of Minnesota Press, 1987.

Verdon, Jean. *Les Françaises pendant la guerre de Cent Ans*. Paris: Perrin, 1991.

———. *Isabeau de Bavière*. Paris: Jules Tallandier, 1981.

Veyne, Paul. "Le Folklore à Rome et les droits de la conscience publique sur la conduite individuelle." *Latomus* 42, no. 1 (January–March 1983): 3–30.

Villedieu, Eugène. "Marguerite de Surville: Sa vie, ses oeuvres, ses descendants devant la critique moderne." *Bulletin de la société des sciences naturelles et historiques de l'Ardèche* 7 (1873): 8–177.

Viollet, Paul. *Histoire du droit civil français*. Paris: L. Larose & L. Tenin, 1905.

Vitz, Erika. *Women in the Medieval Town*. Trans. Sheila Marnie. London: Barrie and Jenkins, 1990.

Wahrmund, Ludwig. *Quellen zur Geschichte des Römisch-Kanonischen Processes im Mittelalter*. 2 vols. Innsbruck: Wagner, 1913.

Waller, Margaret. "*Cherchez la femme*: Male Malady and Narrative Politics in the French Romantic Novel." *PMLA* 104, no. 2 (March 1989): 141–51.

Walters, Lori. "Fathers and Daughters: Christine de Pizan as Reader of the Male Tradition of Clergie in the *Dit de la rose*," in *Reinterpreting Christine de Pizan*, ed. Earl Jeffrey Richards. Athens: University of Georgia Press, 1992, 63–76.

———. "The Woman Writer and Literary History: Christine de Pizan's Redefinition of the Poetic Translatio in the *Epistre au dieu d'amours*." *French Literature Series* 16 (1989): 1–16.

Walther, Hans. *Das Streitgedicht in der lateinischen Literatur des Mittelalters*. Munich: Beck, 1920.

Walzer, Richard. "Aristotle, Galen, and Palladius on Love," in *Greek into Arabic: Essays on Islamic Philosophy*. Cambridge, Mass.: Harvard University Press, 1962, 48–59.

Wauters, Alphonse. *Le Duc Jean Ier et le Brabant sous le règne de ce prince (1267–1294)*. Mémoires couronnés et autres mémoires publiés par l'Académie Royale des sciences, des lettres, et des beaux-arts de Belgique 13 (Brussels: Académie royale, 1862).

———. *Les Libertés communales: Essai sur l'origine et leurs premiers développements en Belgique, dans le nord de la France et sur les bords du Rhin*. Brussels: A. N. Lebègue, 1878.

Willard, Charity Cannon. "Christine de Pizan: The Astrologer's Daughter," in *Mélanges à la mémoire de Franco Simone: France et Italie dans la culture européenne*. Geneva: Slatkine, 1980: 95–111.

———. *Christine de Pizan: Her Life and Works*. New York: Persea Books, 1984.

———. "The Remarkable Case of Clotilde de Surville." *L'Esprit Créateur* 6, no. 2 (summer 1966), 108–16.

Williams, Steven J. "The Scholarly Career of the Pseudo-Aristotelian 'Secretum Secretorum' in the Thirteenth and Early Fourteenth Century." Ph.D. diss., Northwestern University, 1991.

Wippel, J. F. "The Quodlibetal Question as a Discursive Literary Genre." In *Les Genres littéraires dans les sources théologiques et philosophiques médiévales: Définition, critique, et exploitation*. Actes du Colloque international de Louvain-la-Neuve, May 25–27 1981. Publications de l'Institut d'études médiévales, 2nd series. Textes, études, congrès 5. Louvain-la-Neuve: Institut d'études médiévales de l'Université Catholique de Louvain, 1982: 67–84.

Witt, Ronald G. *Hercules at the Crossroads: The Life, Works, and Thought of Coluccio Salutati*. Durham, N.C.: Duke University Press, 1983.

Wolf, Ferdinand. "Über einige altfranzösische Doctrinen und Allegorien von der Minne." *Denkschriften der Kaiserlichen Akademie der Wissenschaften in Wien* (Philosophische-Historische Klasse) 13 (1864): 135–92.

Zumthor, Paul. *Essai de poétique médiévale*. Paris: Seuil, 1972.

———. "Notes en marge du traité de l'amour d'André le Chapelain." *Zeitschrift für romanische Philologie* 63 (1943): 178–91.

Index

Compositor:	G&S Typesetters
Text:	10/13 Aldus
Display:	Aldus
Printer and binder:	BookCrafters

FRANKLIN PIERCE COLLEGE LIBRARY

00106716

DATE DUE

NOV 1 0 2003

GAYLORD

PRINTED IN U.S.A.